T0358875

HANDBOOK OF THE ECONOMICS AND POLITICAL ECONOMY OF TRANSITION

Transition from central planning to a market economy, involving large-scale institutional change and reforms at all levels, is often described as the greatest social science experiment in modern times. As more than two decades have passed since the fall of the Berlin Wall and the collapse of the Soviet Union, it is now an excellent time to take stock of how the transition process has turned out for the economies that have moved on from socialism and the command economy.

This new Handbook assembles a team of leading experts, many of whom were closely involved in the transition process as policymakers and policy advisors, to explore the major themes that have characterized the transition process. After identifying the nature of initial conditions and the strengths and weaknesses of institutions, the varying paths and reforms countries have taken are fully analysed – from the shock therapy, privatization or gradualism of the early years to the burning issues of the present including global integration and sustainable growth.

Topics covered include the socialist system pre-transition, economic reforms, institutions, the political economy of transition, performance and growth, enterprise restructuring, and people and transition. The country coverage is also extensive, from the former socialist countries of the USSR and the satellite states of Central and Eastern Europe to the Asian countries of China, Vietnam and others. The rise of China as a key actor in the drama is chronicled, along with the emergence of a new, more confident, oil-rich Russia. The comparative prosperity of the Central European countries such as Poland and the Czech Republic is contrasted with the mixed fortunes of the former USSR, where some countries are stagnating while others boom.

This *Handbook of the Economics and Political Economy of Transition* is the definitive guide to this new order of things in the former Communist World.

Paul Hare has been Professor of Economics at Heriot-Watt University, Edinburgh, since 1985 and has worked on Eastern Europe and the former Soviet Union since the early 1970s. At Heriot-Watt University he established the Centre for Economic Reform and Transformation in 1990 and this rapidly became a leading centre for research on the transition economies. Professor Hare has had many research grants and consultancy contracts, including with all the leading international financial institutions, and has published widely on transition and other topics. He is the author of *Vodka and Pickled Cabbage: The Eastern European Travels of a Professional Economist,* which was published in 2010.

Gerard Turley is at the J.E. Cairnes School of Business and Economics at the National University of Ireland, Galway. Formerly he was a Research Associate at the Centre for Economic Reform and Transformation, Edinburgh. He has worked on various transition-related projects funded by the EBRD, UK Department for International Development (DFID) and EC EuropeAid. He is the author of *Transition, Taxation and the State* (2006) and co-author of *Transition Economics: Two Decades On* (2010). He has taught in universities in Eastern Europe, Russia and Central Asia, and also in the United States at the University of California, Berkeley.

HANDBOOK OF THE ECONOMICS AND POLITICAL ECONOMY OF TRANSITION

Edited by
Paul Hare and Gerard Turley

Routledge
Taylor & Francis Group

LONDON AND NEW YORK

First published 2013by Routledge

2 Park Square, Milton Park, Abingdon, Oxfordshire OX14 4RN
52 Vanderbilt Avenue, New York, NY 10017

Routledge is an imprint of the Taylor & Francis Group, an informa business

First issued in paperback 2019

Copyright © 2013 selection and editorial material, Paul Hare and Gerard Turley; individual chapters, the contributors

The right of the editors to be identified as the author of the editorial material, and of the authors for their individual chapters, has been asserted in accordance with sections 77 and 78 of the Copyright, Designs and Patents Act 1988.

All rights reserved. No part of this book may be reprinted or reproduced or utilised in any form or by any electronic, mechanical, or other means, now known or hereafter invented, including photocopying and recording, or in any information storage or retrieval system, without permission in writing from the publishers.

Notice:
Product or corporate names may be trademarks or registered trademarks, and are used only for identification and explanation without intent to infringe.

British Library Cataloguing in Publication Data
A catalogue record for this book is available from the British Library

Library of Congress Cataloging in Publication Data
Handbook of the economics and political economy of transition/edited by Paul Hare and Gerard Turley.
p. cm.
Includes bibliographical references and index.
1. Former communist countries–Economic conditions. 2. Former communist countries–Economic policy. 3. Post-communism–Economic aspects. 4. Mixed economy. I. Hare, P. G. II. Turley, Gerard.
HC59.15.H34 2013
330.9171'7–dc23
2012036097

ISBN: 978-0-415-59112-6 (hbk)
ISBN: 978-0-367-86543-6 (pbk)

Typeset in Bembo
by Taylor & Francis Books

To my family

G.T.

To my wife, Cindy

P.G.H.

This publication was grant-aided by the Publications Fund of the National University of Ireland, Galway.

CONTENTS

ILLUSTRATIONS

Tables

Figures

CONTRIBUTORS

Vladimír Benáček entered Academia with the fall of Communism by co-establishing CERGE-EI and the Faculty of Social Sciences at Charles University (Prague, Czech Republic). He still serves in the latter as Associate Professor in International Economics, specializing in the problems of economic adjustment in small open economies.

Josef C. Brada is Professor Emeritus in the Department of Economics at Arizona State University (Arizona, USA). He has written extensively on the economies of Eastern Europe and the Soviet Union, and he served as a consultant to the United Nations, the OECD and the World Bank and to governments in Eastern Europe and Latin America. He served as Editor of the *Journal of Comparative Economics* and is currently the editor of *Eastern European Economics* and *Comparative Economic Studies*.

Pauric Brophy is Managing Director of GDSI Limited (Galway, Ireland), a firm of development consultants specializing in transition economics. He has worked as a policy advisor to national and regional governments in Central and Eastern Europe and the CIS since 1992.

Nauro F. Campos is Professor of Economics and Finance at Brunel University (London, UK). His research interests focus on the political economy of the transition, with emphasis on economic growth, structural reforms, financial liberalization and their contribution to the process of European integration as a whole.

Wendy Carlin is Professor of Economics at UCL (London, UK). She has studied the East German economy since reunification and has worked extensively on aspects of enterprise restructuring, privatization and the business environment in transition more broadly. She is co-managing editor (with Philippe Aghion) of the *Economics of Transition*.

Julian Cooper OBE is Professor of Russian Economic Studies at the Centre for Russian and East European Studies, University of Birmingham (Birmingham, UK), where he has worked since 1971 and for 11 years was Centre Director. His research has focused on the Russian economy, in particular issues concerning defence, industry, science and innovation. For many years he has been an advisor to the Stockholm International Peace Research Institute on the Russian military economy and a regular contributor to their *Yearbook*.

Fabrizio Coricelli is Professor at the Paris School of Economics (Paris, France). He has not only published extensively on transition issues but he has also had extensive work experience on transition countries in positions held at international institutions, such as the World Bank, the European Commission and the EBRD.

László Csaba is Professor of International Political Economy at the Central European University and Corvinus University of Budapest, as well as a member of the Hungarian Academy of Sciences (Budapest, Hungary). In 1999–2000 he was President of the European Association for Comparative Economic Studies, and he is on the editorial board of many international and Hungarian academic journals. His recent books include: *Crisis in Economics?* (2009) and *The New Political Economy of Emerging Europe,* 2nd revised edition (2007), both Akadémiai Kiadó/W. Kluwer.

Michael Cuddy is Professor Emeritus at the School of Business and Economics at NUI Galway (Galway, Ireland). He is Director of GDSI, Galway, an international consulting company. He held the Established Chair of Economics from 1982 to 2008. He specialized in regional and rural development and transition economics.

Marek Dabrowski, Fellow at CASE – Centre for Social and Economic Research (Warsaw, Poland), former Poland's First Deputy Minister of Finance (1989–90). Since the end of 1980s he has been involved in policy advising and policy research in more than 20 countries of Central and Eastern Europe, former USSR and Middle East and North Africa. He is author/ co-author of several papers and books on transition and development.

Rumen Dobrinsky is Senior Research Associate of the Vienna Institute for International Economic Studies (WIIW). Until 2012 he was Director of Economic Cooperation and Integration Division at the United Nations Economic Commission for Europe (Geneva, Switzerland). Between 1996 and 2005 he was responsible for the analytical reporting on transition in the UNECE flagship publication *Economic Survey of Europe*. He has also participated in a number of transition-related projects in Central and Eastern Europe, with a focus on economic transformation in Bulgaria.

Zdenek Drabek is currently a member of the Scientific Council of the Faculty of Social Sciences at Charles University (Prague, Czech Republic) and an independent consultant. He was previously with the WTO and the World Bank, Oxford and Buckingham Universities, and acted as Chief International Negotiator for the Czechoslovakian Government with the EU and in GATT.

Saul Estrin is a Professor of Management and Strategy in the Department of Management at the London School of Economics (London, UK). He was formerly the Adecco Professor of Business and Strategy at London Business School. He has worked for more than two decades on the economies in transition, with particular reference to privatization. He is on the Board of Review of the *Journal of Business Venturing*.

László Halpern is Deputy Director at the Institute of Economics of the Hungarian Academy of Sciences (Budapest, Hungary) and research fellow at the Centre for Economic Policy Research (London). He has been dealing with exchange rates of transition economies, international trade and corporate performance.

Jan Hanousek is a Professor of Economics at Charles University, CERGE-EI, and a Senior Researcher in the Economics Institute (EI) of the Czech Academy of Sciences (Prague, Czech Republic). His research interests include applied econometrics and corporate finance.

Philip Hanson is Professor Emeritus of the Political Economy of Russia and Eastern Europe at the University of Birmingham (Birmingham, UK) and an Associate Fellow of the Russia and Eurasia Programme at Chatham House (London, UK). He has worked mainly on comparative economic systems and on the political economy of Russia.

Paul Hare is a Fellow of CASE (Poland, Warsaw), and Professor Emeritus in the School of Management and Languages, Heriot-Watt University (Edinburgh, UK); he was Professor of Economics at the university from 1985 until his retirement in 2010. There he established the Centre for Economic Reform and Transformation in 1990 and this rapidly became a leading centre for research on the transition economies. For most of his career, he studied the transition economies of Central and Eastern Europe, and the former Soviet Union.

Oleh Havrylyshyn is Visiting Scholar at Munk School of Global Affairs, University of Toronto (Toronto, Canada). Until 1992 he was Professor of Economics at George Washington University (Washington, DC, USA), then Deputy Minister of Finance, Ukraine, its representative at the IMF Board of Directors, and until 2007, Deputy Director at the IMF dealing with FSU countries. He has been involved with transition economies as an academic, consultant, government official and IMF official, and has published many books and articles on transition.

Evžen Kočenda is a Professor of Economics at Charles University, CERGE-EI, and a Senior Researcher in the Economics Institute (EI) of the Czech Academy of Sciences (Prague, Czech Republic). His research interests include corporate performance and governance, international money and finance, and European integration.

Grzegorz W. Kolodko, Professor and Director of TIGER, teaches at the Kozminski University (Warsaw, Poland). Intellectual and politician, he was a key architect of Polish economic reforms, a former Deputy Prime Minister and Minister of Finance, and author of the international bestseller *Truth, Errors, and Lies: Politics and Economics in a Volatile World*.

David M. Kotz is Professor of Economics at the University of Massachusetts Amherst (Massachusetts, USA) and Distinguished Professor in the School of Economics at the Shanghai University of Finance and Economics (Shanghai, China). He is the co-author, with Fred Weir, of *Russia's Path from Gorbachev to Putin: The Demise of the Soviet System and the New Russia*, Routledge, 2007.

Hartmut Lehmann is Professor of Economic Policy in the Department of Economics at the University of Bologna (Bologna, Italy) and Programme Director of the research area Labour Markets in Emerging and Transition Economies at the Institute for the Study of Labour (IZA) (Germany, Bonn). His areas of research are labour economics, applied econometrics and the economics of transition.

Hongmei Liu is Associate Professor in City College, Kunming University of Science and Technology (Yunnan, China). Her research works mainly focus on rural development in China, in relation to technology transition, project evaluation and poverty alleviation.

Peter Luke has previously worked as an economic consultant in Russia working with the Employment Service in Smolensk Oblast and the Regional Administration of Kaliningrad Oblast. He has taught economics at universities in Scotland and England and spent two years teaching economics in Beijing to Chinese students before returning to the UK where he worked as an economic advisor at the Home Office. He is currently principal lecturer and subject group leader in economics at London South Bank University (London, UK).

John Marangos is Associate Professor of Political Economy at the Department of Economics, University of Crete (Crete, Greece). Focal points for John's research include economic transition processes in the Balkans, Eastern Europe, in the former Soviet Union, and in Asia; international development; and innovative methodologies for teaching economics.

Paul Marer is Professor of Business at the Business School of the Central European University (Budapest, Hungary). Previously, he was Professor of International Business at the Kelley School of Indiana University (Indiana, USA). For most of his career, his research has focused on the economies of Central and Eastern Europe.

Vladimir Mau is the Rector of the Presidential Academy of National Economy and Public Administration (Moscow, Russia). Since 1991 Professor Mau contributed to the development and implementation of Russian economic reforms. He served as an advisor and aid to the Russian Deputy Prime Minister and Prime Minister (1991–94), then was a director of the Working Centre for Economic Reforms of the Russian Government (1997–2002).

Tomasz Mickiewicz is a Professor of Economics at Aston University (Birmingham, UK) and an honorary research fellow at University College London (London, UK). He is also Vice-President of the European Association for Comparative Economic Studies and serves on the editorial board of *Post Communist Economies*. He publishes on entrepreneurship, institutions and institutional change.

Jeffrey Miller is a Professor of Economics at the University of Delaware (Delaware, USA). His research has been in the area of comparative economics. He directed a masters level economics programme in Bulgaria in the early 1990s and was editor of *Comparative Economic Studies* from 2001–07.

Mojmir Mrak is Professor of International Finance at the Faculty of Economics of the University of Ljubljana (Ljubljana, Slovenia). He has been involved in transition related projects in Central, Eastern and South Eastern European countries. *Inter alia*, he has co-edited the book *Slovenia: From Yugoslavia to the European Union*.

Alexander Muravyev is Associate Professor at the Graduate School of Management, St. Petersburg University (St. Petersburg, Russia) as well as Senior Research Associate and Deputy Programme Director for Labour Markets in Emerging and Transition Economies at the Institute for the Study of Labour (Bonn, Germany). His main research fields are corporate governance, labour economics and economics of transition.

D. Mario Nuti was Professor of Comparative Economics at Rome University 'La Sapienza' (Rome, Italy) until retirement in 2010. Formerly he taught at Cambridge University (Cambridge, UK); CREES (Birmingham, UK); EUI (Florence, Italy); and LBS. He also served as economic advisor to the European Commission on Central and Eastern Europe, and to the post-socialist governments of Poland, Belarus and Uzbekistan.

Gur Ofer is Professor Emeritus at the Department of Economics, The Hebrew University of Jerusalem (Jerusalem, Israel). He received his PhD at Harvard University (Massachusetts, USA) in 1969. Ofer has worked and published extensively on the Soviet economy, socialist economics and the transition. He was a founder of the New Economic School (NES), in Moscow, Russia, and chair of its international advisory board (1991–2004). Ofer served as chair of the Economics Department at the HU (1985–86), and as the President of the Israeli Economic Association (1998–99).

Richard Pomfret is Professor of Economics at the University of Adelaide (Adelaide, Australia) and Visiting Professor of International Economics at the Johns Hopkins University Bologna Centre (Bologna, Italy). He has been working on the economies of Central Asia and Azerbaijan since 1993, when he worked for the United Nations as regional advisor to the governments of the new independent countries and Mongolia.

Vladimir Popov is an Interregional Advisor in DESA, UN (New York, USA). He has published articles in the *Journal of Comparative Economics, Comparative Economic Studies, World Development, Post Communist Economies, New Left Review* and many other academic journals. His books and articles were published in Chinese, English, Italian, Japanese, Korean, Norwegian, Portuguese, Russian, Spanish and Turkish. He is the author and editor of 11 books; the most recent is *Strategies of Economic Development*. Moscow, Higher School of Economics, 2011 (in Russian).

Matija Rojec is Research Professor at the Faculty of Social Sciences of the University of Ljubljana (Ljubljana, Slovenia). He has been involved in transition-related projects in Central, Eastern and South Eastern European countries. Inter alia he has co-edited the book *Slovenia: From Yugoslavia to the European Union*.

Steven Rosefielde is Professor of Economics at the University of North Carolina, Chapel Hill (North Carolina, USA), a member of the Russian Academy of Natural Sciences (RAEN), and Director of the Japan Foundation Project on the Global Financial Crisis's Impact on Asia. His most recent books include *Russian Economy* (Wiley, 2008); *Russia Since 1980* (with Stefan Hedlund) (Cambridge University Press, 2009) and *Two Asias: The Emerging Postcrisis Divide* (edited with Masaaki Kuboniwa and Satoshi Mizobata) (World Scientific, 2011).

Peter Sanfey is Deputy Director of Country Strategy and Policy within the EBRD's Office of the Chief Economist (London, UK). He has published widely in international journals on transition, macroeconomics and labour economics, and is the co-author of *In Search of the Balkan Recovery: the Political and Economic Reemergence of South-Eastern Europe*.

Mark E. Schaffer is Professor of Economics in the School of Management and Languages, Heriot-Watt University (Edinburgh, UK), and a Research Fellow at the Centre for Economic Policy Research, London and at the Institute for the Study of Labour (Bonn, Germany); he is also a Fellow of the Royal Society of Edinburgh. He has written widely on the economics of transition, with a particular focus on the enterprise sector and the labour market.

Anna Shabunina is an economist at the Fiscal Affairs Department at the International Monetary Fund (Washington, DC, USA). She has worked on transition-related projects at the Centre for Economic Reform and Transformation at Heriot-Watt University (Edinburgh, UK), where she also completed her doctorate degree.

Pekka Sutela is Adjunct Professor at the Aalto University School of Economics (Helsinki, Finland) and Visiting Professor at the Paris School of International Affairs, Sciences Po (Paris, France). He worked from 1990 to 2011 at the Bank of Finland, most recently as Principal Advisor, Monetary Policy and Research.

Daniel Treisman is Professor of Political Science at the University of California, Berkeley (California, USA). He has written three books on the politics and economics of Russia's transition from communism, including most recently *The Return: Russia's Journey from Gorbachev to Medvedev*, and has consulted on aspects of economic transition for the World Bank, the European Bank for Reconstruction and Development and USAID.

Gerard Turley is at the J.E. Cairnes School of Business and Economics at NUI Galway (Galway, Ireland). He has worked on various transition-related projects in Eastern Europe, Russia and Central Asia. He is the author of *Transition, Taxation and the State* and co-author of *Transition Economics: Two Decades On*. He has taught in universities in Eastern Europe, Russia and Central Asia, and also in the United States at the University of California, Berkeley (California, USA).

Milica Uvalic is Professor of Economics, University of Perugia (Perugia, Italy), Member of the UN Committee for Development Policy, former President of EACES. She has worked on transition economies, particularly the Balkans. Recent (2010) books: *Serbia's Transition Towards a Better Future*, and with B. Cerovic (eds), *Western Balkans' Accession to the European Union. Political and Economic Challenges*.

Wing Thye Woo is Professor of Economics at the University of California in Davis (California, USA), Fudan University (Shanghai, China) and Central University of Finance and Economics (Beijing, China); and Executive Director of the Penang Institute (Penang, Malaysia). He specialized in macroeconomics, international economics and growth economics, especially for the Chinese, Indonesian, Malaysian and US economies.

ACKNOWLEDGEMENTS

There are a number of people whom we wish to thank. In particular, we wish to pay a special word of gratitude to Robert Langham, Senior Publisher at Routledge whose idea it was to write a handbook on transition. His tenacity, patience and encouragement were invaluable and we hereby wish to acknowledge his contribution to this volume. To all others at Routledge involved in the publication of this book, and, in particular, to Natalie Tomlinson, we are very grateful. We are very pleased with the final outcome and we hope our readers are too.

An edited volume is only as good as its contributors, not only in terms of their expertise and knowledge, but also in terms of their dedication and commitment. We were very fortunate with the team of colleagues who contributed to this handbook. Aside from the extraordinary knowledge and remarkable experience that our colleagues have, among them former Deputy Prime Ministers and Finance Ministers, special advisors to Prime Ministers, policy advisors to governments and international organizations, chief international negotiators, etc., they also managed to deliver their papers on time and within tight guidelines. Given the very busy lives that they lead, it is a testament to their knowledge of, and commitment to, the subject area that we, as editors, were able to deliver the handbook, more or less on time, to the publishers.

One of the difficulties with a commissioned work like this is that submissions are likely to be very diverse not only in the views they take of transition, but also in style, format, layout, etc. As regards our contributors' views about transition, we have not acted as censors. At times, of course, we have queried certain conclusions, arguments and findings, not least to ensure clarity in the final product. But none of the authors were asked to change their stated views to fit in with some pre-ordained ideas of the editors.

As regards the more technical aspects of this production, we have endeavoured to abide by Routledge's style guidelines as far as possible as we edited the various chapters. We also wish to thank Weibo Xiong, a PhD graduate of Heriot-Watt University (Edinburgh, UK). Weibo did a very fine job in editing an enormous number of tables and figures from all the 37 papers (from 45 contributors), in a consistent and professional manner. We are very grateful to Weibo and we wish him all the best in his future career.

We also wish to thank our colleagues at Heriot-Watt University and, in particular, those in the School of Management and Languages; and staff at the National University of Ireland, Galway, including colleagues in the J.E. Cairnes School of Business and Economics. A special word of thanks to the NUI Galway Grant-in-Aid of Publications Committee who awarded us a subvention to help in the publication of the book.

For granting us permission to reproduce material and data, we are grateful to a number of organizations and publishers, including the Journal of Economic and Social Policy, Taylor & Francis, Springer Science+Business Media B.V., Nomos Publishers, the China Data Centre at the University of Michigan, Palgrave Macmillan, Goskomstat, National Bureau of Statistics of China, United Nations, OECD, EBRD, The World Bank and the International Monetary Fund.

Finally, we wish to acknowledge all the people of the former socialist countries of Eastern Europe, the Soviet Union and East Asia who witnessed extraordinary changes, both positive and negative, in the transition from plan to market that they have been living through. We trust that this volume properly reflects the diversity of country experience across our region of interest, and we hope that it does some justice to the large-scale systemic changes that have been evident since transition began – over two decades ago in Central and Eastern Europe and the former Soviet Union, and over thirty five years ago in China.

As usual, we accept full responsibility for any errors that may remain in this volume, while also acknowledging that there may be some omitted issues and topics that readers would have liked us to include. In selecting material to include, however, we inevitably had to make some extremely difficult choices.

ABBREVIATIONS

AD	Aggregate Demand
ALMP	Active Labour Market Policies
AS	Aggregate Supply
BEEPS	Business Environment and Enterprise Performance Survey
BIT	Bilateral Investment Treaties
CAP	Common Agricultural Policy
CARDS	Community Assistance for Reconstruction, Development and Stabilization
CBA	Currency Board Arrangement
CBR	Central Bank of Russia
CCP	Chinese Communist Party
CEB	Central Europe and the Baltics
CEE	Central and Eastern Europe
CEECs	Central and Eastern European Countries
CEFTA	Central European Free Trade Agreement
CHIP	China Household Income Project
CIA	Central Intelligence Agency
CIS	Commonwealth of Independent States
CLV	China, Laos, and Vietnam
CMEA	Council for Mutual Economic Assistance
CPE	Centrally Planned Economy
CPSU	Communist Party of the Soviet Union
CPV	Communist Party of Vietnam
DTPS	Dual-Track Price System
EBRD	European Bank for Reconstruction and Development
EC	European Community
ECA	Europe and Central Asia
ECB	European Central Bank
ECJ	European Court of Justice
EEC	European Economic Community
EEFSU	Eastern Europe and the Former Soviet Union

EFTA	European Free Trade Association
EMU	Economic and Monetary Union
EPL	Employment Protection Legislation
ERM	Exchange Rate Mechanism
EU	European Union
FDI	Foreign Direct Investment
FH	Freedom House
FPR	Financial Participation Ratio
FR	Federal Republic
FSU	Former Soviet Union
GATT	General Agreement on Tariffs and Trade
GDP	Gross Domestic Product
GDR	German Democratic Republic
GEM	Global Entrepreneurship Monitor
GNI	Gross National Income
GNP	Gross National Product
GSP	General Social Product
GWP	Gross World Product
HDI	Human Development Index
HF	Heritage Foundation
HRS	Household Responsibility System
IBRD	International Bank for Reconstruction and Development
ICT	Information and Communications Technology
ICTY	International Criminal Tribunal for the former Yugoslavia
IFIs	International Financial Institutions
IFRS	International Financial Reporting Standards
IMF	International Monetary Fund (the Fund)
IPA	Instrument for Pre-Accession Assistance
ISPA	Instrument for Structural Policies for Pre-Accession
LiTS	Life in Transition Survey
M&A	Mergers and Acquisitions
MNC	Multinational Corporation
MOD	Ministry of Defence
NATO	North Atlantic Treaty Organization
NEP	New Economic Policy
NIS	Newly Independent States
NIT	Nation in Transit
NMP	Net Material Product
NMS	New Member States
NPF	National Property Fund
NPLs	Non-Performing Loans
NT	Non-tradeable
NTE	Non-transition Economy
OECD	Organisation for Economic Co-operation and Development
PAYG	Pay As You Go
PHARE	Poland and Hungary: Assistance for Restructuring their Economies
PPF	Production Possibility Frontier
PPP	Purchasing Power Parity

PRC	People's Republic of China
PSA	Production Sharing Agreement
PSUs	Primary Sampling Units
R&D	Research and Development
RCA	Revealed Comparative Advantage
REER	Real Effective Exchange Rate
RMB	Renminbi
SAA	Stabilization and Association Agreement
SAP	Structural Adjustment Programme
SAPARD	Special Accession Programme for Agriculture and Rural Development
SCBs	State-controlled Banks
SCEs	State-controlled Enterprises
SEE	South East Europe
SFR	Socialist Federal Republic
SMEs	Small and Medium-sized Enterprises
SOE	State Owned Enterprise
SPS	Socialist Party of Serbia
TEs	Transition Economies
TFP	Total Factor Productivity
TI	Transparency International
TPR	Trade Participation Ratio
TR	Transition Report
TVEs	Township and Village Enterprises
UK	United Kingdom
UN	United Nations
UNCTAD	UN Conference on Trade and Development
UNDP	UN Development Programme
UNECE	United Nations Economic Commission for Europe
US	United States
USDA	US Department of Agriculture
USSR	Union of Soviet Socialist Republics
VAT	Value Added Tax
WB	World Bank (the Bank)
WDR	World Development Report
WTO	World Trade Organization

INTRODUCTION TO THE HANDBOOK[1]

Paul Hare and Gerard Turley

The background

Until the early 1990s, transition economics was not a recognized sub-branch of economics. Instead, we had an economics for the advanced/developed countries, which is essentially what was taught as 'economics' in most Western universities then (and for the most part, still is); and an economics of developing countries, mostly taught as a specialist option within mainstream economics courses and forming the major concern of leading international financial institutions (IFIs) such as the World Bank, various Regional Development Banks and the International Monetary Fund (IMF). In addition, there was a diverse and lively sub-branch known as the 'economics of socialist countries', which sought to understand how central planning worked, and explored issues of incentives and enterprise behaviour in that context.

Then in 1989 the communist Polish government, shortly followed by the Hungarian one, announced that free elections would be held, the Berlin Wall that had divided the city of Berlin for decades was suddenly opened (and thereafter was rapidly demolished) and within months almost the whole of Eastern Europe had ended one-party, communist rule. There was no longer an 'iron curtain' between East and West in Europe. For many people living in the region, this was an extremely anxious period as the Soviet Union was still in place, largely unreformed either politically or economically; and despite President Gorbachev's assurances that his erstwhile socialist partners were free to choose their own development paths, no one was quite sure whether he could be trusted, given the country's past history of military and political intervention in the affairs of Eastern Europe, and given the presence of tens of thousands of Soviet (mostly Russian) troops at bases throughout the satellite states. Luckily, there was no intervention, as President Gorbachev remained true to his word.

Meanwhile, the Soviet Union itself was proceeding towards its own collapse. In late 1990 the USSR, having stagnated economically for at least a decade, took the surprising step of seeking advice on economic reform from the G7 governments, and many of those who took part in the ensuing study (including one of the editors – Hare) sensed that the old central planning system was no longer functioning properly, that the country was drifting economically and that there were real dangers of political disintegration. This indeed happened the following year, in 1991, with a failed coup in August, and the formal dissolution of the Soviet Union announced on (the Western) Christmas Day. Since the Union was, constitutionally, a federation, it broke up into

1

15 successor states, the Russian Federation (or Russia) being easily the largest in terms of population, land area, economic strength and military capability. The other 14 states were Estonia, Latvia and Lithuania; Belarus and Ukraine; Moldova; Armenia, Azerbaijan and Georgia; Kazakhstan, Kyrgyzstan, Tajikistan, Turkmenistan and Uzbekistan.

These rapid, largely unexpected, and world-changing developments gave rise to an enormous response from the international community, struggling both to understand the new configuration of the world economy and to assist the new countries to reform their economies. In parallel, and in support of this international effort, economists and others were quick to undertake a huge volume of new research on what were quickly termed 'the economies in transition'. This stimulated new research centres, new journals and hundreds of studies, both by those familiar with the old communist/central planning systems, and by many newcomers to the region. Quite soon, the field of transition economics widened out to take in other countries that seemed to be moving away from old-style central planning and performing well economically – for instance China, and later Vietnam. By now, over 20 years from the start of transition, we probably have enough perspective on the process to understand the key issues and challenges, while acknowledging that much of the process continues to surprise us, that many mistakes were made along the way by all those involved and that there is still much to learn.

Transition

Let us now sketch out some of the key aspects of the transition process as it has actually unfolded, in order to illustrate some of this.

The state

Economists tend to take the existing states, and the established political configuration, as essentially given when they are thinking about economic policy issues, and this was initially the case when communist regimes collapsed over the years 1989–91. For the transition, however, this proved to be a bad assumption for at least five reasons:

(a) Fifteen new states were created from the Soviet Union (as noted above).
(b) Yugoslavia broke up into several states, with wars going on until the Dayton Peace Accords stopped the fighting in Bosnia in 1995. The final configuration of states in south-eastern Europe is still not fully settled, though by now Yugoslavia itself has been replaced by seven new states (Slovenia, Croatia, Serbia, Bosnia-Herzegovina, Montenegro, Macedonia and Kosovo[2]).
(c) Several successor states from the Soviet Union were involved in wars with neighbours over territory and ethnicity, e.g. Armenia, Azerbaijan.
(d) Several of these successor states experienced civil conflict, often with breakaway regions not recognising the writ of the central government, e.g. Tajikistan, Moldova, Georgia.
(e) Czechoslovakia broke up peacefully to form two new states from January 1993: Slovakia and the Czech Republic.

Hence, unexpectedly (for economists), a great deal of attention has had to be paid to state-building in transition.

Aims of transition

Right from the start it was taken for granted that the transition countries were doing two things: (a) moving away from communist dictatorship and adopting democratic politics; and (b) ending central planning and seeking to build well-functioning, competitive, market-type economies. Neither of these assumptions turned out to be right for all the countries concerned, with Turkmenistan and Belarus remaining largely one-party states; and Uzbekistan, Belarus and some others showing little interest in markets. Politically, too, getting democracy established and working well has proved harder than expected in many countries. Further, countries such as Vietnam and China have pushed ahead rapidly with very successful market-oriented economic reforms while still maintaining socialist rhetoric and remaining one-party states.

What does transition involve?

Leaving aside these political challenges, it was assumed early on that the economic dimension of transition necessarily entailed seven elements:

(a) dismantle the old system (central planning, etc.);
(b) macroeconomic stabilization;
(c) domestic price liberalization;
(d) trade liberalization;
(e) privatization and restructuring of the inherited state-owned enterprises;
(f) social safety net (including reforming labour markets);
(g) diverse institutional reforms.

A high proportion of the academic research and policy analysis of transition focused on topics (b) to (f), especially in the first decade of transition. Topic (a) received little attention since it was assumed to be quick and easy, involving little more than closing down the old planning offices and related administrative units. Topic (g) was initially quite neglected by mainstream economists, partly because its importance was underestimated, and partly because it was thought to be slow and difficult and would therefore come later.

This simple picture of the transition misses out a great deal, but gradually both policy-makers and researchers took on a much wider range of topics. Some of these sought to explain new and unexpected phenomena that affected the whole region, such as explaining the post-socialist recessions. Others were more concerned with the new policies and reforms that transition entailed, such as introducing new currencies; exchange rate policy; creating a good business environment that would encourage a lot of new firm starts (surprisingly neglected initially); building new labour market institutions and associated social policy measures (e.g. unemployment benefits), far more difficult and controversial than the simple heading of topic (f) might suggest; reforming the banks and creating new financial institutions; reforming and rebuilding the tax system and the structure/scale of public expenditure; encouraging foreign direct investment; and many others. The field soon became amazingly diverse and extremely interesting.

Given the rapidly growing complexity and range of the field, researchers often looked for alternative principles to help provide some structure. Thus many people have found it useful to think of transition in terms of three broad areas: macroeconomic reforms, structural reforms and institutional change.

Aid to the transition countries

Of course, right from the start there was the question of aid, that is, how best should the international community support the transition process? This, too, turned out to be remarkably diverse, with aid (both loans and grants) coming from the European Union (EU), many national governments, the established IFIs (the World Bank and IMF) and a newly created IFI, the European Bank for Reconstruction and Development (EBRD) based in London, UK. While often offered for genuinely altruistic reasons, some early aid was offered to Eastern Europe in response to fears of mass migration from East to West if economic conditions became too difficult in the East. In the event, though much migration did take place, and continues to do so, it was never on the scale that the more alarmist reports suggested.

From the EU in particular, aid also took the form of policy initiatives such as the gradual incorporation of many transition economies into the EU's free-trade area. For an important subset of transition economies, too, there was the goal of eventual full membership of the EU, completing their return to Europe. This turned out to take far longer than many transition economies hoped or expected, but in May 2004 eight of them joined the EU (Estonia, Latvia, Lithuania, Poland, Czech Republic, Slovakia, Hungary and Slovenia), followed in January 2007 by two more (Bulgaria and Romania). More states have been accepted as candidates by the EU, but further enlargement is unlikely for some years (with the exception of Croatia, due to join in July 2013, once its accession protocol has been ratified).

Institutions

Gradually, in most of the transition economies, the institutions needed to support well-functioning markets were established (or re-established, for the countries that had had market-type economies between the two world wars). Most fundamental was the recognition and protection of private property rights, since in most of the region most private property, especially of business-related assets, had been illegal. Second was the protection of business contracts between private parties, both from dishonest business partners, other private agents and from state predation. Central Europe was quick to establish this basic framework for private-sector business activity, whereas in most of the former Soviet Union progress was much slower. The importance of the issue was not so well understood there, and the ensuing private-sector 'solutions' to business disputes were at times quite unpleasant. Even today, when the right laws are largely in place, their enforcement is often slow and uncertain, and can sometimes depend on a given firm's personal links with the political élites. Accordingly, in these countries the 'rule of law' cannot yet be said to prevail.

At first, many observers/analysts of early transition were not concerned about market-type institutions, as there was a fairly widespread belief or hope that as soon as central planning was dismantled, the needed institutions would rapidly come into being through private initiative. Sometimes no doubt this happened, but for some markets it was unrealistic to expect such a benign outcome and more active state intervention was needed to get them working well: such 'difficult' markets included the housing market (requiring proper title, registers of ownership, etc.); the labour market; markets for many consumer durables (consumer protection and the like); banks and financial markets.

While in Europe we tend to think of institutions in terms of specific organizations or their legal and regulatory underpinnings, as just noted, it is important to remember that institutions can be either formal or informal, the latter depending on such intangible 'assets' as trust, expectations, local custom and practice, and all sorts of informal understandings. For example, how else can we explain the spectacular success of China's economy since the ending of the hugely disruptive Cultural Revolution in the mid-1970s? The upsurge of township and village enterprises (TVEs) in the late 1970s, started as a series of local experiments by China's pragmatic leadership and rapidly spreading to the whole country, took outside observers and, we suspect, China's rulers, completely by surprise. So how and why did they work? By the late 1970s, a tacit understanding between China's Communist Party and ordinary people seems to have evolved, the key tenets of which were no more political campaigns, and a focus on economic development. At local level, this translated into informal understandings between local officials and those wanting to start new businesses, what became the TVEs. They enjoyed no formal private property rights, but understood that they would be allowed to keep their profits for reinvestment or personal income, paying only local taxes. Entry and exit were quick and easy, there was little or no protection for established firms that couldn't make money (so a tough, competitive environment), and the symbiotic relationship between local government and business helped finance the former while protecting the latter. And it all worked!

Energy resources

The countries of the former Soviet Union fall into two groups, namely those possessing plentiful energy supplies, notably of oil and/or natural gas, and those not so endowed. Thus, Russia and Kazakhstan belong in the first group, Ukraine and Armenia in the second. These disparities in their natural endowments initially gave rise to balance of payments deficits for those lacking energy resources, and structural surpluses for the energy rich. Leaving aside these initial imbalances, much attention has focused on the energy-rich group of successor states, not least because empirical studies have often shown the possession of abundant energy resources to be detrimental for a country's economic growth. This is because the possession of energy has often proved conducive to weak and corrupt government, not particularly oriented towards the development of the country concerned; in addition, energy exports have often been said to push up exchange rates, making non-energy sectors of the economy relatively uncompetitive – this is the so-called 'Dutch disease' phenomenon. Hence researchers and policy analysts have been interested to study how well (or otherwise) the transition economies would manage their energy resources.

China and Russia

Among the plethora of interesting economic and political economy issues that arose in the course of transition, it is understandable that the experiences of certain key countries should have attracted special attention from researchers. The case of China, with its unusual characteristics, was already referred to above. But Russia, too, has been the focus of many studies, owing to its size and geopolitical importance, and some idiosyncratic features of its transition path. Russia's political and economic instability, especially during the 1990s, was a continuing source of concern to Western policy-makers. More recently, the country appears more stable and has enjoyed a decade of quite rapid economic growth but questions still arise about the sustainability of the country's current policies, operating in an incompletely reformed economy.

Financial crisis

Lastly, despite writing this in early 2012, it is impossible not to mention the world financial crisis that began in the USA in 2007 and which soon led to recession conditions in the major developed economies of the world. In the advanced countries, recovery is still in its early stages, and there are still fears of renewed recession across the eurozone. What started as a collapse of the US property market shifted rapidly to become a very serious banking crisis, and now, as a direct result of state-sponsored rescues of major commercial banks in several countries, the banking crisis has been transformed into a fiscal crisis, and for some countries, a sovereign debt crisis.

The crisis has not left the transition economies untouched, with several countries already needing IMF rescue packages to support their banking systems and their public finances. Many countries not already helped in this way appear quite fragile, implying that the reforms of the past two decades have not always put the transition economies in a position to cope with a major crisis unaided. Several of the new EU member states that were doing well in terms of their gradual convergence to EU incomes and living standards have now gone into reverse – hopefully only temporarily – and at the very least convergence will suffer some delay. This recent experience forces us to revisit some of the aspects of macroeconomic policy in transition economies that many observers thought were essentially solved during the first decade of transition. The policy environment needs rethinking to help the economies operate more robustly in the face of external shocks and crises.

What is transition economics?

The above introduction to some of the major issues that arose during the first two decades of transition studies does not quite suffice to define what we mean by the subject area of 'transition economics'. It seems to us to make sense to approach the matter from three directions; taken together, the relevant subject matter can then be defined fairly well.

Why is transition economics not just a variant of development economics?

For the most part (leaving aside later additions to the group), the transition economies are not seriously poor countries. Mostly they are middle-income countries, usually quite heavily industrialized, and with populations that were mostly well educated. Although services tended to be under-developed, and agriculture generally accounted for a higher share of output (GDP) than in the highly developed countries of Western Europe, the economic structure of transition economies was a good deal closer to that of the developed world than it was to a typical developing country. Hence a large part of the subject matter and key issues in development economics would have had at best very limited resonance for most transition economies. Asian entrants to the transition process, notably China and Vietnam, were of course rather different; for they were initially very poor, and agriculture did account for a large fraction of their economies.

Why not just apply mainstream economics and the policy tools of developed countries?

To a large extent that was done, but doing so resulted in a number of mistakes and misunderstandings, and in the end a lot of new thinking, modelling and analysis was required. For instance, when we think about macroeconomic policy in the UK, we take for granted both the existence of liquid and active financial markets for government bonds and other financial assets, and the established governance framework involving the Treasury, the Bank of England and the Financial Services Authority (or its successor). True, this failed to work well in the early stages of the 2008/09 financial crisis, but it is there, and macroeconomic modelling takes it as given.

In the transition economies, none of this framework was in place, neither markets nor the supporting institutions. Thus, at least for the first decade, macroeconomics in the transition economies was not at all the same as the subject we are used to in the developed world, and attempts to treat it as the same led to mistakes, misunderstandings and policy errors.

Similarly, since the early 1980s many developed countries, notably the UK, have gained considerable experience of privatization, especially of public utilities, and have devised interesting frameworks and models to govern the subsequent regulation of such utilities once they are in the private sector. Unfortunately, this vast experience counted for very little when people first sought to apply it in the transition economy context. The UK privatization model involved a separate Act of Parliament for each firm that was privatized, which is fine when only a small fraction of an economy is to be privatized, and that in a moderately leisurely fashion. But in the transition economies, virtually everything was state owned at the start and there was a strong sense that privatization ought to be accomplished rapidly. True, there were debates about the proper speed, but few thought the process should extend over several decades. Consequently, the UK model was a non-starter, and much creative thinking was devoted to the task of devising new approaches to privatization including the creation of privatization agencies and diverse methods of 'sale'.

When public utilities were privatized, there was a presumption that this would be accompanied by the establishment of independent regulators, very much on the model followed by the UK and other developed countries. However, this also mostly failed for two reasons. First, independent regulators can only function properly when the politicians trust them to do so and refrain from interference, a condition that was not often fulfilled in the transition economies. Second, some of the analytical models used in utility pricing in the UK, for example in the electricity wholesale market, were much too complex to be adopted in transition countries with little or no recent experience of operating markets of any kind.

So in these and many other instances, mainstream economics might at best provide a starting point, but much new thinking and new analysis was needed to come up with useful tools and models for transition.

What was special or different about the transition economies?

Here a short list conveys the principal characteristics of these countries:

(i) They began as communist controlled, one-party dictatorships operating their economies using central planning, and with limited or no use of markets (albeit parts of Central Europe had started to introduce more market-friendly reforms).

(ii) Virtually the whole of production was in state ownership.

(iii) Many markets we take for granted in developed countries were absent or functioned under severe constraints, notably the labour market, key financial markets, markets for housing and land.

(iv) Many institutions familiar in western economies performed different functions under central planning and were therefore ill adapted to the needs of a market economy, e.g. the banks (which essentially allocated funds for investment to projects approved in the central plan, not in accordance with their own independent assessments of profitability), the system of taxation (which gained most revenue by creaming off above-plan profits from state-owned enterprises).

(v) The economies lacked dynamism because old firms rarely closed (no bankruptcy) and few new ones were established. Moreover, innovation was weak in these supply constrained economies. Most firms possessed only a rudimentary financial function, and little or no sales and marketing expertise.

(vi) Important economic institutions needed for a well-functioning market economy were absent or functioned badly, including much of the law as it related to business.

(vii) Last, and in keeping with the theme of this volume, political economy aspects of the transition turned out to be more complicated and more difficult than most participants, observers or advisors could have imagined at the start. Transition was never 'just' an economic problem, entailing a variety of more or less technical economic reforms to assure success. Right from the start reformers had to build political coalitions to support the measures they needed to push through; they had to think about the politics of possible reform reversals; and sometimes effective coalitions simply could not be assembled, so reforms were delayed, implemented in a poor sequence, or implemented incompletely.

What have we learned about transition, and what lessons does transition hold for economics?

Surprisingly, perhaps, despite the huge volume of work that has been done on transition by economists, finance specialists, political scientists and many others, there is still no agreed model or theory of the transition. We have a pretty good idea about the 'ideal' end point of the process – in other words, a well-functioning market-type economy, generating economic growth and improving living standards – but how best to get there from a starting point of central planning is still hotly debated among economists. Some of this debate is often cast in terms of the 'big bang' versus 'gradualism' issue, contrasting economic reforms introduced, as far as possible, all at once, with a more step-by-step approach. In practice, however, the difference between these two approaches is far less than one might suppose, since many of the reforms commenced at the start of a 'big bang' might still take years to implement, while even those countries that went for gradualism mostly dismantled central planning and introduced, for example, price and trade liberalization extremely rapidly.

We also know a good deal about the main conditions that need to be in place for an economy to be able to achieve sustained economic growth. The first of these conditions is 'simply' to maintain sound macroeconomic conditions, which essentially means keeping inflation down to manageable levels, keeping the government budget balance under control, and paying careful attention to the balance of payments to avoid the accumulation of excessive and unsustainable external debt. Ideally, it also means keeping unemployment down to levels that are socially tolerable, even while massive structural change in the economy is going on. Once an economy has settled down along a path of steady growth, governments usually find that they can meet such conditions without too much trouble most of the time, but at the start of transition when a lot was changing very fast and economies experienced massive shocks, it was a very different story.

Virtually all the transition economies experienced an initial burst of inflation when they relaxed price controls, accompanied by severe foreign trade shocks as the old socialist trading networks disintegrated and new markets had to be found. However, different countries in the region managed these events very differently. Most of Central Europe and the Baltic States were commendably quick to get a grip on the situation by operating quite tough macro-policies that soon brought inflation under control, and stabilized the government and external accounts. Elsewhere, both in south-east Europe (as Yugoslavia split into several new states) and in the countries of the Commonwealth of Independent States (CIS), attention to sound economic policy was seriously distracted by engagement in various civil and regional wars; and even where there were no wars (as in Ukraine and Kazakhstan, for instance), the new leaders understood little or nothing about, or perhaps had no interest in, how to run a market-type economy. In effect, they experienced a 'baptism of fire', a learning process during which they made many terrible mistakes. The result was that most countries experienced inflation that roared ahead to reach 1000 per cent or even more in the worst year, 1993. Finally, thereafter, the new governments had all introduced new currencies and gradually brought their economies under more effective macroeconomic control. It was a horribly painful and expensive process. But by now it is well understood that a market-type economy (or any kind of economy, actually) will simply not work if the basic macroeconomic foundations are not in place.

For the transition economies, the second condition for getting sustainable growth going again was to build substantial private sectors. At the start of transition, the private sector was tiny in most countries, though Polish agriculture had remained in private hands, albeit mostly comprising very small-scale and inefficient farms; Hungary had allowed a variety of small private businesses to operate from the early 1980s; and even Russia, from the late 1980s, was allowing small co-operatives and leasehold enterprises to be established. So some countries had the beginnings of a private sector, but mostly not very much. At the start, then, the question was how to go about building a private sector.

The obvious answer was to privatize all those state-owned enterprises that had long dominated production in the former socialist countries, and the faster the better. Indeed, so 'obvious' did this answer appear that quite a few eminent economists, not previously known for their work on Eastern Europe and hence not really knowing very much about the region, rushed in to offer their advice to the new governments. The message was privatize, privatize! And logically, if it was to be accomplished quickly, in countries with no stock markets or other functioning financial institutions, and with limited personal savings, most of the old state-owned enterprises would have to be more or less given away to the population at large, or to workers and managers. It could even be argued that this approach was in some sense fair, since under socialism all productive assets were already supposed to be 'owned by the people', whatever that might mean aside from being an appealing slogan.

Several countries, notably the Czech Republic (which did it relatively well) and the Russian Federation (which did it quickly, but badly), thus embarked on various forms of so called voucher privatization whereby vouchers were issued to the population either for free or for a very nominal price. The vouchers were then used to purchase shares in firms being privatized. The big problem with this approach is that it usually did little or nothing to address key problems of these firms, namely their weak management and corporate governance structures, their poor and outdated technology, their need for investment to restructure and their lack of access to (or even knowledge of) alternative markets. However, much privatization did indeed get done, and at least this process did remove many businesses – both bad ones and good ones – from the suffocating clutches of the state.

Interestingly, though, if one examines statistics for various countries on the growth of the private sector during the 1990s, one certainly finds the expected rapid growth; but rather than being a consequence of privatization, much of the observed growth resulted from huge numbers of entirely new private firms, created since the end of communism. In other words, while privatization can no doubt contribute something towards private sector growth, and did so, a large and surprisingly quick contribution can also come from the formation of wholly new firms. This suggests that rather than concentrating on rapid privatization, and frequently doing it badly, it would have been far better for many countries to focus on creating good conditions for new businesses to be set up. That should have been their priority – paying attention to fostering what is often called a 'good (or conducive, or enabling) business environment'. This is not necessarily an easy thing to do, especially in countries where state control has long been all pervasive, and where the authorities are still reluctant to place much trust in what they continue to think of, rather pejoratively, as 'uncontrolled' private sector activity.

A third condition for growth was the restructuring of much of the old (socialist) production, and a fourth was a wide range of institutional developments to support the operation and proper functioning of markets. Restructuring is a controversial and widely misunderstood topic. Some restructuring is going on all the time in all reasonably dynamic and progressive economies. Old industries slowly decline and die, new ones emerge to take their place, often in places and sectors that no one would have imagined a decade or two earlier. Meanwhile, some production stays pretty much the same for long periods, but to prosper it usually needs to modernise to improve productivity. Even within a generally successful sector, there is commonly a lot of change going on. Thus, for example, in the food-processing sectors of the developed countries, tinned and pickled foods have, in recent decades, largely given way to frozen food, while in Central and Eastern Europe this same transformation was just getting started back in 1990 and has now advanced considerably.

So in 'normal' economies, perhaps 2–3 per cent of private-sector production is disappearing each year, while thousands of new firms in a wide range of sectors start up, most of which will fail quite rapidly, a few of which will grow to be the star performers of the future. Hence by the end of a decade of such gradual structural change, perhaps 25–30 per cent of the production that was going on at the start will have gone forever. It will have been replaced by something, but at the beginning of the decade no one could have predicted what (which is why detailed production planning rarely works). A well-functioning economy can adapt to this sort of change, and since new jobs are typically being created as rapidly as old ones are lost, there is no need for it to be accompanied by rising unemployment.

The transition economies in the early 1990s, though, were most definitely not 'normal' economies in this sense. Their economic environment changed very abruptly, and firms that had been protected under socialism for many years, often decades, suddenly found that their formerly guaranteed markets had vanished or declined, and that much of their technology was quickly revealed to be totally out-dated. In these circumstances, it was not just 2–3 per cent of production that needed to 'disappear' each year, but much more, perhaps adding up to as much as half of existing production in the country concerned over a fairly short period – there is a wide range of estimates in the relevant literature, so it is hard to be more precise. This prospect of, effectively, an economic 'meltdown' was quite terrifying for the new governments of the transition economies, especially those that lacked any confidence in the ability of new private sector firms to fill most of the resulting employment gap.

Some countries dealt with the problem by adopting quite tough policies right from the start, cutting subsidies and directed credits to business as fast as they could, thus signalling that enterprises would only survive through their own efforts; such policies were usually accompanied by rapid moves to facilitate setting up new businesses. Others were more cautious, continuing to protect some major firms while still leaving most to the vagaries of the new market forces. These two groups include most of the countries that joined the EU in 2004. Their restructuring has been extremely painful, and has been accompanied by a good deal of unemployment and other forms of social and economic distress. Nevertheless, for the most part these economies are now well placed to grow quite normally, gradually catching up with the more prosperous EU partners, and with restructuring in the future proceeding at normal and therefore perfectly manageable rates. Investment rates in profitable businesses have long been high enough to support such a process.

Other countries, notably Russia and several other CIS members, proceeded with restructuring far more circumspectly, fearing the social and political effects of large-scale unemployment and being slow to create good conditions for new business. The result was often a longer period of stagnation and even decline before growth resumed again, and even 15 years after the start of transition there remained a huge backlog of unfinished restructuring from the socialist period. This approach therefore delayed some of the pain of restructuring, spread the burden over a much longer period, but in the end might easily cost more than the faster restructuring undertaken elsewhere. That said, restructuring is undoubtedly a difficult and politically risky aspect of the transition, and too much of the external advice to the region took insufficient account of the difficulties and costs.

Last, we comment on some aspects of institutional reforms in the transition economies. Their importance was again often misunderstood or underestimated at the start of transition, at least in part because we teach so little about such matters in standard Western-style economics courses. As a result, in both East and West, few economists – or anyone else for that matter – were particularly well equipped to offer good advice about building institutions, so this aspect of transition was a learning process for everyone. The institutional reforms needed to build a market-type economy are both complex and diverse, as well as sometimes being highly technical and rather boring. The latter points sometimes made it hard to mobilize effective political support even for rather important reforms, since politicians didn't find them interesting enough and most of their constituents didn't understand them anyway. In this category would come such reforms as the adoption of international accounting standards for firms; the introduction of VAT and other standard types of tax; the development of effective competition policy; developing laws to define and protect private property rights; protection for minority shareholders in companies; improvements in banking regulation; and so on. Even in the more developed countries, hardly anyone knows much about such arcane issues and policies, and mostly they are just 'there', quietly working away in the background of our lives, given little or no thought. For the transition economies, almost everything had to be created *ab initio*, and it proved a difficult business, fraught with risks, delays and mistakes.

Outline of the book

With 37 contributions from very diverse authors, all acknowledged experts in their respective fields, it is no easy task to pull all their ideas and findings together into a short summary. To assist our readers, we have grouped all the contributions into nine broad areas, and comment briefly on each area below. Not surprisingly, some authors do not fit neatly under a single heading, but we have done our best to place each contribution into the most appropriate section.

The first part, Introduction, provides an overview of the transition process, with Turley (Chapter 1) summarising the experience of the first two decades of transition, followed by Hare (Chapter 2) highlighting key institutional features of transition, often neglected in early discussions of building a market economy. Nuti (Chapter 3) asks whether transition was conducted in the right way, suggesting that the timing – starting in the years 1990–92 – meant that much external advice was heavily influenced by the so called Washington Consensus. Havrylyshyn (Chapter 4) assesses where we are now, and considers whether transition is essentially over. For those countries that joined the EU in 2004, he finds that it largely is.

The next part, Background, steps back in time to the period of central planning, helping us to understand the initial conditions from which transition to a market-type economy developed. All four chapters focus on the Soviet Union and Russia. Ofer (Chapter 5) and Mau (Chapter 6) both discuss Soviet-type central planning, thinking about its strengths and limitations, possible development strategies, and the reasons why economic growth gradually slowed down after the 1960s. Cooper (Chapter 7) studies a particular sector of the economy, namely defence and production for the military. Under central planning this became an extremely large sector and it enjoyed high priority, ensuring that it had access to the best people and resources to support its production targets. Hence once the USSR disintegrated, this sector faced especially challenging problems of adaptation and adjustment, a process still not completed two decades later. Kotz (Chapter 8) reviews the diverse explanations that have been proposed to explain the apparently sudden collapse of the USSR in 1991, arguing that the contradictions between a socialist system aiming to deliver economic benefits to the population and its control by a small, self-perpetuating party elite lie at the heart of the story.

Part III, Beginnings, covers earlier aspects of transition that continued to prove interesting to observers and analysts, often highly problematic for the countries themselves. Thus, Popov (Chapter 9) examines the transformational recession that affected all transition economies (except those in East Asia) in the early years. For many economists, the recession came as a surprise, especially when, in many countries, it turned out to be deep and enduring. Privatization has always been viewed as a core aspect of transition, since at the start nearly all production was in state hands. Hence, Miller (Chapter 10) has an important topic to summarise. Interestingly, though, since transition is really about building a new private sector economy, it turned out in many countries that starting up lots of new firms was at least as effective as privatization *per se* in accomplishing that. Marangos (Chapter 11) reviews various models of the transition process with a view to establishing a framework for understanding the truly momentous changes that have occurred in Central and Eastern Europe. One of the critical issues for transition was to establish a sustainable fiscal policy that would keep budget deficits within manageable limits and avoid the accumulation of excessive debts. At the start, the importance of all this was poorly understood, and in some countries seriously underestimated, resulting in some terrible consequences. Shabunina (Chapter 12) explains what is needed in this area and outlines where various countries stand.

The international dimension of transition forms the subject of Part IV, Integration. Drabek and Benáček (Chapter 13) deal with the vital issue of foreign trade, something that was massively disrupted at the start of transition since the former socialist modes of trade integration were quickly abandoned. A huge reorientation of trade took place towards western trade partners. This was accompanied, as Brada (Chapter 14) shows, by large flows of foreign direct investment (FDI) into the region. Brada also explores the alternative exchange rate policies that were followed by different countries. The next two chapters deal with EU enlargement, with Csaba (Chapter 15) explaining how the process worked and sketching the political background against which it took place. Mrak and Rojec (Chapter 16) show how the prospect of EU accession actually facilitated transition in some countries, by providing a kind of external anchor for reforms.

This political theme is pursued further in Part V, Political Economy. Treisman (Chapter 17) reminds us that the interest groups and well-connected individuals that emerged from communism had plentiful opportunities to engage in corruption. Some countries were able and willing to put controls and constraints on this process, others much less so, depending on the political configurations in the countries concerned. Bulgaria has been a particularly interesting case, as Dobrinsky (Chapter 18) shows. Political conflicts in the early transition years made it hard to agree on sound macroeconomic policies, and only a major crisis in the late 1990s compelled the politicians to find a better way forward for the country. China has grown rapidly since the late 1970s, and a major puzzle has been to understand why, given the lack of political reform and the absence – until quite recently – of any legal protection for property rights. Woo (Chapter 19) offers explanations in terms of local political configurations, with often tacit understandings that developing new firms would be tolerated and even encouraged by a pragmatic national party leadership. Marer (Chapter 20) shows that Eastern Europe had developed, by the first decade of the 2000s, a fairly effective market-type economic model that was resulting in some degree of catching up to the living standards of western Europe. However, the model proved to incorporate several vulnerabilities which came to the fore once the financial and economic crisis hit the region in 2008 and 2009. Hence, it is time to rethink the model, to make it more robust to economic shocks.

In all economies, the firm is the basic unit of production, and this is the theme of Part VI, Firms. Since it had been largely suppressed under central planning, it is interesting to think about the revival of entrepreneurship as transition proceeds, as Estrin and Mickiewicz (Chapter

21) do. Likewise, under central planning firms could not freely engage in foreign trade, so Halpern (Chapter 22) throws some light on the behaviour of firms once they are indeed able to trade without restriction. Although much privatization took place, the state often retained ownership shares in firms, and ownership structures quickly became quite complicated. Kočenda and Hanousek (Chapter 23) illustrate this for the Czech Republic, though a similar picture would hold for many other countries. Drawing on large enterprise datasets, Carlin and Schaffer (Chapter 24) study aspects of the business environment and its impact on firm behaviour, looking for differences between transition and non-transition economies.

Ultimately, what really matters in transition is how ordinary people fare, what their lives are like, and this is the theme of Part VII, People. Sanfey (Chapter 25) draws on the Life in Transition Survey to show how people feel about transition and their lives after 20 years or so. Views are quite diverse, though not many people – notably among the young – would wish to return to the old system. Under communism, great play was often made of the idea that women were equal to men. Reality was often less impressive than the theory, but there is no doubt that women could do well under communism. Hence once transition got under way, there was concern that women might lose out relatively badly compared to men, as traditional prejudices and customs reasserted themselves. This is what Luke (Chapter 26) reviews. How people fare in rural areas compared to urban dwellers is another interesting aspect of debates about living standards. Cuddy *et al.* (Chapter 27) examine this issue by comparing the experience of rural dwellers in China and Russia. Labour markets as we know them hardly existed before transition, so an important feature of transition has been the emergence of what we might think of as more 'normal' labour markets, with individuals free to come and go between jobs, and free to choose what skills they wish to acquire. Accompanying this has been the development of labour market institutions that we tend to take for granted in Western countries; these are reviewed by Lehmann and Muravyev (Chapter 28).

Next, we have Part VIII, Country Studies. This could have been an enormous section, since each country is different, each has its own idiosyncrasies. We have chosen to focus on four particularly interesting and intriguing countries, plus a group of countries, namely those endowed with abundant natural resources (mostly energy). Our chosen countries are: Serbia, by Uvalic (Chapter 29); Estonia, by Sutela (Chapter 30); Russia, by Hanson (Chapter 31); and East Germany, by Carlin (Chapter 32). Countries rich in natural resources are often thought to have special problems, not least because when institutions are weak the revenue streams generated by natural resources provide massive opportunities for corruption. Hence it is of great interest to consider how the transition economies have managed these challenges, and Pomfret (Chapter 33) reviews that for us.

The final part presents some assessments of transition. Campos and Coricelli (Chapter 34) review transition over the past 20 years, looking at the post-socialist recession, subsequent recovery, and the diverse impact on different countries of various crises. Overall, they find that while Eastern Europe has done moderately well, the CIS region rather less so. The next chapter by Dabrowski (Chapter 35) complements this analysis by considering where Eastern Europe and the CIS countries now stand in the world economy, and what challenges they face. It covers progress in economic transition and political reforms, as well as the role of external anchors. Moving East, Rosefielde (Chapter 36) investigates the transition progress achieved by China and Vietnam (and briefly, Laos and Cambodia). Clearly these countries have grown rapidly and living standards have improved, but there is reason to question how sustainable these achievements might prove to be. Last but not least, Kolodko (Chapter 37) asks whether transition has been worth it, especially for the people of the countries concerned. He shows that with the possible exception of Poland and one or two other countries, overall economic growth since the late 1980s for most transition countries averages out at a very low rate, sometimes even a negative rate. Would people have opted to abandon communism and embark on transition to a market-type economy had they realized how rocky and difficult the subsequent two decades would prove to be? We leave the final judgment about this to our readers.

Notes

1 Some of the points made in this chapter draw on thoughts and observations developed in our own recent books, namely Hare (2010), and Turley and Luke (2010).
2 The status of Kosovo remains complicated. It declared its independence in 2008 following a vote in the Kosovo Assembly and this has been recognized by over 90 states, not including its neighbour, Serbia, which still regards the declaration as illegal. Kosovo is not a UN member (owing to opposition from Russia, among other countries), though it does belong to the IMF and the World Bank.

Bibliography

Hare, Paul G. (2010), *Vodka and Pickled Cabbage: Eastern European Travels of a Professional Economist*, London: Athena Press (reissued 2012, by Create Space).
Turley, Gerard and Luke, Peter J. (2010), *Transition Economics: Two Decades On*, London: Routledge.

Part I
Introduction

1

TRANSITION ECONOMIES

The first two decades[1]

Gerard Turley

With the first two decades of transition over, we can now identify the most important stylized facts of transition from plan to market. Some of these patterns of transition were expected, while others happened as generally predicted but the degree of the change was unexpected. Other developments were altogether surprising. The general patterns of transition are outlined in Table 1.1.

We examine these patterns using data from the transition economies (TEs) for the 20-year period 1989–2008. As many other assessments of transition, quantitative or otherwise, covered only the first decade, there will inevitably be differences in terms of the facts and patterns identified. For example, Campos and Coricelli (2002) limited their analysis of the first decade to seven stylized facts. Although there are some similarities between their magnificent seven and our transition 10, most notably with respect to output and sectoral changes, trade, social costs and institutions, there are also differences in that we highlight additional patterns during transition, pertaining to prices, private sector activity and the role of the state.

Output

All of the former Soviet Union (FSU) countries with the exception of Estonia witnessed an output decline during the first decade of transition. Whereas Latvia and Lithuania experienced relatively mild declines in output, Moldova, Tajikistan and Ukraine suffered average annual declines in excess of 9 per cent, resulting in a GDP level, at the end of the first decade of transition, equal to or more than 50 per cent below what it officially was at the outset of transition. At the other end of the scale, Poland and Slovenia performed the best of the former Soviet bloc countries. Overall, the performance of other Central and Eastern European (CEE) countries in this decade was mixed, with some recording small but positive annual growth rates as against those recording negative average annual growth rates. Output in Russia, at least officially measured, fell by 4.7 per cent per annum, but as with other FSU countries not all of the 1990–2000 decline is owing to transition as the former Soviet Union was already in economic decline before its demise in late 1991. In contrast, for the same period China and Vietnam recorded annual average growth rates of 10.6 per cent and 7.9 per cent, respectively. The difference in performance between China/Vietnam and former Soviet bloc countries has attracted much attention with different views cited on the relative importance of determinants such as initial conditions, market versus institutional reforms, foreign trade and external aid, and political change.

Table 1.1 Two decades of transition: the transition 10

With respect to	Stylized fact
Output	Output declines and then recovers
Prices	Inflation soars and later moderates
Sectoral share of GDP	Major sectoral changes in the composition of GDP, with large increases in services
Private enterprise	Private sector share of GDP rises
Investment and consumption	Investment falls and then recovers, consumption falls and then rises
Foreign trade and FDI	International trade initially falls and then increases, FDI flows increase
Labour market	Participation rates fall as does employment which later increases, unemployment rises
Government revenue and public spending	Role of the state declines as the share of tax and public spending in output falls
Demographics	Demographics deteriorate, then stabilize
Institutions	Institutions initially collapse and are then rebuilt

As for the 2000–08 period (that is, prior to the late 2000s financial crisis), this is recognized as the recovery phase (with the output decline in CEE countries ending well before 2000). Countries that recorded some of the largest output falls in the previous decade were, not surprisingly, the same countries that recorded the biggest annual average growth rates in this period (namely, Azerbaijan, Kazakhstan and Tajikistan, albeit countries that were growing from relatively low bases). Georgia, Moldova and Ukraine also performed well but this only goes some way towards recovering the output loss of the previous decade. Although China and Vietnam continued to perform remarkably well, many of the other TEs, both CEE and FSU countries (including Russia), also performed well in terms of economic growth. Not surprisingly, the countries with the highest initial GDP per capita levels, most notably, the Czech and Slovak Republics, Hungary, Poland and Slovenia, were, more or less, the countries that recorded the lowest annual average growth rates for the period 2000–08. However, we need more data for more years before we can conclude that there is evidence of a 'catch up' or convergence effect.

Prices

The trend in inflation during the transition period was one of rising prices followed by a period when inflation rates fell and then stabilized at, in the majority of cases, single-digit inflation rates. After the initial years of rapid price increases, inflation had peaked by the early to mid-1990s and, thereafter, the rate of price increase decelerated in the majority of cases. For some countries, a second bout of inflation occurred in the late 1990s, coinciding with the 1998 Russian crisis and its aftermath. Inflation rates were highest among FSU countries and the Balkans with Central European economies recording the lowest inflation rates of former socialist countries.

For the majority of TEs, the peak of inflation was early on in transition and coincided with liberalization policies. All countries except Bulgaria recorded their highest annual inflation rate in the period 1989–94, with the majority (including all FSU countries) witnessing a peak in inflation between 1992 and 1994. The maximum inflation rate varied from a moderate 24 per cent and 35 per cent in China and Hungary respectively to hyperinflation rates in excess of 4,500 per cent per annum in Armenia, Croatia, Georgia and Ukraine, with Georgia's 1994 inflation rate one of the world's highest rates of inflation in modern times (Table 1.2).

Table 1.2 Inflation in transition economies

Country	Inflation rate at outset of transition (1991)	Maximum inflation rate (annual average)	Year in which inflation peaked (1989–2008)	No. of consecutive years in which annual inflation exceeded 40%	Year in which inflation rate first fell below 40%	Inflation reversal[b]	Year(s) of reversal	Inflation in 2008[c]
Albania	35.5	226	1992	2	1994	Yes	1997/08	3.4
Armenia	274	4,964	1994	5	1996	No	na	9.0
Azerbaijan	107	1,664	1994	5	1996	No	na	20.8
Belarus	94.1	2,220	1994	12	2003	Yes	1999/2000	14.8
Bosnia and Herzegovina	:	:	:	:	:	:	:	7.4
Bulgaria	334	1,058	1997	7	1998	Yes	1996/07	12.4
China[a]	0.7	24	1994	0	na	No	na	5.9
Croatia	123	6,674	1992	4	1995	No	na	6.1
Czech Republic	52	52	1991	1	1992	No	na	6.4
Estonia	211	1,076	1992	4	1995	No	na	10.4
FYR Macedonia	115	1,511	1992	4	1995	No	na	8.3
Georgia	79	22,286	1994	5	1996	Yes	1999	10.0
Hungary	35	35	1991	0	na	Yes	1995/06	6.1
Kazakhstan	78.8	1,877	1994	5	1996	No	na	17.2
Kyrgyzstan	85	855	1992	5	1996	Yes	1999/2000	24.5
Latvia	172	951	1992	3	1994	No	na	15.4
Lithuania	225	1,021	1992	4	1995	No	na	10.9
Moldova	98	1,276	1992	4	1995	Yes	1999/2000	12.8
Mongolia	20.2	268	1993	5	1997	No	na	25.1
Montenegro	:	:	:	:	:	:	:	9.0
Poland	70.3	586	1990	4	1993	No	na	4.4
Romania	170	255	1993	4/8 in total	1995	Yes	1997	7.8
Russia	92.7	1,526	1992	6/7 in total	1997	Yes	1999	14.1
Serbia	:	:	:	:	:	:	:	12.4
Slovak Republic	61.2	61	1991	1	1992	No	na	4.6
Slovenia	118	1,306	1989	4	1993	No	na	5.6

(continued on next page)

Table 1.2 (continued)

Country	Inflation rate at outset of transition (1991)	Maximum inflation rate (annual average)	Year in which inflation peaked (1989–2008)	No. of consecutive years in which annual inflation exceeded 40%	Year in which inflation rate first fell below 40%	Inflation reversal[b]	Year(s) of reversal	Inflation in 2008[c]
Tajikistan	112	2,885	1993	8	1999	Yes	1995	20.9
Turkmenistan	103	3,102	1993	7	1998	No	na	14.5
Ukraine	91	4,735	1993	6	1997	Yes	1999/2000	25.2
Uzbekistan	82.2	1,568	1994	7	1998	No	na	12.7
Vietnam[a]	487	84	1991	1	1992	Yes	1995	23.1

Sources: UNECE Statistical Division Database, compiled from national and international (CIS, EUROSTAT, IMF, OECD) official sources; ESCAP.

Notes:

a Economic transition in China and Vietnam began in 1978 and 1986, respectively. The inflation rates in column two are for these respective years.

b Excluding the impact of the 2008/09 financial crisis.

c The trend of single-digit inflation rates was halted, temporarily at least, in 2008 by the financial crisis when transition (and non-transition) countries witnessed a general rise in inflation rates.

Despite the common trend of a peak in inflation in early years, economies in transition experienced much cross-country variation. This is evident in the number of years in which inflation was high, measured at above 40 per cent, ranging from (aside from non-reforming Belarus and Turkmenistan) zero years in China and Hungary to eight years in Romania and Tajikistan. It is also evident in the occurrence of inflation reversals, defined as a reversal in a downward trend. In the case of the TEs, it is evenly split between countries that did not experience an inflation reversal and those countries that did. Half of the inflation reversals were in the years 1999/2000, with inflation rates in most of the Commonwealth of Independent States (CIS) countries, including Russia, related to the aftermath of the 1998 Russian crisis and the subsequent boost in economic activity and prices.

By 2007 the average inflation rate for TEs was about 7.0 per cent, representing significant progress from the early years. The highest inflation rate in 2007 was a moderate 16.6 per cent, in Azerbaijan, a country that witnessed extraordinary output growth (oil-related) in those years. Unfortunately, these numbers do not tell the full story, as events were to unfold a short time later. Many of the TEs, and particularly in Eastern Europe, were overheating by the late 2000s, reflected in large current account deficits and rising debt levels. With fixed exchange rates the preferred currency policy of a number of TEs, short-term inflows and a credit boom led to a surge in money supply growth and inflation by 2008. More than half of the 31 TEs had double-digit inflation rates in 2008. These weaknesses were further aggravated by the global crisis of 2008/09, with financial markets turning their attention to the most vulnerable Eastern European nations. By the end of the second decade, output decline, recession and deflation rather than inflation had become the main concern for many of the Eastern European transition countries.

Sectoral shares of GDP

The sectoral shares of output are only one of a number of measures that can be used to capture the economic structure of a country. Given that structural changes are central to the transformation process, large changes in the sectoral composition of output were to be expected. In socialist times, industry shares in excess of 50 per cent were common whereas only Croatia and Slovenia had a services share in excess of 50 per cent, typical levels of services for upper-middle-income countries. These high industry shares combined with relatively low services shares were viewed as a serious structural distortion, reflecting a degree of over-industrialisation that required correction.

The reallocation of resources during transition did see, as was predicted, a decline in the industry shares in value added and an increase in the services share, reflecting a catching up with market economies. The evidence indicates that large-scale de-agrarianization (but not in all TEs as we will see later), deindustrialization and tertiarization did indeed take place in transition countries since 1989 (Landesmann 2000). Within five years of the start of transition, the industry share had declined to, on average, 35 per cent (from an average of 42 per cent at the outset) and there was a steady but slow decline to just under the 33 per cent average that transition countries witnessed by 2008.

The deindustrialization that is a common feature in market economies over time as they become more developed appears to have been accelerated in TEs, i.e. the rate of decline in CEE countries (from, on average, 46 per cent in 1990 to, on average, 30 per cent in 2008) is greater than the rate of decline in either upper-middle-income or high-income countries. With respect to industry shares in China, it remains relatively high, with a 47 per cent share in 1979 when reforms began and after three decades of transition, the industry share remains, as a percentage of GDP, in the high 40s, second only to oil-rich Azerbaijan. Vietnam has witnessed an even larger increase since reforms began, from a 28 per cent share in 1987 to a 40 per cent share of GDP in 2008, with much of that increase occurring in the past decade or so.

As for services, at the beginning of transition, the services share of GDP was, on average, only 34 per cent for TEs, as compared with, on average, 43 per cent in low-income countries and 45 per cent in middle-income countries. After two decades of transition and structural change, the services share of GDP in TEs has increased, on average, to 57 per cent in 2008. Again, this is more in line with the 53 per cent average rate for middle income countries but still below the figure of about 60 per cent for upper-middle income countries. With respect to regional differences between CEE and CIS countries, the gap that existed between the two groups of countries at the start of transition has widened after two decades: 39 per cent compared with 32 per cent in 1989 whereas in 2008 it was 64 per cent for CEE countries as against a lowly 51 per cent for CIS countries. Indeed, four CIS countries still had, as of the late 2000s, an agriculture share of GDP equal to or in excess of 20 per cent. As for East Asian countries, the services share of GDP was low at the outset of transition. Despite some increases, it remains relatively low by international standards: in 2008 the services share in value added is 42 per cent and 38 per cent in China and Vietnam, respectively, below the, on average, 46 per cent share for low income and lower-middle income countries.

Private enterprise

With the exceptions of Hungary and Poland, private-sector activities in socialist countries accounted for, on average, no more than 5–10 per cent of GDP. By the mid-1990s, however, the private sector/GDP ratio had risen to in excess of 40 per cent, on average. Given the emphasis on early privatization in CEE and FSU countries, much of the increase in the early years of transition was due to the rapid implementation of privatization programmes. In other countries, particularly Hungary and Poland, the increase was due largely to *de novo* new private firms, the vast majority of which were SMEs in the services sector. Indeed, the importance of new firm formation was widely underestimated in the early years of transition.

By the end of the first decade, the private sector share of GDP was 60 per cent, on average, and rising. Second and third wave privatizations, in addition to new private firms, have seen the private sector account for two-thirds of all economic activity by 2005. In some cases, namely the Czech and Slovak Republics, Estonia and Hungary, the private sector share of GDP is 80 per cent, in excess of the equivalent figure for many well established Western European countries. Even more remarkable, and despite some setbacks, was the extent of the increase in private sector activity in both Russia and China.

In the case of Russia, the most important successor state to the Soviet Union where the ideological opposition to private ownership was the strongest, the private sector share of GDP was reported to be 70 per cent at the end of the first decade of transition. Given the history of communism and the Marxist-Leninist ideology, this level of private ownership is remarkable. Unfortunately, this quite astounding transformation is not the full story as the broad numbers do not tell us much about the quality of the private sector. Given the insider privatization of the early 1990s, the much needed enterprise restructuring and improvement in corporate governance and firm performance that was to follow from the change in ownership did not materialise in all cases. In more recent years, the increase in the share of private sector activity was halted, and possibly slightly reversed, by Putin's efforts to renationalise parts of Russian industry. Despite this recent trend and the oligarchic nature of many sectors that typify Russian industry, the Russian economy today, at least in terms of the division of ownership between private and public, resembles, more or less, other middle-income market economies where private enterprise dominates.

The process was very different in China. For one, reforms initially took place in agriculture with the household responsibility system. In contrast, privatization (of industry, at least) was not formally part of the reform agenda, until some time later. The large state-owned enterprises (SOEs) were not initially slated for privatization. Yet, market reforms did result in an initial increase in private enterprise, although small and often rural in nature. The emergence of small private firms and household business activities, combined later with the privatization of many township and village enterprises (TVEs), saw the private sector share of GDP in China exceed 50 per cent by the mid 1990s. This privatization from below was initially tolerated by government officials and later encouraged, given the apparent increases in output generated by these private enterprises. Of course, China has had a long tradition of entrepreneurship and private enterprise. Before 1949 China had a history of small rural private businesses, which distinguishes it from Russia where in pre-Soviet Union times, the Russian Tsars ruled over their fiefdoms and permitted little or no private enterprise as we know it today. In China, as in many Central European countries, what we witnessed in the first two decades of transition is simply a revival of the private enterprise that flourished pre-socialism.

Investment and consumption

One of the features of the socialist system was high levels of investment expenditure, at the expense of consumption. Investment ratios in 1989 were high in socialist countries, at 34 per cent of GDP in Russia and CEE countries, 26 per cent in China and 31 per cent in other Newly Independent States (NISs) and Mongolia. Benchmark rates for the industrialized world were lower, at 25 per cent for middle-income countries and 22 per cent for OECD countries (World Bank, 1996).

Investment rates were at their highest in the early years of socialist development but by the end of the socialist regime, investment had started to decline. Prior to transition, with the Soviet Union and its satellite states in a deep malaise, and with a looming budgetary crisis across the socialist world, investment expenditure was falling. Much of the capital stock on the eve of transition was in need of serious upgrade; some was simply obsolete. With transition looming, and economic reforms accelerating, the investment expenditure share was expected to decline (but with an improvement in investment efficiency), accompanied by a large boost in the consumption expenditure share of GDP.

Prior to transition, the investment ratio for TEs was, on average, 28 per cent. This compares to average rates of less than 20 per cent for low-income countries, and low to mid 20s for middle- and high-income countries. Within TEs there were sizeable differences, with a rate of 32 per cent in Russia to only 13 per cent in Vietnam. The last few years of the socialist system witnessed a sharp decline in the investment rate, to an average rate of 20 per cent, with these low levels persisting throughout the early years of transition. Although there was a slight recovery in the mid-1990s, levels for TEs remained, on average, low throughout the first decade of transition and even into the early years of the 2000s. However, by the mid-2000s, investment rates had recovered, so that by 2005 the investment ratio had reached, on average, 25 per cent (close to the average rate for middle-income countries). Some cross-country comparisons are worth noting. For example, investment in Russia, as a percentage of GDP, fell from a high of 32 per cent in 1989 to a low of 14 per cent in 1999 before recovering to 22 per cent in 2008. In contrast, investment in China has remained high, from 26 per cent in the late 1980s rising steadily to over 40 per cent in 2008.

As for consumption, prior to transition, consumption expenditure as a proportion of GDP for TEs was, on average, less than 60 per cent. This compares to an average rate, in 1989, of 79 per cent for low-income countries and 60 per cent for middle-income countries. As predicted, transition to the market economy, involving early reforms of liberalization and marketization, resulted in a rise in consumption expenditure relative to GDP levels. Throughout the first decade of transition, the consumption/GDP ratio rose steadily, from 62 per cent, on average, in 1992 to 68 per cent, on average, in 1999. Since then, with the main market reforms already in place, and with the reallocation of goods from investment to consumption already completed, the consumption ratio has tended to remain steady, in the 65–67 per cent range, with sizeable cross-country variations persisting.

Foreign trade and foreign direct investment

The collapse of the Council for Mutual Economic Assistance (CMEA) in 1991 had a detrimental effect on trade flows in the region – a region of the world whose share of global trade was in decline long before 1990/91 – and, in turn, on economic activity. With the disintegration of inter-republic trade links and a collapse of the payments system, it is not surprising that trade volumes in TEs fell early on in transition. Nevertheless, by the mid-1990s, there was a recovery in trade volumes across the TEs, although the 1998 Russian crisis was to prove a further setback for many of the CIS countries. CEE countries began to witness an increase in trade flows and greater diversification of trade, both in terms of export markets (with a surprisingly rapid redirection of trade towards EU markets) and the commodity composition of exports. Reorientation of trade by CIS countries was much slower. Many of the richer CIS countries still tended to export fuels and primary commodities, while importing mainly manufactured and consumer goods.

Foreign direct investment (FDI) flows to socialist countries were virtually absent prior to transition, largely owing to the Communist regimes and associated policies that were in place across the region. One of the expectations of transition was for a flow of FDI to TEs once reforms had begun. Indeed, FDI did flow to former socialist countries but not by as much in the early years as had originally being predicted. There was also a large cross-country variation, with the Czech Republic, Estonia and Hungary doing best and the least reforming economies or countries engaged in civil or international war faring the worst. Despite Russia's great potential, FDI flows in the first decade of transition were low, outstripped by massive capital flight. Political and economic uncertainty, an unfavourable business climate, fears of default, a burdensome government bureaucracy, insecure protection of property rights and weak contract enforcement were often cited as reasons why foreign investors were reluctant to invest in Russia. By the end of the first decade, however, FDI flows to some TEs were relatively large overall, but were still highly concentrated with just three CEE countries accounting for two-thirds of total FDI investment.

The two trends identified above, notably the greater trade openness and the increase in FDI flows are confirmed by the data. However, as with other data for TEs, trade statistics, whether it is for cross-country comparisons or country comparisons before and after transition, need to be treated with caution. As transition has progressed, the trade ratio for TEs has increased to over 100 per cent by the mid-2000s. Although this trade/GDP ratio appears to be high as compared with average ratios for World Bank income classification country groupings, the group of TEs, compared with low-income or lower-middle-income groups, contains many small countries *and* many developed countries, both of which generally tend to have high trade/GDP ratios.

As for FDI flows, expressed as a percentage of GDP, very low levels of FDI pertained at the outset of transition. However, within a few years, FDI flows in some countries, most notably some of the more advanced, reforming EU accession countries were close to, and in some cases exceeded, 5 per cent of annual GDP. In addition, both the East Asian countries of China and Vietnam and oil-rich Azerbaijan, Kazakhstan and Turkmenistan fared well in attracting FDI. As stated earlier, FDI flows to Russia, despite the attraction of natural resources and minerals, were low throughout most of the transition period, with some minor improvement in later years. Indeed, China has done consistently better than Russia in attracting FDI and this factor may partly explain differences in performance between the two big transition countries (acknowledging that the causation may be two-way, i.e. high and improving levels of economic activity may lead to higher flows of FDI).

Labour market

Transition from plan to market involves a reallocation of labour across locations, jobs, sectors and occupations. In their account of transition, Campos and Coricelli (2002) identify changes in the labour market as one of transition's stylized facts. Ironically, and as acknowledged by the authors, labour in CEE/FSU countries did not move much in the literal sense, that is, geographically. Although EU accession did see an increase in migration from the EU accession countries to EU-15 member states, labour mobility within former Soviet bloc countries has been relatively low by international standards. Of course, labour mobility within China has been far greater, with tens of millions moving from rural to urban areas. In other respects, labour in TEs did indeed move, but again, whether it is inter-industry or inter-occupational mobility, worker flows in TEs were somewhat low compared with mobility in some other regions.

In the early years of transition, there were significant labour flows out of the labour force. A feature of the socialist system was high labour force participation rates. In 1989 the labour force participation rate for the TEs was, on average, close to 70 per cent, well above the average rate for upper-middle and high-income countries and similar to average rates for lower-middle and low-income countries. Moreover, female participation rates, by international standards, were high in former socialist countries ranging from, in per cent of the working-age population group, on average, the high 50s in some CEE countries to rates in excess of 70 per cent in some of the Central and East Asian countries. During the first two decades of transition, labour force participation rates fell in the vast majority of TEs. By 2007/08, the labour force participation rate for TEs was, on average, almost 10 percentage points lower than at the start of transition. This decline was not uniform across all transition countries. In many TEs the fall in participation rates was greater for females than for males, indicating that women, at least in those early years of transition, suffered disproportionately from the deteriorating conditions in the labour market.

Labour moved into unemployment (or inactivity), with a subsequent rise in unemployment rates throughout the transition region. With output falling, drastically in some TEs, in the early years of transition, the adjustment in labour markets came in the form of falling employment (and rising unemployment), reductions in real wages or a combination of both. On average, in CEE countries, employment took the brunt of the labour market adjustment. In contrast, CIS countries witnessed a large reduction in real wages. As a result, joblessness has been much more of a feature in CEE countries than CIS countries, during transition.

Employment losses as opposed to gains dominated the early years of transition but there was a welcome reversal of that trend in the second decade, associated with the recovery in output. Aside from Turkmenistan (where data are unreliable) and Uzbekistan (where the output collapse was relatively small), only the East Asian countries of China and Vietnam recorded any significant increases in employment by 2000/01. Employment reductions in the first decade of transition were very large in some countries, both for males and females.

Labour moved from the state sector to the private sector, from large enterprises to SMEs and self-employment, and from agriculture (but not in all TEs as some FSU countries – mainly the Caucasus and Central Asian republics – witnessed an increase in numbers engaged in subsistence farming) and industry to services. These reflected considerable changes in the sectoral distribution of employment (and by occupation), corresponding to the major sectoral changes in the composition of output already alluded to. Differences between the transition experiences of CEE and CIS countries are again evident here with respect to labour market adjustment trajectories, with the CEE countries witnessing swift structural change, sizeable labour adjustment and high unemployment rates whereas, in contrast, the CIS countries have seen slower structural change, sluggish employment response to output changes, and a more gradual rise in (official) unemployment.

Government revenue and spending

The fiscal system that existed under the socialist command economy was very different from the system common in market economies. Once the socialist system collapsed, TEs had to build a market-oriented, rule-based tax system from scratch. Partly because of this, coupled with the collapse in output and incomes, the first decade of transition witnessed a sharp fall in government revenues. This is a trend that had started before the demise of the socialist system, with revenues falling relative to output in the last few years of the centrally planned economy.

Cross-regional variation was evident, with revenues in CEE countries in some years 10 percentage points of GDP higher than in CIS countries in the early years of transition. With the SOEs' losses mounting, and with the more profitable new private firms, mainly SMEs, difficult to tax, government revenues fell. The fiscal crisis that many CIS countries experienced culminated in the 1998 Russian crash. Revenues did improve somewhat after that, owing primarily to the recovery in output experienced by all TEs. The East Asian countries of China and Vietnam tended to have lower levels of government revenue, as one might expect from countries at lower levels of economic development, as measured by income per capita.

Given the high levels of public expenditure during Soviet times, it was expected that the former socialist countries when embarking on transition would experience a fall in government spending, to more 'normal' levels. This indeed was the case. In many countries (CEE countries in particular) budgetary subsidies and military spending fell to the much lower levels common in mature market economies. In the majority of TEs the fiscal contraction did not materialise from a concerted effort to rationalise spending priorities or a systematic reassessment of government obligations. Much of the fiscal adjustment on the expenditure side, and especially so in CIS countries, came about through sequestration, non-payment and expenditure arrears.

Government expenditure as a percentage of GDP was high (much less in China and Vietnam), close to 50 per cent (as it was in the last few years of the Soviet Union) and 55 per cent (as it was, on average, in Eastern European countries) and, in some cases, even higher (with rates of close to 60 per cent in Czechoslovakia and Hungary, pre-transition). Given the level of development, that was unusually high (what Kornai called the 'premature welfare state') and comparable to levels found in the high tax-high spending Nordic countries whose level of income per capita is much higher.

At the beginning of transition, government spending, despite the turmoil of the years preceding the demise of the socialist system, was still high by international standards. Within a few years, that ratio had fallen below the 40 per cent threshold. After twenty years of transition, government spending as a percentage of GDP has fallen about 10 percentage points, on average, to 35–37 per cent of GDP, a figure more in line with levels found in countries at similar levels of economic development and income per capita. There is still much cross-country variation, with the high income countries of Croatia, the Czech Republic, Hungary and Slovenia all with government spending/GDP ratios of 40 per cent or higher. Although there may be an issue over the sustainability of these expenditure levels, it is nevertheless true that in the early and difficult years of transition these levels of social expenditure and investments were important in maintaining public support for market reforms (often in the face of much criticism from vested interests) and did manage to partly cushion the worst effects of transition. In contrast, at the other end of the spectrum are countries such as Armenia, China and Turkmenistan with a government spending/GDP ratio of 20 per cent or less.

Demographics

One of the surprises, and most alarming trends, of transition has being the change in demographics. Since transition began in CEE/FSU countries, a disturbing pattern of falling fertility rates, rising mortality rates, falling life expectancy at birth rates and overall, a decline in population has emerged. This compares sharply with transition in the East Asian countries of China and Vietnam where population numbers keep on rising. The decline in population in Soviet bloc countries over this period is contrary to what one expects for middle income countries whose demographics, on average, tend to improve.

Excluding China and Vietnam, the population of CEE/FSU countries on the eve of transition, taking 1989 as a reference point, was 402.5 million. By 2008 the population had fallen to 396.5 million, a decline of 1.5 per cent, with most of that occurring in Eastern Europe. The decline in FSU countries was even greater. Of the non-war-torn CEE countries, Romania and Bulgaria have recorded the largest declines, 7 per cent and 15 per cent, respectively. It is, however, the FSU countries that have witnessed the largest declines in population numbers. Taking 1991/92 as the start of transition for FSU countries, the majority of former republics of the Soviet Union witnessed a fall in population. In terms of percentages for the period 1991–2008, Georgia suffered a decline in excess of a 20 per cent with Armenia, Estonia, Latvia, Moldova and Ukraine all suffering population declines in excess of 10 per cent (Table 1.3). Although some of these countries did witness conflict early on in transition, others did not, indicating that the reasons for their decline in population lie elsewhere.

In terms of numbers, the majority of the population decline in TEs was in Russia and Ukraine. The population of Russia fell from 148.6 million in 1991 to 142 million by 2008; in Ukraine, the population declined from 52 million in 1991 to 46.3 million in 2008. In contrast, all the most advanced CEE countries (with the exception of Hungary) witnessed over the period 1989–2008 either no change in population, or in the case of the Slovak Republic, a small increase. Interestingly, of the four least advanced reforming TEs only Belarus suffered a decline in population with the other three countries recording large increases. It is difficult to establish how much, if any at all, of the rise in population in these countries is owing to delayed reforms (and less subsequent economic disruption and social upheaval) as opposed to other non-policy factors, such as, for example, all three having large Muslim populations.

With respect to fertility rates, a downward trend was evident *before* the collapse of the socialist system: aside from the trend in middle and high income countries for lower fertility rates, the decline, accelerating in the 1989–91 years, may have been the result of the stagnation and the deepening economic and social crisis emerging in the Soviet Union and its satellite states in the late 1980s. By the mid-1990s many former socialist countries, particularly in Eastern Europe, had some of the lowest fertility rates in the world. The rapid decline in fertility rates continued, with cross-country variations increasing, as the social upheaval persisted and poor economic conditions continued for many of the transition countries and its peoples. Rising unemployment and poverty, falling real wages and declining state supports to the family may have depressed fertility further as family circumstances remained uncertain. However, with the recovery of output well underway in all transition countries by the late 1990s the decline in fertility rates noticeably decelerated.

Table 1.3 Population changes[a]

Country	1989	1991 (for FSU and Mongolia)	2008	1989–2008, +ive % Δ[d]	1989–2008, –ive % Δ[d]	Transition period % Δ (for FSU and East Asian countries)[e]	Number of years of decline	Year(s) of largest decline	Largest yearly decline, %	Years of consecutive decline
Albania	3,256,484		3,143,291		-2		8	1994	-1.4	1992–1999
Armenia	3,542,717	3,512,056	3,077,087		-12	-12	15	1994	-2.4	1991–2005
Azerbaijan	7,085,000	7,271,000	8,680,100	24		19				
Belarus	10,170,000	10,194,000	9,680,850		-5	-5	15	1998; 2002–2005	-0.5	1994–2008
Bosnia and Herzegovina	4,367,068		3,773,100		-13		8	1991–1995	-5.1	1990–1995; 2007–2008
Bulgaria	8,877,000		7,623,395		-15		20	2001	-1.9	1989–2008
China[b]	1,118,650,000		1,324,655,100	20		38				
Croatia	4,767,000		4,434,000		-7		6	1991	-5.8	1991–1992
Czech Republic	10,362,000		10,424,336	no change[f]			18	1993		1991–2008
Estonia	1,568,000	1,561,000	1,340,675		-14	-14	18	1993	-2.6	1991–2008
FYR Macedonia	1,893,436		2,041,342	9						
Georgia	5,466,122	5,418,451	4,307,011		-21	-21	19	1994	-2.0	1990–2008
Hungary	10,398,261		10,038,188		-4		18	1989	-0.4	1989–1990; 1993–2008
Kazakhstan	16,249,500	16,450,500	15,674,000		-3	-5	10	1995	-1.8	1992–2001
Kyrgyzstan	4,340,000	4,495,000	5,277,900	24		17				
Latvia	2,684,000	2,662,000	2,266,094		-15	-15	19	1993	-1.8	1990–2008
Lithuania	3,691,000	3,704,000	3,358,115		-8	-9	17	2000	-0.9	1992–2008
Moldova	4,345,161	4,375,424	3,633,369		-16	-17	15	2001–2003; 2006	-1.4	1994–2008
Mongolia	2,171,336	2,243,379	2,641,216	25		18				
Montenegro	582,633		622,344	7						
Poland	37,963,000		38,125,759	no change[f]						
Romania	23,152,000		21,513,622		-7		18	1992	-1.7	1991–2008

Table 1.3 (continued)

Country	1989	1991 (for FSU and Mongolia)	2008	1989–2008, +ive % Δ[d]	1989–2008, −ive % Δ[d]	Transition period % Δ (for FSU and East Asian countries)[e]	Number of years of decline	Year(s) of largest decline	Largest yearly decline, %	Years of consecutive decline
Russia	147,721,000	148,624,000	141,950,000		-3	-4	15	2003–2006	-0.5	1993–1999; 2001–2008
Serbia	..		7,350,221							
Slovak Republic	5,297,000		5,406,626	2						
Slovenia	1,999,400		2,021,316	no change[f]						
Tajikistan	5,170,280	5,419,016	6,836,083	36		26				
Turkmenistan	3,570,616	3,772,488	5,043,618	45		34				
Ukraine	51,773,000	52,000,470	46,258,200		-10	-11	15	2000–2002	-1.0	1994–2008
Uzbekistan	20,033,394	20,952,000	27,313,700	40		30				
Vietnam[c]	64,774,000		86,210,781	36		43				
Total for TEs (excl. China and Vietnam)	402,496,408		396,505,337		-1.5					
Total for FSU countries		290,411,405	284,696,802							

Source: World Bank Development Indicators.

Notes:

a Midyear estimates.

b China's estimated population in 1978 at the start of reforms was 958.8 million.

c Vietnam's estimated population in 1986 at the start of reforms was 60.2 million.

d The percentages reported here are for the 20-year period 1989–2008, with 1988 (not reported here) as the base.

e Only reporting TEs with a transition start date other than 1989.

f No change is reported when the population changes by one per cent or less.

Is transition a killer? was a question posed by the 1996 World Bank Development Report, *From Plan to Market.* This was in response to rising mortality rates in FSU countries, particularly in Kazakhstan, Russia and Ukraine, but also in the three Baltic States, indicating that despite much of the media attention directed toward the Russian mortality crisis, it was as much a post-Soviet crisis and post-socialist phenomenon, affecting many FSU countries. Identifying precise causes for falling male life expectancy rates and rising mortality rates is a highly complex question. As with fertility, mortality rates were on the increase in the Soviet Union long before transition and, indeed, the upward trend goes as far back as the Brezhnev era. Other than the small reversal in the trend in the mid 1980s, the pattern has been one of rising mortality rates, accelerating from the years 1989–91 onward. With the rise in death rates particularly prevalent among males of working age, various well documented explanations have been cited in the literature for the rise in mortality rates. It remains a vexed topic.

Institutions

In any setting, a stable society requires a set of rules and social norms for behaviour. Measuring institutions empirically is a difficult task where despite recent research and some advances there is no consensus on a precise metric. As of now, there is no universal measure (nor is it clear that there should be) that captures the different aspects of institutions and institutional change. Although there is great temptation to report some of the actual numerics of the different dimensions of institutional change during transition (as, for example, for the period 1996–2008 in Kaufmann *et al.*, 2009), we provide, as an alternate, a descriptive account of developments with respect to institutional quality and change. We reproduce, in Table 1.4, an updated version of a table from Murrell (2003) where, using the World Bank Governance Indicators, the direction of change for each of the six indicators for all TEs is given (where I = improvement; D = Deterioration). The overall evidence is mixed, with sizeable improvements in some dimensions (particularly government effectiveness and regulatory quality) and some countries (most notably in Croatia, Estonia, Latvia, Serbia, the Slovak Republic and Tajikistan) and, in contrast, less so in other dimensions (rule of law, and voice and accountability) and other countries (China, Hungary, Kyrgyzstan, Moldova, Mongolia and Vietnam).

After over two decades, although much progress has been made, there is still a long way to go in improving the institutional quality in many former socialist countries and, most especially, the CIS countries. Nevertheless, given an earlier view that institution building is inevitably a slow process, many countries did manage their institutional construction surprisingly quickly and successfully (Murrell 2003).

In sum, with the notable exception of China, transition witnessed the destruction of the institutional structures of the socialist system and an institutional vacuum for much of the early years of transition. As time passed and state capacity improved, institutions were developed and rebuilt, with more progress in CEE than in CIS countries. By the end of the second decade, a majority of the former socialist countries had many of the market-supporting institutions common in other non-socialist emerging markets and countries at similar levels of development. The question of how the quality of institutions can be improved in the laggard CIS countries remains an outstanding issue.

Conclusion

Some of the stylized facts or patterns of transition as witnessed in the first 20 years were expected, such as the rise in services and private sector activities, the fall in government expenditure, the rise in foreign trade and FDI, and the increase in unemployment. Others happened generally as

Table 1.4 Institutional change 1996–2008[a,b,c,d]

Country	Voice and accountability	Political stability and absence of violence	Government effectiveness	Regulatory quality	Rule of law	Control of corruption	Number of institutional dimensions improving
CEE and Baltics							
Albania	I	I	D	I	D	D	3
Bosnia and Herzegovina	I	D	I	I	D	D	3
Bulgaria	I	I	I	I	no change	I	5
Croatia	I	I	I	I	I	I	6
Czech Republic	I	D	I	I	no change	D	3
Estonia	I	I	I	I	I	I	6
FYR Macedonia	I	D	I	I	D	I	4
Hungary	D	D	no change	I	D	D	1
Latvia	I	I	I	I	I	I	6
Lithuania	D	I	I	I	I	I	5
Poland	D	I	D	I	D	D	2
Romania	I	D	I	I	I	I	5
Serbia	I	I	I	I	I	I	6
Slovak Republic	I	I	I	I	I	I	6
Slovenia	D	I	I	no change	I	D	3
CIS							
Armenia	I	D	I	I	I	I	5
Azerbaijan	D	I	I	I	I	I	5
Belarus	D	I	I	I	D	I	4
Georgia	I	D	I	I	I	I	5
Kazakhstan	D	I	I	I	I	D	4
Kyrgyzstan	no change	I	D	I	D	D	1
Moldova	D	D	D	D	D	D	0
Russia	D	I	I	D	D	D	2
Tajikistan	I	I	I	I	I	I	6
Turkmenistan	D	I	I	I	D	I	4
Ukraine	I	I	I	I	D	I	5
Uzbekistan	D	D	I	I	D	D	2

(continued on next page)

Table 1.4 (continued)

Country	Voice and accountability	Political stability and absence of violence	Government effectiveness	Regulatory quality	Rule of law	Control of corruption	Number of institutional dimensions improving
East Asia							
China	D	D	I	D	D	D	1
Mongolia	D	D	D	I	D	D	1
Vietnam	D	no change	no change	D	I	D	1
Number of TEs for which the institutional score has improved	15	17	23	25	14	16	
% of TEs improving	50%	57%	77%	83%	47%	53%	

Sources: Adapted from Murrell, 2003; Kaufmann et al., 2009.

Notes

a Choosing 2006 (as opposed to 2008 when the global crisis may have had an impact on the numbers) as the end-year makes little difference in terms of overall results.

b 1996 is the earliest year for which the WGI are available.

c No change is when the score moves up or down by 0.03 or less between the years 1996 and 2008.

d The decline in institutional quality that is evident in some countries over time requires careful interpretation. For example, whereas the decline in Hungary is from a position where the institutional quality was relatively high in the mid-1990s, the decline in Kyrgyzstan and Moldova reflects a continuous deterioration from levels that were already very low at the outset. The Chinese case is different again as many of its institutions differ from the standard institutions and this is reflected in its low scores.

predicted but the degree of the change was unexpected, such as the rapid rise in prices and the sudden collapse in revenues. Other developments were simply unexpected. This includes the decline in output and most alarmingly, the fall in population associated with the unprecedented, at least in peacetime in industrialized nations, rise in mortality rates.

As regards these patterns of transition, there are differences between regions/countries and over time. In respect of the latter, the early years recorded the worst features of transition whereas, in general (and before the 2008/09 financial crisis), the second decade of transition witnessed a recovery. In respect of country and regional differences, the biggest difference is between Soviet bloc countries and the East Asian countries of China and Vietnam. Aside from some similarities (increase in services, private enterprise, trade), many of the most disturbing trends (unexpected fall in output and population, big rise in prices) were not experienced in either China or Vietnam. Within the Soviet bloc countries, there are also differences, along the lines of CEE (including the Baltic states) versus CIS countries, with the CEE countries doing much better in terms of output, inflation, private enterprise and demographics.

Note

1 My thanks to Peter Luke, Paul Hare, John McHale and Robert Langham for reading an earlier version of this paper. I am grateful to Taylor & Francis for giving us permission to reprint this paper, albeit in a much shorter form, which first appeared as a chapter in Turley and Luke (2010), *Transition Economics: Two Decades On*, London: Routledge. The longer version included other patterns, in relation to corruption and the informal economy, poverty and inequality. They are excluded from this paper not because they are less important but largely because they are, by their very nature, more difficult to measure and quantify, with more recent data (that is, for the late 2000s) difficult to obtain and verify. Finally, this paper deliberately excludes the 2008/09 financial crisis and its aftermath as it distorts the intended purpose of our analysis, namely the performance of and outcomes in transition countries arising from the transition process, systemic change and subsequent market and institutional reforms.

Bibliography

Campos, Nauro F. and Coricelli, Fabrizio (2002), 'Growth in Transition: what we know, what we don't, and what we should', *Journal of Economic Literature*, vol. 40(3).

Kaufmann, Daniel, Kraay, Aart, and Mastruzzi, Massimo (2009), 'Governance Matters VIII: aggregate and individual governance indicators 1996–2008', *Policy Research Working Paper 4978*, Washington, DC: The World Bank.

Kornai, János (1992), 'The Postsocialist Transition and the State: Reflections in the Light of Hungarian Fiscal Problems', *American Economic Review, Papers and Proceedings*, vol. 82(2).

Landesmann, Michael (2000), 'Structural Change in the Transition Economies, 1989–99', *Economic Survey of Europe*, No. 2/3, Geneva: UNECE.

Murrell, Peter (2003), 'The Relative Levels and the Character of Institutional Development in Transition Economies', in Campos, Nauro F. and Fidrmuc, Jan (eds), *Political Economy of Transition and Development: Institutions, Politics and Policies*, Dordrecht: Kluwer Academic Publishers.

Turley, Gerard and Luke, Peter J. (2010), *Transition Economics: Two Decades On*, London: Routledge.

World Bank (1996), *World Development Report 1996: From Plan to Market*, New York: Oxford University Press.

2

INSTITUTIONS IN TRANSITION[1]

Paul Hare

Introduction

In the early years of transition – after 1989 for Central and Eastern Europe (CEE), after 1991 for the former Soviet Union – reformers in the new governments, as well as their external advisors, commonly advocated a 'standard reform package' that consisted of the following elements: (a) macroeconomic stabilization; (b) price and trade liberalization; (c) privatization and enterprise restructuring; and (d) institutional reforms. In this contribution I shall focus entirely on the last element of the package, *institutions*. It has always seemed to me that the institutional aspect of reform programmes aiming to build well-functioning market-type economies from the ruins of central planning was both very important and difficult to get right.

However, in practice its importance was often underestimated, as was the sheer difficulty of successfully implementing market-oriented institutional reforms and making them work well enough to deliver growth and higher living standards. An important reason for the under-estimation of institutions in early transition reform programmes is, sadly, that in our economics courses – at all levels and in much of the world – we teach next to nothing about institutions. Consider the simplest possible *supply and demand model* as an illustration of what we normally take for granted:

- At the start of a transaction, the seller has ownership in the product being sold, say a consignment of small electric motors, for the sake of specificity.
- The transaction is essentially a transfer of ownership from seller to buyer, against payment of an agreed price, or the prevailing market price.
- At each stage of the transaction, the relevant ownership rights are protected.
- We assume buyer and seller to be honest and not to seek to cheat – to ensure this there might be some enforcement mechanism in the background (police, courts, legal system, etc.).
- The seller is expected to offer some guarantees of product quality and other technical characteristics – this might need inspection and verification services.
- The buyer is expected to pay using a valid means of payment, if need be supported by credit, and receipt of full payment might need to be verified.
- Because enforcement and verification are always costly, transactions are always facilitated (and are cheaper) if there is a high degree of trust between buyer and seller.

Normally when we discuss markets, we just assume, if we think about it at all, that these types of institutional arrangements, are in place and functioning 'normally'. However, we don't often tend to discuss or analyse how they arose, and what makes them work (some discussion can be found in Hare, 2010).

In what follows, I start with some definitions and concepts, simply to clarify what it is we have in mind when we talk about economic institutions and the political economy of transition. Much discussion of the area is characterized by ambiguity and confusion, and while there are many partial theories of institutions covering specific cases, we still lack an all encompassing theory. The institutions important for transition are introduced next, this discussion helping to make clear the critical distinction between institutions *per se*, and the concrete organizational and legal forms through which they are implemented in particular country settings. For those transition economies that have already joined, or wish to join the EU, this includes some remarks on the *acquis communautaire*. I then review a range of empirical evidence on the role of institutions in facilitating transition and fostering post-socialist economic growth, finding support for the rule of law, secure property rights (ownership and business contracts) and liberal trade. Finally, the concluding section outlines what transition has taught us about the roles of institutions in economic life, and highlights some important unsettled issues, including the problem of embedding new institutions in different cultural settings. (For a broader discussion of institutions, not confined to the economies in transition, see World Bank, 2001.)

Definitions and concepts

Institutions are the relatively stable *social arrangements* in a given society that govern how people behave in a variety of circumstances. They can be formal or informal, state led or private, and embody diverse rules, norms and conventions. In economic life, we generally expect well-functioning institutions to possess the following properties:

- They regulate economic behaviour in ways that often conflict with the short-term preferences of economic agents – be they households, firms or agencies of government.
- They are based on shared expectations and meanings, often drawing on customs and legal provisions that establish trust.
- They are often most usefully thought of as 'repeated games' where most types of interaction are expected to occur many times (this strengthens incentives to follow the 'rules of the game' in many situations).

These features imply that institutions are rather like public goods. Hence the 'supply of institutions' generated by the market mechanism left to itself might not correspond with social efficiency. By 'supply' in this context, we mean both the question whether a given institution or type of institution would be created at all by the market, and more detailed issues such as the scale and coverage of the institution concerned. For instance, wealthy people might well provide themselves with services to protect their property rights, but such services might not extend to the poor (indeed, in the worst case, the property rights of the poor might be neither recognized nor protected).

There is evidently a potential role for the state both in creating institutions which the market does not provide and in regulating in the public interest those which it does. On the other hand, in considering the state we should not assume it to be an inherently beneficent agent, in some sense external to 'the economy' *per se*. What turns out to be critical for successful growth is a state that is effective and competent within its acknowledged spheres of authority, but whose discretion and power are subject to effective institutional constraints.

In thinking about the institutions relevant for economic outcomes, several levels are important. The first is that of *social norms or customs*, which certainly includes the following three aspects:

- Honesty in performing agreed economic transactions or tasks.
- Trust between economic agents.
- Confidence about third-party economic behaviour (incl. behaviour by the state and its agencies).

The second concerns *assets and the rights associated with them*, such as:

- Property and the protection of property rights.
- Business forms (e.g. limited liability firm, co-operative, etc.) and their protection.
- Business contracts, the associated rights and responsibilities, and their protection.
- Freedom to initiate and conduct business, with limitations on state regulation at start-up, freedom from fears of expropriation (especially) in the event of success.

These merge into the third level, comprising the *actual institutional forms* established to protect various rights, limit state behaviour, etc. This includes diverse types of formal constraint on state intervention into the economy (via constitutional provisions, judicial review, appeals to higher courts, or other mechanisms).

To sum up, the institutional framework for a market economy ideally has to serve three key functions, namely: (a) protection of property rights; (b) facilitation of transactions; and (c) supporting economically/socially efficient collective action. The next section makes these general remarks about institutions rather more concrete in the context of transition.

Building a market economy – institutions for transition

In the transition economies, the first task for most of the new governments was to dismantle the institutional infrastructure associated with central planning. In discussions of transition, this key step is commonly overlooked, probably because it was entirely taken for granted. However, it involved two elements, both very important. First, the long-established *rules of the game* associated with central planning simply ceased[2] – so enterprises, for the most part, no longer received plan targets for their output, nor centrally determined supplies of inputs, nor instructions concerning what output to deliver to whom.[3] This was an amazing change, one that happened very rapidly in most countries, leaving in its wake an enormous institutional vacuum. Second, the specific *organizations* through which the central planning system functioned – central planning office, supplies office, and the like – were either closed down quite rapidly, or were assigned new tasks more in keeping with the needs of economic administration in the evolving market economies (e.g. with price liberalization, some price control offices became competition policy offices).

As for the institutional vacuum itself, how was that filled? Mostly, and in most countries, it was filled by deliberate decisions taken by the new post-communist governments, setting up new agencies, passing new laws, cancelling much of the former restrictive legislation that banned nearly all private sector economic activity. However, because of the complexity and urgency of the task, huge gaps were often left unfilled. It was often assumed, and foreign advisors were sometimes complicit in this, that where necessary the private sector – vaguely defined and poorly understood as it then was – would somehow step in to fill whatever institutional gaps might remain. However, the resulting private sector 'solutions' are not always very pleasant or socially desirable, and can be accompanied by threats, intimidation, serious levels of violence and large-scale theft of both public and (already) private assets.[4] A major reason for the importance of institution building for a market economy, I would argue, is to protect society against such very nasty outcomes.

That said, what do we expect the *institutional matrix* for a market-type economy to look like, what are its most important elements? (the idea of such a matrix has been discussed by North, 2010). In terms of our earlier discussion, we need to think of this at three levels: (a) customs and norms of behaviour; (b) assets and associated rights; and (c) specific institutional forms, as well as in relation to the three key economic functions that our institutions serve. In addition, it is vital to keep in mind the political dimension of the needed institutions. Table 2.1 illustrates all this.

Table 2.1 is quite complicated, of course, as it needs to be. Much of it speaks for itself, which is fortunate as we lack the space to discuss it in full. However, a few important points are worth bringing out before we move on.

- Much of what is in the table is about market economy institutions and practices that were absent or severely attenuated under central planning. Hence it is perhaps not so surprising that they did not spring to life instantly once central planning ended. A great deal of deliberate institutional design, with associated implementing legislation, was needed.
- Most items in the right-hand column of the table include an informal component, many of which emphasize the roles of trust, confidence, reputation, ethical behaviour, and the like. For a modern economy to function, these are vital aspects of the institutional matrix, the 'culture'. Formal institutions like police and courts will always be needed, but the less they have to be invoked to enforce transactions and protect property rights, the more smoothly the economy functions. The importance of this aspect of building the right 'culture' for a market economy was both underestimated and often poorly done in the transition economies.
- It will be seen that what market economies require, in order to function well, is a mix of *institutions* in the sense of laws, rules, practices, customs, etc, and *organizations* through which the rules are put into effect, e.g. tax office, central bank, competition office, etc.
- What I consider the two most important elements of institution building for a market economy, two that are often neglected by economists (especially those residing in the already developed countries), are in bold italics in the table: strong and effective government and the rule of law.
- ***Building strong government*** after the demise of central planning was easier for those countries that had started reforming early, and that had a history of independent statehood, e.g. Hungary, Poland, Slovenia, among others. It was far harder for the small states of south-eastern Europe that emerged from the disintegration of Yugoslavia and the Balkan Wars of the early 1990s; and for the republics of the former Soviet Union. They were embarking on state building, largely from scratch. They had limited experience of independent government, low administrative capacity and lacked many important institutions, e.g. currency and central bank; banks capable of handling international trade; familiarity with modern forms of taxation; social safety net and labour market institutions; legal and administrative framework for conducting private business, etc. Since strong governments can operate foolish policies, it is important to add that while they are necessary for successful transition, they provide no guarantee of long-term success.
- The ***rule of law*** is a critical element in the transition, widely misunderstood (see Bingham, 2011, and Dam, 2006). It not only entails private individuals and businesses being subject to the law, but also public agencies, public enterprises and the government itself. In a largely rule-based society, no one can be above the law. For the economy, its importance lies in the view that successful firms, earning decent profits, need to be secure against the risk of expropriation or theft by other firms and individuals, or, most importantly, by a greedy and

Table 2.1 Institutional matrix for a market economy

Group of Institutions	Purpose	Examples	Regulation – formal / Informal
Property rights	Establish rights: decide between competing claims; inform non-owners; police claims and exclude non-owners.	Land tenure	Land registry / *Local customs*
		Housing and personal property	Property registers, insurance and recording of transactions / *Informal customs and trust*
		Business premises – buildings and equipment	Property registers, insurance and recording of transactions / *Customary practice*
		Intellectual property rights – R&D and inventions	Copyright, patents / *Secrecy*
Facilitating transactions	Establish rules of exchange, respect for contracts; provide information; facilitate transactions when some markets are missing or incomplete; reduce or reallocate risk	Contract law and means to handle business disputes	Civil courts / Arbitration panels / *Informal understandings*
		Provision of markets, e.g. commodities, finance, trade networks, auctions, etc.	Regulate business practices / Local authorities and trade associations / *Informal regulation and trust*
		Technical standards, e.g. weights and measures, quality measures, money	Standards offices / Central bank / *Trust in standards and the currency*
		Market information	Media, advertising, public information agencies / *Word of mouth, reputation*
		Accounting and auditing rules	Professional bodies and public regulation / *Trust and reputation*
		Banking and credit	Bank regulation / *Custom and practice, trust*
Supporting collective action	To facilitate large-scale private or collective action, and large business organizations Also to facilitate international engagement	Building large infrastructure projects	Planning rules, building codes, other regulation
		Limited liability and bankruptcy laws	Civil courts, company registers / *Informal understandings*
		Competition policy	Office to regulate competition policy and business practices / *Local conventions, trust*
		Diverse business forms to support flexibility	Partnerships, co-operatives, third-sector firms, etc. / Governance regulation
		Employment protection and wages	Courts and tribunals / Trades unions / *Good will and trust*
		International engagement – trade, FDI, credits, etc.	Exchange rate policy / Banks to manage international transactions / Laws on FDI and trade / Membership of IFIs / *Limited role for informal methods and trust*

Table 2.1 (continued)

Group of Institutions	Purpose	Examples	Regulation – formal Informal
Politics	Democracy, elections and parties; Checks and balances; Accountability; Establish and maintain the rule of law; Public finance.	***Strong and effective government***	**Constitution, supreme court** **Armed forces under political control** **Effective ministries and competent civil service** **Convention and trust**
		Rule of law	**Courts, incl. supreme court** **Government must be subject to law** **Confidence and trust**
		Maintaining public order and security	Police, courts; in extremis, the armed forces *General public, public moral standards, trust*
		Party political competition	Free and liberal media Protection of core human rights Restrictions on lobbying and 'buying' influence *Trust in political system*
		Corruption	Institutions to make public officials and politicians accountable to parliament and the public Stiff penalties and exclusion from office for offenders. *High standards of private morality, a 'culture' of honesty*
		Public spending and taxation: (a) goods and services; (b) transfers; (c) taxes and other revenues; (d) debt and debt servicing.	Parliament, cabinet and ministries to set priorities, manage and administer spending, and collect revenues. Central Bank, Treasury (ministry of finance) and debt management agency to deal with debt. *Public trust in fair taxes and efficient spending*

opportunistic state authority. Rich individuals, too, need to be free from fear of arbitrary imposts on their wealth. Tax rules are fine, and should apply to all, but someone suddenly wealthy should not face extra taxes on that account, outside the established legal framework, unless a case can be made and proved in court that the wealth in question consists of ill-gotten gains. Normally, we think of the rule of law in formal terms, but to some degree, as in China, it can work through informal understandings, a tacit agreement between people and state that making money is legitimate and protected.

Significantly, the aim of reformers was not only to have the transition economies function as 'normal' market economies, drawing on the sort of institutional framework just discussed, but it was widely hoped and expected that they would enjoy rapid economic growth, improvements in living standards and hence catch up with the more advanced countries. This has turned out to be harder to assure, for reasons that are discussed a little further in the final section.

By now, economists know a good deal about the requirements of sustained economic growth[5] (CGD, 2008), and this is normally thought of in terms of achieving high rates of capital formation (investing 25 per cent or more of the GDP), mostly invested in productive projects (rather than presidential palaces), having a sound macroeconomic framework (including a decent banking system), an open economy and having a pro-business political system. In addition, one has to think about the microeconomics of growth, in other words what goes on at the level of individual firms. Under socialism, this could scarcely have been duller, since established firms were not permitted to fail (i.e. there was no provision for bankruptcy), new firms could only commence with ministerial approval, as part of the prevailing plan. The consequence was an incredibly static business landscape with astonishingly few firms, of an average size (e.g. in terms of employment) over 10 times what one would expect in a normally functioning market-type economy. This turned out not to be conducive to innovation, and undoubtedly contributed to the lagging performance of the socialist countries in their final decade or two under communism. At enterprise level, therefore, the *desiderata* for successful economic growth are rather straightforward to summarize:

- Easy entry of new firms, few constraints and little regulation.
- Most new firms will fail quite rapidly, others will grow to become the successes of the future. Credit and well functioning financial markets are needed to support growth where it is profitable.
- The privatization of most state-owned firms in an orderly fashion, in a way that supports future production and employment where possible.[6]
- Easy exit of failing firms, requiring hard budget constraints, and quick and easy bankruptcy so that assets can be used productively elsewhere.

It is often thought that having an economy in which lots of firms fail must be inefficient, but exactly the opposite is the case. The point is that a well-functioning market economy offers lots of highly diverse opportunities for making a profitable business, but *ex ante*, no one can possibly know which will succeed and which not. Thus we need lots of start ups simply in order to allow some to succeed. Otherwise the *information problem* is completely overwhelming. Reflecting these remarks, the early transition years saw massive increases in the numbers of registered businesses (albeit with significant cross-country differences), from a few thousand under socialism, to many hundreds of thousands within two or three years. Within less than a decade, the size distribution of firms in most countries looked increasingly like that of an established market-type economy.[7]

What we have outlined above amounts to a complicated set of institutional requirements or *desiderata*, and one might think that a good approach would be to 'pick and choose', or even 'mix and match'. The former means looking at the list of what institutions a market economy typically possesses, and picking a few to implement, perhaps because they are measures deemed politically acceptable and feasible at the time. Some countries did operate this way for a while, and soon discovered that a well-functioning market economy actually needs an institutional structure whose components hang together in a moderately consistent way. So implementing a few bits and pieces just won't do. Likewise, with the 'mix and match' approach, which takes (i.e. copies) company law from France (say), competition policy from Germany or the EU, privatization policy from the UK, and so on. This, too, does not tend to add up to a coherent institutional framework.

At the other extreme is the comprehensive, ready-made institutional framework implicit in the EU *acquis communautaire*. The *acquis* is the set of rules and regulations to which all EU member states have to sign up and incorporate into their respective domestic legislation; it is variously estimated to run to between 80,000 and 100,000 pages (yes, really!), so even translating it (correctly) into the different community languages must be a logistical and technical nightmare. The *acquis* is split into 30 or so chapters, and covers virtually everything one could think of that concerns running the economy, including also provisions to do with social policy, the political system and the judiciary. Those transition economies that set their sights on EU membership knew that they had to adopt the *acquis* in full, this being one of the key Copenhagen criteria for accession. These countries therefore started to adopt and implement this complex EU framework, in some cases years before formal accession negotiations even got under way.

Without the incentive provided by the prospect of EU accession, I doubt whether many transition economies would have adopted the *acquis* in its entirety, nor indeed would I have advised them to do so. For the *acquis* has evolved to suit relatively prosperous countries with large welfare states, and countries that typically grow fairly slowly. For poorer countries with limited market experience and probably weak administrative capacity, and also wanting to grow fast and catch up, a rather more focused subset of the *acquis* would have made more sense, dealing with the investment climate, free trade, single market issues, competition policy, and the like.

Empirical evidence

Here we review some of the empirical evidence that has been explored to assess the impact of institutions on transition to the market, on recovery from the post-socialist recessions and on longer term growth. The first serious attempts to investigate econometrically the performance of transition economies were associated with the names of Fischer, Sahay and Végh (1996a, b, 1997), abbreviated to FSV below. FSV (1996a) performed a regression on a set of 20 transition economies using data for the years 1992–94 (some countries could not be included owing to data limitations), which examined the impact of macroeconomic stabilization and early reforms on growth. A second equation looked at more conventional determinants of growth that were postulated to come into play once a country was well down the transition path.

The first regression showed the decisive role of high inflation and fiscal deficits in producing deep recession at the start of transition. Conversely, in countries that stabilized rapidly, the importance of early market-oriented – and largely institutional – reforms in kick starting the growth process was evident. After a time, the second equation should be the more relevant one, with institutional changes no longer highlighted. Thus, in the medium and longer term, the message for transition economies wishing to grow rapidly was utterly clear, namely that they must devise policies to raise their rates of investment and then maintain investment at high levels. As FSV (1997) shows, with an investment ratio of 20 per cent it would take transition economies an average of 45 years to catch up to current average OECD per capita income levels, while if investment could be raised to 30 per cent of GDP, the average catch up time would fall to 30 years, just one generation. None of the transition economies of the former Soviet bloc (CEE plus FSU), however, is investing enough to catch up very rapidly.

A few years later, a comprehensive study of the links between institutional change and economic performance was provided by Havrylyshyn and van Rooden (2003). This paper started by explaining the GDP growth of transition economies in terms of three sets of variables: (i) current inflation, INFL, taken to indicate the effectiveness of stabilization; (ii) current and lagged indicators of structural reforms; and (iii) two indicators of initial conditions, one reflecting macroeconomic distortions, the other reflecting the distortions associated with socialism before 1989/91. The empirical work was based on data for 25 countries over the period 1991–98 (with a few missing observations due to incomplete data). The basic regressions found a highly significant impact of the stabilization variable as well as the structural reform indicator, with initial conditions significant but rather less important in explaining GDP growth.

The authors distinguished between what they called *structural reforms* which could be measured by some of the European Bank for Reconstruction and Development's (EBRD) transition indicators to do with price liberalization, trade and exchange rates, banking and financial market reforms, private sector growth, and the like; and measures of *institutional reform*, which they took to be about the basic legal and political framework of the society concerned. The latter they measured using the EBRD's indicators of legal reforms (coverage and effectiveness of legal aspects of business), and measures of the extent of political liberalization. Including such indicators in their original regressions simply as additional variables confirmed that institutional reform was important for growth, but it was overwhelmingly dominated by structural reforms.

Falcetti *et al.* (2006) reviewed and updated estimates of the impact of reforms on growth in the transition economies and also looked for feedbacks in the other direction – growth in one period encouraging further reform in the next. Both types of effect were found, and were also found to be robust to alternative specifications. Not surprisingly, the impact of initial conditions (such as number of years under communist rule) declines over time, and the effects of other factors such as oil prices, growth in principal trading partners, and so on, were generally small or insignificant.

More recently, Commander and Nikoloski (2010) carried out a very careful study to test various hypotheses about institutions and performance. They examined three levels: (a) whether the political system affects economic performance; (b) whether the business and investment environment affects country economic performance; and (c) whether perceived business constraints affect firm performance. In all three cases, their regressions, mostly using data covering much of the world, not merely the economies in transition, found very weak effects. The authors considered why this might be the case, given the prevailing orthodoxy regarding the role of institutions, and concluded that there might well be a mix of data issues and model specification issues underlying the findings. For the transition economies, however, the evidence for a positive impact of institutions is generally clearer and stronger, as noted above, presumably reflecting the fact that institutional change has been at the heart of the whole transition 'project'.

Conclusions and unsettled issues

To conclude, I shall highlight some aspects of institutional change in the transition economies that remain puzzling, or that suggest the need for further research and better models of institutional change.

Institutional change is necessary but not sufficient for sustained growth

The market-type institutional changes discussed above are thought to be necessary for growth because they are conducive to economic flexibility, adaptability and innovation, factors important for continued growth in already high-income economies. However, in poorer countries, far from the technology frontier, there is much scope for growth even when the institutions are much less well developed. Even with apparently 'good' underlying institutions, growth is not guaranteed to occur without sound macroeconomic policy, adequate rates of productive investment, competent (and growth oriented) political leadership, and a good deal of sheer luck.

Formal institutions, informal institutions and culture (East Germany)

When East Germany was formally reunited with West Germany in October 1990, the institutions of the West – including the entire *acquis communautaire* of the EU – were more or less instantly transposed into the East. With such 'good' institutions in place, many observers expected the East soon to flourish, but it has not, or at least not yet. Two levels of explanation have been advanced for this. According to the first, some of the decisions made around the time of reunification, such as how to convert East German money balances and wage rates, were simply 'wrong' in macroeconomic terms, as East German productivity was far lower than had been estimated. According to the second, informal institutions to do with working practices, and the Eastern 'culture' stemming from several decades under communism (including the loss of several decades of market-economy experience), meant that the new institutions transplanted from the West could not work as expected (Carlin, 2011, and this volume).

Formal and informal institutions, and growth (China)

Some countries, notably China, have done astonishingly well despite appearing to have rather 'poor' institutions to support markets, private property, contracts, and the like. In part this reflects our still imperfect understanding of institutions, our lack of a really good theoretical framework to help us think about and analyse them. In part, however, it points to the importance of informal institutions, understanding, trust and confidence in facilitating economic activity. Especially in the early years, for instance, the development of township and village enterprises (the TVEs) in China worked so well because there was a tacit understanding at all levels that economic development was the name of the game – so anyone with a business idea that could make money (and hence pay taxes to the local authority) was to be encouraged, and it was understood that people would be allowed to get rich without fear of expropriation. No laws or formal framework supported this. However, China had suffered the horrors of the Great Leap Forward (with accompanying famine) and the Cultural Revolution, so by the mid- to late 1970s the whole country was ready for economic pragmatism and an end to political/ideological campaigns.

External anchors for institutional change (e.g. EU and WTO)

Many countries have found external anchors helpful in pushing forward reforms; for instance, countries seeking EU membership promoted many domestic reforms because they formed part of the *acquis* and so 'had to be done'. Likewise, countries joining the WTO sign up to a lengthy and complex *accession protocol* that not only requires measures to do with trade (e.g. tariff reductions and the like) but often also requires reforms to many areas of domestic economic policy and institutional arrangements. Perhaps surprisingly, countries – especially the larger and more 'visible' ones, like China – are often quite diligent in implementing the provisions of their *accession protocol*. I would expect Russia, whose admission to the WTO was approved in late 2011 (and was ratified during 2012), to take the provisions in its own *protocol* equally seriously. In this sense, we do indeed live in an increasingly rule-based world economy.

The forms and practice of democracy (e.g. Hungary and Russia)

Having the 'right' institutions in place is no guarantee that they will work as one might like them to, because countries have distinct histories, traditions and cultures. These affect both the functioning of their economies, as well as their political life. Hungary and Russia are interesting, and rather worrying examples of this remark.

Hungary, for instance, was required to establish a 'functioning democracy' as part of the Copenhagen criteria for EU entry, and in any case its last communist government had also sought to bequeath a democratically functioning state to its successors. But the two socialist governments of the past decade were beset by scandals and corruption, paving the way for a

Fidesz victory in the 2010 polls – but with just 53 per cent of the vote, Fidesz secured a more than two-thirds majority in the parliament. The Fidesz government has since been able – and has chosen – to pass laws restricting press freedom, changing the constitution to constrain the judiciary and the Constitutional Court, and introducing a new constitution from January 2012. The European Commission has warned Hungary that its proposed new constitutional framework breaches EU law, and that the country's democratic credentials are being steadily eroded. Hence the stability of new and fragile democratic institutions cannot be taken for granted, it seems.

Russia, too, has the forms of democracy, but with major constraints on their proper functioning. These constraints come from two directions. One is the economic, through the economic power and political influence of the so-called 'oligarchs', the magnates owning and controlling Russia's most valuable productive assets. The other is political, through a variety of channels: voter registration; registration and funding of political parties; ballot rigging, reportedly widespread; a poorly functioning and reportedly quite corrupt judiciary; restrictions on the media; restrictions on political protest and demonstrations; and tendencies towards a Putin 'personality cult'. Despite these serious imperfections, Russian democracy remains far ahead of the single-party state that prevailed until 1991, and may yet advance further in a positive direction. The point, however, is that democracy is not just about the institutional forms, but about their practical functioning.

Notes

1 I am grateful to my co-editor for helpful comments on an earlier draft of this contribution. Remaining errors are my own.
2 Some countries, such as Hungary and Poland, had already moved away from central planning towards a greater role for markets long before the start of transition. They were therefore arguably better prepared for the changes to come, though in the event, a country that had hardly reformed at all, Czechoslovakia, proved able to introduce market-type reforms impressively rapidly.
3 I recall visiting firms in Russia in late 1990, a year before the disintegration of the Soviet Union. Some firms were clearly thinking already about 'life after central planning' and were re-thinking what they produced, seeking new suppliers and markets, and so on. Others seemed to be stuck in limbo. They had not yet received their plans for 1991, and stated that they could do nothing or decide nothing until these plans had been delivered; these firms were not at all ready for the central planning system to collapse.
4 An example of this is Russia's failure to establish adequate formal mechanisms in the early 1990s to facilitate the settlement of private business disputes – some form of commercial court might have sufficed, or agreed arbitration arrangements. Lacking such mechanisms, many disputes were settled violently, and at times businessmen in dispute were shot. As stated in the main text, private sector solutions need not be especially desirable.
5 We also know a great deal about how to ruin an economy. The recent and current examples of Zimbabwe and North Korea, and also Somalia, come to mind, three countries whose natural endowments and human resources could generate much higher living standards than they currently enjoy.
6 Other contributions deal with privatization in some detail. Some of the early stages of privatization in many countries were quite chaotic and uncontrolled, with many transfers of ownership that were little better than outright theft of state property. Moreover, a common, rather naive, assumption at the start was that new owners would always run the newly privatized firms as 'going concerns', whereas they quite often ran them into the ground, stealing assets and revenues through shell companies and the like. Luckily, many firms were run much better.
7 Yet many transition countries still underestimate the critical importance of this change to the business landscape. For instance, in several countries where I have worked recently, officials have emphasized how much their general business environment has improved. They are right, with reference to their own fairly recent past; but in comparison with well performing market economies elsewhere, they still have a long way to go. One simple statistic sums this up, namely the number of registered businesses per 1,000 of population: in long-established market economies this can be around 50, while the countries I just had in mind only had between 10 and 20.

Bibliography

Bingham, Tom (2011), *The Rule of Law*, London: Penguin Books.

Carlin, Wendy (2011), 'Eastern German development: Good institutions are not enough', *Journal for Institutional Comparisons* (CESifo Dice Report), vol. 9(1), pp. 28–34.

CGD (2008), *The Growth Report: Strategies for Sustained Growth and Inclusive Development*, Commission on Growth and Development, Washington, DC: World Bank.

Commander, Simon and Nikoloski, Zlatko (2010), 'Institutions and economic performance: What can be explained?', Working Paper No. 121, London: EBRD.

Dam, Kenneth W. (2006), *The Law-Growth Nexus: The Rule of Law and Economic Development*, Washington, DC: The Brookings Institution.

Falcetti, Elisabetta, Lysenko, Tatiana and Sanfey, Peter (2006), 'Reforms and growth in transition: Re-examining the evidence', *Journal of Comparative Economics*, vol. 34(3), pp. 421–45.

Fischer, Stanley, Sahay, Ratna and Végh, Carlos A. (1996a), 'Economies in transition: The beginnings of growth', *American Economic Review*, vol. 86(2) (Papers and Proceedings), pp. 229–33.

——(1996b), 'Stabilization and growth in transition economies: The early experience', *Journal of Economic Perspectives*, vol. 10(2), pp. 45–66.

——(1997), 'From transition to market: Evidence and growth prospects', in Zecchini, Salvatore (ed.), *Lessons from the Economic Transition: Central and Eastern Europe in the 1990s*, OECD and Dordrecht: Kluwer Academic Publishers, pp. 79–101.

Hare, Paul (2010), *Vodka and Pickled Cabbage: Eastern European Travels of a Professional Economist*, London: Athena Press.

Havrylyshyn, Oleh and van Rooden, Ron (2003), 'Institutions matter in transition, but so do policies', *Comparative Economic Studies*, vol. 45(1), pp. 2–24.

North, Douglass (2010), *Understanding the Process of Economic Change*, Princeton, NJ: Princeton University Press.

World Bank (2001), *World Development Report 2002: Building Insitutions for Markets*, Washington, DC: World Bank.

3

DID WE GO ABOUT TRANSITION IN THE RIGHT WAY?

D. Mario Nuti

The transformation recession

The post-socialist transition that began in 1990–92 in central-eastern Europe and the former Soviet Union (FSU) was widely expected to lead to early significant improvements in the level and growth of people's consumption and income.

It was a plausible expectation: leaving aside its authoritarian drawbacks, the old system – with dominant state ownership and enterprise, central planning and broad insulation from foreign trade and investment – was notoriously inefficient. It neglected consumers' preferences, input substitutability in production, and the opportunities and stimuli of the international division of labour. The system had an autarkic bias, which facilitated central planning but was a source of gross inefficiency, even within Council for Mutual Economic Assistance or Comecon (CMEA), the bloc of socialist countries engaged in a process of planned integration since the end of the 1950s (Lavigne, 1991). For instance, Hare and Hughes (1991) showed that on the eve of transition in Czechoslovakia, Hungary and Poland, between one-fifth and one-quarter of manufacturing production exhibited negative value added at world prices (using 1988–89 data on inputs, outputs and exchange rates). Japan bought Soviet machinery for scrap, and aluminium from the socialist bloc was sold internationally at less than the international price of the energy it embodied.

The Soviet-type system (for short, leaving aside national differences and repeated incomplete attempts at reform, only partly successful) was also unstable and imbalanced, marred by internal and external imbalances, both open and repressed. Endemic excess demand, for both consumption and production goods, prevailed at administered prices artificially held below market-clearing levels and disconnected from opportunity costs in production and trade. Excess monetary balances in the hands of the population resulted in shortages, queues, waiting lists and black markets. So much so that Kornai (1980) could entitle his two-volume treatise on that system, *Economics of Shortage*. Such repressed inflation had doomed to failure the frequent attempts at reform of the system in the direction of 'market socialism'.

The system had achieved rapid industrialization and growth, built military might and conquered space, but in the end it was unable to provide basic necessities to the population, had wasted the windfall of price increases enjoyed by its vast natural resources in the 1970s, accumulated unsustainable foreign debt, and in the 1980s stagnated and often declined. The new system would generate market-clearing prices in domestic and international transactions, revive the incentives to follow them thanks to the appropriation of profits by owners of private enterprises, and unleash and discipline entrepreneurship. The few practitioners of the transition who did contemplate some disruption (e.g. Leszek Balcerowicz in Poland in 1990), anticipated at most a one-digit temporary decline followed by accelerated growth and catching up with other market economies.

Instead of that, the transition process was accompanied by a deep and often protracted 'transformation recession' (Kornai's label). Poland experienced the shortest and smallest fall in income (17 per cent of 1989 GDP in just under three years) recovering its 1989 level in 1996 and moving rapidly ahead, while Georgia had the largest and most prolonged fall (75 per cent by 1994 before reversing, and still below the 1989 level in 2011) – leaving aside the transition countries that experienced war (with Bosnia and Herzegovina at over 80 per cent GDP decline and by 2012 still not fully recovered).

Three reactions: denial, necessity, cock-up

This unexpected statistical record provoked three contrasting reactions: disbelief to the point of denial, belief coupled with acceptance of its necessity, belief coupled with rejection of its necessity.

The initial response, which to this day is still held by a few observers (e.g. Åslund, 2000) is that the transformation recession was by and large a statistical illusion, owing to changes in conventions and enterprise behaviour. In the old system there was universal reporting by enterprises that had an incentive to exaggerate gross production achievements, to avoid penalties involved by failure to reach planned targets and to reap the bonuses deriving from plan over-fulfilment. In the new system there was incomplete sample coverage of producers under-reporting net results in order to avoid tax. Also, a significant amount of production activity took place in the black or grey economy, simply going unreported. And people benefited from an increase of their consumer surplus, simply from having access to a broader range of goods, while price increases were to some extent justified by quality increases.

These considerations cannot be dismissed, but can easily be overplayed. There was a grey/black economy, though illegal, already under central planning; its newly found legality in the transition led to at least some of it surfacing, thus unduly boosting the performance of the new system. Consumer surplus is not and has never been included in national income accounting anywhere in the world, and there is no reason to begin accounting for it in the post-socialist transition. Parallel price and quality increases were not necessarily an improvement for all consumers. The availability and quality of public services plummeted. Transition performance was boosted to a great extent by the growth in formerly underprovided and underpriced services, and by real revaluation of the currency from initial gross undervaluation (see below). A single, exceedingly long queue for jobs replaced the many former queues for goods. Both inequality and poverty increased significantly in most transition economies (World Bank, 2000).

The second response to the transformation recession was that it was indeed real, but unavoidable. It was said that the transition was like 'turning a fish soup back into an aquarium', it had to be costly. In Poland the transition was likened to 'turning vodka back into potatoes'. Except that there had been no actual capacity destruction as there had been in wartime to justify this proposition. Others referred to the recession as a form of Schumpeter's 'creative destruction', also implausible since destruction of value-subtracting activities like those mentioned above should have *boosted* national income instead of reducing it, while competition and investment in innovation were missing anyway. Shleifer and Treisman (2000) justify the recession as due to the unprecedented nature of the transition: they entitle their book on Russian transition *On the Road without a Map*. On uncharted territory we can all easily get lost, but this was not the case. We knew very well where we were, and all the conceivable advantages and drawbacks of the Soviet-type system; we knew what was going increasingly wrong with that system; we had – unlike any earlier transition – complete maps of the alternative points of arrival of the transition, i.e. the various versions of available models of capitalism – from Scandinavian type social-democracy to French indicative planning, from German *Mitbestimmung* to the Japanese neo-corporative model. Therefore we knew what had to be changed to implement the transition from where we were to the target model. What we did not know was the desirable speed of the transition and therefore, in case of a non-instantaneous transition, the appropriate sequencing of the necessary moves.

In one respect, however, the politics of transition rather than its economics necessarily involved disruption and recession to some extent. International trade was greatly disrupted by the economic and monetary disintegration associated with the transition in central-eastern Europe and the FSU. In 1991 the socialist trade bloc, CMEA, disintegrated; the transferable rouble, its purely accounting unit used to register planned trade flows at planned prices and carry over trade imbalances within the bloc for later consensual corrections, was replaced by trade at international prices settled in hard currencies. In 1992 the Soviet Union split into its 15 component Republics, with the rouble being replaced by 15 republican currencies, first as rouble substitutes then as proper domestic currencies. Mundell (1997), who regards the transformation recession as the worst ever, more serious than the 1929–32 recession and even the Black Death recession in the fourteenth century (when population also fell, thus preserving living standards) attributes it to a great extent to such monetary disintegration.

Suddenly, next to the Russian rouble there were Belorussian roubles, Lithuanian litas, Latvian lats, Estonian kroons, Ukrainian hryvnas, Uzbek soms and Kyrgyz soms, Georgian laris, Tajik roubles later followed by the somonis, Azeri manats and Turkmen manats, Kazak tenges, Moldovan leus and Armenian drams – a veritable Babel of currencies. The move to republican currencies, initially with limited convertibility and liquidity, restricted trade to bilateral transactions of balanced barter, or to deficits liquidated in scarce hard currencies. The changeover to international prices, and the end of cross transfers within the trading bloc, were other factors depressing trade and therefore employment and GDP. Should the current eurozone crisis eventually lead to its split into national currencies, the same kind of devastating recession should be expected as a result.

The IMF tried to prevent the FSU monetary disintegration, and was actually accused of holding back the transition. The different target models and stages of transition reached and intended by different republics made the preservation of the Union politically impossible. The same can be said of CMEA: early in 1990 Central-Eastern European members of CMEA had refused to continue planned integration within the trade bloc even if that involved loss of access to oil and raw materials from the Soviet Union at subsidized prices.

Having said that the recession was to some (not very large) extent overstated by national statistics, partly (significantly) the consequence of the politically unavoidable split of CMEA and of the Soviet Union (as well as of the Czecho-Slovak Federation and the Yugoslav Federation), a large residual of the recession was indeed real and due to 'having gone about transition the wrong way', to give a summary answer to the question raised by this volume's Editors.

More precisely, much of what did go wrong was owing to (1) the uncritical acceptance of a particular and controversial model of capitalist market economy, namely hyper-liberalism; (2) the extension to transition economies of the Washington Consensus policies applied in the

1980s in Latin America (price liberalization, trade opening, privatization); (3) misplaced emphasis on the relative merits of gradualism versus 'shock therapy', neglecting actual policy trade-offs and governments' preferences; (4) 'state desertion' of public enterprises and more generally of its role even in a market economy, and, in particular, the neglect of institutions in the naïve belief that they would establish themselves, develop and regulate themselves automatically; (5) various policies that can be regarded as mistakes even without the benefit of hindsight, mostly rooted in ideological dogmatism; (6) eventually, sooner or later, most transition economies especially those that joined the European Union (in 2004 and 2007, and the current candidates) completed the transition and accelerated their catching up with the rest of Europe, but the same factors mentioned here caused a vulnerability to the global crisis of 2007–to date, and a stronger (though later and shorter) fall (with the exception of Poland, Albania and Azerbaijan) than in other European economies and, above all, a marked deceleration of their growth. The same factors are now standing these countries in good stead for the subsequent recovery.

Hyper-liberalism

The target model adopted almost everywhere in the transition countries was that of an open and liberal (in the European sense) market economy that would reap the benefits of markets and private ownership and enterprise. However, the timing of the post-socialist transition coincided with the general domination of a particular and controversial model of capitalist market economy, namely hyper-liberalism, typical of the Reagan–Thatcher era. Under the strong influence of this ideology, the instigation of most foreign advisors, the conditionality imposed by the IMF and the World Bank, and the acquiescence of the European Union, the most widespread model in the transition was a hyper-liberal model that was more fundamentalist than any modern capitalist model in existence, including American capitalism.

The hyper-liberal character of the post-socialist transition model is confirmed by the dominant adoption of the following policies:

- Immediate unilateral opening of foreign trade, frequently revoked and therefore premature.
- Exceptionally rapid liberalization of capital flows, in contrast to the experience of other European economies after the Second World War.
- An unprecedented mass privatization (a notable exception was Hungary), through the distribution to the population of free or symbolically priced vouchers, convertible into state assets or shares in state enterprises – a macroscopic experiment in social engineering of debatable effectiveness.
- The demotion of the state, that led to delays or gaps in market regulation, especially in financial markets (see the disastrous diffusion of banking pyramids in Russia, Romania, Albania, Serbia, Macedonia and elsewhere), for the protection of shareholders and more generally for corporate governance.
- The dismantling of the welfare state, which in these economies was to a large extent the responsibility of state enterprises, without reconstructing it at the central level.
- A costly reform of the pension system from a Pay As You Go, defined benefits, distribution system (whereby pensioners are funded by the contributions of current employees), to a capitalization, defined contributions or funded system (with pensions paid out of the revenue earned on accumulated past contributions).
- A low and uniform rate of direct taxation (flat tax), therefore mildly progressive, on households and companies, mostly without taxation of capital gains but with higher indirect taxation.

- A flexible labour market, with weak trade unions and a low incidence of collective bargaining; the principle of market sovereignty was not applied to the labour market, frequently subjected to widespread wage ceilings enforced through punitive taxes.
- Lack of consultation and concertation between social partners and with the government.
- A central bank not only independent but exceptionally independent and free from any controls, without co-ordination with fiscal policy, pursuing a strict policy of inflationary containment and high interest rates, aiming at positive real rates even in the presence of currency appreciation (therefore attracting foreign capital but making the sterilization of the ensuing monetary expansion very costly).
- In general, a dominant weight of markets as against institutions.

This list could continue. Usually the IMF and the World Bank have been either praised or blamed for their part in imposing economic policies and institutional transformations in extreme forms, through the conditionality of their financial assistance, whose effects were multiplied by other public and private institutions in turn making their assistance conditional on an IMF programme. Sometimes Western advisors have been blamed for recommending policies that they would not have dared propose to their own governments. However, the ultimate responsibility for the policies actually adopted must be attributed to the sovereign governments that adopted those policies, and that were often only too pleased to conform to the requests of international institutions and the advice of some Western consultants.

The hyper-liberal victory in central-eastern Europe has involved a watering down of the European Social Model (ESM) as a result of EU enlargement to the East that began in 2004 and 2007 and is still in progress. A model somewhat closer to the ESM was adopted in Slovenia and Estonia, while Belarus and a few Asian republics adopted a model still close to an etatist one and to the old system, while under Putin's leadership since 2000, especially during his second mandate, Russia has moved somewhat in the same direction, of something approaching a *developmental state*. In view of the bitter reconsideration of hyper-liberalism that followed the global crisis of 2007–to date, we can say that, had the transition taken place 20 years later, post-socialism would have certainly adopted a very different model and policies.

The Washington Consensus

The IMF, the World Bank and the US Treasury applied to transition economies the policies implemented in the 1980s in Latin America with relative success: rapid macroeconomic stabilization, liberalization of prices and foreign trade, privatization. The notion that these policies might be replicated in transition economies in the 1990s ignored fundamental differences between the two groups of countries. Latin America in the 1980s suffered from open inflation and hyper-inflation, state enterprises were a minority and were familiar with the market economy including international markets. Transition economies, on the contrary, suffered from repressed inflation (see above); state enterprises were dominant and were not used to a market environment; the bulk of foreign trade was planned and the preserve of state monopoly.

These differences had profound implications. In the transition economies the price increase towards market-clearing level – which was the first necessary step towards a market economy, and indeed would have been necessary for the orderly and efficient running of a planned economy – was naturally bound to overshoot. Faced with a sudden new, unusual state of market balance, at uniform prices higher but necessarily lower than those previously prevailing in the black market, and with expectations of accelerating inflation, economic subjects were bound to reduce their demand for money below its equilibrium level at the new prices. The successive replenishment of liquid resources therefore had to depress the current demand for goods and services. Latin American consumers, instead, faced with a slowing down of open inflation were induced to maintain higher monetary resources than they would have done otherwise.

Looking at it in another way, repressed inflation could be deconstructed, as was usual in Polish literature, into: an inflationary gap (*luka inflacyjna*), i.e. the price increase that would make the current flow of real goods equivalent to the current flow of monetary incomes; and the stock (*nawis*) of accumulated past inflationary gaps. In theory there were ways to eliminate both, in the necessary advance to market clearing. For instance, a confiscatory currency reform at different rates for prices, incomes and cash (as in the late 1950s in the Soviet Union, many central-eastern European countries and China); but this was not politically feasible. Alternatively, a burst of imported consumption financed by foreign loans and aid, but this was not available at the time. Or a front-loaded privatization of state assets, but this was still controversial and a simple announcement would have been hardly credible before the start of the transition.

The choice of price liberalization was the simplest, fastest and most expedient way to clear markets, as a by-product of changing *relative* prices.[1] However, it necessarily involved overshooting: price rises that were practically irreversible had to absorb both the current inflationary gap and its past cumulation; in the following period (defined as the weighted average of the intervals at which markets were restocked) there would be lower demand than sustainable and consequent unemployment (Nuti, 1986).

Overshooting in price liberalization from a repressed inflationary state appears as unplanned fiscal surpluses and massive exchange-rate devaluations with respect to purchasing power parity (PPP) (with the US dollar worth 32 times its Russian rouble PPP equivalent, 20 times its Polish złoty equivalent, eight times its Hungarian forint equivalent when prices were first liberalized). Supply elasticities being low, these devaluations did not always work, but sometimes produced unplanned trade surpluses and reserves accumulation (e.g. in Poland).

This is not a good reason not to undertake price liberalization, for a market economy cannot exist without market clearing. But it makes a strong case for subsequent fiscal and/or monetary stimulus, and parallel price and wage subsidies of the sort introduced in Czechoslovakia and in the early stages of German unification, instead of wage controls and punitive taxation on wage rises (the Polish *popiwek tax*) and the abolition of price subsidies.

Both Latin American and transition economies had inefficient state enterprises, but in transition economies, moreover, they had a dominant position and were centrally planned, without the experience of adjusting to internal and international prices. Thus, the organic growth of new enterprises and the restructuring and commercialization of state enterprises were more important than their instantaneous privatization, and it was unlikely that liberalization could stimulate a rapid supply response, although it was important as a source of greater competition.

Neglect of the *repressed* nature of their inflation caused transition economies significant losses in terms of employment and output, in an economy shifting from supply-side constraints to Keynesian lack of effective demand. The overshooting implied by this approach was aggravated by fiscal and monetary policies more restrictive than intended, and by central controls over wages. The transformation recession was not, or should not have been, a surprise, but a mathematical certainty, although only a Kaleckian economist such as Laski (1990) was able to anticipate it, forecasting correctly a range of 15–20 per cent GDP fall in Poland.

Gradualism versus shock therapy

Since the early stages of the transition there have been endless and lively debates on the relative merits of gradualism versus 'shock therapy' (Kolodko, 2000; Popov, 2007). In truth the scope for government choice in the transition is rather narrow in this respect, and the emphasis on this issue was misplaced. In the transition there are measures that can and must be introduced instantaneously and simultaneously, such as:

- Raise prices to market-clearing levels (see above).
- Legalize private ownership and enterprise.
- Allow all economic subjects – individuals and enterprises – free access to international trade.
- Eliminate quantitative restrictions on imports and exports.
- Unify exchange rates.
- Establish convertibility for current account transactions (not yet for capital account transactions) by residents.

All these changes can and should be made by decree, literally from one day to the next, at a stroke. Temporizing is counterproductive. At the other extreme there are measures that need time for their realization and therefore they should be given all the time that they reasonably require. Such measures include to (i) draft and introduce legislation; (ii) establish a properly functioning legal/judicial system separated from politics; (iii) break-up monopolies and establish competition; (iv) restructure productive capacity; (v) create financial markets; and (vi) establish relations of reputation and trust between government and private sector agents. It does not make sense, indeed it is counterproductive, to pretend that these changes could be accelerated, let alone be instantaneous.

The cases where there is a possible choice between shock therapy and gradualism can literally be counted on the fingers of one hand, namely trade liberalization; the elimination of subsidies; privatization; convertibility on capital account; and, especially, dis-inflation. I consider this an exhaustive list of policy areas where there is no absolute superiority of either gradualism or shock. Their relative merits depend on their respective costs and benefits, i.e. the trade-offs that the economy offers between government objectives, and the actual government preferences between those objectives.

For instance, alternative methods of privatization have costs and benefits (World Bank, 1996); mass privatization can be rapid and equitable, but with some associated costs: losing the fiscal revenue that would result from the sale of state assets, establishing weak corporate governance, leaving an unchanged management and poor access to new investment funds. Privatization via sales to employees and managers is less rapid and obtains some additional revenue for the budget, at the cost of less equity, here as well without managerial improvements and access to investment funds (provided not only by buyers but also through credit). Privatization via sales to the public is slower but involves greater revenue for the state budget, better governance, better management and greater access to investment funds. Sales to foreigners have the advantages of a capital inflow, better access to new technologies and investment funds, trade outlets, at the cost of losing national control and the risk of future capital losses via profit repatriation and capital sales at times of crisis. On the other hand, delaying privatization often creates unprecedented opportunities for self-appropriation of state assets by managers and party officials, and straight corruption (see for instance the 'loans for shares' scheme that gave a few Russian banks a large stake in privatization at rock-bottom prices).

Similar considerations – of costs and benefits subject to government valuation – apply also to the other four areas indicated above. Thus, dis-inflation, from hyperinflationary rates to single-digit inflation, can be tackled gradually or rapidly; the benefits of price stability must be offset against the costs of associated unemployment. External tariffs can be eliminated rapidly and unilaterally or negotiated more slowly; the positive impact on competition and prices must be offset against the possible adverse effect on government revenues and unemployment; it is no accident that countries that opened trade fast, as did Poland, Czechoslovakia and Hungary, subsequently backpedalled and reintroduced tariffs and surcharges. Subsidies can be eliminated gradually (as in the Czech Republic, in spite of Vaclav Klaus's hyper-liberal rhetoric) or quickly (as in Poland); the benefits in term of inflation control must be offset against the claim on government expenditure. Currency convertibility on capital account can be introduced quickly, gaining from capital inflows but risking their volatility, or slowly, avoiding both benefits and risks.

There is perhaps a presumption against instantaneous privatization (in comparison to the birth and growth of *de novo* enterprises), against the rapid introduction of convertibility on capital account (see the Czech koruna crisis of 1997 and the Russian rouble crisis of 1998), against the rapid lowering of trade tariffs (for the resulting loss of government revenue, as lamented even by the then head of IMF Fiscal Affairs, Vito Tanzi, in 1997). And against rapid dis-inflation: Poland's star performance is probably owing among other things to its particularly slow dis-inflation, taking 10 years to go from three digits to single-digit inflation in spite of its shock rhetoric; Slovenia also benefited from slow dis-inflation.

'Clearly a generalised and unconditional "shock therapy" approach is facile and superficial. Just as for Lenin in December 1920, *communism = electrification + Soviet power*, we can say that for the initial Washington Consensus, *transition = liberalization + privatization*. Both equations have a doubtful theoretical foundation and have borne poor results' (Nuti, 2007).

State and institutions

On the rebound from the experience of a totalitarian state, transition leaders went to the opposite extreme of wanting to contain state activity to the minimum and destroy state institutions in order to allow the free play of market forces. Policy interventions appeared as undue interferences with market forces: in 1990 the Polish Minister for Industry and Trade, Tadeusz Syryjczyk, argued that 'The best industrial policy is no industrial policy' (Kolodko and Nuti, 1997). In the still large public sector, pending privatization, 'state desertion' of public enterprises occurred and led to continued inefficiency and to the appropriation of state assets by managers and *apparatchiks*. The weakening of state institutions made it possible for private subjects and enterprises to benefit from 'state capture', effectively a form of corruption.

In particular, the role of the state in the establishment, monitoring and regulation of institutions was neglected, in the naïve belief that institutions would establish themselves, develop and regulate themselves automatically. Sachs (1993) typically asserts that 'markets spring up as soon as central planned bureaucrats vacate the field'. Markets are self-regulating (homeostatic) mechanisms in the sense of adjusting prices to demand, supply to prices, actual to desired capacity; but they are not generated automatically, nor are they self-disciplined. They are social artefacts that rely on state authority for their validation and regulation, and often for their very existence. The kind of markets that moved in when central planners left at the beginning of the transition were the wretched people who lined up in Moscow streets to offer a few individual items for sale or barter, not the fabric of a market economy. When central planners move out, unless the state creates and controls markets, they leave a vacuum, and what moves in is disorganization and chaos (Blanchard and Kremer, 1997): former backward and forward planned linkages are broken, and a supply multiplier leads to chain losses of output and unemployed inputs. Unfortunately the importance of institutions (stressed by North, 1990) came too late to influence transition policy-making.

Ellman (2012) stresses 'The need for an effective and accountable state', compared with the Friedmanite notion that 'the state is not the solution but the problem'. He quotes the World Bank's 1997 *World Development Report* recognizing that 'An effective state is vital for the provision of the goods and services – and the rules and institutions – that allow markets to flourish and people to lead healthier, happier lives. Without it, sustainable development, both economic and social, is impossible' (p. 1). And the 2002 *World Development Report* was entitled *Building institutions for markets*. Ellman regards the official acceptance of these principles, that were not new, as one of the lessons of the transition, and reviews a number of adverse effects of their earlier neglect, such as the accumulation of payment arrears in the Russian economy, a new institution generated in the transition but actually incompatible with a market economy.

The quality of policies

The quality of transition policies is usually judged by the speed and intensity with which a country has followed the prescriptions of the Washington Consensus, or by the indices of transition progress assessed by the EBRD in their annual *Transition Reports*, or their cumulation over time. It seems necessary, however, to consider instead the consistency and feasibility of policy targets; the choice and intensity of qualitative and quantitative policy instruments and packages with respect to those targets, the co-ordination of policies delegated to different agencies; the continuity of policies, in the sense of their inter-temporal consistency, the possible undesirable side-effects. We have already discussed the necessary overshooting of price liberalization without subsequent fiscal or monetary stimuli. Two other examples are given here: central bank independence and pension reform.

Central Bank independence

The principle of Central Bank independence rests on very shaky theoretical foundations, namely rational expectations. These are supposed to eliminate the trade-off between unemployment and inflation, to the point that inflation can be targeted by an independent Central Bank while the government is supposed to take care of unemployment.

In the transition this principle was implemented with mixed results. Some central bank governors were not really independent (Belarus 1994–98); others followed their own personal political agenda (in Poland in 1995 the Central Bank governor stood for election as President without resigning beforehand and resumed her position after a resounding defeat); others aimed at targets different from price stability, such as the support of state enterprises (Russia 1992).

In the fight against inflation, the Central Bank sometimes fixed real interest rates at usurious levels (Russia 1994, with a real annual rate of the order of magnitude of 200 per cent, or Poland towards the end of the 1990s and early 2000s). Such rates became a residual form of central planning that necessarily caused deflation. There was no co-ordination with fiscal policies, which involved interest rates, exchange rates and fiscal deficits all higher, with less inflation but higher unemployment and lower net exports and lower incomes, than would otherwise have been possible and desirable.

In Russia in 1998 the containment of inflation led to overvalued exchange rates, maintained thanks to high interest rates which were not consistent – given the burden of public debt – with fiscal balance. The bubble exploded in August 1998: the Russian government defaulted in spite of the massive financial support of the IMF, the World Bank and the G8; the banks that had sold credit default swaps to cover investors against the risk of devaluation were unable to meet their obligations; those investors who were not favoured by the government with the early redemption of government bonds lost most of their investment; and the rouble was massively devalued.

A policy of excessively high real interest rates naturally encouraged the postponement of payments of purchases, wages and taxes on the part of enterprises, and eventually the postponement of all payments (including salaries and pensions) on the part of the government, also in view of the IMF unwisely setting limits on the government deficit in cash instead of on an accruals basis. This form of de-monetization and accumulation of payment arrears, which in Russia reportedly reached something like 40 per cent of industrial transactions, was an unnecessary recessionary factor.

Pension reform

Imagine that a PAYG pension system is introduced where there was none before. Pensions begin to be paid instantly, out of the current contributions of those currently employed, while making sure, however, that the following condition is continuously satisfied:

$$p.P = a.w.L$$

where p is the average pension, P are the old age pensioners, w is the average wage, L are those currently employed, and a is the fraction of their wage that they contribute to the pension system. As long as:

$$a = p.P/w.L = (p/w).(P/L)$$

the system is balanced, does not absorb any resources from the state budget and can be deemed to 'yield' pensioners a rate of return equal to the growth rate of the wage bill. Certainly it is like a Ponzi scheme, in that payments out are funded by payments in. However, it is a *viable* Ponzi scheme, in that there are always new depositors (as long as there are *some* current employees), withdrawals are restricted (to pensioners, monthly) and are orderly (i.e. not exceeding new payments in). Population ageing can be anticipated, dealt with by prior accumulation of reserves, or by raising pension contributions, by lowering pensions or extending the retirement age.

A capitalized, fully funded, defined contributions system, by definition, does not cost anything to the budget – until there is a serious financial crisis in which the state cannot leave the elderly destitute. It yields whatever rate of return is earned by the investment of employee contributions; it promotes 'choice' and the development of financial markets. However, the switch from the first to the second pension system has an *unnecessary cost*, i.e. the emergence of a pension debt that – as long as the equilibrium condition mentioned above is satisfied – could otherwise remain conveniently buried for ever, until the end of the world.

A PAYG system has an implicit hidden debt, equal to the present value of the pension rights already matured by current employees and pensioners, but such a debt only has to be paid if there is a transition to a capitalized, fully funded, defined contribution system (see Chapter 8 of Eatwell *et al.*, 2000, Barr and Diamond, 2008).

Paradoxically, the reversal of such a reform, with a return to PAYG (partial or full, temporary or permanent), would free fiscal resources equivalent to the pension contributions of those currently employed for the entire period during which the reversal lasts (see the recent examples of Poland, Hungary, and other transition economies), without resorting to unnecessary and illegal confiscation of pension funds already accumulated.

The current crisis

The global crisis of 2007 to date struck transition economies in the middle of a process of rapid growth and robust catching up with the rest of Europe. In 2000–07, central-eastern Europe grew at an average yearly rate of 6.3 per cent, south-eastern Europe at an average of 5.0 per cent, and the CIS at 8.3 per cent, while the EU-15 grew at an average of 2.6 per cent, thus leading to progress in convergence towards average EU-15 income levels, from 39 per cent in 1995 to 57 per cent in 2005 (Connolly, 2010). The crisis hit them: (1) *with a 1-year delay* compared to the global economy, in the last quarter of 2008 after the collapse of Lehman Brothers (simply because of the relative under-development of their financial systems, for they were not involved in the sub-prime crisis); (2) *with particular intensity*, not so much compared to other country groups but rather with respect to their earlier performance before the crisis and especially contrasting with previous forecasts of their performance. Against this background, therefore, the actual income falls (with the exception of Poland in the EU, Albania and Azerbaijan, with positive though slow growth in 2009) are an under-estimate of the impact of the global crisis in the region. What counts is the *deceleration* (i.e. the growth rate decrease) involved; and (3) was followed by a *more rapid recovery* compared to the rest of Europe (though not as fast as other emerging countries), resuming the earlier convergence process with the EU-15 but still with modest and intermittent progress. There has been a great diversity among these countries, depending on their economic policies and in particular their exchange rate regime, their dependence on foreign trade, and their integration in global financial markets.

The Bruegel-WIIW (2010) report gives great importance to the exchange rate regime: floating rates have fared better than fixed. This is true – with two qualifications. First, a floating exchange rate can maintain international competitiveness through devaluation – up to a point, for competitive devaluations make every competitor worse-off. If trade flows are sufficiently elastic and there is appropriate spare capacity, this improves trade balances. However, devaluation raises the value of all debt denominated in foreign exchange – which is most of it in these countries, in view of higher interest rates in a fairly stable domestic currency and the difficulty of borrowing in domestic currency. Thus, devaluation may turn private and public loans into sub-primes, raising both the risk of default and interest rates.

A fixed exchange rate does not have this negative impact on debt, but loses international competitiveness and causes unemployment, and is still exposed to the risk of sudden devaluation, all the more damaging as it is less expected; the very prospect of a possible devaluation may raise interest rate spreads and the price of Credit Default Swaps. Every exchange rate regime has both costs and benefits, but there is no regime that protects a country fully from a crisis.

Second, the orthodox 'bi-polar' view of exchange rates typified by Fischer (2001), namely that a fixed or adjustable peg should be avoided in favour of either a flexible or hyper-fixed regime (Currency Boards, or the unilateral adoption of a foreign currency), has been falsified by the transition countries in the economic crisis. In particular the Baltic sstates have suffered greatly – from the straitjacket of a hyper-fixed misaligned parity – in terms of output and interest rates, and from the alternative 'internal' devaluation in the form of a severe deflation, which was forced upon them as the only remedy to restore competitiveness.

The EU has not allowed its members and accession candidates to adopt unilateral euroiza-tion, but has allowed Currency Boards (e.g. Bulgaria, Latvia), inexplicably because their success is subject to the achievement of at least the fiscal and monetary convergence conditions required before adopting the euro. A Currency Board simply reduces the probability of a crisis at the very considerable cost of making the crisis catastrophic if and when it occurs (as in Argentina in 2002).

The adoption of a hyper-liberal economic system, which had partly contributed to the transformation recession, subsequently facilitated their integration in the European economy, their growth and convergence. Openness to trade and dependence on external finance made them particularly vulnerable in 2009, with the collapse of world trade (the first episode of de-globalization since global integration resumed its course after the last War) and the slow-down and often the reversal of capital flows (often referred to as their 'sudden stop'). There was also the impact of worsening terms of trade, which on average was almost as large as that of the reduction in trade volume, and worse for primary products exporters (primarily Russia, Azerbaijan and Kazakhstan).

Financial integration promoted growth and convergence, but in the crisis it became a channel for contagion. Large capital inflows (flowing 'downhill' in this case, not 'uphill' from emerging to advanced economies as is often the case globally; reaching 11 per cent of their GDP before the crisis) made these countries vulnerable to flow reversals. Moreover, the composition of capital inflows in many transition economies was often inappropriate, focusing on real estate and financial services rather than on manufacturing tradeables.

Transition economies on average had a high share of foreign ownership of banks, growing especially in 1999–2001 from an average 40 per cent to over 70 per cent (except Slovenia), mostly by EU-15 groups, approaching 100 per cent in some countries of Central-Eastern Europe. Foreign banks provided personnel, know how, funds, credibility and expanded the volume of credit. At the beginning of the global crisis, however, in a framework of lower capital inflows, these countries suffered initially from the frequent capital repatriation by foreign banks, also because national government support for EU-15 banks was not extended to their eastern operations. This was a typical prisoner's dilemma, i.e. there was a collective advantage if all banks kept lending, an individual advantage for one bank that did not while all the others did, and a collective loss if all banks withdrew. However, the EBRD and the IMF provided funds and incentives that kept this adverse development under control through the European Bank Co-ordination Initiative (the so-called 'Vienna Initiative') between international banking groups, home and host-country authorities, IFIs and the EU (see the EBRD's *Transition Report*, 2009). The Initiative is being replicated in 2012, with lower prospects of success.

The Bruegel–WIIW (2010) report stresses the need for regulation and supervision of financial markets, such as constraints on leverage, regulation of derivatives, better capitalization, counter-cyclical macroeconomic policies, Glass–Steagall-type legislation, consumer protection, transaction taxes, provisions for systemic risk. That all this was needed was already well known before the crisis, except that the hyper-liberal approach that had dominated the global economy since the late 1980s shaped the financial systems of transition countries even more forcefully than those of advanced countries.

Those transition economies that joined the EU did not – with the exception of Slovenia and to some extent Estonia – adopt the institutions of the European Social Model; it was not part of the institutional convergence required by the EU of new members. This resulted in the inadequacy of social safety nets, to protect the population from unemployment, poverty, illness and old age. Such inadequacy raised the social cost of the economic crisis when it happened and disabled some of the mechanisms that dampen economic decline (they are usually called 'automatic stabilizers', improperly because they can slow down the decline but cannot reverse it on their own).

On the positive side, the same deep and possibly premature integration with the global real and financial economy is bound to lead to economic recovery in these countries if and when – sooner or later – the global economy bounces back.

Note

1 There were three gradual alternatives, all of them inferior to instant change. First, sequential price rises initially short of equilibrium (involving lower inflation but persistent disequilibrium and expectations of further inflation). Second, a two-track price system (China 1980s, part controlled part free, but in

transition economies imbalances were too large, there was no time and too little administrative capacity). Third, sequential price liberalization of groups of commodities (which would have led to adverse forced substitution). Price liberalization was preferable to the uncertain guesswork of an arbitrary and inefficient system of market-clearing administered prices.

Bibliography

Åslund, A. (2000), *The Myth of Output Collapse after Communism*, Washington, DC: Carnegie Institute.

Barr, N. and Diamond, P. (2008), *Reforming Pensions: Principles and Policy Choices*, New York and Oxford: Oxford University Press.

Blanchard, O. and Kremer, M. (1997), 'Disorganization,' *The Quarterly Journal of Economics*, vol. 112(4), pp. 1091–1126.

Bruegel-WIIW Expert Group on Central-Eastern Europe (2010), *Whither Growth in Central and Eastern Europe? Policy lessons for an integrated Europe*, Brussels and Vienna, June.

Connolly, R. (2010), 'The determinants of the economic crisis in emerging Europe', CREES, University of Birmingham, December.

Eatwell, J., Ellman, M., Karlsson, M., Nuti, D.M. and Shapiro, J. (2000), *Soft Budgets, Hard Choices: the future of the welfare state in central eastern Europe*, London: IPPR.

EBRD (various years), *Transition Report*, London: European Bank for Reconstruction and Development (annual publication since 1994).

Ellman, M. (2012), 'What did the study of transition economies contribute to mainstream economics?', JACES Conference Paper, June.

Fischer, S. (2001), 'Exchange Rate Regimes: Is the Bipolar View Correct?', *Journal of Economic Perspectives*, Vol. 15(2), Spring.

Hare, P. and Hughes, G. (1991), 'Competitiveness and Industrial Restructuring in Czechoslovakia, Hungary and Poland', *CEPR Discussion Paper No. 543*, London, April.

Kolodko, G.W. (2000), *From Shock to Therapy. The Political Economy of Postsocialist Transformation*, Oxford and New York: Oxford University Press.

Kolodko, G.W. and Nuti, D.M. (1997), 'The Polish Alternative – Old myths, hard facts and new strategies in the successful Polish economic transformation', *UNU/WIDER Research for Action series no. 33*, Helsinki, May.

Kornai, J. (1980), *Economics of Shortage*, 2 Vols, Amsterdam: North Holland Pub Co.

Laski, K. (1990), 'The stabilisation plan for Poland', *Wirtschaftspolitische Blatter* n.5 37 Jg., pp. 444–57.

Lavigne, M. (1991), *International political economy and socialism*, Cambridge: Cambridge University Press.

Mundell, R.A. (1997), 'The great contractions in transition economies', in Blejer, Mario I. and Skreb, Marko (eds), *Macroeconomic Stabilisation in Transition Economies*, Cambridge: Cambridge University Press, pp. 73–99.

North, D.C. (1990), *Institutions, Institutional Change and Economic Performance*, Cambridge: Cambridge University Press.

Nuti, D.M. (1986), 'Hidden and repressed inflation in Soviet-type economies: definitions, measurements and stabilization', *Contributions to Political Economy*, 5, pp. 37–82.

——(2007), 'Managing Transition Economies', in White, Stephen, Batt, Judy and Lewis, Paul (eds), *Developments in Central and East European Politics*, No. 4, Durham, NC: Duke University Press.

Popov, V. (2007), 'Shock therapy versus gradualism: lessons from transition economies after 15 years of reforms', *Comparative Economic Studies*, 49, pp. 1–31.

Sachs, J. (1993), *Poland's Jump to the Market Economy*, Cambridge, MA: MIT Press.

Shleifer, A. and Treisman, D. (2000), *On the Road without a Map, Political Tactics and Economic Reform in Russia*, Cambridge, MA: MIT Press.

World Bank (1996), *From Plan to Market. World Development Report*, Oxford and New York: Oxford University Press.

——(1997), *The State in a Changing World. World Development Report*, Vol. 1, Washington, DC: World Bank.

——(2000), *Making Transition Work for Everyone: Poverty and Inequality in Europe and Central Asia*, Washington, DC: World Bank.

——(2002), *Building institutions for markets*. World Development Report, Washington, DC: World Bank.

4

IS THE TRANSITION OVER?

A definition and some measurements

Oleh Havrylyshyn

Introduction[1]

While many observers thought it was premature for Czech Prime Minister Václav Klaus to suggest in 1995 the transition was over except for fine-tuning,[2] nearly 25 years after the fall of the Berlin Wall it is worth asking the question again. The main contribution of this chapter is to show that, for all practical purposes, the post-communist transition is over in most of the early reformers of Central Europe and the Baltic states; but it is *not over* for other transition countries – though many are well advanced, and only three or four remain far behind. The reasons why some are still lagging behind are not investigated, save for a few telegraphic remarks.

Earlier studies addressing this question did not define the end of transition rigorously, but were more often qualitative judgments.[3] Here, a precise definition of transition and its end point is proposed, as well as some practical ways of measuring it. Coverage is for the period 1990–2010 in post-communist Europe and Eurasia, excluding China and Vietnam as the they are not only still communist regimes, but the transformation they faced was different, more akin to an economic development problem for a still agricultural economy.

The next section defines transition theoretically as the attainment of an efficient market allocation equilibrium. Then the end point is defined as the correction of socialism's main distortions to arrive at a position similar to properly functioning market economies. To assess this, a number of quantitative indicators are presented. The final section summarizes the evidence on completion of transition, noting the differences across countries and measures used.

Defining the end of transition

The meaning of transition and its aims differs for different individuals. For citizens of the former communist countries, transition was seen as a way to overcome the backward economic conditions of the socialist world, and its end was catching up to income levels of the EU; define this as *POP1*. The transition was also viewed as the return to 'civilized European society' with democratic and personal freedoms, *POP2*, with more or less equal weight given to each element. For academics, views differed but overlapped; political scientists and historians focused more on democratization and freedoms: *POL*. These political aspects of transition are not discussed further below.

Economists were most interested in the transition to a market economy with private ownership, comprising two steps which form the focus of this contribution: achieving market rules (*MRULE*), and attaining optimal efficiency (*MEFF*).[4]

A theoretical definition of economic transition and its end point

Two main schools of thought developed on how to do transition: the rapid or big-bang reforms, versus gradual reforms. In the early years of the transition many said that knowing exactly how to proceed was difficult because 'when the Berlin Wall fell there was no theory of transition' (Roland, 2001, p. 9). The concern that one needed more time to think it through and do it right was itself an argument for gradual reforms, but the main rationale was to avoid the social costs of high unemployment during the time it took for new efficient industries to develop. Paradoxically, both big-bang and gradualism proponents based their arguments on the same theoretical principles of efficient resource reallocation. However, neither school explicitly specified a comprehensive model of transition, whence the contentious view, 'there is no theory'.

For the present purpose of defining an end point of transition, it is proposed here that a sufficient theoretical basis is provided by combining Kornai's (1994) partial definition (changes of rules and incentives by eliminating the central plan, price liberalization, allowing private ownership and imposition of hard-budget constraints), with Blanchard's (1997) also partial

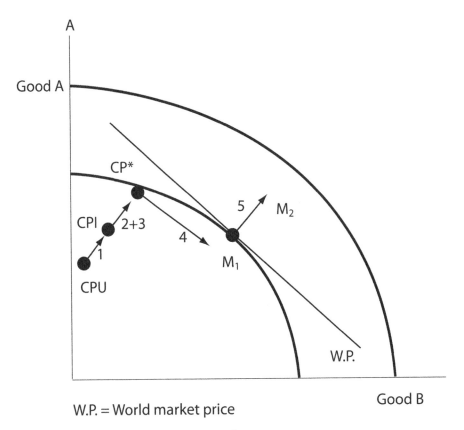

Figure 4.1 How the PPF defines transition and its end
Copyright © 2008 by Nomos Publishing, Baden-Baden/Germany.

definition (resource reallocation and efficiency improvements in response to new incentives). Call this the KB theory of transition and define Kornai's changes as the *MRULE*, and Blanchard's as *MEFF*. Broadly, most writings on transition, whether espousing big-bang, gradualism or institutions first, all implicitly worked in this theoretical context: *change the rules, then reallocate resources to achieve efficiency*.[5]

This KB theory can be represented in a simple Production Possibility Frontier (PPF), Figure 4.1 showing the conventional production trade-off between two goods, say A, machinery, and B, consumer goods, assuming full and efficient employment of all resources, and world prices WP. A second PPF is shown further out from the origin; this represents the basis for new growth after transition has been completed.

Take CP★ as the Central Planner's optimum combination of A and B, which historical consensus agrees was not achievable in practice owing to various socialist inefficiencies. With the actual position inside the PPF at CPI (inefficient), Kornai (1994) argued the first step in transition – *MRULE* – will create a transition recession with output declining to CPU (underemployment). Whether one starts here or at CPI does not materially affect the argument, for in either case the system in under-producing relative to potential, and is generally biased towards a high ratio of machinery to consumer goods. Once *MRULE* is achieved, corrections take place reducing socialist inefficiencies and underutilization of capacity, i.e. recovering from the transition recession and moving towards the PPF.[6]

The actual steps taken by the economy in reaction to *MRULE* may be simultaneous but are usefully distinguished as follows: (1) output decline due to hard-budget from CPI to CPU; (2) recovery of output with socialist capacity back to CPI; (3) efficiency improvements to move economy towards PPF; and (4) movement along PPF, reallocating resources among goods to reflect preferences and comparative advantage in an open economy. Thus, the ultimate end of transition is market equilibrium, and it is reached at M1.[7]

MRULE, involves changing the rules from central planning to competitive market decision-making and allowing private ownership. Popularly, this is often described as creating capitalism, which can be misleading and the source of disagreements about outcomes. Formally, capitalism refers only to the 'ownership' aspect, with state-guided capitalism, monopoly capitalism or competitive capitalism all possible. In this spirit, it has been said that capitalism has now been achieved in Russia or Ukraine, suggesting transition is over. But in fact their non-competitive 'oligarch' capitalism is an incomplete transition relative to the open and competitive market rules benchmark. An alternative interpretation for such countries is that transition is frozen part-way towards a competitive and open market economy.[8]

From the economist's perspective, achieving *MRULE* is just the first step, a necessary but not sufficient condition for the end of transition. The end point and sufficient condition is *MEFF* (at M1); once it is achieved it must have been the case that *MRULE* was also achieved. Nevertheless, it is very useful to track achievement of the *MRULE*, as is done by the EBRD's annual Transition Indicators, as shown below.

Deriving measures of the MEFF end point

Direct measurement of the PPF is not possible, and even efficiency frontier estimates for a single product require a massive econometric exercise. Here proxy indicators for M1 are proposed, *measuring how far the well-known faults of socialism have been corrected relative to the benchmark, average value for 'similar' market economies*.

It is widely agreed that the main shortcomings of economies based on Soviet-type central planning were: (1) anti-consumer bias as seen, for example, in the very low level of automobile and telephone ownership; (2) over-industrialization and its mirror image, a very low share of services activity in GDP; (3) a relatively closed economy with low ratio of trade to GDP; (4) inward orientation of trade within the socialist bloc; (5) goods-specific allocations that were not reflective of comparative advantage. For the first four the consensus is strong; but less so for the comparative advantage issue; furthermore, it is very difficult to determine a country's comparative advantage and judge how much correction there has been, hence this measure will be treated more qualitatively and conclusions will be less certain.

Considering what each of these faults implies about the correction allows one to derive a practical measure of the end point. Correcting the anti-consumption raises the share of personal consumption in GDP, and the most sensible benchmark is middle-income market economies. Data on major consumer goods like automobiles are also available for illustration.[9]

Correcting the over-industrialization means that the GDP share of manufacturing or industrial sectors should fall over time. The benchmark for M1 here can be more rigorous than a simple comparison with similar market economies: it is well known in development theory going back to Clark (1940) that this share at first increases as an economy develops with the counterpart share of agriculture declining. At some middle-level of income the manufacturing share begins to decline, with agriculture continuing to decline but services increasing. Econometric cross-country analysis of this relationship was done by Chenery, Robinson and Syrquin (1986), and recent estimates for transition countries will be summarized in the next section.

The closed and inward-oriented economy of the socialist period should become more open during the transition, so that its trade/GDP ratio rises, and each country's trade should become more geographically diversified, with the share of exports outside the (former) socialist bloc rising. Openness ratios are readily calculated and cross-country comparisons are summarized below. For geographic diversification, the benchmark is based on available gravity model estimates for transition countries.

Finally, there is the product misallocation fault, not being at the comparative advantage equilibrium on the PPF at world market prices. Most outside experts held this view, but some were less sure suggesting that, for example, the concentration of Eastern European satellites on small and medium manufactures, while the USSR concentrated on natural resources and heavy industry, was not altogether wrong. This is also far more difficult to measure, short of the extensive factor endowment estimates as in Leamer (1984), which do not appear to exist for transition countries, hence prudence might suggest omitting this indicator. However, it has become a central policy issue in many CIS countries (Russia, Ukraine, Kazakhstan) with concerns that transition has 'hollowed out' the strong manufacturing capacity of the socialist period and pushed countries backward to the status of resource-based economies. Therefore some analysis of this is attempted here, but warily and less rigorously than for other measures.

Evidence on completion of transition

MRULE: CEB completed, others advancing, a few laggards

Before assessing attainment of *MEFF*, it is useful to ask how close countries are to completing the first step, *MRULE*. The EBRD provides a widely used set of annual transition indicators (TIs), each assessed on a scale running from 1.0 (indicating next to no change from central planning) to 4+ (often interpreted as 4.3, representing a fully functioning market economy). The indicators comprise three groups: market liberalization (*LIB*), market institutions (*INST*) – the EBRD labels these second-generation measures – and infrastructure reform. Here, the average of the first two is used to indicate the extent of attainment of *MRULE*. Since the EBRD does not score existing market economies, it is a little unclear what the top score of 4.3 really represents. Hence, here the attainment of *MRULE* is considered more or less complete at indicator values of 4.0.

Three of the indicators comprise the main liberalizing measures (*LIB*): liberalization of prices, trade, and small scale privatization. The other five are akin to institutional rule changes (*INST*): firm governance, entry and competition, financial market development, etc. How good is this measure? Shortcomings of the TIs have been noted by many, but no alternatives are available for the full period. The above definition for *INST* is far from ideal and much less comprehensive than others like the World Bank Governance Indicators or Doing Business Indices. However, its advantage is the full coverage from 1990. Furthermore, Havrylyshyn (2009) shows a very high correlation (0.90 or more) between *INST* and other measures.

Table 4.1 presents data for 27 countries in five groups showing the following: the year *LIB* reached 4.0, the year in which the TIs (*LIB* + *INST*) reached 4.0; if still below 4.0, actual 2010 values are shown in brackets. *INST* values for 2010 are in the last column.

Countries are grouped to reflect similar reform progress,[10] central Europe and the Baltic states (CEB) are the most advanced, with south-east Europe (SEE) now catching up, more reformist FSU countries (CISM) close behind, with Belarus, Turkmenistan, Uzbekistan (CISL) little advanced.[11] Table 4.1 suggests *MRULE* for the *LIB* subset was largely achieved in CEB as early as 1992–94, with one exception, Slovenia in 1996. The Baltic countries, starting only about 1992 had completed these by 1994, no later than most of Central Europe. Only Poland and then Czechoslovakia were earlier.[12] *INST* values increased much more slowly for all, and even the fastest CEB countries are still short of a 4.0 value.

Most SEE and CISM countries have by now reached the 4.0 threshold for *LIB*, with Bosnia-Herzegovina, Montenegro and Tajikistan just short. But apart from Bulgaria and Romania (EU members), none has come at all close in the *INST* category, thus these countries, despite considerable policy changes, are far from completing even the first Kornai step. Even farther behind are the three CISL countries, still remaining with socialist rules rather than the market.

Significantly, the broad picture of CEB near completion, SEE and CISM moving forward but still short, and CISL virtually unchanged from the socialist period, presages the results below for indicators of *MEFF* completion.

Indicators for attainment of MEFF

Here we show values by country groups of *MEFF* proxies related to major distortions of socialism. The CISL laggards and SEE are excluded for some indicators; and in CISL the *MRULE* is so little advanced that progress to *MEFF* is hard to judge; SEE are more advanced on the *MRULE*, but political and civil instability through the nineties has doubtless delayed adjustments, especially on the structure of production and exports.

Anti-consumer bias corrected for most

To assess how much anti-consumer bias has been corrected it suffices to observe trends in the share of personal consumption in GDP, as shown in Figure 4.2 and the comparable benchmark Middle Income Countries (MIDINC) as defined by the World Bank.

Both CEB and CISM show an increase in the consumption share within the first five years already from below 50 per cent of GDP to a little under or over 60 per cent, bringing them close to the MIDINC average of about 60 per cent. Lazarev and Gregory (2007), in a study of

Table 4.1 Attainment of *MRULE*

Country	Year LIB=4	Year TI=4	Inst (2010)
Croatia	1994	[3.7]	3.3
Czech Republic	1992	2007	3.7 (2007)
Hungary	1994	2005	3.8
Poland	1993	2007	3.7
Slovakia	1992	2007	3.5
Slovenia	1996	[3.5]	3.0
Central Europe			3.5
Estonia	1994	2006	3.8
Latvia	1994	[3.8]	3.3
Lithuania	1994	[3.8]	3.5
Baltic states			3.6
Albania	2000	[3.2]	2.5
Bosnia-Herzegovina	[3.8]	[3.0]	2.5
Bulgaria	2000	[3.8]	3.4
Macedonia	1994	[3.4]	2.8
Montenegro	[3.9]	[3.0]	2.4
Romania	1998	[3.5]	3.2
Serbia	2007	[3.1]	2.5
South-Eastern Europe			2.8
Armenia	2001	[3.3]	2.7
Azerbaijan	2007	[3.2]	2.1
Georgia	1997	[3.5]	2.6
Kazakhstan	1997	[3.2]	2.5
Kyrgyzstan	1995	[3.2]	2.4
Moldova	2005	[3.1]	2.5
Russia	2007	[3.1]	2.7
Tajikistan	[3.8]	[2.6]	1.9
Ukraine	2007	[3.2]	2.5
CISM			2.4
Belarus	[2.6]	[2.2]	1.9
Turkmenistan	[2.3]	[1.5]	1.0
Uzbekistan	[2.7]	[2.2]	2.0
CISL			1.6

Source: Author's calculations from EBRD Transition Reports

Russia, also conclude the bias is largely corrected. Some overshoot is seen in 1995 for SEE countries, perhaps reflecting the much greater political and economic instability. Broadly it seems that anti-consumer bias has been quickly and probably completely corrected in most transition countries; in Figure 4.1 this would mean that allocation had shifted to the lower right, with more consumer goods being produced.

A dramatic example for a specific item whose consumption was severely constrained under socialism, automobiles, is shown in Figure 4.3, suggesting fulfilment of consumers' pent-up demand, particularly in the CEB countries where economic recovery came soonest.[13] A similar story can be told for telephones, housing space, household appliances, and foreign travel. All this is of more than descriptive interest, since such surges in meeting pent-up demand are probably also associated with the excess-credit and overheating in the second transition decade, which resulted in this region being the hardest hit among emerging markets by the global recession.

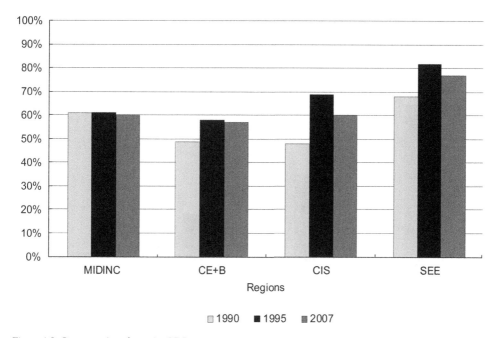

Figure 4.2 Consumption shares in GDP
Source: World Bank, *World Development Indicators*, various years.

Over-industrialization largely corrected in CEB, only partially in CISM

The problem of over-industrialization typically involved an over-emphasis on heavy and military industry compared to light industry and consumer goods, but here only the overall industry share in GDP is analysed. The changes in this share since 1990 are shown in Figure 4.4, for the original EU-15 as a rough benchmark, for the New Member States acceding in 2004 (NMS – the CEB group except Croatia), and Belarus (BY), Russia (RU), Ukraine (UA), Kazakhstan (KZ).[14]

Over-industrialization is evident in the 1990 panel: compared to a share of just over 30 per cent in the EU-15, nearly all the centrally planned economies had values of about 50 per cent. Kazakhstan's 35 per cent reflected its natural resource endowment, which incidentally is consistent with some arguments made that central plan allocations were not entirely out of line with comparative advantage. Within five years these shares fell sharply to levels around 35 per cent, but this may not have been a new equilibrium yet because of the short time for adjustment, and in the case of the CIS countries because their transition policies (*MRULE*) had barely begun. The 2004 values confirm a downward trend for the NMS, and suggest lagging adjustment for the CIS. The NMS countries reached about 32 per cent on average, only somewhat higher than the share for the much higher income EU-15. For CIS countries the share stayed in the range 35–40+ per cent, with some experiencing a slight rebound and Kazakhstan rising to a share even higher than in 1990.

The trend was towards correction, but is it complete, is MEFF attained? The EU-15, with its higher level of development, is not the best benchmark for this: a more rigorous test is provided by estimates of Chenery-type equations as follows:

$$INDSH = a + b.y1 + c.y2 + d.POP + e.SIZE + f.NATRES + g.DUM \quad (4.1)$$

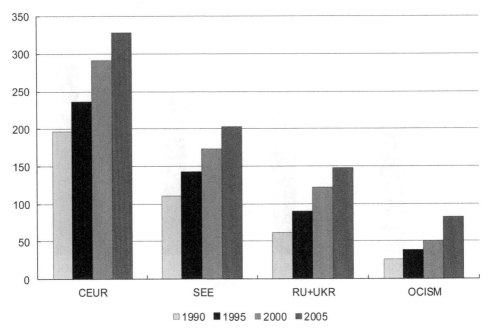

Figure 4.3 Car ownership per 1,000 population
Source: United Nations, *Annual Statistical Yearbook*, various years.

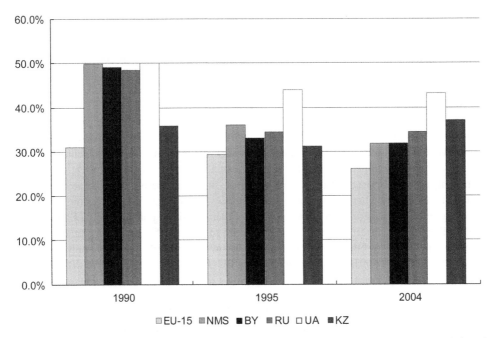

Figure 4.4 Industry and construction as percent of gross value added (Years 1990, 1995, 2005. Selected
        countries and country groups)
Source: Calculations of WIIW INDEUNIS Project: see note 14.

where y = per capita income, POP = population, SIZE = geographic area, and NATRES = some measure of natural resource endowment; some estimates use DUM for special country characteristics.

The available literature generally agrees there has been correction, and more so in CEB, but some find that by 2005 it is not yet complete even there. Gros and Steinherr (2004), using 1997 data, concluded already that in 'Central Europe the transition is nearly over'. More recent estimates for CEB in Döhrn and Heilemann (2005) and Thiessen (2004) find the correction was virtually done. Note that this means it took between 10 and 15 years after *LIB* values reached 4.0. Thiessen and Gregory (2005), looking at the employment share in ten NMS and using a fuller Chenery equation with proxies for resource endowments and institutions, confirm a clear correction trend, but conclude 'transition is not over' as only four of them have reached the MEFF point.

No Chenery estimates for the CIS appear to be available, though Lazarev and Gregory (2007) conclude that 'Russia ... a low-middle income country ... is structurally similar to higher income economies'. They infer that either Russia is approaching high-income status, or past distortions remain; the latter seems more likely, as argued below.

Table 4.2 summarizes the available estimates of Chenery predictions for CEB – shown as a range – while for Russia, Ukraine and Kazakhstan, the values are the author's 'reasoned guess' based on the following assumptions. All three have lower income than CEB, hence shares should not be lower. Ukraine, with limited natural resources save for agriculture, whose exports are constrained by EU policies, is likely to be at the top of the range, say 35 per cent. Russia, with a comparable level of development, is likely to be lower given its strong natural resource endowment, as is Kazakhstan. If the 'reasoned guess' shares are taken at face-value, the three CIS countries are far from completing this part of the transition, with actual share values considerably in excess of the norm for countries at that level of development, and in the cases of Russia and Kazakhstan far more industry than their natural resources would suggest.

Trade orientation: all very open, geographical re-orientation complete for CEB, nearly so for CIS

In the socialist period there was much trade within the Council for Mutual Economic Assistance (CMEA), but standard trade-GDP ratios were far below 'normal', with very little trade outside the bloc save for Russian energy exports. 'Normal' means the expected ratio drawn from a cross-country regression where the trade ratio is a function of income, size, landlocked status, etc. Several such studies have been done with results briefly summarized here. Virtually all transition economies very rapidly opened to trade beyond the old bloc, trade ratios for the smaller countries quickly reached 100 per cent and more by 2005, and on the whole 'fit' well in such regressions.[15] Turkmenistan is an exception, but interestingly the other two CISL laggards have very high openness ratios. The evidence, while incomplete, is enough to conclude that the trade-opening aspect of adjustment is essentially complete.

Table 4.2 Industry shares of GDP, actual and predicted (selected years and countries, groups)

	Actual: 1988–1990	*Chenery: predicted*	*Actual: 2005*
NMS	50	32–35	32
RUS	48	(30? Res)	38
UKR	50	(35??)	43
KAZ	35	(30? Res)	38

Source: As in Figure 4.4 plus author's compilations.

Equally important was the substantial outward shift of trade. A good indicator of this is the share of a country's exports to the EU-15;[16] Figure 4.5 shows the trends from 1990 to 2005, with a dramatic shift evident in all countries and groups. It was most immediate for Central Europe, jumping from 20–40 per cent in 1990 to over 60 per cent by 1995, then stabilizing at about 65 per cent. For the Baltic states it was even more dramatic, from less than 5 per cent to well over 50 per cent. With the exception of Russia, all USSR republics had very limited exports to EU (though some of this was accounting, attributing to state-trading firms in Moscow exports from other republics). It is thus not surprising that the biggest jump was in the Baltic states, followed then by the Ukraine which increased more slowly from 5 per cent in 1990 to about 25 per cent in 2005. Russia started much higher at 20 per cent, and this doubled to more than 40 per cent, however some of the increase was not a volume but a price effect, as the dominant export was energy (mostly oil and gas). The same sharp reorientation is seen in SEE. However, is the reorientation complete?

Analogously to industry share, a rigorous test is whether destination shares are similar to predictions of the well-known gravity model:

$$X_{ij} = a + b.Y_i + c.Y_j + d.DIST_{ij} + e.DUM \quad (4.2)$$

where X_{ij} is exports from country i to country j; Y_i is GDP of each country, and $DIST_{ij}$ is the distance (in kilometres or travel costs) between i and j, and DUM are variables reflecting special relations between i and j such as common language, contiguous borders, free trade arrangements and the like. The coefficients b and c are positive and d is negative. Results for available gravity model estimates are summarized in Table 4.3 showing export shares to the EU before transition, the range of predicted values for this share in various gravity model studies, and the range for actual shares in the period 2000–2005.[17]

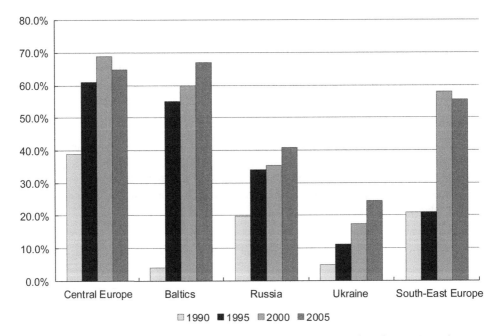

Figure 4.5 Share of total exports to EU (Years 1990, 1995, 2000, 2005. Selected countries and country groups)
Source: as in Figure 4.4.

Table 4.3 Share of exports to the EU: actual and gravity estimates

	EU share: 1987	EU Share: predicted by models	EU share: 2000–05 actual
Central Europe	35	70–80	65–70
Baltic states	4	60–70	55–65
Russia	20	35–40	40–45
Ukraine	5	30–35	20–25

Source: Author's compilations for Column 2; and WIIW INDEUNIS calculations.

Clearly, the CEB countries have essentially completed their geographic orientation towards Europe; Russia exceeds the estimated norm but perhaps only because energy prices have been very high; Ukraine has not yet reached the 'normal' despite its huge shift. There is no hard evidence for other CIS countries or SEE, but it is likely that, as in Ukraine, the shift has been substantial if still incomplete.[18]

Has the comparative advantage equilibrium been reached? Maybe, maybe not

As already noted, determining the new comparative advantage equilibrium is far more difficult than for the other indicators. Leamer endowment models are a vast undertaking, and even more feasible measures such as comparisons of RCA (revealed comparative advantage) values is still a large exercise, though some of this has been done.[19] An alternative approach here is to ask two questions: have some countries seen *greater* shifts in export structure; is there evidence of shifting up the technological ladder-of-comparative-advantage? Culling the literature on the above still allows use of the best available quantitative evidence.

Consider first the broad categories, agricultural, natural resource, and manufactured goods. Figure 4.6 shows that for Central Europe (= NMS5 excluding the Baltic states) the manu-facturing share has risen steadily, albeit from an already high level over 70 per cent. In contrast SEE, Russia and even Ukraine show a slight decline, offset by the rise for natural resources. For Ukraine natural resource content is understated, included in major exports like chemicals and metallurgy. Kazakhstan is not shown but exhibits the same trend as Russia, based on energy.

The increased emphasis on resources in the large CIS countries has generated heated debates about industrial policy,[20] an issue not pursued here. But does this evidence say anything about a new equilibrium? Unfortunately, not definitively. Arguably – and contentiously – one might conclude that the observed movement is *towards* a new equilibrium and not away from it, given the socialist over-emphasis on heavy-industry and the unsurprising outcome that countries with rich natural resources – energy in Russia and Kazakhstan, cotton in Uzbekistan, mild climate in Moldova (suited to fruit orchards).

Having said this, the opposite case can also be made: one should have expected the strong scientific and educational endowment of the USSR to bring about an increasing export of more high-tech products, based on radical rationalization of a large industrial capital endowment, at least after some time. In fact, a sharply increasing sophistication of exports is clearly observable in the CEB countries. Numerous studies have looked at the changed composition in terms of capital-intensity, skill-intensity, low versus medium versus high technology content, and have generally found this very quickly changed in an upwards direction already in the nineties.

Table 4.4 summarizes the widely used measure of Intra-Industry Trade (IIT), usually thought to reflect technical sophistication. In Central Europe, IIT is now in the same range or higher than in 'similar' emerging market economies, Russia and Ukraine are still much lower. This too

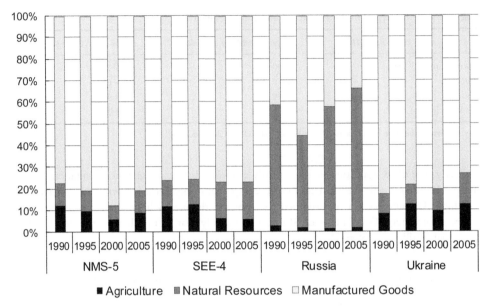

Figure 4.6 Sectoral structure of exports (Years 1990, 1995, 2000, 2005. Selected countries and country groups)
Copyright © 2008 by Nomos Publishing, Baden-Baden/Germany.

Table 4.4 Intra-industry trade index. Selected comparisons

Industrial 1978 (1995)	59 (75)
East Asia 1991–94	48
Latin America 1991–94	35
Turkey 1991–94	28
Central Europe 2000–02	55–60
Russia 2000–02	20–25
Ukraine 2000–02	38–40

Source: Author's compilations.

confirms that there was a much more dynamic structural change in Central Europe, and perhaps an approach to their new comparative advantage equilibrium.

It is not our purpose to seek the causes of the CIS lagging behind CEB in the attainment of the transition end point, but a short remark is warranted. Proponents of industrial policy contend that over-rapid reforms killed off the existing industrial potential. Perhaps more compelling are two other explanations: first the *MRULE* reforms came much later and are still incomplete; second the CIS export patterns may in fact be the new equilibrium given their large natural resource endowments.

Summary and conclusions

To answer the question, 'is transition over', it is necessary to define transition; this is best done in the context of a conventional production possibility frontier, as the movement from the socialist inefficiency position inside the frontier towards the frontier and finally to a market efficiency equilibrium point, *MEFF*, the end of transition. Direct measurement of a PPF being impossible, it is instead proposed to measure how much correction has occurred in the main faults of socialism, with the end point reached when these take values similar to comparable market economies. The first conclusion is that for Central Europe and the Baltic states transition is essentially over, elsewhere some of the shortcomings of central planning have been corrected or nearly so, but many have not, and at least three former USSR republics lag very far behind.

It is important to distinguish between two steps of the transition process: first are the changes in policy to establish market rules, *MRULE*. While this is *not* in itself a measure of the end of transition, it is a necessary condition to motivate the reallocations which lead to the *MEFF* end point. The annual transition indicators of the EBRD show that the CEB group completed the market-liberalizing parts of the rule changes by as early as 1992–94, and the remaining institutional dimensions of reforms were very close to completion by about 2010. SEE countries took much longer just for the liberalization elements, but by 2010 were close to completion. The same is true for nine CIS countries with moderate reform effort; though some achieved this well before 2000, most did so later. However, for both these groups, progress on the institutional elements was much slower, and only two (EU members Bulgaria and Romania) are approaching the CEB. Entirely *sui generis* are three laggards, Belarus, Turkmenistan and Uzbekistan, still scoring much closer to values representative of centrally planned economies. That these rankings are echoed in the measurement of *MEFF* achievement is probably not a coincidence, though the causal relation is not explored in detail.

For two of the socialist shortcomings measured here – anti-consumer bias and low trade-GDP ratios – a strong conclusion emerges that nearly all transition countries have completed this correction, with consumption-GDP ratios rising to levels comparable to middle-income countries, and openness-ratios rising sharply to fit well in cross-country regressions. Only Turkmenistan remains an exception. Over-industrialization, defined as the share of industry to GDP, was largely corrected in CEB before 2000, and may be incomplete but moving downward in most others. This is seen not only in the simple trend values of the ratio, but is confirmed by econometric estimates of the Chenery equation across a large sample of countries. The inward orientation of trade within the bloc has shifted rapidly and dramatically. Gravity model predictions of exports by destination show that CEB had reached a new equilibrium probably before 2000, with the large CIS countries approaching but not all yet at their expected values.

It is generally agreed that central planner's product allocations were not in accord with what world market prices might have implied, though some argued that comparative advantage within the socialist bloc was partially reflected, as evidenced by the concentration of the USSR on heavy industry and resources, and of the satellites on lighter manufacturing – though the latter's global non-competitiveness was revealed immediately at the start of transition and opening up to the world economy. In any event some analysis of changes in export structure is worth attempting, though precise identification of comparative advantage is not feasible. Instead, two less rigorous questions are posed: did some countries or groups show greater changes? And how much shifting occurred up the comparative-advantage ladder (towards higher technical sophistication)? Once again the CEB saw much greater changes with a continual rise of manufactures' share, with increased skill and technical content, while CIS exports continued to have a high resource content, and little movement up the technical ladder. Many different measures have been used in the literature to analyse export content, but one, the share of IIT, reflects them as if a 'tip-of-the-iceberg': CEB with values around 60 per cent, similar to those in East Asia, while Russia and Ukraine (30–40 per cent) remain at or below Latin American values.

Our results do tentatively allow the conclusion that CEB seemed to have reached a new equilibrium in its global trading relations. Many observers both inside and outside the CIS insist that the results also mean, at least for the large countries like Russia, Ukraine, Kazakhstan –

perhaps even Uzbekistan – that they are moving away from rather than towards a new comparative advantage equilibrium, and that supportive industrial policy is needed to overcome the 'hollowing out' of the manufacturing sector caused by transition. The available evidence cannot refute this view, but neither does it confirm it. Direct estimates of what is the optimal comparative advantage were not (and cannot) be done, and qualitative interpretations can go either way. On the one hand, given the strong skill and human-capital base of the USSR, and a large, albeit inefficient, capital stock, one might expect eventual export success in many technically advanced areas. On the other hand, the large resource endowments, and the very delayed and still incomplete achievement of *MRULE*, might well explain the actual outcome.

These findings point to a few key areas for further research. First, the issue of what is or is not comparative advantage merits much more investigation in future research, with more emphasis on its dynamics, especially to address the heated debates in Russia and Ukraine about 'Industrial Policy' to speed the process of moving up the ladder of comparative advantage. Second, the issue of partial reforms and their sequencing merits considerable research effort, not merely for its historical interest to the transition debates, but also for the valuable lessons it could surely provide for emerging markets with non-socialist but very involved governments, like the new Arab regimes. It is evident in this analysis that movement to *MRULE* involved partial reforms, some more delayed than others, and in all cases even slower implementation of good institutions – yet recovery came early in CEB, elsewhere it was later but did come with a surge, and seems to continue in the post-crisis period with solid if not astronomical growth. The conclusion is inescapable: you do not need the full complement of reforms to get good performance. But then what is it you do need? Is there a *de minimis* combination, or does it vary by country? Last, the fact of different speeds to implement *MRULE* raises a central political-economy question: why? How much was happenstance, historical endowment and memory, the incentive of EU membership, anti-liberal preferences of new vested interests, oligarchs?

As one approaches the 25th anniversary of the opening and dismantling of the Berlin Wall, the amount of data and experience from the transition will be vast, covering a few complete business cycles, and numerous regimes. Economists should not overlook the opportunity this wonderful laboratory provides.

Notes

1 A detailed analysis with fuller references but earlier data is in Havrylyshyn (2009).
2 The reference is to Svejnar (1999), p. 78 who questioned 'declarations such as that of the Czech Prime Minister in 1995'.
3 I accept that many experts have the ability to make such a judgment and this can be valuable.
4 Svejnar (1999) presages these distinctions, which he describes as 'two conditions' that must hold for transition to be completed, but does not define them rigorously.
5 Roland (2001) makes a similar argument about the underlying aims and concepts of all three schools of thought. He also shows without elaborating the same PPF representation.
6 A second-best question, and a key aspect of the sequencing debates is: if all the rule changes are not yet in place what combination of partial reforms gives fastest adjustment? One example of such an analysis is Zinnes *et al.* (2001), who show econometrically that efficiency improvements of privatized firms were greatest where liberalization was accompanied by good institutions.
7 Figure 4.1 can also depict the *POP1* definition of transition's end: a movement to a higher level of production for all goods (the higher PPF and an analogous equilibrium M2), hence a higher per capita income. This is not explored further here.
8 Åslund (1997), in my view, misleadingly titles his otherwise excellent book 'How Russia Became a Market Economy'.
9 Others like telephones, housing space and quality, clothing variety, video and audio equipment, could be measured as well, but the results for autos are sufficiently representative.

10 The original analysis is in Havrylyshyn (2006). While the rationale for groupings was not geographic, it is not coincidental that the results show regionalism, because there certainly were geography, proximity and historical inertia effects behind the differential progress of countries – not least EU membership incentives.
11 Arguably, Tajikistan is more like the CISL group – but this is not material to the present analysis.
12 It is likely this is what Klaus had in mind in his 1995 statement; indeed *LIB* for CZ had reached 4.0 as early as 1992.
13 Some of the country groups in Figure 4.3 for cars are different because of data availability in the source; Baltic states not shown, Russia–Ukraine shown separately and OCIS (other CIS) does not include all countries.
14 Their study compares average industry share averages for the World Bank's broad income groups.
15 Broadman (2005, p. 297, Fig. 11.1); he also gives great detail on other aspects of trade.
16 EU-15 exports are, unsurprisingly, given proximity, the predominant share for exports outside the old bloc, and thus serve as a good proxy for the geographic reorientation in transition.
17 Actual values and references to gravity model studies are in Grinberg *et al.* (2008), Ch. 2.
18 Havrylyshyn (2009) elaborates on causes for a faster or slower adjustment.
19 Another difficulty with RCA comparisons is that per capita income similarity is not an adequate benchmark: high RCA for narrow product definitions is due to many factors such as inertia, tradition, specific resources, human capital, and foreign investment.
20 Much of Grinberg *et al.* (2008) addresses these debates; it also discusses the most relevant studies from the vast literature on measuring skill-intensity and quality of exports in Central Europe.

Bibliography

Åslund, A. (1997), *How Russia Became a Market Economy*, Washington, DC: Brookings Institution.
Blanchard, O. (1997), *The Economics of Post-communist Transition*, Oxford: The Clarendon Press.
Broadman, M. (2005), *From Disintegration to Reintegration: Eastern Europe and the Former Soviet Union in International Trade*, Washington, DC: World Bank.
Chenery, H., S. Robinson, and Syrquin, M. (1986), *Industrialization and Growth. A Comparative Study*, Oxford: Oxford University Press (published for the World Bank).
Clark, G. (1940), *The Conditions of Economic Progress*, London: MacMillan.
Döhrn, R. and Heilemann, U. (2005), 'Sectoral Change and Economic Integration: Theoretical and Empirical Aspects of the Eastern Enlargement of the European Union', pp. 79–96 in Welfens, P. and Wziatek-Kubiak, A. (eds), *Structural Change and Exchange Rate Dynamics. The Economics of EU Eastern Enlargement*, Berlin: Springer Verlag.
EBRD (Various years), *Transition Report*, London: European Bank for Reconstruction and Development.
Grinberg, R., Havlik, P. and Havrylyshyn, O. (eds) (2008), *Economic Restructuring and Integration in Eastern Europe*, Baden-Baden: Nomos Publishers.
Gros, D. and Steinherr, A. (2004), *Economic Transition in Central and Eastern Europe*. Cambridge: Cambridge University Press.
Havrylyshyn, O. (2009), 'Is The Transition Over?', *Economics Department Working Paper* 1209, Queen's University, Kingston, Ontario.
——(2006), *Divergent Paths in Post Communist Transformation: Capitalism for All or Capitalism for the Few?* Houndmills: Palgrave MacMillan.
Kornai, J. (1994), 'Transformational Recession: The Main Causes', *Journal of Comparative Economics*, vol. 19, pp. 34–63.
Lazarev, V. and Gregory, P. (2007), 'Structural Convergence in Russia's Economic Transition,' *Economic Change and Restructuring*, vol. 40(3), pp. 281–304.
Leamer, E. (1984), *Sources of International Comparative Advantage: Theory and Evidence*, Cambridge, MA: MIT Press.
Roland, G. (2001), 'Ten Years After … Transition and Economics', *IMF Staff Papers*, vol. 48 (special issue), pp. 29–52.
Svejnar, J. (1999), 'The Transition Is Not Over, But Note The Merits of the Central European Model,' in Brown, A. (ed.), *When Is The Transition Over?*, pp. 77–98, Kalamazoo, MI: W.E. Upjohn Institute.
Thiessen, U. (2004), 'Modelling Structural Change: Assessing the Likely Sectoral Pattern of Structural Changes in the NMS,' DIW Berlin, Working Paper.
Thiessen, U., and P. Gregory (2005), 'Modelling the Structural Change of Transition Countries, *Discussion Paper* 519, DIW Berlin.
Zinnes, C., Eilat, Y. and Sachs, J. (2001), 'Benchmarking competitiveness in transition economies', *Economics of Transition*, vol. 9(2), pp. 315–353.

Part II
Background

5

SWITCHING DEVELOPMENT STRATEGIES AND THE COSTS OF TRANSITION

The case of the Soviet Union and Russia

Gur Ofer

A short way that is long and a long one that is short.

(Talmud Bavli, Massechet Eruvin, *daf 53 page b*)

Introduction

The literature on modern economic growth and on economic development discusses a large number of cases where pairs of growth strategies follow each other, one strategy fits better the takeoff and the early stages of economic development while the other follows at a later stage (Rodrik, 2005). First-stage strategies, 'takeoffs', are typically specific to certain periods, to groups of countries in a region or even to individual countries.[1] The main features of the earlier strategy are typically heterodox in nature, they violate some of the main 'classical' principles: private property, free and open markets, less government intervention, and a democratic regime; principles at the base of the social system and economic growth in the developed world and that usually underline the second-stage strategy of developing countries.

Among the main takeoff or first-stage strategies one can list the choice of labour intensive production with 'appropriate technology' imported from developed countries; various kinds of industrial policies, dubbed 'imbalanced', in contrast with 'balanced' growth, focusing on industrial growth, even producers' goods industries, over agriculture; then there are various internal market constraining arrangements, the creation of large financial-production conglomerates, designed to provide financing and focus on industrial policy goals, as in Japan, South Korea, Taiwan and across East Asia. Takeoff strategies related to foreign trade and openness, range from virtual or functional autarky, *à la* Communism, to 'import substitution' – in Latin America, India and other countries – and up to 'export-led growth' as originated in Japan and spread throughout east and south-east Asia and beyond. Finally, there are policies of direct government interventions, culminating in full nationalization of all production via central planning and authoritarian regimes, such as under Soviet Communism.

The development literature that deals in great detail with the different nature of the two stages, paid little attention, until recently, to the transition between them, its nature and cost. Most of this literature is embedded in the theory and practice of the development of institutions, the main tools that translate growth strategy into programmes of action. While institutional economics has deep roots in the past (North, 1990), it received a boost following the transition of the Communist countries during the late 1980s and 1990s.[2] The main points in the literature relevant to this contribution are that the takeoff strategy establishes institutions that are different from those that facilitate growth in the second stage. Furthermore, according to Gerschenkron (1962), the deeper the relative economic backwardness of a country, the harsher may be the institutional tools used for the takeoff, hence the more difficult and possibly longer the transition.[3]

The shift from stage 1 to stage 2 can be thought of as being composed of two parts or two sub-periods: a period of delayed reform, during which a new strategy and institutions can already serve economic growth better. They are not installed at the right time, mostly because of the resistance of interest groups, including the old leadership, who stand to gain, economically and/or politically from the *status quo* and to lose so much from the shift, but are strong enough to resist changes. This period of delay, dubbed 'institutional' or 'convergence traps' is very costly in terms of lost growth and resources that could have supported the transition. The second period of the shift is when the transition to a new strategy and the institutional shift are taking place. The extent of economic losses connected with the transition depends on the required institutional changes, on the need to 'import' new institutions, on the level of tension between the newly installed 'formal' institutions and the existing 'informal' ones, those based on 'trust', the quality of 'social capital' and of 'civil society' and other 'cultural' attributes related to the conduct of business (North, 1990), and to a large extent also on the quality of policy making of the government in charge.

Communism is an extreme case where the growth strategy is just one part of a wider, holistic scheme of social organization. In such cases a full-fledged ideology is covering all spheres of life and economic development is only one goal, albeit a prominent one. What we call a first stage is designated by the Communist regime as an alternative social strategy for the long run with no 'second stage'. Such a doctrinal constraint creates an added barrier to change when it is warranted. Within Communism, the Soviet Union is an extreme case of a combination of a harsh autocratic regime and a highly ambitious growth strategy.

At the other extreme of the two-stage development strategy is what may be called the 'evolutionary' or 'balanced growth' strategy where more or less uniform policy tools are implemented along the way and where changes are typically small and gradual, accompanying and responding to the needs of the development process. Both a market economy and the democratic regime are gradually evolving, sometimes in a framework of a 'dual economy' where the new institutions of market economy and democracy are gradually established as economic activity moves away from the 'traditional' sectors to the modern ones. The evolutionary strategy was followed mostly by the already developed countries and a few developing ones. This group included developing countries that followed a relatively short-lived first-stage strategy, implementing 'light' and 'heterodox' tools for a few years, and moved quickly to the second stage of balanced growth with limited transition costs (a number of such cases are listed by Rodrik, 2005, Table 9).[4]

The main goal of this contribution is to study the nature and extent of the costs that are involved in a two-stage development strategy, specifically those that are caused by the transition from one stage to the other. We proceed as follows: the next section is devoted to the experience of the Soviet/Russian case, and discusses the initial decisions about growth strategy taken in the 1920s and their consequences, the appropriate time for change that was missed during the mid–1960s, and the nature of the postponed transition in the late 1980s and early 1990s. The last section offers a number of estimations and counterfactuals related to the transitional costs, and provides a short concluding discussion.

The case of the Soviet Union/Russia

Here we review in a summary fashion the considerations that led to the decision on strategy in the 1920s, the main characteristics of this strategy, the missed appropriate time for change, the forces that caused the postponement of the transition and that made it so difficult, and the main barriers confronted by the transition. Even if justified to some extent as a proper takeoff strategy, the appropriate time for change was clearly a few decades earlier than when it actually happened. The extreme nature of the strategy, and the long delay in the change, made the cost of the transition extremely high, offsetting a significant portion of what may be considered its positive achievements.

The decision on the Soviet growth strategy

The growth strategy of the Soviet Union was decided upon in the late 1920s, following a rather prolonged, well-articulated debate, concentrating mostly on the economic aspects of the alternatives presented. This may have been the earliest open debate on growth strategy in modern times. The final decisions on full public ownership, on collectivization of agriculture and on central planning and a harsh authoritarian regime, while based on political and ideological grounds, were motivated also by important economic considerations. This 'first stage' lasted almost six decades with relatively minor changes on the way.

The debate during the second part of the 1920s was between the supporters of a version that was later dubbed 'balanced growth' and those advocating faster growth based on the prime development of heavy industry. 'Balanced growth' was to be based on simultaneous development of agriculture and all branches of industry and services, with the help of foreign technology, investment and trade, with only partial government ownership of key industries. The main growth engine of the alternative, fast growth strategy was to be high investment rates focused on heavy and producers' goods industries, a growth model in line with Marxist thinking.[5] Central planning would become the main operational tool and regulator of all transactions, and most markets would be eliminated. The economic growth strategy was embedded in an authoritarian regime that also reflected Stalin's quest for absolute power, and with military considerations in mind.

Was the Soviet version of the first stage worthwhile? There is no argument that the price paid in terms of human suffering and lost life of the cruel Stalinist version of this strategy was extremely high, and not worth paying. Stalin's rule shaped the first part of the 'first stage' as an even more extreme institutional pattern and structure than a more moderate variant of a similar strategy might have produced. Yet, even so significant economic outcomes were achieved in growth of output, in structural changes, urbanization and modernization and in an impressive accumulation of human capital. Following the period of reconstruction in the aftermath of the huge human losses and devastation of the Second World War, the Soviet Union emerged as a nearly modern industrial economy and as a strong military power, with some surplus product to spare in order to moderately raise the standard of living of the population and (under Khrushchev) some ability to relax the political pressures.[6]

There is more scope for discussion on the potential economic outcomes of a counterfactual story had the Soviet Union followed the alternative strategy of balanced growth. The point I would like to make here, however, is that it is much more likely that a transition towards a more democratic pattern and a market economy, had it happened during the mid-1960s, might have produced a much better record for the Soviet Union. The 20th Congress of the Communist Party in 1956 could have been the first signal for the turning point. We shall come back to this below.

Growth deceleration since the mid-1960s

The Soviet Union didn't turn around at that time but instead experienced a process of declining growth rates, lagging behind instead of catching up with the developing countries, wasting more than 20 years on what eventually proved to become an end game for its growth strategy and the Soviet Union and empire. The poor economic performance during this 'stagnation period' imposed additional hardships on the transition that followed. This extra burden can be thought of as a debt left by the old regime, not only to the London and the Paris clubs, but also in the form of highly damaged institutions and decaying physical infrastructure. Had the transition started sometime during the 1960s, it probably could have been done in a more gradual way and it could have started from agriculture through decollectivization, possibly along the Chinese way of the late 1970s.

The decline in performance of the Soviet economic system during the last two decades until the fall can be explained mostly by the fact that its growth strategy was not replaced in time. The change was called for, among others, by the changes in the nature of the mission, the exhaustion of the old growth formula, and the attrition and fatigue of the system. This is a well-known story, extensively described in the literature (Ofer, 1987; Easterly and Fischer, 1995; Hanson, 2003; Popov, 2007, and many others) but let us outline it in a summary fashion here. Around 1970 the Soviet per capita GDP reached its peak relative to the US level, at 37.1 per cent (Maddison, 2006, pp. 459–89; see also Note 13). The average growth rate of per capita GDP during 1970–90 declined to just 1 per cent (zero if 1991 is included).

The main factor that contributed to the declining growth was the near exhaustion of the 'extensive' model, based on growth of labour and capital, and later on capital alone, and the need to move to an 'intensive' growth version, based to a larger extent on increased productivity. The main mechanism of extensive growth blocked productivity improvements. The command system of management and control, the coercive discipline, the emphasis on quantities produced, the simple incentives, all performed relatively well in order to move resources and to achieve major structural changes. The ideological over-coating helped in this too, at least for a while. These tools were also more appropriate for a simple economy, the creating of new enterprises rather then their replacement 30 years later when they became obsolete (Popov, 2007). All these instruments were orthogonal to the requirements of improved efficiency and technological changes which call for creativity at all levels, managerial autonomy, flexible incentives, a market-oriented and open economy, and a free society. The result was sharply declining capital productivity. The leading technologies of the early period, concentrating around steel, transportation equipment and heavy machinery were much more suitable to the old strategy than the high-tech, ICT and related technologies of the later years.

Then there is the heavy economic price paid for the mistakes of the old system, collectivization of agriculture and the allocation of many industries to 'cold' and remote areas of the Soviet Union (Gaddy and Ickes, 2010); the heavy burden of increasing defence outlays, in particular its negative effect on the technological capabilities for (civilian) growth; the extra price paid for the efforts of 'haste' or catching up, the race to achieve faster growth early at the expense of growth in the future. Such policies resulted in rapid decline in demographic fertility, fast depletion of natural resources, the neglect of infrastructure, tight secrecy, etc. Finally, attrition, fatigue, declining motivation and cynicism started to creep in. How long could the harsh discipline of the early years be sustained? How long could one preserve the motivating power of ideology?

All these aspects of the decay of the old growth strategy continued, even more intensively during the last phase of the Soviet Union. These are the costs of postponement of the switch to a more appropriate strategy.

The 1960s as the right time for change and why it didn't happen

The period under Khrushchev, especially following his famous de-Stalinization speech of 1956, was one of a relatively moderate political and cultural thaw, including the opening up of a lively discussion on economic issues, the first more or less free one since the 1920s. The ills of the Soviet economy at that stage were more openly exposed and discussed and solutions were offered. While this episode is mostly connected with the name of Evsey Liberman, most other leading economists participated and contributed, and the leaders listened. While only a few economists went that far, the 'light at the end of the tunnel' for some among them was provided by Oscar Lange's model of 'market socialism' and/or by the implementation of some of its features, as in the Yugoslav version of communism.

This was also a period of a number of economic reforms, mostly though of an administrative nature; the most notorious among them was the shift of the management of the economy from a central ministerial system to regional councils (the *Sovnarkhozy*), a change that threw the system into a considerable degree of 'disorganization'. This was also when more attention was directed at the well being of the population, to the point that when agriculture didn't produce the required amount of output, imports of significant amounts of grain were ordered for the first time (and continued since then). The early 1960s saw also the first decline in the rates of growth of the economy, a deceleration that motivated much of the economic discussions mentioned above.

It all culminated, paradoxically enough, in a sort of a coup that replaced Khrushchev, pro- mised the most radical economic reform of the Soviet economy up till then, the notorious 'Kosygin reforms' but ironically enough evolved to the domination by Brezhnev over what was later dubbed the 'stagnation era'.[7] The hopes for significant reforms turned into what was dubbed by Gertrude Schroeder 'the treadmill of reforms' for the rest of the Soviet period.

The power and prestige of the Communist party at the time was strong enough to oversee such a process of a real transition if the leadership could have been convinced that this was the right way. While it is not simple to explain why such a desirable development did not take place, it is quite clear that at the mid-1960s the power of inertia of the system was still very strong, the institutions too rigid and the state of mind of the leadership too fixed and con- fident, just a few years after Sputnik, in order to allow any kind of a radical change. The old structure secured their power. Central planning was also needed very much in order to provide for the defence requirements of the cold war. Here Khrushchev helped to throw more gaso- line at the fire with the Cuban crisis. Indeed, the 1960s witnessed a further rise of the defence budget and its share in GDP (Ofer, 1987, pp. 1787–88). The energy crisis of 1973 and a second one at the end of the 1970s, served as 'manna from heaven'; they helped to paper over, even in the eyes of the leadership, the even faster declining growth rates and the structural difficulties, and allowed the Soviet system to continue to 'muddle through' for a few more years.[8] One has to remember that the initial growth strategy was never thought of as a 'first stage' but rather as an alternative permanent ideology and growth strategy.

The accepted view of the immediate reason and timing of the fall of the Soviet system in the late 1980s and early 1990s was the outcome of the 'disorganization' caused by partial, badly coordinated and erroneous reforms implemented by Gorbachev (Ellman and Kontorovich, 1998, ch.2). Can one assume that the same might have happened had the coup against Khrushchev failed as a result of a combination of similar factors, and a similar dynamics develop? Alternatively, one may conceive of an orderly, gradual and controlled reform that could have started with a process of decollectivization, improving the supply of food and creating popular support for the reforms. The rolling back of collectivization at that stage could have been much more promising (even more feasible?) than nearly three decades later. The reform could have continued with a series of international agreements on arms control and disarmament and a gradual policy of opening up and a moving towards a market economy.

In contrast to developments in the Soviet Union, the Chinese Communist leadership did find a way to introduce gradual changes under the title of the 'The Chinese version of Communism' that just recently includes even the legalization of private property rights, probably also under the same umbrella. The Chinese leadership gave priority, and in a better chosen time, to the economic prosperity of China and at the same time managed to stay in power. Only later, when Gorbachev was convinced that he must act, and when his earlier moves had backfired, he also preferred the preservation of the Soviet Union and its economy over continued adherence to the letter of the communist system, and at the end even of the Communist party (Hanson 2003, pp. 253–54).

The challenges of the transition[9]

When the transition arrived, following the collapse of the old regime, Russia (and the other transition countries) found itself facing difficult challenges related to the needed systemic shift. Two main clusters of problems should be considered: one is the need to replace the institutional edifice of central planning and the authoritarian regime with that of a market economy and democracy; and the other is the required changes in the industrial structure of the economy, replacing high public investment, defence and heavy industry, with more consumption, light industry and services; a shift driven by the changing origins of demand and of the opening up of the economy. Both the qualitative and quantitative dimensions of the required changes are immense, possibly the most extreme case of systemic switching.

The inherited set of institutions, formal and informal (North, 1990), that served the old regime with variable efficiency, were diametrically orthogonal to those needed for the emerging market and democratic regime. Their entrenchment in the public sector and in all segments of the society created a formidable barrier for change. Many of the new needed formal institutions had to be imported from the West and 'transplanted' into an unfamiliar, even hostile environment, an additional challenge (Djankov *et al.*, 2003).

Even more problematic was the transformation of the informal institutions, the norms and culture of behaviour of agents across the economy. Such changes, which normally lag behind those in formal institutions, lag even further when new institutions are installed abruptly and still more so when they are transplanted from the outside. Additional difficulties to endogenize the proper informal institutions were imposed by the tension between formal and informal institutions under the old regime, tensions that widened further during the stagnation period: erosion of the 'civic society', depletion of social capital and the deterioration of trust.

The transition in Russia can be divided so far into three sub-periods, the second period identified with Yeltsin (1991–99) and the third with Putin (and Medvedev). Gorbachev recognized the crisis and decided to meet it with radical reforms within the Communist system, initially even using traditional communist tools like the acceleration (*Uskorenia*) and the anti-alcohol campaigns. Other, more radical reforms, albeit partial and inconsistent, drove the economy into high inflation, shortages and 'disorganization' and in a way forced the leadership to take more radical measures. The 1990s under Yeltsin saw the main systemic changes, price and trade liberalizations, privatization and major changes in the structure of production, as well as the disintegration of the Soviet Union and the establishment of democratic institutions and freedom. All these were accompanied by sharply declining output, high inflation and severe macroeconomic imbalances: and high levels of 'disorganization' caused mostly by the poor performance of the government itself.

The following decade, under Putin was different: Growth was resumed, owing to consolidation of the main reforms, some improvements in the functioning of the government and increasing revenues from the export of energy. The improved government performance was achieved mostly through acts of recentralization of control at the hands of the national government, including over the media, some renationalization of strategic industries and restrictions on political and personal freedoms, even some use of methods of the old regime; what was dubbed by Gaidar as 'soft authoritarianism' (Gaidar and Bouis, 2007, p. 255). Yet, both transition decades suffered from high levels of corruption, during the 1990s with more emphasis on government capture and plunder, while during the 2000s with ample government corruption and rent seeking. While the last decade saw a measure of stabilization and increasing output and living standards, it is the view of many that further growth is conditioned upon the resumption of major structural economic reforms. The institutional retreat and the postponement of the needed reforms further extend the transition period and its economic costs (Ofer, 2010; Gaidar and Bouis, 2007, 'Afterword', pp. 250–56).

Calculations and concluding discussion

Did the *short*, more assertive and dictatorial 'takeoff' or 'first stage' of development strategy in the Soviet Union (and other countries) pay off; or did it turn out to be *long*, as in the Talmudic story quoted above (and below)? In the case of the Soviet Union this may be paraphrased, following Nove (1964), into the extreme question, 'was Stalin really necessary'?

Given that the two-stage strategy was much more costly than otherwise assumed, a question that may be raised is whether there could have been a hypothetical, alternative strategy that could have achieved the desired takeoff with somewhat 'softer' means? And would that have made the future shift to stage two less costly? Given the personality of Stalin, one may assume that such a takeoff variant might well have been possible. Robert Allen (2003, Ch. 4) answers this question in the negative for the Soviet Union. He argues further that the chosen takeoff strategy saved the Soviet Union from the dismal fate of many developing countries, and that no alternative strategy could have accomplished such a feat. Harrison seems also to agree. He sees the cruel Stalin's version of discipline as necessary to achieve the goals of the regime (Harrison, 2000; see also Hanson, 2003, pp. 252–53). On the other hand, Hunter and Szyrmer (1992, pp. 257–65) produce a better counterfactual record for the Soviet Union during 1928–40 (and beyond), a strategy much closer to 'balanced growth'. I am ready to leave this question unresolved at this point. Then there is the question, given the choice of a first stage strategy, whether the transition took place on time. Was it well designed and executed? Not in the Soviet Union. Is China a good example of such a case? Is the crisis that so many experts have been predicting for China for quite some time, still looming ahead?

Finally there is the question of 'how much?' What are the actual additional costs of the shift? Here again one has to differentiate between costs in the form of lives lost and human hardship and suffering of the 'desert generation', including during both the first stage and the transition, and the economic costs of lost growth. An estimate of the last part of the losses is attempted here based (mostly) on data compiled by Maddison (2006).[10]

The annual per capita rate of growth of the Soviet economy during 1950–70 was 3.5 per cent and during 1928–50 (leaving out the war years) about 3.7 per cent. This range of growth rates represents the gross achievements of the first stage. These rates have to be adjusted by: (1) the lower growth rate of one per cent annually during the period of delayed transition, 1970–90; and (2) the negative and/or lower growth rates during the transition years. This period can be determined in a number of ways: one is the period of declining output, under the 'transformational recession' in Russia during 1990–98, when aggregate output declined by about 40 per cent. Another approach is to consider the period that it took for Russia to regain its pre-transition GDP level, around 2005 (*Transition Report*, various years). The rate of growth of per capita GDP during such a period is set by definition at zero.[11] Combining together the delay and the transition periods gives (under approach 2) a period of 35 years with an average annual growth of around 0.5 per cent (even lower under approach 1). Finally, per capita economic growth over 1950–2005, first stage plus delay and transition, was approximately 1.5 per cent and for 1928–2005 (again the war years excluded), a fraction higher. Much less impressive and not much to boast about, especially in view of the large unaccounted for costs.[12]

Under a third alternative one can ask how long it may take for Russia to regain its *relative* level of per capita GDP, that reached its highest level of 39.4 per cent of the US level back in 1973. According to estimates worked out by Maddison (2006, pp. 461–68, 475–79), Russia reached a relative level of income per capita of just 19.4 per cent of that of the USA by 2001, the last year of his calculations. Based on *World Development Report* and *Transition Report* data (various years) this ratio may have reached one-third by 2008 and may perhaps regain the 1970 level within a few years. This approach extends the duration of the between-stages delay and transition period to more than 30 years![13]

In view of all the above, can one conclude that even if a forceful takeoff strategy of one sort or another is warranted, or even necessary, that a 'softer' version of such a strategy would be more cost effective in the longer run when the costs of the 'switch' are taken into account? And that such a 'softer' approach would have been worthwhile trying, even at the expense of somewhat lower growth rates early on?

The Talmudic story whose essence is quoted above goes as follows (my translation):

> Once I was walking along a road and saw a young child sitting at a crossroads and I asked him, 'which way should we go to the town?' He said to me: 'This way is short and long and that one long and short'. I walked along the short and long. As I approached the town I discovered that it was surrounded by gardens and orchards. I turned back and said (to the child), 'son, didn't you say 'short'?' He responded, 'and didn't I say 'long'? ...

Notes

1 Rodrik (2005) differentiates between strategies needed for takeoff and those that provide for sustained long-term growth. Indeed in many cases takeoff strategies may last much longer.

2 Recent literature surveys include Acemoglu *et al.* (2005), Rodrik (2005), Aghion and Howitt (2009).

3 An earlier version of this contribution adapted a model presented by Djankov *et al.* (2003) for the two-stage growth case. More ambitious growth policies during the first stage imply higher levels of 'dictatorship' and 'disorder' and hence higher economic losses along the way, losses that manifest themselves when the transition comes.

4 The longer version of this paper includes short descriptions of a number of cases, Japan and East Asia, Latin America, India, where the periods of delayed reform, and then of transition, were quite costly in terms of overall long term growth.

5 A model developed by a Russian economist, G.A. Feldman, in the late 1920s followed Marx and showed how high initial investment in producer goods industries can produce high rates of growth and, later, high consumption levels.

6 A book by Robert Allen (2003) reopens the debate over the merit of the Soviet development record.

7 During 1965–70 GDP growth rates were equal to those during the previous five-year period, mostly owing to late arrival of benefits of changes in agriculture made by Khrushchev. The rate of growth of industrial output continued to decline (Hanson, 2003, pp. 248–53).

8 See Gaidar (2007, Ch. IV) and Gaddy and Ickes (2010) on the effect of high energy prices on the need for economic reforms in the eyes of the Soviet leadership.

9 For an expanded discussion of these issues see Ofer (2010).

10 Data for years past 2001 are from the World Bank, *World Development Report* (WDR), various recent years and (for Russia) EBRD, *Transition Report* (TR), various recent years.

11 By 2005 Russian GDP reached 88 per cent of its 1989 level, a few points higher when compared with 1990, and still a few points higher when per capita GDP levels are compared, this last point owing to the decline of the Russian population during this period (2007 TR, Table A.2.1, p. 35).

12 In addition the above calculations are biased upward for the Soviet period owing to lack of consumer sovereignty, limited variety, shortages and long queues, and over-spending on inefficient capital goods. All these were eliminated under the transition.

13 Maddison, 2006, pp. 459–89, various tables. The figures of the relative GDP per capita in the text refer to Russia in both 1973 and 2001. Maddison also calculated a series for the Soviet Union, with the corresponding relative GDP per capita for Russia in 1970 37.1 per cent and for 2001 16.6 per cent of the US levels respectively.

Bibliography

Acemoglu, D., Johnson, S. and Robinson J.A. (2005), 'Institutions as a Fundamental Cause of Long-Run Growth', in Aghion, P. and Durlauf, S. (eds), *Handbook of Economic Growth*, London: Palgrave-McMillan, Ch. 6.

Aghion, P. and Durlauf, S. (eds) (2005), *Handbook of Economic Growth*, London: Palgrave-McMillan.

Aghion, P. and Howitt, P. (2009), *The Economics of Growth*, Cambridge, MA: MIT Press.

Allen, CR (2003), *From Farm to Factory: A reinterpretation of Soviet industrial Revolution*, Princeton, NJ and London: Princeton University Press.

Djankov, S., Glaeser, E., La Porta, R., Lopez-de-Silanes, F. and Shleifer, A. (2003), 'The New Comparative Economics', *Journal of Comparative Economics*, vol. 31, pp. 595–619.

Easterly, W. and Fischer, S. (1995), 'The Soviet Economic Decline', *The World Bank Economic Review*, vol. 9(3), pp. 341–71.

EBRD (2003), *Transition Report 2003*, London: European Bank of Reconstruction and Development.

Ellman, M. and Kontorovich, V. (eds) (1998), *The Destruction of the Soviet Economic System: An Insiders' History*, Armonk, NY: M. E. Sharpe.

Gaddy, C. and Ickes, B.W. (2010), *Russia's Addiction: The Political Economy of Resource Dependence*, Washington, DC: Brookings Institution.

Gaidar, Y. and Bouis, A.W. (2007), *Collapse of an Empire: Lessons for Modern Russia*, Washington, DC: The Brooking Institution.

Gerschenkron, A. (1962), *Economic Backwardness in Historical Perspective*, New York: Praeger.

Hanson, P. (2003), *The Rise and Fall of the Soviet Economy*, London: Longman.

Harrison, M. (2000), 'Coercion, Compliance and the Collapse of the Soviet Command Economy', mimeo, University of Warwick.

Hunter, H. and Szyrmer, J.M. (1992), *Faulty Foundations: Soviet Economic Policies 1928–40*, Princeton, NJ: Princeton University Press.

Maddison, A. (2001), *The World Economy: A Millennial Perspective*, Paris: OECD.

——(2006), *The World Economy: Vol. 1: A Millennial Perspective; Vol. 2: Historical Statistics*, Paris: OECD.

North, D.C.(1990), *Institutions, Institutional Change and Economic Performance*, Cambridge: Cambridge University Press.

Nove, A. (1964), *Was Stalin Really Necessary?*, London: Allen and Unwin.

Ofer, G. (1987), 'Soviet economic Growth: 1928–85', *Journal of Economic Literature*, vol. 25(4), pp. 1767–1833.

——(2008), 'Soviet growth record', in Durlauf, Steven N. and Blume, Lawrence E. (eds), *The New Palgrave Dictionary of Economics,* 2nd edn, London: Palgrave Macmillan.

——(2010), 'Twenty Years Later and the Socialist Heritage is still Kicking, The case of Russia', *UNU-Wider,* Working Paper 2010/59.

Popov, V. (2007), 'Life cycle of the centrally planned economy: why Soviet growth rates peaked in the 1950s', in Estrin, S., Kolodko, G. and Uvalic, M. (eds), *Transition and Beyond: A Tribute to Mario Nuti,* Basingstoke: Palgrave Macmillan.

Rodrik, D. (2005), 'Growth Strategies', in Aghion, P. and Durlauf, S. (eds), *Handbook of Economic Growth,* London: Palgrave-McMillan, Chapter 14, (earlier draft, September 2003).

World Bank (2003), *World Development Report 2003*, Washington, DC: World Bank.

6

CENTRAL PLANNING IN THE SOVIET SYSTEM

Vladimir Mau

Well intentioned people have begun advocating supervision and control of the economy by the state and even the supplanting of private enterprise by state enterprise. We have already gone quite far down this route: it is being suggested that the state should play an important part in the grain trade and in supplying grain to a population numbered in millions … doubtless we shall next be told that the state should not only plough the land and sow and harvest the grain but also publish all newspapers and journals, write novels and short stories, and offer its services to the arts and the sciences.

(Nikolai Bunge, 1890)

Introduction

It was always maintained by Soviet theorists that the distinguishing feature of the Soviet socialist or Communist economy would be centralized economic planning. This was their *sine qua non* and all discussions over the Soviet economic model revolved around two questions: what should be the nature of economic planning and how was an effective centrally planned economy to be constructed? These were two sides of the same problem but historically solutions were sought along different lines of enquiry.

At the beginning of the 20th century, following the establishment of the industrial economy with its characteristics of large-scale machine production and a strong tendency towards the creation of ever-larger dominant firms in key branches of production and distribution, it seemed to many economists that, as a consequence of objective economic forces, market competition would inevitably be replaced by central planning. Such ideas were especially popular in countries that were 'catching up', such as Germany and then, later, Russia. The First World War gave an impetus to central planning, and the instruments of economic management that emerged at that time were looked upon by many economists and politicians not as emergency war-time measures but as portents of the economic system of the future. At the time the advantages of a planned economy seemed to these individuals to be self-evident, and they viewed their main task as being to develop the methodology of planning and to acquire practical experience of implementing the plan.

Later on, as the deficiencies of the planned economy became more apparent, new issues became topical – how to achieve efficiency in a planned economy and how to combine centralization with incentives that would promote the economic growth of individual firms. After the Second World War, when the market economies in democratic countries entered a period of stable and dynamic growth, finding answers to these questions became a matter of urgency.

Formation of the planned economy

At the end of the 19th and the beginning of the 20th centuries, in a number of European countries, ideas of centralized economic planning acquired increasing popularity. This was associated with the growth of large scale machine-based industry and with the processes of centralization of production and capital on the one hand, and with the recurrence of serious economic crises on the other. In the Russian economy, where there was a significant state sector and where a long-standing tradition of 'étatism' existed, these views were particularly widespread. In political and economic circles there were ever more frequent demands for the 'operation of market forces' to be limited and for a strengthening of the role of central government in the economy.[1] The opinion of Nikolai Bunge, the Chairman of the Russian Council of Ministers and former Minister of Finance, cited above, was remarkably prophetic. No less prophetic were the words of the major oil entrepreneur, P.O. Gusakov: 'Here in Russia the view is firmly established that the state can act in the economic sphere just as a private entrepreneur does … This kind of thinking can very easily lead to state socialism.'[2]

Tendencies leading towards a planned economy obtained a powerful impetus with the coming to power in Russia of the Bolsheviks. A planned, moneyless economy was one of their programmatic objectives and the crisis of the money economy during the war and revolution was interpreted by many Bolsheviks as heralding the future Communist economy.[3] During the years 1918–20, Russia, in conditions of severe budgetary crisis and steep inflation, was subjected to an experiment aimed at achieving within a short time span a planned economy, the abolition of money and a transition to commodity exchange. It was during these years that a debate began over the role, forms and mechanisms of realization of a single economic plan.[4] The ideas that were put forward were based on the realities of 'War Communism', and for the most part they did not venture beyond the limits of that economic doctrine. The planned economy was conceived as being a strictly centralized natural economy, analogous to a huge trust, and the plan was conceived as a kind of prescription that laid down the parameters of economic activity for every producer.[5] Attempts at implementing this policy resulted in severe poverty and in an acute political crisis, and it was for these reasons that the New Economic Policy (NEP) was introduced in 1921.

The NEP (1921–29) was an attempt at creating a socialist market economy in which state property dominated, large industry was centrally administered (the 'commanding heights') and private property and market anarchy (as it was usually described) were tolerated in the agrarian sector, in services, in small and medium-sized enterprises, and in construction.

During the 1920s, debates continued over the methodology of planning and several drafts were produced of the first national annual and long-term economic plans.[6] These debates in many respects predetermined the future model of centralized economic planning of the Soviet type. A conception of planning emerged that was in fundamental contradistinction with the doctrine of War Communism: in place of the notion of the 'prescriptive plan' there arose a concept of the plan as the choice of an optimal trajectory for the progress of the economy towards a specified goal. The logic of the plan was now predicated upon the economic independence of enterprises and upon their accountability for the effectiveness of their decision-making. The realization of this system presupposed a transition from crude administrative methods of planning to more economic methods, and the disappearance in due course of the directive character of the projects of the central planning organs. Market mechanisms were to operate in conjunction with planned regulation, enterprises and their workers were to be motivated by economic stimuli.[7]

The 1920s were a most productive period in the development of the theory of economic planning. Brilliant economists and leading industrial managers contributed to the debate. These included Bazarov, Bukharin, Ginzburg, Groman, Kondratiev, Krzhizhanovsky, Sokol'nikov, Strumilin and Yurovsky. A number of government institutions – the State Planning Agency (*Gosplan*), the Supreme Council of the National Economy (*VSNKh*), the Commissariat of Finance (*Narkomfin*) and the Commissariat for Agriculture (*Narkomzem*) – not only drafted the planning documents that belonged to their spheres of competence but put forward alternative conceptions for the long-term socio-economic development of the country. This open confrontation between different points of view made a positive contribution to the attempt to build a planning system that would really work.

During the 1920s extensive research was carried out into a whole range of aspects of economic planning. Planning methods such as the use of dynamic coefficients (obtained by analysing the actual development of the economy), the development of methods of balances, expert evaluations, the estimation of alternative plan variants, and techniques of mathematical modelling were worked out theoretically and tested in practice. Questions of plan optimality, the appropriate relationships between territorial and branch planning, the inter-relationships between the national economic plan and the financial plan were all studied. Work undertaken at this time to draw up a balance of the national economy was of great importance.

An understanding of the economic conjuncture and of the laws of development of the Soviet economy were considered to be important prerequisites of planning. Since the principal goal of the period was considered to be economic reconstruction, which would be followed only later by economic development, a number of researchers undertook the analysis of 'reconstruction processes'.[8]

The work that was done on the First Five-Year Plan occupied an important place in the history of the theory and practice of planning. Between 1925 and 1928 several variants of the Plan were elaborated by different groups of economists. The purpose of this long-term or 'perspective plan' was to plot a course for the industrialization of the economy. However, as work on the Five-Year Plan progressed, profound disagreements arose among leading economists as to the role, content and methodology of perspective planning. With the reconstruction period coming to a close, the main disagreements were over the sources for future economic growth. Inside *Gosplan* the view came to prevail that 'the creative will of the revolutionary proletariat' would be the decisive factor in the management of the economic plan: it would be sufficient, in order to ensure that the plan achieved its targets, to involve the workers in its realization. Furthermore, an idealization of the capabilities of government made for a dismissive attitude towards prudent management of the budget and of the monetary system. Budgetary expansion led to inflation and the central fixing of prices in particular areas resulted in shortages.

Proponents of an alternative model argued that the perspective plan should aim for the creation of conditions favourable to the accumulation and utilization of capital and emphasized the importance of economic equilibrium in a planned economy. The debate became structured around the issue of 'genetic' as opposed to 'teleological' planning. The ideas put forward in 1923 and 1924 by Bazarov for the organic fusion of these two concepts at first encountered almost no criticism. What Bazarov argued was that in the process of formulation of the perspective plan it would become necessary to combine the search for ways of realizing set goals (the teleological imperative) with a projection into the future of current economic trends (the genetic imperative). However, Bazarov's conception begged one important methodological problem – namely, by what mechanisms should goals actually be set, how should one choose between alternative models of development of the economy, and how much discretion should be accorded for choosing between available alternatives. At the time, however, discussions focussed on the relationship between directive planning and forecasting, that is upon the inter-action between government directives on the one hand and the results obtained from analysis of tendencies within the economy and economic forecasting on the other.[9]

At the end of the 1920s and beginning of the 1930s, the issue of the relationship between genetic and teleological imperatives, which had been compressed into the dichotomy 'prognosis versus administrative command', and which had been confined essentially to the realm of theory, acquired a political dimension. The idea that the administrative command was an inherent attribute of planned economic management became set in ideology and this was accompanied by a rejection of the pursuit of balanced economic growth and the adoption of a policy of 'whipping' the country forward. Efforts at applying real planning guidelines now collapsed. The Communist leadership of the USSR was afraid that the development of market relations would demonstrate that the state sector of the economy was uncompetitive and that this would ultimately lead to the overthrow of the political regime.

With the destruction of NEP and the consolidation of a strict administrative system, the practice of directive planning, in which there was no place for market stimuli, became entren-ched. It was by these methods that the Soviet leadership achieved the rapid industrialization that to a significant degree made possible the victory of the USSR in the Second World War. For several decades, this decisive victory conferred political inviolability and legitimacy upon the model of centralized planning and greatly restricted the scope for any questioning of its economic effectiveness.

The search for an improved planning model

The low level of effectiveness of the central planning system gradually became apparent and by the 1950s discussions were taking place over how to improve it. These discussions took place not only in the USSR but also in other countries with Soviet-type economies, particularly Hungary and (the then) Czechoslovakia.

The Soviet economy had a powerful capacity for mobilizing resources but proved to be economically ineffective in peace-time. The main problem was the absence of economic incentives within the system encouraging growth and efficiency, responsiveness to consumer demand, and innovation. The principal motive of Soviet managers was to acquire the lowest possible plan targets from central government and the maximum amount of resources for the fulfilment of these objectives. This 'de-stimulation' operated at all levels of the hierarchy: thus, enterprises lobbied to be issued with a minimal plan by the Ministry and the Ministries then lobbied to obtain a minimal plan from *Gosplan*.

There were no incentives for innovation, for the renewal of products and improvements in the quality of output. The principal goal of enterprises was not increases in the productivity of labour, but the fulfilment and over-fulfilment of their centrally planned targets. Whereas the USSR surpassed the USA at the beginning of the 1970s in terms of gross capital investment, the productivity of labour in industry in the USSR in 1970 was 53 per cent and in 1975 55 per cent of that of the USA.[10]

Economic agents (households and enterprises) had no incentive to save or to invest. Growth was obtained by extra-economic methods, namely coercion, including the use of force. A shortage of goods and the secondary role played by money in the economy significantly cur-tailed the interest of citizens in working more effectively and in obtaining higher incomes. As a result, the rates of growth of industrial output gradually declined – from 16.5 per cent per annum in 1929–33 to under 1 per cent in the 1980s.

The Soviet economic model relied, essentially, upon a kind of 'fetishism of the plan'.[11] The plan was handed down by some higher power that was deemed to be capable of managing everything. The presumption was that every aspect of socio-economic development could be covered by including an appropriate indicator in the plan. This was very astutely noted by the first Chairman of *Gosplan*, Krzhizhanovsky, who wrote:

> Reading these programmes, one has the impression that when they were drawn up it was implicitly assumed that government possesses some miraculous power enabling it to cater for every need to every conceivable extent … In the final analysis, this has transformed production plans into projects for which no one is accountable. They have doubtless been drawn up with the best of intentions, but from the standpoint of economic management they are suspended in mid-air.[12]

In these circumstances, of course, the performance of all participants in the economic plan (branches of the economy, enterprises, workers) could only be assessed in terms of the fulfilment or over-fulfilment of plan targets.

The first attempts that were made to improve the planning system (during the 1930s–1950s) were imprisoned within this logic and merely sought ways of improving planning methods. The failures of the planned economy were attributed, at worst, to the sabotage of bourgeois economists, to the personal shortcomings of individual economic managers, to conservatism, bureaucratism, incompetence and low levels of accountability. At best, they were attributed to imperfect methodologies, to the absence of technical resources (computers) that would facilitate the calculation of all needs and resources and enable these to be matched. It was felt that any improvement in the functioning of planning in the socialist economy could only come from a tightening of the administrative and legal controls over enterprises.

The limitations of this approach, which essentially identified the planning system with administrative commands, became more and more evident towards the middle of the 1950s. Attention was then switched to the problem of planning indicators. It was argued that emerging problems could be solved simply by designing more appropriate indicators for measuring the performance of the enterprise. Economists criticized the use of gross output indicators as the key measure of performance; there were multifarious proposals for perfecting the system by introducing indicators measuring the volume of work completed in an enterprise. In other words, the plan was represented as being an agglomeration of indicators centrally imposed upon the enterprise and motivating it to achieve its plan targets.

In due course it became clear that there were more profound reasons for the ineffectiveness of the planned economy. Economists now focused on plan fulfilment as an indicator of the successful functioning of the enterprise. However, if plan fulfilment was a criterion for the payment of wages and bonuses then all participants had a vested interest in a lowering of the assessment of their production potential, in obtaining both low plan targets and increased allocations of resources for plan fulfilment. Efficiency of production and the interests of consumers took second place to the fulfilment of planning targets. The planning indicators become an end in themselves.

Elevation of the plan to the status of the key indicator of economic performance at times produced absurd and at other times even tragic results. A classic example of the latter is the attempt of the leaders of Ryazan Oblast in 1959 to obtain all kinds of rewards and bonuses for rapidly implementing the Party's slogan for increasing the production of meat. In pursuit of this goal almost every herd of cattle in the farms of the Oblast was put to the knife. Cattle were then purchased from other Oblasts and even from Kazakhstan. Of course, there was recourse to false accounting and all kinds of other machinations. The outcome was a massive destruction of livestock, including that of thoroughbred and breeding stock. For sure, the plan was over-fulfilled and the First Secretary of the Oblast Committee of the Communist Party of the Soviet Union, Larionov, received the award of Hero of Socialist Labour. However, within a year, when the catastrophic results of this planning bacchanalia were exposed, he committed suicide.[13]

In their efforts to achieve improved growth rates from enterprises, the highest government bodies of the Soviet system attempted to regulate not only the outcomes of the activity of enterprises but also their means of achieving these outcomes, deploying to this end an ever-increasing number of supplementary indicators. An illustration of this tendency is the uninterrupted increase in the number of indicators imposed on enterprises from above from the 1960s to the 1980s despite the fact that during this same period the government issued a number of directives opposing this practice. And so, whereas at the beginning of the 1960s enterprise activity was regulated by several tens of indicators imposed 'from above', by the beginning of the 1980s there were several hundred such indicators. In 1986, for example, the enterprises of the Ministry for Electro-Technical Production (*Minelektrotekhprom*) had to report annually on around 500 indicators, the Ministry of Instrumentation and Control Systems (*Minpribor*) on 450; the Ministry of Agricultural Machinery (*Minselkhozmash*) on 600 and the Ministry of the Machine Tool Industry (*Minstankoprom*) on 400.[14] There developed a vicious circle: the more the activity of an enterprise was regulated, the more energetically it sought to lower its planning targets, the easier it became for the enterprise to create the impression that it had fulfilled its plan by improving its interim performance. Conversely, the more the assessment of the performance of an enterprise became divorced from its real contribution to the output of the national economy, the more pronounced became the drive for centralization, since the predominant method of influencing the behaviour of the enterprise had become the imposition of ever more planning targets.

Having become aware of this phenomenon, Soviet economists engaged in stormy debates over which indicators were the 'correct' indicators: which indicators would more accurately describe the performance of enterprises, branches of the economy and individual workers and in so doing bring about a qualitative improvement in the effectiveness of the planning system. Various clusters of indicators were compiled; many pilot studies were launched.[15]

At the end of the 1950s a number of economists put forward a fundamentally different solution which consisted not in any permutation of indicators but in the abandonment altogether of assessment according to plan fulfilment.[16] This was a radical turn in the debate, but the Soviet system could not, as a matter of principle, abrogate assessment by the plan: the only alternative was assessment by profit or profitability and this would have entailed a transition to market price formation, which was perceived as being absolutely inimical to the survival of the Soviet system.[17]

Economic stimulation was understood in this context as a problem specific to planning, in so far as the system of socialist economic management needed to motivate the enterprise not only to fulfil the plan but to co-operate in the formulation of 'taut' plans. This approach attempted to link the planned management of the economy with mechanisms for harmonizing the interests of the subjects of socialist production. In reality, this was a new understanding of planning, whereby planning was conceived as a mechanism for reconciling the activity of enterprises and individual workers with national economic objectives.

The reform measures introduced in Hungary, Czechoslovakia and the Soviet Union during the 1960s were a landmark in the modernization of the planning system of the Soviet type. In the USSR the reform was launched in 1965 and has become known as the 'Kosygin Reform', in honour of the Chairman of the Council of Ministers of the USSR. A number of leading

Soviet economists of a liberal persuasion worked on key elements of the reform. They included Nemchinov, Novozhilov, Liberman and Birman.[18]

The reform entailed an increase in the independence of enterprises, a reduction in the number of planning indicators imposed from above, a reorientation of the system of stimulation away from plan fulfilment indicators that provided the enterprise with incentives to restrict the scope of its activity and to maximize its resource requirements towards outcome performance indicators based on profit and volume of production. The most radical proposals envisaged stimulating competition and allowing the possibility of bankruptcy for socialist enterprises. All of this, however, took for granted the absolute domination of state ownership of the means of production and the continuation of centralized price formation.

The economic reform produced ambivalent results: economic growth between 1965 and 1970 was around 8 per cent compared with less than 5 per cent for the previous five-year period. However, even these figures contained a significant degree of inflation. Enterprises had used their greater freedoms mainly to make formal changes to the assortment of their output and to increase the prices of their 'new' goods, in the final analysis with a view to increasing wages (instead of capital accumulation and investment) – behaviour that was natural given the absence of any real owner of the enterprise who might have given some thought to strategic investment. The political crisis in Czechoslovakia (1968) demonstrated that the consistent implementation of market reforms could sweep away the Communist Party's monopoly hold on power. By the end of the 1960s, the economic reforms had been wound up; it had become clear that the Soviet system had exhausted its potential for development. The need to find a way of enabling the system to evolve and adapt to the requirements of a new age had become evident and the economic reforms had been an opportunity to begin this process of transformation. With the termination of the reforms in 1965 the Soviet economic model gradually descended into a profound systemic crisis.

Centralized planning and the post-industrial challenge

The crisis of the planning system was accompanied by a political crisis but this was not the root of the matter. Fundamental was the need to transcend the established industrial system. As long as it operated within the straightjacket of centralized planning, the USSR was incapable of responding to the challenges of post-industrial society.

With the advent of post-industrialism an increasing degree of 'uncertainty' permeates all social activities. This results from two aspects of post-industrial society that radically differentiate it from the traditional and more familiar industrial society. Firstly, there is a sharp increase in the rate of technological change, which, in turn, makes for a dramatic curtailment of the time horizons available for economic and technological forecasting. Secondly, a virtually unlimited increase in the demands of consumers is accompanied by a dramatic increase in the ability to satisfy these demands (in respect of both material resources and technological capabilities). The scale of economic production increases many times whilst at the same time the economy becomes highly individualized (one could say personalized or even 'privatized'): consumer demands and technological decisions become increasingly *individualized* and this makes for an increase in levels of uncertainty.

The process of *individualization* enhances the importance of *decentralization*. Whereas large-scale production was a key feature of industrial society, its importance in the post-industrial world diminishes. Of course, in branches of the economy where production on a massive scale persists, huge centralized firms continue in their usual role. However, as science advances and finds increasing application in economic and social life, large-scale economic production recedes and there is less need for the centralizing principle in the organization of the economy.

Whereas in the past the key function of the state was to concentrate resources in priority areas, it now acquires the role of creating the conditions that will enable economic agents (firms) to comprehend the latest shifts in the development of productive forces and to take account of the latest challenges as they move forward. The adaptability of an economic system becomes a far more important condition of its success than its ability to mobilize material and human resources – the particular claim to fame of the USSR.

All of this entails a sharp reduction in the time horizons available for forecasting the special needs and dominant trends in technological development in any country and any individual sectors of an economy. Whereas in the industrial era it was possible to identify what should be developmental priorities for the next 20–30 years and, having achieved specific objectives, enter the ranks of the advanced countries (this was the achievement in the 19th century of Germany and in the 20th century of Japan and Russia), now priorities are rapidly changing. In the present day, a country that attempted to overtake the rest of the world in the number of computers produced per head of population, develop programmes for the production of world-class aircraft and telephones could well discover when these projects had been completed that technology had moved a step forward. It might not have realized at the time the projects were approved that universal computerization lay ahead. What this means for the future is that it is not hardware that is important (even in the sphere of so-called 'hi-tech') but the flow of information. The abuse of central planning by the state is *the fatal conceit* (to use the expression of Friedrich von Hayek) and can result only in perpetual economic backwardness.[19]

Despite all this, it seems that the global financial and economic crisis (that began in 2008) has revived interest in central planning. This is evident in Russia, especially on such occasions as when government departments come to prepare their performance budgeting reports. They are required to devise specific indicators for use in measuring the effectiveness of their performance. Once again we seem to be succumbing to the fetishism of the plan. It is practically impossible, in the first place, to devise indicators that will clearly and unambiguously measure the attainment of desired results. Many indicators either do not lend themselves to unambiguous interpretation or will produce very unreliable results.

Not only does the selection and definition of performance indicators present difficulties, such indicators are subject to the interplay of many complex factors operating on different time scales. On the one hand, the results of the activity of a given management team (branch or regional) become apparent only with the passage of time, and these time lags are, as a rule, not known in advance. In some circumstances, the efforts of one management team may only become apparent when a new management team has taken over. There are many examples of this in economic history and in present-day political and economic practice.

Besides, expecting results continually to improve is a throw-back to the Soviet economic system. When assessing the performance of government departments or regions we cannot expect to be able to identify trends for every conceivable indicator. Infatuation with performance assessment carries with it the additional risk that quantitative measurement will inexorably acquire greater importance than the assessment of qualitative improvements, for example in the structure of the economy or in the morale of institutions. Here is a relevant example from the 1970s. At that time the Soviet economy achieved a steady rate of growth, albeit at the rather low rate of around 3 per cent per annum. By contrast, the Western economies were stagnating and, furthermore, experiencing high inflation. Soviet economists and politicians pontificated on the appearance of a hitherto unknown phenomenon – 'stagflation'. Western economists, for their part, produced pessimistic forecasts of 'zero growth'. Yet within a relatively short period of time it transpired that the Western economies, in the very throes of the crisis, had been developing resources that would in due course facilitate a dramatic break through into the post-industrial phase of development. And of course, this was not achieved by planning. In the meantime, the USSR headed for national catastrophe, diligently fulfilling its targets according to plan.

Conclusion

One of the most important developments of the 20th century was a significant increase in the role of the state in the economy, which culminated in the creation of a completely centralized national economy managed according to the requirements of a single central economic plan. The ideas of 'statism' and of state regulation, of limiting the operation of market forces, acquired ascendancy in almost all countries with developed market economies. However it was in the Soviet Union that the ideology and practice of planning reached their apogee, with the abolition of private property and the introduction of an economy wholly within the public sector.

We must distinguish between the ideology of communism and the ideology of central planning: the first is an abstract social and political doctrine with claims to 'universal' validity; the second emerged at a particular stage of development of the technical base of society, in the specific conditions of industrial development based on mass production. It was during this period, as large scale production units came into operation, that centralized management of the economy and the abolition of competition (perceived as being wasteful and inefficient) were judged by some to be not only feasible but also necessary.

The communist idea and the idea of a centrally planned economy coalesced during this period and they found their practical implementation when Soviet leaders proceeded to construct an economy on completely new foundations. Over almost a century of development, the planned economy, in both theory and practice, went through several stages of development:

The first was that of the widespread enthusiasm for planning of the beginning of the 20th century, when efforts were made to implement the idea, whilst at the same time retaining market relations. This was the model of the war economy in Germany during the First World War and the model of market socialism in the USSR between 1921 and 1929.

The next stage of the development of planning involved an intensification of central control, in defiance of market forces or by means of the almost complete abolition of the market (though money continued to play a role at all times). At first, this policy yielded positive results in the form of the accelerated industrialization of the USSR. However, there were enormous costs in terms of the expenditure of resources, which is to say that even if the policy was effective then it was effective only politically and militarily – the Communist Party was able to remain in power and the Soviet Union prevailed in the Second World War. However, it was not successful economically: the productivity of labour in the USSR significantly lagged behind that of the developed countries and never really caught up.

From the very earliest stages of the development of the planned economy, economists and politicians were aware of the defects of the system and sought ways of overcoming these defects. Discussions around this theme persisted during the years that followed the Second World War.

There were three basic approaches to improving the planning system. The first sought to improve the quality of the planning process, to recruit more able planners and to utilize contemporary computer technology. In the mid-20th century it seemed that genuinely scientific planning could be achieved with the assistance of computers that would at least provide complete information and make it possible to balance needs with resources. Paradoxically, however, it was the vigorous growth of information technology that aggravated the profound crisis of the centralized economy.

The second approach favoured improving the system of planning indicators, reducing their number and devising a key, integral indicator that would measure the contribution of a given enterprise to the general weal. Debates over how to improve indicators were never-ending, throughout the entire history of the planned economy.

The third approach focused on improving the management of centralized planning and the advocates of this approach spoke of the need to reform the system by increasing the role of market incentives. Here the emphasis was not on indicators but on the use of market mechanisms, including market processes of price formation. As experience would show, this approach was incompatible with the existence of a system of central planning.

In an era of technological progress, as development ceased to rely on large scale machine production and the production of goods and services became increasingly individualized, the inadequacies of the centralized planning became more and more evident. This led to the collapse of central planning and of the Soviet political and economic model.

Notes

1 Typical for the beginning of the 20th century was this pronouncement published in the principal journal of Russian entrepreneurs: 'We urgently require a business plan for our financial and economic life … The plan does not require any deliberation by any new agency and it certainly does not require any additional state regulation. The economic conditions of our time have been so well studied and the financial and the economic circumstances of Russia are so well understood that in order for Russia to be transformed from an ignorant, hungry and deprived country into an enlightened, well-fed and confident one very little is required: the merger of all of the programmes that are scattered across individual departments into a single, common … plan for the economic and financial development of Russia.' ('Minuvshii god', *Promyshlennost' i Torgovlya*, (1909), No. 1, p. 3).

2 P.O. Gusakov, 'Speech to the Conference of the Council of Congress on the oil problem', (*Promyshlennost' i Torgovlya*, (1908), No. 6, p. 351).

3 L. Kritsman, *The single economic plan and the Commission for Resource Utilization* (Moscow, 1921). Alexander Bogdanov was one who took issue with this, arguing that the war economy could in no way serve as the prototype of a planned socialist economy. See A. Bogdanov, *Problems of Socialism* (Moscow, 1918, pp. 44, 87).

4 See S.I. Gusev, *The single economic plan and the single economic apparatus* (Kharkov, 1920); A. Katyn, *The single economic plan and the single economic centre* (Moscow, 1920); L. Kritsman, *The single economic plan and the Commission for Resource Utilization* (Moscow, 1920).

5 L. Kritsman, *The single economic plan and the Commission for Resource Utilization* (Moscow, 1920), p. 7.

6 The first annual plan was the *Control figures for the national economy in 1925/1926* (Moscow, Leningrad, 1925). The drafting of perspective plans began in 1926 and the work undertaken then served as the basis for the five year plans. The First Five-Year Plan applied to the years 1929–33.

7 See A.M. Ginzburg, *Introductory sketches: Legislation on Trusts and Syndicates* (Moscow/Leningrad, 1926), pp. xi–xiii; A. Katyn, *Essays on the organization of the national Economy* (Moscow, 1922), pp. 21–22; V. Bazarov, 'On the question of the economic plan', *Ekonomicheskoe Obozrenie*, 1924, No. 6; V. Sarabyanov, *Key issues of the NEP* (Moscow/Leningrad, 1925), p. 194.

8 V.A. Bazarov, *Towards a methodology of perspective planning* (Moscow, 1924), p. 13; V. Bazarov, 'Concerning the "reconstruction processes" in general and the "prospects for emission" in particular', *Ekonomichesko Obozrenie* (1925, No. 1); V.O. Groman, 'Concerning a number of empirically observed regularities in our national economy', *Planovoe Khozyaistvo*, 1925, Nos 1, 2 and *passim*).

9 See V.A. Bazarov, *Towards a methodology of perspective planning* (Moscow, 1924), pp. 8–9 and 'On the methodology of drafting perspective plans', *Planovoe Khozyaistvo* (1926), No. 7, p. 9–10; N.D. Kondtratiev, 'The plan in relation to forecasting', *Puti Sel'skogo Khozyaistva* (1927), No. 2 and 'Critical comments on the plan for the development of the national economy', *Planovoe Khozyaistvo* (1927), No. 4; N.P. Makarov, 'Some current methodological problems in the drafting of perspective plans for agriculture', *Puti Sel'skogo Khozyaistva* (1927), No. 2; S.G. Strumilin, 'On the drafting of the perspective Five-Year Plan', *Planovoe Khozyaistvo* (1927), No. 3 and 'The industrialization of the USSR and

the epigones of Populism', *Planovoe Khozyaistvo* (1927), Nos 7, 8; L.K. Leontiev, 'On the problem of setting targets in planning', *Planovoe Khozyaistvo* (1928), No. 1.

10 Even these figures, based on official data of the period, were almost certainly rather over-optimistic estimates (editors' note).

11 For a detailed analysis of this phenomenon, see V. Mau and I. Starodubrovskaya, 'The fetishism of planning: a necessary political-economic commentary', *Ekonomicheskie Nauki* (1988), No. 4.

12 G.M. Krzhizhanovsky, Works, Vol. 2: *Problems of Planning* (Moscow/Leningrad, ONTI, 1934, p. 103).

13 See *Ryazanskie Vedomosti* (1998), 27 November. http://r-starina.chat.ru/3a.htm.

14 See *Pravda*, 22 September 1986.

15 Soviet discussions on the perfecting of planning and of the system of management of the economy are reviewed in V.A. Mau, *In search of the plan: A contribution to the history of Soviet economic thought from the 1930s to the 1960s* (Moscow, Nauka, 1990).

16 E.O. Liberman, 'On the planning of industrial production and material incentives for its development', *Kommunist* (1956), No. 11; V.S. Nemchinov, 'Fulfilling the plan and material incentives', *Pravda,* 21 September 1962.

17 V.A. Mau, *In search of the plan: A contribution to the history of Soviet economic thought from the 1930s to the 1960s* (Moscow, Nauka, 1990).

18 In some foreign publications the reform is described as the 'Liberman Reform', following the publication in 1962 of the article that initiated the most serious economic discussion since the 1920s: E. Liberman, 'Plan, profit and premia', *Pravda,* 9 September 1962.

19 F.A. Hayek (1990) *The Fatal Conceit. The Errors of Socialism.* London: Routledge.

7

FROM USSR TO RUSSIA

The fate of the military economy

Julian Cooper

Introduction

One of the factors complicating post-communist economic transformation in the Russian Federation from the beginning of 1992 was the existence of an extremely large military sector employing many millions of people in the armed forces, the defence industry and agencies concerned with the planning and management of this hypertrophied system for the defence of the country. It was not only the scale of this military capability that presented a problem, but also its structure and mode of functioning. For decades this had been the highest priority sector of the Soviet economic system, used to working with the best-quality resources available, relatively generous funding and strong political support at the highest levels of the Communist Party and state. The collapse of the USSR and communist rule at the end of 1991 had a profound impact on the military economy, with powerful echoes even two decades later.

The USSR military economy

The core of the defence industry of the USSR was administered, for most of the final 25 years of the country's existence, by nine industrial ministries, often referred to simply as the 'nine', overseen by a high-level co-ordinating agency, the Military-Industrial Commission. In addition, some industrial enterprises of nominally civilian ministries also produced armaments alongside civil goods such as tractors, motor vehicles and energy sector equipment. However, most of the enterprises of the defence industry proper also produced civilian products, including consumer goods (mainly electrical and electronic) and certain material inputs and equipment required in the manufacture of armaments, such as special steel and machine tools, which the civilian industrial ministries concerned were unable to supply to adequate quality and precision. This in-house supply of inputs also reduced the vulnerability of the defence industry to the supply breakdowns endemic in the Soviet economy: in 1990 approximately 60 per cent of total output was military, i.e. armaments and other military hardware made to the order of the armed forces or produced for export, the rest civilian. The activities of the defence industry were shrouded in an extraordinary level of secrecy, only relaxed to a modest degree in the final years when Mikhail Gorbachev was leader.[1]

The defence industry was indeed of a massive scale. By 1990 it employed over 8 million people, including almost 1.5 million in research and development (R&D). This was over 19 per cent of total industrial employment. Its output represented 12 per cent of the total output of industry as a whole. However, as noted, the defence industry also manufactured many civilian goods, in particular those of a relatively high technological level. Indeed, almost all high technology industry in the USSR was undertaken within the defence sector, so much so that in 1990 half the industry's total production was of civilian goods. In the same year almost 80 per cent of all industrial R&D undertaken in the country was performed by the defence industry and almost 70 per cent of this was for military purposes.[2]

The work of the defence industry was coordinated by a small (in terms of personnel) but powerful agency, the Military-Industrial Commission. Just as the Soviet economy as a whole was producer-driven, with very weak customer power, this was also true of the defence industry, which to a large extent was able to determine the types of weapons supplied to the armed forces and their volume. Only in the late Gorbachev years were the military able openly to voice their discontent with this one-sided arms procurement system.

The USSR was a very large-scale exporter of armaments. During the 1980s the volume of arms exports approached US $20 billion a year. In principle, the earnings from these exports should have strengthened the trade balance and permitted more imports, including consumer goods. In practice, many of the arms were supplied on very generous credit terms with little expectation of full repayment, or given away as gifts. Thus in 1986–90, according to official sources, only a third of arms were sold for cash, 40 per cent were supplied on credit and 27 per cent were given away or transferred at heavily discounted prices.[3] Arms were transferred to Warsaw Treaty Organization partners, nations regarded as close political friends, and to less developed countries in the hope that they would support Soviet policies and, perhaps, take the path of socialism. Only towards the final years of the Soviet Union did a more commercial approach begin to develop, with arms being sold for hard currency to some Middle Eastern oil-rich nations.

For most of the post-war years, Soviet military spending was totally non-transparent and the official figure for budget spending on defence in the annual State Budget covered only personnel and maintenance, the financing of all arms procurement, R&D, nuclear weapons, construction being hidden in other budget chapters. With *perestroika* and *glasnost*, the Soviet leadership began to publish a more comprehensive version of the defence budget. For 1989 the USSR declared a figure of just over 8.0 per cent of gross national product (GNP) but this referred to the Ministry of Defence (MOD) forces only.[4] For the same year the Central Intelligence Agency (CIA) estimated a total spending on the entire military effort of almost 18 per cent GNP.[5] In the present author's view, 14–16 per cent represents a more credible share of GNP in 1988–89.[6] In 1988 the Soviet leadership decided to reduce military spending and, at the same time, embarked upon a policy of 'conversion', meaning, in principle, replacement of military production by civilian, with a direct re-orientation of production capacities to alternative uses.

However, it was not the scale of the military effort alone that had a deleterious impact on the performance of the Soviet economy. This was a point that many liberally minded critics during the Gorbachev years failed to grasp, sometimes leading them to propose wildly exaggerated estimates of the size of the 'monster', as the military-industrial complex was often termed. The first important issue is the one that the economist Yurii Yaremenko (1981) understood: the fact that the defence industry, the highest priority branch of the economy, was allocated the best available quality material inputs and provided with funding allowing it to offer favourable conditions of employment, permitting it to employ the most highly skilled personnel. Lower priority sectors were deprived of quality inputs, material and human, and were unable to work as effectively or to produce high quality products. Over time, this structural distortion of the Soviet economy became ever more pronounced and became a factor inhibiting the overall development of the economy. This argument relates to that of Kornai (1980): the defence industry of the USSR became habituated to very soft budget constraints. Finance as such was a secondary factor, what mattered was access to real human and material resources of adequate quality, and these were assured.

Yaremenko's argument was taken further by a leading Soviet authority on military matters, Vitalii Shlykov, a former military intelligence officer. It was Shlykov who coined the term 'structural militarisation' to characterise the state of the Soviet economy (Shlykov, 1995). He was the first in the USSR to focus public attention on the extraordinarily elaborate system of mobilisation preparation that had developed in the country from the 1930s. In Shlykov's view, this system had become the 'sacred cow' of Soviet national security policy (Khrapovitskii, 1991). In the USSR countless enterprises, military and civilian, were obliged to maintain substantial spare production capacities to be engaged rapidly in the manufacture of armaments or other military-related goods in the event of war or national emergency, the so-called 'special period'. In order to undertake such production, enterprises were also required to stockpile materials, components and other inputs, and to ensure that workers were properly trained to switch to military work if required. In the European part of the country, these reserves had to be sufficient for three months of wartime production; in the Asian part, six months. This extraordinarily elaborate and costly system was shrouded in almost total secrecy.[7]

As Shlykov has persuasively argued, this system had an impact on the whole economy, not just the defence industry. Mobilization plans could involve preparation for potential increases in military output of 10 times or more. In order to supply this production, the metals industry, chemical industry, civilian machine building and energy sector, and other industries providing inputs also had to maintain spare capacities and in some cases keep them in operation in the event of need. This was an extraordinarily wasteful system, giving rise to massive spare capacity and low levels of productivity, over time deepening the structural distortions of the economy. In Shlykov's opinion this 'structural militarisation' played a significant role in the weakening and eventual failure of the Soviet economic system.[8] Interestingly, this view has been echoed more recently by none other than the head of the leading economic research centre of the MOD, the 46th Central Scientific Research Institute, the responsibilities of which include drawing up the long-term armaments programme. After an overview of the Soviet mobilization preparation system, Vasilii Burenok concluded that the demands of attempting to guarantee the security of the country in this way had consequences: 'The breakup of the USSR and the destruction of its economy are explained, not in the last instance, by the efforts to fulfil demands of this type, that overstrained the capacities of the state and brought it to a catastrophe.'[9]

In March 1989 there was a decision to reduce Soviet military expenditure by 14 per cent over the period 1988–91, including a reduction of spending on arms procurement by 19.5 per cent and on military R&D by 15 per cent. According to data published later, this intention was over-fulfilled: in the event, the reductions were 29 per cent for procurement and 22 per cent for R&D.[10] As spending was being reduced, many defence enterprises were under pressure to increase their civilian output, in particular their manufacture of televisions, washing machines, refrigerators and other household goods, the government seeking to expand the output of goods in demand that would absorb some of the rapidly growing monetary overhang. Meanwhile, *Gosplan* and the defence industry ministries worked on a highly ambitious state conversion programme for the years 1991–95, which was eventually approved in December 1990.[11] By this time the ministries of the defence industry had already been allocated enterprises from the disbanded Ministry of Machine building for the Light and Food Industries and some plants making medical equipment. The programme was elaborated in typical Soviet fashion with detailed targets and investment allocations on the assumption that the traditional planning system would continue to function, but by the time it had been approved this was no longer the case. The economic system was in crisis and the conditions for the realization of the conversion programme had to a large extent disappeared. In the event, many defence enterprises did start new civilian production but this usually did not involve any conversion of capacities previously devoted to military work; instead, these capacities, if no longer receiving orders, were mothballed in order to retain production capabilities in the event of mobilization for war.

After the attempted coup of August 1991, the leaders of which included three prominent figures of the defence industry, the administrative structures of the military economy rapidly unravelled. *Gosplan* had already been transformed into the Ministry of the Economy, and in November the Military-Industrial Commission was abolished and all but one of the industrial ministries dissolved, the only one to be retained, on security grounds, being that for the nuclear industry. By this time an increasing number of defence industry organizations in the republics, which had declared their sovereignty, adopted a republican status and no longer recognized the authority of Moscow. The highly disciplined and coherent Soviet military-industrial complex, to a large extent, had already ceased to exist before the final end of the USSR in December 1991.

The 1990s: transformation and contraction

In independent Russia from the beginning of 1992, the military economy underwent far-reaching transformation, just as the economy as a whole underwent market transition. Firstly, the scale of budget funding of the armed forces contracted rapidly and to a very considerable extent; secondly, spending on arms procurement and R&D was cut even more radically than total spending on defence, with extremely severe consequences for the defence industry; thirdly, the defence industry was not immune to privatization and the general 'disorganization' that characterized the economy as a whole. The impact of these factors was unambiguous: the output of the defence industry, especially of armaments and other military hardware, collapsed, with a rapid shrinkage of employment. To some extent the blow was cushioned by arms exports, but overall the principal motivation of defence industry managers became survival. The dramatic downsizing of the vast Soviet defence sector was not undertaken to any coherent plan, but was overwhelmingly a spontaneous process of adaptation to rapidly changing economic conditions.

In the early months of 1992 the new Gaidar government wrestled with the problem of drawing up a feasible budget for the year, initially for the first quarter only, in an attempt to reduce the massive deficit which developed during the final years of the Soviet Union. This followed price liberalization at the beginning of the year, a process that had an immediate, negative, impact on the defence industry. It was decided to reduce military expenditure but to focus the cuts on procurement and R&D, in recognition that manpower reductions could not be implemented immediately. As a result, expenditure on arms procurement was cut by two-thirds at a stroke.[12] In taking this action the government received support from the military leadership, which acknowledged that there were vast stocks of weapons available, supplemented by equipment withdrawn from countries previously in the now dissolved Warsaw Treaty Organization. The scale of the cuts caused panic in the defence industry, which pressured the government, not without success, to pursue an active arms export policy. In reality, results were modest but to some extent production levels were maintained during 1992, most of the finished arms finding no buyers.[13] In the expectation that the policy of reduced procurement would be reversed, heightened by the dismissal of Gaidar as acting Prime Minister in December 1992, enterprises endeavoured to retain their employees. As argued by the above-mentioned Shlykov, this was done in part by disposing of stockpiles of non ferrous metals and other materials held under the Soviet system of mobilisation preparation.[14] The export of mobilization reserves, strictly forbidden but possible in the circumstances of fragmented authority in the early 1990s, was a profitable business that helped to keep many enterprises afloat, at least in the short term.

Military expenditure remained severely constrained until the 1998 financial–economic crisis and beyond, only easing to some extent after the year 2000. To make matters worse for the defence industry, allocations to defence in budget laws were increasingly subject to sequestration. By 1997 the military output of the defence industry had fallen to less than one-tenth of its 1991 level. Civilian output held up more strongly, but the overall output of the industry was still less than one-fifth of its level in the final Soviet year.[15] By 1997 total employment in the defence industry in Russia, excluding the nuclear weapons sector, was almost 2.8 million, including 600,000 in R&D, compared with over 6 million in 1990, 1.3 million of whom had been in R&D.[16]

As the privatization campaign gathered pace in 1992, Anatolii Chubais, chair of the State Committee for the Management of State Property (GKI), made it clear that the defence industry would not be immune. As part of preparation for possible privatization, many of the production associations and research–production associations, groupings of enterprises into corporate structures that had been created in the USSR from the early 1970s, were disbanded, on the principle that enterprises and R&D organizations would be privatized as separate units. Many defence industry directors vigorously opposed possible privatization and succeeded in diluting the GKI's original intentions.[17] As a result, by the end of the 1990s three-quarters of all defence industry enterprises and organizations remained in full state ownership or had state shareholdings, of varying size, from a single 'golden share' to 75 per cent or more, and just one-quarter were fully privatized joint stock companies.[18] By branch, the electronics and aviation industries had the largest share of fully privatized companies, the munitions, ground forces equipment, and shipbuilding industries had the smallest.

In privatizing defence companies, two considerations complicated the process. Firstly, a feature of such enterprises in Soviet times was the attachment to them of extensive provision of housing and diverse social assets considered vital in maintaining stable, suitably skilled, labour collectives. Secondly, notwithstanding market transformation and the new post-Cold War security situation, the elaborate system of mobilization preparation inherited from Soviet times remained intact, albeit with somewhat reduced expectations as to the scale of reserve capacities that had to be maintained. Officially, these obligations extended equally to both state and privately owned enterprises fulfilling state defence orders, although in practice they proved more difficult to enforce at the latter.

With Vladimir Putin as President from early 2000, following the initial post-crisis recovery fuelled above all by the sharp devaluation of the rouble from August 1998, the economy began to revive and prospects for the military sector began to improve for the first time in almost a decade. Military expenditure on the MOD forces as a share of GDP stabilized at around 2.5–2.7 per cent.[19] Gradually, budget allocations on the annual state defence order, covering the procurement of new armaments, the repair and modernization of existing arms, and military R&D, began to increase, permitting the purchase of modest volumes of new strategic missiles, tanks and armoured vehicles, and by the end of the decade a few combat aircraft, helicopters and naval vessels.

This increased domestic acquisition improved the economic situation of some enterprises, but for most of the decade from 2000 it was growing arms exports that kept key enterprises alive and permitted some new investment. The volume of arms exports increased from US $3.7 billion in 2000, to US $6.2 billion in 2005 and US $10.4 billion in 2010.[20] However, these exports were heavily focused on a limited range of systems and companies, in particular combat aircraft (Sukhoi and to a lesser extent MiG), helicopters, air defence systems, supplied by the 'Almaz-Antei' corporation, some diesel-electric submarines and surface naval ships, and tanks and other armoured vehicles. Some strategically important companies were unable to benefit from export orders because of the nature of their work, in particular those involved in building strategic nuclear missiles.

During the 1990s the defence industry underwent numerous administrative changes, ranging from initial leadership by a Committee for the Defence Industry, to a Ministry in 1996, then the Ministry of the Economy, followed by a number of specialized agencies. During the late 1990s some stability was finally achieved, with oversight of the industry being vested in the Ministry of Industry.[21] The Federal Space Agency (*Roskosmos*) was responsible for the missile-space industry, the Federal Nuclear Agency (*Rossatom*) for nuclear weapons, and from the end of 2007 some 330 enterprises and organizations of the defence industry were transferred to a state corporation, *Rostekhnologii* ('Russian Technologies'), although remaining subject to the general oversight of the industry ministry. In 2006 a new Military-Industrial Commission was organized, headed by a deputy prime minister, but while taking responsibility for the state defence order and the system of mobilization preparation, it was not granted the strong powers to command lower level organizations enjoyed by its Soviet predecessor.

From 2000 there was a concerted effort by the government to group defence industry organizations into a limited number of corporations, so-called 'integrated structures'. This proved to be a difficult, protracted process as many enterprises resisted incorporation, often backed by regional authorities, concerned that tax revenues obtained from local enterprises would be centralized in Moscow. As of 2011 this state-led process of restructuring was still underway but many free-standing enterprises still remained. However, by then several significant corporate structures had been formed, including the above-mentioned 'Russian Technologies', the 'United Aircraft Corporation' (all fixed-wing aircraft building), the 'United Shipbuilding Corporation' (the majority of shipyards) and 'Almaz-Antei' for air defence systems. As a result, the Russian defence industry is now dominated by a relatively small number of monopoly, or near-monopoly, producers, a process justified by the government in terms of the need to respond to international competition. However, the absence of competition in the domestic market has generated problems, as discussed below.

From 2000 the output of the defence industry steadily increased on an annual basis, but even by 2010 the level of 1991 had still not been recovered. Thus, for military goods, barely half the 1991 output had been reached, for civilian goods, 70 per cent.[22] In 2010 almost 70 per cent of total output was of a military character, a share somewhat larger than that in late Soviet years, in part because of the inadequate competitiveness of many of the sector's products, but also because by this time some predominantly civil enterprises had left the defence industry.[23] The employment of the industry had almost stabilized, with some 1.6 million in industrial activity and 500,000 in R&D.[24] The large number employed in R&D can be explained in part by the low productivity characteristic of this sector in Russia, but also by the fact that budgetary funding of research is less rigorously monitored than budgetary funding of production activities, leading to the suspicion that military-related R&D is characterized by considerable waste of resources. But in individual branches the loss of personnel had been dramatic, for example, the electronics industry, responsible for components, by 2007 had 100,000 employees, compared with 724,000 in 1990.[25]

However, with only modest recruitment of new workers, largely because of relatively low pay compared to the average for industry as a whole, not to speak of more dynamic sectors such as financial services, the defence industry's personnel have aged: in 1990 the average age was 39 years, by 2008 approaching 50.[26] Of all the sectors of the defence industry, it is electronics that exhibits the most serious loss of capability. Notwithstanding an official policy, at least until the late 2000s, of almost total reliance on domestic sources of supply for all armaments delivered to the Russian armed forces, there has been a mounting dependence on imported electronic components.

One significant aspect of the Soviet military economy, inherited by Russia, remained virtually unchanged for many years and began to be reformed only in recent years: this was the system by which the military procured new armaments. In the USSR the military was a relatively passive customer for armaments, with the defence industry able to a large extent to dictate what weapons were supplied and also the quantities delivered. This was a producer driven system and the memoir literature suggests that this bias became even more pronounced after the appointment of Dmitrii Ustinov, with a background in defence industry management and oversight, as defence minister in 1976. However, the military were able to exert some influence on the quality of weapons through its network of 'military representatives' who were located at enterprises and development organizations to monitor their work on behalf of the customer. In addition, the technical specifications of new armaments were partly determined by the staff of the ordering agencies of the military. In independent Russian in the early 1990s when a civilian, Andrei Kokoshin, a specialist on the USA, was first deputy defence minister, there was interest in moving towards a US-style customer-driven procurement system, but practical results were minimal.[27]

Central to the system of arms procurement are the ten-year state armaments programme and the annual state defence order. The programme, updated every five years, sets out the military's requirements, with funding estimates based on the economic forecast of the economics ministry and the budget forecast of the finance ministry. The programme does not have legal force but to a considerable degree is supposed to determine the state defence order, which in recent years has been drawn up by the Military-Industrial Commission and signed into law by the President. Russia's experience with the armaments programme has been negative. The programmes adopted to 2005, 2010 and 2015 were all abandoned as unrealizable, largely because they were elaborated on the basis of over-optimistic economic forecasts, including inadequate allowance for inflation.

At the end of 2010 the latest programme, to 2020, was adopted. This proved to be extraordinarily ambitious, with total spending of almost 21 trillion roubles (*c.* US $700 billion), including 19 trillion roubles for the MOD, in order to secure a fundamental modernization of the equipment of the country's armed forces.[28] The preparation of this programme was in part a response to the experience of the Russian armed forces in the brief war with Georgia of August 2008. This exposed some serious deficiencies in the armaments deployed and focused the attention of the political leadership on the need for decisive action.

The war with Georgia also prompted a far-reaching reform of the MOD forces to give them 'a new face', to use the term adopted by the civilian minister, former chief of the Federal Tax Service, Anatolii Serdyukov. As part of this reform there have been vigorous efforts to transform the arms procurement system, with two main directions. First, the ordering of armaments and the conclusion of contracts with the defence industry contractors is being civilianized, with the creation of a new agency, *Rosoboronpostavka*, the head of which, Nadezhda Sinikova, is a former deputy leader of the tax service. The ordering process is being monitored by another civilian agency, *Rosoboronzakaz*.[29] Second, the military's role in implementing the annual state defence order has undergone a significant change. Whereas in the past the military simply accepted the terms offered by industry, in particular the prices charged for armaments, with the order for the year 2011, the MOD, backed by President Dmitrii Medvedev and Prime Minister Vladimir Putin, played the part of a tough and demanding customer, refusing to accept prices it considered to be excessively high. To some extent the high prices being demanded by some defence enterprises reflects a Soviet-era legacy: they have extraordinarily high overheads because they seek to maintain the inherited social infrastructure, retained in the defence industry to a greater extent than in other sectors, and also to finance the retention of substantial unused capacities, kept to meet possible mobilization demands. However, they also reflect the monopoly position of many suppliers. The tough negotiations resulted in long delays in placing orders but the move signalled a fundamental change in the balance of power: producer dominance is over, now the MOD is to be a demanding customer, very much on the lines of the acquisition system of the USA, although, as is well known, such a system is also not without problems.

In making this belated reform the MOD, backed again by the government, made it clear to industry that in the event that it failed to meet the military's requirements, armaments would be imported. To underline the point, in June 2011 a deal was signed with the French company DCNS for the purchase of two 'Mistral' class helicopters carrying amphibious assault ships, at a cost of €1.2 billion.[30] However, this was not the only acquisition of foreign military technology: Russia has also purchased armoured vehicles from Italy, unmanned aviation vehicles from Israel, night vision systems from France and light armour from Germany. Until recently the defence industry always knew that the military would procure its products, even if they did not meet requirements, because there was no alternative, a strict policy of domestic supply only being observed.[31]

Conclusion

In retrospect it is difficult to see how the downsizing of the military economy could have been achieved by other means. The institutional conditions for an orderly, programmed, process were lacking. The administrative capacities of the Russian state were extremely weak during the 1990s and the organizational structures that had managed the military economy in Soviet times had been liquidated or, if they still existed, failed to function with any effectiveness. The sharp contraction was painful and costly, but what is striking is the extent to which many of the relatively highly-skilled labour force of the defence industry proved able to find alternative employment on their own initiative. However, the fact remains that for almost twenty years the Russian armed forces received very few new weapons and the stock of equipment inherited from Soviet times degraded inexorably. By 2010 re-equipment had become a necessity and it is not surprising that the political and military leadership embarked upon an ambitious state armaments programme. However, over a 20-year period much of the defence industry had also been starved of investment and hired only a limited number of new personnel. Its ability to meet the new challenge must be in serious doubt. In a few years time, Russia may have little choice but to open up the military economy and promote large-scale international cooperation. By 2011 this process had started but on a very cautious basis. Its further development will mark the true end of the USSR military economy.

In assessing the extent of transformation since the end of the USSR it is relevant to consider the present-day Russian military economy from the perspective of the analyses of Kornai, Yaremenko and Shlykov. Firstly, it is clear that soft budget constraints, though less prevalent and not as soft as in Soviet times, still exist. One of the factors promoting the creation of large corporate structures such as *Rostekhnologii* and the 'United Aircraft Corporation' was the fact that many enterprises working for the state defence order are loss making. By grouping them with profitable enterprises, cross subsidisation became possible, just as it was within Soviet industrial ministries. In the case of *Rostekhnologii*, according to its general director, Sergei Chemezov, one-third of the enterprises entering into the corporation when it was created in late 2007 were bankrupt or in a near-bankrupt state.[32] During the 2008–09 financial-economic crisis, a quite large number of defence enterprises received budget support to keep them functioning.

Secondly, the structural regime, with its associated price distortions, as conceptualized by Yaremenko, has largely disappeared. Indeed, some of the cost and pain of transformation experienced by the military economy can be explained in part by its adaptation to the loss of the administratively secured special conditions that it enjoyed in Soviet times. Now, if a defence industry enterprise wishes to secure highly skilled personnel or acquire high grade production equipment, it has no choice but to provide competitive remuneration or pay the ruling market price.

Thirdly, the structural militarization, as analysed by Shlykov, has to a large extent disappeared, but not completely. The elaborate system of mobilization preparation still exists but on a reduced scale and appears to be restricted more narrowly to the immediate defence sector rather than ranging widely over the civilian economy. However, since responsibility for management of the mobilization system was switched in 2008 from the Ministry of Economic Development to the Military-Industrial Commission it has once again become a matter of high-level state secrecy, making an assessment of its status almost impossible.

Overall, it can be concluded that the two decades since the Soviet system began to collapse have seen a substantial systemic transformation of the military economy. It is no longer the 'monster' or 'state within the state' as it came to be regarded in the final years of the USSR, but with its nuclear capability and role as the world's second largest arms exporter, it is by no means a minor actor in present-day Russia. However, the capability of the defence industry is extremely uneven and future development is likely to involve increased international engagement.

Notes

1 For an overview of the Soviet defence industry, see Cooper (1991).

2 Data from Cooper (2006), pp. 132–33.

3 Data from *Nezavisimaya gazeta*, 29 September 1992 (P.Fel'gengauer). The latter category may have included arms supplied according to barter arrangements, but details are lacking.

4 Calculated from Alexashenko (1993), p.7 and Goskomstat SSSR (1991), p.5.

5 Firth and Noren (1998), p. 130.

6 Cooper (1998), p. 246. Note, the military share of GDP in the USA in 1989 was 5.8 per cent; in the UK, 4.0 per cent (SIPRI (1991), p. 174).

7 Significantly, when a fuller version of the defence budget was eventually published in 1989, it did not include spending on the mobilization preparation.

8 Shlykov (2002), p. 149 ('… the economic collapse of the USSR was a consequence in the first instance of the system of mobilization preparation of the economy.')

9 Burenok (2011), p. 6.

10 See Vinslav (2006), part 1, p. 45.

11 Vinslav (2006), part 1, p. 51.

12 See Cooper (2001), p. 246.

13 See Cooper (1997), pp. 174–95 on Russian arms export policy in the early 1990s.

14 See Shlykov (1995), pp. 27–29.

15 Cooper (2001), pp. 317–19.

16 Cooper (2010), p. 156 and Cooper (2006), p. 133,

17 On defence industry privatization, see Sánchez-Andrés (1995) and (1998).

18 Http://ia.vpk.ru/vpkrus, accessed 11 February 1999 (Information Agency TS VPK).

19 Cooper (2010), p. 147.

20 *Ibid.*, p. 153, and www.vpk.name/news/5180, 18 April 2011.

21 See Cooper (2010), p.155.

22 Calculated by the author from data of Information Agency TS VPK (www.vpk.ru) and, for 2010, www.rosprep.ru/news, 19 April 2011.

23 www.minpromtorg.gov.ru/special/gov/20/36, accessed 23 April 2011.

24 *Ibid.*, p.156.

25 *Strategiya razvitiya elektronnoi promyshlennosti Rosii na period do 2025 goda*, Moscow, 2007, p.13 and *Sovestskaya Rossiya*, 17 April 1999.

26 Cooper (2006), p. 133, and http://nvo.ng.ru/concepts/2008=06=20/1_opk.html, 20 June 2008.

27 See Cooper (1993), pp. 152–54.

28 http://nvo.ng.ru/armament/2011-03-11/8_opk.html, 11 March 2011, Vladimir Shcherbakov, 'Bol'she zhelaniya i skromnye vozmozhnosti'.

29 See http://rosoboronpostavka.ru and http://www.fsoz.gv.ru.

30 www.rg.ru/2011/06/14/mistral-anons.html, 14 June 2011.
31 The only exception was supply from other former Soviet producers in countries of the Commonwealth of Independent States considered reliable, in particular Belarus.
32 www.rostechn.ru/archive/3/detail.php?ID=7403 (from *Novaya gazeta*, 21 April 2010, interview with Sergei Chemezov).

Bibliography

Alexashenko, S. (1993), 'The budgetary system in the USSR: impossibility of transformation', *European Economy*, no. 49.

Burenok, V.M. (2011), 'O podkhodakh k mobilizatsionnoi podgotovke promyshlennosti v sovremennykh usloviyakh', *Vooruzhenie i ekonomika*, no. 2(14), pp. 5–8.

Cooper, J. (1991), *The Soviet Defence Industry: Conversion and Reform*, London: Royal Institute for International Affairs/Pinter.

——(1993), 'Transforming Russia's Defence Industrial Base', *Survival*, vol. 45, no. 4, pp. 147–62.

——(1997), 'Russia' in Pierre, Andrew J. (ed.), *Cascade of Arms*, Washington, DC: Brookings Institution Press, pp. 173–202.

——(1998), 'The military expenditure of the USSR and the Russian Federation' in *SIPRI Yearbook 1998*, Oxford: Oxford University Press, pp. 243–59.

——(2001), 'Russian military expenditure and arms production' in *SIPRI Yearbook 2001,* Oxford: Oxford University Press, pp. 313–22.

——(2006), 'Society-military relations in Russia: the economic dimension' in Webber, Stephen L. and Mathers, Jennifer G. (eds), *Military and society in post-Soviet Russia*, Manchester: Manchester University Press, pp. 131–56.

——(2010), 'The "Security Economy"' in Galeotti, Mark (ed.), *The Politics of Security in Modern Russia*, Farnham: Ashgate, pp. 145–70.

Firth, N.E. and Noren, J.H. (1998), *Soviet Defense Spending. A History of CIA Estimates, 1950–1990*, College Station: Texas A&M University Press.

Goskomstat SSSR (1991), *Narodnoe khozyaistvo SSSR v 1990g. Statisticheskoe ezhegodnik*, Moscow: 'Finansy i statistika'.

Khrapovitskii, D. (1991), 'Dvazhdy mertvyi kapital'. *Soyuz*, no. 24 (June), p. 11 (interview with Vitalii Shlykov).

Kornai, J. (1980), *Economics of Shortage*, Amsterdam: North Holland Publishing.

Sánchez-Andrés, A. (1995), 'The First Stage of Privatisation of the Russian Military Industry', *Communist Economies & Economic Transformation*, vol. 7, no. 3, pp. 353–67.

——(1998), 'Privatisation, Decentralisation and Production Adjustment in the Russian Defence Industry', *Europe-Asia Studies*, vol. 50, no. 2, pp. 241–55.

Shlykov, V. (1995), 'Economic Readjustment within the Russian Defense-Industrial Complex', *Security Dialogue*, Vol. 26, no. 1, March, pp. 19–34 (and comment by Julian Cooper, pp. 35–39).

——(2002), 'Chto pogubilo Sovetskogo Soyuza? Genshtab i ekonomika', *Voennyi vestnik*, No. 9 (Mezhregional'nyi fond informatsionnykh tekhnologii).

SIPRI (1991), *SIPRI Yearbook 1991*, Oxford: Oxford University Press.

Vinslav, Y. (2006), 'Konversiya otechestennogo oboronno-promyshlennogo kompleksa: fragment retroanaliza i nekotorye aktual'nye vyvody', *Rossiiskii ekononomicheskie zhurnal*, no. 3, pp. 37–52 (Part 1) and no. 4, pp. 42–54 (Part 2).

Yaremenko, Y. (1981), *Strukturnye izmeneniya v sotsialisticheskoi ekonomike*, Moscow: Mysl.

8

WHY DID TRANSITION HAPPEN?

David M. Kotz

Introduction

In the mid-1970s Soviet-type systems occupied a major part of the world. The list of states with Soviet-type economic and political systems, characterized by state ownership, central planning, and rule by a Communist Party, included the USSR, Bulgaria, Czechoslovakia, the German Democratic Republic (GDR), Hungary, Poland, Romania, Albania, China, Mongolia, Vietnam, Cambodia, Laos, North Korea and Cuba. A number of other states in Asia and Africa had adopted some features of the Soviet-type system, although not rule by a Communist Party.[1]

At that time, the Soviet-type system appeared stable and even unassailable. Under that system, often called 'state socialism', the USSR had developed rapidly from a rural, agricultural country in the late 1920s to an urban, industrial society. It had become one of the world's two superpowers. The USSR was a world leader in science and some areas of technology, launching the world's first space satellite. According to estimates by the US Central Intelligence Agency, in 1975 Soviet GNP was about 60 per cent of that of the USA. If Soviet and US GNP growth rates had both remained at their averages during 1950–75 that were widely accepted at the time, then in 36 more years Soviet GNP would have surpassed that of the USA, in 2011 (Kotz and Weir, 2007, pp. 33–37).[2]

China, starting from an underdeveloped economy in 1949, had, despite periodic disruptions from political-economic zigzags, built a significant industrial base through central planning by the mid-1970s. The Vietnamese Communists in North Vietnam had just expelled the USA from Vietnam, uniting the whole country under Communist Party rule. At that time Cuba's version of state socialism attracted wide interest in Latin America and Africa and among intellectuals in many countries.

In a remarkable historical turnaround, some 15 years later state socialism had vanished, or was gradually disappearing, in almost every state on the above list. State socialism was abandoned and was replaced by an effort to build the rival system of capitalism. The most powerful of that group of states, the USSR, disintegrated into 15 separate countries. Such a sudden collapse of a mighty economic, political, and social system, absent either violent revolution or external invasion, is unprecedented in modern history. Why did such a remarkable transition happen?

The demise of state socialism occurred very rapidly, in 1989–91, in the USSR, the seven Communist-ruled states in East/Central Europe, and Mongolia. In those states, within a few short years the institutions of state socialism were dismantled and Communist Party rule was overthrown, with a quick shift to building a capitalist system. In China the process was one of gradual evolution over several decades starting in 1978, with the Communist Party holding onto power while the key economic institutions of state socialism – state-owned enterprises and central planning – were gradually replaced by those of capitalism, namely private enterprise and production for profit in the market. The share of industrial output produced by state-owned enterprises did not fall below 50 per cent until the early 1990s. A similar gradual transition began somewhat later in Vietnam.

This contribution examines the reasons why this transition took place in one particularly important state, the USSR. In March 1985 Mikhail Gorbachev became General Secretary of the Soviet Communist Party and soon launched an effort to reform and democratize Soviet socialism, known as *perestroika*. Six years later state socialism was dismantled and replaced by an effort to build capitalism, the Soviet state ceased to exist on December 31 1991, and Gorbachev's opponent, Boris Yeltsin, was in charge of the newly independent Russian state. Analyzing this process in the USSR during the period 1985–91 helps to understand, not just that specific case, but the entire process of transition in all of the countries. State socialism first arose in the USSR, and that model was copied, more or less closely, by all of the other Communist-ruled states. Each individual case of transition had its own particular features and developments. Nevertheless, it will be argued here that the key to understanding why the entire momentous, and largely unforeseen, transition occurred can be found in the process that emerged in the USSR during 1985–91.

Contending explanations

There remain many contending explanations 20 years after the demise of the Soviet Union. This is not surprising – historians still debate the reasons for the decline and fall of the (Western) Roman Empire roughly 1,600 years ago. The contending explanations of the Soviet demise fall into several distinct and sometimes contradictory categories. Some authors cite factors external to the USSR while others point to internal developments. Some focus on chance, or accidental, occurrences, while others emphasize systemic factors. Among the explanations that centre around systemic factors, some claim that an irresolvable flaw was present in state socialism from the start, while others assert that problems arising from the evolution of the system account for its demise. Some stress economic factors, some political factors, and still others point to cultural factors.

This section reviews several widely disseminated explanations for the Soviet demise, arguing briefly that none of them can adequately account for it. The following section proposes an explanation that, in our view, fits the historical evidence in the Soviet case, explains otherwise puzzling features of the Soviet demise, and can also explain why (and to some degree, how) a similar process, of either a rapid or gradual character, took hold in almost all of the other state socialist systems – as well as explaining why that process has not so far spread to Cuba.

Two related explanations start with an assumption that the centrally planned economy contained irresolvable contradictions that caused an economic collapse, leaving no choice but to adopt the only alternative system for a large-scale state capitalism. The first version of this explanation asserts that central planning can work only for the basic industrialization stage of economic development. According to this view, initial industrialization involves a few key tasks – constructing the necessary transportation, power, and other infrastructure; building a few basic producer goods and consumer goods industries; and shifting the labour force from agricultural work to the various new non-agricultural pursuits. Central planning can effectively mobilize resources to accomplish such key tasks.

According to this view, once industrialization is completed central planning becomes unworkable in the face of the more complex economic demands of a post-industrialization economy. However, this explanation has a problem. By the eve of the Second World War, the Soviet Union had, in record time, completed basic industrialization. Nevertheless, the Soviet economy continued to grow relatively rapidly following postwar reconstruction from 1950 to 1975, with an average annual GNP growth rate of 4.8 per cent in that period based on CIA estimates (Kotz and Weir, 2007, p. 35). Soviet central planning did not collapse after basic industrialization was completed; rather, it continued to function remarkably effectively.

The second version of this explanation holds that central planning can work both for indus-trialization and for the following stage of the initial building of an urban consumer society. The latter second stage, like industrialization, still has a few key goals – building apartments for the rising urban population, producing basic consumer amenities such as refrigerators and television sets, and producing the infrastructure and public goods for the new urban population (transportation, sanitary facilities, educational institutions, parks, and so forth). However, according to this explanation, once the initial building of an urban consumer society is completed, consumer needs become much more complex, as do the number and quality requirements for producer goods, and central planning becomes unworkable in the face of this third stage of economic development.

The assumptions behind this version appear plausible. The economic performance of the Soviet economy did sharply deteriorate after 1975, with the estimated GNP growth rate falling to the 1.8–1.9 per cent range in 1975–85 (prior to the major economic reform efforts that followed). However, slow economic growth indicates stagnation, not economic collapse. The flaw in this explanation is, once again, a problem of timing. The Soviet economy did not have a single year of economic contraction after the Second World War until 1990, when GNP fell by 2.5 per cent, followed by a precipitous double-digit fall in 1991. However, the final appearance of something like economic collapse came only when political developments in the USSR led to the dismantling of central planning and the separation of the 15 constituent republics of the economically highly-integrated USSR in 1990–91 (Kotz and Weir, 2007, Ch. 5). Central planning in the USSR never did produce the predicted economic collapse – instead, economic collapse came only when central planning was dismantled by its political opponents, leaving a disin-tegrating USSR with no functioning system of economic coordination in place, neither market forces nor central planning. In other words, disintegration left behind an institutional vacuum.

Another explanation cites a loss of legitimacy of the state socialist system in the USSR as the cause of its demise (Fukuyama, 1993; Kontorovich, 1993). There is ample evidence that a major part of the Soviet population became disenchanted with the official ideology. There were many glaring contradictions between the official ideology and the readily observable reality of Soviet life, such as that between the pretension of economic equality and the special privileges of the ruling elite. The promised world revolution, after seeming to progress for a time at least in the less economically developed part of the world, appeared to stall after the 1970s. The pre-1975 economic catch-up with the West seemed to go into reverse after 1975.

However, in capitalist states the official ideology has, at times, also lost much of its influence, as occurred during the Great Depression of the 1930s when capitalism seemed to be failing. Again, in 2008 the sudden financial and economic collapse in the advanced countries led to widespread questioning of the dominant free-market ideology. However, in neither case did system collapse follow. Gorbachev tried to renovate the official ideology of the Soviet system while also seeking to jettison the features of the Soviet system that were in conflict with socialist ideals – yet that effort did not succeed. One has to ask why it did not.

Some analysts attribute the Soviet demise to the costs to the Soviet economy of keeping up with Western military spending, claiming that such costs led to the Soviet economic slowdown after

1975 that ultimately undermined the USSR. However, the evidence about Soviet military spending does not support this explanation. In 1950 Soviet military spending absorbed about 17 per cent of GNP, a much larger share than for the USA. However, while military spending rose during 1950–80, it rose more slowly than GNP, falling slightly to 16 per cent of GNP in 1980 (Ofer, 1987). Since the military burden did not prevent rapid economic growth during the 1950s and 1960s, it is not plausible that it could explain a growth slowdown in the mid-1970s. Under Gorbachev military spending was reduced as a share of GNP as relations with the USA improved.

An influential explanation is that nationalism destroyed the Soviet system. According to this view, once political repression was lifted and the system was liberalized under *perestroika*, the drive for independence of the various nationalities that made up the USSR could not be contained. Nationalist movements of growing strength did arise in some of the Soviet republics in the late 1980s, and the final collapse of the USSR did take the form of the dissolution of the Union into the 15 republics that had constituted the USSR. However, there are two serious weaknesses in this explanation for the Soviet demise.

First, while nationalism might be able to account for the disintegration of the Soviet state, it cannot explain why the social system was changed from state socialism to capitalism. While some other states disintegrated in this period (the GDR and Czechoslovakia), most did not. Second, a careful analysis of the political process in the USSR during 1989–91 does not support the claim that a drive for independence stemming from nationalism explains the Soviet demise. In a referendum in March 1991, held in 9 of the 15 republics representing 92.7 per cent of the Soviet population, 76.4 per cent supported preservation of the Soviet Union. It was the determination of the group led by Boris Yeltsin to attain state power that led to the disintegration of the USSR, not nationalist pressures. Yeltsin was unable to push aside Gorbachev and his backers in the largely democratic new Soviet governing institutions created in 1989. Instead, Yeltsin had to shift to a strategy of taking power in the Russian Republic of the USSR, from which position he was able to dismantle the USSR.[3]

The key event was Yeltsin's success in getting the Russian parliament to pass a sovereignty resolution on June 8 1990. This asserted that control over Russia's vast natural resources, previously provided to the whole USSR at subsidized prices, belonged to the Russian government, not the Union state. While this could not be enforced yet, its passage propelled the other 14 republics on the road toward leaving the USSR, including the majority that had previously had no significant nationalist movement. In August 1991 Yeltsin seized the power that would soon enable him to dismantle the USSR when, following the failure of a coup attempt by members of Gorbachev's cabinet, Yeltsin, without any legal basis, shifted control over all Soviet assets in the Russian Republic to that republic's government and banned the Communist Party on Russian territory, causing the other republics to flee the Union.[4]

Another explanation claims that popular opposition to socialism and support for capitalism overthrew the system. According to this view, once Gorbachev's *perestroika* instituted free elections and the right to engage in political activity, the majority voted in capitalism by voting for Boris Yeltsin, at least in the Russian Republic where Yeltsin won the republic presidency with 57.3 per cent of the votes in June 1991. However, Yeltsin never stated that he favoured capitalism. He campaigned for office stressing opposition to the privileges of the elite and support for democracy, 'market reform', and more rights for the Russian Republic within the USSR. Some introduction of markets was part of Gorbachev's plan for the reform of Soviet socialism. Public opinion surveys showed that a majority of the Soviet population continued to support some form of socialism through 1991, with only between 3 per cent and 17 per cent supporting the introduction of capitalism, depending on the wording of the particular survey (Kotz and Weir, 2007, pp. 132–34). While Yeltsin did become popular with most sections of the Russian Republic population in 1989–91, the public never endorsed the introduction of capitalism or the dismantling of the USSR.

Many analysts argue that the Soviet demise was owing to accidental developments rather than any systemic factor. There are two main variants of this explanation. The first is the 'Andropov's kidney' explanation – that Yuri Andropov, the first post-Brezhnev General Secretary and a tough and practical former KGB head, would have been able to maintain the system through modest reforms had his rule not been cut short by him dying of kidney failure after 15 months in office in February 1984. According to this view, it was Gorbachev's impetuous, ill-thought-out transformation of every aspect of the Soviet system within a very short period that produced a cascade of unforeseen consequences that rapidly destabilized the system (Ellman and Kontorovich, 1998). While it is difficult to deny that Gorbachev conducted the reform in ways that unexpectedly caused serious economic problems and that enabled the groups favoring capitalism to come to power, the fact that a similar transition occurred in almost all of the other Communist-ruled states strongly suggests that some systemic factor was at work, making this explanation unpersuasive.

A second version of this explanation, popular among supporters of the pre-*perestroika* Soviet system and among some analysts in China, holds that Gorbachev had a secret plan from the beginning to dismantle socialism, which he was finally able to carry out once he became the General Secretary. There is no evidence to support this view of Gorbachev, apart from a supposed claim that has circulated on the internet since the early 1990s in which Gorbachev is quoted from a media interview as admitting that he had wanted to destroy socialism, the Communist Party, and the USSR from the beginning (with his wife and Western powers influencing his decision) – a quote which Gorbachev has several times stated is a fake. In any event, if a single individual could destroy the Soviet system by reaching the top of the political hierarchy, that implies a serious systemic weakness in that system, which must be explained.

Explaining the Soviet demise

The explanation that seems to fit the historical process in the USSR during 1985–91 is based on a contradiction in state socialism that was present from the start and whose effects intensified over time as the system evolved. That is the contradiction between a system designed to deliver economic benefits to the population on the one hand and the control of that system by a small self-perpetuating élite on the other. The Soviet system was built by socialist revolutionaries seeking to replace capitalism, which they saw as based on the exploitation of labour by a small wealthy class, by a system of production designed to meet the needs of the producers. All the major means of production were state owned, and production was guided by an economic plan that was supposed to be aimed at meeting individual and social needs. The system provided the population with full employment, almost guaranteed lifetime jobs, guaranteed pensions, free education and medical care, inexpensive vacations, and subsidized housing.

However, the system was, from the beginning, run by a small and self-perpetuating 'party-state élite', with power flowing from the top down rather than from the bottom up. The elite ruled in a dictatorial and repressive manner. Before the Russian Revolution all socialists had expected that socialism would be democratic, more so than was possible under capitalism with its small class of wealthy owners of the means of production. However, that is not the way it turned out.

This contradiction meant that the group that held a monopoly on power – the officials who ran the system – had no collective or individual interest in maintaining the system. The founding generation of leaders were committed to what they thought of as socialism. However, over time, as the founding generation was replaced by individuals who had risen within the system, the ruling elite changed from a group of dedicated revolutionaries to a group consisting primarily of people seeking power and privilege. The successor generations of high officials learned to mouth the official socialist ideology, but studies of the Soviet élite in the 1980s show that only a few actually took it seriously.

The Soviet elite was a materially privileged group. Its members had exclusive access to the best housing and consumer goods. However, the material privileges of the ruling elite were restricted by the socialist features of the system. Members of the élite could not legally own any property, beyond a home and an automobile. Most of their privileges were attached to their position in the hierarchy, not their person as is the case in capitalist systems. While they could use their connections to get their children into the best schools and then into comfortable jobs, they could not pass on any significant wealth to their children or even assure them entry into the ruling élite.[5] Even accounting for the special perks of members of the Soviet élite, their consumption level was far below that of high level officials in Western capitalist systems, both absolutely and relative to the average consumption level of the society. The official incomes of the highest paid members of the elite were only about eight times that of the average worker – far from equality but even farther from the huge multiple found in capitalist systems.[6]

Because of the very hierarchical structure of the élite of the state socialist system, with power concentrated in the top leader or a small group of top leaders, there was no opportunity for members of the elite to openly question the system. However, as the system evolved, the basic contradiction between a privileged, self-perpetuating élite and a system that provided no legitimacy for their privileges – and indeed served to limit them – was bound to eventually undermine the elite's support for the system. Once Gorbachev's *perestroika* democratized the system, it freed the party-state elite to ponder the future of the system.

Few members of the élite found Gorbachev's vision of a democratized socialism appealing – it was likely to reduce the élite's privileges and power. Few found a return to the pre-*perestroika* system attractive, since it was that system that had limited their privileges. Capitalism soon emerged as the most appealing future to a majority of the party-state élite.[7] That direction of change would position them to shift from the managers of the valuable assets of the Soviet system to becoming the owners.[8] Once a large majority of the ruling elite turned against the existing system and came out in support of capitalism, they constituted a powerful force for transition.[9]

By 1991 most of the party-state élite had shifted their allegiance to Boris Yeltsin, who, despite his refusal to state publicly that he favored capitalism, clearly signaled to the sophisticated that a transition to capitalism was exactly his aim. Yeltsin's success at winning support from the great majority of the party-state élite was the key to his rise to power in the Russian Republic. In 1990 he was narrowly elected chairman of the new Russian Republic parliament – making him the chief executive of that republic – only by winning support from a large part of the Communist Party deputies. His top advisors and inner circle were made up, not of dissident democrats, but of people from the Soviet élite who were rejecting Gorbachev's plan for the reform of socialism (Kotz and Weir, 2007, p. 131). While, as was noted above, the majority of the Soviet public continued to favour some form of socialism, the Soviet system had bred passivity into the population, and the outcome was decided by struggles within the elite (Kotz and Weir, 2007, Ch. 8).

This explanation of the demise of the Soviet system accounts for its rapid and relatively violence-free character. Once a large majority of the élite, which had run the USSR since the 1920s, decisively threw its support behind a shift to capitalism, it was very difficult to stop the transition. As Soviet expert Jerry Hough has noted, Gorbachev, who officially retained control of the coercive apparatus of the state to the end, could have ordered Yeltsin's arrest for violation of Soviet laws, but he never did so (Hough, 1997, Ch.10). Gorbachev's method of political operation had always been manoeuvre within the elite, and once he lost its support, he seemed to give up.

Implications of the reasons for the Soviet demise

The way in which the demise of the state socialist system and the shift to building capitalism took place in the Soviet case differed in various respects from the other cases of transition. However, the same underlying contradiction was operating in all of them.[10] In some countries in East/Central Europe, a powerful opposition movement arose outside the Communist Party in the late 1980s, but in most cases the Party gave up power without much if any resistance. In Poland and Hungary, successor parties to the Communist Party soon emerged as able managers of the transition to capitalism, with their original base in the former state socialist élite enthusiastically supporting the transition.[11]

China has followed a different path of transition since 1978, yet it has been driven by the same underlying dynamics. In China the Communist Party has held onto power while supervising a gradual transition to a market economy with predominantly private ownership of enterprises. China's élite has been enriched by this process, and many of the wealthiest new capitalists are connected, by blood or other ties, to party officials. In 2002 the party changed its rules to admit 'entrepreneurs', meaning capitalists, to membership in the party. While this process is officially described as 'socialism with Chinese characteristics', few believe this characterization, with most observers viewing it as 'capitalism with Chinese characteristics'.[12]

The Cuban leadership's resistance to a transition to capitalism, despite its weak economy and enormous pressure from the USA, can be explained by the continuing presence in power of the founding revolutionary generation, which has not given up on socialist ideals. It is likely that, once the founding generation passes from the scene, Cuba will follow some path to capitalism. However, such an outcome might not be uncontested, despite the serious economic difficulties in Cuba, since Cuba's version of state socialism, while sharing the feature of concentration of power in a few hands, has probably been the most successful one at engaging the population in active participation and winning active support in the population for socialist ideals.

The explanation for transition proposed here has implications for evaluating the advice on transition strategy given by Western institutions. Among the main reasons that most Western advisors recommended a rapid transition, including immediate liberalization and quick privatization, was the belief that the old Communist élite was liable to stage a return to the old system if given an opportunity. Many Western advisors thought it was necessary to 'make the transition irreversible' whatever the cost of rapid transition might be. This meant freeing prices in the face of huge excess money demand, which was bound to unleash a burst of rapid inflation that caused many problems. It meant quick privatization in societies having no legitimate wealthy class that could buy the privatizing enterprises, which had many negative results, including that in many cases well-connected individuals or criminal elements obtained the enterprises for next to nothing. Had the Western advisors better understood the process that led to transition, including the support for this process by most of the old élite, more consideration might have been given to a more gradual path of transition, which the case of China suggests can be far more effective.

Notes

1 This chapter does not consider the case of Yugoslavia, despite the fact that a Communist Party held power there until the 1980s. Although the new states that emerged from the former Yugoslavia are often included in the list of transition countries, Yugoslavia adopted the Soviet model of state ownership and central planning only for a few short years in the late 1940s and soon shifted to a quite different system – a market system with worker managed enterprises. Thus, the 'transition' that occurred in Yugoslavia starting in the 1980s was not a transition from the Soviet model.

2 Claims that US Central Intelligence Agency estimates of Soviet economic growth rates were exaggerated arose after the Soviet demise, but no serious evidence was ever found to support such assertions. See Kotz and Weir (2007, pp. 37–39) and Millar *et al.* (1993).

3 The Russian Republic, one of 15 making up the USSR, had about half of the Soviet population and three-fourths of its land area. The official name for the Russian Republic was the Russian Soviet Federated Socialist Republic.

4 For a full analysis of these events, see Kotz and Weir (2007, Ch. 8).

5 One study found that, in the late 1970s 70 per cent of ministers and heads of state committees and over 50 per cent of the directors of the largest state enterprises began as workers or peasants (Kotz and Weir, 2007, p. 309 note 71).

6 For evidence about the limited material privileges of the Soviet elite, see Kotz and Weir (2007, pp. 106–10) and Hough (1991, pp. 276–77).

7 A focus group survey of a sample of the Moscow elite in June 1991 found 76.7 per cent to have a pro-capitalist ideology, while 12.3 per cent favoured democratic socialism and 9.6 per cent the old regime (Kotz and Weir, 2007, pp. 110–11).

8 One study found that 62 per cent of the 100 top post-Soviet Russian businessmen in 1992–93 were from the Soviet party-state elite (Kotz and Weir, 2007, pp. 113–14). For an account of the transformation of members of the Soviet party-state élite into capitalists, see Kotz and Weir (2007, pp. 111–21).

9 A full account of the transition to capitalism in the USSR is more complex, in that other groups in Soviet society became important supporters of transition to capitalism, including much of the intelligentsia, many of the most influential economists, and a newly emerging class of capitalist owners of enterprises. However, the elite played the decisive role (Kotz and Weir, 2007, Chs 5–7).

10 In addition, Gorbachev's decision to announce a non-interventionist policy in other Communist Party ruled states made it possible for transition to occur in East/Central Europe.

11 The demise of state socialism followed a somewhat different path in the GDR, where a democratic reformist group inside the Communist Party pushed the old party leadership aside at the last moment. However, the new reformist leadership lost the support of the majority of the population, who voted for merger with the Federal Republic, lured by the prospect of the West German consumer lifestyle.

12 In 2006 the author asked a provincial party official, who was talking about the many Western investments in the area, what made China 'socialist'. After a few minutes of puzzled silence, she replied, 'The government does things that benefit the people.'

Bibliography

Ellman, M., and Kontorovich, V. (eds) (1998), *The Destruction of the Soviet Economic System: An Insider's History*, Armonk, NY and London: M.E. Sharpe.

Fukuyama, F. (1993), 'The Modernizing Imperative', *The National Interest*, vol. 31 (Spring), pp. 10–18.

Hough, J.F. (1991), 'The Politics of Successful Economic Reform', in Hewitt, E.A. and Winston, V.H. (eds), *Milestones in Glasnost and Perestroyka: Politics and People*, Washington, DC: Brookings Institution Press.

——(1997), *Democratization and Revolution in the USSR 1985–1991*, Washington, DC: Brookings Institution Press.

Kontorovich, V. (1993), 'The Economic Fallacy', *The National Interest*, vol. 31 (spring), pp. 35–45.

Kotz, D.M., and Weir, F. (2007), *Russia's Path from Gorbachev to Putin: The Demise of the Soviet System and the New Russia*, London and New York: Routledge.

Millar, J.R., Berkowitz, D.M., Berliner, J.S., Gregory, P.R. and Lintz, S.J. (1993), 'An Evaluation of the CIA's Analysis of Soviet Economic Performance, 1970–90', *Comparative Economic Studies*, vol. 35(2), pp. 33–57.

Ofer, G. (1987), 'Soviet Economic Growth: 1928–85', *Journal of Economic Literature*, vol. 15(4), pp. 1767–1833.

Part III
Beginnings

9

TRANSFORMATIONAL RECESSION[1]

Vladimir Popov

Introduction

From 1989 to 1998 Russia experienced the transformational recession – GDP fell to 55 per cent of the pre-recession 1989 level. During the second transition decade, 1999–2008, the Russian economy was recovering at a rate of about 7 per cent a year and barely reached the pre-recession peak of 1989 (Figures 9.1 and 9.2).[2] However, another recession – this time a cyclical one – followed, and Russian GDP fell by nearly 8 per cent in 2009. Only in 2012 was the country's pre-recession (1989) GDP finally surpassed again. In sum, therefore, for two decades, there has been no overall increase in output.

Typology of recessions

Economists distinguish between supply-side and demand-side recessions, the former being caused by supply shocks, the latter by demand shocks. The framework is the Aggregate Supply-Aggregate Demand (AS-AD model): the AS curve characterizes a positive relationship between output and prices (the higher the prices, the larger the supply of goods), whereas the AD curve characterizes the negative relationship between the demand for goods and prices. The demand is the *aggregate* demand; it could be increased (AD moves to the right) by expansionary fiscal and monetary policy. The supply is the *aggregate* supply; in the long-run the AS curve is vertical (given full utilization of production capacities and labour, and the level of productivity), but in the short-run the AS curve is positively sloped (firms respond to growing prices by expanding output and employment, but eventually this causes wages to increase, so costs catch up with growing prices and output returns to the equilibrium level).

The negative demand shock occurs, when there is a decline in the demand for the country's exports, or when investors decide to cut spending on new projects, or when consumers decide to save more and spend less – the AD curve moves to the left, as shown in Figure 9.3. Fortunately, the government and the Central Bank can respond to the shock by expansionary fiscal and monetary policy, and can return the AD curve back to its initial position. There is an agreement among economists that the Great Depression of the 1930s was caused by demand factors (the debate is mostly about whether it was poor monetary or fiscal policy that failed to return the AD curve).

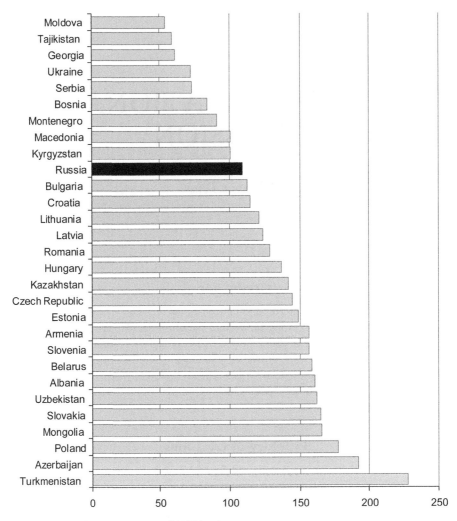

Figure 9.1 2008 GDP as a percentage of 1989 level
Source: EBRD *Transition Report.*

The supply shock occurs when costs increase – either the workers ask for higher wages or fuel producers abroad increase prices for fuel that is imported into the country, or the bridge collapses due to an earthquake. The AS curve then moves to the left (adverse supply shock), and the government does not have the power to affect its position in the short run. The only thing the authorities could do to restore output is to absorb the supply shock by increasing aggregate demand (moving the AD curve to the right, restoring output at a cost of higher prices – Figure 9.4).

Structural recession – caused by the decline of one (non-competitive) sector and the rise of another (competitive) sector – would not be a recession at all, if the transfer of resources (capital and labour) from the first sector to the second sector were instant and effortless. However, in reality such a transfer of resources is associated with higher costs (retraining of employees, replacement of fixed capital stock) and takes time, so the structural recession (whatever the reasons are – supply side or demand side) becomes a typical supply-side recession.

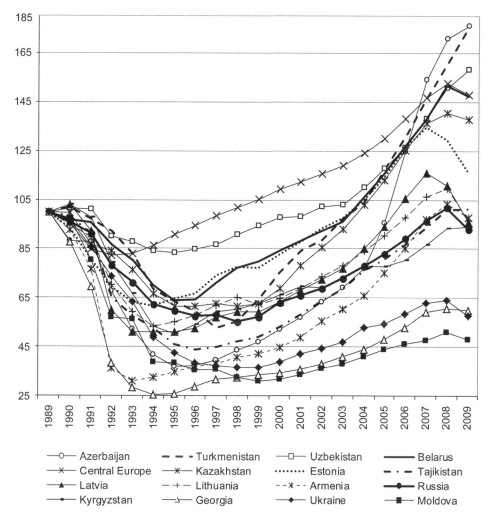

Figure 9.2 GDP change in FSU economies, 1989 = 100%
Source: EBRD *Transition Report*, various years.

This is not to say, however, that all supply side recessions are structural. Imagine that workers ask for higher wages in all regions and industries, so that profits contract by the same amount in all companies, so they fire employees and cut output. When unemployment grows, real wages fall, profits increase and output is gradually restored to the previous level. We have a supply-side recession and a recovery without the reallocation of capital and labour from one sector (industry, region) to another.

This is true with respect to demand-side recessions as well. There may be a fall in demand for the products of a particular industry and then there is a need to reallocate resources from this industry to the other sectors. However, one could imagine a demand-driven recession, caused by an absolutely even contraction of demand for all products (say, due to the excess tightening of monetary policy) – in this case we have a temporary decline in output (and prices) that comes to an end as wages fall and the previous profit rate is restored at the new (lower) level of prices and wages.

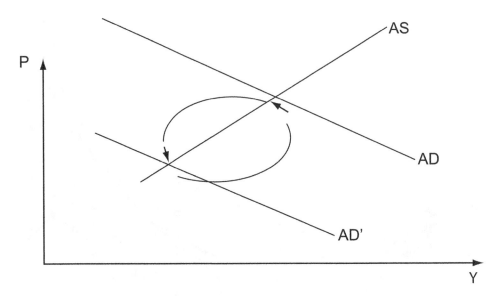

Figure 9.3 Adverse demand shock and government reaction.

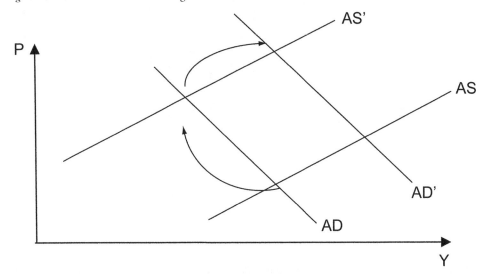

Figure 9.4 Absorption of the adverse supply shock.

So, there may be recessions, supply-driven and demand-driven, not associated with the need to reallocate resources between sectors. The important difference between these 'structural' and 'general' recessions is that in the latter case there is no need to reallocate resources, so there is no need for new investment. First, contraction of output occurs across all industries, so that there is unemployment and underutilized production capacities; later, during the recovery, employment and capacity utilization rates increase universally across industries.

For instance, recessions in post-communist countries were mostly structural supply side – due to changes in relative prices after deregulation (Popov, 2007). But the appropriate (inappropriate) government policies could have eased (aggravated) this structural recession. Thus, it has been argued, for instance, that the impact of demand-side factors (excessively tight demand management) on output decline in Poland has been much more pronounced than the impact of supply-side factors (Rosati, 1994).

For non-(former) communist countries, the same question – whether the recession is supply side or demand side – is of course of major importance as well. If the former, an increase in inflation rate may be warranted (to absorb the adverse supply shock); if the latter, the good policy would be to stick to the pre-recession inflation rates.

There are objective constraints for the transfer of resources from one sector to the other, in particular the size of savings and investment that could be used to reallocate capital (Popov, 2007).

Consider a country where deregulation of prices (or elimination of trade tariffs/subsidies) leads to a change in relative price ratios and thus produces an adverse supply shock for at least some industries. Capital should be reallocated from industries facing declining relative prices and profitability to industries with rising relative prices. Assume that 50 per cent of the total output is concentrated in non-competitive industries: this whole sector should disappear either gradually or at once depending on how fast relative prices will change; capital is not homogeneous and cannot be moved to the competitive sector, whereas labour (for the sake of argument) can be reallocated to the competitive sector without costs.

If prices are liberalized instantly, then the whole non-competitive sector becomes unprofitable overnight and output falls immediately by 50 per cent; later savings for investment are generated only by the competitive sector, so it takes a number of years to reach the pre-recession level of output. If reforms are carried out slowly (gradual price deregulation or elimination of tariffs/subsidies), so that every year output in the non-competitive sector falls by, say, 10 per cent, this fall could be largely compensated by the increase in output in the competitive sector. *The best trajectory, of course, is one that deregulates at a pace that leads to the reduction of output in the non-competitive sector at a natural rate, i.e. as its fixed capital stock retires in the absence of new investment.*

The example illustrates that there is a limit to the speed of reallocating capital from non-competitive to competitive industries, which is determined basically by the net investment/GDP ratio (gross investment minus retirement of capital stock in the competitive industries, since in non-competitive industries the retiring capital stock should not be replaced anyway). It is not reasonable to eliminate output in non-competitive industries faster than capital is being transferred to more efficient industries.

Market type reforms in many post-communist economies created exactly this kind of a bottleneck. Countries that followed the shock therapy path found themselves in a supply-side recession that is likely to become a textbook example: an excessive speed of change in relative prices required a volume of restructuring that was simply impossible with the limited pool of investment. Up to half of their economies were made uncompetitive overnight owing to the change in relative prices after deregulation. Output in these uncompetitive industries was falling for several years and fell in some cases to virtually zero, whereas the growth of output in competitive industries was constrained, among other factors, by the limited investment potential and was not strong enough to compensate for the output loss in the inefficient sectors.

Hence, at least one general conclusion from the study of the experience of transition economies appears to be relevant for the reform process in all countries: *provided that reforms create a need for restructuring (reallocation of resources), the speed of reforms should be such that the magnitude of the required restructuring does not exceed the investment potential of the economy.* In short, the speed of adjustment and restructuring in every economy is limited, if only due to the limited investment potential needed to reallocate capital stock. This is the main rationale for gradual, rather than instant, phasing out of tariff and non-tariff barriers, of subsidies and other forms of government support of particular sectors.

Analysis: why did Russia perform worse than other post-communist economies during transition?

The debates of the 1990s juxtaposed the shock therapy strategy with gradualism. The question why Russia had to pay a greater price for economic transition was answered differently by those who advocated shock therapy and those who supported gradual, piecemeal reforms. Shock therapists argued that much of the costs of the reforms should be attributed to inconsistencies of policies followed, namely to slow economic liberalization and to the inability of the governments and the central banks to fight inflation in the first half of the 1990s. On the contrary, the supporters of gradual transition stated exactly the opposite, blaming the attempt to introduce a conventional shock therapy package for all the disasters and misfortunes.

In Popov (2000, 2007) various explanations of the transformational recession are discussed and an alternative explanation is suggested: the collapse of output was caused primarily by several groups of factors. First, by greater distortions in the industrial structure and external trade patterns on the eve of the transition. Second, by the collapse of state and non-state institutions, which occurred in the late 1980s – early 1990s and which resulted in chaotic transformation through crisis management instead of organized and manageable transition. Third, by poor economic policies, which basically consisted of bad macroeconomic policy and import substitution industrial policy. Finally, *fourth*, the speed of reforms (economic liberalization) affected performance negatively at the stage of the reduction of output because enterprises were forced to restructure faster that they possibly could (due to limited investment potential), but positively at the recovery stage.

To a first approximation, the economic recession that occurred in former Soviet Union (FSU) states was associated with the need *to reallocate resources* in order to correct the inefficiencies in industrial structure inherited from the centrally planned economy (CPE). These distortions included over-militarization and over-industrialization, perverted trade flows among former Soviet republics and Comecon countries, excessively large size and poor specialization of industrial enterprises and agricultural farms. In most cases these distortions were more pronounced in Russia than in Eastern Europe, not to speak about China and Vietnam – the larger were the distortions, the greater was the reduction of output. The transformational recession, to put it in economic terms, was caused by an adverse supply shock similar to that experienced by Western countries after the oil price hikes in 1973 and 1979, and similar to the post-war recessions caused by conversion of the defence industries.

As Figure 9.5 shows, the reduction of output in Russia during the transformational recession was to a large extent structural in nature: industries with the greatest adverse supply shock (deteriorating terms of trade – relative price ratios for outputs and inputs), such as light industry, experienced the largest reduction of output. The evidence for all transition economies is in Table 9.1: the reduction of output by country is well explained by the indicator of distortions in industrial structure and trade patterns (it remains statistically significant no matter what control variables are added). The magnitude of distortions, in turn, determines the change in relative prices, when they are deregulated.

The nature of the recession was basically an adverse supply shock caused by the sudden large change in relative prices. However, such a reduction of output owing to the inability of the economy to adjust rapidly to new price ratios is by no means inevitable, if the deregulation of prices proceeds gradually (or if losses from deteriorating terms of trade for the most affected industries are compensated by subsidies). The pace of liberalization had to be no faster than the ability of the economy to move resources from non-competitive (under the new market price ratios) to competitive industries.

Therefore, it should be expected that there is a negative relationship between performance and the speed of liberalization. It should be also expected that the larger magnitude of distortions in

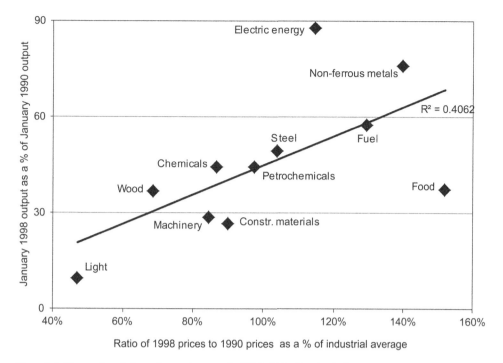

Figure 9.5 Change in relative prices and output in 1990–98 in Russian industry
Source: Popov (2007).

industrial structure and trade patterns would lead to the greater reduction of output during the transformational recession, but would not have much of an impact on performance during the recovery stage (once the non-competitive sector had been shut down completely).

An additional reason for the extreme depth of the transformational recession was associated with the *institutional collapse* – here differences between EE countries and the FSU are striking. The adverse supply shock in this case came from the inability of the state to perform its traditional functions – to collect taxes and to constrain the shadow economy, to ensure property and contract rights and law and order in general. Naturally, poor ability to enforce rules and regulations did not create a business climate conducive to growth and resulted in increased costs for many companies.

One measure of institutional strength is the dynamics of government expenditure during transition. This factor seems to have been far more important than the speed of reforms. In Kolodko's words 'there can be no doubt that *during the early transition there was a causal relationship between the rapid shrinkage in the size of government and the significant fall in output*' (Kolodko, 2000, p. 259). Keeping the government big does not guarantee favourable dynamics of output, since government spending has to be efficient as well. However, the sharp decline in government spending, especially for the 'ordinary government', is a sure recipe to ensure the collapse of institutions and the fall in output accompanied by the growing social inequalities and populist policies.

When real government expenditures fall by 50 per cent and more – as happened in most CIS and south-east European states in a short period of time, just a few years – there was practically no chance to compensate the decrease in the volume of financing by the increased efficiency of institutions. As a result, the ability of the state to enforce contracts and property rights, to fight criminalization and to ensure law and order in general declined dramatically (Popov, 2009).

Table 9.1 Regression of change in GDP in 1989–96 on initial conditions, policy factors, and rule of law and democracy indices, robust estimates

Equations, number of observations/variables	1, N=28	2, N=28	3, N=28	4, N=28	5, N=28	6, N=28	7, N=28
Constant	5.3***	5.4***	5.2***	5.4***	5.4***	5.5***	5.7***
Distortions, % of GDP[a]	-0.005**	-0.005**	-0.003	-0.006**	-0.007***	-0.007***	-0.007***
1987 PPP GDP per capita, % of the US level	-0.009**	-0.006*	-0.007**	-0.007**	-0.009***	-0.008***	-0.008***
War dummy[b]				-0.19[c]	-0.36***	-0.37***	-0.45***
Decline in government revenues as a % of GDP from 1989–91 to 1993–96					-0.011***	-0.011***	-0.011***
Liberalization index			.05			-0.02	0.03
Log (Inflation, % a year, 1990-95, geometric average)	-0.16***	-0.20***	-0.18***	-0.17***	-0.13***	-0.13***	-0.14***
Rule of law index, average for 1989–97, %	0.008***						
Democracy index, average for 1990–98, %	-0.005***						-0.003**
Ratio of the rule of law to democracy index		0.07***	0.07***	0.06***	0.05***	0.05***	
Adjusted R², %	82	83	83	85	91	91	90

Dependent variable = log (1996 GDP as a % of 1989 GDP). For China – all indicators are for the period of 1979–86 or similar.
*, **, *** Significant at 10, 5 and 1% level, respectively.
Notes: a Cumulative measure of distortions as a % of GDP equal to the sum of defence expenditure (minus 3% regarded as the 'normal' level), deviations in industrial structure and trade openness from the 'normal' level, the share of heavily distorted trade (among the FSU republics) and lightly distorted trade (with socialist countries) taken with a 33% weight – see Popov (2000) for details.
b Equals 1 for Armenia, Azerbaijan, Croatia, Georgia, Macedonia, and Tajikistan and 0 for all other countries.
c Significant at 13% level.

Thus, the story of the successes and failures of transition is not really the story of consistent shock therapy and inconsistent gradualism. The major plot of the post-socialist transformation 'novel' is the preservation of strong institutions in some countries (very different in other respects – from Central Europe and Estonia to China, Uzbekistan and Belarus[3]) and the collapse of these institutions in the other countries. At least 90 per cent of this story is about the government failure (strength of state institutions), not about the market failure (liberalization).

It is precisely this strong institutional framework that should be held responsible for both – for the success of gradual reforms in China and shock therapy in Vietnam, where strong authoritarian regimes were preserved and CPE institutions were not dismantled before new market institutions were created; and for the relative success of radical reforms in EE countries, especially in Central European countries, where strong democratic regimes and new market institutions emerged quickly. And it is precisely the collapse of strong state institutions that started in the USSR in the late 1980s and continued in the successor states in the 1990s that explains the extreme length, if not the extreme depth of the FSU transformational recession.

To put it differently, the Gorbachev reforms of 1985–91 failed not because they were gradual, but owing to the weakening of the state institutional capacity leading to the inability of the government to control the flow of events. Similarly, the Yeltsin reforms in Russia, as well as the economic reforms in most other FSU states, were so costly not because of the shock therapy, but owing to the collapse of the institutions needed to enforce law and order and carry out a manageable transition.

It turns out that the FSU transition model (with the partial exceptions of Uzbekistan, Belarus and Estonia) is based on a most unfortunate combination of unfavourable initial conditions, institutional degradation, and inefficient economic policies, such as macro-economic populism and import substitution.

What leads to the institutional collapse and could it have been prevented? Using the terminology of political science, it is appropriate to distinguish between strong authoritarian regimes (China and Vietnam and to an extent Belarus and Uzbekistan), strong democratic regimes (Central European countries) and weak democratic regimes (most FSU and Balkan states). The former two (strong regimes – democratic or authoritarian) are politically liberal or liberalizing, i.e. protect individual rights, including those of property and contracts, and create a framework of law and administration, while the latter regimes (weak regimes), though democratic, are politically not so liberal since they lack strong institutions and the ability to enforce law and order (Zakaria, 1997). This gives rise to the phenomenon of 'illiberal democracies' – countries where competitive elections are introduced before the rule of law is established. While European countries in the 19th century and East Asian countries recently moved from first establishing the rule of law to gradually introducing democratic elections (Hong Kong is the most obvious example of the rule of law without democracy) in Latin America, Africa, and now in CIS countries democratic political systems were introduced in societies without the firm rule of law.

Authoritarian regimes (including communist), while gradually building property rights and institutions, were filling the vacuum in the rule of law via authoritarian means. After democratization occurred and illiberal democracies emerged, they found themselves deprived of old authoritarian instruments to ensure law and order, but without the newly developed democratic mechanisms needed to guarantee property rights, contracts and law and order in general. Not surprisingly, this had a devastating impact on both the investment climate and output.

There is a clear relationship between the ratio of rule of law index on the eve of transition to democratization index, on the one hand, and economic performance during transition, on the other. To put it differently, democratization without the strong rule of law, whether one likes it or not, usually leads to the collapse of output. There is a price to pay for early democratization, i.e. the introduction of competitive elections of government under the conditions when the major liberal rights (personal freedom and security, property, contracts, fair trial in court, etc.) are not well established.

Finally, performance was of course affected by *economic policy*. Given the weak institutional capacity of the state, i.e. its poor ability to enforce its own regulations, economic policies could hardly be 'good'. Weak state institutions usually imply populist macroeconomic policies (budget deficits resulting in high indebtedness and/or inflation, overvalued exchange rates), which have a devastating impact on output. On the other hand, strong institutional capacity does not lead automatically to responsible economic policies. Examples range from the USSR before it collapsed (periodic outbursts of open or hidden inflation) to such post Soviet states as Uzbekistan and Belarus, which seem to have stronger institutional potential than other FSU states, but do not demonstrate higher macroeconomic stability.

Regressions tracing the impact of all the mentioned factors are reported in Table 9.1 (Popov, 2000). 80 to 90 per cent of the variations in the dynamics of GDP in 1989–96 could be explained by the initial conditions (distortions and initial GDP per capita), institutional capacity of the state (decline in government revenues and rule of law and democracy indices), and macroeconomic stability (inflation). If the rule of law and democracy indices are included in the basic regression equation, they have the predicted signs (positive impact of the rule of law and negative impact of democracy) and are statistically significant (equation 1 in Table 9.1), which is consistent with the results obtained for a larger sample of countries.[4]

The best explanatory power, however, is exhibited by the index that is computed as the ratio of the rule of law index to democracy index: 83 per cent of all variations in output can be explained by only three factors – pre-transition distortions, inflation, and rule-of-law-to-democracy index (Table 9.1, equation 2). If a liberalization variable is added, it turns out to be statistically insignificant and does not improve the goodness of fit (equation 3). At the same time, the ratio of the rule of law to democracy index and the decline in government revenues are not substitutes, but rather complement each other in characterizing the process of the institutional decay. These two variables are not correlated and improve the goodness of fit, when included together in the same regression: R^2 increases to 91 per cent (equation 5) – a better result than in regressions with either one of these variables alone. The liberalization index, when added to the same equation, is not statistically significant, and has the 'wrong' sign.

To test the robustness of the results, another year for the end of the transformational recession was chosen – 1998, so the period considered was 1989–98. (By the end of 1998 the absolute trough was reached in 24 countries out of 26 that experienced the recession.) The adjusted R^2 is slightly lower, but the statistical significance of coefficients remains high (with the exception of the initial GDP per capita). The best equation is shown below:

$$Log(Y98/89) = 5.8 - 0.006DIST - 0.005Ycap87 - 0.39WAR - 0.01GOVREVdecline - 0.17logINFL - 0.003DEM$$

$$(-2.48) \quad (-0.09) \quad (-3.22) \quad (-2.94) \quad (-4.60) \quad (-1.74)$$

(N = 28, Adjusted R^2 = 82 per cent, T-statistics in brackets, all variables are shown in the same order as in equation 7 from Table 9.1 (liberalization variable is omitted.)

Once again, if a liberalization variable is introduced in this equation, it turns out to be insignificant.

Finally, to deal with the *endogeneity problem* (liberalization affects performance, but is also affected by performance – if output falls, liberalization very likely, would be halted) the liberalization variable was instrumented with the democracy level variable (Popov, 2007). The results are in Table 9.2: the main difference from Table 9.1 is that liberalization now affects performance significantly and negatively.

As argued in Popov (2007), at the recovery stage (1998–2005), the impact of distortions on performance disappears, but the influence of institutions persists, and the impact of the speed of liberalization (increment increase in liberalization index) becomes positive and significant. This is very much in line with intuition: after the non-competitive sector is eradicated during the transformation recession, further liberalization (which inevitably becomes gradual at this point) cannot do much harm, whereas institutional capacity always affects growth.

To sum up, the following scheme summarizes the principal factors affecting performance during transition (Figure 9.6): the FSU in general (there are some exceptions) and Russia in particular had poor initial conditions (allocation of resources by industries and regions under central planning was very different from market type, so when prices were deregulated and allowed to govern the allocation of capital and labour, sizeable restructuring occurred leading to a recession). To add insult to injury, there was also a dramatic decline in the institutional capacity of the state.

Institutional Capacity \ Distortions	Low	High
High	China, Vietnam	Eastern Europe
Low	Albania, Mongolia	FSU

Figure 9.6 Initial conditions (distortions) and institutions – classification of countries

Table 9.2 2SLS robust estimates – regression of change in GDP in 1989–96 on initial conditions, institutional capacity, liberalization and rule of law and democracy indices (Liberalization index instrumented with the democracy level variable)

Equations, number of observations/variables	1, N=28	2, N=28	3, N=17	4, N=17
Constant	6.4***	6.3***	6.0***	6.0***
Pre-transition distortions, % of GDP	-0.01***	-0.02***		-0.004
1987 PPP GDP per capita, % of the US level	-0.007**	-0.01***		
War dummy[a]	-0.45***	-0.29[b]		
Liberalization index in 1995	-0.18**	-0.39*	-0.19***	-0.19***
Decline in government revenues as a % of GDP from 1989–91 to 1993–96	-0.02***	-0.02***		
Log (Inflation, % a year, 1990–95, geometric average)	-1.7***	-0.22***	-0.22***	-0.19***
Rule of law index, average for 1989–97, %		-0.01[c]		
Increase in the share of shadow economy in GDP in 1989–94, p.p.			-0.02***	-0.015***
R^2, %	86	77	88	90

Dependent variable = Log (1996 GDP as a % of 1989 GDP).
For China – all indicators are for the period of 1979–86 or similar.
*, **, *** significant at 10, 5 and 1% level respectively.
Notes: a Equals 1 for Armenia, Azerbaijan, Croatia, Georgia, Macedonia, and Tajikistan and 0 for all other countries.
b Significant at 12% level.
c Significant at 16% level.

Conclusions

After allowing for differing initial conditions, it turns out that the fall in output in transition economies was associated mostly with their poor business environment, resulting from institutional collapse. Liberalization alone, when it is not complemented with strong institutions, cannot ensure good performance. Institutional capacities in turn, depend to a large extent on the combination of the rule of law and democracy: the data seem to suggest that both authoritarian and democratic regimes can have strong rule of law and can deliver efficient institutions, whereas under the weak rule of law authoritarian regimes do a better job in maintaining efficient institutions than democracies. To put it more succinctly, the record of illiberal democracies in ensuring institutional capacities is the worst, which predictably has a devastating impact on output.

Notes

1 This chapter uses extensively papers previously written by the author: Popov (2000), Popov (2007, 2009).
2 Figure 9.1 is based on GDP indices (2008 as a percentage of 1989) reported in the EBRD *Transition Report* 2009, whereas Figure 9.2 reports chain indices (based on annual growth rates) from the same source. The discrepancies are not that substantial.
3 Countries like Belarus and Uzbekistan fall into the same group with central European countries and Estonia – with a small reduction of state expenditure as a per cent of GDP during transition, good quality of governance, little bribery, small shadow economy and low state capture index (Hellman, Jones and Kaufmann, 2000). In 2005 Belarus and the Slovak Republic were the only two countries out of 25 surveyed in EE and FSU (Business Environment and Enterprise Performance Survey – BEEPS), where significant improvement was registered in 2002–05 in all seven areas of economic governance (judiciary, fighting crime and corruption, customs and trade, business licensing and permits, labour regulations, tax administration) – EBRD, 2005.
4 For a larger sample of countries (all developing and developed countries, not only transition economies), the result is that there is a threshold level of the rule of law index: if it is higher than a certain level, democratization affects growth positively, if lower – democratization impedes growth (Polterovich and Popov, 2007). For the regressions reported in Table 9.1 (to explain changes in output in 1989–96) averages of rule of law and democracy indices were used for the longer period (1989–98) to account for the fact that business agents often anticipate changes in business climate that are captured in experts' estimates only later.

Bibliography

Hellman, J., Jones, G. and Kaufmann, D. (2000), 'How Profitable is Buying the State Officials in Transition Economies?', *Transition: The Newsletter about Reforming Economies*, April, pp. 8–11.
Kolodko, G.W. (2000). *From Shock to Therapy. Political Economy of Postsocialist Transformation*. Oxford and New York: Oxford University Press.
Polterovich, V. and Popov, V. (2007), 'Democratization, Quality of Institutions and Economic Growth', in Dinello, N. and Popov, V. (eds), *Political Institutions and Development. Failed Expectations and Renewed Hopes*, Cheltenham: Edward Elgar.
Popov, V. (2000), 'Shock Therapy versus Gradualism: The End of the Debate (Explaining the Magnitude of the Transformational Recession)', *Comparative Economic Studies*, vol. 42(1), pp. 1–57 (www.nes.ru/%7Evpopov/documents/TR-REC-full.pdf).
——(2007), 'Shock Therapy versus Gradualism Reconsidered: Lessons from Transition Economies after 15 Years of Reforms', *Comparative Economic Studies*, vol. 49(1), pp. 1–31.
——(2009), 'Lessons from the Transition Economies. Putting the Success Stories of the Postcommunist World into a Broader Perspective', *UNU/WIDER Research Paper No.* 2009/15.
Rosati, D.K. (1994), 'Output Decline during Transition from Plan to Market: A Reconsideration', *Economics of Transition*, vol. 2(4), pp. 419–41.
Zakaria, F. (1997), 'The Rise of Illiberal Democracies', *Foreign Affairs*, vol. 76(6), pp. 22–43.

10

PRIVATIZATION

Jeffrey Miller

Introduction

A major difference between capitalism and socialism is the ownership of non-labour productive resources. Before the transition began, the state owned most of the non-labour productive inputs in the Communist economies. Since a central feature of capitalism is the private ownership of productive resources, the ownership of these non-labour assets needed to be transferred into private hands. While there were examples where state-owned companies had been privatized in Western capitalist economies before the transition began, there had never been a privatization programme of the magnitude and scope that was required if the former Communist countries were to achieve the transition to capitalism.

A major challenge in carrying out the privatization process was to privatize these assets in a way that both created efficient institutional arrangements and was a fair distribution of the new private ownership rights. While the capitalist model of small firms in perfect competition leads to efficient outcomes, the Communist model had involved creating large enterprises that could more easily be controlled by central planners. If large state-owned enterprises were to be privatized, and not broken up into small enterprises, institutions needed to be created that would align incentives for the managers of large enterprises with their owners. In mature capitalist economies, these governance institutions had evolved over time and differed significantly across countries. Although these governance institutions in mature capitalist economies do not always perform well, their absence in Communist economies and, therefore, the need to create some form of governance institutions, made the goal of private sector efficiency much more difficult to achieve.

Ownership of non-labour assets is a form of wealth and while these assets were state owned, there was a sharing of this wealth across the community. Communist countries, consistent with the Communist ideology, had relatively equal distributions of income, even though political power within these countries, and the advantages of power, were not so equally distributed. One objective of privatization was, therefore, to establish a fair distribution of the ownership rights of the newly privatized assets. If the assets were sold on the market, then getting a fair market price for the assets was also important since such benefits would accrue to everyone through the government. Selling assets to political insiders at prices far below their market value, as was the case in transfers to oligarchs in Russia, was a clear violation of this principle.

In addition to these challenges, the environment within which the privatization needed to take place added to the problems of moving privatization forward. Because the state owned almost all property in Communist countries, people had little non-human capital wealth. Furthermore, the high inflation levels which accompanied the release of prices at the beginning of the transition in many countries wiped out much of the savings that people had accumulated in the banks. As a result, if governments tried to sell state property, foreigners could easily outbid domestic bidders or the amount obtained from the sales would be far below the real value of the assets.

There were also economic reasons for the rapid sale of these assets. When enterprises remained in the hands of the state, it was difficult to control the actions of enterprise managers. When the inputs and outputs of state enterprises were sold on free markets (in contrast to allocation through a planning process at fixed prices), there was room for managers of state enterprises to exploit their positions to enhance their wealth at the expense of the enterprise and their state owners. By setting up 'shadow' firms they could sell their output at low prices or buy inputs at inflated prices from these shadow firms and capture these income flows for themselves.

While the East German privatization programme was exceptional in many respects, a more detailed look at the programme can illustrate the problems faced by these countries as they transitioned from state ownership to private ownership. East Germany was about the size of Czechoslovakia before it was broken up into the Czech Republic and Slovakia. The Germans had many advantages that other countries in the region lacked. West Germany provided financial support that could not be matched elsewhere. Furthermore, the West German legal and institutional structure could be transposed on the East German situation in a way that was not possible in other countries. In spite of these advantages, the privatization programme in East Germany proved very difficult to implement.

To carry out their programme the Germans quickly set up the *Treuhand Anstalt*, an independent government agency, whose purpose was to carry out the privatization over a four-year time period. The *Treuhand* took over about 12,400 firms with approximately four million employees. Early in the process, the *Treuhand* did an assessment and classified the firms into categories. It was determined that 26 per cent of the firms could not survive, and an additional 24 per cent would not be profitable in the short run. Only 2 per cent of the firms could be privatized immediately (Dyck and Wruck, 1998). Given that East Germany was one of the more successful Communist countries, these latter figures are an indication of the problems that had to be faced by other countries as well.

The *Treuhand* largely completed its assigned task within the four years of its mandate. By 1994 it had been engaged in more than 14,000 privatization transactions that involved 1.5 million job guarantees. Most of the firms were sold to West Germans (70 per cent) and East Germans (20 per cent). While initial expectations were that the process would generate income, in fact the subsidies amounted to about DM 200 billion (Dyck and Wruck, 1998).

The changes that took place in East Germany during this period led to significant increases in unemployment and a reallocation of workers away from agriculture and industry towards services and construction. These difficulties were ameliorated by migration to West Germany, unemployment benefits and pension support from the West, but it was a difficult period for the East. When it came to privatization, other Communist countries faced equally daunting challenges without the financial resources provided by the West Germans.

Methods of privatization

In the face of these difficulties, five general methods of expanding the private sector were proposed: (1) encouraging entry of new firms into the private sector; (2) restitution of property to former owners; (3) management–employee buyouts; (4) voucher privatization; and (5) direct sale of state assets to private citizens. The use of one of these methods did not exclude the use of the others and in most countries a combination of these methods was used.

In the early years of transition Murrell (1992) and others argued for the importance of small firm entry as a means of privatization of the economy. Entry was promoted by trying to reduce the cost of registration and starting up new firms. Restitution of property also aided this process as restitution often provided physical locations where new small firms could start their businesses. An important advantage of entry and restitution is that the firms tended to be small and competitive forces were sufficient to align incentives so that these firms would operate efficiently. A disadvantage is that these firms often needed external financing to grow and the financial sector was at a very primitive stage of development during the early years of transition.

Restitution had its limitations, however. Records of previous owners were limited and the economies of Communist countries had gone though a great transformation over the 45–70 years since the imposition of major nationalization programmes. Identification of previous owners was difficult or impossible in many situations. While restitution was used to privatize agricultural land, apartments and retail properties, it was not possible to use this approach to privatize the large enterprises that had come into being during the Communist period. Furthermore, if the goal of privatization is to make more efficient use of available resources, restoring property to previous owners who are not prepared to make effective use of the property would not lead to higher productivity.

Privatizations through management–employee buyouts were part of the process in many countries. While management–employee buyouts could be done quickly, there were many problems with this approach. Fairness was one of the first issues. Workers who happened to be working at a profitable enterprise would be much better off than workers who happened to be working at an enterprise that was not viable in the new environment. If the enterprise was viable, managers were able to exploit their position to take advantage of workers either by buying up shares from workers at low prices or by conducting market transactions through shadow firms which they controlled.

Management–employee buyouts also left the existing managers in control of the firm. These managers had been placed there during the central-planning regime and were not necessarily the best people to manage the transition of the enterprise to the new environment.

Voucher privatization was proposed to privatize large enterprises quickly in an environment where there was little private financial wealth. In a voucher privatization citizens bought vouchers for a nominal fee. The voucher points (as a substitute for money) could then be used to bid for shares in enterprises that were being privatized. Czechoslovakia was the first country to implement a large-scale voucher programme, although Russia also implemented a programme during the first years of its transition that had many of the characteristics of a management–employee buyout.

There were many variants of the voucher approach. These different approaches reflected concerns about enterprise governance post-privatization. Having many small shareholders creates the Berle and Means (1932) problem of the separation of ownership from control. Even in capitalist economies where stock markets and their regulation have developed over long periods of time, these conditions present serious challenges to the efficient operation of companies. Creating the needed governance institutions in an environment where large enterprises were suddenly privatized and their shares dispersed among many small shareholders was an even more daunting challenge.

To deal with these problems, Poland, for example, created National Investment Funds that received 33 per cent of the shares and representation on the board of a privatized company

(Brada, 1996). In other countries (e.g. Czech Republic and Bulgaria) mass privatization funds were created by private firms. These funds collected vouchers from individuals and then bid in the auctions for shares of the firms. Because they were able to buy many more shares than individuals could purchase, these funds were able to purchase substantial ownership shares in the enterprises that were being privatized. The problem was that these new funds also needed to be regulated and in some cases the managers exploited their situation to steal money from their funds (Wallace and Stojaspal, 1996).

Another problem with voucher privatization is that it does not generate any revenue for the government. This was particularly problematic because during the first phases of transition, tax collection was difficult. Standard capitalist-type tax systems did not exist before the transition began, so many countries had problems in raising sufficient revenue to support government services. Privatization represented a potential source of additional revenue and if countries used voucher privatization, these sources of revenue had to be foregone.

Sales of enterprises thus represented an attractive alternative for many governments, but as mentioned above, the only way to get a reasonable price for enterprises was to include foreign bidders. This many countries did; Hungary being an important early example. Still, there was initially strong political opposition to having foreigners gain control of important enterprises. Another problem with sales of enterprises is that assessing the market value of these enterprises was difficult and so many sales were highly controversial.

Evaluation of privatization

By 2010 the private sector had become an important part of the economy in most transition countries, as Table 10.1 reveals. In 13 of 28 countries in the European Bank for Reconstruction and Development (EBRD) studies, the private sector represented at least 70 per cent or more of GDP by 2010. In several other countries, the private sector share was between 60 per cent and 70 per cent (Bosnia/Herzegovina, Moldova, Montenegro, Russia, Serbia and Ukraine). In a few countries the private sector share was much lower (Belarus (30 per cent), Tajikistan (55 per cent), Turkmenistan (25 per cent) and Uzbekistan (45 per cent)). Despite these differences across countries, the percentage share of the private sector in almost all countries has been remarkably stable over the past few years – an indication that the big push towards privatization is largely over, even in countries where the share of the private sector is still low.

The EBRD has also developed a series of indicators designed to measure progress in developing a healthy private sector (EBRD, 2000). The three indicators most relevant to the privatization process are: (1) the index of small-scale privatization; (2) the index of large-scale privatization; and (3) the index of enterprise reform. These indices are scaled from 1 to 4+ where 1 stands for little progress (away from central planning) and 4+ is a situation close to the standards of an advanced market economy. In the index of small-scale privatization almost all the countries with the exception of Turkmenistan (2.7), Bosnia/Herzegovina (3.0) and Belarus (2.3) had very high scores. Some countries had scores of 4.3. On the index of large scale privatization, the scores were considerably lower but still reasonably high in a number of countries. The average score was about 3.2, with Turkmenistan (1.0) and Belarus (1.7) showing little if any progress.

The development of good governance institutions has been much more difficult. The average score on the index of enterprise reform is 2.5 with only Estonia, Hungary and Slovakia getting a score as high as 3.7. While the private sector has become an important part of most transition economies, there is still room for improvement of the associated governance institutions. First, bankruptcy laws need to improve. For these scores to really move up, the EBRD is

Table 10.1 Private sector share in GDP (in per cent)[a]

	1994	1999	2008	2009	2010
Albania	50	75	75	75	75
Armenia	40	60	75	75	75
Azerbaijan	20	45	75	75	75
Belarus	15	20	30	30	30
Bosnia and Herzegovina	na	35	60	60	60
Bulgaria	40	70	75	75	75
Croatia	35	60	70	70	70
Czech Republic[b]	65	80	na	na	na
Estonia	55	75	80	80	80
FYR Macedonia	35	55	70	70	70
Georgia	20	60	75	75	75
Hungary	55	80	80	80	80
Kazakhstan	20	60	70	70	65
Kyrgyz Republic	30	60	75	75	75
Latvia	40	65	70	70	70
Lithuania	60	70	75	75	75
Moldova	20	45	65	65	65
Mongolia	na	na	75	75	75
Montenegro	na	na	65	65	65
Poland	55	65	75	75	75
Romania	40	60	70	70	70
Russian Federation	40	70	65	65	65
Serbia	na	na	60	60	60
Slovak Republic	55	75	80	80	80
Slovenia	30	55	70	70	70
Tajikistan	15	30	55	55	55
Turkmenistan	15	25	25	25	25
Ukraine	40	55	65	60	60
Uzbekistan	20	45	45	45	45

Notes:

a These statistics come from the EBRD tables. The share of the private sector in GDP is only an estimate so the figures probably look more stable than they actually are, but it is clear that the size of the private sector has stabilized in nearly every country.

b The Czech Republic 'graduated' from EBRD programmes in 2007, so statistics for the Czech Republic are not available after 2007.

looking for evidence of more investment by minority shareholders as a signal that they feel protected. With these improvements, financial markets should be able to expand and financial market forces should play a bigger role in influencing firm governance.

There have been many studies analysing whether the privatization process has actually improved production efficiency. There are several extensive surveys of this literature. Using meta-analysis, Djankov and Murrell (2002) surveyed more than a hundred studies and found:

> that privatization is strongly associated with more enterprise restructuring. Economic effects are quite often very large, for example adding several percentage points to enterprise growth rates. The privatization effect is, however, statistically insignificant in the Commonwealth of Independent States (CIS).
>
> *(Djankov and Murrell 2002, p. 740)*

They also found that performance varies depending on the new ownership type. When outsiders gain control, there is more restructuring than when insiders gain control. When ownership is more concentrated (i.e. investment funds, foreigners and other block-holders), there is significantly more restructuring than when the ownership is diffuse. They found that greater competition and hardening of budgets also create more restructuring, although competition did not have a positive effect in CIS countries.

A later survey by Estrin *et al.* (2009) looked at more recent studies, including studies of Chinese privatization. They found that as time has passed differences in performance have shifted from questions of insider/outsider control and domestic/foreign ownership, to a more focused issue of domestic versus foreign ownership. Whereas the productivity of domestic private firms does not differ significantly from that of state firms, foreign ownership has a positive effect. They suggest that a possible reason for this is that foreign firms bring better corporate governance to firms where the legal structures in these countries is underdeveloped. They concluded their survey by stating:

> The most important policy implication of our survey is that privatization *per se* does not guarantee improved performance, at least not in the short run. Type of private ownership, corporate governance, access to know-how and markets, and the legal and institutional system matter for restructuring and performance. Foreign ownership tends to have a positive effect on performance. The positive effect of privatization to domestic owners, to the extent that it exists, takes a number of years to materialize.
>
> *(Estrin* et al. *2009)*

Improved firm performance is only one criterion for judging the success of privatization programmes. A major reason that privatization programmes were so politically difficult to implement was that privatization involved a transfer of wealth. The economics literature has paid less attention to this issue, but it has been an important issue for those who live in the transition economies. Particularly important is people's perceptions of the legitimacy of the privatization, regardless of the actual methods used to privatize assets.

Denisova *et al.* (2010) have used the 'Life in Transition Survey' of 28,000 individuals from 28 transition countries conducted by the World Bank and EBRD to evaluate attitudes towards privatization. They look at different demographic groups to determine whether age, occupation, income and other socio-economic factors affect attitudes towards privatization. They do find that these factors can influence the way people view privatization, but they also find that more than 50 per cent of the respondents in each one of the transition economies and 80 per cent of the total survey participants support some kind of revision of the privatization process. Possible choices for redoing the process include everything from additional taxation to renationalization and then reprivatization. They also find that these negative views about privatization are not reflected in negative views about a private market economy. People do see the advantages of a private market economy. However, they commonly do not see the privatization process as it has been carried out in their country as legitimate.

Summary

From the beginning, transferring property rights from the state to the private sector was seen as an essential part of the transition process. The privatization process turned out to be a very complex process. Citizens had little non-labour wealth and the institutions needed to support good corporate governance in a market system did not exist. The latter issue was particularly problematic because an important part of the privatization process involved transferring large enterprises from state control to private citizens, and good governance of large corporations requires sophisticated institutional arrangements.

In spite of these difficulties most transition economies in the Former Soviet Union and Eastern Europe now have private sectors whose relative size is comparable to the private sectors in Western European countries. The results, however, are mixed. Governance structures have not developed as quickly as privatization itself. Enterprises have been restructured and performance has improved, but privatization has not led to the dramatic changes that were anticipated by some analysts when the process began.

The process is also perceived to have been illegitimate by the vast majority of people living in the region. Historically, it has been very difficult to establish new property rights in a fair and equitable manner. While programmes, like voucher privatization, attempted to provide a fair distribution of the privatized property, new arrangements were often manipulated by those who were able to translate their power under the Communist system into wealth under the new arrangements. In the rapidly changing environment where governments were weak, fraud was also difficult to police.

At this juncture in many countries, the large-scale privatization process has largely been completed. Governance structures still need to be greatly strengthened before the full potential benefits of privatization can be realized. Whether there will be a political backlash because of the widespread perceptions of illegitimacy is still an open question.

Bibliography

Berle, A.A. and Means, G.C. (1932), *The Modern Corporation and Private Property*, Reprint, Piscataway, NJ and London: Transaction Publishers.

Brada, Josef C. (1996), 'Privatization is Transition – Or is it?' *The Journal of Economic Perspectives*, vol. 10(2), pp. 67–86.

Denisova, I., Eller, M., Frye, T. and Zhuravskaya, E. (2010), 'Everyone hates privatization, but why? Survey evidence from 28 post-communist countries,' *Centre for Economic and Financial Research at New Economic School*, Working Paper No. 143, May.

Djankov, S. and Murrell, P. (2002), 'Enterprise Restructuring in Transition: A Quantitative Survey,' *Journal of Economic Literature*, vol. 40, pp. 739–92.

Dyck, I.J.A. and Hopper Wruck, K. (1998), 'Organization structure, contract design and government ownership: A clinical analysis of German privatization,' *Journal of Corporate Finance*, vol. 4, pp. 265–99.

EBRD (2000), *Transition Report 2000: Employment, Skills and Transition*, London: European Bank for Reconstruction and Development.

Estrin, S., Hanousek, J., Kočenda, E. and Svejnar, J. (2009), 'Effects of Privatization and Ownership in Transition Economies,' *Journal of Economic Literature*, vol. 47(3), pp. 699–728.

Murrell, P. (1992), 'Evolution in Economics and in the Economic Reform of the Centrally Planned Economies', in Clague, Christopher and Rausser, Gordon C. (eds), *The Emergence of Market Economies in Eastern Europe*, Cambridge, MA and Oxford: Blackwell, pp. 35–53.

Wallace, C.P. and Stojaspal, J. (1996), 'The Pirates of Prague,' *Fortune*, vol. 134(12), pp. 78–86, (23 December).

11

THEORIES AND MODELS OF ECONOMIC TRANSITION

John Marangos[1]

Introduction

The collapse of centrally administered socialism in the Soviet Union and Eastern Europe initiated the movement from a centrally administered economy towards a market economy, commonly referred to as the transition process. The word 'transition', the passage from one state to another, might seem appropriate; nevertheless, it did not explicitly capture all the complexities involved. The transition process entailed superseding the essential properties of the centrally administered economy, consequently further destabilizing the former economic system, and replacing it with a market economy.

Any exposition of the transition problem in the economic literature must necessarily be a simplification of the complexities involved. One approach taken in writings on the transition process reduced the issues to an isolated variable of the economic sphere. The various aspects of the transition problem were pigeon-holed in thematic sub-categories, thus avoiding the inter-related nature of economic institutions and behaviour. Others took an alternative approach, and provided a solution to the problem by explicitly or implicitly favouring specific behavioural assumptions and/or economic relationships. Furthermore, others omitted the impact of the political process, ideology, institutions or the initial conditions on the transition process, showing little or no interest in the political, ideological, institutional outcomes of the economic policies implemented and whether the initial conditions influenced those outcomes. Thus, modelling of the transition process was highly subjective and based on value judgements.

The aim of this contribution is to overcome those weaknesses by proposing an alternative conceptualization of the transition process. This involves substituting a more holistic approach for the 'pigeon-hole' methodology adopted by most writers. The elements of the reform programme are interdependent, mutually supportive and interactive. This paper emphasizes the interrelated nature of the reforms which results from the interrelated nature of economic institutions and behaviour. Because of this interrelatedness, there were grave dangers associated with making one or more elements of the reform programme central, while discounting others. But despite the limitations of economic analysis, the transition process itself was never restricted to the economic field. The development of market relations is not independent of other social relations. It would seem that political, ideological, institutional aspects and the initial conditions of the transformation were fundamental. Indeed, economic reforms cannot be understood or assessed solely in narrow economic terms.

The chapter is restricted to the development of theoretical and conceptual models of transition. Each model is a construction based on the values and beliefs, which most economists adopting the particular model, subscribe to. Each model is a stylized version of the view of how the economy operates, with reference to the transition from a centrally administered economy to market economy, suggested by the economic analysis in question.

What follows is structured in the following manner. First, an answer is provided to the question of what the transition process entailed. Next, I argue that a political economy approach is most suitable in analysing the transition process. However, a political economy approach gives rise to alternative theories and models of transition, which are then presented. Non-market alternatives are not considered. Finally, the practicality and usefulness of the political economy approach, as adopted herein, is expounded in the conclusion.

What did the transition process entail?

During the transition process, there is a co-existence of elements of centrally administered socialism and market relations; thus, traditional economic theory based on the presence of market relations was most likely not appropriate. As such, the transition was effectively implemented in the dark. Thus, while not only the collapse and the timing of the collapse of centrally administered economies surprised economists, many aspects of the transition process also did. The transformation was one of the most dramatic non-marginal adjustments in economic systems ever experienced. The complexities involved did not have any historical parallels and people's desire for quick results caught economists unprepared. In the end, economic science responded by developing an appropriate body of economic analysis – transition economics – to facilitate and provide some form of direction to the aforementioned process.

An attempt to solve the transition problem involved several questions, of which the most important were:

(i) *What should the end state be?*
    While most economists agreed on the introduction of market relations in the Russian and Eastern European economies, the market as such is not a homogeneous entity. Experience shows that market capitalist economies are not all identical.

(ii) *What is the process by which the desirable end state will be achieved?*
    This question included reference to the speed and sequencing at which the necessary reforms should be implemented.

(iii) *What are the means that should be used to induce the reforms?*
    This question reflected the choice of policy instruments.

(iv) *What elements, if any, of the existing structure of the centrally administered economy should remain?*
    This question asked whether any aspects of the centrally administered economy were consistent with and desirable in a market economy.

The answers to these questions could not be derived by using mainstream economic analysis alone, but also depended on one's perception of social reality. Given assumptions about economic behaviour, the questions arose of how the economic system functions and responds to changes, and what is a good society? The answers to these questions reflect one's assessment of each economic and non-economic performance dimension, as well as the weights one assigns to these performance dimensions. In addition, alternative economic theories, mostly conflicting, utilize criteria for determining how society and the economy function and how society should distribute responsibilities between the market and the state, with the purpose of solving economic problems. Thus, different views on social reality and the nature of a good society are associated with distinct methodologies and a particular set of social values which have implications for economic policy formulation. This gives rise to alternative theories and models of transition, based on different assumptions, diverse methods of analysis and different goals.

A political economy approach to transition

The success of the transition reforms depended not only on specifying the necessary economic conditions, but also on whether certain conditions were satisfied with respect to the non-economic elements. In general, reformers are constrained by the lack of sufficient information, the social, legal, cultural and economic institutions, the physical environment and systemic factors. For this reason, the analysis adopted in this paper is in the tradition of political economy, which incorporates the interaction between political institutions, social consciousness and ideas within the framework of economic relationships. The transition process is holistic, historical, dynamic and comparative in nature and, as such, a political economy approach would seem appropriate. Political economy stresses that making economic sense and understanding economic relationships are not feasible without explicit awareness of power, institutions and values. A political economy approach to the transition process contests the belief that economics and politics are interested in distinct terrains within the society and that they employ different methods of analysis. Consequently, the analysis of the transition process was consistent with the tradition of political economy, as economics alone is and was not enough (Murrell, 1991, p. 62). However, a political economy approach generates disagreement and results in alternative transition theories and models. For economists disagree over what defines a good society and thus they disagree about the different weights assigned to economic performance indicators.

A political economy approach to the transition process gives rise to alternative theories and models of transition. The distinguishing features of the different transition theories and models based on each set of unique elements are presented in Table 11.1.

Theories and models of transition

Economic paradigm

This contribution develops five alternative theories and models of transition, based on three distinct views of economic paradigms: the neoclassical, post-Keynesian and market socialism. The neoclassical model of transition encompasses an approximation of competitive capitalism as the desired outcome and uses the neoclassical economic paradigm. The fact that there is disagreement about whether competitive capitalism is an appropriate goal, and whether it is feasible, gives rise to the need to consider alternative theories and models. Consequently, a critique of the neoclassical model which assesses its weaknesses and inadequacies gives rise to an alternative model based on post-Keynesian propositions. The aim here is to develop a model of transition, broadly defined as 'social democratic', which overcomes the weaknesses of the neoclassical model and is also both realistic and feasible, as argued by post-Keynesian economists.

In this context, it would also be appropriate to consider a market socialist model of transition. As the designation of the model implies, it is a combination of a market system and socialist principles. The market socialist model is concerned with the optimal combination of centralization and decentralization, of markets and planning, of individualism and the common good, and of public and private property. The market socialist model incorporates the Marxist economic paradigm and thus takes a different view of the way the economic system functions.

Table 11.1 Alternative theories and models of transition

Primary elements	Models of transition				
	Shock therapy	*Neoclassical gradualism*	*Post Keynesian*		*Market socialism*
Economic paradigm	Neoclassical		Post Keynesian		Marxism
What is a good society?	Competitive capitalism		Social democratic capitalism		Market socialism
Speed	Shock therapy	Gradualism			
Political structure	Pluralism				Non Pluralism
Ideological structure	Self-interest		Self-interest Common good	Self-interest Common good Participation	Self-interest Common good Participation through the party
Institutions	Product of market forces		Product of state action		
Initial conditions	Not a concern	Some concern	Important		Extremely important

Source: Adapted from Marangos (2003).

The issue of speed

The movement towards a market economy may take two forms: the shock therapy approach and the gradualist approach. Within the neoclassical model we can distinguish between shock therapy and the gradualist model of transition. The shock therapy approach requires an immediate and rapid transition to the market, while the gradualist model favours an evolutionary process towards a market system. The issue of speed addresses the issue of human consciousness and perceptions when a dramatic change in behaviour is required, such as the transition from central administration to markets. The opposing views, with regard to speed, reflected the different beliefs about individual responses, which can either be rapid or time-consuming. The distinction with regard to speed was relevant only for the neoclassical model, since both post-Keynesians and market socialists were in favour of a gradual approach. They agreed with the neoclassical gradualist economists that change had to be slow since institutions, organizations and patterns of behaviour and thinking could not be changed immediately. In the following, an analysis of the alternative adjustment paths takes place.

Shock therapy

The shock therapy approach was characterized by a rapid implementation of reforms, minimization of time intervals between measures, and fast correction of policy mistakes. 'The main issue is to cross the rising river as fast as possible in order to reach the other shore and establish a firm foundation for the construction of a new economic system based on the market' (Åslund, 1992, p. 87). The shock therapy approach assumed that the transition process did not necessarily imply a reduction in output as important reforms in economic structures were not necessarily associated with a reduction in living standards. Thus, it was argued that the stabilization programme and the institutional reforms should have taken place at the same time. Lipton and Sachs (1990, p. 100) quoted Gonzalo Sanchez de Losada, Bolivia's former Planning Minister, who in 1986–89 administered the reform process in his country and stated that, 'if you are going to chop off a cat's tail, do it in one stroke, not bit by bit'. Getting the prices right from the beginning would encourage entrepreneurship under hard budget constraints. The underlying assumption was that individuals would always respond quickly to the incentives provided, even when dramatically new behaviour was required. Most importantly, a gradual process would have resulted in the wastage of the precious reserve of political capital developed after the collapse of centrally administered socialism. At the time, people were willing to accept radical solutions to the difficult economic problems they faced, providing a window of opportunity for reforms, that might not last for long.

Gradualism

Neoclassical economists who were in favour of the gradualist approach, along with the post-Keynesians and the market socialists, argued that the changes in the economic system, which were required to complement the introduction of market relations, could not be introduced rapidly: these changes inherently take time. There was need for gradual change, since institutions, organizations and patterns of behaviour and thinking would not change immediately. These elements could only take shape and function after an 'organic historical development' (Kornai, 1990, p. 52). So the process of change had to be slow. It could be speeded up, but nevertheless needed to be gradual. Otherwise 'artificial transplants hastily forced upon these societies will be rejected by their living organisms' (Kornai, 1990, p. 20). Gradualists insist that complementarity between reforms requires gradualism as institutional reforms are slow-moving processes. The gradual approach allows people to adjust their behaviour and thinking with minimum psychological costs; thus reducing their resistance to change. In contrast, the shock therapy supporters argue that the longer the transition process, the more time available for self-interested pressure groups to regroup and use their monopoly and political power to oppose the reforms.

The political structure

The transition process also depended on developments in the political structure. 'In the transition, the liberalization of political markets is often as important as the liberalization of economic markets' (Parish and Michelson, 1996, p. 1043). This is because market reforms initiated 'modern' civil societies, stimulating the emergence of autonomous interest groups, political parties, independent media, and opportunities to participate in political processes. Political legitimacy and cohesion were essential elements of the reform process, which was so extensive and radical.

The political structure determines the decision-making process in society, and this has consequences for the structure and function of the central authorities. It also determines the bureaucratic constraints, that is, formal and informal orders or prohibitions enforced through pressures or threats upon the individual by the bureaucracy. Political decisions would influence market structures. There is a link between economic and political structures. Once a society has chosen its economic structure, this will have consequences for the decision-making processes, and especially for the structures and functioning of the central authorities. In terms of political structure, we can distinguish between two alternatives, namely the pluralistic and non-pluralistic structure. In particular:

Political pluralism

A transitional model with political pluralism introduces fundamental changes with consent, debate and discussion, agreement and compromise. With pluralism there is recognition that antagonism and conflicting interests exist in society, based on the diversity of human beings. There is no single correct line, no sole and invariably correct perception of issues. It means that the common good will not be laid down in an authoritarian or totalitarian manner by the state, but is determined through a plethora of different opinions which are freely discussed. However, the adoption of pluralism would also result in changes in the economic model which reformers strive to introduce. The transition process based on pluralism may influence the model itself. Such changes may be of a minor nature and could be incorporated without altering significantly the basic model. For example, the acceptance of multi-party politics, the concessions for private property and hiring labour were not included in the original Gorbachev market socialist model, but were added at a later stage. However, pluralism exacerbated the difficult situation of transition in the Soviet Union by allowing the people to show their dissatisfaction. The attempt to keep the Union together in a political pluralistic environment resulted in large concessions to the republics, which ultimately resulted in the break-up of the Soviet Union. It was a 'cost' that the reformers had to pay, if pluralism was to be an essential precondition for the implementation of the model. The neoclassical, post-Keynesian and pluralistic market socialists incorporate pluralism in their theory and model of transition.

Non-pluralism

This is where the transition to a market economy is characterized by a non-pluralistic process, based on a political party which is a leading role party (with a monopoly of power), which adopts a leading position (its views determine most decisions) and a correct line (the party scientifically derives the correct understanding of things). Those in favour of a non-pluralistic process argued that the implementation of such radical reforms required a politically stable and powerful government that had enough authority to implement the reforms, independent of public opinion and vested interests. In this way, the government would be able to concentrate on the reform process and avoid any problems associated with the political process, thus formulating unconstrained economic policy. Authoritarian rule may likewise be capable of achieving a dynamic improvement in the standards of living. A transition process based on non-pluralism would have avoided the problems that Gorbachev had to face, according to non-pluralistic socialists. In broad terms, the Chinese transition process uses a non-pluralistic process; the Chinese transition process, however, is also multi-level, characterized by competition between districts, provinces, etc.

The choice between pluralism and non-pluralism effectively had to do with the nature of economic and political power and whether the central authority was willing to relinquish some of its power in favour of participation by the people through pluralism. Accordingly, it depended on whether the reformers were willing to accept the input of the people in the development of the transition programme, at the cost of altering the model significantly.

Ideology

Ideology refers to a cohesive set of values and beliefs about others, the world, and ourselves. It embodies a distinct 'world view' as to how society and, thus, the economic system functions. 'Ideas and ideologies shape the subjective mental constructs that individuals use to interpret the world around them and make choices' (North, 1990, p. 111). The introduction of market relations in the former centrally administered economies unavoidably eventuated in a change in the dominant ideology. This was because human behaviour takes place within a given ideological framework, with its specific values, beliefs and worldview. Ideology is a set of directives for activity as well as the means for rationalizing human behaviour assisting in overcoming the free-rider problem.

Ideology advocates a particular pattern of social relationships and arrangements, and determines the goals of human activities and the moral standards of human behaviour. Ideology determines and creates human personality, which influences the identity of a society. Thus, we should regard ideology as a set of directives for activity, as well as the means for rationalizing human behaviour. It is used to justify a specific economic structure, which its supporters seek to promote, realize, pursue or maintain. The economic, political, legal, moral and religious institutions are what they are because they facilitate and uphold the ideological framework of the society. Ideology can encourage within a market system:

a   *Self-interest*. With respect to the ideological structure, market economies have developed an ideology that emphasizes and encourages self-interest and self-help based on Adam Smith's famous arguments. Neoclassical economists stress that in order to be able to understand social phenomena we need to understand individual actions. Individuals are allowed, within defined limits, to follow their own values and convictions rather than somebody else's, and individuals should not be subject to coercion. The neoclassical model would be in favour of stimulating a self-interest ideology.

b   *Common good*. The question arose whether there was a need to bring together the goals of the individual and society. Should there be any restriction on individual behaviour in a market system in the name of the common good? If the answer were 'yes', then how would the common good be determined? Perhaps by an open pluralistic process where individuals come together to plan for the common good, or through a leading-role, leading-position and correct-line party? The answer needs to be incorporated in each transition model. The post-Keynesian model combines a self-interest ideology with the common good within a pluralistic political environment.

c   *Participation*. The decision-making process does not only involve the formulation of the common good, but may also involve the breakdown of hierarchical relations within the enterprise and society. The question then arises whether the transition theory and model will allow the effective participation of the workforce in the decision-making process of the enterprise. The market socialist theory and model integrates self-interest, common good, and participation. While the pluralistic market socialist model would encourage participation in all aspects of decision-making, the non-pluralistic Chinese model encourages participation only through the party mechanism.

The role of institutions

A radical change such as moving towards a market economy required a reform in the institutional structure consistent with the institutional arrangements fundamental for the proper functioning of a market economy. This was because any 'attempt to account for the diverse historical experience of economies or the current differential performance of advanced, centrally planned economies and less-developed economies without making the incentive structure derived from institutions an essential ingredient appears to me a sterile exercise' (North, 1990, p. 134).

The role of economic institutions is to make individuals responsive to the economic environment and make the economic environment responsive to individual actions. The institutional structure determines the rules of the game in a society, which are human-devised restrictions that mould human interaction (North, 1990, p. 3). It identifies the constraints in that rational economic actors comprehend, plan and endeavour to achieve their goals. Institutions encourage competitive or co-operative behaviour, reduce or increase transaction costs and provide the organizational foundation for production and exchange. In addition, society's interests are embedded in the institutional structure and change as institutions change in accordance with customs, regulation, ideology and *ad hoc* decisions by those who hold power. Hence, under the new economic conditions of emerging markets, economic actors struggle to establish institutions to facilitate competition and to serve their interests through both informal arrangements and formal institutions.

The question that had to be answered by the transition theories and models was how would an appropriate institutional structure be developed in transition economies. Does it involve government action, as Kregel *et al.* (1992, p. 28) argued that institutions 'often emerge spontaneously and through repeated social interaction but in many cases they have to be made by conscious action', a statement with which the post-Keynesians and the market socialists would agree. However, Rapaczynski (1996, p. 87) differs, stressing that institutions are ' … largely the product of market forces, rather than government fiat'. Neoclassical economists, following Hayek, interpret the presence of institutions as an outcome of 'human action' rather than 'human design'. As such, the likelihood of designing institutions, as post-Keynesians and market socialists argue, is regarded as utopian, an immaterial exercise, that not only will not work but will be counterproductive.

Initial conditions

While the Russian and Eastern European economies were structured on the basis of a central administration, this did not mean that these economies were identical. The need for change was recognized long ago and the political authorities in these countries had experimented, to varying degrees, with reform. In addition to each country's initial economic structures and economic conditions, there was a need to incorporate their own political, cultural, ideological, and institutional elements, power relationships and the role of the state. All these elements were unique to each country. Therefore, the question arose: 'What is the impact of strategy and policy, and sequencing, as opposed to country-specific initial conditions such as politics, pattern of industrialisation, or institutional structure?' (Parker *et al.*, 1997, p. 3).

The shock therapy supporters argued that the transition programme they proposed had general application across economies with immensely different initial conditions and political environments. The basic elements of a market economy could have been adapted to different historical and cultural environments. For the remaining theories and models, to varying degrees, the efficiency and feasibility of any transition strategy depended on the specific conditions prevailing in the individual countries. The neoclassical gradualist economists showed some concern for the initial conditions, since they shaped the gradual transformation of the society. However, they argued that this should not have been used as a pretext to substantially delay the reforms and distort the achievement of a free market. The post-Keynesians considered the initial factors important, while for the market socialists they were extremely important in shaping socialism, because of the hostile capitalist world the transition countries would be surrounded by if they chose the socialist path.

Conclusion

A political economy approach to the transition process gives rise to alternative theories and models of transition. The development of each theory and model is based on a set of ideas, to most of which individual economists who subscribe to the particular body of analysis would conform. The shock therapy theory and model is based on neoclassical economic analysis, has a goal of competitive capitalism, it uses a shock therapy approach towards speed, the political structure is pluralistic, the ideology encourages self-interest, the necessary institutions will be the result of market forces and the initial conditions were not a concern (Marangos, 2002).

The neoclassical gradualist model is based on neoclassical theory, has a goal of competitive capitalism, it uses a gradual approach to reforms, the political structure is pluralistic, the ideology encourages self-interest, the necessary institutions will be the result of market forces, and there was some concern for the initial conditions (Marangos, 2005).

The post-Keynesian model uses post-Keynesian theory and has social-democratic capitalism as a goal; it adopts a gradualist approach towards speed, the political structure is pluralistic, the ideology encourages self-interest and the common good, the necessary institutions will be the result of state action and the initial conditions were important (Marangos, 2004).

The pluralistic market socialist model uses Marxist economic analysis and has market socialism as a goal; it uses a gradualist approach towards speed, the political structure is pluralistic, the ideology encourages self-interest, the common good and participation, the necessary institutions will be the result of state action and the initial conditions were extremely important.

Finally, the non-pluralistic market socialist model uses Marxist economic analysis and has market socialism as a goal; it uses a gradualist approach towards speed, the political structure is non-pluralistic, the ideology encourages self-interest, the common good and participation through the party, the necessary institutions will be the result of state action and the initial conditions were extremely important.

In this way, a political economy approach makes it possible to understand the transition process from a new and more enlightened perspective. With this approach, we are better able to comprehend the complexities involved and the disagreements between social scientists about the transition process.

Note

1 Part of this chapter is based on John Marangos (2003), 'Alternative Politico-Economic Models of Transition', *Journal of Economic and Social Policy,* vol. 8(1), pp. 52–71; see journal website, epubs.scu. edu.au/jesp. I would like to thank the Managing Editor of JESP, Associate Professor Jeremy Buultjens, for allowing me to use elements of the published paper.

Bibliography

Åslund, A. (1992), *Post–Communist Economic Revolutions. How Big a Bang?* Washington, DC: Centre for Strategic and International Studies.

Kornai, J. (1990), *The Road to a Free Economy,* New York: W.W. Norton.

Kregel, J., Matzner E. and Grabher, G. (1992), *The Market Shock,* Vienna: AGENDA Group.

Lipton, D. and Sachs, J. (1990), 'Creating a Market Economy in Eastern Europe: The Case of Poland', *Brookings Papers on Economic Activity,* No. 1, pp. 75–147.

Marangos, J. (2002), 'The Political Economy of Shock Therapy', *Journal of Economic Surveys,* vol. 16(1), pp. 41–76.

——(2003), 'Alternative Politico-Economic Models of Transition', *Journal of Economic and Social Policy,* vol. 8(1), pp. 52–71.

——(2004), 'A Post-Keynesian Approach to the Transition Process', *Eastern Economic Journal,* vol. 30(3), pp. 441–465.

——(2005), 'A Political Economy Approach to the Neoclassical Gradualist Model of Transition', *Journal of Economic Surveys,* vol. 19 (2), pp. 263–293.

Murrell, P. (1991), 'Can Neoclassical Economics Underpin the Reform of Centrally Planned Economies?', *Journal of Economic Perspectives*, vol. 5(4), pp. 59–76.

North, D.C. (1990), *Institutions, Institutional Change and Economic Performance*, Cambridge: Cambridge University Press.

Parish, W.L. and Michelson. E. (1996), 'Politics and Markets: Dual Transformations', *American Journal of Sociology*, vol. 101(4), pp. 1042–1059.

Parker, S., Tritt, G. and Woo, W.T. (1997) 'Some Lessons Learned from the Comparison of Transitions in Asia and Eastern Europe', in Woo, W.T., Parker, S. and Sachs, J.D. (eds), *Economies in Transition: comparing Asia and Eastern Europe,* Cambridge, MA: MIT Press.

Rapaczynski, A. (1996), 'The Roles of the State and the Market in Establishing Property Rights', *Journal of Economic Perspectives*, vol. 10(2), pp. 87–103.

12

FISCAL POLICY IN TRANSITION ECONOMIES

Sustainable public finance as a measure of successful transition[1]

Anna Shabunina

Starting from zero

Planned economies neither had nor needed either comprehensive fiscal policy or strong fiscal institutions. The share of the private sector was small and official unemployment did not exist, since government enterprises often employed more people than they needed. Strict tax rules or consistently applied tax codes were rarely in place. Often the governments negotiated tax payments with large enterprises and used the resulting revenue stream to redistribute resources between government-owned entities. Tax administration was easy since the exact information on prices and output was available, and a small number of large entities usually made their transactions via the single state-owned bank. Explicit taxes on individuals did not exist (Tanzi, 1992).

Transition to the market economy has drastically changed the situation. A small number of government-friendly agents were replaced by a large number of private actors with high incentives to avoid payments to the government. In addition most social expenditures (schools, hospitals, kindergartens) that were previously on the balance sheets of the public enterprises were transferred to the government liabilities list (Cheasty and Davis, 1997). Previously hidden unemployment became apparent and quickly surged to high levels in many transition countries. The newly established governments urgently needed to develop fiscal policy as well as to establish the institutions needed to implement it.

The challenges facing policymakers were colossal—fiscal institutions, including tax and customs administrations, budget office, budget law, and treasury had to be created from scratch under circumstances of high uncertainty and lack of information, widespread corruption and strong vested interests. It was clear that the role of the state in the economy should be reduced, but no clear vision or agreement existed among the new stakeholders on how large the changes should be: what functions the state should give up? what new ones it should take on? etc. Conducting fiscal policy in these circumstances was highly challenging.

A decade of fiscal adjustment: expectations met and missed

As a result of falling budget revenues, deficits initially widened in most transition economies, setting the public debt on an unsustainable trajectory. This was especially severe in the former Soviet Union countries (FSU), where deficits ballooned after 1991, on average exceeding 15 per cent of GDP by 1993. The combination of a shrinking revenue base and a diminishing propensity to pay taxes was among the principal reasons for the widening fiscal gap. Again, the situation was considerably worse in the FSU countries, where revenues declined by 11 per cent of GDP on average during the first three years of transition. In central European countries, revenues fell significantly during the first year but recovered somewhat afterwards, reducing the total shortfall to 4 per cent of GDP by 1994 (Figure 12.1).

Central European countries that were quick to adjust expenditure in the first few years had stabilized and even expanded it again after 1995. The relatively high share of the private sector that these countries had initially gave them an advantage in establishing effective tax collection systems. The FSU countries experienced a more severe GDP downfall and for this reason supported higher levels of government spending (as a ratio of GDP) for longer, but they had to continue reducing it up to 1997 in their attempts to control the ballooning government deficits. Their failure to reprioritize and adjust public expenditure levels contributed to the abrupt deterioration of the public finances. One of the contributing factors was the practice of keeping old subsidies and entitlements in place while allowing price liberalization to expand the resulting charges on the budget.

At the starting point, the share of government expenditure in GDP in the transition economies significantly exceeded that of market economies with similar levels of GDP per capita (Figure 12.2), often by a margin that was clearly unsustainable in the medium term. Collecting sufficient tax revenue to finance this level of expenditure would be incompatible with the goals of developing the private sector and boosting economic growth.

Additionally, most transition economies faced tough financing constraints that made fiscal adjustment not only unavoidable but painfully abrupt. Most countries had to undergo fiscal adjustment during the earlier years of transition. FSU countries had to reduce their deficits by an average of 10 percentage points over a two to three year period. Unfortunately, fiscal consolidation was largely achieved by expenditure cuts across the board without prioritization, with cuts largely falling on capital and infrastructure spending. In addition, the instruments that were used often undermined normal budget procedures. Arrears in government current expenditure were common, including public employees' salaries in education and the health sectors (Gupta *et al.*, 2003).

Moreover, disappointingly small privatization revenues did not aid the deteriorating fiscal position and contributed to negative perceptions of the law and "rules of the game" in the new democracies. Inadequate tax administration and institutional response, failure to tap revenues from the energy sector, and widespread corruption of the budget processes resulted in the failure of several governments to perform their expected redistributive role (Tanzi, 1999; Gupta *et al.*, 2003). The huge increase in income inequality became one of the enduring negative outcomes, giving rise to a social and political backlash that would impede future reforms.

In some cases, the rapid increase in state indebtedness and the failure of the government to implement needed policy adjustments to set the state finances on a sustainable path resulted in default on sovereign obligations (Russia, Ukraine, Bulgaria). The Russian default of 1998 had large negative spillovers on the region via financial markets contagion as well as through regional trade channels.

At the same time, the fiscal stabilization achieved by some transition economies during the first decade of transition (namely Slovakia, Slovenia, Estonia, etc. Figure 12.3) opened the way for sustainable economic growth. The results of Giavazzi and Pagano (1996) showed that fiscal adjustment can have an expansionary effect on the economy, mainly operating via reducing the extent of debt monetization, restraining inflation, and hence boosting the credibility of economic policies. A few years after the Asian crisis and Russian default, sustainable fiscal adjustments paid off in terms of higher growth, with better outcomes for those countries that had badly needed to achieve macroeconomic stability (Segura-Ubiergo *et al.*, 2006).

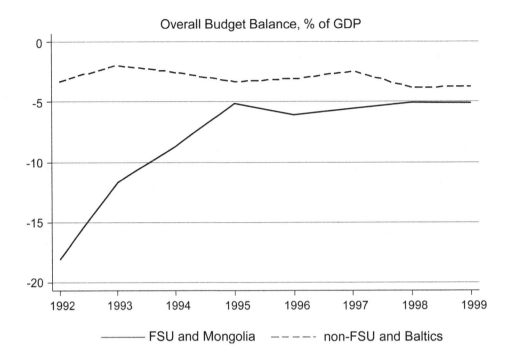

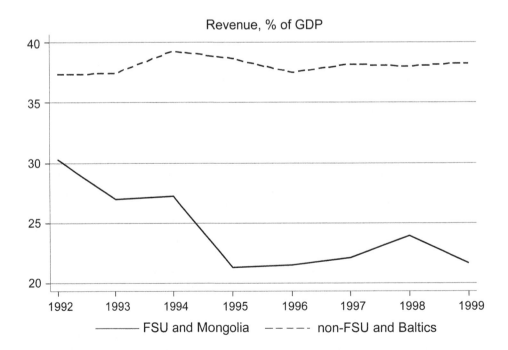

Figure 12.1 Fiscal stance in transition economies 1991–99
Source: IMF *World Economic Outlook* 2009.

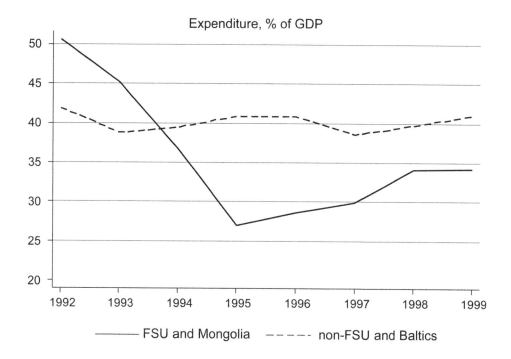

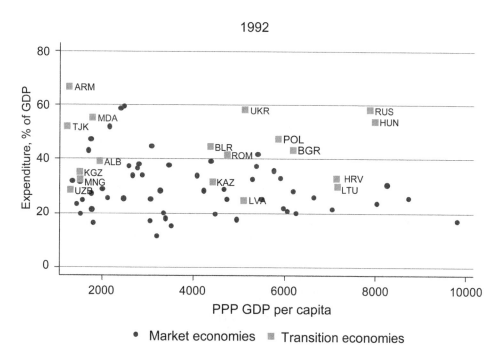

Figure 12.2 Government expenditure in transition economies
Source: IMF *World Economic Outlook* 2009 and author's estimates.

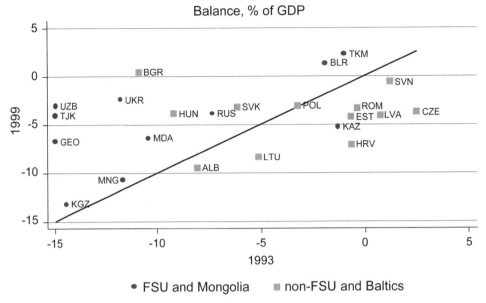

Figure 12.3 Budget balance dynamics in 1993–99 by country, per cent of GDP
Source: IMF *World Economic Outlook* 2009.

An important measure to deal with the revenue shortfall was the adoption of value-added tax (VAT). The rate initially adopted has generally been reduced, and in most Central and Eastern Europe (CEE) states VAT now provides about the same proportion of total fiscal revenue as in most Western European states (i.e., 15–25 per cent). Moreover, a number of CEE and South East Europe (SEE) economies have introduced flat-rate personal income taxes (World Bank, 2007).

Gradually, important progress was made in creating vital fiscal institutions. By 1999 modern treasury reforms had been adopted in many transition economies, with Latvia and Kazakhstan leading the way, and with Armenia, Azerbaijan, Estonia, Georgia, and Lithuania not far behind. In the Kyrgyz Republic and Turkmenistan, a substantial share of government finances remained outside of the treasury system. In the remaining countries, apart from some improvements in the management of external debt, little reform of financial planning and management has occurred.

When interpreting government statistics on the early years of transition, an important caveat should be added. Widespread barter operations, payment arrears to suppliers and wage arrears that created gaps between commitment and cash basis government budget indicators, methodological difficulties when measuring arrears, all implied that the accurate measurement of government financial accounts became very difficult (Gupta *et al.*, 2003).

Great moderation of the 2000s and an underestimated need for fiscal prudence

Most transition economies experienced a setback in growth after the 1997 Asian crisis and the Russian default. However, in many cases currency devaluation triggered a faster recovery than expected and the lesson that sound fiscal policies are essential for economic growth has been learned by many—or at least to some extent.

The large group of former socialist economies—already with heterogeneous structures right at the start of transition—diverged into three separate groups with distinct 'models' of economic growth. The 10 countries (soon to be 11, with Croatia) that joined the European Union (EU) enjoyed relatively high economic growth driven by the accession process. This meant trade and financial integration in the first place, but also convergence on the fiscal stance, especially for the countries that have joined the monetary union. A second group of transition countries, those with rich natural resource endowments, also benefited from strong global economic growth. The ever-rising commodity prices of the mid-2000s fuelled an economic boom and filled the state coffers of commodity exporters. Traditional trade and financial links, including remittances, have channeled the spillovers of this growth towards the third group. While some of the legacies of the socialist economies still exerted their influence in all countries, fiscal developments in these groups are worth analyzing separately. Figure 12.4 shows the dynamics of the budget balance according to these groups of countries.

The fiscal stance in the new EU members strengthened ahead of EU accession with eight out of 10 countries in the sample achieving a budget balance above -3 per cent of GDP by 2007. A notable exception to this prudent fiscal behavior was Hungary, which ran fiscal deficits above 3 per cent of GDP in most years, and as a result did not succeed in reining in the debt-to-GDP ratio. The Czech Republic on the other hand, has adjusted by more than 10 per cent of GDP within a decade, managing to reach -0.7 per cent of GDP by 2007 (Figure 12.5).

All new EU members experienced a revival of the state share in the economy: both revenues and expenditures have risen as a share of GDP. While the expenditure growth was often permanent (for instance, Figure 12.6 shows the wage bill increase having the largest contribution to government expenditure) and driven by the income catch-up process with the EU, part of the boost in revenues appeared to be temporary, driven by domestic credit, and demand booms. This often resulted in overestimated potential output and misjudgments over the cyclical position of the economy. Adequate fiscal buffers were not accumulated.

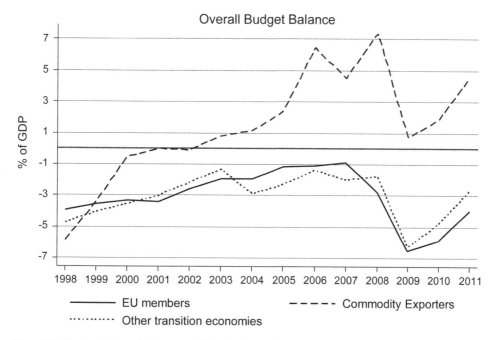

Figure 12.4 Budget balance during second decade of transition
Source: IMF *World Economic Outlook* April 2012.

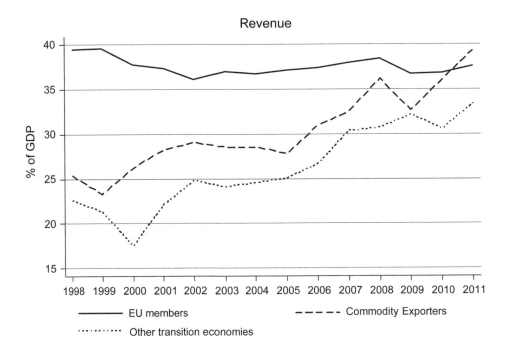

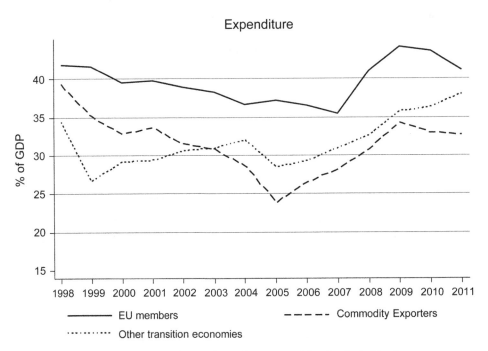

Figure 12.5 Government Revenue and Expenditure during second decade of transition by country group
Source: IMF *World Economic Outlook* April 2012.

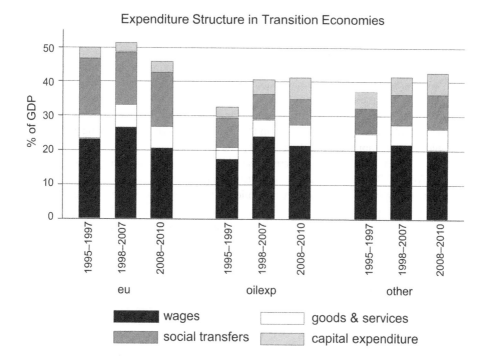

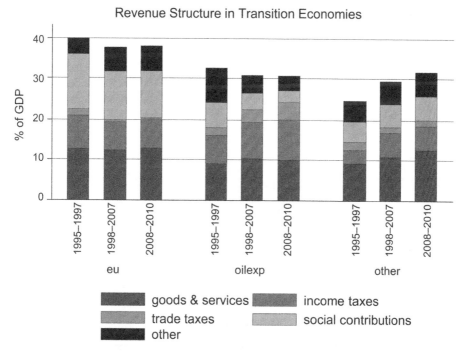

Figure 12.6 Expenditure and Revenue Structure Change
Source: IMF *World Economic Outlook* April 2012 and author's estimates.

Even the countries that had seemingly sound public finances witnessed large deficits when their revenues collapsed with the implosion of the credit boom. Figure 12.7 shows that it was not the fiscal balance itself, but rather the rapid expenditure growth, that characterized countries that had to request external official assistance. Some countries, more so when the monetary policy was constrained by exchange rate targeting, failed to use fiscal policy actively and prevent their economies from overheating. Latvia represents a more classic example of the Eastern European model of development. It had sound fiscal indicators; however, they were based on large external and internal imbalances accumulated in the pre-crisis times. Hungary is primarily an example of fiscal imprudence (Fabrizio *et al.*, 2009).

Rising oil and gas prices in the pre-crisis years helped the resource-rich economies of Azerbaijan, Kazakhstan, Russia and Turkmenistan to strengthen their fiscal positions, moving from fiscal deficits to significant surpluses by the mid-2000s. The average revenue-to-GDP ratios have increased, bridging the gap with the more economically advanced new EU members. Commodity-related revenues went up from 4 and 5 per cent of GDP in Kazakhstan and Russia in 2002 to 11 and 12 per cent in 2008, respectively. While estimation of the structural fiscal balances for commodity exporters presents a methodological challenge, historical memories of the dangers of dependence on highly volatile hydrocarbon prices generated the needed political will to save the windfall gains. Sovereign wealth funds were created in Russia, Kazakhstan, and Azerbaijan. Subsequent use of these funds made it possible to mitigate the effects of the economic downturn and the related fall in commodity prices, while sustaining a counter-cyclical fiscal policy stance.

The third group of countries was hit harder by the crisis and did not have sufficient buffers to respond to the downturn. Most of the countries in this group had to seek external international assistance and introduce fiscal consolidation without having the possibility of conducting counter-cyclical fiscal policy.

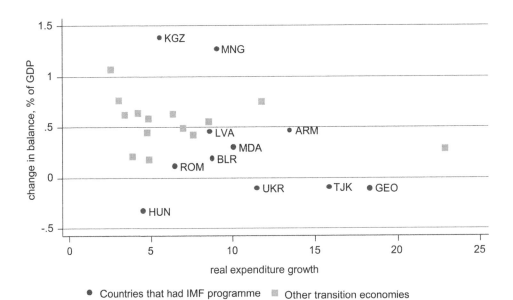

Figure 12.7 Annual change in fiscal balances and expenditure growth 2001–07
Source: IMF *World Economic Outlook* October 2009 and author's estimates.

Overall, the transition economies were more resilient in the face of the global financial crisis than they had been a decade earlier at the time of the Asian crisis. However, for some countries, insufficient fiscal consolidation during the boom years resulted in the lack of vital budgetary buffers when the crisis hit. The specific reasons were different in different countries—but the most common case was the underestimation of the positive output gap. Often a temporary shock caused by high capital inflows was considered as a permanent boost in potential GDP and therefore the need for fiscal 'cooling' was neglected.

Fiscal responses to global crisis by the transition economies

As the waves of financial crisis moved from the advanced to the emerging economies, destroying the myth of economic decoupling along the way, policymakers in many transition economies were faced with capital flight to safety, which was not always correlated with country fundamentals. Commodity prices declined. Previously abundant financing by the Western banks was also sharply reduced. Countries with significant vulnerabilities had to resort to external official assistance, while others tried to implement counter-cyclical fiscal stimulus to varying degrees.

There are several factors that limit the scope of counter-cyclical fiscal policy in a given country: (1) debt sustainability considerations; (2) macroeconomic vulnerability, e.g., high inflation, high current account balance, low reserves; (3) absorption capacity; and (4) institutional factors. These factors are more prominent in emerging and transition economies. Historical studies show that emerging economies, including those in transition, are more prone to pro-cyclical fiscal policy (Baldacci *et al.*, 2006). Figure 12.8 shows the number of transition economies that were able to conduct counter-cyclical fiscal policy[3] during the decade 2001–10. Fiscal policy responses during the crisis were a new venture for most countries, and the effectiveness of the implemented measures remains to be assessed. Among the transition economies,

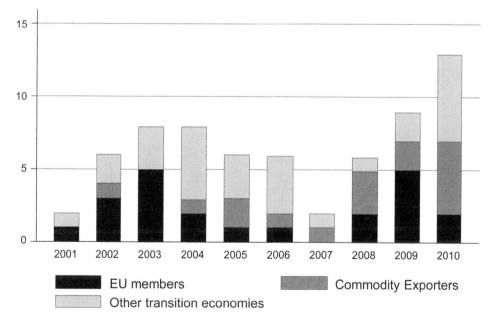

Figure 12.8 Transition economies and counter-cyclical fiscal policy
Source: IMF *World Economic Outlook* April 2012 and author's estimates.

commodity exporters implemented the largest fiscal stimuli. A large part of this stimulus turned out to be permanent increases in expenditure, with the result that medium-term structural deficits have deteriorated; e.g., the non-oil deficit in Russia has expanded from below 4 per cent to around 13 per cent of GDP. As a result of these measures fiscal buffers were used up in most countries and the average debt-to-GDP ratios have increased by 15 per cent of GDP in new EU members, 3 per cent of GDP in commodity exporters and 11 per cent of GDP in the other transition economies.

Fiscal challenges in the post-crisis world

At the time of writing (early 2012), the attention of the financial markets is fully captured by the question of debt sustainability in a number of advanced European countries. And while deficits and debts in many transition countries are not high compared to the advanced European countries, they are approaching thresholds widely regarded as rather dangerous for emerging markets. As markets grow more sensitive to sovereign debt risks, the question of sustainable debt dynamics in many transition economies will come to the fore. Market sentiment can shift very rapidly, especially towards countries with a poor record of fiscal discipline (e.g., those with a history of sovereign debt default).

Figure 12.9 shows that most countries had reduced their debt levels during the pre-crisis years. However a large part of this favourable dynamic could be attributed to the negative interest rate growth differentials (*r-g*) that many of them enjoyed during this period (Abbas *et al*, 2011)

When compared to advanced economies, all three groups of transition economies enjoyed a lower interest rate——growth differential. Figure 12.10 shows the decomposition of these

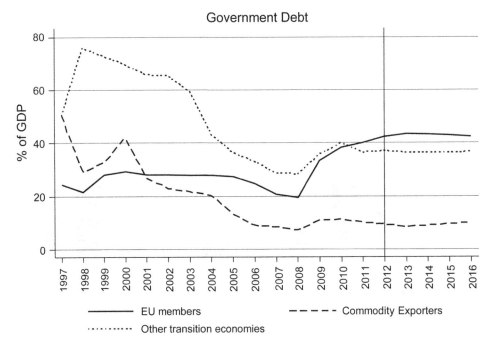

Figure 12.9 Debt dynamics in transition economies, by country group
Source: IMF *World Economic Outlook* April 2012 and author's estimates.

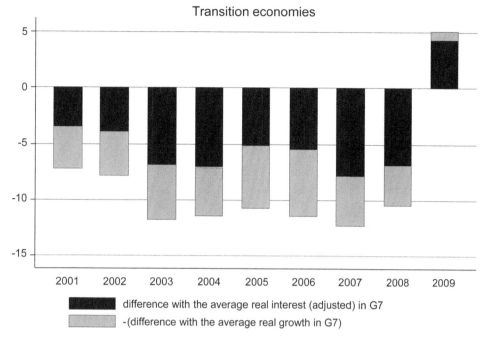

Figure 12.10 Difference in r-g in the G7 economies
Source: Escolano *et al.*, 2011.

differences into the difference in the real effective interest rates paid on government debt and real growth rates. While high growth rates are expected from theoretical analysis, the lower real interest rates need explanation. Part of it can be traced back to the restricted or underdeveloped financial sector that allowed the state to borrow at low or even negative interest rates in some countries. In others, large capital inflows and expectations of exchange rate appreciation contributed to this phenomenon (Escolano *et al.*, 2011). In the post-crisis global environment, interest rates will be higher; debt sustainability analysis should address these risks and guide the policymakers towards creating adequate fiscal buffers. Additional consideration should be given to the adverse impact of debt on growth, which is estimated to be higher for emerging economies (Kumar and Woo, 2010).

Medium- and long-term fiscal challenges

Medium- to long-term fiscal stability requires countries to address their age- and health-related expenditures. The legacies of socialist economies are still lingering, with low retirement ages and higher life expectancy after retirement, especially so in countries that still have a different retirement age for women. Most countries face unfavourable demographic trends, partially caused by the legacy of the first decade of transition which will take its toll on the financing of state pension liabilities. Some transition economies, like Bulgaria, the Czech Republic, Estonia and Poland, provide examples of appropriate reforms in this direction, with increased retirement ages and declining projected expenditure (Figure 12.11). Others, in particular Russia and Ukraine, face huge increases in liabilities, amounting to 31.5 and 49.3 per cent of GDP, respectively, in the next 20 years if nothing is done (IMF, 2011c). While the current levels of

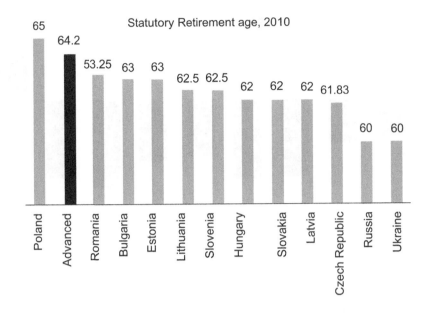

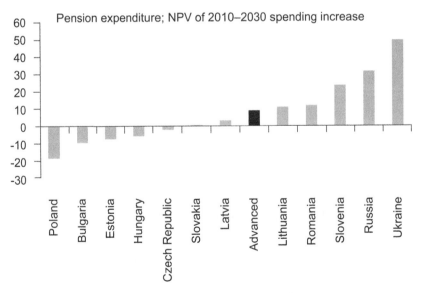

Figure 12.11 Pension Expenditure and Pension Age comparative statistics
Source: IMF (2011c), *The Challenge of Public Pension Reform in Advanced and Emerging Economies.*

government debt remain low in these countries, the rising liabilities of the state, if left unaddressed, will quickly raise the issue of fiscal sustainability.

Figure 12.12 shows government expenditure in GDP in the transition economies in 2009 compared to that of market economies with similar levels of GDP per capita. When compared to the corresponding graph for 1992 (Figure 12.2), we see that many countries will need leaner governments. In particular EU members remain at the upper frontier in terms of government expenditure compared to their level of GDP. For other transition economies, more effort should be devoted to rationalizing government expenditure rather than reducing its overall size. Reassessment of government expenditure priorities, better targeting of social expenditure and more growth friendly tax systems are all urgently needed.

Many transition countries have conducted comprehensive tax reforms, often successfully simplifying their tax systems and reducing tax evasion. Flat income taxes worked well in many countries, resulting in increases in revenue (World Bank, 2007). However, labour taxes, mainly high social security payments, remain an issue, especially in the new EU members. Tax wedges are often close to those of Western European countries and are higher than in emerging Asia. In many of these countries, the social security system still bears the legacies of the former socialist economy and needs comprehensive reform to improve targeting and efficiency. Tax administrations also have great potential for improvement. All this will be a prerequisite for improving competitive positions in the globalized world and would create more space for short-term support in the event of future economic downturns.

Most transition economies have enjoyed favourable interest rate—growth rate differentials during the last decade. The new EU member states, associated with their accession, benefited from substantial credibility premia in the form of lower sovereign yields (Hauner *et al.*, 2010). Going forward this is likely to change as global risk aversion increases and markets become

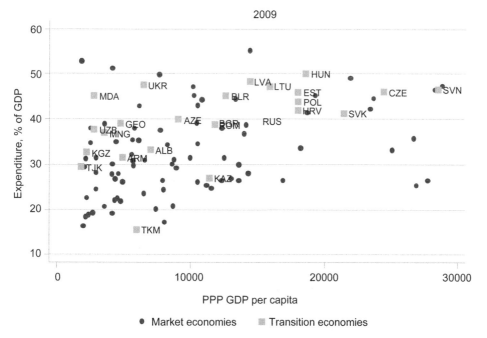

Figure 12.12 Government Expenditure and GDP per capita level
Source: IMF *World Economic Outlook* 2009 and author's estimate.

more discriminating as regards the (perceived) health of fiscal balances in individual countries. While current market attention is largely focused on some of the advanced economies, the fiscal balances of emerging Europe and other transition economies will be subject to increased scrutiny by the markets.

Some transition economies have been pursuing the right steps in the direction of increased fiscal responsibility and improved budgetary frameworks. Hungary has introduced a balanced budget rule; Serbia introduced a balanced budget rule adjusted for the business cycle; Hungary, Serbia and Slovakia introduced the debt rule; and Poland and Romania established expenditure rules (IMF, 2012). While fiscal rules cannot provide a complete guarantee of fiscal prudence, they do help to establish the credibility of fiscal policy and make irresponsible fiscal measures more costly—both economically and politically.

Many transition economies entered this crisis less vulnerable than they had been 10 years earlier; however, the global scale and magnitude of the current recession is taking its toll even on those countries that had strong fundamentals and limited vulnerabilities on the fiscal front. In particular, commodity exporters still need to diversify their economies and their tax base. New EU members, especially those with larger current account deficits, are vulnerable to negative spillovers from the advanced European economies. More medium- and long-term fiscal planning should be introduced and fiscal transparency should also be revamped in all these countries.

Going forward, debt ratios in transition economies are projected to start declining from 2014. However, this expectation is often based on the continuing favourable dynamics of low or negative interest rate growth differentials. Many of the vulnerabilities listed above threaten to undermine such benign debt dynamics. Hence comprehensive and credible medium-term fiscal strategies are needed to mitigate these risks and preserve the sustainability of government finances.

Notes

1 The views expressed herein are those of the author and should not be attributed to the IMF, its Executive Board, or its management.
2 In this figure and others, group median data are displayed for country groups.
3 Fiscal policy response is considered counter-cyclical in year t if the change in the cyclically adjusted primary balance (CAPB) compared to year t-1 has the same sign as the output gap change, defined as the current output to potential output ratio minus one.

Bibliography

Abbas, S.M.A., Belhocine N., El-Ganainy, A. and Horton, M. (2011), 'Historical Patterns and Dynamics of Public Debt: Evidence from a New Database', *IMF Economic Review*, revised and resubmitted.

Alam, A. and Sundberg, M. (2002), 'A Decade of Fiscal Transition', *Policy Research Working Paper No. 2835*, Washington, DC: World Bank.

Aristovnik, A. and Bercic, B. (2007), 'Fiscal Sustainability in Selected Transition Countries', *MPRA Paper No. 122*.

Baldacci, E., Clemens, B., Gupta, S. and Mulas-Granados, C. (2006), 'The Phasing of Fiscal Adjustments: What Works in Emerging Market Economies?' *Review of Development Economics*, 10(4), pp. 612–31.

Cheasty, A. and Davis J. (1997), 'Fiscal Transition in Countries of the Former Soviet Union: An Interim Assessment', in MOCT/MOCT.

Escolano, J., Shabunina, A. and Woo, J, (2011), 'The Puzzle of Persistently Negative Interest Rate–Growth Differentials: Financial Repression or Income Catch-Up,' *IMF Working Paper No. 11/260*, Washington, DC: International Monetary Fund.

Fabrizio S., Leigh D. and Mody A. (2009), 'The Second Transition: Eastern Europe in Perspective,' *IMF Working Paper No. 09/43*, Washington, DC: International Monetary Fund.

Giavazzi, F. and Pagano, M. (1996), 'Non-Keynesian Effects of Fiscal Policy Changes: International Evidence and the Swedish Experience', *Swedish Economic Policy Review*, Vol. 75, November, pp. 75–111.

Gupta, S., Leruth, L., de Mello, L. and Chakravarti, S. (2003), 'Transition Economies: How Appropriate is the Size and Scope of Government', *Comparative Economic Studies*, 45, pp. 554–76.

Hauner, D.A., Jonas J. and Kumar M. (2010), 'Sovereign Risk: Are the EU's New Member States Different?' *Oxford Bulletin of Economics and Statistics*, 72(4), pp. 411–27.

International Monetary Fund (2012), *Fiscal Monitor*, Washington, DC: International Monetary Fund, May.

——(2011a), *World Economic Outlook*, Washington, DC: International Monetary Fund, September.

——(2011b), *Fiscal Monitor—Addressing Fiscal Challenges to Reduce Economic Risks*, Washington, DC: International Monetary Fund, September.

——(2011c), 'The Challenge of Public Pension Reform in Advanced and Emerging Economies', *IMF Policy Paper, December 28, 2011*, Washington, DC: International Monetary Fund.

——(2010a), *Fiscal Monitor*, Washington, DC: International Monetary Fund, November.

——(2010b), 'From Stimulus to Consolidation—Revenue and Expenditure Policies in Advanced and Emerging Economies', *IMF Policy Paper 10/64*, Washington, DC: International Monetary Fund.

Kumar, M.S. and Woo, J. (2010), 'Public Debt and Growth,' *IMF Working Paper 10/174*, Washington, DC: International Monetary Fund.

Purfield, C. (2003), 'Fiscal Adjustment in Transition Countries: Evidence from the 1990s,' *IMF Working Paper No. 03/36*, Washington, DC: International Monetary Fund.

Segura-Ubiergo A., Simone, A. and Gupta, S. (2006), 'New Evidence on Fiscal Adjustment and Growth in Transition Economies,' *IMF Working Paper No. 06/244*, Washington, DC: International Monetary Fund.

Tanzi, V. (1992), 'Fiscal Policies in Economies in Transition', Washington, DC: International Monetary Fund.

——(1999), 'Transition and the Changing Role of Government,' *Finance and Development*, vol. 36, Washington, DC: International Monetary Fund.

World Bank (2007), *Fiscal Policy and Economic Growth. Lessons for Eastern Europe and Central Asia*, ISBN: 0-8213-7181-9.

Part IV
Integration

13

TRADE REORIENTATION AND GLOBAL INTEGRATION

Zdenek Drabek and Vladimír Benáček[1]

Introduction

It is difficult to think of historical cases when countries were subjected to more dramatic external shocks and had to undergo more fundamental reorientation of their external trade as was the case for the transition economies following the collapse of the Berlin Wall. Simultaneously, they had to face deep internal shocks originating in the demise of central planning. The shocks led to fundamental changes in the system of resource allocation, leading to dramatic changes in the system of ownership, industrial organization, legal and administrative institutions, incentives and in the role of economic policy.

The external economic shock was brought about by the breakdown of the Council for Mutual Economic Assistance (CMEA)[2] trading arrangements and the diversion out of the CMEA markets, which accounted for the bulk of trade of all transition countries. Suddenly, the transition economies (TEs) found themselves without reliable external markets. This had serious adverse effects on their exports, aggregate demand and on domestic production owing to the disruption in the supplies of imports. Moreover, all these shocks took place during the Gulf War, which led to big increases in world energy prices and a sharp deterioration in the terms of trade of most TEs. The effects of the shocks were equally dramatic, as we shall see below.

With the benefits of hindsight of more than 20 years since the collapse of central planning, we now know that several TEs have succeeded in the adjustment process very well. This clearly raises the question how these TEs managed to do so and what were the challenges for policy makers. Hopefully, the experience of those countries will be helpful to other countries facing similar adjustment challenges and difficulties, and the need for policy reforms in the external sector of their economies.

The main aims of this contribution are threefold: (1) to identify the main problems and challenges of adjustment in TEs; (2) to assess the success with which the TEs have been able to address those challenges through domestic restructuring and better integration into the world economy; and (3) to evaluate the factors explaining their success in general.

A few remarks on our methodology should be noted. Transition countries cover a highly diversified group of countries not only in terms of their size, endowments and location, but also in terms of their policies. For reasons of space, therefore, we limited our study to the countries in Eurasia, with a strong orientation on central and eastern Europe. Our descriptive approach is relatively simple and eclectic, and we shall primarily draw on the existing literature with only a small part constituted by our own research. However, we shall also make a normative assessment in the final section of the key factors explaining the success of trade adjustment. We proceed by only outlining the main arguments, and the reader will have to consult other relevant literature for the details. Our emphasis in the study of adjustment is put on the performance measured in terms of trade volumes and their geographical and sectoral distributions, leaving aside such important issues as costs of adjustment, the impact of trade on income distribution and poverty or the interdependence of policies.

Difficult initial economic conditions and policy challenges

The initial conditions for adjustment were extremely difficult. The difficulties can be divided under two separate headings – policy challenges and deteriorating economic performance. The fundamental policy challenge was the need for a complete dismantlement of a system in which markets had been almost completely eliminated and replaced by an administrative system of economic governance (Appendix 13.1). Since the very inception of the centrally planned system, international trade became its weakest point – a place where all the shortcomings of the administrative system became most apparent. The major task was to restore, and in some cases introduce afresh, the operation of markets. In the area of international trade this meant opening up the economy to foreign competition and to new markets, and integrating the countries into the global economy.

Economic difficulties faced by policy makers in the early 1990s were also daunting:

- Prior to 1989–91, TEs experienced a prolonged economic slowdown which was reflected in the stagnation of their international trade (Appendix 13.2). Persistent problems of inefficiency resulted in a continuous departure of effective real exchange rates from equilibrium, requiring increasing subsidization of exports and taxation of imports in order to maintain a degree of trade balance.
- The immediate effect of the 1989 political changes was a decline in domestic production, spending and external trade (Drabek and Smith, 1995), which led to lay-offs, falling fiscal revenues and to monetary easing.
- Mobilization of domestic resources and financial intermediation were poor owing to the extremely weak and under-capitalized financial sector. Commercial banking in communist countries was rudimentary. On the other hand, most TEs had a relatively low level of external debt exposure and could, therefore, facilitate their adjustment through external borrowing.
- The introduction of market-based prices, the loss of external markets, the distorted tax system and large government expenditures led to the emergence of 'twin deficits' – on fiscal and current accounts (Drabek, 1995). This, in turn, led to a large financing gap, which required a radical government response aimed at domestic resource mobilization, restraint of domestic spending and access to external borrowing. This pressure shaped the new economic strategy, which had to be built on increased openness to world markets, strict financial and macroeconomic discipline and well-functioning product and factor markets.
- The price interventions and currency controls prior to the transition resulted in a serious over-valuation of the official exchange rate.
- The ongoing Gulf War in the Middle East led to a further deterioration of terms of trade of the TEs, as already noted above.

- Once domestic markets were opened up to world markets and prices liberalized, no TE could resist the pressure of open inflation, which was previously suppressed by price controls (Drabek, Janacek and Tuma, 1994). The physical infrastructure supporting the external sector (roads, railroads, ports, airlines, telephones and other related services) was in an extremely poor state, and had to be revamped by extensive investments. Moreover, much of the infrastructure was directed towards the CMEA markets rather than the West and the global markets.

- There was a critical shortage of skills in financial, business, accounting and legal services. On the other hand, most enterprises were overmanned and government bureaucracy greatly overstaffed.

Policy adjustment to shocks in more detail: radical trade restructuring in the TEs

The range of policy interventions required to address the challenges listed above was vast. Policy design could often be 'imported' but what actually matters in such situations is the quality of policy implementation and enforcement, which must be masterminded at home. Brand new legislation or extensive amendments were needed with regard to domestic and foreign commercial transactions, thousands of state corporations had to be placed on a commercial basis and, in most cases, privatized. New start-up companies had to be established and legal coverage had to be provided for service industries which were historically neglected and they were, therefore, in a nascent state. New financial institutions (e.g. money and stock markets) had to be created and the commercial banking transformed by massive takeovers by foreign banks. Another immediate task was to introduce proper market-consistent policy instruments such as taxation, public procurement and allowing free price formation in the markets for goods, services and factors (Falcetti *et al.*, 2000; Fischer and Sahay, 2000).

During the 1990s trade protection was substantially reduced (e.g. completely phased out with the EU-15 and slashed by converging to the level of the EU external tariff). Tariffs were either kept low in low-tariff countries or set at fairly low levels in high-tariff countries (Drabek and Bacchetta, 2004). Foreign exchange transactions were liberalized, state trade monopolies eliminated, foreign trade activities and decisions decentralized. Domestic competition was greatly increased through a wide-ranging privatization of state production and trading enterprises, and the establishment of foreign companies was greatly liberalized. New markets were opened up by signing Europe Agreements (precursors of the Agreements of Accession to the European Union) and either by joining or renegotiating the membership in GATT/WTO. In 1992 the Visegrad countries also signed the Central European Free Trade Agreement (CEFTA) with a very liberal programme (Kaminski, 1999). As we shall see below, the signing of these agreements created powerful incentives for closer trading links with the EU and for trade reorientation from the East to the West.

TEs established laws and institutions facilitating international trade and investment. The system of various surcharges, levies, subsidies and bureaucracies was simplified or eliminated altogether. Corporate taxation was relatively modest. Assistance was offered to firms with the provision of information on foreign markets complemented with trade insurance and guarantees. Physical infrastructure improved with the access to EU cohesion funding, expanding bank finance and with the entry of foreign investors. Another central issue was the exchange rate policy when nearly all countries allowed an initial sharp devaluation of currency, stimulating exports and curbing imports (Drabek and Brada, 1998).[3] Foreign currency restrictions on the current account were eliminated almost immediately.[4]

Another element of the trade policy reforms was membership in multilateral institutions – the IMF and IBRD (Drabek 1995, 1996) and in the WTO (Michalopoulos, 2000). Furthermore, the integration of TEs into the global economy was enhanced through membership in other global and regional economic and political organizations, such as the European Bank for Reconstruction and Development (also the Asian Development Bank in the case of countries in Central Asia) and the Bank for International Settlements. The main economic objectives of these policy initiatives were to: (1) increase the credibility of government policies; (2) improve access to foreign markets for exports; (3) improve access to foreign financial markets; and (4) increase the effectiveness of capital and labour markets by enhancing the mobility of capital and labour.

In a particularly important step towards attracting FDI into the region, TEs signed numerous bilateral investment treaties (BIT) in order to provide security of property rights and a degree of transparency with internationally binding legal commitments to their policies. Many of these measures have been taken autonomously by the countries themselves, but many measures resulted from the countries' membership in international organizations (such as provisions concerning foreign currency restrictions regulated by the IMF Articles of Membership) or in the European Union (such as regulations concerning SPS and TBT measures under the *acquis communautaire*). Moreover, the domestic reform process was also probably accelerated by indirect pressures from abroad, such as the conditioning of MFN market access in the USA by the Jackson-Vanik Amendment. These policy initiatives also anchored trade policy commitments to more realistic exchange rates and increased their transparency.[5]

Empirical evidence on trade restructuring

How successful have the TEs been in adapting to new market conditions and to serious domestic economic disequilibria? An answer to this question, using several criteria, is in short – 'very successful' even though the performance obviously varied from country to country. The empirical evidence on the salient features of trade reorientation and adjustment is provided in Table 13.1 and in Appendix 13.3.

The following changes and conditions can be considered as crucial for the success of the transition in foreign trade:

Geographical reorientation. Given the sudden collapse of the intra-CMEA trade, the most immediate task for TEs was to reorientate their trade from 'lost' to new markets. The effectiveness of the process and, in particular, the speed with which the reorientation took place was quite remarkable, as documented by the example of Czech exports (see Figure 13.1). The most dramatic change was the sharp drop in the share of markets in Russia and the Ukraine on the one hand, and the dramatic gains of Germany and Austria on the other. After the economic stabilization at the turn of the millennium there was a slight rebound and return to some of the 'abandoned' markets of the former Soviet Union. Similar conclusions about the intensity and speed of market reorientation can be reached in the majority of TEs, as can be seen in rows 3–7 of Table 13.1.

Trade openness and intensity. The second remarkable feature of the reorientation process was the change in trade intensity. Reconstructing trade data for the early 1990s and making them comparable with pre-1990 data is an extremely complex and difficult task, as already noted. Nevertheless, it is safe to suggest that any decline of trade – to the extent that it occurred – was temporary and short lived. Moreover, the trade reorientation took place extremely fast. The high speed of trade adaptation allowed the domestic adjustment to take place at higher levels of trade and income and, therefore, with lower social costs relatively than would otherwise have

Table 13.1 Review of the indicators of international trade development: comparison of TE with the developed market economies in different periods of time

Row no.	Indicator	Region or country	Year	Value	Year	Value	Source
1	Exports/GDP ratio (nominal)	EU-15	1992	19.8%	2010	29.2%	IMF, OECD
2	Exports/GDP ratio (nominal)	EU-10 access.	1992	24.2%	2010	49.3%	IMF, OECD
3	Exports/GDP ratio (nominal)	Russia	1994	22.9%	2008	27.9%	Rosstat
4	Annual growth rates of all exports	EU-15	1992–1999	4.4%	1999–2010	4.5%	OECD
5	Annual growth rates of all exports	EU-10 access.	1992–1999	11.3%	1999–2010	12.7%	OECD
6	Annual growth rates of exports with EU-15	EU-10 accession	1992–1999	14.2%	1999–2010	11.2%	OECD
7	Share of exports to the EU-15	Visegrad 4 (PL, H, CZ, SK)	1990	34.1%	2010	60.6%	UNECE and Eurostat
8	Unit nominal price in EUR per kilogram of exports of EU-15	EU-15 to EU-15 (intra-region)	1999	€1.22	2010	€1.55	Eurostat
9	Unit nominal price in EUR per kilogram of exports of EU-15	EU-15 to non-EU-15	1999	€1.92	2010	€2.52	Eurostat
10	Unit nominal price in EUR per kilogram of exports to EU-15	EU-10 to EU-15	1999	€0.66	2010	€1.67	Eurostat
11	Unit nominal price in EUR per kilogram of exports of EU-15	EU-10 to non-EU 15	1999	€0.43	2010	€1.17	Eurostat
12	Annual growth rates of technologically advanced exports	EU-15 versus EU-10	1999–2010	4.3%	1999–2010	14.1%	Eurostat
13	Shares of sophisticated manufacturing products on total exports*	EU-15	1999	68%	2010	67%	Eurostat
14	Shares of sophisticated manufacturing products on total exports*	EU-10 accession	1999	58%	2010	68%	Eurostat
15	Kilogram prices of exported sophisticated manufacturing products*	EU-15	1999	€3.62	2010	€4.45	Eurostat
16	Kilogram prices of exported sophisticated manufacturing products*	EU-10 accession	1999	€1.34	2010	€3.47	Eurostat

Sources: IMF, *World Economic Outlook Database*, June 2011; OECD, International Trade by Commodity Statistics (ITCS), June 2011; Eurostat, External Trade Database, http://epp.eurostat.ec.europa.eu/newxtweb/, July 2011; Rosstat, Russian Federation Statistics Service, Moscow, June 2011; UNECE, Geneva, Statistical database of the Economic Commission for Europe, 1991, 1995 and 2005. Note: * For the purpose of this article, 'sophisticated' manufacturing products include chemicals, rubber, plastics, metals, machinery, transport equipment and controlling and optical instruments.

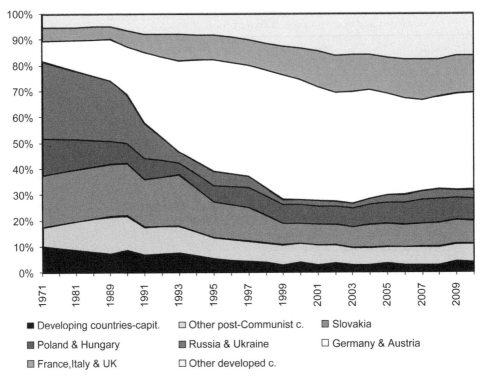

Figure 13.1 Changes in geographical distribution of Czech Exports, 1971–2010
Source: The CSO Yearbooks of 1973, 1983, 1993 and trade databases of 1999 and 2010.

been the case. The increase in trade openness can be seen from the data in rows 1 and 2 of Table 13.1. One most notable exception has been Russia whose trade openness hardly changed during the 1990s (row 3 of the same table).

Exports as drivers of economic growth. The rapid trade recovery also played an extremely important role in the TEs as a driver of economic growth. From the very beginning of transition, exports turned from economic 'laggards' into an important segment of aggregate demand and a factor of GDP growth in nearly all TEs. For example, the Czech export/GDP ratio rose from 37 per cent in 1990 to 77 per cent in 2008. To put it differently, Czech exports increased nearly 11-fold during that period while the Czech nominal GDP in USD terms increased six-fold. After deducting the value of the import content from exports, the share of exports in GDP increased from 28 per cent to 40 per cent.

Imports as drivers of competitiveness. Imports have also played an extremely important role in TEs. The effect has been both direct and indirect. The direct impact was generated through imports of key inputs for production and from imports as a means of technology transfer (Halpern *et al.*, 2011). The indirect effect came from the strong links between the growth of exports and that of imports, reflecting a growing dependence of export competitiveness on the latter via external outsourcing. Using once again the example of the Czech Republic, the Czech total exports had a 24 per cent import content in 1990, and the share increased by 2008 to 48 per cent.[6] It should also be noted that imports also played an important role in stimulating domestic competition and thus increasing the countries' competitiveness and efficiency. In some of the smaller TEs, this contribution could turn out to become the decisive growth factor (e.g. Slovakia, Hungary, Estonia), forcing domestic firms to achieve world standards of competition.

Sustainability of adjustment in quality. Poor quality of manufactured exports characterized exports of the TEs prior to the changes in 1990. Achieving qualitative changes in the commodity structure of exports was, therefore, a crucial condition for a breakthrough in the ability of TEs to adapt to the new market conditions by reshaping their comparative advantages. This would put the countries on a more sustainable path of growth which, too, should bode well for the future. The competitiveness of countries' exports is often assessed in terms of their ability to diversify exports towards higher value-added commodities and gains in terms of trade by exporting 'quality'. The latter is sometimes assessed by kilogram prices. Although this technique of measuring quality must be used cautiously, it provides useful indications of long-term trends.

The TEs other than those exporting natural resource-based products typically 'specialized' in low value-added products for export, which were associated with low dollar average unit prices of exports. In order to capture the evolution of 'quality' changes over time, we proxied unit prices by the kilogram prices of exports in time series. For example, as shown in Figure 13.2, in 1988 the kilogram price of average Czech exports to the EU-15 was US $0.31 (adjusted for inflation). This was a mere 17 per cent of the kilogram prices of its EU-15 imports, while in 1948 (the year of the Communist takeover) there was no evidence of any difference between the unit prices of exports and imports. The traditional interpretation of these numbers has been that:

1. The products exported from those countries were sold on world markets with a large discount, compensating for their technological backwardness, lack of goodwill, poor marketing, reliability and prestige.

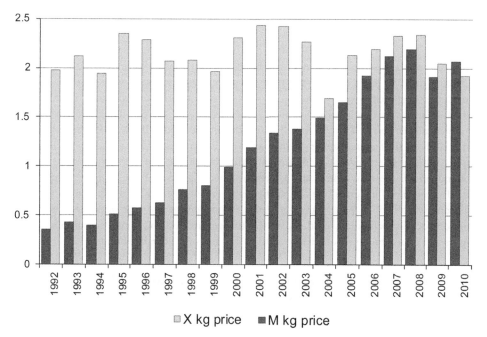

Figure 13.2 Unit (kilogram) prices of Czech exports and imports with the EU-15, 1992–2010 (in EUR and in constant prices of 2009)
Sources: Czech Statistical Office, Prague, Trade Statistics of the Czech Customs, database of March 2011 and CPI indices of Eurostat, 2010. Authors' estimations.

2. The structure of exports was biased towards less sophisticated products and products with a high content of natural resources and unskilled labour, reflecting a structural rigidity.

The process of trade adjustment had to be three-pronged: (a) upgrading the quality of products by increasing the value-added content through R&D and capital-intensive technologies. This process was greatly helped by substantial inflows of FDI and technology transfer; (b) a better management of firms achieved through privatization and integration of local businesses with global markets; and (c) giving more weight to more profitable exports. The radical liberalization of trade policy was the key instrument in guiding business decisions in that direction. A similar picture signalling improvements in export structure and in the quality of production can be found in Hungary, Poland, Romania and Latvia, among others. Corresponding improvements in unit and kilogram prices for other TEs can be seen in rows 8–11 and 15–16 of Table 13.1.[7] Furthermore, the qualitative changes in the structure of production and exports can also be documented by fundamental changes in the integration of local firms into global production networks, especially those originating in the EU area.

Spinoffs from increasing returns to scale. The predominance of inter-industry specialization has gradually turned in TEs into intra-industry trade (IIT) and specialization with a rising share of exchanges of similar products (Drabek and Smith, 1995). Moreover, the participation of local firms in global supply chains has also increased (Fidrmuc, 2001). After just a decade of transition, some smaller economies reached degrees of IIT comparable to advanced market economies. Initially, TEs could not but compete in the so-called horizontal IIT, i.e. by exporting low quality products and importing sophisticated products, which belonged to a similar product classification. In the later stages of transition we could observe the convergence to vertical IIT where TEs gained from direct R&D spillovers to trade (Damijan *et al.*, 2003; Besedes, 2011).

The mixed blessing of natural resource endowments

Russia, Ukraine and other countries of the Commonwealth of Independent States (CIS) have followed a different path: by retaining their specialization in products with a high content of natural resources (such as oil, gas, iron ore, steel). Unable to attract significant volumes of FDI into other industries, their export growth depended highly on the natural resources (with accompanying dangers of 'Dutch disease'). Using the gravity model, Babecka-Kucharcukova *et al.* (2010), analysed the factors shaping the trade of these TEs and found that exports were essentially supply constrained, impeded by inefficient infrastructure, shortage of capital and credit, volatility of world prices, the slow and costly process of diversification of the manufacturing sector, unresolved problems in agriculture and in the management of property rights. They argued that each country's ability to benefit from globalization depended on their internal progress with transition, focusing particularly on the quality of the legal framework, improved transport, energy supplies and education, and compliance with WTO rules for liberalized trade.

Assessing the adjustment performance: factors explaining success or failure

The early 1990s witnessed a major debate among economists about the adjustment of TEs to the external and internal shocks following the collapse of central planning. There were two critical issues at stake in the debates – one was related to the magnitude in the decline of output in the immediate post-1990 period and the other concerned the success of adjustment policies in those countries (Winiecki, 2002). The magnitude of the decline of output was partly a statistical problem owing to serious shortcomings in the national income accounting and in trade statistics during the central planning period.

The debate about the latter issue – the success of adjustment policies – was far more complicated and controversial. Many observers thought that the decline of output was too drastic and a result of policy failures. Some even argued that the decline was preventable since the adjustment did not necessarily require strict fiscal and monetary tightening as is normally the case in countries with balance of payments difficulties.

Drawing on the literature and more recent empirical evidence, our conclusion concerning the adjustment performance is straightforward: contrary to the views of the 'transition optimists' we do not find any major surprise in the performance of the TEs. The adjustment took place as would be predicted by trade theory. Fundamental changes had to be expected in the process which greatly resembled a form of 'creative destruction'. It is only the magnitude of the decline in individual countries that still needs to be explained. The drop in exports to CMEA countries could not be immediately replaced by an increase of exports to other markets, whose comparative advantages had to be discovered and adjustments had to be made on the supply side. Hence their decline added to a drop in domestic aggregate demand, linked to the disruption of production, growth of unemployment and tight public finances.

Nevertheless, the performance of countries differed. For example, the Visegrad-4 countries experiencing a 56 per cent drop in their CMEA exports during 1989–92, but recovered these losses by nearly doubling their exports to OECD countries in the same period. We can identify seven main areas, which could explain why the various countries' trade adjustment performance differed from one another:

1. *Speed and effectiveness of macroeconomic and financial stabilization.* Macroeconomic and financial stability was critical for the design and implementation of liberal trade policies (Drabek, 1995). In some TEs, trade liberalization was held back by uncertainties about inflation, exchange rate, external debt, taxes and access to credits.[8]

2. *Increase in competitiveness.* Poor export competitiveness of TEs prior to 1990 was a particularly serious issue as we have argued above (Hughes and Hare, 1992; Dulleck *et al.*, 2005). The critical factor for rising productivity, efficiency and increased competitiveness of local firms was privatization and entrepreneurship. All TEs have experienced improvements in the competitiveness of their firms even though the improvements differed from country to country, depending on the speed and effectiveness of institutional reform.[9]

3. *Effective export diversification.* The speed of export diversification differed from country to country. For example, the process was much faster in the countries of Central Europe and the Baltic states in comparison to most other European TEs. This was reflected in the different degree of integration of countries into global supply chains (greatly facilitated by the prospects for the EU accession), increases in intra-industry trade, the explosion of tourism-related services, and the emergence of successful SME start-ups.[10]

4. *Efficiency of markets.* Given the countries' different history, their experience with operations of product and factor markets was clearly different. This created different conditions for legislative and institutional reforms and it affected the efficiency of market operations. For example, labour markets in countries such as Poland, the former Yugoslavia and Romania had been more flexible than those of other TEs. Labour mobility between enterprises and jobs was important particularly in view of the large disruptions following the changes in 1990. The differences in labour mobility could be among the explanations of different patterns of adjustments to the shocks (Jurajda and Terrell, 2002; Fidrmuc, 2002).

5. *Trade adjustment and positive role of foreign investment.* Industrial and financial restructuring – two major challenges of TEs at the time – required considerable new investment into fixed and financial assets. FDI could provide access to new foreign markets, bring new technologies, new management techniques, help raise depleted reserves of international currency and mobilize new resources without a corresponding increase in domestic taxation. The available empirical evidence confirms the positive role of FDI in the process of adjustment (Javorcik, 2004) and different perceptions of risks by foreign investors of investing in TEs (Lankes and Venables, 1997), which led to different rates of FDI inflows in TEs. Nevertheless, the extent of spillovers continues to be debated even though the presence of spillovers is not disputed (Havranek and Havrankova, 2011).

6. *Imports and productivity.* As noted above, Halpern *et al.* (2011) stress the role of imports in the process of stimulating productivity growth. This explains why raising the import content of exports became so important in transition. The argument is interesting in itself because both theory and empirical evidence usually emphasize other factors of productivity growth such as investment, better management, and technology or labour skills.

7. *Incentives.* What probably characterized the post-1990 policy most was the changes in incentives for firms and households, with significant effects on international trade. Price liberalization, the enforcement of property rights, attractive taxation, rationalization of the exchange rate regimes, competition policies, privatization and changes in corporate management, financial restructuring and, last but not least, open trade policies played an extremely important role in stimulating investment, increasing corporate efficiency and their profitability.

We believe that local combinations of the above factors were the main explanations for the different degrees of success in the adjustment performance achieved by different countries. An attempt to generalize the performance of individual TEs was made by some economists who tried to capture the role of policy and other factors on the adjustment performance but, ultimately, the performance will depend on the specific conditions of each country. It will be up to the individual researchers to determine which of these factors was important in each particular country.

Appendix 13.1 Systemic shortcomings of centrally planned foreign trade

Domestic prices in the formerly centrally planned economies were poorly linked to costs of production and utilities. The link between domestic relative prices of traded goods and relative world prices was extremely weak, and changes in world prices were not automatically transmitted into changes in domestic prices. Exports and imports strongly depended on international barter agreements, especially within the CMEA with exports typically only seen as payments for imports. The official exchange rates were 'artificial' and domestic currencies not freely convertible. Foreign currency was administratively rationed and subject to wide-ranging restrictions. A complex system of taxes and subsidies was used to isolate domestic prices from changes in world market prices, thus forming a myriad of *de facto* multiple exchange rates pertinent to specific product categories or even producers. Foreign trade was carried out by monopolies formally separated from domestic firms which eliminated competition, protected domestic firms and undermined the processes that would normally stimulate greater efficiency.

While formally in place, tariffs had no economic effect on domestic prices and had, therefore, no allocative function. They were only used in international negotiations as a (weak) bargaining instrument. The allocation of imports was determined by plan targets and administrative decisions, which in effect constituted quantitative restrictions. Exports were also subject to strict administrative controls. Trade financing by credit was virtually non-existent as financial transactions were essentially used only to monitor the physical movements of goods and services. The decision-making of trading companies and domestic firms was subject to the demands of planners and government officials rather than to the dictum of profitability.

Appendix 13.2 Trade performance prior to 1990

An assessment of trade performance of TEs prior to 1990 is extremely difficult owing to serious problems of trade statistics (their coverage and valuation). According to most experts, however, growth rates of exports were generally extremely low. During the period of 1975–88, for example, the nominal growth of CPEs' exports only reflected the dollar inflation in world markets. According to the UN, the conversion of CPEs' exports in intra-regional trade into nominal dollars yielded the value of US $48.5 billion for 1975 and US $47.5 billion for 1988.[11] The much more reliable data for exports to developed countries based on 'mirror statistics' of the Western partners revealed that the CPEs' average annual nominal growth rate for the same period was 6.9 per cent. However, allowing for high dollar inflation during the 1970s and 1980s, even that real growth was negligible. The mire of foreign trade statistics in 'socialist' countries is also revealed by frequent revisions and by conflicting reports of different national institutions. For example, the 1988 total exports of the Soviet Union were reported by the UNECE in 1989 to be US $110.5 billion while the updated statistics published in 1992 slashed that figure right down to US $62.02 billion.[12]

The quality of statistics did not improve during 1990–93 when the data were affected by liberalization of foreign trade, and when the deep depreciation of exchange rates led to tax evasion, under-reported exports and imports and speculative commercial transactions. The poor growth of trade performance reflected the extremely low efficiency of their countries' economies (Hughes and Hare, 1992). The low economic efficiency resulted in persistent losses through the deterioration in the terms of trade with market economies and to a lesser extent in trade with the Soviet Union.

Appendix 13.3 The break-through in the views on trade reorientation and growth

Further supporting evidence for the success of trade reorientation in the TEs comes from studies assessing the adjustment process with the help of gravity models. The most prominent was the study of Hamilton and Winters (1992), who used the gravity model to predict trade volumes of TE under the assumption of liberalized international trade driven essentially by fundamental economic factors such as level of income, distance from markets, and diversification of production structure. Their hypothesis was that the Cold War and the central planning system deeply distorted the 'normal' flows of trade, and that liberalization of trade policy should lead to much higher trade levels at a given GDP than without the policy changes. Using a sample of 76 well-performing market economies, they estimated the model coefficients characterizing the pattern and intensity of such trade. Despite serious data problems,[13] their most important conclusions have withstood the scrutiny of time. They predicted a considerable expansion of trade even without any changes of output (GDP), and that the core countries of the EU-15 would become the main trading partners of the TEs after their liberalization. They also predicted significant shifts in the commodity structure of trade. As the level of education and skill levels of employees were comparable to those of the less developed West European countries, the trade creation would be in sectors producing goods embodying medium-level and, partially, high level technology.

These conclusions implied that the fall in the total trade of the TEs would be short-lived and that a boost of their trade volumes to 'normal' levels could be expected quite rapidly. They also implied that the specialization in exporting labour-intensive products would be short-lived. As the firms restructured, there would be a tendency to reallocate production to more capital (including human capital)-intensive industries. The gains from more trade with Western countries would more than compensate for the losses from less trade with the former socialist countries. The drive towards more trade in technologically more sophisticated products would be enhanced by intensive inflows of FDI.[14]

Ultimately, the success of trade reorientation was even more spectacular than what Hamilton and Winters (1992) predicted. Their predicted volumes of trade (adjusted for inflation) of the TEs with the EU-15 were reached in the majority of analysed countries during the first 10 years of transition. Some countries achieved it even faster: Hungary and Poland in 1995, Czech Republic and Slovakia in 1998 (which required boosting their exports to the EU-15 nearly six-fold in real terms relative to 1985!). The targets for the trade openness ratios relative to the world and EU-15 were achieved only somewhat later, approximately in the period 1997–2003, by which time the total exports of the TEs actually accelerated and doubled.

Russia, as well as some other countries of the former Soviet Union, fell behind the predicted trade volumes for much longer. Relying largely on exports of natural resources, Russia could not expand its exports at the rates akin to those for manufacturing exports of Central Europe. Russia's development is driven by domestic demand, and exports do not take the role of drivers of innovation and entrepreneurship, as became the rule in smaller TEs and in China.

Notes

1 The financial support from the Grant Agency of the Czech Republic no. P402/0982 to Vladimír Benáček is gratefully acknowledged.

2 CMEA (also called Comecon) was the economic integration bloc of eleven Communist countries under the hegemony of the Soviet Union.

3 The policy debate and the actual policies are discussed in Rosati (1997).

4 The importance of currency convertibility for the TEs is discussed in Flemming and Rollo (1992), in papers included in their Part I.

5 What role was played in the adjustment process by these organizations is not entirely clear. Membership was clearly essential even though the rules of these organizations may not always be conducive to adjustment. See Bown and McCulloch (2005). For more relevant discussion, see also Drabek (1995; 1996).

6 See *Measuring Globalization: OECD Economic Globalization Indicators*. Paris: OECD, 2010.

7 Carlin and Landesmann (1997) provided a systematic analysis of the conditions in TEs that strengthened the competitiveness of TEs in the sector of tradeables. For more recent evidence see Besedes (2011).

8 The role of exchange rate policy was particularly important. One of the critical issues was the question of stability of nominal exchange rates that accompanied appreciation in the real exchange rate. Much of the debate at the time was whether government should pursue a more flexible exchange rate policy. Halpern and Wyplosz (1997) argued that such appreciations should not be resisted because of their wider effects on efficiency and productivity.

9 The literature looking at the improvements in export competitiveness is fairly large and covers different methodologies ranging from changes in real effective exchange rates, net value added in world prices to kilogram prices. It generally supports the conclusion reported herein. See, for example, Landesmann and Stehrer (2002).

10 The rise of entrepreneurship and start-up firms is explained in Winiecki *et al.* (2004). For a discussion of determinants of export structure of TEs in the post-1989 period, see Hoekman and Djankov (1997) and Crespo-Cuaresma and Wörtz (2005).

11 Source: *Economic Bulletin for Europe*, UNECE, Geneva (44), 1992, p.132. In reality there was no reliable system of comparing the evolution of their mutual trade; 'convertible rubles' were actually not convertible internationally, trade statistics in nominal domestic currency were distorted by an unknown inflationary bias, and the value of barter lacked any informational content.

12 Compare *Economic Survey of Europe 1989–90*, UNECE, Geneva, Appendix Table C.4 with *Economic Bulletin for Europe*, UNECE, Geneva (44), 1992, p. 132.

13 As we have already noted, both GDP figures and exchange rates available to Hamilton and Winters were seriously distorted, which also distorted their estimated intensity of trade among the TEs. We have updated the 1985 data used by these authors by drawing on the latest reconstructed data at the UNECE in Geneva. We have found that the GDP data for TEs used by Hamilton and Winters were slightly overvalued, and that their real trade with market and developing economies was underestimated by about 15 per cent, and that the trade among TEs was overestimated by approximately 40 per cent. In brief, we presume with our revised estimations that the movement towards the potential (or 'normal') trade of TEs after liberalization would be somewhat less dramatic and that the intra-CMEA trade (among TEs) did not drop as sharply as Hamilton and Winters (1992) suggested.

14 See, for example, Damijan *et al.* (2003).

Bibliography

Babecka-Kucharcukova O., Babecky, J. and Raiser, M. (2010), *A Gravity Approach to Modelling International Trade in South-Eastern Europe and the Commonwealth of Independent States: The Role of Geography, Policy and Institutions*. Prague, Czech National Bank, Working Papers Series No. 4.

Besedes, T. (2011), 'Export Differentiation in Transition Economies', *Economic Systems,* vol. 35(1), pp. 25–44.

Bown, C.P. and McCulloch, R. (2005), *Facilitating Adjustment to Trade in the WTO System.* Brandeis University, mimeo.

Carlin, W. and Landesmann, M. (1997), 'From Theory into Practice? Restructuring and Dynamism in Transition Economies', *Oxford Review of Economic Policy,* vol. 13(2), pp. 77–105.

Crespo-Cuaresma, J. and Wörz, J. (2005), 'On Export Composition and Growth', *Review of World Economics,* vol. 141(1), pp. 33–49.

Damijan J., Knell, M., Majcen, B. and Rojec, M. (2003), 'The Role of FDI, R&D Accumulation and Trade in Transferring Technology to Transition Countries: Evidence from Firm Panel Data for Eight Transition Countries', *Economic Systems,* vol. 27, pp. 189–204.

Drabek, Z. (1995), 'IMF and IBRD Policies in the former Czechoslovakia', *Journal of Comparative Economics,* vol. 20, pp. 236–64.

——(1996), 'The Stability in Trade Policy in the Countries in Transition and Their Integration into the Multilateral Trading System', *The World Economy,* vol. 19(6), pp. 721–45.

Drabek, Z. and Bacchetta, M. (2004), 'Tracing the Effects of WTO Accession on Policy Making in Sovereign States', *World Economy,* vol. 27(7), pp. 1083–1125.

Drabek, Z., Janacek, K. and Tuma, Z. (1994), 'Inflation in Czechoslovakia 1985–91', *Journal of Comparative Economics,* vol. 18, pp. 146–74.

Drabek, Z. and Smith, A. (1995), *Trade Policy and Trade Policy in Central and Eastern Europe.* London: CEPR Discussion Papers, No. 1182.

Drabek, Z. and Brada, J. C. (1998), 'Exchange Rate Regimes and the Stability of Trade Policy in Transition Economies', *Journal of Comparative Economics,* vol. 26, pp. 642–68.

Dulleck, U., Foster, N., Stehrer, R. and Wörz, J. (2005), 'Dimensions of Quality Upgrading in CEECs', *Economics of Transition,* vol. 13 (1), pp. 51–76.

Falcetti, E., Raiser, M. and Sanfey, P. (2000), *Defying the odds: initial conditions, reforms and growth in the first decade of transition.* London: EBRD Working Paper, No. 55.

Fidrmuc, J. (2001), 'Intra-industry Trade Between the EU and the CEECs – The Evidence of the First Decade of Transition', *Focus on Transition,* no. 1, pp. 65–78, Vienna: Austrian National Bank.

Fidrmuc, J. (2002), *Migration and Regional Adjustment to Asymmetric Shocks in Transition Economies.* William Davidson Working Paper, No. 441.

Fischer, S. and Sahay, R. (2000), *The Transition Economies after Ten Years.* IMF Working Paper WP/00/30.

Fleming, J. and Rollo, J.M.C. (eds) (1992), *Payments and Adjustment in Eastern Europe.* London: Royal Institute of International Affairs and EBRD.

Halpern, L., Koren, M. and Szeidl, A. (2011), 'Imports and Productivity', *American Economic Review*, forthcoming. Also published in London, CEPR, DP No. 5139.

Halpern, L. and Wyplosz, C. (1997), 'Equilibrium Exchange Rates in Transition Economies', *IMF Staff Papers*, vol. 44(4), pp. 430–61.

Hamilton, C. and Winters, A. (1992), 'Opening up Trade in Eastern Europe', *Economic Policy*, no. 14, pp. 78–116.

Havranek, T. and Irsova, Z. (2011), 'Estimating Vertical Spillovers from FDI: Why Results Vary and What the True Effect Is', *Journal of International Economics*, vol. 85 (2), pp. 234–44.

Hoekman, B. and Djankov, S. (1997), 'Determinants of the Export Structure of Countries in Central and Eastern Europe.', *World Bank Economic Review*, vol. 11 (3), pp. 471–87.

Hughes, G. and Hare, P. (1992), 'Trade Policy and Restructuring in Eastern Europe', in Fleming, J. and Rollo, J.M.C. (eds), *Payments and Adjustment in Eastern Europe*. London: Royal Institute of International Affairs and EBRD, Chapter 9.

Javorcik, B. (2004), 'Does Foreign Direct Investment Increase Productivity of Domestic Firms: In Search of Spillovers from Backward Linkages', *American Economic Review*, vol. 94 (3), pp. 605–27.

Jurajda, S. and Terrell, K. (2002), *What Drives the Speed of Job Reallocation During Episodes of Massive Adjustment?* William Davidson Institute, WP 432.

Kaminski, B. (1999), *The EU Factor in Trade Policies of Central European Countries*. Washington, DC: World Bank Policy Research Working Paper, November.

Landesmann, M., and Stehrer, R. (2002), 'Evolving Competitiveness of CEECs in an Enlarged Europe', *Rivista di Economia Politica*, vol. 92(1), pp. 23–87.

Lankes, H.-P. and Venables, A. J. (1997), 'Foreign Direct Investment in Eastern Europe and the Former Soviet Union: Results from a Survey of Investor', in Zecchini S. (ed.), *Lesson from the Economic Transition*. London: Kluwer Academic Press and OECD, pp. 555–65.

Michalopoulos, C. (2000), 'WTO Accession for Transition Economies. Problems and Prospects', *Russian and East European Finance and Trade*, vol. 36 (2), pp. 63–86.

Rosati, D. (1997), 'Exchange Rate Policies in Post-Communist Economies', in Zecchini S. (ed.), *Lesson from the Economic Transition*. London: Kluwer Academic Press and OECD, pp. 481–502.

Winiecki, J. (2002), *Transition Economies and Foreign Trade*, London: Routledge

Winiecki, J., Benáček, V. and Laki, M. (2004), *The Private Sector after Communism. New Entrepreneurial Firms in Transition Economies*. New York: Routledge.

Zecchini S. (ed.) (1997), *Lesson from the Economic Transition*. London: Kluwer Academic Press and OECD.

14

THE EXCHANGE RATE AND FOREIGN DIRECT INVESTMENT

Two paths to globalization

Josef C. Brada

Introduction

A major objective of the transition economies was to put their external economic relations on a new footing by replacing central planning and trade agreements with other communist countries with market forces to determine trade flows. Doing so required creating a functioning exchange rate, one that translated foreign prices into domestic ones, allowing domestic consumers to purchase from abroad what could be had more cheaply on the world market and producers to export what they could profitably sell on world markets.

Also absent in the pre-transition economies was the multinational corporation (MNC), whose role in transferring capital, technologies, skills and products to all corners of the globe had grown rapidly in the post-Second World War period. If the transition was to integrate the countries of the former Soviet Bloc into the global economy, establishing a functioning exchange rate and finding ways for MNCs to play a constructive role in the transition were critical.

The exchange rate

Early steps to create an exchange rate regime

The currencies of the communist countries were inconvertible; despite various efforts at reform, they could not be freely converted into other currencies, nor was it possible to purchase goods with them in the domestic economy without the consent of the planners. Moreover, the exchange rate did not play its fundamental role of translating foreign prices into domestic prices. Rather, imported goods were sold on the domestic market at prices set by planners that did not reflect the prices of these goods on the world market. Similarly, producers of exports received arbitrary domestic prices for their products regardless of what these exports sold for on world markets.

In the Central European countries, eliminating the trade apparatus that had existed during the communist regime so that all firms could freely engage in international trade, and reorienting their trade away from an excessive dependence on trade with other socialist countries, became an important early priority, along with price liberalization and stabilization. In the case of the former Soviet states, there was an initial effort to maintain old trade ties with other Soviet Republics through the creation of a rouble sphere, but this proved unworkable.

Trade was to be determined by the forces of supply of exports and demand for imports, and these forces had to be mediated by a functional exchange rate, something that had not existed in the planned era. The problem facing the reformers was what sort of exchange rate regime to adopt and how to set the exchange rate. While the problem of choosing an exchange rate could be left to the market if a country adopted a freely floating exchange rate, some transition countries were reluctant to adopt such a regime because they believed that, owing to economic and political uncertainty, the exchange rate would be too low and too volatile, hampering trade and investment. Moreover, a floating exchange rate could not serve as a nominal anchor to promote domestic anti-inflation policies.

A number of East European countries adopted exchange-rate pegs. Since there had been no functioning exchange rate in the past, the rate at which to peg was controversial. Purchasing power parity suggests that an exchange rate that equalizes the price of a bundle of tradeable goods valued in domestic prices and in the domestic currency to the price of the same bundle of goods priced at foreign prices and in a foreign currency is a good approximation of a sustainable rate. However, domestic prices in the transition economies were badly distorted by various subsides, the quality of goods was not comparable to goods available in market economies, there was a large monetary overhang and pent up consumer demand that threatened massive domestic inflation, and some of the transition economies were deeply indebted, so they needed trade surpluses rather than balanced trade. Some observers recommended adopting the black market rate of exchange as a better benchmark, although the nature of that market implied a serious undervaluation of the currency.

In the event, East European peggers set exchange rates that significantly undervalued their currencies, with convertibility for the current but not the capital account (Czechoslovakia being an exception, with early capital account liberalization). This excessive undervaluation was seen as useful in that it would both restrain imports of consumer goods to satisfy household demand and enable socialist-era firms to redirect their exports to the West and to improve their products and technologies in order to become more competitive on world markets. A cost of this was that imports of consumer goods and intermediate products such as fuels, components and machinery rose sharply, raising the level of retail prices and the operating costs of firms, thus providing an additional inflationary impetus to the economy. Combined with the high levels of inflation set off by domestic price liberalization, this led to an instantaneous and sustained real appreciation of the peggers' currencies, which continued for some years as inflation in these countries remained high.

Hungary and Poland adopted crawling pegs to accommodate their high levels of inflation, Czechoslovakia a deeply depreciated peg to the DM and US$. By the mid-1990s, as inflation declined, these countries expanded the band around the fixed or crawling rate to give market forces a greater role in setting the exchange rate. The Czech Republic faced a currency crisis in 1997 that forced it to float the koruna, and the Russian crisis of 1998 put pressure on the zloty and forint as well. While the pegged exchange rate functioned as a nominal anchor to give credibility to anti-inflation policies, tight monetary policy led to high interest rates and large capital inflows that had to be sterilized.

The Baltic states faced the additional problem of eliminating the Soviet rouble from circulation and introducing their own currencies. Once this was accomplished, they pegged their currencies, Estonia and Lithuania through currency board regimes, and these arrangements survived the rouble crisis of 1998. Bulgaria was noteworthy for switching from a floating exchange rate to a currency board arrangement in 1997 to give credibility to its hitherto unsuccessful stabilization efforts.

Most of the CIS countries adopted a managed float with heavy government control, including requirements that exporters sell their foreign currency earnings to the central bank. Russia experienced a crisis in 1998 when the government was unable to borrow sufficient funds to service its debt and finance its operations. The rouble was driven out of its trading band, floated and declined in value from about 5–6 roubles/US\$ to as much as 30 roubles/US\$. While other countries that have floated their currencies have not experienced crises of similar magnitude, the Russian experience does suggest that the lack of an nominal exchange rate anchor to prop up anti-inflation policies contributed to the persistence of inflation. In some countries with flexible rates the sustained depreciation of the currency has led to dollarization or Euroization of the economy and to capital flight as residents seek a more stable repository for their liquid assets.

The exchange rate and EU accession

Transition economies that join the EU will have to adopt the Euro as their currency at some point in the future, and to do so they have to meet numerical targets, *inter alia*, for inflation, the interest rate and exchange rate stability. Thus the nexus between inflation and the exchange rate will become more critical for these countries. As the transition economies grow more rapidly than the 'old' EU members, they have higher inflation due to the Balassa–Samuelson effect, which posits that higher income countries have higher price levels and that real convergence must therefore lead to price convergence and thus to higher inflation rates in the countries that are catching up. This creates an advantage for countries that have chosen to float their currencies because they can offset part of domestic inflation through the appreciation of their currencies. For example, Horváth and Koprnická (2008) estimate that, for the Czech Republic, a 5 per cent appreciation of the koruna reduces inflation by 1 per cent. The Czech Republic, Slovakia and Romania have experienced both real and nominal appreciation post-accession, but Hungary and Poland have experienced nominal depreciation, possibly the result of poor macroeconomic policies that exacerbated their inflation rates.

If the Maastricht criteria are met, then the country must spend two years in the European Exchange Rate Mechanism (ERM2) regime before it can adopt the Euro. During that time, the country is required to keep its currency from fluctuating no more than 15 per cent against the Euro, with intervention mandatory at the limits of the band; not to devalue its currency against any EU member; and to eschew the use of currency controls. Countries are free to assume more stringent obligations if they wish. If a country does not meet the Maastricht criteria, then it has greater latitude in its exchange rate regime outside the framework of ERM2, thus enabling it to deal with domestic and external shocks by means of both macroeconomic policies and changes to its exchange rate.

Three transition countries have already met the Maastricht criteria and successfully completed two years in ERM2, enabling them to adopt the Euro as their currency: Slovenia in 2007, the Slovak Republic in 2009 and Estonia in 2011. Latvia and Lithuania are currently in ERM2 and thus may be able to adopt the Euro in the near future. The other new members of the EU have not as yet become part of ERM2. In some cases, this is because they do not yet meet the Maastricht criteria and because they still need to catch up with the EU levels of per capita GDP, a process that will continue to keep inflation rates high. Poland and the Czech Republic appear reluctant to make concrete commitments to Euro adoption, and other countries such as Bulgaria and Hungary do not meet the Maastricht criteria.

The global crisis of 2008 and the subsequent debt crises within the eurozone have negatively impacted transition economies' progress toward Euro adoption in several ways. First, the global recession has worsened government finances, making it harder to meet the Maastricht criteria relating to the government deficit. Second, policy makers and the populations of the transition economies view the eurozone much less favourably than they did before the crisis hit, and, third, policy makers now see some value in retaining an independent monetary policy and exchange rate flexibility to cushion external shocks to their economies.

Foreign direct investment

Introduction

Foreign direct investment (FDI) means investments in foreign countries that enable home-country investors to acquire control over productive assets in the host countries. Such investments, which have given rise to the multinational corporation (MNC), take two forms. One is the so-called greenfield investment, where the foreign investor builds a completely new factory or other productive facility in the host country. The other way of undertaking FDI is through a merger or acquisition (M&A), where the foreign firm purchases a controlling interest in an existing firm in the host country. FDI has been a major engine of globalization in the post-Second World War period, growing much faster than global output and international trade, and it has extended the reach of some MNCs to virtually all countries. The attractiveness of FDI for MNCs is two-fold. On the one hand, it enables the MNC to benefit from firm-specific advantages in new markets without transferring those advantages to potential rivals, and, on the other hand, it enables the MNC to break up its production process so that different components are produced in countries where it is cheapest to do so, while retaining a measure of control and coordination over the production process that would not be possible through subcontracting or international trade alone.

The communist countries missed out entirely on this development. This was partly due to ideology; the presence of privately owned capital meant the exploitation of labour, which they could not allow. Moreover, foreign control over domestic economic activity was inconsistent with central planning. True, the Soviet Union had briefly experimented with 'concessions' to foreign firms for the development of natural resources in the 1920s, and, starting with Yugoslavia in 1967, East European countries passed legislation allowing joint ventures between state-owned enterprises and Western firms, but these few experiments were more curiosities than effective means of globalizing the communist economies. As a result, the countries of East Europe and the former USSR began the transition without the presence of inward FDI or multinational firms. This section reviews the volume and pattern of FDI inflows into the transition economies and then examines the contribution that FDI made in three areas: privatization, capital accumulation and economic performance.

The volume and distribution of FDI in transition economies

Investment in the transition economies was attractive to MNCs for a number of reasons. On the one hand, the region represented a potentially large and untapped market. Consumers in the region had suffered from poor quality, lack of variety, obsolescence and shortages of consumer goods. Even through incomes in the region were low, the potential was great. Other MNCs were interested in the region as a place where they could locate production facilities that would capitalize on the region's proximity to the EU market and on the presence of skilled workers who were paid a fraction of the wages paid to workers in Western Europe. In addition there were opportunities for investment in franchise sectors such as telecommunications and banking, and, in some countries, in the exploitation of natural resources.

Investment flowed first and in greatest amounts to the countries of Eastern Europe, because of their more successful efforts at both political and economic transition, because they had more attractive industrial assets to offer foreign investors, because they offered relatively large domestic markets with higher incomes than did the transition economies farther to the East and because they were close to EU markets and thus their products could be more easily integrated into MNCs' supply chains. Table 14.1 shows the magnitude of the inflows both in absolute amounts and, to put them in perspective, in relationship to their GDPs. Those transition economies that have joined the EU have clearly received massive inflows of FDI, so that their stock of FDI relative to GDP is higher than the EU average of 42 per cent despite the fact that the old EU members have been receiving FDI for many more years. The countries of

Table 14.1 Inward FDI of transition economies

Country	Stock of inward FDI in 2010 (mill US$)	Stock of inward FDI as % of GDP in 2010
EU members		
Bulgaria	47,971	100.2
Czech Republic	129,893	67.6
Estonia	16,438	85.6
Hungary	91,933	71.0
Latvia	10,838	45.2
Lithuania	13,449	37.1
Poland	193,141	41.2
Romania	70,012	43.9
Slovakia	50,678	58.1
Slovenia	15,022	31.5
South-east Europe		52.0
Albania	4,355	36.7
Bosnia and Herzegovina	7,152	42.5
Croatia	34,374	56.8
Montenegro	5,456	138.2
Serbia	20,584	46.5
Macedonia	4,493	48.0
CIS		31.4
Armenia	4,206	44.7
Azerbaijan	9,593	17.6
Belarus	9,940	18.3
Georgia	7,821	67.1
Kazakhstan	81,352	61.1
Kyrgyzstan	974	21.6
Moldova, Republic of	2,837	49.2
Russian Federation	423,150	28.7
Tajikistan	915	16.2
Turkmenistan	8,186	40.7
Ukraine	57,985	42.5
Uzbekistan	4,460	11.7

Source: UNCTAD, FDI/TNC database (www.unctad.org/fdistatistics).

south-east Europe have fared less well, in part due to regional instabilities, to their distance from the EU market and the relatively small size of their domestic markets.

The CIS countries present a more diversified picture. Some, such as Georgia or Kazakhstan, have benefited from major investments in oil and natural resource exploitation and the construction of oil and natural gas pipelines. Other countries, lacking resources or controlled by elites who wish to keep foreign investors out, have received only minor inflows of FDI. Nevertheless, in 2000–09 only the emerging countries of Asia saw greater inflows of FDI.

FDI and privatization

At the start of transition, many countries looked to foreign investors to purchase state-owned firms and to restructure them, in the process raising money for the state. Hungary was the most aggressive in seeking out 'strategic investors' who would purchase state-owned enterprises (SOEs), upgrade their technologies, restructure their operations and turn them into viable businesses, and as a result, was an early leader in FDI inflows. Most privatization programmes allowed for the participation of foreign investors in some way, but FDI inflows were slowed by economic nationalism, with concerns that valuable assets were being sold to foreigners at excessively low prices or that land and natural resources should not be sold to foreigners and by debates over whether SOEs should be restructured to make them more attractive to buyers and thus fetch a higher price or sold on an 'as is' basis. Privatizations that left insiders, either former managers or workers, in control of privatized firms tended to limit possibilities for foreign investors to purchase newly privatized firms from local owners. Many countries created Ministries or special units to sell off SOEs to foreign investors, the most prominent of them being the German Treuhand, charged with selling off the SOEs of the former East Germany.

Among the more noteworthy of the early acquisitions were General Electric's purchase of the Hungarian light bulb manufacturer Tungsram and Volkswagen's purchase of the Czech car maker Skoda. Despite many successful acquisitions, there were also conflicts between foreign investors and the host country when foreign investors shut down local research facilities, reduced production and employment, scaled back product lines, or failed to make promised investments in the firms they had acquired. The number of SOEs that were attractive to foreign investors was also limited, and thus mergers and acquisitions as a form of privatization declined in importance through the 1990s.

M&A activity was particularly important in the telecommunications and banking sectors. In the case of telecommunications, the communist-era national telecom monopolies were sold off to foreign telecommunications firms, usually in a bidding process organized by the home-country government. Improvements in the telecommunications infrastructure were seen as critical for economic restructuring, and the existing networks were outdated and inadequate in coverage. These multi-billion dollar transactions were particularly complex because the buyers had to commit to large investments in upgrading the network while the governments had to make promises about the future regulatory environment, tariffs and the introduction of competition from new entrants.

Commercial banks emerged in the transition economies from the breakup of the communist-era State Banks. As a result, the new commercial banks also inherited the debts that SOEs had owed to the State Bank, and many of these loans became non-performing as the transition recession deepened. Governments were concerned that the state-owned banks needed injections of capital as well as of expertise in evaluating and making loans, so that they would not continue to finance loss-making firms. Foreign banks, while realizing the potential of the transition economy market, were concerned about the quality of the assets that their acquisition targets held, and in many cases governments had to expend significant sums to clean up the banks' balance sheets before they could be sold to foreign investors. Nevertheless, in the EU member transition economies, foreign-owned banks, especially those owned by banks from Austria, Germany, Italy and France (and Sweden in the Baltic states) dominate the banking sector, holding no less than two-thirds of all banking assets, and in many cases more (Slovenia is an exception). Much the same pattern holds for Southeast Europe, but, in the CIS, the role of foreign banks in the privatization of the banking sector was much less.

FDI and capital formation

Because FDI takes two forms, M&A and greenfield investments, its contribution to capital formation is difficult to judge. If foreigners acquire an existing local firm by, say, buying it from the government through privatization, no increase in the country's capital stock takes place. In the case of greenfield investments, the foreign investor does build a new facility, and thus the country's stock of productive capital increases by the amount of greenfield FDI.

The overall ratio of FDI to fixed capital formation in the transition economies has varied widely over time, but for those transition countries that have joined the EU, the ratio in many years has been in excess of 30 per cent and at times even higher; for south-east European countries, it has rarely exceeded 20 per cent per year and for the CIS countries it has come to exceed 10 per cent only since 2003. At the same time, as privatization has run its course in these countries, investment has increasingly taken the form of greenfield investment, thus affecting capital formation more directly. In CIS countries that are rich in energy and natural resources, foreign investments have been largely for energy exploration, development and transportation, with much less interest in industrial projects. Most of the transition economies invest more than they save, and thus FDI has been an important source of financing to close this gap and an important contributor to their efforts to catch up to living standards in more advanced countries.

FDI and economic performance

FDI has important effects on economic performance, and evidence of this can be seen in the transition economies. FDI has both a direct and an indirect effect on capital formation. The direct effect is the greenfield (and to a lesser extent M&A) FDI itself, and the indirect effect is the impact of FDI on the volume of domestic investment, known as crowding-in and crowding-out. Crowding-in is the result of domestic investments that are induced by FDI inflows. Such induced investment can be infrastructure investments or capacity expansion by domestic businesses who supply parts, components or business services to the foreign investor or who use or distribute its output. Crowding-out results when the foreign investor pre-empts business opportunities that might have been seized by domestic firms or when the foreign investor competes directly with domestic firms, reducing their profit and market share and thus driving down their willingness and ability to invest. The magnitude of these two effects, of course, depends to some extent on the nature of the investments coming into the country and on the ability of domestic firms to respond to both opportunities and threats. Mileva (2008) finds that, in the transition economies, the crowding-in effect is quite significant, with US $1 of FDI inducing US $1 of domestic investment. Moreover, studies of the crowding-out effect (Mišun and Tomšík, 2002; Mileva, 2008) find it to be non-existent or negligible in these economies.

Foreign investors are also expected to bring with them skills, new technology and products, and connections to global markets. This should make foreign-owned firms more productive, thus raising the overall productivity of the economy. Early studies of foreign-owned firms, mainly in the East European transition economies, found them to be more profitable, more export oriented and faster growing than domestically owned firms. Later studies confirmed that this was not just the result of foreign investors purchasing only the best-performing firms available in the privatization process but rather of the advantages conferred by foreign owners on their affiliates. FDI also produces productivity spillovers to domestic firms. Suppliers of inputs to the foreign firm as well as users of the firm's products experience productivity gains; the former from the need to upgrade their products to meet the MNCs higher standards, the latter from the availability of higher quality inputs supplied by the foreign-owned firm. Additional productivity gains occur from the knowledge that the MNC brings which is diffused in various ways, such as the hiring of its workers and managers by local firms or by the imitation of its better business practices.

Finally, foreign investments can promote structural change, creating or restructuring entire sectors of the economy. Perhaps the most striking example of this effect is in the motor vehicles sector. Although a number of East European countries had indigenous car manufacturing capacity prior to the transition, this was badly outdated and had little chance of surviving in a global market; other transition economies had no such capacity. Investments by car makers from both Europe and Asia have made automobiles and automobile parts the leading export category from most of the Central European countries. In the Czech Republic, this occurred through Volkswagen's acquisition and complete revamping of Skoda, but other countries such as Hungary and Slovakia, which started with little or no car manufacturing capacity, also benefited greatly in terms of exports and jobs from foreign investments in the automotive sector.

Conclusion

While the transition economies are now globalized to different degrees, with some being highly integrated into the global economy and others less so, the differences appear to be much more due to their level of economic development, endowments of natural resources, location and domestic policies and politics than to the specifics of either what exchange rate regime to choose or how to allow for inflows of foreign direct investment. In the case of the exchange rate, countries with fixed exchange rates have borne higher costs due to the need to sterilize capital inflows and to use fiscal policy to offset external shocks, suggesting that once inflation was tamed and the national currency's credibility was established, floating the currency may have been a preferable policy.

In the case of foreign direct investment, differences in national strategies toward privatization did result in some differences in the volume of FDI at the beginning of the transition process, but over time, fundamentals, including location, market size and overall business climate have come to the fore in determining each country's ability to attract foreign investors. Especially for the Central European countries, FDI has been a major force for their integration into the global economy and their convergence to the living standards that prevail in more developed EU member countries.

Bibliography

Estrin, S., Hanousek, J., Kočenda, E. and Svejnar, J. (2009), 'Effects of privatization and ownership in transition economies', *Journal of Economic Literature*, vol. 47(3), pp. 699–728.

Hanousek, J., Kočenda, E. and Maurel, M. (2011), 'Direct and indirect effects of FDI in emerging European markets: A survey and meta-analysis,' *Economic Systems*, vol.35(3), pp. 301–22.

Hanousek, J., Kočenda, E. and Svejnar, J. (2007), 'Corporate ownership, control and performance after mass privatization', *Economics of Transition*, vol. 15(1), pp. 1–31.

Horváth, R. and Koprnická, K. (2008) 'Inflation Differentials in New EU Member States: Empirical Evidence', *Czech Journal of Economics and Finance*, vol. 58(7–8), pp. 318–328.

Mileva, E. (2008), 'The Impact of Capital Flows on Domestic Investment in Transition Economies', *European Central Bank Working Paper* 871, Frankfurt.

Mišun, J. and Tomšík, V. (2002), 'Does Foreign Direct Investment Crowd In or Crowd Out Domestic Investment?' *Eastern European Economics*, vol. 40(2), pp. 38–56.

15

ENLARGEMENT OF THE EUROPEAN UNION

László Csaba

Introduction

The European project has been, from the very outset, *deeply political*. The idea of eternal appeasement, rooted in the experiences of the three devastating wars of the 1870–1945 period, has paved the way to an idealist–constructivist rethinking of the dismal experiences with the *Realpolitik* of the entire post-Westphalian period, starting with the peace treaty concluding the Thirty Years War in 1648. The founding fathers of the European project, Adenauer, Schuman and de Gasperi, were deeply convinced of the need to rebuild Europe from scratch. This reconstruction was meant to be material, ideational, institutional and policy level, so that it would affect the everyday lives of citizens, and would result in peace and prosperity on the old continent. For subsequent generations, including that of Helmut Kohl, François Mitterand and Jacques Delors, i.e. until the 1990s, this emotional and political commitment dominated other, including economic considerations (Delors, 2004).

The European project as a moving target

European integration could never have become a reality without two *external conditions*. One was uncontested Soviet/Russian military hegemony, especially in terms of ground troops and traditional weapons, lasting at least until 1990. This made the joining of forces imperative for the political class of the non-Sovietized part of Europe. And similarly, the emergence of the cold war, the antagonism of the two military blocs, NATO and the Warsaw Pact, created incentives for implementing European integration in more than one area. The second factor was thus the USA. It has been, from the very outset, a silent but indispensable third party to the interaction of Europeans. Providing a strategic umbrella over a militarily inferior and factional community of democratic states was thus vital. However, so was ideological support for Europeans joining forces and 'taking care of their own business'. Both have long been instrumental in pushing the often lukewarm, nationalist and hesitating European leaders towards more rather than less co-operation in a number of areas.

The European project started with the European Defence Initiative of 1950, quickly voted down by both the French and German legislatures. Ever since this first debacle, the *modus operandi* of European integration has been *incrementalism and partial solutions*, rendering the usual yardstick in social sciences, coherence, irrelevant for each and every area and at all times. Meanwhile, the original objective of creating a federal state – commonly dubbed as *finalité politique* – has been pushed back to a remote historical perspective. As a consequence, both the unfinished nature and the internal contradictions, as well as the ensuing *constant compromises and crises*, are among the fundamental features defining what the EU is all about. Therefore the move towards an 'ever-closer Union', as well as the constant enlargement of the club with more and more new members, both count among the factors defining how the European project is being implemented on the ground.

The move from the European Coal and Steel Community (1951) to the Common Agricultural Policy (1957), common market – first only in industrial goods (1970) – and common external tariffs, common external trade policy (1975) and single market (1986), single currency and early proposals about political union (1992), all constitute milestones on a bumpy, but clear road towards a constitutionally limited central power.[1] While the EU has never intended to be a state *strictu senso* – as it does not possess either a monopoly over the use of force or a monopoly right to impose taxes – it is clearly more than a free market or even a mere commonwealth of fully independent states. Supranational arrangements, especially those such as the European Court of Justice (ECJ) and the European Central Bank (ECB), but in part also the directly elected European Parliament with its prerogatives to co-decide over a number of vital issues, constitute a *halfway-house solution between a federation and a club*. The supranational organs may decide, without the consent of member-state legislatures, on concrete issues. European law, in a number of areas, is directly enforceable within the nation states. In theory, European law enjoys pre-eminence over national legislation, while in practice, the transposition of European stipulations into national rules is often a complex and controversial process.

Being concerned with enlargement, we omit any discussion of how and why the European Economic Community (EEC) has been deepening, why and how it has extended the competences of common policies over more and more areas, as listed above, and why it has transformed itself into a political, economic, legal union and adopted joint arrangements on such policy areas, which were traditionally seen as the heart of national sovereignty.[2] If we merely list monetary policy, centralized in the hands of an ECB, not directly responsible to any of the national legislatures, or common foreign and security policy, justice and home affairs, or the imposition of the rulings of the supranational European Court of Justice, overruling on occasion major economic and policy decisions of national elected governments, we can get the picture.

In this context, the gradual but steady *expansion of Community competences,* both by the individual area of activity, and by including new members, is the name of the game. This is not something that is in need of explanation, quite the contrary. It has been felt, from the very outset, that the six nations setting up the EEC in 1957 were just the vanguard, not the entirety of Europe. With reference to the then recent uprisings in Hungary and Poland, the Treaty of Rome, adopted in 1957, explicitly stated that the EEC was '*open to all European democracies*'.

This has proven to be a truly strategic statement. First and foremost, it reflected the deep conviction that the division of Europe into democratic and Communist halves was unsustainable in the historic perspective. It provided hope and orientation for generations, for a brighter future and for the possibility to change that which, at times, was portrayed and perceived as eternal, namely the Soviet conquest of Central and Eastern Europe. However, equally importantly, *it provided an anchor for democratization in the South of Europe.* It helped Turkey to move away from military rule, through the first Europe Agreement in 1963, that offered the promise of eventual full membership, albeit in the possibly rather distant – and unspecified – future. It helped Greece to restore democracy and stabilize a restive population via the fast-track entry of Greece to the EC in 1981. It also assisted and even anchored the democratization processes in

Spain and Portugal, two countries with limited democratic credentials and relatively closed economies in the pre-1986 decades.

However, the most formative – and indeed *transformative* – *enlargements have been those to the north*. Taking Britain on board from 1 January 1973 – together with Ireland and Denmark – has truly changed the nature of the entire European project. It is unsurprising that the founding members – and France in particular – would have been reluctant to allow the UK to join the European project. If for no other reason, Great Britain, a former imperial power and an island state, never having been enthusiastic about the federalist project on the continent, is itself a bulwark against turning Brussels into a super-state, now or at any time in the future. *Incorporating Britain has made the Community project truly European,* by neutralizing EFTA and other, in theory, competing structures. Letting the British in has lent additional weight – financial, military and political – to the Community. However, it has also *watered down the ambitious original project*. It warranted a go-slow strategy, lack of idealism and enhanced materialist–pragmatist approaches for decades to come, until the collapse of Communism led to changed hearts – at least for some time.

The second, and no less transformative enlargement, has also been to the north, i.e. by the accession of *three neutral countries, Austria, Finland and Sweden in 1995*. On the surface, it looked quite easy. All three countries were in good shape, enjoyed high productivity levels, were rich welfare states and, by the same token, net contributors to Community coffers. No ethnic divisions, no conflicts with neighbours, no threats to their respective democracies by extremist forces or an authoritarian past. However, in reality these countries *formed a new core,* a hard nut to crack. These countries have never been emotionally committed to the idea that combining armed or other forces might be a good thing in its own right. On the contrary, they tended to ask for the palpable material additional benefits any joint project may or may not deliver.

As a result the new members of 1995 tended to be quite sceptical towards the evolving project on political union, and especially of developing the European Security and Defence Policy. They were critical about the efficiency of major spending areas, like farming and infrastructure. They were uncomfortable about the lack of transparency that featured in community decisions reached in Brussels in most areas. These nations also distrusted the various 'grand bargains' struck among the big countries, especially over military involvement, or setting major expenditure priorities for the financial guidelines. In other words, they *strengthened the intergovernmentalist trend* in EU affairs, emphasized the materialistic and de-emphasized the idealistic elements. Besides*, new priority areas,* such as gender equity, environmental protection, social standards and research and development were put on the agenda.

Eastward enlargement – too early or too late?

When the Soviet Empire collapsed in 1989/91, this dramatic historic turn took most analysts and policy-makers by surprise. What mattered from our perspective was the fact, that *the EC was completely absorbed in its own internal affairs: in implementing the single market project of 1986 and preparing itself for the monetary union/EMU,* to be launched from 1992. Therefore the historic earthquake, rendering *inter alia* the reunification of Germany a reality by October 1990, was met with scepticism and resentment. 'Digestion' of the previous southern enlargement was still far from complete.

'Deepening first, widening next' was the basic maxim of decision-makers. Also, most of them became quite fearful, having experienced southern enlargement, about taking on board more poor countries. With only 30–50 per cent of the per capita GDP of the EU-12, combined with assertive nationalist economic platforms, *eastward enlargement to bring in the new democracies was perceived as a real threat to the EU.* The would-be candidates, calling for generous measures of redistribution, or threatening to send millions of migrants to the wealthy core EU, were not really welcome. The Nordic enlargement by three rich countries with no great power aspirations – and an associated reluctance to spend on strategic grounds – had only exacerbated the situation. The debates over the need to cap Community expenditures at a very low fraction of Community GDP (no more than about 1.25 per cent) had a major influence on budgetary outcomes for the entire 1991–2011 period.

It is perhaps unsurprising, that not only did deepening – EMU and the political union envisaged by the Maastricht Treaty – take precedence, but also the seemingly smooth Nordic enlargement did so as well.[3] While the latter required the pronounced Russian interest in keeping the neutrality and non-alignment of those three countries to be disregarded, taking on board the poor and unstable Eastern economies, ruined by decades of Communism, seemed a lunatic idea for the Community of the 1990s, by then driven more by interest than by the initial idealism. To be fair, enthusiasm for democratic and market transitions did in due course create a major strategic impetus leading to the eventual enlargement. While the Commission itself tended to be pro-active ever since the 1989 launch of the PHARE assistance programme, member-states, who have the final say, were less enthusiastic. Fears of mass migration and inflated transfer claims, as well as caution against what seemed the extension of the German sphere of influence at the expense of French and British interests, have slowed down the process (as is nicely documented in Winters, 1994).

Judging by the fact that the journey lasted 15 years and in the case of Romania and Bulgaria 17 years, it must have been an arduous trip. Indeed, this process had a number of layers (cf. Balázs, 2002). At square one, we find the success of West European integration in the 1951–91 period, providing a decisive challenge to the *outright and visible economic failure* and eventual dissolution *of its alternative,* the eastern integration bloc of countries, CMEA. Second, the abolition of Soviet tutelage across the region did open up some geopolitical room for manoeuvre, as would be needed for a major change of trade and political orientation. Against this background – and especially observing the re-emergence of Russia asserting claims for privileged partnership with its 'Near Abroad' ever since 1993 – *the integration of the former socialist countries with the EU was alarmingly slow.* Third, it took about four years for the EU even to spell out the criteria for accession, in the June 1993 Copenhagen Council. It took a further six years until the Berlin Council of March, 1999, for the financial framework for the eventual and gradual eastward enlargement to be created, in the shadow of the 'humanitarian intervention' in the former Yugoslavia.[4]

But judging by other criteria, however, enlargement might still be seen as premature. Adopting new institutions, whether an independent judiciary, or a competition agency, has often remained formal and rudimentary. Harmony between home-grown solutions and the joint accomplishments, i.e. rules and regulations enshrined in the 100-thousand pages of the *acquis communautaire,* has been less than perfect. This is understandable if for no other reason than that the Union rules were devised by and for more advanced economies, where transition-related issues were simply non-existent. To give just one example, creating contestable markets has not been regarded as a government job in the old EU countries, it is mostly a given. By contrast, wholesale privatization in Central and Eastern Europe was an opportunity to create competition and de-monopolize production in the former Socialist economies. Failing to do so inevitably created efficiency losses.[5]

Likewise, copying social standards – e.g. early retirements, disability compensation, wage legislation – typical of the old EU countries translated into lastingly high unemployment and low labour market activity levels, with an extended presence of the informal economy as a lasting phenomenon. True, the extension of the universalist welfare state had been a product of the late socialist period (Berend, 2009). Later it was trimmed back rather than revoked during two decades of transition. Still, this relatively generous welfare state was premature (Kornai, 1992) and bore no relation to the productivity levels actually achieved by those economies.

It is natural to ask whether there is anything for which the EU might/should be 'blamed'? The answer is non-trivial, for more than one reason. First, during the 1990s, there was a tendency on the part of local élites to do whatever they could to show themselves as 'good Europeans', implying a degree of over-zealousness to adopt EU arrangements locally. Second, EU officials often tended to be patronizing and required compliance with the pettiest detail of their 'rules of the game'. Third, during the association and later accession negotiations, EU partners did have a trump card of not accepting local suggestions, ranging from conditions in detention centres to such trivialities as the regulations on tea boilers.[6] Fourth, especially in the phase preceding accession, via the so-called *acquis screening*, the Commission had an instrumental way of checking in enormous detail how legislation was being applied on the ground.

Overall, the *involvement of the Commission was far greater,* and owing to the fluidity of transition societies, *its influence exceeded anything comparable to the Northern and Southern enlargements.* Notwithstanding this, the outcome was predetermined primarily by the domestic balance of forces. However, especially in comparison to countries with no immediate EU perspective, such as Ukraine, Russia or Serbia at the time, or the even poorer and conflict-ridden Caucasian countries, it is difficult to ignore the fact that *the EU perspective and perceptions in Brussels really mattered.* Both played a significant and progressive role in shaping the actual outcomes in the countries which eventually joined the EU. We may observe similar improvements in the cases of Croatia and Serbia as soon as their eventual membership had moved within reach. And unsurprisingly, some *regression is clearly demonstrable among those left out from the enlargement process,* since 2000 (Haukkala, 2009).

Enlargement has proved to be premature in more than one dimension. First, improvements on the fiscal front, accompanied by early accession to the eurozone, have yet to materialize. If the EU has indeed served as a disciplinary device on a number of occasions and for diverse countries, EMU and the rules of fiscal surveillance have fallen well short of pre-empting suboptimal policies. And even though the major derailments happened in Greece, Ireland, Italy and Portugal, rather than in the new members, *it is difficult to see how EU rituals contributed to improved fiscal and macro-economic performance.* True, three tiny states, Slovenia, Slovakia and Estonia managed to adopt the Euro in 2007, 2009 and 2011, respectively, but larger countries continued to drift and no quick fixes are in sight for the current decade.

Likewise, there is not much sign of those decentralizing and marketizing reforms, which, in theory, could have been triggered by prospective EMU membership, and which are needed anyway to create sustainable public finances for the long run. Among the non-economic issues, improvements in the rule of law, or better respect for the environment, or improved social rights for citizens are yet to materialize in the new member states. In each of the listed areas, domestic commitment, rather than external coercion is the real measure of what has or has not been delivered. *If countries do not spend voluntarily on issues that figure high on the Community agenda, it is a clear indication of their divergent priorities – in other words, their lack of maturity in regard to the joint agenda.* This is perhaps one of the reasons, why – *unlike in any preceding enlargement* – neither new policy agendas, nor new volumes and objectives of funding, and also no change in the ways of functioning of the common institutions, could be observed. If anything, this no-change scenario has been the *differentia specifica* of the eastward enlargement.

Who transforms whom and why?

Conventional wisdom at the onset of transition was simple. Countries coming from the distorted world of the Soviet Empire would become 'normal European nations'. In concrete terms this seemed straightforward, namely a one-way street to Europeanization. This meant no more and no less than *copying the well-functioning arrangements from Western Europe,* from macroeconomic textbooks to the opening hours of tiny shops in downtown areas.

As experience has amply demonstrated, things have evolved otherwise. First, as was only to be expected on the basis of an analogy with the medical sciences, any implant tends to function in the context of the recipient organism. The latter may absorb, transform or even reject the former. Arrangements that could not be integrated into local conditions, tend to remain formal or ineffectual. Second, as in nature, any action triggers a reaction. Countries that joined the EU on the base of given arrangements have developed expectations based on those. The latter relate primarily to transfers, their size and scope. One of the most frequently cited references was that of the southern enlargement. Then a combination of lavish transfers, aggressive bargaining positions of the new members, and inefficient uses were the rule, rather the exception, as documented by a series of *ex post* Cohesion Reports of the Commission. While new eastern members wished to replicate the precedent, this was a nightmare scenario only to be avoided by the old and rich members – which they actually have averted.

Third, new members have developed an assertiveness of their own, following the – often bad – example of old members, whenever it came to discussing visions, strategies or issues other than their immediate material or power interest. The decline in popularity of the European project, demonstrable via surveys like the Eurobarometer, is largely due to the decline in idealism, in the over-selling of the material content of integration, which remained rather limited.

Fourth, *new members remained net contributors for several years,* since their limited administrative capacity constrained their ability to draw on Community funds of various sorts, while contributions up to one per cent of GNI had to be made in full. By redistributing such a tiny fraction of overall income, a number which is to be sustained in the 2014–20 budget period, the EU funds are unlikely to work miracles in any area that one might mention. By contrast, institutional anchoring and involvement in Community policies are likely to remain formative for the concluding phases of transition.

In more general terms, this implies that new members were perhaps too eager to copy the preoccupation of old members with issues of low politics. In so doing they also contributed to the strengthening of inter-governmentalism in the EU. The latter is a euphemistic term for describing the demise of most, if not all, visionary and long term projects, and the stagnation in terms of moving towards *finalité politique.*

Fifth, the latter must be seen as a novelty against the overall historic dynamism of the EU that we discussed earlier. Despite all of its ills, the project of 'ever-closer Union' continues to be in the making, implying also more political, economic, financial and legal co-operation, especially in areas relating to the lives of everyday citizens, like money and migration.

Sixth, *attempts to 'politicize' the Union* by allowing for the more abstract and less down-to-earth issues to capture the agenda, *have actually backfired.* The latter is well symbolized in the ill-fated project to create a basic law for the Community, an initiative started in 1997. This idea has clearly overdone the parallel of the EU to the nation-state. The project, which was aborted by referenda rejecting the incomprehensible and practically irrelevant deals struck by representatives of the political class, ended in the Lisbon Treaty of 2009, 'de-constitutionalizing' the EU (Reh, 2009).

What has been the contribution of the new member-states to this modest outcome? Formally speaking, their representatives were involved already prior to accession in the work of the Constitutional

Convention convened in Laeken in 2002–03. Furthermore, since 2004, their representatives sit on all EU fora, from Ecofin to ECJ. Still, the input of the new members, other than voicing their immediate material and power interest, has largely remained negligible.[7]

The sheer increase in numbers as well as in diversity calls for new ways of operation in the EU. *Europe 2020*, a strategic document adopted in June, 2010, is an attempt to give an answer to those new challenges, bringing the Union closer to citizens and allowing for more flexible and less bureaucratic forms of co-operation. However, it is hard to overlook the fact that *crisis management, first in the old members, and later in Greece, Portugal and Ireland, has overshadowed any strategic thinking, let alone action.* The foot-dragging over the priorities of the financial guidelines for 2014–20 does not suggest any sign of fundamental reform, either in terms of spending priorities, or in terms of operation.

As a consequence, and quite paradoxically for the non-participant observer, new members have by no means become agents for change (cf. also Csaba, 2009), either within the EU itself, or more widely; thus they *have not adopted a stance of advocacy for further enlargements.* In isolated cases, such as Austrian, Italian and Hungarian support for Croatia finally has led to the conclusion of all negotiating chapters by the end of the Hungarian EU Presidency in late June 2011. Granting candidate status to Serbia, Macedonia and Montenegro in 2009 were thus steps in the right direction. They have already exerted major influence on those nations, including giving rise to the extradition of respective national heroes, such as generals Gotovina and Mladić, to the International Criminal Court in The Hague, Netherlands.

It goes without saying that *by far the most challenging and immediate task for further eastward enlargement is that of Turkey.* Half a century of partnership, and six years of membership talks have yielded some important insights (for details, cf. Philippidis and Karaca, 2009).

From the practical perspective Turkey has made major advances, from being a military dictatorship with an inward looking economy to a multi-party system, with a pluralist press and an economy functioning in a customs union with the EU. Over 5 million persons of Turkish origin live in Western Europe. Thus, from the economic perspective, enlargement is by and large a done deal, save for EMU. On the other hand, political developments in Turkey, moving towards a more authoritarian and more Eastward looking set of policies since 2006,[8] the tiptoeing over human rights issues and limitations on freedom, have repeatedly raised fundamental questions. Namely: *Does the largest secular state in the Near East indeed share what is termed for shorthand 'European values';* or does it pay lip service to them as long as its economic interests are best served this way.

This dilemma shows in its entirety why the question raised in the title of this section is critically important for the future of the EU. In the case of Turkish membership, a country of 74 million people, the EU's traditional 'take it or leave it' approach of unilateralism makes little sense and in any case could probably never succeed. An EU including Turkey will never be like the EEC of the Six. The latter was a small club, whose leaders were anchored in the Catholic tradition, and wished appeasement and unity, on both political and moral grounds. The Community of 30+ is going to be a broad commonwealth of secular nations, with policies based on interest rather than ideas. Conversely, Turkey within the EU will no longer resemble the state created by Mustafa Kemal Atatürk, based on the four core principles of: (a) the leading role of the army as a general and final arbiter; (b) nationalism; (c) the presumption of a single, indivisible Turkish nation defined by citizenship, not ethnicity or religion; and (d) state ownership and economic self-sufficiency.

This author certainly does not possess the answer to the open-ended debate over where the ultimate boundaries of Europe should be drawn. One may or may not want to jump into the emotional debate over Turkish membership, its terms and timeline. What is most relevant, from the academic perspective, is that we have managed to illustrate and perhaps demonstrate: *joining the EU is not comparable to joining 'just another international organization'*. If for no other reason, this is because EU membership has been, and also will be, transformative of the society and economy of any acceding nation.

Notes

1 This is enshrined in the Lisbon Treaty, effective from 2009.
2 For details of both policies and institutions, see the monographic accounts by Wallace *et al.* (2010); and Moussis (2006).
3 Maastricht, institutionalizing monetary union putting forward the first proposals towards political union, was adopted in 1992, Northern enlargement materialized in 1995, while EMU was launched in 1999; Eastern members joined in 2004 and 2007, respectively.
4 It seems that NATO membership was taken – informally – as a pre-condition for EU membership.
5 'Privatizing' Hungarian energy providers to foreign state-owned firms, while retaining their monopoly position, creates the weird situation that a unit of electric energy costs about 40 per cent more in Budapest than in Paris, despite the quite different income levels in the two capitals.
6 These are areas where the Community does not possess immediate competences for supranational action.
7 For instance, one of the initiatives of then President Prodi to cut back the number of Commissioners to six, encountered vocal resistance from the new members, each sticking to an 'own' place in the Commission. Thus, one of the few truly supra-national bodies of the EU had to develop portfolios for which there is no Community competence, such as protecting small languages or taxation, just to be filled by a representative of each member. Workability of such committees, let alone the cosiness of the top decision-makers in a minimum circle of 90 persons, needs no further elaboration.
8 While the first AKP government of the moderate Islamists tended to overdo European expectations, the tide and related practices have changed in their second and third term in office. Membership negotiations move, if at all, at a snail's pace.

Bibliography

Balázs, P. (2002), *Az EU külpolitikája és a magyar-EU kapcsolatok fejlődése* [External policies of the EU and the Hungarian-EU relationship]. Budapest: KJK-Kerszöv.

Berend, T.I. (2009), *From the Soviet Bloc to EU: the Economic and Social Transformation of CEE since 1973.* Cambridge and New York: Cambridge University Press.

Csaba, L. (2009), *Crisis in Economics? Studies in European Political Economy.* Budapest: Akadémiai Kiadó.

Delors, J. (2004), *Memoires.* Paris: Plon.

Haukkala, H. (2009), 'Lost in translation? Why the EU has failed to influence Russia's development,' *Europe-Asia Studies*, vol. 61, no. 10, pp. 1757–76.

Kornai, J. (1992), 'The postsocialist transition and the state: reflections on Hungarian fiscal problems,' *American Economic Review,* vol. 82, no. 2. pp. 1–15.

Moussis, N. (2006), *Acces to European Union: Law, Economics, Politics.* 15th revised edition. Geneva: Euro-confidentiel.

Philippidis, G. and Karaca, O. (2009), 'The economic impacts of Turkish accession,' *World Economy*, vol. 32, no. 12, pp. 1706–29.

Reh, C. (2009,) 'The Lisbon Treaty: de-constitutionalizing the European Union?' *Journal of Common Market Studies*, vol.47, no. 3, pp. 625–50.

Wallace, H., Pollack, M. and Young, A. (eds) (2010), *Policy-Making in the European Union* 6th revised and extended edition. Oxford: Oxford University Press.

Winters, L.A. (1994), 'The Europe Agreements: with a little help from our friends', in Wang, Zh.K. and Winters, L.A. (eds), *Eastern Europe's International Trade.* Manchester and New York: Manchester University Press.

16

EU ACCESSION AS AN INSTRUMENT FOR SPEEDING UP TRANSITION

Mojmir Mrak and Matija Rojec

Introduction

EU accession and transition processes are two sides of the same coin. The heart of the transition process is a transformation from a one-party political system and a centrally planned economic system to a democratic, multi-party political system and a functioning market economy. This is also the heart of the EU accession process. According to the June 1993 Copenhagen European Council 'accession will take place as soon as a country is able to assume the obligations of membership by satisfying the economic and political conditions. As far as economic conditions are concerned, the membership requires: (i) that the candidate country has achieved stability of institutions guaranteeing democracy, the rule of law, human rights and respect for and protection of minorities; (ii) the existence of a functioning market economy, as well as the capacity to cope with competitive pressure and market forces within the EU; (iii) the ability to take on obligations of membership, including adherence to the aims of political, economic and monetary union'.

The aim of this contribution is to assess how far the EU – and specifically the realistic prospect of accession – has been an instrument for speeding up transition. The first impact of the EU accession on launching of the transition processes dates back to the pre-transition era. At the political level, the idea of EU membership was often an important factor motivating populations in the still communist and centrally planned economies to support systemic changes of their socio-economic and political systems and in some cases also to create new sovereign states.[1]

Later on, the EU accession has helped in speeding up transition via processes of nominal and real convergence of the EU candidate countries. In terms of nominal convergence, the speeding up of transition by EU accession has proceeded via the instruments of economic policy dialogue between the Commission and candidate countries. By achieving candidate status, a country in fact decides to adopt the EU type of market economy, the instruments of economic policy dialogue assure more efficient and thorough implementation of the reform processes due to the external pressures of the European Commission, and the provision of pre-accession assistance (funds and technical assistance) also provides some push to the reform processes. In terms of real convergence, preferential access of candidate countries to the internal market of the EU has provided them with an important lever of growth and economic restructuring, the same goes for the increased interest of multinational companies (MNCs) from the EU (and elsewhere) to invest in acceding countries. Below we provide arguments in favour of these channels of positive impact of EU accession for the transition process.

EU accession process as a means of speeding up transition reforms

The fact that a transition country decided to apply for EU membership and its consequent achievement of candidate status meant that the country had opted for a specific type of market economy, i.e. for the EU type of market economy with all its specifics and institutional arrangements. This fact quite precisely defined the type of transition reforms the country would have to go through. It also helped a candidate country to avoid, or at least to ease, some of the normally long-running and difficult political discussions over the concept, content and implementation of every single reform. The decision in favour of EU accession, more or less also meant a decision about the basic concepts of reforms, including the legal and institutional system. What remained was mostly the political will to implement these reforms, which has never really been questioned in most of the candidate countries. In this way, many unknowns about the direction and intensity of reforms have been avoided and, as a result, the risks and the time necessary for the preparation and adoption of reforms were reduced.

Gaining EU candidate country status also meant that a country undertook commitments *vis-à-vis* the European Commission as far as the implementation of the reforms was concerned. The economic content and pace of reforms was planned and monitored via the economic policy dialogue between the European Commission and candidate countries. The two main instruments of this dialogue were Progress Reports and the so called Pre-Accession Economic Programmes.[2] In Progress reports, which assess candidate countries' accession progress in the previous year, the Commission used the so called Copenhagen criteria as a yardstick to judge their readiness for EU membership. The Copenhagen criteria – existence of a functioning market economy, capacity to cope with competitive pressure and market forces within the EU – are in fact nothing else but a list of transition reforms to be implemented by countries in order to become viable EU member states.

In the Pre-Accession Economic Programmes, the candidate countries conveyed to the Commission the main characteristics of their next two–four years of economic policy measures, both as regards their macroeconomic policies, with special emphasis on their fiscal policy, and concerning their proposed structural reforms. In this way, the economic policy dialogue speeded up transition reforms as the Commission exerted pressure on the candidate countries, and provided financial and technical assistance related to the implementation of the mutually agreed reform programmes. Candidate countries also tended to use the argument of 'Commission's pressures' as an excuse to push forward unpopular domestic reforms and to neutralize internal opposition to reforms.

In the above context, we claim that the EU accession process both speeded up transition reforms in the candidate countries and also ensured that the pace and content of transition reforms would converge. This is not the case for other transition countries that are not on track for EU membership. The result is that they lag behind in their transition processes and that the pace of their respective transition reforms diverges considerably. Assuming that the extent to which transition reforms in a given country have been accomplished can be objectively measured, we test this proposal by looking at the most commonly used indicators of reform progress, namely the EBRD Transition Indicators. We use three different summary transition indices: (i) overall transition index as average for all nine reforms taken into account by the EBRD Transition Index; (ii) Stage 1 reforms index, which we calculate as an average of the indicators of price liberalization, trade and foreign exchange system, and small privatization; and (iii) Stage 2 reforms index, which we calculate as an average of the indicators of large scale privatization, enterprise restructuring, competition policy, banking reforms and interest rate liberalization, securities markets and non-bank financial institutions, and infrastructure reform. It is the Stage 2 structural reforms which represent the core of the transition process, the difficult and time-consuming part of it. We claim that it is here in particular, where the EU accession process makes the biggest contribution to speeding up the reforms.

To test this we compare trends in EBRD Transition Indicators for nine new member states (NMS-9: Bulgaria, Estonia, Hungary, Latvia, Lithuania, Poland, Romania, Slovak Republic and Slovenia), seven formal and informal candidate countries (CC: Albania, Bosnia and Herzegovina, Croatia, Macedonia, Moldova, Montenegro and Serbia) and three European CIS countries (Belarus, Russia and Ukraine). Each index ranges from 1 to 4+: 1 meaning only the initiation of transition reforms (little or no change from central planning) and 4+ meaning more or less the situation in advanced market economies. Thus, once a country approaches level 4, its institutional setting is near to that in the advanced market economy countries (EBRD, 1999).

Figure 16.1 shows average transition indices for overall, Stage 1 and Stage 2 reforms and within-group standard deviations of these averages for NMS-9, CC and European CIS countries. *Averages* show the pace of reforms, while *standard deviations* show whether the level of transition reforms tended to converge or not. The EU accession process was supposed to contribute positively to the pace as well as to the convergence. In Stage 1 reforms, the NMS-9, by the late 1990s, had almost achieved the maximum possible value of the transition index. The increase in the Stage 1 reforms index for CC countries was more gradual and still rising, but they gradually caught up with NMS-9 countries. The situation in European CIS countries shows that Stage 1 reforms lagged behind the CC and especially the NMS-9 countries, and that since 2003 there has not been much further progress with these reforms. The standard deviation of the Stage 1 reforms index has been almost zero for the NMS-9 since the late 1990s, the standard deviation for CC countries was higher, but has been decreasing quickly since the late 1990s and gradually approached the level of the NMS-9. The situation is again very different for European CIS countries, where the standard deviation was initially quite high and showed little real tendency to decrease.

The situation is very different as far as the Stage 2 reforms index is concerned. Here, all three groups of countries still show increasing trends in the average values of the index and obviously need more time to reach the maximum level of the index of around 4. More interesting is the point that, somewhere in the second half of the 1990s, the NMS-9 had reached a certain level of advantage over CC, which they have held onto until the present day. In other words, after gaining an initial advantage over the CC countries, the NMS-9 countries maintained their lead over the CC countries in implementing Stage 2 reforms. The trend and the level of the average Stage 2 reforms index of European CIS countries is surprisingly similar to that of CC countries. As far as the standard deviation is concerned the situation is similar, as it is least in the case of NMS-9, followed by CC and the European CIS countries. The level of these differences is somehow kept in the last five years, but while the standard deviation for NMS-9 and CC countries has been constantly decreasing, this is not so for European CIS countries. It thus seems that EU accession process has given an important initial push to the Stage 2 transition reforms of NMS-9 and somewhat later to CC countries and it also makes the pace and level of their transition indicators converge.

These trends in averages and standard deviations of transition indices support the proposal that the EU accession process has been an instrument for speeding up transition reforms in NMS and candidate countries. To some extent it is surprising that this impact has been more apparent for Stage 1 reforms, meaning mostly liberalization and stabilization, than for the more difficult and time consuming structural and institutional reforms of Stage 2. It seems that the European

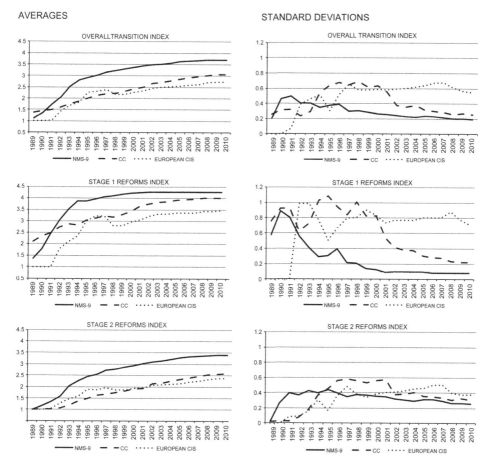

Figure 16.1 Overall Transition Index, Stage 1 reforms Index and Stage 2 reforms Index for NMS-9, CC and European CIS countries: Group averages and standard deviations in 1989–2010

Source: Calculated from EBRD Transition Indicators by Country, www.ebrd.com/pages/research/econom ics/data/macro.shtml#ti

Commission has been more successful in promoting stabilization and liberalization than structural and institutional reforms. This highlights the problem of a possible implementation gap.

Provision of pre-accession assistance (funds and technical assistance)

In 1989, when the process of transition started in the countries of Central and Eastern Europe, the EU responded impressively quickly with financial aid to Poland and Hungary aimed at assisting their efforts to restructure and reform their economies (Programme PHARE: *Pologne-Hongrie Aide à la reconstruction économique*). During its initial years, PHARE primarily took the form of technical assistance, while already by 1991, the programme had become a technical assistance and know-how transfer programme covering a wider range of transition economies in the region. The second important reorganization of PHARE occurred in the mid-1990s when PHARE was turned into an actual pre-accession instrument adapted to the priorities and needs of each individual recipient country. As progress was made and the demand for technical assistance declined, the programme was reoriented towards investment aid, particularly in areas such as infrastructure and environmental protection. Further, the programme started to be operated on the basis of instruments from the Structural Funds.

The third major reorganization of PHARE accompanied the beginning of the EU accession negotiations. Following the Commission discussions around Agenda 2000, PHARE was redirected towards two crucial priorities associated with the adoption of the *acquis communautaire*, namely institution building and investment support. The instrument was accompanied by two new pre-accession instruments – the Instrument for Structural Policies for Pre-accession (ISPA) and the Special Accession Programme for Agriculture and Rural Development (SAPARD). Some 3.1 billion Euros a year was made available from these funds for the 10 Central and Eastern European candidate countries during the 2000–06 period, with some additional pre-accession funds available also to Malta, Cyprus and Turkey as well as to Western Balkan countries through the Community Assistance for Reconstruction, Development and Stabilization (CARDS) programme.

In the current financial perspective of the EU covering the period 2007–13, pre-accession assistance has been integrated into a single instrument called Instrument for Pre-accession Assistance (IPA). In a similar way to the previous programming period, the pre-accession assistance has two basic objectives: first, to assist candidate countries in their transposition of the *acquis*, and, second, to assist the candidate countries in the efficient use of Structural Funds and the Cohesion Fund. For the IPA, amounting to around 1.5 billion Euros a year, all seven EU candidate and potential candidate countries from the western Balkans plus Turkey are eligible. The programme is made up of five components: (i) support for transition and institution building; (ii) cross-border co-operation; (iii) regional development; (iv) human resource development; and (v) rural development. The first two components are available to all the candidate and potential candidate countries while only the candidate countries enjoy access to the remaining three components.

Preferential access to the internal market of the EU

Preferential access to the EU internal market has helped transition countries to strengthen their competitive position and exports to the EU markets and thus to advance their real convergence. In the period 1990–2004, i.e. from the beginning of transition to their accession to the EU, eight transition countries which acceded to the EU in 2004 (NMS-8: Czech Republic, Estonia, Hungary, Latvia, Lithuania, Poland, Slovakia and Slovenia) recorded an extremely high growth of exports in absolute as well as in relative terms, that was accompanied by increasing market shares abroad and by the domination of the EU-15 as the main market (see Table 16.1). Most of this development is explained by gravity theory, i.e. by the fact that pre-transition trade with CMEA countries, was much above the 'normal' level and with the EU-15 much below the 'normal' level. Size, proximity and the development level of the EU-15 add up to an extremely strong gravity force for transition countries' exports. Additionally, the EU integration process provided these countries with preferential access to EU-15 markets. The literature suggests that preferential market access, especially the Europe Agreements, has clearly been an important additional factor in increasing the volume of NMS-8 trade (particularly with the EU-15).

The access of transition countries to OECD markets has evolved in three stages. The first stage was the removal of discriminatory measures (non-tariff barriers) aimed specifically against state-trading economies, in fact the granting of Most Favoured Nation status. The EU was the first to do that. The second stage was granting preferential market access under the General System of Preferences, which put transition economies on a par with developing countries with quota-limited free access for most products. Again, the EU was the first to take that step. The

Table 16.1 Main exports related indicators of NMS-8 in 1990–2004

	1990	1995	2000	2001	2002	2003	2004
Exports of goods (billion EUR)	31.4	61.7	129.1	148.1	159.7	173.1	209.2
Exports index (1990 = 100)	100.0	196.8	411.6	472.1	509.4	552.1	667.2
Exports as % of GDP	n.a.	29.3	36.7	37.4	37.8	41.5	46.0
Exports as % of World imports	1.11	1.54	1.80	2.08	2.28	2.55	2.81
Exports to EU-15 as % of EU-15 total imports	n.a.	2.53	3.69	4.19	4.57	4.94	5.38
Exports to EU-15 as % of total exports	46.0	60.6	68.4	67.8	67.5	67.1	65.9

Sources: UNCTAD, World Bank and WIIW (The Vienna Institute for International Economic Studies) databases.

third stage was the conclusion of Europe Agreements between the EU-15 and most of the NMS-8 by the mid-1990s, and their anticipated accession to the EU after the Copenhagen EU summit. General System of Preferences represented a big step in tariff liberalization, but there is little evidence that, 'with its limitations and exclusions (quantity limits, special treatment of sensitive products, uncertainty of access), it alone can explain changes in transition economies' shares in OECD imports' (Kaminski *et al.*, 1996).

Clearly, the Europe Agreements have been far more important than General System of Preferences. Kaminski *et al.* (1996) analysed the effects of the Europe Agreements with Czechoslovakia, Hungary, Poland, Romania and Bulgaria signed in 1991 and 1992. They claim that provisions on trade with industrial products, which affected about 80 per cent of the exports of these five countries to the EU, significantly improved their access to EU markets. In 1992 the first year they were in force in Hungary, Poland and former Czechoslovakia, the Agreements freed slightly less than 50 per cent of total exports to the EU from import duties and non-tariff barriers. According to the Agreements, these shares were to increase over five years to about 80 per cent for the former Czechoslovakia, 60 per cent for Hungary and 70 per cent for Poland. Apart from that, tariffs were reduced for a number of other products, and the Copenhagen summit further cut the time to reach the top of the EU preferential trade pyramid, at that time occupied by the EFTA countries. These reductions in trade barriers translated into a competitive edge over suppliers from other countries. Still, the Europe Agreements retained a number of restrictions characteristic for the General System of Preferences (delays in liberalizing imports of sensitive products, tight rules of origin, continuing threats of antidumping, and the virtual exclusion of agriculture), which were then gradually removed in the process of EU integration.

Increased interest of MNCs to invest in acceding countries

The opening up of transition countries for inward FDI has been one of the most visible effects of the transition process. At the same time, the EU accession process fundamentally changed the position of transition countries in MNCs' considerations and reduced the perception of investment risks. This increased the interest of foreign investors from the EU (and elsewhere) to invest in the transition countries, which in turn speeded up their real convergence. Why was that so?

Economic theory suggests that economic integration increases FDI inflows in the region because: (i) the size of the market increases, and this led to the replacement of exports with FDI; the consequence was an increase of FDI inflows in the NMS; (ii) MNCs reorganized their investments in the region in response to the new configuration of locational advantages (new structure of costs, benefits, economies of scale) among member countries; the consequence was increased FDI in some old and new member states, and even some retreat of FDI from others;

and (iii) new investment opportunities arising from the restructuring of activities between countries, sectors and firms triggered by economic integration. The consequence was an increase of FDI inflows in NMS (Dunning, 1993). In the case of transition countries, EU accession itself also reduced transaction costs and perceptions of investment risks because it gave important assurances to foreign investors about the timing of accession, as well as about the type of economic and legal system the transition countries were heading towards (Baldwin *et al.*, 1997).

Empirical evidence (Table 16.2) quite clearly confirms the above pattern, i.e. the tremendous increase of absolute and relative (increasing inward FDI stock to GDP ratio, increasing share of NMS-8 in world inward FDI stock, and increasing NMS-8 to EU-15 inward FDI stock ratio) values of FDI in the NMS-8, and the major importance of EU investors in this increase. In this context, it is important to note that the relative increase of FDI inflows in NMS-8 (measured by NMS-8 to EU-15 FDI inflows ratio; Table 16.2) happened before their accession in the EU, indicating that the impact of EU accession on FDI inflows was already anticipated to a considerable extent before accession. In other words, foreign investors tended to plan on the basis of a country's likely future membership of the EU.

This positive impact of the EU accession process on inward FDI is important for the transition process, as FDI has traditionally been seen as an important means for structural upgrading and increasing the productivity of transition economies and, thus, for their catching up with the EU. Most of the relevant literature tends to confirm these expectations, more precisely: (i) foreign subsidiaries in transition countries deepen trade linkages by having disproportionately high shares in exports and imports; (ii) direct effects of FDI are significantly higher productivity of acquired companies/greenfields than of domestic firms; (iii) in terms of industrial and market structure, FDI plays a dual role as restructuring agents by building new sectors (electronics, automotive), and as market seekers (food, banking, telecoms); and (iv) the effects of FDI are mostly concentrated on the acquired or newly erected plants, with the extent of spillovers generally rather limited, depending on local companies' absorption capacity (Djankov and Hoekman, 2000; Hunya, 2000; Damijan *et al.*, 2008; Smarzynska, 2003).

Conclusions

The process of transition of the centrally planned economies from Central and Eastern Europe into market economies has been implemented simultaneously with the accession of these

Table 16.2 Main indicators related to inward FDI stocks in NMS-8 in 1990–2004

	1990	1995	2000	2001	2002	2003	2004
Value (billion EUR)	4.0	32.1	93.4	112.1	146.8	187.7	257.1
FDI stock index (1990=100)	100	803	2335	2803	3670	4693	6428
FDI stock as % of GDP*	7.3**	12.3	30.0	32.2	37.4	40.9	45.9
NMS-8 in World inward FDI stock (%)	0.19	0.95	1.26	1.50	1.95	2.00	2.33
NMS-8 to EU-15 inward FDI stock ratio (%)	0.52	2.88	4.22	4.77	5.27	5.12	5.78
Share of EU-15 investors in NMS-8 inward FDI stock (%)	n.a.	n.a.	n.a.	n.a.	87.2	80.3	80.5
NMS-8 to EU-15 FDI inflows ratio (%)	0.9	13.7	3.5	6.7	8.0	5.3	16.4

Sources: UNCTAD, FDI/TNC (www.unctad.org/fdistatistics) and WIIW (The Vienna Institute for International Economic Studies) databases.
Notes: * Non-weighted average.
** Data for 1993.

countries to the EU. The two processes have been strongly intertwined and it can be empirically confirmed that those countries of the region which became members of the EU during the 2004/07 enlargement have by and large also come closer to completion of their transition process than those transition countries that are still EU candidate countries. Interestingly, though, many of the new member states of the EU continue to experience considerable problems with actual implementation of the *acquis communautaire*. This is also the main reason why EU accession negotiations are now even more structured than they were during the big Eastern enlargement.

Moreover, the current financial and economic crisis has interrupted the almost two-decades long period of real convergence of the new EU member states. There is a growing consensus that the pre-crisis model of economic growth in most countries of the region, based on strong domestic demand and large capital inflows, is not sustainable any more and needs substantial adjustment. The key elements of a revised economic growth model will have to incorporate the following three components: first, the increase of domestic savings and consequently a reduction of these countries' reliance on foreign savings. Second, adjustments in macroeconomic and financial policy oriented towards more proactive channeling of capital inflows towards tradeable, export-oriented activities. And third, radical Lisbon Strategy-type structural reforms aimed at increasing productivity, that is needed to restart a dynamic and sustainable economic growth in the region.

Notes

1 In Slovenia, for example, a slogan of the Slovenian Communist Party in the later 1980s, i.e. at the time when the winds of change began to blow, was 'Europe now'. It may be said that some mention of EU membership was never omitted whenever requests for independence, a democratic parliamentary system and a market economy were put forward.
2 Pre-Accession Economic Programme is a policy dialogue instrument for candidate countries, while the respective instrument for countries which have not yet acquired formal candidate status is an Economic and Fiscal Programme. Their content, however, is more or less the same.

Bibliography

Baldwin, R.E., Francois, J.F. and Portes, R. (1997), 'The Costs and Benefits of Eastern Enlargement: The Impact on the EU and Central Europe', *Economic Policy*, April, pp. 127–76.
Damijan, J.P., Rojec, M., Majcen B. and Knell, M. (2008), 'Impact of Firm Heterogeneity on Direct and Spillover Effects of FDI: Micro Evidence from Ten Transition Countries', *LICOS Discussion Paper Series*, Discussion paper 218/2008. Leuven: LICOS Centre for Institutions and Economic Performance.
Djankov, S. and Hoekman, B. (2000), 'Foreign Investment and Productivity Growth in Czech Enterprises', *World Bank Economic Review*, vol. 14(1), pp. 49–64.
Dunning, J.H. (1993), *Multinational Enterprises and the Global Economy*, Wokingham: Addison-Wesley.
EBRD (1999), *Transition Report 1999*. London: EBRD.
Hunya, G. (ed.) (2000), *Integration through Foreign Direct Investment*, Cheltenham: Edward Elgar.
Kaminski, B., Wang, Z.K. and Winters, L.A. (1996), *Foreign Trade in The Transition: The International Environment and Domestic Policy*, Studies of Economies in Transformation, No. 20, Washington, DC: World Bank.
Smarzynska, B. (2003), 'Does Foreign Direct Investment Increase the Productivity of Domestic Firms? In Search of Spillovers through Backward Linkages', *The American Economic Review*, vol. 14(1), pp. 49–64.

Part V
Political economy

17

CORRUPTION IN THE POST-COMMUNIST TRANSITION

Daniel Treisman

Introduction

Among scholars, journalists and the general public, it is widely believed that the frequency and scale of corruption increased dramatically in the post-communist countries after they began their transition. Corruption is usually defined as the misuse of public office for private gain. It comes in many varieties – from the extortion of bribes and kickbacks from businessmen and citizens to the embezzlement of budget funds, the stripping of state assets, nepotistic hiring and violations of electoral and party finance rules. That said, the prototypical case that informs most research is that of a state official who demands an informal additional payment from citizens in return for providing some public service – in other words, a bribe.

The post-communist transition of the last 20+ years coincided in time with the emergence of a new literature in economics and political science on the empirics of corruption. Scholars have used survey-based measures of the perceived or experienced incidence of bribery to try to answer questions about why corruption is more widespread in some countries and in some years than in others. In this note, I review their early efforts to assess and explain the variation in corruption among post-communist countries. As will become clear, the measures available are problematic, and for that reason the results of this work have been rather frustratingly inconclusive.[1]

How corrupt?

Since corrupt transactions are illegal, assessing their frequency and scale presents an obvious challenge. Since the mid-1990s, the campaigning NGO Transparency International (TI) and the World Bank have constructed and published measures of subjective perceptions of corruption, which aggregate the ratings of country experts, risk analysts' evaluations, and polls of business executives and citizens. The aim is to determine how corrupt experts, businessmen and citizens *think* a given country is in a given year and to turn such opinions into a cross-nationally comparable index. TI's 'Corruption Perceptions Index' and the World Bank's 'Control of Corruption' indicator are highly correlated with each other, which is not surprising since the sets of surveys and ratings used to construct the respective measures typically overlap.

Some studies have analysed the cross-national variation in these indexes, treating them as perhaps noisy but probably unbiased estimates of countries' actual levels of corruption (e.g. Treisman,

2000; Milanovic *et al.*, 2010). However, concern has grown in recent years that these indexes may reflect stereotypes and 'folk theories' about the causes of corruption rather than measuring the actual incidence of corrupt transactions (Treisman, 2007; Donchev and Ujhelyi, 2010). More recently, an alternative type of data has become available – 'experience-based' indicators derived from survey questions that ask respondents about their own experience with officials demanding bribes. Since 2004 TI has surveyed the populations of a large number of countries, and asked among other questions whether the respondent or a household member had paid a bribe in any form during the previous 12 months. Since 1999 the European Bank for Reconstruction and Development and the World Bank have periodically polled executives of firms in post-communist countries in their Business Environment and Enterprise Performance Survey (BEEPS). In 1999, 2002, 2005 and 2008–09 they asked the executives how common it was for 'firms like theirs' to have to make unofficial payments to officials to 'get things done'.

Measures of the frequency of bribery derived from such questions about local experience correlate with those derived from expert ratings and opinions. However, among countries thought to have high corruption, the correlation between experience-based and perceptions indicators is relatively weak. Moreover, while the perceptions indicators are correlated with a long list of plausible determinants of corruption – from authoritarian rule to a lack of women in government – such correlations for experience-based measures are much weaker, suggesting perhaps that experts and media opinion-formers simply assume corruption to be frequent in places where its supposed causes are visible (Treisman, 2007; Donchev and Ujhelyi, 2010). Perceptions of corruption also appear to be much stickier than reported experience of it. Among the post-communist countries, the correlation between the World Bank's perceptions indicator in 2000 and 2009 (r = 0.90) is much higher than that between the experience-based BEEPS measure of bribe frequency in 1999 and 2009 (r = 0.56).[2]

Recently, certain scholars have devised creative ways to measure corruption in particular countries (Italy and Indonesia), but these techniques have not yet been extended to the post-communist world (Golden and Picci, 2005; Olken, 2009). Both the techniques provide snap-shots rather than a means of assessing corruption over time, and in the Indonesian case the measure was only available at the very micro level.[3] Data are available from some countries on prosecutions for bribery and embezzlement, but the problems in interpreting such data are so great as to render their use highly problematic. Different rates of registered crimes and prose-cutions may reflect differences in the zeal or budget of enforcers, and in any case only a fraction of actual transactions is probably detected.

The unfortunate conclusion is that we lack a credible method and data source to assess change in the incidence of corruption in the post-communist countries in the late 1980s and early 1990s. If one ignores the problems with perceptions-based measures, these are available for a number of transition countries from 1996. However, for experience-based measures, one must wait until 1999 for the first BEEPS survey of business executives and until 2004 for the first TI Global Corruption Barometer survey of national populations. Thus, what happened to corruption in the years right after the fall of communism will remain a subject of surmise, anecdotes and suggestive case studies.

More data are available regarding the second decade of transition. Table 17.1 shows an experience-based measure of corruption derived from the BEEPS surveys from 1999–2009. Specifically, I show the percentage of business executives interviewed in each country who said it was always, usually, or frequently true that firms like theirs had to make additional irregular payments or gifts to officials to get things done. (Other possible answers were 'sometimes', 'seldom', 'never' and 'don't know'.)

Several points are clear from this table. First, there is a great deal of variation, both across countries and over time.[4] The proportion who said it was always, usually, or frequently true

Table 17.1 Percentage of firm executives who said it was always, usually, or frequently true that firms like theirs had to make additional irregular payments or gifts to officials to get things done (BEEPS)

	1999	2002	2005	2009
E. Europe				
Albania	47	36	46	13
Bosnia and Herzegovina	29	22	20	12
Bulgaria	24	33	16	9
Croatia	18	13	11	9
Czech	26	13	10	5
Hungary	31	23	12	5
Kosovo				1
Macedonia		23	25	9
Montenegro				6
Poland	33	19	14	5
Romania	51	37	21	20
Serbia and Montenegro		16	33	
Serbia				20
Slovakia	35	36	11	8
Slovenia	8	7	5	3
*Average**	30	24	16	9
Baltic states				
Estonia	13	12	6	3
Latvia		18	7	7
Lithuania	23	21	24	2
*Average**	18	16	15	3
Other FSU				
Armenia	40	14	10	15
Azerbaijan	59	27	30	22
Belarus	14	24	22	9
Georgia	37	38	7	4
Kazakhstan	24	30	24	17
Kyrgyzstan	27	44	53	25
Moldova	33	34	19	15
Russia	29	39	39	24
Tajikistan		35	21	19
Ukraine	35	35	28	24
Uzbekistan	47	20	21	34
*Average**	35	31	25	19
Memo: Turkey	37	24	13	9
*Average post-communist**	31	26	20	13
*Median post-communist**	30	26	19	11

Source: BEEPS data downloaded from EBRD at: www.ebrd.com/pages/research/analysis/surveys/beeps.shtml.

Note: ★ All averages calculated for only those countries that had data in all years. Percentages are unweighted, since weights only available for 2009.

that firms needed to make informal payments ranged from a high of 59 per cent in Azerbaijan in 1999 to a low of 1 per cent in Kosovo and 2 per cent in Lithuania in 2009.[5] Second, between 1999 and 2009 there was a very consistent fall in the proportion of businesses reporting that bribery was common. This was true across the various sub-regions. (It was also true of Turkey, which was included as a comparator country, suggesting the change may not be a specifically post-communist phenomenon). For 2002–09, the BEEPS survey also included comparable questions that asked what percentage of annual sales revenues a typical firm paid in unofficial payments/gifts to public officials.[6] The average amounts (not shown here) fell consistently in this period across the post-communist countries (but not in Turkey). Of course, rapid economic growth was simultaneously increasing the value of firms' revenues, so the absolute amounts paid may not have decreased.

Thus, although we cannot know whether the frequency of bribery increased in the 1990s, there is evidence that the frequency among businesses fell in the 2000s, and in many countries by large amounts. Improvements were not uniform across policy areas. Between 1999 and 2005, there were significant reductions in corruption related to taxes, customs, and business licensing, but no improvement in government procurement and the judiciary (Anderson and Grey, 2006). The burden of corruption was also heavier for some firms than for others: newer, smaller, privately owned, domestic firms tended to report that bribes were necessary more frequently and for larger amounts than older, state-owned, and foreign-owned firms (*Ibid.*).

What about bribes extracted from the population? Data from TI's Global Corruption Barometer on the proportion of respondents who said a household member had paid a bribe in the previous 12 months are available only from 2004. These percentages also vary considerably both across countries and over time. In a given year, the indicators of bribery for the population (TI) and bribery for firms (BEEPS) are correlated, but far from perfectly (Figure 17.1). Among those post-communist countries included in the survey in all years, the reported frequency of bribery dropped on average from 2004 to 2007, before rising again in 2010. There were some positive stories – countries where the frequency fell throughout the period (e.g. Croatia, the Czech Republic) – but there were also some where the reported frequency was higher in 2010 than in 2004 (e.g. Bosnia and Poland).[7]

Explaining the pattern

What might explain variation in corruption levels, both cross-nationally and over time? Scholars have suggested a variety of possible causes. A first set has to do with countries' pre-transition characteristics – economic, geographical and cultural. Worldwide, there is a strong correlation between higher economic development and lower reported corruption. Thus, we might expect those countries that were most developed at the start of transition to report less bribery. Some have argued that more plentiful natural resources create battles over rents, corrupting the state. Some former communist countries – e.g. Azerbaijan, Turkmenistan, Kazakhstan, and Russia – are rich in oil, gas, and other minerals. Culturally, the post-communist countries inherited quite different religious traditions, a factor some have linked to variation in corruption worldwide. Four major religions – Islam, Eastern Orthodoxy, Catholicism and Protestantism – are represented, along with many minor ones. The timing of communization might also matter. Communist regimes co-opted and destroyed autonomous civic organizations. If such policies had gradual, cumulative effects, more remnants of civic culture might have survived in countries that became communist later.

A second set of possible determinants relates to the political and civic institutions created during the transition period. The post-communist countries vary in the extent of democracy and constraints on the executive that emerged. They also differ in the independence and vigour

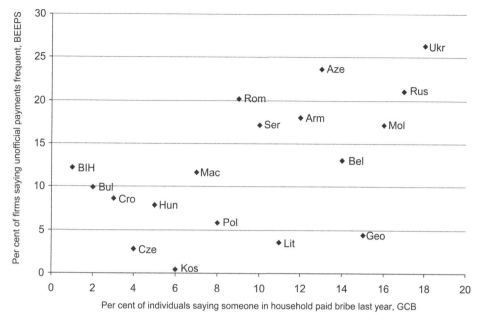

Figure 17.1 Frequency of bribery reported by citizens and firms, transition countries, 2009
Sources: EBRD data download (BEEPS), Transparency International, Global Corruption Barometer 2009,
www.transparency.org/news_room/in_focus/2009/gcb2009#dnld, p.32.
Note: Weighted averages (both surveys), excluding 'don't knows'; because of weighting, percentages differ
slightly from those in Table 17.1.

of the press, which is important for exposing corruption, as well as in key details of their constitutional structure such as whether they have parliamentary or presidential regimes and the
extent of decentralization. Besides political institutions, differences in political practices during
the transition period could have consequences for corruption. Some have argued that turnover
of government officials was crucial for improving governance (Shleifer, 1997). More frequent
turnover between political parties or leaders might reduce the incentive for firms to invest in
clientelistic protections, reducing bribery (Milanovic *et al.*, 2010).

Third, economic performance during the transition might affect corruption. In conditions of
rapid growth, citizens, appeased by rising incomes, might be less motivated to monitor and
punish officials who enrich themselves. On the other hand, if economic development brings
with it increases in state capacity and modernization of society, this might reduce corruption.
Fourth, the policies enacted in the transition period might be important. Faster deregulation
might reduce the number of licenses and permits in return for which officials can extract bribes.
Some argue that rapid privatization increased corruption (although proponents of this view
rarely compare the extent of corruption observed during privatization to that which might be
expected had the assets remained under the control of the bureaucrats). Some countries moved
faster than others to enact policies specifically aimed at reducing corruption (Rousso and Steves,
2006). Finally, for those countries with a realistic hope of joining the EU, this was said to create
incentives to clean up governance (although improvements might slow after a country was
actually admitted, as some believe happened in Bulgaria and Romania).

Surprisingly few studies have examined which of these factors correlate with perceived corruption
levels in the post-communist countries, and even fewer look for links to experience-based

measures. Treisman (2002) analysed two perceptions measures of corruption and one experience-based one (the percentage of revenues reportedly paid by firms in unofficial gifts and payments from the 1999 BEEPS survey).[8] I found that four factors, already fixed at the start of transition – initial GDP per capita, the number of years the country had been communist, a measure of the country's natural resource endowment, and the percentage of the population that adhered to Protestantism – could explain from 62 to 87 per cent of the variation among post-communist countries in perceived corruption and 64 per cent of the variation in the bribe burden. (In fact, natural resources were never statistically significant, so the other factors were doing the work.) Those countries that were initially more developed, that had become communist later, and that had a sizeable share of Protestants (Estonia and Hungary) had both lower perceived corruption and a lower reported burden of bribery. A few of the variables included to capture aspects of the transition (measures of democracy and decentralization; leadership turnovers; polarization of executive and parliament; the extent of market reform, privatization and legal reform) were significant in regressions of corruption perceptions, but none was significantly related to the experience-based measure of the bribe burden.

One interpretation of this is that any relevant differences in policies or political and economic performance during the transition were themselves predetermined by differences in a country's initial levels of economic development and duration of communist domination. Both of these were, in turn, highly correlated with a country's location – in general, the further east the country was, the lower the initial income and the earlier the communist takeover – and consequently also with the odds of quick admission to the EU. Another interpretation is that I failed to find results because of the crudeness of available data and problems of reverse causation that I was not able to address.

I also found that perceived corruption was significantly higher (as of 1998–2001) in post-communist countries than the average in other parts of the world, but that most of this difference could be eliminated by controlling for income and years of democracy since 1950. Thus, it was not the communist legacy *per se*, but rather the relatively lower income and lack of democratic experience (itself a consequence of communist rule) that made post-communist countries stand out. One can now examine the same question using the experience-based measure from TI's Global Corruption Barometer. In 2004 respondents in post-communist countries were significantly more likely to say that a household member had paid a bribe during the previous year: the post-communist average was about nine percentage points higher than the average for other countries. However, this difference steadily decreased over the years. By 2010 the post-communist effect had turned negative, although not statistically significant.[9]

Milanovic *et al.* (2010) explore the effect of leadership turnover on perceived corruption (using the World Bank measure). They find that more turnovers of power between opposed parties in the early years of transition correlate with lower perceived corruption as of 2006. An interesting question not answered in the paper is whether this effect would remain significant using experience-based corruption measures.

To assess the effectiveness of policy, Rousso and Steves (2006) constructed measures of the extent to which post-communist countries introduced explicit reforms to fight corruption. They focused on three common types of anti-corruption measures: the adoption of integrated anti-corruption programmes, the passage of legislation to enhance governance institutions and accountability, and the signing of international anti-corruption conventions. They then looked at how the intensity of corruption fighting, thus measured, correlated with the main experience-based corruption indicators from the BEEPS survey. They found that, although the apparent levels of corruption in 2002–05 declined significantly, the change was 'not associated with the intensity of anti-corruption activity in the preceding period' (1999–2002).' They conclude that the apparent reduction in frequency of bribery in the transition region 'is not necessarily related to the high-profile anti-corruption initiatives adopted in so many of these countries' (*Ibid.*, p. 266).

In an extended analysis of the BEEPS data from 1999 to 2005, Anderson and Grey (2006) sought to explain the trend of improvement visible in Table 17.1. They suggested that deregulation and simplification of rules may have helped to reduce corruption. In cross-section, they found a negative correlation between a measure of 'ease of paying taxes' from the World Bank's *Doing Business* indicators and the reported frequency of bribery related to taxation. However, they lacked the data to test for dynamic effects, and the cross-sectional relationship was not robust to inclusion of other controls (Anderson and Grey, 2006, p. 94). They also found that the more cumbersome and costly it was to enforce a contract, the greater was the reported frequency of bribery with regard to courts (*Ibid.*, p. 96).

Besides this, Anderson and Grey (2006) endorse the notion that prospects of joining the EU helped. Dividing countries into different groups on the basis of their closeness to EU admission, they conclude that those countries whose accession in a given period was 'probable but not certain' were the most active in enacting anti-corruption legislation (*Ibid.*, p. 81). Of course, this relationship also might not survive the inclusion of controls. Also, based on the study of Rousso and Steves just cited, one might wonder whether enacting such legislation had any clear effect on the corruption level.

Their other findings are mostly negative. Faster economic growth between 2002 and 2005 was not related to change in reported corruption (p. 29); nor did the length of time the country's leader had been in power seem to matter. They suggest that there may be an inverted U-shaped relationship between civil liberties or constraints on the executive and corruption: more authoritarian countries like Belarus and Uzbekistan and more democratic ones like Slovenia and Estonia tend to have lower reported corruption than those in between them. As they acknowledge, however, lower reported corruption in authoritarian states might reflect 'the strong control environment, the low level of private-sector activity, different conceptions of what constitutes corruption, or the hesitation of respondents to answer questions freely'.

Conclusion

The lack of quantitative data makes it difficult to test the widespread view that corruption spread and intensified in the first decade of transition from communism. During the second decade, more survey data on respondents' concrete experiences with corruption have become available. These data suggest that the frequency of corruption varied a great deal, both across countries and in a given country over time. The extent of bribe extraction from businesses fell quite dramatically after 1999, and bribe extraction from citizens may have fallen at least until 2007. In 2004 the citizens of post-communist countries were more likely than their peers elsewhere to report that a household member had paid a bribe in the previous year; by 2010 this was no longer the case.

Evidence about why reported bribery is much more frequent in some post-communist countries than in others is limited. Most of the variation in a given year maps onto the East-West divide: countries further east – which were mostly less developed at the start of transition, had been communized for longer, and had poorer prospects of rapid EU accession – generally have higher corruption levels. Attempts to identify effects of policies enacted during the transition – whether aspects of economic reform or explicit anti-corruption measures – have not been successful. It is possible that once scholars have enough data to look for dynamic effects in multi-year panels they will find more evidence for such influences. In the meanwhile, a great deal remains unknown about the path and logic of corruption in the post-communist world.

Notes

1 A sizeable literature has already developed on governance in the post-communist countries. Limited by the genre to a very short list of references, I apologize to the authors whose contributions I am unable to cite.

2 My calculations from the respective databases. Across all countries, the correlation between the World Bank's 2000 and 2009 measures is r = 0.93.

3 Golden and Picci (2005) compared the estimated value of the stock of public infrastructure to the value of past investments in it. Olken assessed the level of corruption in a road building project by having engineers analyse samples of the materials used.

4 There were some changes in the details of the BEEPS questionnaire and implementation over these years, but not significant enough to explain large differences.

5 The figure for Kosovo is surprising, given the common perception that corruption remained quite widespread (see, for instance, 'Corruption in Kosovo: Time to Go Straight,' *The Economist*, March 18, 2010, www.economist.com/node/15731392). Large-scale incidents of embezzlement and grand corruption would not necessarily be captured by the enterprise survey.

6 The same question was also asked in 1999, but the answers were coded as falling within a number of unequally spaced ranges; from 2002, the actual percentage was recorded.

7 Lack of data precludes any serious consideration of the Asian communist countries of China and Vietnam in this article; neither was included in the BEEPS survey, and they were only included in the Global Corruption Barometer in recent years. For what it is worth, the percentage of respondents who said in 2010 that a household member had paid a bribe during the past year was 44 per cent in Vietnam (almost as high as Azerbaijan) and 9 per cent in China, the same level as in Austria (Transparency International, *Global Corruption Barometer 2010*, p. 46). I would like to see some more years of data before accepting the China figure at face value.

8 This study also examined a measure of 'state capture' – i.e. the percentage of firms who said that firms like theirs often had to 'make extra, unofficial payments to public officials to influence the content of new laws, decrees, or regulations'.

9 My calculations using data supplied by TI.

Bibliography

Anderson, J.H. and Grey, C.W. (2006), *Anticorruption in Transition 3: Who Is Succeeding and Why?* Washington, DC: World Bank.

Donchev, D. and Ujhelyi, G. (2010), 'What Do Corruption Indices Measure?' University of Houston, www.class.uh.edu/faculty/gujhelyi/corrmeasures.pdf.

Golden, M. and Picci, L. (2005), 'Proposal for a New Measure of Corruption, Illustrated with Italian Data', *Economics & Politics*, vol. 17 (March), pp. 37–75.

Milanovic, B., Hoff, K. and Horowitz, S. (2010), 'Turnover in Power as a Restraint on Investing in Influence: Evidence from the Postcommunist Transition', *Economics & Politics*, vol. 22, pp. 329–61.

Olken, B. (2009), 'Corruption Perceptions vs. Corruption Reality,' *Journal of Public Economics*, vol. 93(7–8), pp. 950–64.

Rousso, A. and Steves, F. (2006), 'The Effectiveness of Anti-Corruption Programs: Preliminary Evidence from the Post-Communist Transition Countries', in Rose-Ackerman, S. (ed.), *International Handbook on the Economics of Corruption*, Cheltenham: Edward Elgar, pp. 247–77.

Shleifer, A. (1997), 'Government in Transition', *European Economic Review*, vol. 41, pp. 385–410.

Treisman, D. (2000), 'The Causes of Corruption: A Cross-National Study', *Journal of Public Economics*, vol. 76(3), pp. 399–457.

——(2002), 'Post-communist corruption', in Campos, N. and Fidrmuc, J. (eds), *Political Economy of Transition and Development: Institutions, Politics, and Policies*, Boston, MA: Kluwer, pp. 201–26.

——(2007), 'What have we learned about the causes of corruption from ten years of crossnational empirical research?' *Annual Review of Political Science*, vol. 10, pp. 211–44.

18

BULGARIA AND POLITICAL ECONOMY OF TRANSITION

Rumen Dobrinsky

Introduction and conceptual framework

Economic and political transformation in Bulgaria has been rather uneven and often changed direction. Compared to the countries in central Europe, it took much longer to define the course of reforms and until 1997 Bulgaria was a laggard in the reform process. In 1996–97 the deepening macroeconomic imbalances escalated into a severe financial crisis combining a crash in public finances, a run on the banks and a collapse of the currency, all of which gave rise to a hyper-inflationary hike in early 1997.

However, after 1997 the situation changed radically: the course of economic and political reforms was firmly set and the policy orientation towards a pluralistic democracy and market economy gained support among a wide majority of the society. In political terms, this was a definitive shift in values embodied in a firm orientation towards EU membership. In terms of economic policy, the emphasis was placed on fast macroeconomic stabilization (based on a currency board arrangement) and acceleration of structural reforms. There was a remarkable turnaround in economic performance: inflation rapidly fell to low single digits, public finances were brought under firm control and the economy grew steadily at a relatively rapid pace, which allowed for the recovery of real incomes and private consumption. The successful institutional reforms culminated with EU accession on 1 January 2007—which is also the end point of the narrative in this contribution.

Bulgaria's economic and political transformation has been the subject of extensive research. An overview of the political developments during the first phase of transition at the onset of transition can be found in Koford (2000). The initial stop-and-go reform effort, its policy rationale and macroeconomic outcomes are analyzed in Bristow (1996) and Jones and Miller (1997). The policies and the sequence of events that lead to the crisis are addressed in Avramov and Sgard (1996), Dobrinsky (1994, 1996), OECD (1997). Minassian (2001) addresses Bulgaria's relations with the IMF and summarizes the outcomes of the Fund-supported programmes. The nature of the crisis itself and its various facets are analyzed in Berlemann and Nenovsky (2004) and Dobrinsky (2000). The change in the policy course in the post-crisis period is analyzed in Dobrinsky (2001) and Nenovsky and Hristov (2002). Nenovsky and Rizopoulos (2003) analyze different aspects of the political economy of the regime change in this period. A few studies have attempted a synopsis of longer periods in Bulgaria's transition: Mihov (2001) provides an overview of the economic policies and changes during the first decade of transition. Miller and Petranov (2000) look at the process of privatization in Bulgaria and its outcomes.

Bulgaria's peculiar path towards the market economy reflects, *inter alia*, the intricate and strenuous political economy of the process of transformation. This contribution presents a concise overview of the political economy of the transition in the country focusing on the motivation and driving forces of Bulgaria's reform process.

The political economy of the transition has been about the political decisions on reform policies: How do these decisions take shape? What motivates such decisions? What are the driving forces (and actors) behind the decisions on reforms (or non-reform)? How are reforms implemented? When implemented, how successful are the policies in achieving their objectives? Why are some attempted reforms successful while others fail?

The theoretical literature also provides clues to some of these questions. Oddly enough—and somewhat disappointingly—the transition from plan to market *per se* did not motivate many new developments in the theoretical political economy literature. Most of the theoretical essays in this area were based on the application of already existing theoretical models of the political economy of economic reforms or their extensions.

Roland (2002, 2000), following Rodrik (1993), distinguishes between two main strands in the related literature: normative (which seeks to rationalize the decision-making problem of reformers subject to political constraints) and positive (which looks at the reform process as the outcome of a clash—or a deal—among interest groups).

A key specificity of the recent literature is the understanding of the endogeneity of the political process in a situation of a dynamic political equilibrium. It has been pointed out (Krueger, 1993) that, on the one hand, market responses to economic policies affect the political equilibrium and can induce changes in policy; on the other hand, economic interests are often a function of past policies.

Another key notion in the literature is that of political constraints, which by and large determine the space of feasible reforms as well as the degrees of freedom of policy makers. Roland (1994, 2000) points to the need to distinguish between *ex ante* political constraints (political factors that may block the adoption of reforms) and *ex post* ones (possible reversals after the reforms are implemented and their outcomes are known).

Another important feature of these models is the focus on the re-distributional nature (related to costs and benefits) of most economic reforms which gives rise to 'winners' and 'losers' of the reforms (Fernandez and Rodrik, 1991).

Notably, theoretical models are often put forward with the benefit of hindsight. In reality, most transition reforms were performed as trial and error. The same applies to the related political process which at best was promoted by visionary politicians and at worst, was captured by interest groups (Hellman *et al.*, 2003).

We illustrate some of the above concepts and the dynamics of transformation reforms with the case of Bulgaria, one of the most intriguing cases of the political economy of the transition from plan to market.

The political economy of non-reform leading to crisis (1989–97)

The context

Several major factors shaped the course of reform policies in Bulgaria: the specificity of the context; the acute political constraints at the onset of transition; the controversial process of stakeholder formation; a peculiar institutional dynamics; inefficient external anchors.

The specificity of the context played an important, if not a dominating, role in the initial phases of Bulgaria's reforms. A multiplicity of contextual factors—such as the extremely difficult initial economic conditions compared to other former communist countries (Dobrinsky, 1997), specific cultural and historic legacies, unfavorable geography, low state capacity, etc.—entailed path dependence and *de facto* acted as deterrents to market reforms. Importantly, in the case of Bulgaria, the inherited large macroeconomic imbalances were coupled with a severe foreign debt problem which led to a default in 1990.

The start of transition was marked by a collapse of the previously existing institutional structures. The speed of institutional destruction in Bulgaria by far exceeded the speed of creating new institutions. Ironically, the attacks on the public institutions of the communist state often degenerated into an attack on the institutions of the state *per se*. This forced retreat by the state resulted in an 'institutional hiatus,' with severely negative consequences for the reform process (Kozul-Wright and Rayment, 1997). It bred perverse incentives at the micro level, giving rise to adverse side effects such as financial indiscipline, rent seeking, and corruption.

The first phase of transition was characterized by amorphous and unstable stakeholder groups as well as by frequent changes of government representing different sides of the political spectrum. The short planning horizon essentially pre-empted polices targeting the medium or long-term horizon as a rational choice for politicians.

External factors also strongly affected the dynamics of Bulgarian reforms. The only important external actor in this period was the IMF. But the IMF as an institution was unprepared for the unprecedented challenges of the transition from plan to market. Being dominated by the spirit of the 'Washington Consensus,' the first IMF-supported programmes put too much emphasis on neo-liberal macroeconomics and too little on the context and the institutional environment and structural issues (Rodrik, 1996). These policies did not enjoy sufficient support from the Bulgarian government bureaucracy and were largely mistrusted by the Bulgarian public (Minassian, 2001). Programmes largely missed their targets and goals and as a result none of the four consecutive funding agreements subject to IMF conditionality between 1991 and 1996 was brought to a successful end (Table 18.1).

Lasting political polarization pushed the reform agenda in different directions, with dismal outcomes. On the macroeconomic front little was done to address the underlying causes of macroeconomic instability. No significant structural and institutional reforms were initiated in this period. Little progress was made in privatization (Figure 18.1) and enterprise restructuring. Soft budget constraints took various forms (Schaffer, 1998) leading to an escalating bad loans problem (Dobrinsky, 1994; Dobrinsky *et al.*, 2001).

Delayed reforms as a rational choice

At the start of transition, Bulgaria was facing the combination of a complex reform agenda and an extremely painful adjustment effort, compounded by the default on the foreign debt. Political support for the needed reforms was weak, indeed absent, due to high uncertainty about their distributional outcomes. Different interest groups feared, and were unwilling to accept, a disproportionate share of the costs of reforms. The political incentives for reforms were further reduced by the short lifetime of governments. The needed adjustment effort was hardly marketable to an electoral constituency as it involved painful measures with uncertain outcomes in a highly polarized society with heterogeneous stakeholder groups. One of the main societal failures in this phase was the inability to establish a core agreement on a coherent reform programme addressing both the adjustment effort and the basic market reform agenda. In the technical sense this was equivalent to a co-ordination failure among stakeholders and politicians.

Table 18.1 The two periods in Bulgaria's transition

	Reform failure	Reform success	
	1990–1997	1998–2003	2004–2008
Real GDP growth, average annual rate, %	−4.5	4.4	6.5
Real gross fixed capital formation growth, average annual rate, %	−10.8	18.7	18.6
Growth of total employment, average annual rate, %	−3.7	0	3.2
Rate of registered unemployment, period average, %	13.3	15.5	9.1
Growth of industrial labour productivity, average annual rate, %	0	4.7	4.6
Consumer prices inflation, average annual rate, %	174.7	7.7	7.7
Growth of average real wages, average annual rate, %	−15.2	5.4	5.7
Average share of food expenditure in household budget expenditure, %	47	42	38
BNB basic interest rate, %	99.6	4.2	4
Average short-term commercial lending interest, %	130.4	11.8	9.4
Commercial rate on (one-month) time deposits, %	71.8	3.1	3.4
Consolidated government balance (deficit), % of GDP (period average)	−6.3	−0.5	2.7
Total public debt, % of GDP (period average)	139.8	70.4	24.7
FDI annual flow, % of GDP (period average)	1.3	5.6	19.6
Share of private sector in GDP, % (period average)	46	69	75
'Progress in transition', EBRD (period average score)	2	3	3.38
Memo: Best performing country 'Progress in transition' (period average score)	3.01	3.79	3.9
IMF funding agreements brought to a successful end (number)	0 (out of 4)	3 (out of 3)	–
Average term in office of governments (years)	<1	4 (as law)	4 (as law)

Source: Author's calculations on the basis of national statistics, EBRD Transition Reports.

The required reforms in this period can be broken down into two broad categories: macro-economic stabilization and systemic reforms. Without looking into the aspect of sequencing, we try to interpret the rationale for delayed reforms in the context of some theoretical models.

One of the key related questions is why it took so long—compared to other countries with similar starting positions in the reform process—to introduce and sustain policies guaranteeing macroeconomic stability. The 'war of attrition' model suggested by Alesina and Drazen (1991) provides a rational explanation of delayed stabilizations in a similar macroeconomic setup. One of its results is that macroeconomic stabilization can be delayed because of significant distributional implications of the needed policy reform. In a heterogeneous society, when

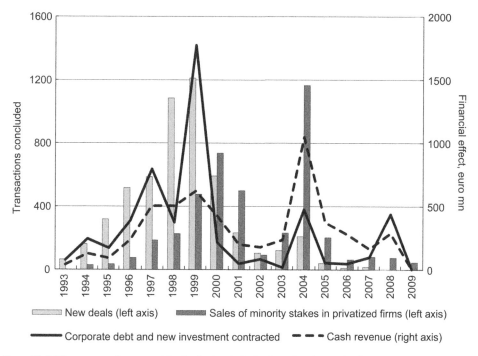

Figure 18.1 The process of commercial privatization in Bulgaria and its financial effect, 1993–2009
Source: Bulgarian Privatization Agency.

certain socio-economic groups may have to bear a disproportionate share of the reform burden, each group attempts to shift the burden of stabilization onto other groups ("war of attrition") and this delays the implementation of the reform.

As to systemic reforms, the prevailing socio-economic and political environment in Bulgaria in that period was consistent with the framework of the model of resistance to reform in the presence of individual uncertainty developed by Fernandez and Rodrik (1991). According to this model, some reforms that would have been popular *ex post* may not enjoy support *ex ante* depending on the uncertainties regarding the identities of the gainers and losers from the reforms.

In principle, the reform package facing Bulgaria's policymakers combined trade liberalization (as in the original Fernandez–Rodrik model) with enterprise restructuring and restructuring of foreign debt. All these policy measures were expected to affect post-reform relative prices and can thus be interpreted in the framework of the above model. The main theoretical outcome is that a situation when the individual gainers or losers of the reform cannot be clearly identified in advance is likely to be associated with the inability to form a voting majority in support of the needed reform. Hence, the likely policy outcome in this situation is preservation of the *status quo*.

While looking at the reform agenda from two different angles (that of their implied uncertainty and that of their distributional consequences) both models provide a rational interpretation of the reluctance of policy makers to go ahead with the needed reform agenda.

In fact, the socio-economic and political context in Bulgaria, the policy course, and the observed outcomes of (the lack of) reforms are also consistent with other models in this strand of the literature. Thus, Cukierman *et al.* (1992) derive the result that political polarization (very pronounced in Bulgaria in this phase) increases the probability of blocking the reforms Similarly, Murphy and Sturzenegger (1996) arrive at the result that the more ideological the political parties are (another typical feature of the Bulgarian political system at the time), the more likely it is that reforms would be blocked (as indeed happened).

The outcomes

The uneven course and piecemeal nature of Bulgarian reforms in the early phases of transition is reflected in the country's dismal economic performance in this period (Table 18.1). Bulgaria experienced one of the worst transformational recessions in Eastern Europe. The first phase of transition was characterized by a chronic large fiscal deficit (Figure 18.2), persistently high inflation and very high unemployment. The toleration of non-payments among economic agents (an important institutional failure) instigated widespread financial indiscipline in the economy. Ultimately, the negative consequences of non-reform accumulated in the banking system in the form of an escalating stock of bad loans. The banking system itself was institutionally weak: bank supervision was poorly designed and not endowed with sufficient power to enforce prudential banking regulations and practices (OECD, 1997).

The situation with banks' portfolios rapidly deteriorated: at the end of 1995, some 75 per cent of the outstanding commercial bank loans were classified as sub-standard or non-performing. Public confidence in the banking system started to erode in late 1995. The panic gradually escalated with the subsequent closure of several banks and towards mid-1996 took the form of a full-scale run on the banking system. The collapse of the banking system provoked massive currency substitution and capital flight, exerting a strong downward pressure on the currency and causing a drain of official forex reserves. Money supply was out of control. Attempting to save the banking system, the central bank increased uncollateralized refinancing of the commercial banks. Finally, a special law was passed in December, obliging the central bank to

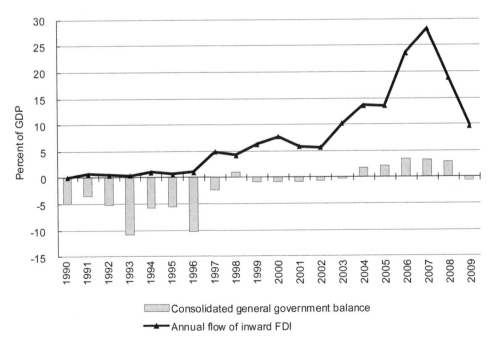

Figure 18.2 Fiscal deficit and inward FDI in Bulgaria, 1990–2009 (per cent of GDP)
Source: Author's calculations on the basis of national statistics.

extend a huge credit line to the budget (equivalent to 45 per cent of GDP in 1996). This enormous monetary injection spurred a hyperinflationary hike at the turn of 1996.

The chaos in the financial system, as well as in the economy as a whole, the eroding real incomes and the steadily deteriorating expectations triggered a plunge in economic activity: the cumulative GDP drop in 1996–97 amounted to some 15 percent. The crisis resulted in a significant loss of financial wealth for a great number of people and provoked mass street riots. In January 1997, the ruling government was forced to resign. A caretaker government took office to prepare early parliamentary elections, which were held in June 1997.

The political economy of successful reforms (1997–2007 and beyond)

The new context

The 1996–97 crisis was a dividing line in Bulgaria's reforms. It resulted in further impoverishment and deepening of the social stratification, and brought about widespread frustration with the policies pursued during the first phases of transition. The biggest losers were the low- and middle-income classes, those who had held assets and savings in domestic currency. By the time of the crisis and during its course, many of them lost a major share of what they had to lose, in terms of both wealth and jobs.

The general disillusion with the previous policy stance translated into broad public support for a radical change in the course of economic reforms. The reform drive was supported by a process of consolidation of stakeholder groups. During the course of transition, small entrepreneurs gradually emerged as one of the most influential stakeholder groups. Foreign investors and the emerging class of big domestic entrepreneurs and executives also gained in importance. Private entrepreneurs had a vested interest in a stable and predictable economic environment, transparent policy, and political stability.

Equally important, significant changes took place in the country's external environment. In the first place this was the IMF, which intervened during the crisis offering financial support, but under the conditions of a clear role in macroeconomic management. The other major external agent that entered into play was the EU. The actual turning point in the relations with the EU was the decision to start accession negotiations with Bulgaria in 1999. These important external signals provided a powerful support for those domestic political forces with a pro-market political orientation.

All these changes in the context amounted to a 'structural break' in the driving forces of Bulgarian reforms in the sense of a major change in the underlying structural relations that drove the reform process and determined its direction.

The political economy of policy change

The political economy of this second phase of transition can also be interpreted within the strand of literature on the positive economics of policy reform. The models of Drazen and Grilli (1993) and Drazen (1996) suggest rational choice theoretical arguments why major economic crises may serve as catalysts of reforms. They conclude that the welfare losses associated with crises mobilize societies to put in place measures that would otherwise be impossible to enact. In such a framework, if there is no consensus between interest groups over the reform path and the distribution of the costs and benefits associated with it (as was the case in Bulgaria), a crisis may be the only way to induce necessary policy changes. Put differently, in a situation of a crisis, the costs incurred by the population, including the interest groups most affected by reforms, become comparable to the costs of reforms and political support for reforms starts to grow. The Drazen and Grilli interpretation is fully consistent with the situation in Bulgaria at the peak of the financial crisis in 1996–97. It was the deep economic and financial crisis that finally motivated a political agreement on the future reform course.

Taking into consideration the endogeneity of the policy process in a situation of a dynamic political equilibrium (Krueger, 1993) adds another nuance. As noted above, in such a framework, both policies and the political equilibrium (support of or resistance to policies) can change endogenously over time. In the case of Bulgaria, the attitude of the main interest groups, including those that resisted reforms most fiercely in the first phases of transition, were rapidly changing during the crisis as they were beginning to realize that past policies of non-reform were leading to a catastrophe. This was equivalent to a major shift in the political equilibrium in the country towards reform-oriented policies.

And finally, one cannot ignore the importance of the external agents in legitimizing the change in policy direction and in providing an anchor to local reform-minded politicians after 1997. The IMF had a prominent role in instituting policies of fiscal restraint under extremely harsh economic conditions, which has been the key factor of macroeconomic stability after 1997. In turn, the realistic prospects for EU membership (regarded by local politicians as an impending reward for policy success) and the disciplining role of accession negotiations have been a crucial vehicle for pushing through a broad institutional, legislative and regulatory reform agenda. It would be fair to say that the risks of abandoning the reform course and slipping back into policy havoc would have been much greater in the absence of these strong external anchors.

The outcomes

The key component and instrument of the policy approach towards macroeconomic stabilization in Bulgaria was a currency board arrangement (CBA) which started operation in July 1997 with the nominal exchange rate fixed against the Deutsche mark (subsequently to the euro). Under this arrangement, there was no room for sovereign monetary policy: the central bank was banned from open market operations and refinancing of commercial banks.

Under the CBA the instruments of fiscal policy, in principle, remained available to policy makers; however, in practice, the degrees of fiscal policy freedom were limited by long-term fiscal sustainability concerns (Dobrinsky, 2001). Indeed, Bulgaria's fiscal policy under the CBA was set up under a medium-term fiscal framework that would guarantee fiscal sustainability (Horvath and Székely, 2003). This framework was a major technical innovation in Eastern Europe and its implementation proved a success.

A major focus of the accompanying reforms was placed on institutional strengthening. New technical criteria regulating risky exposure of commercial banks and very tight capital adequacy requirements as well as stringent requirements on bank reporting to the supervision authority were put in place.

During the years that followed, a number of important structural reforms were also given a start. These included a tax reform whose main direction was towards lowering the tax burden as well as reforms of the pension and health care systems; other components of the social security system were also reorganized.

Privatization was finally given a solid start. Sales to strategic foreign investors were declared as high priority targets and this period saw several landmark sales of large SOEs. The years between 1997 and 1999 were the period of most intensive ownership transfer combining commercial privatization (Figure 18.1) and several waves of mass privatization that mostly involved small and medium-sized SOEs (Miller, 2011; Miller and Petranov, 2000). Bank privatization was also assigned high priority and by 2004 all state-owned banks had been privatized to strategic foreign investors.

The process of accession negotiations with the EU which started in 1999 played a very important role in speeding up market reforms, especially in their institutional aspect. This preparation of EU accession involved negotiations on the 30 'chapters' which make up the EU's *acquis communautaire*. EU accession implied a considerable widening and deepening of the reform process with the goal, within a relatively short historic time span, to upgrade market institutions to a status typical of a mature market economy.

In the period after 1997, Bulgaria's macroeconomic performance improved considerably, especially when compared to the preceding period (Table 18.1). The major improvements in the fiscal system brought about a remarkable consolidation in public finances (Figure 18.2) and a sharp fall of public debt as a proportion of GDP. Macroeconomic stabilization was finally achieved. The initial stagnation that accompanied enterprise restructuring was followed by years of strong growth.

The fast reform progress in these years is also evidenced by EBRD's assessment of 'progress in transition' (Table 18.1). In these assessments Bulgaria moved from being one of the laggards in reforms before 1997, to one of the more advanced reformers in the period thereafter. Another sign of positive change has been the surge in the flow of inward FDI after 1997, in contrast to the anemic inflows prior to that (Table 18.1 and Figure 18.2). Foreign investors 'vote with their feet' and this change was a clear indication of the improvement in the investment climate and the business environment in general.

Concluding remarks

Bulgaria's experience in economic and political transformation is one of failure and success: a first phase characterized by a series of failures and relatively successful reforms in later stages. Political economy factors played a key role in the dynamics and outcomes in both phases of Bulgaria's transition. Moreover, Bulgaria's experience in both phases is consistent with the theoretical predictions of a number of models of the political economy of economic reforms.

A variety of intertwined factors and developments (from context, to institutions, to design, to political constraints, to implementation) undermined Bulgaria's first reform efforts. This experience confirms that disregarding or underestimating the importance of any of these components can drive a reform effort to failure. From a political economy point of view reform failure in this period highlights the role of uncertainty about the outcomes of reforms and their distributional implications. Such an analytical insight helps to understand better why policies that worked in other transition economies turned out to be unsuccessful (or non-starters) in Bulgaria: while a number of countries attempted similar reform programmes at the start of transition, the outcomes were very different due to a different context and/or country-specific structural and institutional characteristics.

The reform programme in the second phase of transition owes much of its success to the fact that it addressed some of the institutional failures of the first phase of transition: both institutional strengthening and improving governance were important factors for the acceleration of the ongoing structural reforms. From a political economy point of view reform success in this period underscores the role of a major crisis as a catalyst of reforms. Bulgaria's experience in the second phase also suggests that in a situation of amorphous and unstable stakeholder groups external anchors can substitute as a co-ordinating factor in the design of reform policies.

Bibliography

Alesina, A. and Drazen, A. (1991), 'Why Are Stabilizations Delayed?' *American Economic Review*, vol. 81(5), pp. 1170–88.

Avramov, R. and Sgard, J. (1996), 'Bulgaria: From Enterprise Indiscipline to Financial Crisis,' *MOCT-MOST*, vol. 6(4), pp. 71–102.

Berlemann, M. and Nenovsky, N. (2004), 'Lending of First versus Lending of Last Resort: The Bulgarian Financial Crisis of 1996/1997', *Comparative Economic Studies*, vol. 46(2), pp. 245–71.

Bristow, J. (1996), *The Bulgarian Economy in Transition*, Cheltenham: Edward Elgar.

Cukierman, A., Edwards, S. and Tabellini, G. (1992), 'Seigniorage and Political Instability', *American Economic Review*, vol. 82(3), pp. 537–55.

Dobrinsky, R. (2001), 'Fiscal Policy under a Currency Board Arrangement: Bulgaria's Post-Crisis Policy Dilemmas,' *Russian and East European Finance and Trade*, vol. 37(2), pp. 36–77

——(2000), 'The Transition Crisis in Bulgaria,' *Cambridge Journal of Economics*, vol. 24(5), pp. 581–602

——(1997) 'Transition Failures: Anatomy of the Bulgarian Crisis,' *The Vienna Institute for Comparative Economic Studies* (WIIW), Research Report No. 236, April.

——(1996), 'Monetary Policy, Macroeconomic Adjustment and Currency Speculation under Floating Exchange Rate: The Case of Bulgaria,' *The Economics of Transition*, vol. 4(1), pp. 185–210

——(1994), 'The Problem of Bad Loans and Enterprise Indebtedness in Bulgaria', *MOCT-MOST*, vol. 4(3), pp. 37–58

Dobrinsky, R., Dochev, N., Markov, N. and Nikolov, B. (2001) 'Corporate Financial Flows and Access to Bank Finance under Distorted and Perverse Incentives: Bulgarian Firms in the Eve of the Financial Crisis', *Russian and East European Finance and Trade*, 37(2), pp. 78-114.

Drazen, A. (1996) 'The Political Economy of Delayed Reform', *The Journal of Policy Reform,* 1(1), pp. 25-46.

Drazen, A. and Grilli, V. (1993), 'The Benefit of Crises for Economic Reforms,' *American Economic Review*, vol. 83(3), pp. 598–607

Fernandez, R. and Rodrik, D. (1991), 'Resistance to Reform: Status Quo Bias in the Presence of Individual-Specific Uncertainty', *American Economic Review*, vol. 81(5), pp. 1146–55.

Hellman, J., Jones, G. and Kaufmann, D. (2003), 'Seize the State, Seize the Day: State Capture and Influence in Transition Economies', *Journal of Comparative Economics*, vol. 31(4), pp. 751–73.

Horvath, B. and Székely, I. (2003), 'The Role of Medium-Term Fiscal Frameworks for Transition Countries: The Case of Bulgaria', *Emerging Markets Finance and Trade*, vol. 39(1), pp. 86–113.

Jones, D. and Miller, J. (1997), *The Bulgarian Economy: Lessons from Reform during Early Transition*, Aldershot: Ashgate.

Koford, K. (2000), 'Citizen Restraints on "Leviathan" Government: Transition Politics in Bulgaria', *European Journal of Political Economy,* vol. 16(2), pp. 307–38.

Kozul-Wright, R. and Rayment, P. (1997), 'The Institutional Hiatus in Economies in Transition and Its Policy Consequences', *Cambridge Journal of Economics*, vol. 21(5), pp. 641–61.

Krueger, A.O. (1993), 'Virtuous and Vicious Circles in Economic Development', *American Economic Review* (AEA Papers and Proceedings), vol. 83(2), pp. 351–55.

Mihov, I. (2001), 'Bulgaria: Ten Years of Economic Transition', in Blejer, M. and Skreb, M. (eds), *Transition: The First Decade*, Cambridge, MA: MIT Press, pp. 401–39.

Miller, J. (2011) 'Evaluation of Mass Privatization in Bulgaria', *Comparative Economic Studies*, vol. 53(4), pp. 621–646.

Miller, J. and Petranov, S. (2000), 'The First Wave of Mass Privatization in Bulgaria and Its Immediate Aftermath', *Economics of Transition*, vol. 8(1), pp. 225–50.

Minassian, G. (2001), 'Bulgaria and the International Monetary Fund', *Russian and East European Finance and Trade*, vol. 37(2), pp. 7–35.

Murphy, R.L. and Sturzenegger, F. (1996), 'The Feasibility of Low Inflation: Theory with an Application to the Argentine Case', *Journal of Policy Reform*, vol. 1(1), pp. 47–74.

Nenovsky, N. and Hristov, K. (2002), 'The New Currency Boards and Discretion: Empirical Evidence from Bulgaria', *Economic Systems*, vol. 26(1), pp. 55–72.

Nenovsky, N. and Rizopoulos, Y. (2003), 'Extreme Monetary Regime Change: Evidence from Currency Board Introduction in Bulgaria', *Journal of Economic Issues*, vol. 37(4), pp. 909–41.

OECD (1997), *OECD Economic Surveys Bulgaria*, Paris: Organisation for Co-operation and Development.

Rodrik, D. (1996), 'Goodbye Washington Consensus, Hello Washington Confusion? A Review of the World Bank's Economic Growth in the 1990s: Learning from a Decade of Reform', *Journal of Economic Literature*, vol. 44(4), pp. 973–87.

——(1993), 'The Positive Economics of Policy Reform,' *American Economic Review* (AEA Papers and Proceedings), vol. 83(2), pp. 356–61.

Roland, G. (2002), 'The Political Economy of Transition', *Journal of Economic Perspectives*, vol. 16(1), pp. 29–50.

——(2000), *Transition and Economics. Politics, Markets, and Firms.* Cambridge, MA and London: The MIT Press.

——(1994), 'The Role of Political Constraints in Transition Strategies', *Economics of Transition*, vol. 2(1), pp. 27–41.

Schaffer, M. (1998), 'Do Firms in Transition Economies Have Soft Budget Constraints? A Reconsideration of Concepts and Evidence', *Journal of Comparative Economics*, vol. 26(1), pp. 80–103.

19

INTERPRETING CHINA'S ECONOMIC GROWTH AND PREDICTING ITS FUTURE COURSE

Wing Thye Woo

It is not a matter of great contention that China is the star performer amongst the transition economies. What is highly contentious, however, are the reasons that have been proposed to explain China's stellar growth. Because China avoided the prolonged recession of eastern Europe and the former Soviet Union (EEFSU) in the beginning of their transitions, it was fashionable almost up to 2000 to attribute China's success in economic transition to the particular set of reform policies that China implemented. The most enthusiastic contributors to this laudatory literature would even trumpet the inevitable appearance of a new set of economic practices that was based on neither Soviet-style socialism nor free-market capitalism, e.g. Nolan (1993) and Rawski (1995). The whiff of a forthcoming revolution in economic theory was certainly in the air as the bulk of the economic transition literature that related to China in the first-half of the 1990s expounded various lessons that EEFSU should learn from China's seemingly unorthodox approach to economic transition.

By 2000, however, the praise for the 'China Way' has largely been muted because virtually all of the much-ballyhooed, innovative, non-capitalist policies of the 1980s had been abandoned by then. The stance of the Chinese economic policy regime had not only become recognizably similar to those in the capitalist East Asia, but it was also on course to become even more similar to them – a commitment that China made when it agreed to the conditions imposed on its application for World Trade Organization (WTO) membership. Also, the sustained economic growth in much of EEFSU after 1995, and more careful comparative analyses of a larger set of transition economies, had undermined the veracity of the so-called 'lessons from China'. In fact, the end of the 1990s saw the appearance of a number of influential studies that predicted 'the coming collapse of China', e.g. Chang (2001).

This chapter will focus on two issues: (a) the debate on China's growth mechanisms; and (b) the prospects for continued high growth in China.

The first phase of the debate on China's growth mechanisms

There have been two phases in the debate over why China has performed better than EEFSU. The analytical divide focused in its first phase on the speed and the scope of the reform programme:

gradual, piecemeal reform versus fast, comprehensive reform. Then in its second phase it focused on the epistemological origin of the reform strategy: institutional experimentalism to produce new non-capitalist institutional forms versus institutional convergence to best international practices in the advanced capitalist economies.

The first phase of the debate arose from the contrast between the slow and partial liberalization of prices by China in the 1978–91 period and the overnight deregulation of virtually all prices by Poland on 1 January 1990. For example, in 1979, China had two prices for most agricultural products – low-plan prices in state-owned stores where ration coupons were required for purchase of products, and market-determined prices in the farmers' markets – and had plan prices for most industrial goods. Since China had experienced immediate output growth upon the implementation of market-oriented reforms while Poland had an immediate output decline, some observers even saw the set of fast, comprehensive reforms (big-bang reforms) as a shock to the economy, e.g. Lin *et al.* (1994).

To many of these observers, the secret of China's sustained high growth with satisfactory price stability was that China implemented the correct sequence of reforms. Gradual reform was the strategy of sequencing reforms. For example, Griffin and Khan (1993) held that the brilliance of the Chinese reformers lay in liberalizing the economy before liberalizing the politics (*perestroika* first and *glasnost* later), while McMillan and Naughton (1992) contended that the brilliance of China lay instead in liberalizing the agricultural sector before liberalizing the industrial sector. For McKinnon (1991), the key to ensuring growth-with-stability was to restore macroeconomic balance and reform the fiscal and financial institutions before undertaking microeconomic liberalization like price deregulation. Then, according to Olson (1992: ix), unless the economic reforms were preceded by institutional reforms (e.g. establishment of a legal system), the output response to the economic liberalization would be low, if not negative.

The fact that different economists have identified different sequences as the optimal sequence reveals that the 'correct' sequence is far from obvious. It is also not obvious whether there is a correct sequence that applies to every transition economy. For example, contrary to Olson's thesis, the high Chinese growth was certainly not preceded by any great changes in Chinese legal institutions governing contract implementation and property rights.

Fan and Woo (2009) rejected the sequence interpretation of gradualism because it does not characterize the reform process in China correctly and does not recognize adequately the interaction among reforms that sustains the progress of each individual reform. To see this second point, consider the reform of state-owned enterprises (SOEs). Because SOEs were used to guarantee full employment during the central planning period, market-oriented reforms of the SOEs (which could involve privatization of the SOEs) could lead to the shedding of surplus workers and the termination of company-based pensions to retired workers. If the state does not already have social welfare programmes in place to provide relief payments to the displaced workers and pensioners in the respective forms of unemployment insurance and welfare, then there would be a drastic fall in their standard of living. A social cost is incurred when the SOE reform runs ahead of the reform in social safety nets.

Similarly, a welfare loss is also produced when we reverse the above sequence of reforms. Specifically, the new state-funded welfare programmes will induce the SOE managers to unload surplus workers and pensioners into these programmes without necessarily making any reforms in the operations of the SOEs themselves.

The optimal solution is of course to privatize the SOEs and establish the state-funded social safety nets simultaneously, but these simultaneous reforms are unlikely to be in the feasibility set because each of them takes a different length of time to accomplish, and, more relevantly, it would be beyond the capability of the state to handle both large projects at the same time. In short, optimal sequences exist only when the policy-maker is constrained to introduce one new policy measure at a time (i.e. so-called optimality disappears once simultaneous implementation of policies is technically possible).

In the above two examples, sequencing will always result in a social cost because of the incoherence between the reforms in these two sectors. One way of avoiding this social cost is to undertake simultaneous *partial* reforms that will maintain coherence between the two reforms. The key is to keep the pace of SOE reform consistent with the pace of the reform of social safety nets. This is the *Parallel Partial Progression* approach that Fan and Woo (2009) have proposed as the alternative conceptual framework for the gradualist approach. Parallel Partial Progression is not the same as the step-by-step sequencing approach, because a 'partial reform' is not a 'completed step'. Simultaneous partial implementation is preferable to policy sequencing because it eliminates the costs of incoherence among policies. The inter-dependence between reform of the SOEs and reform of the social safety net system means that a lack of progress on either reform could constrain the continued progress of the other. This incoherence between the two reforms could be described as a 'reform bottleneck'.[1]

Perhaps, the most important reason why the debate on China's growth mechanisms stopped using the dichotomy in policy implementation (gradual versus fast) as its focus is because this policy dichotomy did not correspond to the dichotomy in output response (growth versus decline). Within EEFSU, initial output decline was the norm regardless of the speed of marketization. Output fell in slow reformers like Ukraine and Romania, in moderate-speed reformers like Russia and Hungary, and in big-bang reformers like Poland and Estonia. Within communist East Asia – China, Laos and Vietnam (CLV) – sustained higher output growth was achieved immediately with the initiation of gradual reforms in China in December 1978 and with the unleashing of big-bang reform in Vietnam and Laos in March 1989.[2]

Sachs and Woo (1994) have proposed that the marketization of transition economies in EEFSU and CLV had different output consequences because the marketization initiated different economic processes in EEFSU and CLV. The marketization of EEFSU economies unleashed the economic restructuring of distorted industrialized economies, whereas the marketization of CLV economies allowed the economic development of subsistence peasant agricultural economies. Poland in 1990 and Russia in 1992 had bloated heavy industries, and their task was to move labour and capital away from the heavy industries to the light industries and the services sector.[3] China in 1978 and Vietnam in 1989 had surplus agricultural labour and the task was to industrialize and to legalise the private service sector to absorb this surplus labour.[4] The immediate outcome of economic restructuring in EEFSU was job loss (economic pain!), and the immediate outcome of economic development in CLV was output growth (economic gain!). In short, the dichotomy in output response to marketization in EEFSU and CLV resided in the dichotomy of their initial economic structures – industrialized urban economies in EEFSU versus subsistence rural economies in CLV.

The second phase of the debate on China's growth mechanisms

With the de-emphasis on the primacy of (a) slow implementation of marketization measures and (b) the confinement of these measures to a few areas at a time, a second strain of gradualism came to the fore in the debate. Gradualism was no longer described as a strategy in itself but as the by-product of a strategy of experimentation to find a third way between state-plan socialism and free-market capitalism. Gradual reform was re-interpreted to be the technical outcome of a three-step reform process. First, different implementation protocols for any particular policy were tested in different locations; second, the results were evaluated; and, third, the central government propagated the best implementation protocol (which has to be at least as good as the free-market protocol) for nation-wide adoption. In short, this second strain of gradualism claims that the dichotomy in initial growth performance between EEFSU and China follows from the dichotomy between the Washington Consensus policies implemented in EEFSU and the innovative, non-capitalist-biased policies implemented in China.

We call this type of gradualist perspective the Experimentalist School (E-school) because it views China as groping, with considerable success, towards a unique Chinese economic model. According to Naughton (1995):

> Reforms have been gradual and evolutionary ... Reforming without a blueprint, neither the process nor the ultimate objective was clearly envisaged beforehand ... It can be seen, *ex post*, that there is substantial coherence to these different elements. Reduction of the state's monopoly led to rapid entry of new firms. Entry of new firms, combined with adoption of market prices on the margin, led to enhanced competition, and began to get state-sector managers accustomed to responding to the marketplace. Gradual price decontrol was essential. Competition eroded initially high profit margins for state firms, and induced the government, as owner of the firms, to become more concerned with profitability. The government experimented with better incentive and monitoring devices, and this improved state-sector performance ... [5]

In Woo's (1999) opinion, Naughton's reasoning is guilty of *post hoc ergo propter hoc*, and he argued against the E-school's claim of China's economic exceptionalism:

> [In the marketization of centrally planned economies] little institutional experimentation is needed or desired. The long-run goals of institutional change are clear, and are found in the economic models of existing market-based economies. ... [The] sense of wonderment about China's 'institutional innovations' and Rawski's [1995] claim that China's reform experience challenges the 'fundamental tenets of economic theory' derive from an inadequate understanding of growth experiences elsewhere in the world.

We call this second viewpoint the Convergence School (C-school) because it holds that Chinese economic success is the outcome of Chinese institutions gradually converging with those of non-socialist market economies, especially those in East Asia.[6] The C-school believes that China's rapid growth reflects the same forces that have underpinned rapid growth throughout East Asia – market-based, export-led growth of labour-intensive manufactures – and that the 'innovative institutions' so admired by the E-school are simply imperfect substitutes for normal market institutions that would have provided China with at least as rapid growth, and at less cost in terms of long-run distortions. Gradualism, in this view, has not been a strategy so much as a result of continuing political conflict and other difficulties inherent in setting a policy course in a country of some 1.3 billion people. According to the C-school, China has achieved the greatest success in precisely the areas (e.g. agriculture and coastal provinces) where market reforms have gone the furthest.

Table 19.1 sums up the key differences between the E-school and the C-school in how they interpret China's achievements. We will select for discussion two of the more unusual claims: (a) partial price deregulation is superior to complete price deregulation; and (b) localized collective ownership, as opposed to centralized collective ownership, generates enterprise performance that is at least equal to private ownership.

Table 19.1 Experimentalism versus Convergence

	E-school	C-school
Speed of reform	Sequential trial-and-error	Rapid and comprehensive liberalization of agriculture, and of international trade in coastal provinces; slow deregulation of SOEs and of international trade in interior provinces
Reasons for gradualism (incrementalism)	Economic experimentation	Political compromise; ideological commitment to state ownership
Sources of rapid growth	Unintended virtuous cycle, and few dislocations from large shifts in policies	Existence of surplus agriculture labour; East Asia pattern of labour-intensive export-led growth
Outcomes in the SOEs	Substantial improvements in production efficiency	Little technical progress; and over-compensation of SOE personnel and over-investment that weaken the fiscal situation
Interpretation of the TVEs	Adaptations to China's economic conditions of still-developing markets	Continuing legal restrictions on private ownership
Future directions and pace of reform	Policies will change to reflect evolution in material conditions and lessons from continuing experiments	Policies will push China toward a normal private market economy with characteristics similar to other East Asian economies

Is the dual-track pricing system superior to complete price liberalization?

Lau, Qian and Roland (LQR, 2000) have claimed that the dual-track pricing system (DTPS) is the reason why China avoided the transformational recession of EEFSU. The LQR thesis of 'gain without pain' can easily be understood by using a two-sector general equilibrium model of heavy industries and light industries.[7] Under centrally planned socialism, the heavy industry SOEs and the light industry SOEs would each be given a total output target that is, respectively, larger and smaller than what output would have been under the free market; and there would be excess demand in each market because of the artificially low plan prices. To cover the total cost, the plan price of each good equals the average cost of producing the target output, and is hence below the marginal cost of the final units of targeted output. Certain privileged individuals would be given ration coupons that entitle the holder to buy a fixed quantity at the plan prices, and, needless to say, there would be a black market in ration coupons. Now, if the prices were to be freed completely in this setting, there would be an increase in welfare (measured as the sum of consumer surplus and producer surplus in the two markets) but there would be losers because the former recipients of ration coupons would have to pay higher prices.

According to LQR, China achieved a Pareto-improving outcome when it implemented the DTPS. China continued to issue the same number of ration coupons (i.e. set the same output target) at the low plan prices, but if a firm produced above its output target, the firm could sell the excess output at market-determined prices. As DTPS could increase the output of the light industrial good only with a decrease in the output of the heavy industrial good in a general equilibrium setting, what made this situation Pareto-improving? LQR answered this question by claiming that the light industry SOE manager in China had executed the following sequence of actions: (i) went into the black market for ration coupons for heavy industrial good and bought coupons for some of the planned output; say, X units of the heavy industrial good;

(ii) informed the manager of the heavy industry SOE that he would not exercise his right to buy the X units if the heavy industry SOE would release the inputs for these X units for employment in the light industrial good sector (The heavy industry SOE manager was happy to cooperate because, with the marginal cost of the final units of his output target above the plan price, the reduction of output by X units increased his profits); and (iii) hired the newly released inputs from the heavy industrial sector and expanded the production of the light industrial good.

The above LQR account of how DTPS worked in China is consistent with a theoretical general equilibrium model of Pareto-improving sectoral adjustment but it is empirically inconsistent with the facts. LQR's theoretical model required the heavy industrial sector to shrink as the light industrial sector expanded but the empirical record shows that output of both the light and heavy industrial sectors went up every year following the introduction of the DTPS in 1985. Light industrial output increased 64 per cent in the 1984–87 period, and heavy industrial output increased 55 per cent.

What really happened was not that DTPS reallocated industrial production within the SOE sector as LQR had suggested but that the DTPS, *together*[8] with the partial liberalization of (a) agriculture, (b) ownership forms (i.e. entry into the industrial sectors by domestic non-SOEs and foreign non-SOEs), and (c) foreign trade, caused a rapid increase in industrial output; most of which came from the new non-SOEs. Furthermore, the labour that fuelled the fast expansion of the non-state industrial sector did not come out from the SOEs[9] but from agriculture, a sector that was not identified by LQR as an important contributor to China's high growth rates after 1984.

Woo (2001) has argued that dual-track pricing was an unsustainable economic mechanism, not just because of the technical difficulties in its administration, but also because of the political difficulties in maintaining the cohesion of the ruling coalition. The plan track for inputs conferred instant black market profits on the privileged recipient of the quota. The resulting outcry over the 'middleman' role of many children of top leaders led Hu Yaobang, then head of the Communist Party of China (CPC), to arrest the children of several top conservative (pro-planning) leaders. This crackdown aggravated the infighting inside the ruling coalition, and this contributed significantly to the dismissal of Hu Yaobang as head of the CPC in 1987. The choice facing the CPC élite was to either maintain the political coalition or maintain the dual track price system. Political reality is the reason why the plan track was ended quickly in the 1990–91 period when the conservative faction was in charge of the economy, even though this action was not Pareto-improving and was against its ideological precepts.

Is localized socialism the viable form of socialism?

The single largest contributor to China's economic growth in the 1985–93 period was the collectively owned sector, which consisted mostly of rural industrial enterprises that were registered as owned collectively by villages, townships, or counties, and were hence called township and village enterprises (TVEs). According to E-school literature in the first half of 1990s, TVEs represented localized socialism just as SOEs represent centralized socialism, i.e. TVEs meant ownership by the local community instead of ownership by the national community, and (certainly) not private ownership.[10] The E-school argued that collective ownership is an effective way to raise capital funds for rural enterprises and to reduce the principal-agent problem by shortening the distance of supervision, e.g. Naughton (1994) interpreted the TVE ownership structure as a good adaptation to market failures caused by China's underdeveloped markets for factors of production.

The C-school was sceptical of the E-school's functionalist explanation of the TVE ownership form because the collective ownership structure of rural industry is highly unusual by international standards, e.g. the rural industries in Indonesia, Taiwan and Thailand are mostly family owed. The basic distinction in TVE ownership between the E-school and the C-school is that the former takes the formal registration status as the real situation, while the latter regards the formal registration status to be the cover for an evolving ownership pattern. The C-school rejected the E-school's emphasis on the state's superiority in financial intermediation because Taiwan's small and medium-sized private enterprises exhibited dynamic growth in the 1960–85 period even though they were heavily discriminated against by Taiwan's wholly state-owned banking system. Taiwan's rural firms thrived because informal financial markets emerged to cater to their needs.[11]

The C-school saw the TVE ownership structure as the product of political and not economic circumstances. First, private ownership was heavily discriminated against (if not, banned) in many areas until about 1993, and thus collective ownership of rural industry arose as the primary response to the profitable niches created by central planning. Many private enterprises evaded discrimination by registering themselves as collectively-owned, a charade that Chinese observers called 'wearing the red cap'. Second, the collective ownership of TVEs was rendered more manageable by the low labour mobility in the countryside, which, in turn, was the result of the system of political control known as the household registration system (*hukou*) that tied the peasants to the land. Community ownership was hence workable because the community members expected to remain in the same place indefinitely, and there was also no complicating factor of inward migration until the late 1990s.[12]

The debate on the nature of the TVEs started waning around 1995 because, by then, many legal restrictions against private ownership of enterprises had been removed and the process was widely expected to strengthen, and the privatization of collectively-owned TVEs was happening in the richest coastal provinces. While the final fate of TVEs was not clear in 1995, Putterman (1995), who believed 'that some form of market socialism could be [economically] viable', was pessimistic about the future of collective ownership because he viewed global and Chinese political trends as unjustifiably favouring private enterprises.

In 2012 the rural firms that are still registered as collectively owned are no longer a significant economic force; and most of the rural firms registered as TVEs are shareholding co-operatives that are indistinguishable from private enterprises. We think that this change has occurred not because CPC stands for the 'closet party of capitalists' as some members of the E-school have implied but because the collective ownership structure was not compatible with the efficient operation of enterprises, even small and medium-sized ones. Once the political discrimination against capitalist ownership forms was reduced substantially, there was no longer the need for the charade of 'wearing the red hat'.

The road to prosperity might not be a smooth one

China's economy has been like a speeding car for the past 30 years. Its GDP per capita (PPP in US$) overtook India's in 1979, the Philippines' in 1992 and Indonesia's in 1999. It is revealing, however, that the CPC has become cautious about the continuation of high growth since 2006 when it replaced 'economic construction' with 'the establishment of a harmonious society by 2020' as its primary mission.[13] The obvious implication from this change is that the present major social, economic and political trends within China are unlikely to lead to a harmonious society.

To return to the analogy of China's economy being like a speeding car, we could classify the high-probability failures that could cause a car crash in the future into three analytical categories: hardware failure; software failure; and power supply failure (Woo 2007).

A *hardware failure* refers to the breakdown of an *economic mechanism* – a development that is analogous to the collapse of the chassis of a car. Examples of hardware failures are a banking crisis; a budget crisis; and a productivity growth crisis. Specifically, the huge macro-stimulus that the Chinese government had implemented in 2008–10 in response to the global financial crisis could well cause a hardware failure to occur. The success of the stimulus programme was ensured by ordering (1) the state-controlled enterprises (SCEs) to undertake huge investments regardless of anticipated future demand, and (2) the state-controlled banks (SCBs) to extend the necessary loans for these investments.[14] Because the SCEs and the SCBs had implemented a state-assigned mission, their managers cannot rightly be held responsible should the assigned projects turn out to be financial busts in the future.

Many of these industrial and infrastructure investments were undertaken by the 8,000 local investment companies established by the local governments; and the loans of these investment vehicles had amounted to 51 per cent of GDP by the end of 2009 and the debt of the central government amounted to 20 per cent of GDP.[15] Given the many anecdotes about new investments in industries plagued by overcapacity (e.g. steel, cement and aluminium); trophy investments (e.g. grand town centres, high-speed rail and stately administrative buildings); and spontaneous privatization of project funds (e.g. massive purchase of cars by state bodies), much of the bank loans to the stimulus programme could end up as non-performing loans (NPLs) – which would then cause either a banking crisis or a fiscal crisis.

A second concern about China's stimulus programme is that the SCBs had channelled the flood of liquidity to the SCEs and neglected the increased financing needs of the private sector brought on by the global financial crisis. Examples abound of private companies that closed or were acquired by their state-controlled counterparts, and this expansion of the state firms at the expense of the private firms is likely to lower future productivity growth.

A *software failure* refers to a flaw in *governance* that creates frequent and/or widespread social disorders, a situation akin to a car crashing because of a fight among the people inside the speeding car. Software failures could come from the present high-growth strategy worsening inequality and corruption significantly, and from the state not being responsive enough to rising social expectations. The satisfactory functioning of a market economy requires a wide array of regulatory institutions that range from straightforward law-and-order administration to complicated legal adjudication. China's strategy of incremental reform combined with the fact that institution building is a time-consuming process meant that many of its regulatory institutions are either absent or ineffective. The results have been governance failures on many important fronts, e.g. tainted food products, unsafe working conditions and corruption.

The process of trickling down of income appears to have weakened in the last decade. In the first half of the 1990s, the US $0.75 poverty rate (i.e. the proportion of rural population receiving a daily income of US $0.75 or less) dropped rapidly from 15 per cent in 1990 to 5 per cent in 1998. However, in the following seven years, the decline was less than one percentage point. The progress in poverty alleviation in the last decade is particularly unimpressive when the poverty line is lowered to US $0.50 per day, i.e. truly hardcore poverty. The truly hardcore poverty rate actually increased from 1.9 per cent in 1998 to 2.8 per cent in 2005. In short, because the high growth rate in the 2000–05 period did not cause income to trickle down to the poorest 5 per cent of the rural population, income inequality has worsened considerably.

Furthermore, income inequality has been increased by the embezzlement of state assets, seizure of farmlands for industrial development and corruption because of the absence of effective mechanisms to supervise government employees. Wang and Woo (2011) have found that urban residents have substantial unreported (hidden) income. Table 19.2 reports their estimates of official income and true income in each income group. The official income per capita and true income per capita in the richest 10 per cent of households in 2008 was 43,614 RMB and 139,000 RMB, respectively; official income being one-third of true income. Total household

Table 19.2 Disposable income per capita in each income category in 2008

Category	% of urban households	Official income (RMB)	'True' income (RMB)	Distribution of hidden income (%)
Lowest income	10	4,754	5,350	0.4
Low income	10	7,363	7,430	0.0
Lower middle income	20	10,196	11,970	2.3
Middle income	20	13,984	17,900	5.1
Upper middle income	20	19,254	27,560	10.9
High income	10	26,250	54,900	18.8
Highest income	10	43,614	139,000	62.5
All urban dwellers	*100*	*16,885*	*32,154*	*100.0*

Source: Tables 5 and 6 in Wang and Woo (2011).
Note: Hidden Income = Total True Income - Total Official Income.

disposable income in 2008 was 14.0 trillion RMB according to the official data but 23.2 trillion RMB according to the Wang and Woo estimate. As 63 per cent of the total unreported income went to the richest 10 per cent of urban households, the income of the richest 10 per cent of Chinese households is really 65 times that of the poorest 10 per cent instead of the 23 times reported in the official data. In short, the Gini coefficient is clearly much higher than the Asian Development Bank's (2007) figure of 0.47 for 2004.

As effective governance for equitable growth has now become much more challenging, social harmony has been diminished. The incidence of public disorder, labelled 'social incidents', rose steadily from 8,700 in 1993 to 32,500 in 1999 and then to 74,000 in 2004; and the average number of persons in a mass incident has also risen greatly, from eight in 1993 to 50 in 2004.

The third kind of failure that the Chinese economy is vulnerable to, *power supply failure,* refers to the economy being unable to move forward because it hits either *a natural limit* or *an externally imposed constraint* – a situation that is akin to the car running out of fuel (a natural limit) or running into a roadblock (an externally imposed constraint). Examples of power supply failures are an environmental collapse or a collapse in China's exports because of a trade war.

How credible is the environmental threat to China's economic growth? The present mode of economic development has given China the dirtiest air in the world; it is polluting more and more of the water resources, and, possibly, changing the climate pattern within China. Water shortage appears to pose the most immediate environmental threat to China's continued high growth. The extended period of semi-drought in northern China combined with the economic and population growth have caused more and more water to be pumped from the aquifers, leading the water table to drop by 3–6 metres a year.

While northern China has been getting drier and experiencing desertification, nature as if in compensation (or in mockery) has been blasting southern China with heavier rains, causing severe floods that have brought considerable deaths and property damage almost every summer since 1998. The sad possibility is that the northern droughts and southern floods may not be independent events but a combination caused by the large emission of black carbon in China; Streets (2005). Clearly, without water, growth cannot endure.

The second type of power supply failure arises from the fact that China's quest to build a harmonious society internally would not be possible without a harmonious world externally. China's emergence as a major trading nation has been accompanied by increasing conflicts with the European Union and the USA about China's trading practices and its exchange rate policy. A trade war with the developed economies would certainly end China's high growth.

China's chronic trade surplus reveals a deep-seated serious problem in China's economy, its largely unreformed financial system. This problem is revealed by the aggregate-level accounting identity that the overall current account balance is determined by the fiscal position of the government, and the savings–investment decisions of the SCEs and the private sector. Specifically:

$$CA = (T - G) + (S_{SCE} - I_{SCE}) + (S_{private} - I_{private})$$

where CA = current account in the balance of payments; $CA = (X - M) + R$; X = exports of goods and non-factor services; M = imports of goods and non-factor services; R = net factor earnings from abroad (i.e. export of factor services); T = state revenue; G = state expenditure (including state investment); S_{SCE} = saving of the SCEs; I_{SCE} = investment of the SCEs; $S_{private}$ = saving of the private sector; $I_{private}$ = investment of the private sector.

Because the Chinese fiscal position $(T-G)$ has nearly always shown a small deficit, the current account surplus reflects primarily the savings of SCEs and the private sector being larger than the sum of their investment expenditures. Why has China's financial system failed to translate the savings into investments? Such an outcome was not always the case. Before 1994 the voracious absorption of bank loans by SCEs to invest recklessly kept the current account usually negative and the creation of NPLs high. When the government implemented stricter controls on the SCBs from 1994 onward (e.g. removing top bank officials whenever their bank lent more than its credit quota or allowed the NPL ratio to increase too rapidly), the SCBs slowed down the growth of loans to SCEs. This cutback created an excess of savings because the SOB-dominated financial sector did not then re-channel the released savings (which were also increasing) to finance the investment of the private sector.

This failure in financial intermediation by the SCBs is quite understandable. Firstly, the legal status of private enterprises was, until recently, less secure than that of the state enterprises; and, secondly, there was no reliable way to assess the balance sheets of the private enterprises, which were naturally eager to escape taxation. The upshot was that the residual excess savings leaked abroad in the form of the current account surplus. Inadequate financial intermediation has made developing China a capital exporting country and put it in conflict with its trade partners.[16]

Understanding the past and dealing with the future

Gradualism in China is not so much the result of a particular theory of reform, as it is the result of political deadlock and compromises within the CPC between the conservative reformers and the liberal reformers, and a general lack of consensus in the society at large. With these basic differences in economic strategy, it is not surprising that partial reform was the compromise solution – both conservative reformers and liberal reformers were able to implement part of their programmes, e.g. all the Special Economic Zones were located in southern China, far away from the important political centres. This repeated factional struggle and compromise is the primary reason why the CPC has continually altered its stated goals for economic reform, which has progressed from the 1979 ideal of 'a planned economy supplemented by market regulations' to the 1992 ideal of 'a socialist market economy with Chinese characteristics'.

The key question in the debate about China's economic growth is whether the growth was generated by the appearance of new, non-capitalist economic institutions or by the convergence to a private market economy. The important issue is not speed but the direction of reform. China's accession to the WTO constitutes a watershed in the debate between the C-school and the E-school. To appreciate this point fully, the WTO membership must be viewed in the context of the comprehensive transformation of China's economy and society that began with the 12th Party Congress in 1982, and accelerated after the 17th Party Congress in 2007. The constitution has been amended to accord legal protection to private property; and capitalists can now become members of CPC. WTO membership is, hence, only one of the many policy actions led by the state to promote the continued convergence of China's economy to the norms of its East Asian neighbours so that economic growth would be sustained. More importantly, China's leaders know that explicit embrace of capitalist institutions under WTO auspices would be welcomed by the general Chinese public as a step forward in the reform process, rather than as a surrender of China's sovereignty in economic experimentation.

In thinking about how susceptible China's growth is to the three types of failures that the economy could encounter, first, we consider that the incomplete marketization of China's economy has increased the probabilities of the three classes of failure. For example, the unreformed financial sector threatens the fiscal balance with potential NPLs, facilitates corruption with selective credit practices, and generates trade tensions with chronic trade imbalances.

We also think that the probabilities of either a software failure or a power supply failure are higher than the probability of a hardware failure. This is because the first two are harder problems to deal with. For most hardware problems, China can learn from the experiences of the rest of the world, especially those of the richer countries in East Asia, as long as ideological constraints on methods of economic management continue to wither. The 1868 insight of the Meiji reformists that success in economic catch-up largely involves a willingness to adopt and adapt to 'best international practices' will continue to apply to China until its per capita GDP converges with that of Japan and Western Europe.

Dealing with software failure is harder than dealing with hardware failure for two major reasons. The first is that development policymaking in China has become more challenging because popular expectations of administrative performance have risen dramatically with income growth and, more importantly, with increasing knowledge of the outside world. A Chinese government that consistently fails to produce results in line with the rise in social expectations runs an increasing risk of being challenged by internal factions within the CPC, culminating in an open split, with each side seeking the support of non-party groups.

The second reason is that successful reconfiguration of the administrative software requires not just highly developed political skills but favourable circumstances in the domestic political arena and a benign international environment – both of which are normally beyond the reach of most politicians. What happens in the future will depend on whether the CPC is sufficiently confident and politically skilful to lead the democratic transition and emerge afterwards as the most important political force. History tells us that the French and British monarchies reacted very differently to popular requests for reform of the administrative software – and the outcomes were very different in each case. The practical issue is whether the CPC can do a better job in political transition than the Kuomintang did in Taiwan during 1983–88.

Dealing with power supply problems is much harder than dealing with hardware problems because power supply problems are often issues of which the world has few (mostly, no) successful experiences (for example, a global carbon dioxide emission pact), or it involves powerful foreign partners where differentiation between well-meaning cultural misunderstanding and unstated national rivalry is not easy. Most solutions to power supply failures require a mobilization of international effort, and China has generally been either a free rider or an unenthusiastic participant in such mobilization efforts, e.g. the Copenhagen Summit in 2009. The fact is that China and the other major powers will need to have a similar opinion of China's responsibilities in the world economy before there can be significant cooperation on common problems.

China's economy has now become an important shaping force of the global economy and, Chinese civil society has come to possess more and more of the middle-class aspirations common in the industrialized world. China's continued high growth now necessitates a new development strategy that also emphasises the creation of a harmonious society and a harmonious world – and this will require an improvement in its administrative software and in its contributions to the protection of the global environmental commons, of the global trading system, and of global security.

Notes

1 In Fan and Woo's opinion, the two major bottlenecks to growth that China is facing are financial reform and political reform.

2 The official start date for Vietnam's economic reform is the end of 1986 when Vietnam implemented partial reforms under the prodding of Gorbachev. The GDP growth rates in 1986 (3.4 per cent) and 1987 (3.9 per cent) were in fact lower than in 1985 (5.7 per cent). What went up substantially upon the initiation of the partial reforms was the rate of increase in retail prices: from 192 per cent in 1985 to 487 per cent in 1986, and 372 per cent in 1987. In March 1989 Vietnam implemented drastic macroeconomic stabilization (immediate slashing of the budget deficit and bank credits to SOEs), almost complete price deregulation overnight, discrete devaluation of the currency to the black market level, and relaxed control over private ownership. The GDP growth rate increased from 5.9 per cent in 1988 to 8.6 per cent in 1989; and the inflation rate fell from 374 per cent in 1988 to 95.8 per cent in 1989. Laos followed a course that was parallel to Vietnam and so did its inflation rate.

3 The unusually large heavy industrial sector in the USSR is nicely captured by the fact that, for every US$ 1 million of GDP, the USSR produced 280 metric tons of crude steel while the USA produced 18.5 tons, West Germany 34.4 tons and Japan 36.5 tons.

4 The agricultural sector held over 70 per cent of the Chinese labour force in 1978, almost 80 per cent of the Vietnamese labour force in 1989, and about 90 per cent of the Laotian labour force in 1989. The Chinese farmers received a net income that was about one-third of what the urban SOE worker received. Russian farmers in 1989 accounted for less than 20 per cent of the labour force and received a net income that was comparable to the Russian factory worker.

5 Rawski (1995) also provided a similar unintended virtuous cycle description of China's reform process. Other members of the E-school include Nolan (1993), and Lin, Cai and Li (1994).

6 Members of the C-school include Bruno (1994), Fan (1994), and Xiao (1997).

7 See detailed exposition in Woo (2001).

8 This is hence the Parallel Partial Progression of reforms at work, and not the correct sequencing of reforms at work.

9 State employment was 17.9 per cent of the labour force in 1984 (the eve of the introduction of dual-track pricing in the industrial sector) and it rose to 18.3 per cent in 1989. The state sector in 1989 employed 14.7 million workers more than in 1984. In employment, China was certainly not growing out of the plan either in absolute or in relative terms.

10 Examples of such sentiments are:

- 'China's "collectively"-owned enterprises are not cooperatives ... All members of the local community are *de jure* owners of "collectively"-owned enterprises.' (Nolan, 1993, p. 297)
- 'The surprising thing about TVEs is not that they function without clearly specified property rights, but rather the fact that local government ownership turns out to be a fairly robust ownership form ... ' (Naughton, 1994, p. 268)
- 'An elaborate vocabulary of denial obscures the uncomfortable reality that these firms, widely described as collectives, TVEs, non-state, quasi-private or even private enterprises, are typically owned and controlled by local governments.' (Rawski, 1995, p. 1172)

11 The power of market forces, when tolerated by the local authorities, to induce financial institutional innovations was also seen in Wenzhou city when economic liberalization began in 1979; see Liu (1992).

12 Weitzman and Xu (1994) have argued that collective ownership reflected the deep Chinese social sense of brotherhood (*gemenxing*) but this hypothesis is at odds with the dominance of small private enterprises in rural Taiwan, and the prevalence of Chinese-owned private firms in Southeast Asia.

13 The CPC's description of the desired harmonious socialist society is certainly convergence to a G7-type of society: a democratic society under the rule of law; a society based on equality and justice; an

honest and caring society; a stable, vigorous and orderly society; and a society in which humans live in harmony with nature.

14 'State-controlled' and not 'state-owned' because most state-owned firms have now been listed on the stock exchange and the state is their biggest shareholder.

15 The 51 per cent figure is from combining information in Shih (2010) who reported the debt of the central government to be 20 per cent of GDP, and the information in the *Financial Times* ('China warned of growing 'land loan' threat,' March 28, 2010) that the combined figure was 71 per cent.

16 See Woo (2008). Savings behaviour is not independent of the sophistication of the financial system. An advanced financial system will have a variety of financial institutions that would enable pooling of risks by providing medical insurance, pension insurance, and unemployment insurance; and transform savings into education loans, housing loans, and other types of investment loans to the private sector. *Ceteris paribus*, the more sophisticated a financial system, the lower the savings rate.

Bibliography

Asian Development Bank (2007), *Key Indicators: Inequality in Asia*, Manila: ADB.

Bruno, Michael (1994), 'Our Assistance Includes Ideas As Well As Money,' *Transition*, World Bank, Vol. 5 (1), pp. 1–4.

Chang, Gordon (2001), *The Coming Collapse of China*, New York: Random House.

Fan, Gang (1994), 'Incremental changes and dual track transition: understanding the case of China,' *Economic Policy*, Vol. 19 (supplement), pp. 99–122.

Fan, Gang and Woo, Wing Thye (2009), 'The Parallel Partial Progression (PPP) Approach to Institutional Transformation in Transition Economies: Optimize Economic Coherence Not Policy Sequence,' *Modern China*, Vol. 35(4), pp. 352–69.

Griffin, Keith, and Khan, Azizur Rahman (1993), 'The Transition to Market Guided Economies: Lessons for Russia and Eastern Europe from the Chinese Experience,' University of California at Riverside, paper presented at the Conference on *The Transition of Centrally-Planned Economies in Pacific Asia* held at the Asia Foundation in San Francisco, May 7–8, manuscript.

Lau, Lawrence J., Qian, Yingyi and Roland, Gerard (2000), 'Reform without Losers: An Interpretation of China's Dual-Track Approach to Transition,' *Journal of Political Economy*, Vol. 108 (1), pp. 120–43.

Lin, Justine Yifu, Cai, Fang and Li, Zhou (1994), 'China's Economic Reforms: Pointers for Other Economies in Transition,' *Policy Research Working Paper No. 1310*, World Bank.

Liu, Yia-Ling (1992), 'Reform From Below: The Private Economy and Local Politics in the Rural Industrialization of Wenzhou,' *China Quarterly*, No. 130, pp. 293–316.

McKinnon, Ronald (1991), *The Order of Economic Liberalization: Financial Control in the Transition to a Market Economy*, Baltimore, MD: Johns Hopkins University Press.

McMillan, John and Naughton, Barry (1992), 'How to Reform a Planned Economy,' *Oxford Review of Economic Policy*, Vol. 8, No. 1, pp. 130–43, Spring.

Naughton, Barry (1994), 'Chinese Institutional Innovation and Privatization from Below,' *American Economic Review*, Vol. 84(2), pp. 266–70.

——(1995), *Growing Out of the Plan: Chinese Economic Reform, 1978–1993*, Cambridge: Cambridge University, Press.

Nolan, Peter (1993), *State and Market in the Chinese Economy: Essays on Controversial Issues*, London: MacMillan.

Olson, Mancur (1992), 'Preface' in Claque, Christopher and Rausser, Gordon (eds), *The Emergence of Market Economies in Eastern Europe*, Oxford: Basil Blackwell.

Putterman, Louis (1995), 'The Role of Ownership and Property Rights in China's Economic Transition,' *The China Quarterly*, No. 144, December, pp. 1047–64.

Rawski, Thomas (1995), 'Implications of China's Reform Experience,' *The China Quarterly*, No. 144, pp. 1150–73.

Sachs, Jeffrey and Woo, Wing Thye (1994), 'Structural Factors in the Economic Reforms of China, Eastern Europe and the Former Soviet Union,' *Economic Policy*, April, pp. 102–45.

Shih, Victor (2010), 'China's 8,000 Credit Risks,' *The Wall Street Journal*, February 8, 2010.

Streets, David (2005), 'Black Smoke in China and Its Climate Effects,' *Asian Economic Papers*, Vol. 4(2), pp. 1–23.

Wang, Xiaolu and Woo, Wing Thye (2011), 'The Size and Distribution of Hidden Household Income in China', *Asian Economic Papers*, Vol. 10(1), pp. 1–26.

Weitzman, Martin and Chenggang Xu (1994), 'Chinese Township Village Enterprises as Vaguely Defined Cooperatives,' *Journal of Comparative Economics*, Vol. 18, pp. 121–45.

Woo, Wing Thye (1999), 'The Real Reasons for China's High Economic Growth,' *The China Journal*, Vol. 41, January, pp. 115–37.

——(2001), 'Recent Claims of China's Economic Exceptionalism: Reflections Inspired by WTO Accession,' *China Economic Review*, Vol. 12(2/3), pp. 107–36.

——(2007), 'The Challenges of Governance Structure, Trade Disputes and Natural Environment to China's Growth,' *Comparative Economic Studies*, Vol. 40(4), pp. 572–602.

——(2008), 'Understanding the Sources of Friction in U.S.–China Trade Relations: The Exchange Rate Debate Diverts Attention Away from Optimum Adjustment,' *Asian Economic Papers*, Vol. 7(3), pp. 61–95.

Xiao, Geng (1997), *Property Rights and Economic Reform in China*, Beijing: China Social Science Press (in Chinese).

20

TOWARDS A NEW GROWTH MODEL IN EASTERN EUROPE

Paul Marer

Why economic growth is important

Economic growth matters not just because it leads to rising prosperity. People living in countries with growing economies tend to be happier and more optimistic. Material improvement leads to general satisfaction; stagnation or decline leads to misery and pessimism. Economic growth matters because its absence causes long-term unemployment and falling living standards for many. Growth is also the only realistic way to generate the tax revenues needed to service the outsized sovereign debts that so many countries have accumulated today, and to fund the obligations of ageing societies.

The growth prospects of a country depend not only on its past, current and future economic policies but also on the kinds of investment that its governments, companies and households have made and will make – or not make – in their economic future. Growth depends also on the economic and political health of a country's neighbourhood, as well as that of the world at large. The external environment is especially important for assessing the growth performance and prospects of the small and medium-sized open economies of Central and Eastern Europe (CEE).

However, generating growth is not easy. It consumes finite resources. It is cyclical and often has adverse environmental impacts. Growth is spurred by innovation and improved productivity, which not only creates jobs but also destroys old ones. Therefore, individuals, organizations and countries must constantly adapt, or face stagnation and decline.

This chapter focuses on the CEE countries – the 10 countries from the region that joined the EU in the 2000s – a group sometimes referred to as the EU-10.[1] The central thesis of this chapter is that the CEE countries must speedily adapt the growth model that had served them well for about a dozen years – from the mid-1990s through to 2007 – until the great global recession of 2008–09 and the eurozone crises that became evident in 2010 and 2011.

The first part of this chapter summarizes the common features of the 'old' growth model that characterized the development paths of the CEE countries up to the Great Recession. Focusing on the EU-10, it also contrasts the CEE model with those pursued by the countries of Latin America and East Asia. The next part calls attention to the vulnerabilities engendered by the CEE growth model. It then suggests that the nature and extent of country-specific vulnerabilities offer plausible explanations for differences in the ten countries' growth performance and prospects. The last part discusses the reasons why the 'old' CEE model needs to be modified, outlines the essential features of the proposed 'new' model, and concludes with policy recommendations.

The 'old' growth model

The CEE 'growth model' story starts around 1995, when the turmoil from the post-Communist 'transformation recessions' was largely over and most CEE countries had reached or passed beyond their lowest output levels following the collapse of the centrally planned system. The classic phase of the model, when its features became the most pronounced, was the 2000–07 period, coinciding with a global economic boom and with the anticipation and then the realization of all ten CEE countries becoming full EU members.

The six distinct features of the CEE growth model were: (1) the fast-paced expansion of domestic demand; (2) this was facilitated by the rapid growth of credit; (3) financed in large part by capital inflows; (4) these allowed the countries to run sustained current-account deficits; (5) made possible by the region's speedy integration into the global economy; (6) while experiencing significant appreciation of their real exchange rates. The application of this model facilitated the *real economic convergence* of the CEE countries with Western Europe through to 2007.

The following paragraphs comment briefly on each aspect. Only summary evidence is given, with detail provided later or in the references. The evidence presented focuses on the EU-10 during 2000–07. However, certain of the reproduced figures (from the IMF, the World Bank, the EBRD, the ECB and other sources) may have country coverage larger or smaller than the EU-10, and periods somewhat longer or shorter than 2000–07.

Fast-paced expansion of domestic demand

Pent-up consumer demand that resulted from perennial shortages under central planning, grossly under-developed service sectors, and under-valued property prices prompted rapid demand growth for consumer goods as well as for retail and financial services, and a boom in construction. Those, in turn, led to surges in investment-to-GDP ratios for a decade. Domestic demand during 2000–08 grew at double-digit rates in the Baltic states, Romania and Bulgaria, while *net* exports were negative for them (as well as for several other CEE countries, as shown on Figure 20.1[2]).

Rapid credit expansion

The granting of credit was facilitated both by the pent-up demand for credit, for the reasons just stated, as well as by the abundant availability and the low cost of credit, largely from foreign sources. The period 2003–06 was one of historically high global liquidity, with fierce competition in international banking and abundant supplies of credit to emerging economies, such as CEE.

Large capital inflows

The inflows were relatively larger in emerging Europe than in other emerging economies. At its peak in 2007, the average inflow in emerging Europe as a share of GDP (20 per cent) was double that in Latin America. Most of the difference was attributable to cross-border loans and deposits from West European parent banks to their affiliates in the East. The relative importance of other types of inflows, like foreign direct investment (FDI) and portfolio debt and equity accumulation, were broadly similar to those in other regions.[3]

Sustained current-account deficits

Each CEE country ran current-account deficits each and every year between 2000 and 2007, ranging between 2 per cent and 22 per cent of GDP annually, depending on country and year.[4]

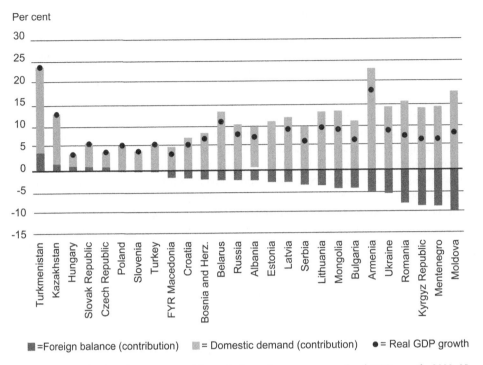

Figure 20.1 Contribution of net exports and domestic demand to average annual real GDP growth, 2000–08
Source: EBRD (2010), Chart 4.1, p. 68, with permission.

Independently of the size of the current-account deficit, it matters a great deal how the deficits are financed. The larger the portion covered by FDI – considered to be a less volatile source of capital inflows than cross-border borrowing by banks and non-financial institutions or portfolio investment – the lower is the vulnerability factor.

Speedy integration into the global economy

The standard way to measure the level and trend of a country's globalization is through its trade participation ratio (TPR): the sum of exports plus imports as a percentage of GDP. Between 1996 and 2007, the average TPR of the EU-15 (Western Europe) rose from about 60 per cent to about 80 per cent. However, during the same period, the TPRs of nine of the 10 CEE countries grew by more than 20 percentage points.[5] Parallel to – and even more dramatic than – trade integration was the CEE's financial integration with Western Europe. The financial participation ratio (FPR) can be calculated analogously to the TPR: the sum of external financial assets and liabilities to GDP. In just over a decade, the ratios had increased in all CEE countries, in several to above 200 per cent. Both the level and the rate of increase of their FPRs were much faster than those of other emerging regions.[6]

One factor greatly facilitating the EU-10's trade and financial integration (mainly) with Western Europe was the effect of political integration between Europe's two regions. Membership in the EU probably encouraged foreign investors, including banks, to pursue long-term investment strategies in the East that otherwise might have been considered too risky.[7]

Real exchange rate appreciation

All CEE countries had experienced appreciations of their 'real effective exchange rates' (REER) between the late 1990s (Latvia after 2004) and the Great Recession.[8] The appreciation took place while the CEE countries had different exchange rate regimes: the Baltic countries and Bulgaria had pegged rates; the rest, managed floating rates (Slovenia, Slovakia and Estonia only until they joined the eurozone in 2007, 2009 and 2011, respectively). In countries with *pegged exchange rates*, REER appreciation was due to domestic inflation (caused in part by capital inflows, which supported a rapid expansion of credit). In countries with *flexible exchange rates*, their rising REERs were due to a combination of appreciating nominal exchange rates and inflation. The rising REERs of these countries also reflected the substantial undervaluation of their currencies during the early stages of transformation.

Real-income convergence. The purchasing-power parity-based real per capita GDPs of the CEE countries, expressed as a percentage of the average per capita GDP of the EU-15, had increased at impressive rates until the Great Recession.[9] Growth theory identifies two factors that drive the convergence of the less-developed towards the more developed countries – provided that the two country groups are reasonably homogeneous, such as East and West Europe are: (1) diminishing returns in the accumulation of capital, giving capital higher marginal productivity in the poorer countries that have much lower capital/labour ratios; and (2) the adoption or adaptation of the wealthier countries' technology, knowledge and institutions, which increases total factor productivity in the less advanced countries.[10] Both factors had apparently supported the convergence of the CEEs toward the more developed West, as evidenced and supported by large net capital flows from West to East Europe. However, growth differentials in favour of the countries of CEE have been more varied than 'normal' convergence alone can explain. For certain CEE countries, there remain unexplained positive and negative 'growth differentials' between 'adjusted' per capita real growth rates – the difference between each country's actual growth tempo and the 'catch-up' growth rates that would have been expected, given initial per capita GDP levels.[11] Hungary was the only country among the EU-10 that during 2000–10 had an average negative growth differential of 0.5 per cent per annum. Each of the other nine countries had positive growth differentials, with Slovakia leading the pack with an average of 2 per cent per annum.[12] Later on, we identify some of the factors that were most likely responsible for such differentials.

Price-level convergence. Real income convergence inevitably means rising average prices towards the price levels of the more advanced countries. This is so because initial price levels in the lesser developed countries are always lower than in the more advanced countries. The logic is as follows. Wages in the tradeable (T) and non-tradeable (NT) sectors are approximately the same *within* any country. Competition for labour makes it so, even though productivity differences between the higher- and lower-income countries' T sectors are much smaller than in their NT sectors. Owing to the much higher level of productivity in the high-income country's T sector, wages – and thus the price level – will also be higher.

Fast-growing emerging economies will typically experience rapid productivity growth in their T sectors, so wage and price levels in the T sectors will increase. Wages in the NT sectors will follow, even though there will *not* be equally rapid increases in productivity in the NT sectors. This will result in inflation (or at least inflationary pressure) since increases in wages in the NT sector are not supported by corresponding increases in productivity. In conclusion, the catching up process will typically involve some extra inflation, adding to whatever other inflationary pressures the economy may be experiencing, so price levels will also be converging toward those in the higher-income countries. This is known as the Balassa-Samuelson effect;

evidence for it has been found in the CEEs, too.[13] Estimating how much of a price-level convergence is due to the Balassa-Samuelson effect as compared to other causes has been extensively debated.[14]

The CEE growth model in global perspective. Three key features of the CEE model – growth driven by domestic demand, supported by the rapid expansion of credit and FDI; large current account deficits; and the real appreciation of the exchange rates – had also characterized the old growth models of Latin America and East Asia (except that East Asia's rapid growth was driven by exports rather than domestic demand). This growth model, whose central feature is persistent current-account deficits, was largely discredited by the collapse of the Latin American economies in the mid-1980s and by the East Asian crisis of 1997–98. Since then, both groups of countries have switched to policies ensuring current account balance or even surplus, reinforced by high savings (thereby accumulating international reserves), and to exchange rate policies supporting *net exports* as the key sources of growth.[15]

As long as the CEE countries could continue to match or exceed the real income convergence records of Latin America (vis-à-vis the USA) and East Asia (vis-à-vis Japan), as emerging Europe has been able to do until recently (vis-à-vis Western Europe), one could not be too critical of the CEE growth model.[16] However, this model will be unable to support further real-income convergence, for reasons discussed below. Let us note that Latin America and East Asia did indeed adjust their similar models, also as a result of the crises they faced.

Model implementation and vulnerability

The CEE growth model helped to engender growth but also created vulnerabilities. Perhaps the most important vulnerability of the model has been to any sudden stop or reversal of capital inflows. To the extent that the flow of domestic credit and the servicing of foreign debt (resulting from cumulative current account deficits) rely on foreign financing, a sudden stop of capital inflows, even a significant slowdown, will cause growth to plummet.

Another vulnerability engendered by the model is the impairment over time of international competitiveness. This is a probable outcome of growth being driven mainly by domestic demand, especially if demand originates disproportionately in the NT sectors. Satisfying such demand will suck in imports and generate inflationary pressures, with adverse consequences for the competitiveness of countries whose main exports are *not* energy and other primary products, as is the case for the EU-10. The appreciation of REERs also has adverse impacts on competitiveness.

The author considers that the degree to which the individual CEE countries had allowed their economies to become vulnerable is the key to explaining differences in their growth performances (including growth volatility) as well as growth prospects.[17] Vulnerability means that an economy will be forced by an external shock to make a sudden, sharp and painful adjustment, or that it will be consigned to a low-growth trap, or both.

The literature identifies a large number of factors likely to shape economic growth; their importance varies across countries. To highlight some of the differences among the CEEs, *six interdependent economic policies* are identified that – in view of the growth model relied upon – had increased or dampened a country's vulnerability to: (a) capital inflow disruptions; and (b) deteriorating international competitiveness. High vulnerability sooner or later adversely affects a country's growth, while low vulnerability is neutral or favourable for growth performance and prospects, other things being equal. The six factors are:

1 The contribution of net exports to growth.
2 The pace and source of credit expansion.

3   Inflation, as measured by comparative trends in unit labour costs.
4   Choice of exchange rate regime.
5   The level and structure of external debt.
6   Fiscal balance and the relative size of the public sector.

The following paragraphs comment briefly on each aspect. Some statistical evidence is presented; fuller details are in the references.

1. The contribution of net exports to growth

Countries that during the boom years of 2000–07 had, on average, substantial import surpluses – so that net exports had made a negative contribution to growth – became especially vulnerable because net imports can become increasingly difficult to finance if the financing sources – be they capital inflows or remittances from migrant workers abroad – dry up, as they had, for several years, after the Great Recession. Sustained net imports are also an indication that a disproportionate share of foreign and domestic capital has gone into the NT sectors, which, over time, weakens international competitiveness. The extent of vulnerability depends on such factors as the country's export dynamics and composition (the more dynamic and high value the exports, the lower the vulnerability), inflation relative to the cost- and price-level changes of competitors, and the relative size and composition of foreign debt (the lower the debt/GDP ratio and the smaller the share in foreign currency, the lower the vulnerability).

Figure 20.1 shows the contribution of net exports and that of domestic demand to average annual GDP growth during 2000–08 for 26 transforming economies, including the EU-10.[18]

The contribution of net exports to real GDP growth is defined as the average change in real net exports between 2000 and 2008, divided by real GDP in 2000. The contribution of domestic demand to real GDP growth is calculated as the difference between the average annual real GDP growth and the contribution of real net exports.

Focusing on the 10 CEE countries, the figure reveals that Hungary, Poland, the Czech Republic and Slovenia had tiny positive or only small negative net export contributions to growth, whereas the three Baltic states plus Bulgaria and Romania had large negative contributions. Thus, this factor appears, *ceteris paribus,* to place the last five countries into relatively vulnerable positions on their post-2008 growth prospects, because it suggests inadequate international competitiveness.

2. The pace and source of credit expansion

While the growth of credit is essential for innovation, investment and economic growth, whether it engenders vulnerability – and if it does, the extent of it – depends on two factors: the pace of credit growth and its sources of funding. The pace of credit growth can be *excessive* (defined by a World Bank study as a tempo much faster than that of the average of all comparable developing nations outside emerging Europe, adjusted for the initial underdevelopment of the financial sectors in CEE) or *convergent* (credit growth rates similar to comparable nations outside the region).[19] Between 2000 and 2008, the three Baltic states and Romania had experienced excessive credit growth (Bulgaria to a lesser extent), while the other five countries had normal (convergent) credit expansion.[20] Excessive credit expansion accelerates GDP growth for a time, but it generates bubbles that eventually burst, creating a GDP slump.

The three main sources of credit are *wholesale funding* (short-term borrowing by domestically owned banks from other banks and financial institutions abroad); local subsidiaries, predominantly funded by their *foreign parent banks*; and *resident deposits*. Wholesale funding has the highest risk because the availability and the cost of such funds are highly sensitive to changing international credit conditions. Foreign parent funding is less risky, at least as long as the parents are reasonably healthy and are willing to support their daughters. Resident deposits entail the least risk because central banks are usually ready to defend the domestic banking system in case of panicky withdrawals.

The three Baltic states, Hungary and Bulgaria had funded their credit growth mainly through the parents of their foreign-owned subsidiaries, making their economies medium-vulnerable. However, the Czech Republic, Slovakia, Poland and Romania had relied largely on resident deposits, making them relatively less vulnerable.

Considering credit vulnerability on both counts (excessive growth of lending and the ultimate sources of those funds), the three Baltic states were clearly the most vulnerable at the onset of the Great Recession.

It is important to stress that the source of the vulnerability has not been the predominant foreign ownership of the banking sectors in CEE. To illustrate, during 2000–06 the share of loans extended by foreign-owned banks in total credits was higher in the Czech Republic (85 per cent) than in Latvia (65 per cent).[21] At the same time, the loan-to-deposit ratio was 280 per cent in Latvia and only 80 per cent in the Czech Republic, implying that an extraordinarily large proportion of loan growth in Latvia was funded from abroad. While Prague's prudent monetary and fiscal policies kept Czech crown interest rates roughly on a par with those in the eurozone, hence providing no incentive to borrow in foreign currency, the combination of Latvia's relatively high inflation and Euro-pegged exchange rate made foreign-currency loans especially attractive.[22] Latvia's excessive credit growth, financed largely from abroad, made the country doubly vulnerable, similarly to those of the other Baltic states.

3. Unit labour costs and inflation

The lower is a country's unit labour cost relative to those of its competitors and the smaller its rate of inflation, the more favourable is its international competitive position, other things being equal. This is a matter of great importance for the open economies of CEE; certainly a key factor in their growth prospects.

Figure 20.2 shows the 2001 unit labour costs of four CEE countries – the Czech Republic, Hungary, Poland and Slovakia – relative to those of 16 competitor countries from around the world. A decade ago the four CEE countries' unit labour costs were at comparable levels; those of the others in the region were, plausibly, at similar levels or lower. Figure 20.2 shows that the CEE countries were quite competitive vis-à-vis the Latin American and Southeast Asian countries, especially if one takes into account the relatively high education and skill levels of the CEE workforces. This was certainly one factor in the EU-10's dynamic export performance, even though it was overshadowed by the even faster import growth in many countries.[23]

Changes in unit labour costs are the outcome of the tempo of productivity improvements (which reduce it) and the rate of increase of nominal wages and wage-related taxes and charges (which raise it). Figure 20.3 reveals that between 2001 and 2008 unit labour costs rose especially fast in the Baltic states and Romania (five to 10 times faster than in the USA), whereas unit labour costs had remained under impressive control in Poland. Therefore, considering this factor in isolation, Poland appears to have secured a sizeable advantage over the other CEE countries in terms of international competitiveness (thus also in terms of growth prospects), while the Baltic states and Romania found their situation increasingly difficult. Loss of competitiveness surely impairs growth prospects at some stage, unless remedial actions are successfully taken to

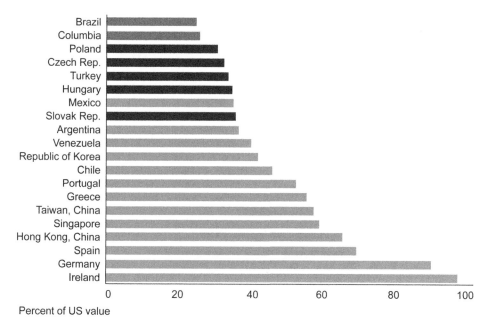

Percent of US value

Figure 20.2 Unit Labour Costs of Poland, Czech Republic, Hungary and Slovakia versus 16 Competitor
Economies
Source: EBRD (2010), Chart 4.4a, p. 70, with permission.

regain competitiveness. The other five CEE countries are in the middle of the pack, suggesting
that changes in their relative unit labour costs neither enhanced nor constrained their growth
prospects in a major way.

4. Choice of exchange rate regime

There is no ideal exchange rate regime, especially for small, open economies. The two basic types are
pegged and flexible regimes (each with variants). Both types have economic and political
advantages and problems. For example, if pegging to another currency or currency basket is credible,
such a regime can stop high inflation in its tracks, as was the situation in the Baltic states and
Bulgaria. Furthermore, pegging to the Euro has been a powerful political signal by the Baltic states of
their strong determination to join the eurozone, an aspect of their further integration with Europe.

At the same time, pegged exchange rates can increase economic vulnerability through several
channels. As a signal of eventual entry into the eurozone (at earlier times, before there was even
a hint of the eurozone crises to come), pegging encouraged capital inflows, and thus credit
expansion. Pegging encouraged capital inflows because it eliminates (or at least reduces) the
currency-risk premium and thus lowers the effective rate of interest. However, when a currency
is pegged, the central bank is unable fully to 'sterilize' the inflow of capital and to rein in the
growth of credit.[24] As inflation accelerates, as the exchange rate remains credibly pegged, and as
there is free movement of capital (full convertibility), domestic interest rates will rise much
above interest rates on comparable assets in foreign currency. That encourages borrowing in
foreign currency, which further promotes capital inflows and excessive credit growth.

A pegged currency can also make a country vulnerable if the exchange rates of its direct
competitors have more flexible regimes (e.g. Poland, Hungary, Romania and the Czech

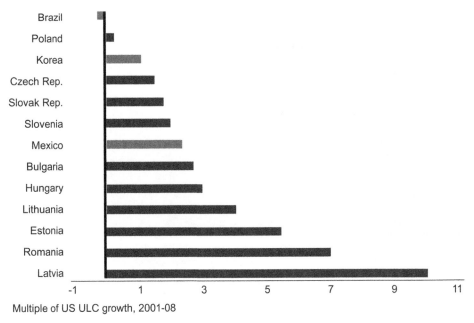

Multiple of US ULC growth, 2001-08

Figure 20.3 Unit labour cost growth of 10 CEE Countries, Mexico, Korea and Brazil, 2001–2008
Source: EBRD (2010), Chart 4.4b, p. 70, with permission.

Republic) whose depreciation further impairs the competitiveness of the former group of countries, as happened early on during the Great Recession.

Because pegging the exchange rate also has significant benefits and because it is not the basic source of inflation – it only makes it more difficult to remedy its causes – this factor has tended to reinforce the already noted high vulnerability of the Baltic states and Bulgaria.

To regain competitiveness, the alternative to currency devaluation is 'internal devaluation', that is, substantial lowering of money wages and prices in the economy. This is exceedingly difficult to do economically, socially, and politically. None the less, large internal devaluations were engineered in the Baltic states as well as in Romania (and to some extent in Bulgaria) during 2009–11.

5. The level and structure of external debt

It is important to make a distinction between *public debt* (sovereign or government) and *external debt*. Public debt can be held by domestic and external lenders while external debt can be owed by governments and by the private sector (i.e. financial and non-financial institutions and households). Therefore, public and external debt sustainability need to be addressed as separate though interdependent issues. One source of interdependence is that large-scale defaults by the private sector tend to increase government debt through lower tax receipts and higher unemployment and other social benefit payments. Public debt also rises if systemically important financial and non-financial firms are bailed out. Another source of interdependence is that a high level of public debt, which needs to be continuously rolled over, displaces credit to the private sector, which after all is the sector that drives an economy forward. And a decline in the sovereign's creditworthiness raises not only its cost of foreign borrowing but also that of the private sector.

No theoretical model can specify what levels of government debt to GDP or private external debt to GDP ratios are 'safe' because sustainability depends on a host of future domestic policies and on unpredictable external environmental variables. However, what has been established, based on the accumulated historical experiences of many countries, are the ranges at which debt burdens clearly become too onerous, significantly reducing GDP growth. And at still higher levels of debt (in some cases even at lower levels), default can be threatened or triggered. Reinhart and Rogoff identified a *sovereign-debt-to-GDP ratio* of 90 per cent as such a threshold.[25] The Maastricht criteria set 60 per cent as the maximum 'safe' sustainable limit for eurozone members. According to Reinhart and Rogoff, emerging markets face even lower thresholds for total external debt (public plus private) – which is usually denominated in foreign currencies. When *total external debt* reaches 60 per cent of GDP, growth declines, on average, by 2 per cent per annum; at much higher ratios, the decline becomes larger and debt sustainability increasingly problematic.[26] Debt sustainability is defined as the ability of a country to permanently cap its debt-to-GDP ratios at current levels or, if they are higher than the threshold, the ability to bring the debt to or below the threshold.[27]

Figures 20.4 and 20.5 show the sovereign debts and the total external debts, respectively, of the CEE countries as a percentage of their GDP in recent years, with regional and international comparisons. Our focus is not so much on sustainability but on the comparative vulnerabilities of the countries on account of differences in their debt levels and structures.

The first thing to note is that sovereign debt levels to GDPs are, on average, much lower in the EU-10 than in Western Europe's EU-17. This is no great comfort, however, to the CEE region, given the severe sovereign debt problems several eurozone countries are currently facing, and considering that most Western European countries can better afford to service larger public debts than the economically and financially weaker countries of CEE.

Also notable is than in every EU country (except in Sweden), debt ratios had risen dramatically between 2007 and 2011. However, most relevant for us are the exceptionally large differences in the sovereign debt levels among the EU-10. Hungary has by far the largest ratio at 80 per cent of GDP. At the other end of the spectrum we find Estonia (with debt levels below 10 per cent) and Bulgaria (20 per cent). The sovereign debt levels of each of the seven other countries lie roughly in the 40–60 per cent range. But external debt-to-GDP ratios are different!

Estonia and Bulgaria – the two CEE countries with the lowest sovereign debt ratios in Figure 20.4 – were among those with the highest external debt ratios in 2008 – indicating that it was excessive foreign borrowing by their private sectors, for the reasons already indicated, that caused their debt explosions. Latvia had the highest external debt ratio, at almost 180 per cent of GDP. By refusing to sever its currency's peg to the Euro, its government was forced to borrow large amounts from the IMF and from other sources to defend the peg. That, in turn, dramatically increased Latvia's sovereign debt from 10 per cent to 60 per cent of GDP in just four years (Figure 20.4), an excellent example of the interconnectedness of private external and public debt.

The level of sovereign debt matters. But for the small, open economies of CEE, the level of external debt matters even more, especially for those with weak domestic financial systems (including capital markets), which means that their main sources of funding have to be external. This makes them highly vulnerable to changes in external credit conditions.

On the eve of the Great Recession, we find the Czech Republic in the most advantageous debt position: It was one of only two EU-10 countries whose 50 per cent external debt ratio had remained substantially below the Reinhart-Rogoff threshold of 60 per cent, as did Poland's at 55 per cent. At the other extreme – clearly in the danger zone – were/are Latvia, Estonia and Hungary, with external debt ratios twice to three times higher than that of the Czech Republic.

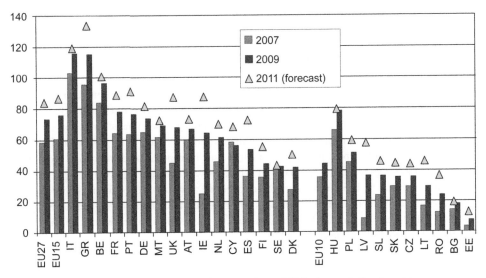

Figure 20.4 Public Debt Level in per cent of GDP in the EU-27 before and after the crisis
Source: Eurostat (2011) and Eurostat forecast.

6. Fiscal balance and the relative size of the public sector

Figure 20.4, which shows sovereign debt as a percentage of GDP, says a lot – but not every-thing – about the comparative cumulative fiscal balances of the countries. A high ratio indicates large cumulative budget deficits. However, the Figure 20.4 does not reveal when the deficits were accumulated and how difficult it will be for the authorities to bring their budgets under control. Were the deficits accumulated mainly during the down phases of the business cycle or during boom times? If during the latter, then deficits will be more difficult to bring under control, other things being equal. Another important factor is the relative size of the public sector in the economy. The higher is the share of budget expenditures in GDP and the higher is the level of public debt, the more difficult it will be to achieve a *primary balance* in the budget (that is, balance before interest payments on outstanding debt), which is a precondition for debt stabilization.

The cumulative government budget surpluses (+) or deficits (-) of the EU-10 during 2001–07, as a percentage of GDP, were[28] Estonia +10.0 per cent; Bulgaria +5.3 per cent; Latvia -8.0 per cent; Lithuania -10.2 per cent; Romania -14.2 per cent; Slovenia -14.5 per cent; Slovakia -27.7 per cent; Czech Republic -8.9 per cent; Poland -31.5 per cent; and Hungary -48.9 per cent. The numbers show that the outlier in the group, Hungary, had unusually large fiscal deficits during the boom years preceding the Great Recession, making it highly vulnerable to the global liquidity crisis in the fall of 2008, following the collapse of Lehman Brothers. This forced Hungary to be the first to turn to the IMF and the EU for a 20 billion Euro emergency aid package, and to undertake a painful retrenchment early on. (Subsequently, Latvia and Romania among the EU-10 also received IMF assistance). Hungary is also a regional outlier on the relative size of its public sector (Figure 20.6).

Figure 20.6 shows individually for 27 EU countries the size of public expenditures in 2007 as a percentage of each country's GDP (vertical axis) against per capita GDP levels (horizontal axis). As the regression line shows, the share of public expenditure in GDP tends to rise as income levels rise. For example, the shares are the highest (just above 50 per cent) in some of the richest EU countries: France, Sweden, and Denmark. The shares tend to be much lower in

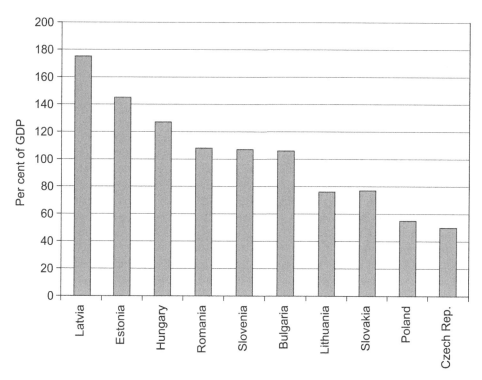

Figure 20.5 External Debt-to-GDP Ratios of the EU-10 Countries in 2007
Source: Calculated by the author, based on USD external debt and GDPs (at current exchange rates), as reported in the *CIA Fact Book*, 2007 or 2008, country pages.

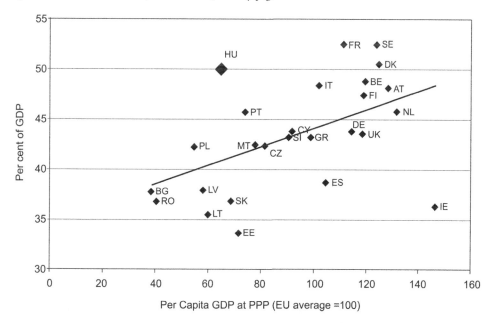

Figure 20.6 Public Expenditure in the EU Countries in 2007 as per cent of GDP
Source: Forthun, C. and R. P. Hagemann (2010), 'Sustaining the Momentum of Fiscal Reform in Hungary', *OECD Economics Department Working Papers*, No. 802, OECD Publishing.

CEE: under 35 per cent in Estonia and between 35 and 40 per cent in Lithuania, Latvia, Slovakia, Bulgaria and Romania.

Hungary is an outlier: at 50 per cent of GDP, its government expenditure level is comparable to those of some of the Western European welfare states and higher than those of Austria, Finland, Italy, Germany and the Netherlands. Hungary is thus what János Kornai called a 'premature welfare state' – premature in the sense that it has a level of government expenditures, spent disproportionately on transfer payments, that the country simply cannot afford. Therefore, taxes are high, which has pushed many individuals and SMEs into the grey economy to avoid taxes, prompting successive governments to raise taxes on those who cannot escape them. That, in turn, has been pushing more people into the grey economy and the authorities into deficit spending, financed at high real rates of interest. Large public expenditures and high local-currency real interest rates crowd out credit that would otherwise be available for the private sector, pushing businesses and households to borrow in foreign currency (which was available before the Great Recession at much lower interest rates than those charged on domestic-currency loans).

The above facts and reasoning suggest, first, that Hungary has not only a short-term but also a longer-term vulnerability to worsening credit conditions in Europe (and globally) and, second, that it will be difficult for the country to find sources of adequate and sustained economic growth.

Summing up

It is the author's contention that the degree to which an individual CEE country had allowed its economy, through policy choices, to become vulnerable prior to the Great Recession, that is, through 2007 – under the growth model outlined earlier – is the key to explaining differences in growth performances (including growth volatility) during the Great Recession as well as differences in medium-term growth prospects from 2011 on. Two types of interdependent vulnerabilities are emphasized: harm to the economy that would be triggered by a sudden stop or reversal of capital inflows and those resulting from a substantial loss of international competitiveness. The two vulnerabilities can reinforce each other: persistent loss of competitiveness hurts the current account whose growing deficits will be increasingly difficult to finance if capital inflows were to decline, stop or be reversed, and/or the cost of foreign financing were to rise significantly.

Table 20.1 summarizes the country-specific vulnerabilities that were induced or avoided by the domestic policy factors discussed: If *net export contribution is negative* and large for an extended period, that makes an economy vulnerable, as does a *credit bubble*, a comparatively high rate of *inflation*, an *inflexible exchange rate regime, high public and/or external debt,* or a *high share of government expenditure* in GDP.

A 'V' symbol indicates vulnerability relative to those of the other countries in the group. A 'P' sign suggests that the country had 'protected' itself comparatively well with respect to the given policy variable against potential adverse impacts. Although the placing of the symbols is evidence based, judgement is also involved.

The patterns shown in Table 20.1 indicate vulnerability to external shocks not just in the absolute sense but (perhaps mainly) the vulnerabilities of the countries relative to each other. The pattern shows that the Baltic states, Bulgaria and Romania became vulnerable owing to several domestic policies having contributed to unsustainable credit bubbles and substantial loss of external competitiveness. These factors had enabled the countries to achieve impressive rates of growth through 2007. However, at the onset of the Great Recession the vulnerabilities came

Table 20.1 Vulnerability of the EU–10 during 2009–10 due to domestic policy choices

Country	Vulnerability factors						
Type of external shock	Exp.	Cr.	High	ER.	High debt		High
	contr.	bubble	infl.	regime	Sov.	Ext.	G/GDP
Estonia							
Δ K inflows		V			P	V	
↓ Competitiveness	V	V	V	V			
Latvia							
Δ K inflows		V				V	
↓ Competitiveness	V	V	V	V			
Lithuania							
Δ K inflows	V					V	
↓ Competitiveness	V	V	V	V			
Bulgaria							
Δ K inflows			V		P	V	
↓ Competitiveness	V	V	V	V			
Romania							
Δ K inflows		V					
↓ Competitiveness	V	V	V				
Hungary							
Δ K inflows					V	V	V
↓ Competitiveness							
Poland							
Δ K inflows							
↓ Competitiveness			P				
Czech Republic							
Δ K inflows						P	
↓ Competitiveness							
Slovakia							
Δ K inflows							
↓ Competitiveness							
Slovenia							
Δ K inflows							
↓ Competitiveness							

Source: Author's construction.
V, highly vulnerable; P, protected well.

big problems for the small, highly open economies (which the Baltic states and Bulgaria certainly are). Their high levels of external indebtedness, mainly by their private sectors, created further vulnerabilities.[29] The high and multiple vulnerabilities of the five countries thus contributed to their rather extreme see-saw pattern of growth: impressive tempo on the way up; followed by painful plunge on the way down.

Responding to the crisis, especially to the loss of competitiveness, each of the five countries had, in fact, taken drastic actions – internal devaluation (a substantial lowering of wages and prices during 2009–10) – which set the stage for their subsequent growth recovery (Table 20.2). Most of the other countries in the EU–10 group also had impressive pre-crisis growth rates and they were also hurt by the crisis. However, in most cases their GDP declines were not as severe as those countries with comparatively greater vulnerabilities.

Table 20.2 Real GDP growth in the EU-10, 2007–11 and estimates for 2012 (in per cent)

	2007	2008	2009	2010	2011	2012*
Bulgaria	6.4	6.2	-5.5	0.4	1.7	0.8
Czech Rep.	5.7	2.5	-4.7	2.7	1.7	0.1
Estonia	7.5	-3.7	-14.3	2.3	7.6	2.0
Hungary	0.1**	0.9	-6.8	1.3	1.7	0.0
Latvia	9.6	-3.3	-17.7	-0.3	5.5	2.0
Lithuania	9.8	2.9	-14.8	1.4	5.9	2.0
Poland	6.8	5.1	1.6	3.9	4.3	2.6
Romania	6.3	7.3	-6.6	-1.6	2.5	1.5
Slovakia	10.5	5.8	-4.9	4.2	3.3	2.4
Slovenia	6.9	3.6	-8.0	1.4	-0.2	-1.0
Ave (not weighted)	7.0	2.8	-8.2	1.6	3.4	1.2

Source: IMF, *World Economic Outlook Europe*, April 2012, Table A-4, p. 194.
Notes: * Forecast. ** Owing to its unsustainable external debt, Hungary was forced to adjust early.

Hungary is the only other country in the group with multiple 'Vs', indicating excessive levels of public and external debt and a grossly oversized public sector. These three vulnerabilities were (and remain) mutually reinforcing. Because Hungary apparently did not experience a big loss of competitiveness, its large GDP decline during the Great Recession was not among the worst in the region (Table 20.2). The main consequences of Hungary's multiple vulnerabilities would seem to be the danger of economic stagnation, of being stuck in a low-growth trap.

The remaining four EU-10 countries – Poland, the Czech Republic, Slovakia and Slovenia – had no glaring vulnerabilities relative to the other six. In fact, Poland has a 'P' in one column, indicating that it appears to have maintained its external competitiveness better than its neighbours. This was probably one of several factors helping Poland to be the only country not only in CEE but in the EU able to sustain growth during the Great Recession (Table 20.2). The Czech Republic also gets a 'P' in one column for having its economy relatively well protected against sudden stops in capital inflows by accumulating only a relatively modest level of external debt.

Adjusting the growth model

Let us recall the main features of the region's pre-crisis growth model: fast-paced expansion of domestic demand, facilitated by rapid credit growth, financed by large capital inflows covering the resulting current-account deficits, made possible by the region's rapid political, trade and financial integration with Western Europe, accompanied by real exchange rate appreciation. This growth model has made the EU-10 economies highly vulnerable to external shocks, especially those emanating from Western Europe. High vulnerability was the inevitable consequence of the model. The only question about it was whether the individual CEE countries' domestic economic policies and institutional choices had increased or dampened their vulnerability; this issue was analysed above and summarized in Table 20.1.

Given recent past and prospective future developments in Western Europe – the linked sovereign debt and banking crises, threatening the very existence of the eurozone as it was constituted more than a decade ago – why East Europe's growth model must now be adjusted is quite evident. So how can and should the model be modified?

The proposed 'new' model should have two strategic priorities. One is to find new domestic sources of growth. The other is to reduce their vulnerability to external shocks, especially those that will continue to be generated by the medium- and long-term economic, financial and political problems in Western Europe. This dual development strategy should rest on three interdependent pillars: macro-stabilization, export promotion so that net exports become a driver of growth and reducing obstacles to sustained domestic productivity improvements.

Macro-stabilization

The experiences of many countries over extensive periods have shown that a stable macro-economic framework is a necessary though not sufficient condition for sustained growth. A stable macro-framework means smoothing macroeconomic volatility, which discourages long-term investment. This includes preventing excessive, credit-driven domestic demand booms, since these encourage the transfer of resources from the generally more productive and productivity-enhancing tradeable to the generally less productive and less innovation-focused non-tradeable sectors.

A stable macro-framework includes prudent fiscal policies, a commitment to which can be strengthened by parliaments adopting fiscal rules that set limits on expenditure growth and deficits, as Bulgaria, Poland and some of the Baltic states have recently done. High public and external debt ratios that are growth limiting, such as those of Hungary, need to be gradually and prudently reduced. This should be facilitated by caps on the size of the public sector relative to GDP agreed upon by the main political parties. When tax burdens on labour and entrepreneurship are excessive, they should be reduced, with the resulting gaps in revenues closed by an equitable widening of the tax base.

Increased trade participation and net exports should be enhanced sources of growth

Among countries of comparable size, those with relatively high and growing TPRs tend to have higher growth rates, *ceteris paribus,* than those where such indicators are lower and growing more slowly. This is because productivity tends to be higher in the tradeable than in the non-tradeable sectors. Relying on net exports as a source of growth promotes this. To be sure, the EU-10 faces a much more difficult environment for achieving this than did the Asian and Latin American countries in past decades. Therefore, geographic and product diversification should be emphasized; both could be helped, for example, by strengthening intra-CEE co-operation and specialization – based on market potential, not on administrative edicts.

Reducing obstacles to productivity growth

Usually enumerated under the label of structural reforms, they include certain standard as well as country-specific measures designed to eliminate obvious domestic bottlenecks to growth. Standard measures include designing, implementing and enforcing industry- and branch-specific competition rules (neither too lax nor excessive); assuring labour-market flexibility, including rules of wage determination that safeguard competitiveness; and improving those many aspects of the business environment where a country suffers competitive disadvantages.[30]

Strengthening institutions can also remove growth bottlenecks. For example, most CEE countries need to establish – and others to improve – well-functioning domestic money and capital markets (which has many aspects) to pool domestic savings and to make available additional sources of finance to the private sector, thereby reducing excessive dependence on the (foreign and domestic) bank-centric nature of their financial systems.

A great deal can be done everywhere in the region to improve the educational systems at all levels, using as models the experiences of countries where improved education and industry-academia co-operation have been major long-term contributors to accelerated economic growth.[31]

* * *

Sustained economic growth is essential for the reasons stated in the introduction of this contribution. The pace of sustainable growth is the outcome of a huge number of interacting variables; there is no single magic bullet that can be fired to achieve it. The growth prospects of a country will of course always be influenced by developments in the external environment. Nevertheless, the immense complexity of sustainable growth can be reduced to two sets of domestic variables. First, policymakers in CEE must achieve a consensus on new growth strategies and policies, along the lines sketched above. Second, a country must have a reasonably stable central power structure to implement the agreed economic strategies and policies, while securing a sustained 'buy-in' for them from the general public.[32]

Notes

1 The Baltic states of Estonia, Latvia and Lithuania, plus the Czech Republic, Hungary, Poland, Slovakia and Slovenia joined in 2004; Bulgaria and Romania in 2007.

2 EBRD (2010), Chart 4.1.

3 IMF-REO, May 2010, p. 28. The IMF definition of 'emerging Europe' excludes two of the most developed CEE countries (the Czech Republic and Slovenia) while it includes Turkey, Russia, Ukraine and the non-EU-member South European countries. However, in this context, the statement about the relative size and composition of capital inflows is valid for the EU-10 group, too.

4 ECB (2009), p. 10.

5 Fabrizio *et al.* (2009, p. 7). Only Estonia, already highly open in 1995, registered a smaller TPR increase.

6 *Op. cit.*, p. 10 and Figure 7 on p. 15. See also IMF-REO, October 2011, Section 4.

7 EBRD (2010), Chapter 4.

8 Jimborean (2011), Figures 4, 5 and 6 (pp. 34–35). The REER is the weighted average of a country's currency relative to an index or basket of other major currencies, adjusted for the effects of inflation. The weights of the different currencies are usually their countries' trade shares. The measure of inflation used – consumer prices, wholesale prices, unit labour costs, or export unit values – will influence the results, although in the case of CEEs, the results were not dissimilar. Comparing the REER trends of several countries will show which have gained or lost international competitiveness. Another source, charting data since 2005, shows that all CEE currencies appreciated until late 2008, declined significantly in the following year, and by and large stabilized during 2010 (Gardo and Martin 2010, Chart 31, p. 37).

9 Fabrizio *et al.* (2009, Figures 1(a) and 1(b), pp. 3–4); Jimborean (2011, Figure 1, p. 6) (in the latter study, the base line is the average per capita GDP of the EU 27). See also *Turmoil at Twenty*, Figure 1.1., p. 26.

10 Institutional adaptation could involve, for example, privatization, the central bank, tax and accounting systems, and commercial law.

11 IMF-REO, October 2011. Estimates of the growth differentials are sensitive to the shape of the calculated convergence line.

12 *Ibid.*, Fig.3.7 (p. 52)

13 Jimborean (2011, Figure 2, p. 7). Bela Balassa and Paul Samuelson developed their quite similar theories, independently, in 1964. The Balassa-Samuelson inflation effect originates in the supply side (cost push). Real income convergence will also generate inflationary pressures from the other side (demand pull) as capital inflows and the resulting expansion of credit lower the real rate of interest and raise asset prices as well as the CPI.

14 BIS (2008).

15 Fabrizio *et al.* (2009, p. 5).

16 *Ibid.*, p. 10.

17 The link between vulnerabilities and performance is not straightforward because the tempo of GDP growth in any period is the net outcome of a complex set of interdependent variables. For an excellent study defining, quantifying and applying a large number of vulnerability indicators to nine CEE countries individually as well as a group, see Gardo and Martin (2010).

18 EBRD (2010), Chapter 4, p. 68.

19 World Bank (2010) *Turmoil at Twenty*, p. 10.

20 For the growth and composition of credit growth to the private sector in each country, see *Turmoil at Twenty*, Table 1.3, p. 50. For comparisons of trends in credit levels relative to GDP, see Gardo and Martin (2010), Chart 7, p. 14. The chart shows that while credit-to-GDP levels in CEE are still modest as compared with averages in the eurozone, per cent changes in the CEE countries since 2002 were dramatically higher than in Western Europe.

21 *Ibid.,* Box Figure 2, p. 67. A different set of data, for different years, can be found in Gardo and Martin (2010), Chart 3, p. 8.

22 *Turmoil at Twenty*, pp. 6–7.

23 EBRD (2010), *Transition Report*, Chapter 4, offers detailed data and analysis.

24 A peg means that the central bank's primary responsibility is to maintain the exchange rate. Since large capital inflows would appreciate the rate, the central bank must 'sterilize' the inflow by selling its own currency for foreign currency-denominated assets, thereby building up its foreign exchange reserves. Since the central bank is releasing more of its currency into circulation, this will expand the money supply, creating inflationary pressures that will erode a nation's export competitiveness just as much as currency appreciation would.

25 *Carmen M Reinhart* and *Kenneth Rogoff*, 'Debt and Growth Revisited', VOX, August 2010. www. voxeu.org/index.php?q=node/5395 (accessed November 1, 2011).

26 *Ibid.* A more recent BIS study identifies the threshold at around 85% of GDP, noting that governments should keep debt levels well below the threshold to have fiscal buffers to deal with extraordinary adverse events (Cecchetti *et al.,* 2010).

27 The conditions for capping debt-to-GDP ratios are the following (Akyüz, 2007, pp. 1 and 5):
A *public debt ratio* stops increasing when the growth rate of the GDP is at least as high as the real effective interest rate on government debt. If the growth rate is lower, then there must be a corresponding primary budget surplus. If the growth rate is higher, the debt ratio can be stable or declining even when there is a primary budget deficit.
An *external debt ratio* stops increasing when there is a sufficient current-account surplus (net transfer of resources abroad) to cover the difference between net capital inflows and interest payment on the debt. The amount of surplus increases with the external debt ratio and the growth-adjusted real interest rate on debt.

28 European Commission, ECOFIN, *General Government Data* (Spring 2011), Table 53b.

29 A partial offset in Estonia and Bulgaria has been their surprisingly low levels of sovereign debt, giving their authorities some room to manoeuvre.

30 The annual *Global Competitiveness Report* and the World Bank's *Doing Business* reports are goldmines for identifying such bottlenecks.

31 The OECD's annual, multi-country Programme for International Student Assessment (PISA) survey results show that an intelligently improved educational system is the greatest contributor to improved economic growth performance.

32 The overwhelming importance of these factors has been documented in the recent cross-country study, *Why Nations Fail*, Robinson and Acemoglu (2012)

Bibliography

Akyüz, Y. (2007), 'Debt Sustainability in Emerging Markets: A Critical Appraisal', *DESA Working Paper* No. 61

Cecchetti, S., Madhusudan, M. and Zampolli, F. (2010), 'The Future of Public Debt: Prospects and Implications', *BIS Working Paper No. 300*

Checherita, C. and Rother, P. (2010), 'The Impact of High and Growing Government Debt on Economic Growth: An Empirical Investigation for the Euro Area', *ECB Working Paper No. 1237.*

Coricelli, F., Driffield, N., Pal. S. and Roland, I. (2010), 'Microeconomic Implications of Credit Booms: Evidence from Emerging Europe', *EBRD Working Paper* No. 119.

EBRD (2010), *Transition Report*, London: EBRD.

Fabrizio, S., Leigh, D. and Mody, A. (2009), 'The Second Transition: Eastern Europe in Perspective', *IMF Working Paper* No. 09/43, Washington, DC: International Monetary Fund.

Forthun, C. and Hagemann, R.P. (2010), 'Sustaining the Momentum of Fiscal Reform in Hungary', *OECD Economics Department Working Papers*, No. 802, OECD Publishing.

Gardo, S. and Martin, P. (2010), 'The Impact of the Global Economic and Financial Crisis on Central and Eastern Europe and Southeastern Europe and Latin America', *Bank of Spain Occasional Paper* No. 1002.

IMF (2010), *Regional Economic Outlook: Europe Fostering Sustainability*, Washington, DC: IMF (May)

——(2011a, b), *Regional Economic Outlook*, Washington, DC: IMF (April and October).

Jimborean, R. (2011), 'The Exchange Rate Pass-Through in the New EU Member States', *Banque de France*, Document No. 341.

Mihaljek, D. and Klau, M. (2008), 'Catching Up and Inflation in Transition Economies: The Balassa-Samuelson Effect Revisited', *BIS Working Paper* No. 270.

Reinhart, C. and Rogoff, K. (2010), 'Debt and Growth Revisited', VOX-EU. www.voxeu.org/index.php?q=node/5395 (accessed November 1, 2011).

Robinson, J. and Acemoglu, D. (2012), *Why Nations Fail*, New York: Crown Publishers.

World Bank (2010), *Turmoil at Twenty: Recession, Recovery and Reform in Central and Eastern Europe and the former Soviet Union*, Washington, DC: World Bank

Zorzi, M., Chudik, A. and Dieppe, A. (2009), 'Current Account Benchmarks for Central and Eastern Europe', *ECB Working Paper* No. 995.

Part VI
Firms

Part VI
Flux

21

ENTREPRENEURSHIP IN THE TRANSITION ECONOMIES OF CENTRAL AND EASTERN EUROPE

Saul Estrin and Tomasz Mickiewicz

Introduction

The willingness of business people to take risks in the formation of new firms is rightly regarded as one of the principal characteristics of a market economy. As risk-takers, entrepreneurs drive innovation and introduce new products and technologies. Moreover, the processes of entry of new firms by entrepreneurs, which reallocate resources from low- to high-productivity uses, is pivotal to achieving efficiency, while the pressures of potential entry push existing firms to minimize their costs and prevent waste. Entrepreneurship is therefore seen as an indicator of national economic health, especially with respect to the ability to grow and to create jobs. Recently, better availability of data on entrepreneurial entry has enabled researchers to test hypotheses on the impact of economic growth on entrepreneurship and to find evidence supporting a positive relationship (Parker, 2009).

The situation at the start of transition in most of the former communist economies was potentially especially conducive to entrepreneurial activity, as was widely recognized by analysts at the time (Kornai, 1990). This was because domestic relative prices, notably for energy, were not aligned with international ones, and trade patterns were severely distorted in the Soviet bloc. This had led to an over-expansion of industry, and especially heavy industry, at the expense of services and consumer products (Estrin *et al.*, 2006). There was therefore a fundamental need for economic restructuring; an activity for which, in a competitive market economy, entrepreneurs would be the primary agents.

However, the environment was not conducive to restructuring through this mechanism. Under communism, entrepreneurial activity was extremely low. Private entrepreneurship was frowned upon and most often outlawed. This exacerbated the fact that most countries in eastern Europe (but not parts of central Europe) did not have an entrepreneurial tradition in the pre-communist period. Moreover, while extending private ownership was seen as a route to building a capitalist class supportive of reform, policies focused on privatization and therefore implicitly favoured restructuring via existing firms or through foreign direct investment (Estrin *et al.*, 2009). Even so, the huge restructuring required for successful transition opened up new areas of profitable opportunity, and in many countries these were seized with alacrity. However, after a surge in entrepreneurial activity in some countries in the 1990s, high rates of entrepreneurship did not last, and, as we will show, entrepreneurship tends to be significantly lower in central and eastern Europe than in comparable economies two decades after the start of the transition.

This chapter discusses the reasons for this finding and illustrates empirically various possible explanations using the Global Entrepreneurship Monitor (GEM) dataset. Among the main causes of low entrepreneurial activity in eastern Europe are comparatively weak institutions (formal and informal). Aidis *et al.* (2010) present evidence that formal institutions have a strong impact on entrepreneurship, notably via the size of the state sector. However, the significantly lower entrepreneurial activity in transition economies cannot be explained by this alone. Informal institutions, or cultural values and norms, are also important. Estrin and Mickiewicz (2011) identify this indirectly through a generational effect; the older generation in eastern Europe that was born and educated under communism is not only less entrepreneurial than the younger generation, but also less entrepreneurial than older generations in other parts of the world. However, this result also offers hope for the future, as the younger generation is shedding the communist-era social norms and values. In the following section, we outline recent developments in measuring entrepreneurial activity internationally before briefly summarising the evidence about the relationship between entrepreneurial activity and the level of development. Having established the very low levels of entrepreneurial activity in most former Soviet bloc transition economies, we go on to consider likely explanations, including institutional quality, corruption and social values. We conclude with a brief discussion of the impact of migration and of the recent economic crisis.

A comparison of the levels of entrepreneurship in transition and other economies

The 2010 GEM Report (Kelley *et al.*, 2010) provides country-level indicators of entrepreneurship for 59 economies. These indicators were constructed from representative samples of at least 2,000 individuals in each country, each from the working age population. The GEM data capture a wide range of entrepreneurial activities and can be used to compare the transition economies with other countries. While the dataset does not provide information on all the transition economies, their coverage is wide enough for interesting comparisons with developed western economies and (non-transition) emerging markets.

We commence by reporting levels of entrepreneurial activity in transition as against other economies in Table 21.1. For entrepreneurship, GEM offers four main measures of entrepreneurial activity, namely:

- The *nascent entrepreneurship rate* (proportion of the population aged 18–64 actively involved in setting up a business they will own or co-own and manage; this business has not paid salaries, wages or payments to the owners for more than three months).
- The *new business ownership rate* (proportion of the population aged 18–64 currently owner–managers of a new business – owning and managing a running business that has paid wages, etc., for more than three but less than 42 months).
- *Early-stage entrepreneurial activity* (proportion of the population aged 18–64 who are either a nascent entrepreneur or a new business owner).
- The *established business ownership rate* (proportion of the population aged 18–64 who are owner-managers of an established business that has paid wages, etc., for more than 42 months).

Table 21.1 Entrepreneurial activity, 2010 GEM Report

	Nascent entrepreneurship rate	New business ownership rate	Early-stage entrepreneurial activity	Established business ownership rate
Bosnia and Herzegovina	4.1	4.1	7.7	6.6
Croatia	3.8	1.9	5.5	2.9
Hungary	4.6	2.6	7.1	5.4
Latvia	5.6	4.2	9.7	7.6
Macedonia	4.4	3.6	8	7.6
Montenegro	12	3.1	14.9	7.8
Romania	3.3	1.1	4.3	2.1
Russia	2.1	1.9	3.9	2.8
Slovenia	4.1	4.1	7.7	6.6
Transition economies	4.7	2.8	7.3	5.3
Factor-driven economies	11.8	12.3	22.8	12.6
Efficiency-driven economies	7.6	6.7	14.0	9.3
Innovation economies	3.0	2.8	5.7	7.1

Source: Kelley *et al.* (2010) plus authors' calculations.
Note that the early stage rate may be lower than the sum of nascent rate and new businesses rate because it avoids double counting: some individuals may be involved in more than one entrepreneurial project in various stages.

We follow the strategic entrepreneurship literature in dividing economies according to their stage of development with respect to innovative processes (Porter, 1990). Thus, the country sample is divided into three groups based on Kelley *et al.* (2010), yet we separated the transition countries into a fourth category:

- *Factor-driven economies* (relatively low-income economies): this stage of development is marked by high rates of agricultural self-employment. Economies compete primarily through low costs of production, the supply of commodities or low value-added products. Most small manufacturing and service firms are run by self-employed workers. In our sample, countries at this stage are Angola, Bolivia, Egypt, Ghana, Guatemala, Iran, Jordan, Syria, Tonga, Uganda, West Bank and Gaza and Yemen.
- *Efficiency-driven economies* (middle-income emerging markets): countries at this stage of development have efficient production techniques in large markets, and so are able to exploit scale economies. Capital and labour play the crucial role in productivity growth and self-employment is declining. This is the closest comparator group for eastern Europe. The economies at this stage in our sample are Argentina, Brazil, Chile, China, Colombia, Costa Rica, Malaysia, Mexico, Peru, South Africa, Taiwan, Trinidad and Tobago, Tunisia, Turkey and Uruguay.
- *Innovation-driven economies* (high-income economies): growth relies primarily upon innovation, and the economy shifts towards higher value-added activities. The role of the entrepreneur as innovator becomes more central. In our sample, countries in this stage of development are Australia, Belgium, Denmark, Finland, France, Germany, Greece, Iceland, Ireland, Israel, Italy, Japan, Republic of Korea, Netherlands, Norway, Spain, Switzerland, the UK and the USA.
- *The transition countries of Eastern and Central Europe*: there are nine transition countries in our sample – Bosnia and Herzegovina, Croatia, Hungary, Latvia, Macedonia, Montenegro, Romania, Russia and Slovenia.

The relationship between the level of development and entrepreneurial activity is not linear because entrepreneurship takes different forms and play different roles as income per capita in an economy increases (Parker, 2009). Thus, low-income countries have a large number of small businesses but as income per head rises, industrialisation and economies of scale increase the role of large firms in the economy. This may be accompanied by a reduction in the number of new businesses. At high levels of income, entrepreneurship begins to increase once again as institutions become more conducive and more individuals can access the resources necessary to start their own business. There is also a structural shift to services leading to an increase in entrepreneurial entry. Thus, the literature proposes that the relationship between entrepreneurial activity and the level of development will be U-shaped. Note that since most transition economies are probably in the second stage of development (efficiency-driven), entrepreneurial activity might be expected to be relatively low.[1]

Table 21.1 shows that our measures of entrepreneurship are usually lower in transition economies than in the other three categories of economy for all four types of entrepreneurial activity. The only exception is in comparison with innovation-driven economies, for which all measures of entrepreneurial activity are very low. Most importantly, entrepreneurship rates in the transition economies are significantly lower than in the key comparator group – the non-transition, efficiency-driven (middle-income) economies. For most indicators, the averages for other middle income economies are about double those of the transition economies. Especially striking are the extremely low entrepreneurial activity rates in Russia – among the lowest in the world. However, Romania docs not score much better.

The issue is illustrated further in Figure 21.1, which plots the relationship between the total entrepreneurial activity rate (nascent plus new business owners) and GDP per capita. The relationship is found to be U-shaped, as predicted, and the highlighted area represents observations within the 95 per cent confidence interval. The transition economies can be seen to be clustered below the regression line and often outside the area of significance, somewhat below the minimum of the curve. The result is confirmed by regression analysis – when running a corresponding regression model with linear and quadratic GDP per capita and including a dummy for the transition economies, the latter is significant at the 1 per cent level and has a negative sign (based on heteroscedasticity-robust standard errors).

The determinants of entrepreneurial activity

The remainder of this contribution is devoted to a preliminary exploration of why levels of entrepreneurial activity have remained so low in transition economies. The academic literature has identified a number of factors that influence the levels of entrepreneurship, including individual attitudes to risk, formal and informal institutions, human capital endowments and the development of the financial sector (e.g. Aidis *et al.*, 2010). We focus on the differences between transition economies and other countries with respect to these determinants.

Human capital

Levels of education and training are important for entrepreneurship and in principle the transition countries fare relatively well in this area. The communist regimes created extensive education and health services. Many central and east European economies continue to invest a high proportion of GDP in education. As a result, educational standards are high and transition economies typically have a high proportion of students in 'hard' subjects such as mathematics and engineering. That however does not imply that the educational systems produce graduates with skills important

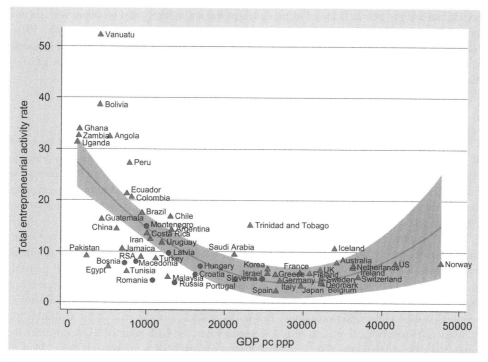

Figure 21.1 GDP per capita (purchasing power parity) and total entrepreneurial activity rate
Sources: Kelley *et al.* (2010) – total entrepreneurial activity (owners-managers of either start-ups or young businesses/working age population); World Bank 'World Development Indicators' – GDP per capita purchasing power parity for 2009, constant 2005 US dollars.

specifically for new entrepreneurs and for the employees they would wish to hire. A closer inspection of surveys of framework conditions for entrepreneurship reveals that in this respect the situation is particularly problematic in Russia, Croatia and Slovenia. In all three countries, inadequate quality of primary and secondary education is listed as one of the three most negative framework conditions, and – unlike the majority of other countries – post-school education is not listed amongst those that have a positive impact (Kelley *et al.*, 2010). The disparity between general high quality of education and the deficiency of skills required for entrepreneurship is particularly striking for Slovenia, the most developed of the transition economies, yet where rates of both economic growth and entrepreneurship are not high.

Finance

Entrepreneurs require financial resources in order to establish and run their firms and they must either provide these resources from their own savings or borrow from financial markets. Private savings were inadequate at the start of the transition and capital market development remained weak in most of these countries (Estrin *et al.*, 2006). Progress in reform of the securities market and non-bank financial institutions was typically slow during the first decade of transition (EBRD *Transition Reports* 1999; and other years). The banking sector was inexperienced in private-sector lending and lacked the organizational capability to finance entrepreneurial businesses, with state-owned banks continuing to favour state-owned firms. However, over the past decade there has been significant progress in financial sector development and reforms, and problems with finance are no longer a factor distinguishing most of the transition economies (Mickiewicz, 2010). Nevertheless, the GEM survey of entrepreneurship framework conditions reveals that in Latvia, Macedonia and Russia, finance is still listed as one of the three most negative factors affecting entrepreneurs (Kelley *et al.*, 2010).

Formal institutions

The institutional environment affects the propensity to start a new business because of its impact on the transactions costs of starting a new firm and on the returns in the early years of the business. Potential institutional obstacles to entrepreneurial activity include the quality of the commercial code, the strength of legal enforcement, administrative barriers to entry and to business activities, the prevalence of extra-legal payments and generally deficient market-supporting institutions (McMillan and Woodruff, 2002).

For the transition economies, a distinction should be drawn between the countries of Central and Eastern Europe (CEE) and those of the former Soviet Union (FSU), excluding the Baltic states. These were only annexed by the Soviet Union in the 1940s, and therefore probably preserved some institutional memory of a market economy; hence they can be regarded as more similar to CEE. Most CEE economies inherited institutions that were more conducive to operating a successful market economy. This initial advantage at the start of the transition was strengthened further by the process of EU accession when the CEE adopted EU legal codes and institutions. By contrast, the FSU had little prior experience of a market economy. Market-supporting institutions had to be developed after 1991 virtually from scratch.

In particular, the Soviet legacy left policy preferences for a large state sector that typically militates against entrepreneurial activity, because of the resulting high taxation, and the associated complexity of the regulatory environment that increases the transaction costs of running independent businesses. Higher taxes and welfare provision may affect entrepreneurial entry via their direct impact on expected returns to entrepreneurial activity and on its opportunity cost. Yet while many transition countries have preserved a large state sector, a significant number of countries such as Russia are characterized by smaller state sectors, which can be dated back to the collapse of tax revenue in the 1990s and tax reforms in early 2000s. Nevertheless, even in Russia the extent of state redistribution is not small when compared with fast-growing Far East Asian economies, including China, South Korea and others.

In many countries in the region, the state also continues to engage in arbitrary interference in enterprise affairs, putting out its 'grabbing hand' to the detriment of new private ventures (Shleifer and Vishny, 1998). Entrepreneurs are the most affected by corruption and ineffective regulatory frameworks since, unlike large firms, they lack bargaining power vis-à-vis the bureaucracy (Aidis *et al.*, 2010).

For entrepreneurship, it is also important to have strong property rights. There is no universally accepted set of country-level measures of institutional quality; we use the Heritage Foundation–Wall Street Journal Economic Freedom Index (Beach and Kane, 2008), which has wide coverage. The enforcement and protection of property rights is correlated with GDP per capita. However, for the overwhelming majority of transition economies, the scores for property rights are still significantly below the scores that could be expected on the basis of their level of development (Mickiewicz, 2010).

These intuitions are supported empirically in the work of Aidis *et al.* (2010), who consider whether differences in the level of entrepreneurial activity between countries can be explained by variation in formal institutions. They use factor analysis to construct synthetic measures of formal institutions. This data reduction technique allows the large number of related institutional indices to be combined into two distinct composite variables: the 'size of the state sector' (clustered around the extent of state spending) and the 'rule of law'. The key components of the latter are the (highly inter-correlated) measures of the protection of property rights and of freedom from corruption based on the Heritage Foundation/Wall Street Journal data.

Figure 21.2 presents the findings for the transition economies covered by the Heritage Foundation 2011 dataset. We utilise the two key institutional dimensions important for entrepreneurship as identified by Aidis *et al.* (2010): the size of the government and property rights.[2] The lower-right hand side of the figure remains empty – this implies that no transition economies are characterized by those institutional characteristics identified as being conducive to entrepreneurship. Central European countries have strong property rights systems but also extensive state sectors. In contrast, Central Asian economies have limited state sectors, but property rights are weak. However, from the point of view of entrepreneurial framework conditions, the worst cases relate to the Balkan states and the CIS countries, where both property rights are weak and state sectors are extensive; Belarus and Bosnia and Herzegovina are the most prominent examples of this combination.

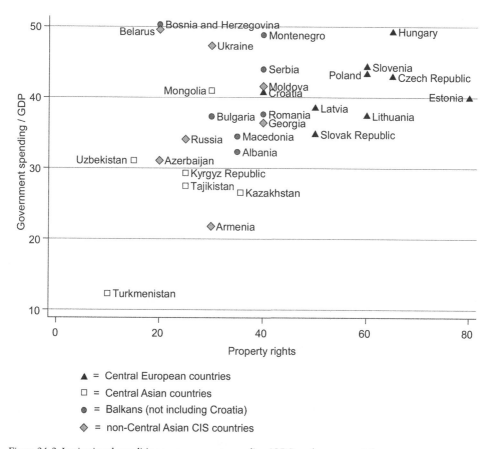

Figure 21.2 Institutional conditions: government spending/GDP and property rights
Sources: Heritage Foundation plus authors' calculation. Here, the property rights index reflects 'the ability of individuals to accumulate private property, secured by clear laws that are fully enforced by the state.' (Beach and Kane, 2008; see further detail there). Note that data on government spending in Turkmenistan may be problematic.

Social and cultural factors

Informal institutions (prevailing norms and values) are as important as formal institutions in shaping the framework for entrepreneurship. Communism left a legacy of values and norms that are not conducive to entrepreneurship (Batjargal, 2003; Hsu, 2005; Ledeneva, 2006). Sztompka (1996) describes this legacy as a 'bloc culture' which comprised priority of dependence over self-reliance; of conformity over individualism; and of rigidity and extremism in beliefs over tolerance and innovation.

Schwartz and Bardi (1997) explain that the norms developed in the communist era were not the result of indoctrination, but rather resulted from social adaptation to the prevailing economic and social conditions. Indeed, their adoption was sometimes in direct contradiction to the official ideology. Thus, while the communist system officially promoted trust and co-operation, the prevailing conditions of surveillance of citizens led to distrust, which became deeply rooted in social attitudes. Values that are critical for entrepreneurship remain much weaker in post-communist societies than in comparable countries. However, the differences between transition and comparator countries are lower for younger people, as the latter have a much greater capacity to adapt to new conditions and are more receptive to new cultural influences (Estrin and Mickiewicz, 2011).

These findings can be confirmed by using the data collected by the World Value Surveys. Trust is an essential prerequisite for entrepreneurship. However, for transition countries the levels of generalized trust in others are relatively low. This creates disincentives to entrepreneurial activity, as developing new business relations is hampered by the perceived risk inherent in dealing with strangers.

In the 2010 GEM study, respondents in various countries were asked to assess the social and cultural norms that correspond to framework conditions for entrepreneurship. The GEM data show striking differences between the transition group and other countries. The social status attached to entrepreneurship is lowest in the transition economies compared to all other groups of countries, and the same relates to positive media coverage. Even if the number of respondents who believe that entrepreneurship is socially perceived as a good career choice is higher than in high income ('innovation driven') economies, it is still almost 10 percentage points lower than in the comparator 'efficiency-driven' group of countries, as Table 21.2 shows.

Corruption

Embedded, widespread corruption becomes another informal institution, and is likely to be damaging to entrepreneurial activity and expansion, as it increases the costs of starting and running a business and reduces entrepreneurial gains. As was the case for property rights, for the overwhelming majority of transition economies, the scores for corruption are significantly worse than could be expected on the basis of their level of development (Mickiewicz, 2010). The level of corruption reflects all the institutional weaknesses in an economy, as it is affected by weak property rights, arbitrariness in state administration, a weak judicial system, and inefficient and non-transparent regulatory frameworks. But it is more than that. It also reflects prevailing social norms and therefore it is characterized by persistence, responding slowly to changes in the formal institutional environment (Aidis *et al.*, 2008, 2010). It can be treated as a proxy for overall institutional quality, both formal and informal. For most transition economies, high corruption is consistent with low scores on levels of entrepreneurship.

Last but not least, all these factors explain only part of the cross-country variation in rates of entrepreneurship. For lack of space we do not comment on all potentially important dimensions. In particular, there is simultaneity between economic growth and entrepreneurship.

Table 21.2 Attitudes to entrepreneurship, 2010

	Entrepreneurship as a good career choice	High status to successful entrepreneurs	Media attention for entrepreneurship
Bosnia and Herzegovina	76.0	63.0	47.6
Croatia	67.1	49.9	41.8
Hungary	55.0	73.7	47.4
Latvia	58.8	64.8	57.2
Macedonia	71.3	66.2	56.0
Montenegro	81.0	68.4	69.5
Romania	66.5	65.5	46.9
Russia	65.4	63.7	46.6
Slovenia	53.2	73.7	56.2
Transition economies	66.0	65.4	52.1
Factor-driven economies	75.3	80.9	65.3
Efficiency-driven economies	75.4	73.0	67.7
Innovation-driven economies	59.5	70.1	55.5

Source: Authors' calculations based on Kelley *et al.* (2010).

Note: Average survey responses on extent to which social and cultural norms are considered to be supportive of entrepreneurship.

While entrepreneurship contributes to economic growth (Parker, 2009), the latter also attracts more entrepreneurial entry via widening the range of profitable opportunities. This may explain some cases in our data, where entrepreneurial entry is strong despite weak institutions, for example Montenegro.

Assessing the impact of values and norms

Estrin and Mickiewicz (2011) investigate the impact of informal institutions indirectly through the age structure of entrepreneurs. They hypothesise that change in informal institutions will be embedded in generational change; acceptance of corruption and non-entrepreneurial attitudes are deeply rooted in the generation brought up under communism. Older people are less likely to be entrepreneurial in all countries but this effect is likely to be stronger in transition economies. To test their hypothesis, they introduce an interaction term defined as the transition dummy multiplied by each individual's age (and age squared). They found that – even after controlling for the size of the state, property rights and a number of macro- and individual-level controls – this effect was negative and statistically significant in regressions of the probability of an individual choosing to become a nascent entrepreneur (new business start-ups). Thus, the negative effect of age on entrepreneurship was found to be significantly stronger in transition countries, even when controlling for variation in individual characteristics such as education and gender, as well as for differences in the formal institutions discussed above. Estrin and Mickiewicz (2011) attribute this result to the negative impact of informal institutions, notably the communist heritage in norms and values, on entrepreneurial activity.

Conclusions

We have shown that entrepreneurial activity rates are lower in transition countries than in comparable middle income economies. In large part, this is the result of deficient formal institutions in central and eastern Europe. In particular, one can point to inadequate property rights protection, regulations that hamper businesses and the relatively large size (controlling for the level of development) of the state sector. Informal institutions, including attitudes and social norms, are also a problem. In the GEM survey, existing social and cultural norms are highlighted as more serious obstacles by respondents in transition economies than in comparator countries. The particular cultural values supporting entrepreneurship are weaker in transition countries than elsewhere.

Generalized trust was severely damaged during the communist era, while other values conducive to entrepreneurship including confidence and autonomy are also weak. Estrin and Mickiewicz (2011) identify a clear-cut generational effect: the older generation born and educated under communism is far less entrepreneurial than its counterpart in other regions of the world. This is both a cause for concern and a source of optimism since the younger generation carries much less of the burden of the past.

The ambiguous effects of migration

Our study suggests that entrepreneurship should increase in transition economies when the new generation born and educated in a market economy grows to maturity. However, even here the auguries are not entirely positive because the demographic structure in Eastern and Central Europe is beginning to converge to that of western Europe, with relatively fewer young people. The impact of this could be amplified by the effects of the wave of migrations of mostly young people from eastern to western Europe. However, hopefully, this will not only enhance entrepreneurship in recipient countries like UK, Ireland and Germany, but also create positive feedback effects by increasing the perceived returns to entrepreneurial behaviour and an increased number of start-ups by return migrants.

The low levels of entrepreneurial activity do not seem to have been a significant constraint on economic growth in central and eastern Europe so far. This is perhaps because of the role of foreign direct investment (in east central Europe; see Bevan and Estrin, 2004) and high resource prices (in much of the former Soviet Union). However, deficiencies in entrepreneurship could become more telling in the future. In addition, the role of policy in improving the situation is likely to be limited in the short term because of the persistent negative impact of informal institutions, which can only change slowly over time. For policy-makers who focus on entrepreneurship, there may, however, be big benefits over the longer term from limiting the size of the state sector, reducing corruption, improving property rights, shaping education so it offers a better match with the needs of business, and from promoting cultural values conducive to economic initiative.

The effects of the global recession

The impact of the 2008/09 crisis on central and eastern Europe has been mixed, with Poland experiencing only a mild slow down, but the small open economies of the Baltic republics sliding into two-digit recessions (meaning that GDP fell by more than 10 per cent). Although crises can sometimes unleash new entrepreneurial energies (as well as boost necessity-driven entrepreneurship), the aftermath of 2009 had a negative impact on entrepreneurship in the region via reduced actual and perceived opportunities and more difficult financing conditions. Nevertheless, as illustrated by Table 21.3, this has been temporary.

The GEM data for 2008 and 2009 show that entrepreneurial activity rates on average did not decline in eastern and central Europe compared with 2008. The two striking cases were Hungary and Latvia, where there were significant increases in activity. These economies were among the worst-affected by the crisis, suggesting that there was an increase in necessity-driven

Table 21.3 The crisis and entrepreneurship

Country group	Year (GEM report)	Early-stage entrepreneurial activity	Nascent entrepreneurship rate
Transition	2007	5.03	3.08
Transition	2008	5.77	3.48
Transition	2009	6.58	3.67
Transition	2010	5.87	3.60
Innovation	2007	6.14	3.84
Innovation	2008	6.73	3.72
Innovation	2009	6.03	3.35
Innovation	2010	5.69	3.16
Efficiency	2007	16.88	8.32
Efficiency	2008	17.43	10.20
Efficiency	2009	16.72	10.13
Efficiency	2010	18.00	10.40

Source: Global Entrepreneurship Monitor (GEM) 2007–10. The country coverage in the regional groups in this table differs from tables 1 and 2 as it is governed by the availability of the same countries in 2007, 2008, 2009 and 2010. Notably, the comparator efficiency group is now composed entirely of Latin American economies and the factor-driven group is absent.

entrepreneurship. In 2010 the entry rates in central and eastern Europe still did not reflect much negative impact of the crisis, in contrast with high income (innovation driven) economies. Transition economies share the pattern of recovery similar to the comparator emerging market economies of Latin America ('efficiency-driven' group in Table 21.3), albeit that the latter region is characterized by much higher entry rates overall.

Notes

1 GEM also distinguishes between necessity-driven (individuals who are involved in entrepreneurship because they have no other option for work) and improvement-driven entrepreneurship (engagement in entrepreneurial activity in order to be independent or to increase income). Necessity-driven activity tends to be higher in less developed economies. As an economy develops, it declines as large firms provide more employment opportunities. At the same time, the proportion of opportunity-driven entrepreneurial activity increases with income per head.

2 Though we use Heritage Foundation data, their indicator of government spending is transformed back to the original figures, reversing the non-linear transformation the Heritage Foundation applies. The latter places a heavy penalty on a high level of spending by introducing a quadratic term (Beach and Kane, 2008).

Bibliography

Aidis, R., Estrin, S. and Mickiewicz, T. (2008), 'Institutions and Entrepreneurship Development in Russia: A Comparative Perspective'. *Journal of Business Venturing*, vol. 23, pp. 656–72.

——(2010), 'Size matters: entrepreneurial entry and government', *Small Business Economics*, DOI: 10.1007/s11187-010-9299-y.

Batjargal, B. (2003), 'Social capital and entrepreneurial performance in Russia: A longitudinal study', *Organization Studies*, vol. 24(4), pp. 535–56.

Beach, W. and Kane, T. (2008), *Methodology: Measuring the 10 Economic Freedoms*. Washington, DC: The Heritage Foundation. www.heritagefoundation.org.

Bevan, A. and Estrin, S. (2004), 'The determinants of foreign direct investment into European transition economies', *Journal of Comparative Economics*, vol. 32, pp. 775–87.

EBRD (1999), *Transition Report 1999; Ten Years of Transition,* London: European Bank for Reconstruction and Development.

Estrin, S., Meyer, K. and Bytchkova, M. (2006), 'Entrepreneurship in Transition Economies', in M. Casson, A. Basu, B. Yeung and N. Wadeson (eds), *The Oxford Handbook of Entrepreneurship,* Oxford: Oxford University Press.

Estrin S., Hanousek, J. Kočenda, E. and Svejnar, J. (2009), 'The Effects of Privatization and Ownership in Transition Economies', *Journal of Economic Literature,* vol. 47(3), pp. 699–728

Estrin, S. and Mickiewicz, T. (2011), 'Entrepreneurship in Transition Economies: The Role of Institutions and Generational Change', in Minniti, M. (ed.), *The Dynamics of Entrepreneurship,* Oxford: Oxford University Press, Chapter 8, pp. 293–338.

Hsu, C. (2005), 'Capitalism without contracts versus capitalists without capitalism: Comparing the influence of Chinese guanxi and Russian blat on marketization', *Communist and Post-Communist Studies,* vol. 38, pp. 309 – 327.

Kelley, D., Bosma, N. and Amorós, J. (2010), *Global Entrepreneurship Monitor. Global 2010 Report,* Babson Park, MA and Santiago, Chile: Babson College and Universidad del Desarrollo.

Kornai, J. (1990), *The road to a free economy: Shifting from a socialist system: the example of Hungary,* New York: Norton.

Ledeneva, A. (2006), *How Russia Really Works. The Informal Practices that Shaped Post-Soviet Politics and Business,* Ithaca, NY: Cornell University Press.

McMillan, J. and Woodruff, C. (2002), 'The central role of entrepreneurs in transition economies', *Journal of Economic Perspectives,* vol. 16(3), pp. 153–70.

Mickiewicz, T. (2010), *Economics of Institutional Change,* Houndmills: Palgrave Macmillan.

Parker, S. (2009), *Economics of Entrepreneurship,* Cambridge: Cambridge University Press.

Porter, M. (1990), *The Competitive Advantage of Nations,* London: Macmillan.

Schwartz, S. and Bardi, A. (1997), 'Influences of Adaptation to Communist Rule on Value Priorities in Eastern Europe', *Political Psychology,* vol. 18(2), pp. 385–410.

Shleifer, A. and Vishny, R.W. (1998), *The Grabbing Hand: Government Pathologies and Their Cures,* Cambridge, MA: Harvard University Press.

Sztompka, P. (1996), 'Looking Back: The Year 1989 as a Cultural and Civilizational Break', *Communist and Post-Communist Studies,* vol. 29(2), pp. 115–29.

22

TRADE AND FIRMS IN TRANSITION

László Halpern

Introduction

International trade and firms are closely related with each other; exporting and importing firms participate directly in trade, while other firms like suppliers or customers of the trading firms are involved indirectly. International trade in the case of open economies shapes the market competition within the country and has a major impact on the technology as well in the form of importing new technologies and creating capacities to meet foreign demand. The collapse of the former politico-economic system and its associated system of regional integration has led to fundamental changes in both international trade and corporate structures in the post-communist countries.

State-owned firms traded within the socialist regional integration framework Council for Mutual Economic Assistance(CMEA) on the basis of strict quotas, centrally imposed bilateral clearing conditions[1] and detailed technical specifications. There were no incentives to upgrade products as the centrally administered prices rewarded neither better inputs nor new technologies that aimed at producing higher quality output. Primary and intermediate inputs and consumer goods imported from the West were allocated by different rationing schemes as the currencies were not convertible. Moreover, firms selling to developed markets were not allowed to retain their earnings in convertible currencies. Multiple exchange rates and widespread export subsidies and import tax schemes were used to keep under some degree of control the ever-growing appetite for valuable inputs from imports and the easy exports to countries of the Eastern trading bloc.

Ever since the process of transition to the market commenced, new firms and restructured old firms have faced much harder budget constraints; firms are trading under market conditions, imports are mostly unrestricted and tariffs and non-tariff barriers are significantly decreased. These firms are now competing with their domestic peers and newly created domestic and foreign firms, which forces them to keep a close eye on market signals and future profits. Consequently, trade has significantly dropped within the former trade integration area for the socialist bloc, and has risen sharply with new partners, especially with Western Europe. Most of the old export products were either dropped or upgraded; as a result, the export bundle has substantially changed.

Trade reorientation

The countries of Eastern Europe and the former Soviet Union all belonged to the regional and international integration system that operated under communism and central planning. The CMEA (or Comecon) imposed an excessive degree of specialization in production and a centrally decided division of labour, which hardly paid any attention to cost and efficiency considerations. This system of planned specialization was sustained economically only by maintaining a high degree of self-sufficiency within the CMEA and by conducting little trade with the rest of the world.

The starting point of transition for all the CEE countries was, therefore, the dual structure of their exports, the composition of commodities which were sold to Western markets being quite different from that which characterized their sales to CMEA markets. Many countries had the characteristics of industrially developed economies in their export shares to other CMEA markets but as exporters to the West their products were less processed, less sophisticated. The structure of trade was predominantly characterized by the legacy of inherited capacities in industries that were most heavily dependent upon selling to CMEA markets in the past (Landesmann and Székely, 1995).

While there was a need for a radical restructuring of production and international and interregional trade in all post-communist countries following the fall of the Berlin Wall and the break-up of the Soviet Union, the nature and difficulty of the required restructuring differed considerably between countries and regions. Of the eight CEE and Baltic countries that joined the European Union (EU) in 2004, all except Slovenia had been part of the Soviet bloc. Together with Bulgaria and Romania, which joined the EU in 2007, they required a drastic reorganization of their external trade directed towards Western Europe.

The countries of the Commonwealth of Independent States (CIS) also needed to reduce their trade dependence on Russia but the latter would continue to play a significant role as an origin and destination of trade. This was due not only to its geographical proximity but also to the high degree of production specialization in the former Soviet republics, and their economic interdependence as a result of the communist system.

The six former Yugoslav republics were already more integrated into the global trading system prior to the break-up of Yugoslavia. Except for Slovenia, however, their further integration into the regional and global economies was delayed by conflicts and sanctions.

Trade liberalization

While their initial conditions varied, all countries were to gain from liberalization – freeing domestic markets from administered prices and opening them to international trade – following the mis-allocated and wasted resources under the old system. Recognizing this potential and the need to weaken state control, many early reformers relied on comprehensive internal and external liberalization. The pace and scope of this liberalization varied widely, however.

In some cases, the collapse of the old regime and national independence resulted in only limited liberalization of domestic markets and the introduction of new artificial barriers to trade and transit. These barriers were either self-imposed or they were the result of barriers erected by others. For example, much of the regional infrastructure in the CIS, including roads, railways and power grids, has been starved of investment and maintenance, often for reasons of political rivalry among countries. Some of these restrictions are due to legitimate concerns about terrorism and drug trafficking, but mutual mistrust, nationalistic rivalry and trade protectionism have also played a role.

In contrast to the retreat towards self-sufficiency in some CIS countries, the expansion of the EU has been central to the reintegration into the global economy of many countries of the region. This is clearly the case for the eight post-communist countries that became members in 2004, and for Bulgaria and Romania, which joined the EU in 2007.

Initial phase reforms included price liberalization, foreign exchange and trade liberalization, and small-scale privatization. Second phase reforms included large-scale privatization, governance and enterprise restructuring, competition policy, infrastructure reforms, banking and interest rate liberalization, and the reform (and sometimes the creation) of non-bank financial institutions.

Building on these reforms, the countries redirected their trade towards existing EU members and away from former CMEA members. They increased significantly their overall openness to trade and attracted large capital inflows primarily in the form of foreign direct investment. These processes of structural and institutional reform, greater openness to trade and increased FDI tend to be mutually reinforcing in terms of their impact on overall economic performance, helping to sustain progress in transition and to support integration into the Single European Market.

International integration places significant demands on a country's economic, political and social institutions. Trade across long distances and between new trading partners requires confidence in the enforcement of contracts. The increased competition resulting from participation in global markets can force costly adjustment on some previously protected sectors. Open trade policies need to be accompanied, therefore, by a strong institutional framework that can enforce contracts and support the process of adjustment – particularly in the labour market – if international integration is to be lasting and successful. The challenge is to find a way of encouraging the developing and post-communist countries to undertake the necessary institutional reforms together with the liberalization of trade.

The link between integration and domestic institutional reform is particularly clear in the requirements for EU accession. The enlargement process has played a crucial role over the past decade in supporting far-reaching institutional reforms in the accession countries and strengthening the foundations for their integration into the EU and the world economy. For those countries of the region for which EU membership prospects are either distant or absent altogether, one should ask whether there are alternative modes of interacting with the wider regional and global communities that would trigger similar institutional reforms. In particular, the question is to what extent improved market access to industrialized countries should be conditional on strengthening domestic institutions. Increased integration with regional neighbours could be another option, although the merit of such regional arrangements requires closer scrutiny.

New trade patterns

Transition economies experienced a significant movement of trade away from the CMEA and towards the OECD and other global markets. Excluding intra-bloc trade, openness to the rest of the world increased in all transition economies. Trade with the rest of the world was the driving force behind the increasing openness of the transition countries, particularly in the accession countries.

What patterns of trade specialization were these countries able to follow in the light of this drastic trade reorientation? The countries of the region were thought to be endowed with relatively cheap and well educated labour and a capital stock of rather uneven quality in different industries as compared to countries at a similar degree of development (see Faini and Portes, 1995). However, as Helpman (in Gács and Winckler, 1994, p. 238–39) commented, remarking on the most likely changes in the patterns of specialization and trade in these countries, some of the initial capital stock was inadequate, while some of the human capital was also redundant. Given the education level of the population and the composition of the employees, though, it seemed that these countries have had the capacity to learn and absorb Western technologies and organizational methods relatively rapidly.

The degree of integration for each country is influenced by a variety of factors, such as its size, its location, its level of income and its level of reform. The impact of these factors on the extent of integration can be estimated in a so-called 'gravity model'. EBRD (2003) presents an empirical model that relates the level of trade between two specific countries to the size of their respective economies and the costs of shipping goods from one country to another. These costs are influenced by geographical distance as well as the actual costs of transport and any policy-related obstacles to trade.

The observed trade in 2003 was only around 60 per cent of the predicted trade in central Europe and Baltic state (CEB), and only around 25 per cent in south eastern Europe (SEE), Croatia and the CIS. Transition economies on average traded between 40 and 75 per cent less than the average non-transition economy when the above factors are taken into account. Then the following factors were added to the baseline estimation to see whether they could account for at least some of the lack of integration of the transition economies: the size of a country; the number of borders a country has to cross to get to a target market; the quality of transport infrastructure; the extent of trade liberalization; the quality of a country's institutions.

For the CEB, the gap between actual and potential trade was not reduced significantly by taking these additional factors into account. The only significant impact came from the number of borders. This suggested that following accession, trade in these countries – in particular, with the EU and among themselves – was likely to increase further as border controls vanished. There was little for the accession countries to gain from policy improvements since they already had better than average trade policies and governance ratings. Overall, there was some potential for increased trade in these countries which then materialized following EU enlargement in 2004.

For SEE, Croatia and the CIS, the introduction of these additional factors had a bigger impact. Taking all of them into account, the gap between actual and potential trade diminished to around 60 per cent for SEE. For the CIS, the combination of geographical constraints, border controls, restrictive trade policies and weak institutions explained almost entirely its lack of integration in the world economy. As the CIS contains the largest group of landlocked countries in the world, it faces the key challenge of overcoming obvious constraints to transit and transport, particularly in Central Asia.

For the CIS the actual level of trade with other CIS countries has been several times higher than the level predicted by the gravity model, and CIS trade with the rest of the world has been correspondingly much lower than predicted. This indicates that mutual dependencies existed and still exist in the CIS. SEE has been significantly below its trade potential even once all the other factors are taken into account. One possible explanation for this gap might be the continuing impact from the break-up of the former Yugoslavia in 1991. Of course, this gap also suggests that there is a significant potential for increased trade from and within SEE as the regional instability in the western Balkans is overcome. Trade within the region should also increase as bilateral relations improve and a network of free trade agreements was to be established.[2]

Restrictive trade policies and the poor quality of governance are key factors in explaining the low levels of integration in SEE and the CIS. The gravity model shows that CIS trade would have increased by around 20 per cent if countries in the region had adopted trade policies similar to those in the accession countries and became WTO members. Moreover, trade would almost double if the CIS also had the same quality of governance as the accession countries. For SEE and Croatia the impact of these factors would be 10 per cent and 50 per cent respectively. This result suggests that trade liberalization alone may be insufficient to improve the economic prospects of these countries.

Corporate structure

The classical enterprise in a communist country was by definition state-owned, large and was oriented to a detailed production plan measured in physical units. Meeting the plan was of prime importance and the plan was normally very ambitious. Therefore, production issues dominated entrepreneurship, marketing and cost minimization in managerial concerns. Consistently, the typical manager was a production engineer and not a businessman. Managers faced a mix of monetary and career-based incentives, which were a function of plan fulfilment and political loyalty. Profits and efficiency considerations could not play any significant role as the administratively fixed prices bore no relation to marginal costs, and investment decisions did not depend on future market and profitability prospects. The enterprise was organized along very hierarchical lines in which local and regional units of the communist party had a pivotal role. Workers had virtually no role in enterprise decisions, except in regard to personnel policy and welfare services. Firing rates were extremely low by any standard, as underemployment was widespread within the firm. The enterprise was not only a producer of goods, but also a provider of welfare services to its employees and to its local neighbourhood. For these reasons, efficiency was not considered in determining the scale of employment.

Multi-level bureaucracy co-ordinated the functioning of state-owned firms. The bureaucracy was in charge of setting prices, establishing delivery links between producer and buyer and of providing the credit necessary for the fulfilment of the annual plan. All in all, the general presence of the soft budget constraint for firms and the overall shortage of production inputs and consumer goods and durables characterized the landscape of these planned economies; bureaucratic co-ordination and rationing were in place, leaving a limited, mostly subordinated role to market mechanisms.

This classical and rigid corporate planning system was softened in a few countries, notably Yugoslavia, Hungary and Poland. Decentralizing reforms reduced the scope and detail of bureaucratic decision making. Markets and competition increased in importance. However, formal planning was supplemented with increased bargaining between the bureaucracy and enterprises over diverse aspects of administrative regulation and prices.

Corporate transition

The enterprises initially functioned in communist economies, and their behaviour was a product of the institutions and policies of those economies. In the 1990s those institutions and policies changed radically. These changes compelled enterprises to adapt their behaviour in order to survive, and perhaps to succeed, in a new, liberalized, market environment. The term enterprise restructuring has come to denote the whole process undertaken by enterprises as they adapt for survival and success in a market economy.

During the first decade of transition, more than 150,000 large enterprises in 27 transition economies went through deep changes in every aspect of their political and economic environments (Djankov and Murrell, 2002). Some enterprises have responded to the challenge, entering world markets with great dynamism and becoming indistinguishable from their competitors in mature market economies. Many others remained stalled in the past, undergoing protracted deaths, delayed at times by their slippage into a world of barter and subsidies. Thus, the radical changes in transition economies were matched by enormous variance in the degree to which enterprises restructured their operations and responded successfully to events.

As Carlin and Landesmann (1997) explain, corporate restructuring in a transition economy can take two main lines: defensive–reactive–shallow on the one hand and strategic–active–deep on the other. Reactive restructuring behaviour, such as labour-shedding or seeking markets for output, so as to contain losses and ensure the survival of the enterprise, took place in enterprises of all kinds in transition. However, deep restructuring involving a forward-looking strategic orientation (e.g. new investment and radical reorganization of product lines and processes) was, at least in the early stages, mainly observed in enterprises owned by foreigners. Further theoretical work suggested that deep restructuring required outside ownership and served to highlight the limitations of privatization strategies based on selling to enterprise insiders.

Corporate performance

Estrin *et al.* (2009) found that the effect of private ownership on corporate performance is positive in CEE but insignificant in the CIS, while there was a strong positive effect of foreign ownership in both the CEE and CIS regions. Privatization to foreign owners was found to result in considerably improved performance of firms virtually everywhere in the transition economies – an effect that is best characterized as a fairly rapid shift in performance rather than a gradual improvement over an extended period of time. The performance effect of privatization to domestic owners was on average less impressive and it varied across regions. The effect was smaller, often delayed, but positive in CEE; it was nil or even negative in Russia and the rest of the CIS. This divergence of findings between CEE and the CIS coincides with differences in policies and institutional development in the two regions, with the former increasingly adopting EU rules and joining the EU, and the latter proceeding more slowly in introducing a market-friendly legal and institutional system.

Firm-level studies suggest that concentrated (especially foreign) private ownership has a stronger positive effect on performance than dispersed ownership in CEE and the CIS. Worker ownership in CEE and the CIS does not seem to have a negative effect. Data from CEE and the CIS suggest that new firms are equally or more efficient than firms privatized to domestic owners and foreign start-ups appear to be more efficient than domestic ones. Contrary to the assumptions of many theoretical models, as well as the evidence from some developing countries, privatization in the post-communist economies is not associated with a reduction in employment. On the contrary, private owners tend to keep employment at higher levels than state-owned firms. Furthermore, macro studies are consistent with micro analyses in that they suggest that privatization, especially when accompanied by complementary reforms, may have a positive effect on the level of aggregate output or economic growth.

Why was the effect of privatization in CEE and the CIS smaller in the case of domestic as against foreign private owners? One reason is the limited skills and access to world markets on the part of the local managers. Domestically owned privatized firms are also the ones where performance-reducing activities such as looting, tunnelling and defrauding minority shareholders have been most frequent. In a number of countries, the nature of the privatization process initially prevented large domestic private owners from obtaining 100 per cent ownership stakes and insiders or the state often owned sizeable holdings. It frequently took these large shareholders several years to squeeze out minority shareholders and in the process the large shareholders sometimes artificially decreased the performance of their newly acquired firms in order to squeeze out the minority shareholders at low share prices.

The importance of good management and corporate governance, access to world markets and the presence of a well-functioning legal and institutional framework were the key factors for success. For the former state-owned firms, restructuring was most easily and effectively achieved by foreign ownership. Foreign firms routinely bring in capable expatriate managers and invest heavily in training local managers. They sell products through their global distributional networks, introduce a relatively advanced system of corporate governance and stress the importance of business ethics. Corporate governance of foreign firms hence compensates to a considerable extent for the underdeveloped legal and institutional system that prevailed in many transition economies. However, the spillover effect of foreign firms on the environment may remain rather limited and can compensate for a relatively short period only. In extreme cases foreign firms may even find it more rewarding to accommodate their pattern of behaviour to that imposed by the domestic legal and institutional system.

While some domestic firms also developed good corporate governance, the underdeveloped legal system allowed local managers in many privatized firms to maximize their own benefits at the expense of corporate performance, and hence the welfare of shareholders as well as stakeholders such as workers and the government treasury. This was likely to account for the limited positive performance effects of privatization to domestic private owners as compared to the performance of firms privatized to foreign investors.

Djankov and Murrell (2002) claim on the basis of a large number of studies that product market competition has been a major force behind improvements in enterprise productivity – the most important indicator of success in restructuring – in the transition economies as a whole. Both import competition and domestic market structure are generally significant in explaining enterprise performance. The effects are strong for CEE countries, but for the CIS countries, increased competitive pressures were not associated with enhanced restructuring.

Import competition in the CIS countries does not have a significant effect on enterprise restructuring. In contrast, import competition is significant in explaining enterprise restructuring in the CEE sample. Changes in domestic market structure are important in explaining enterprise restructuring in both the CIS and CEE samples. These results are confirmed in a study of over 3,300 enterprises in 25 transition economies (Carlin *et al.*, 2001) that shows strong positive effects of the reduction of market concentration on firm efficiency. The significant effect of changes in domestic market structure on enterprise restructuring in the CIS resonates with recent evidence on high barriers to entry in transition economies.

Carlin *et al.* (2001) found that the power of competition in influencing performance is much more important than the effect of ownership itself. In the growth of sales and productivity, as well as in new product restructuring, the presence of some market power together with competitive pressure, especially from foreign suppliers, strongly and robustly enhanced performance. New product restructuring was in turn an important contributor to firm performance, so this character of competition appeared to have both direct and indirect effects. Transition was an investment-intensive process and the descriptive evidence from the BEEPS survey of the EBRD and the World Bank indicated the presence of financing constraints. This supported the interpretation that retained profits, in the presence of competitive pressure, were important for financing the restructuring that helped firms to succeed. The presence of soft budget constraints appeared to have a broadly negative impact, and a favourable business environment a broadly positive impact, on firm performance.

All in all, the transition process can be successful if market structure nurtures rivalry among firms and removes monopolies; budget constraints become hard; the obstacles facing new entrants are removed; and financial systems support major investments in restructuring.

Firm-level performance and exporting

Transition economies established close trade relations with their neighbours and new partners. The resulting export growth during the first decade of transition was mostly owing to low unit labour costs, the initial massive trade liberalization and high world trade growth. Now these factors are unable to ensure the same dynamics of exports in the future. EBRD (2010) presents the results of a regression analysis using annual data for about 130 advanced and emerging-market countries between 1999 and 2009 in order to understand the explanatory factors behind export success. Trade-partner real GDP growth and nominal effective depreciation raise real export growth. The effect of trading partner tariffs is not statistically significant, while non-tariff barriers significantly diminish export growth. Non-tariff barriers are more relevant than tariffs as an obstacle to export growth as tariff barriers are already fairly low, reflecting the trade liberalization that occurred during the 1990s.

Measures of institutional quality also affect export growth. Real export growth is affected by difficulties in clearing customs, lack of corruption, and by the rule of law. It is not the level of these three measures of institutional quality that affects real export growth, but their interaction with non-tariff trade barriers. All three dampen or strengthen the effect of non-tariff trade barriers on real export growth. The rule of law and the lack of corruption mitigate the downward pressure on export growth from non-tariff trade barriers abroad, while cumbersome customs procedures exacerbate their effect.

Based on firm level data, EBRD (2010) endorses the observation that exporters in transition economies are more likely to engage in product innovation, even when the reverse causality from innovation to exporting is stripped out. Lower tariffs and greater export market growth make firms more likely to export, unless markets are very distant. Foreign and larger firms with a better-skilled and educated employees are also more likely to export. Larger firms, younger firms and private firms with better-educated employees are more likely to innovate than their peers. In addition, firms receiving subsidies find it easier to innovate.

After transition

To continue their convergence with advanced economies in the post-crisis world, transition economies will need to rely more heavily on exports as a source of innovation and growth. This will become more difficult as one-off effects from entering free trade areas subside and unit labour costs catch up with those of trading partners. Active policy measures will therefore be necessary to sustain rapid export growth. In particular, policy-makers can support greater export-orientation by lowering non-tariff trade barriers that impede access to new and major existing export markets. They can also improve key aspects of the domestic business climate by reducing corruption and improving the rule of law and customs procedures.

Notes

1 It is worth noting here that within the socialist bloc, the trading currency was the transferable rouble. However, it was in practice neither a rouble – for transferable rouble balances could not be used freely to buy goods for roubles in the Soviet market – nor transferable – since each pair of countries was supposed to maintain (approximate) bilateral balance in their mutual trading accounts. Thus, a firm in Hungary could not freely use a transferable rouble balance to purchase goods in, say, Bulgaria.

2 In the late 1990s and early 2000s SEE saw the establishment of over 20 bilateral free trade agreements. Such a structure of FTAs is administratively cumbersome and not particularly conducive to efficient trade, not least because each agreement tends to have its own list of products where trade remains restricted and rules of origin can be absurdly complicated. Hence the recent agreement to establish a single FTA covering the whole SEE region is greatly to be welcomed.

Bibliography

Carlin, Wendy and Landesmann, Michael (1997), 'From Theory into Practice? Restructuring and Dynamism in Transition Economies', *Oxford Review of Economic Policy*, vol. 13(2), pp. 77–105.

Carlin, Wendy, Fries, Steven, Schaffer, Mark and Seabright, Paul (2001), 'Competition and enterprise performance in transition economies: Evidence from a cross-country survey', *EBRD Working paper No. 63*, London: EBRD

Djankov, Simeon and Murrell, Peter (2002), 'Enterprise Restructuring in Transition: A Quantitative Survey', *Journal of Economic Literature*, vol. 40(3), pp 739–92.

EBRD (2003), *Transition Report*, London: EBRD.

——(2010), *Transition Report*, London: EBRD.

Estrin, Saul, Hanousek, Jan, Kočenda, Evžen and Svejnar, Jan (2009), 'The Effects of Privatization and Ownership in Transition Economies', *Journal of Economic Literature*, vol. 47(3), pp. 699–728.

Faini, Riccardo and Portes, Richard (eds) (1995), 'European Union Trade with Eastern Europe', *Centre for Economic Policy Research*, London.

Gács, János and Winckler, Georg (eds) (1994), *International Trade and Restructuring in Eastern Europe*, Berlin: IIASA and Physica Verlag.

Landesmann, M.A. and Székely, I.P. (eds) (1995), 'Industrial Restructuring and Trade Reorientation in Eastern Europe', *Department of Applied Economics Occasional Papers No. 60*, Cambridge: Cambridge University Press.

23

PYRAMID STATE OWNERSHIP AND CONTROL IN THE CZECH REPUBLIC

Evžen Kočenda and Jan Hanousek[1]

Introduction and motivation

State ownership and its transformation has been a feature that is an inherent part of the transition experience and led to the emergence of corporate pyramid structures in various transition economies (Ma *et al.*, 2006; Chernykh, 2008; Kočenda and Hanousek, 2009). In general, a corporate pyramid is a group of firms whose ownership structure follows a top-to-bottom direction of control, where the ultimate owner is at the top and exerts its control over firms at successive lower levels. This fractal-like pattern of ownership can proliferate to several levels. The key characteristic of a corporate pyramid is a separation between ownership and control, which lends the ultimate owner leveraged power over minority shareholders. La Porta *et al.*, (1999) show that corporate pyramids are widespread around the world but these structures are more often present in emerging markets (Khanna and Yafeh, 2007).

Existing studies report a significant presence of the state in European firms (La Porta *et al.*, 1999), whose control potential further increases when direct control is augmented by control through golden shares (Bortolotti and Faccio, 2006). The literature on the extent of state control in the pyramidal framework in transformation economies is scarce, but for example Chernykh (2008) provides evidence for a dramatically high level (37–48 per cent) of state control over the sampled Russian firms. Ma *et al.* (2006) describe the emergence in China of business groups in which a state-owned firm as the largest shareholder can exert power over the rest of the companies in a business group. The formation of these pyramid-like corporate structures was intentional, to allow the state extensive control as well as to facilitate the transition itself (Yiu *et al.*, 2005).

Following the above account the identification of the extent of integrated state control is important because the state as ultimate owner can exert great political influence over the economy. Properly identifying the extent of state control is also important owing to the potential negative effects stemming from the conflict between political costs and agency costs. For example, when pursuing non-economic objectives, firms with state control would be less likely to innovate and restructure their line of production or they might intentionally delay restructuring.

In this contribution we analyse the development of integrated state control in Czech companies, which also involved the emergence of corporate pyramid structures. Integrated state control can emerge as a result of extensive privatization, which has occurred in numerous countries. Such an arrangement appeared in the Czech Republic, where industrial holding companies emerged out of the former centrally-planned units, sometimes with 15–30 horizontally and vertically linked plants and subsidiaries. These companies were voucher privatized and restructured using government subsidies. The remaining shares were bought at a discount by new management teams and consortia of Czech banks. Voucher privatization led to the creation of large, diversified investment funds, often indirectly run by banks, which controlled linked enterprises (Khanna and Yafeh, 2007).

We complement the existing literature by introducing an accurate method to assess the extent of control by an ultimate owner and by producing evidence of the state being in control of a web of seemingly private companies within a corporate pyramid-like structure in the Czech Republic. Our detailed analysis of the data shows that the direct control of the state was significant and was further enhanced via golden share holdings. We conclude that integrated state control was not effectively used by the state, a finding that indicates the inefficiency of a state bureaucracy. Although the amount of state control is significant in the data, we do not find evidence of integrated state control employed to an extent similar to corporate structures in Russia or China.

Control in the pyramid and data

The interrelated ownership structure within the state pyramid is illustrated in Figure 23.1. On the top layer we identify the three main institutions through which the state is able to execute control. The key institution is a generic 'State Privatization Agency' that was established in all transformation economies under different names in order to administer state property. In the Czech Republic this agency was called the National Property Fund (NPF). Second, municipalities received various ownership stakes as free property transfers and became stakeholders in numerous companies, mainly in utilities and transportation. In many firms the stakes of municipalities were parallel with those of the NPF. Finally, other state agencies became stakeholders in

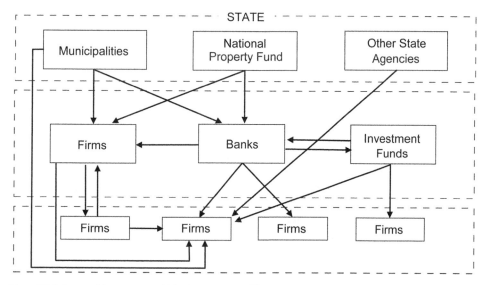

Figure 23.1 Ownership structure within the state pyramid
Source: Springer, *Economic Change and Restructuring*, Aug. 2011, 'State ownership and control in the Czech Republic', Kočenda, E. and J. Hanousek, with kind permission from Springer Science+Business Media B.V.
Note: Investment funds were first established in countries that used a voucher scheme to privatize part of the state assets.

firms where the state needed to protect or to strengthen its interests. The description of the multiple presence of the state via different authorities is similar to that in Russia and China but the use of the control potential is different.

The next layer down shows industrial and financial companies in which the state is an owner. These are standard industrial, manufacturing or trading companies labelled as firms, various financial institutions labelled as banks, and privatization investment funds, specifically set up during the privatization scheme, labelled as investment funds. The ownership rights of the state with respect to the businesses in the three categories are denoted by directional arrows. The lowest layer allows us to begin unveiling the extent of the state pyramid. As a general rule, firms own stakes in other firms but do not own stakes in banks or investment funds. This is a result of the post-privatization arrangements and does not have any natural economic rationale behind it.

A further result of the privatization scheme is the dominant presence of banks in investment funds because it was primarily banks that established the investment funds as a tool to acquire ownership stakes in privatized firms. Stakes of investment funds in banks are less frequent and have developed over time through the process of investment funds rearranging their portfolios. Both banks and investment funds own stakes in firms as a rule, either directly or indirectly. Arrows pointing from banks and investment funds toward firms at the top (first) and lowest (third) levels denote the potential for cross ownership: control in the third-level firm via the first-level firm. Of course, the stylized nature of the arrangement in Figure 23.1 does not preclude the possibility of a stake in a firm on the second level as well.

To analyse the extent of state control we have assembled a data set on the extent of ownership in a large sample of Czech firms over the period from 1996 (one year after the privatization scheme officially ended in February 1995) to 2005 (the dismantling of the NPF). The data come from the archives of the NPF, the former Ministry of Privatization, the Prague Stock Exchange, the Centre for Securities in Prague, the commercial database Aspekt, and the Commercial Register of the Czech Republic. Our dataset was assembled from the above sources based on the unique organization identification number assigned to each firm. From our data we are able to isolate the specific extent of ownership represented by the state corporate pyramid as well as to distinguish various means of state direct and indirect control and the amount of assets under control. In this respect we are able to trace the development of state control in a large number of firms over time. As such, we work with a uniquely large sample that is by its size close to the total population of medium-sized and large firms in the economy. More detailed information on the sample size in each period is provided below along with our results on the extent of state control.

Formally, we describe the chain of control via voting rights in a manner similar to that developed by Chapelle and Szafarz (2007), who, among others, voiced the idea that direct control by any type of owner could be complemented by indirect control rights. To analyse the full extent of a control mechanism we compute the extent of integrated ownership rights from the top of the control chain – the apex of the pyramid – towards each firm. The algorithm allows us to compute the extent of the integrated control of the state as an ultimate owner (top of the pyramid) in companies in our sample. When doing so we consider the succession of ownership levels down to the final potential level (ranging between eight and 12 levels) in a manner similar to Khanna and Yafeh (2007). This way we also control for cross-ownership, potential double ownership, etc. A detailed description of the algorithm to compute the extent of integrated state control is provided in Appendix 23.1.

In measuring the state control over a company we follow the approach of La Porta *et al.* (1999) and use total voting rights. In order to gauge the true control of the state we distinguish between two categories of ownership concentration. First, we use a threshold of 50 per cent, which conforms to the International Financial Reporting Standards (IFRS) as well as to the Czech company law in terms of majority ownership. The second, less conservative, threshold is 25 per cent, which conforms to the methodological approach used by the firm-level database Aspekt. Other studies used a 20 per cent threshold (e.g. La Porta *et al.*, 1999), but we prefer 25 per cent threshold as it is in line with the relatively high ownership concentration present in Czech firms (Hanousek *et al.*, 2007).

Further, besides the direct control associated with the number of shares held, state control may also be executed by other means. The most effective is the 'golden' share. Such an instrument, in the form of a single share with special status, allows the state to use a *veto* right to prevent any major changes in a company where the state holds such a share. Utility companies are a typical example of state control through the golden share, but not the only example, as the golden share has been part of the ownership structure in other industries as well.

Finally, we distinguish the control over smaller and larger firms. The size, and hence the importance, of a company might influence its ability to generate business tax revenues and dividends, to provide employment and therefore income tax revenues, and to provide economic opportunities for suppliers who also provide employment and generate taxes. Thus, control over larger companies creates a potential for achieving various economic and non-economic objectives. We calculate the various degrees of state control using the total assets of a firm as a proxy for its size. The total assets are preferred to sales since firms were privatized (in both privatization waves) in various proportions of their assets (Hanousek and Kočenda, 2008). This approach allows us to infer the extent of state control over the large and important firms in the economy and consequently the extent of wealth that is controlled by the state through direct as well as pyramidal ownership channels.

Specifically, for each year we calculate the summary values of total assets (of firms) under state control. The overall value of these assets V in a given year t is the sum of the absolute values of the total assets of firms where a state position exists:

$$V_t = \sum_{j=1}^{N} V_t^j$$

First, we begin with the sum of the assets under direct control based on majority voting rights. Specifically:

$$V_t^D = \sum_{j=1}^{N} A_{jt}[State \geq 50\%]$$

defines the sum of the absolute values of the total assets of firms in year t in which the state held more than a 50 per cent share (A_{jt} is the accounting value of the total assets of firm j where the state has such a direct stake in year t). Second:

$$V_t^P = \sum_{j=1}^{N} A_{jt}[Pyramid \geq 50\%]$$

defines the sum of the absolute values of the total assets of the firms in year t that were under integrated state control via a pyramid structure. Finally, we define a similar value for a structure that combines control via the pyramid and golden share together as:

$$V_t^{PG} = \sum_{j=1}^{N} A_{jt}\{[Pyramid \geq 50\%] \wedge [GoldenShare]\}$$

Table 23.1 State control over firms (state represented by the National Property Fund)

(a) Majority voting rights of at least 50 per cent

Year	Total Number	Extent of the control		
		Direct	*Pyramid*	*Pyramid and Golden Share*
1996	814 [100%]	102 [13%]	103 [13%]	NA [NA]
1997	479 [100%]	70 [15%]	70 [15%]	158 [33%]
1998	321 [100%]	54 [17%]	54 [17%]	139 [43%]
1999	269 [100%]	53 [20%]	53 [20%]	134 [50%]
2000	241 [100%]	52 [22%]	52 [22%]	130 [54%]
2001	193 [100%]	41 [21%]	42 [22%]	94 [49%]
2002	159 [100%]	35 [22%]	35 [22%]	73 [46%]
2003	143 [100%]	30 [21%]	31 [22%]	63 [44%]
2004	122 [100%]	26 [21%]	26 [21%]	55 [45%]
2005	104 [100%]	25 [24%]	25 [24%]	54 [52%]

(b) Voting rights of at least 25 percent

Year	Total Number	Extent of the control		
		Direct	*Pyramid*	*Pyramid and Golden Share*
1996	814 [100%]	210 [26%]	210 [26%]	NA [NA]
1997	479 [100%]	145 [30%]	146 [30%]	225 [47%]
1998	321 [100%]	96 [30%]	96 [30%]	168 [52%]
1999	269 [100%]	80 [30%]	80 [30%]	150 [56%]
2000	241 [100%]	76 [32%]	76 [32%]	146 [61%]
2001	193 [100%]	63 [33%]	63 [33%]	107 [55%]
2002	159 [100%]	46 [29%]	46 [29%]	82 [52%]
2003	143 [100%]	37 [26%]	38 [27%]	73 [51%]
2004	122 [100%]	31 [25%]	31 [25%]	62 [51%]
2005	104 [100%]	29 [28%]	29 [28%]	60 [58%]

Source: Springer, *Economic Change and Restructuring*, Aug. 2011, 'State ownership and control in the Czech Republic', Kočenda, E. and J. Hanousek, with kind permission from Springer Science+Business Media B.V.
Notes: Total Number denotes number of firms where state has any voting rights. Direct defines control through 50% and 25% voting rights, respectively.
Numbers in brackets denote percentages with respect to the base that is Total Number in respective year.
Pyramid defines control through chain of successive voting rights of 50% and 25%, respectively. Golden Share defines control through this instrument.

Extent of state control

State control over firms

The control potential of the state pyramid is presented in Tables 23.1–23.4. We begin with a simple account and in the first two columns of Table 23.1a, we show the number of firms in which the State, represented by the National Property Fund, had any voting rights. The number in each year constitutes a 100 per cent base for relative comparison, which is presented in parentheses immediately following the absolute numbers throughout the table. As the economic transition progressed the absolute number of firms with a state presence decreases. In the third column we show that the number of firms that the state controlled directly through its (at least) 50 per cent majority voting rights decreases over time as well. The relative proportion increases, though. The control ability of the state in the pyramid is essentially the same as its direct control, both in absolute and relative terms. This indicates that control through the pyramid did not enhance direct control. However, the control ability doubles when golden shares are accounted for.

In Table 23.1b, we present the results of the control potential when a 25 per cent voting-right threshold is considered. As one might expect, the direct control of the NPF increases with this less conservative threshold. The increase is considerable during the second half of the 1990s but after 2001 it is only moderate. Pyramidal control is surprisingly not enhanced by the lower threshold. The golden share, on the other hand, exhibits a strong effect so that the control potential of the NPF over time at least doubles with respect to its direct control (with the exception of 1996). One point we can learn from Table 23.1 is that the pyramid structure in which the NPF represents the state as the ultimate owner does not seem to add much to its direct control potential. On the other hand, the instrument of the golden share is an important mechanism that enhances the control of the state considerably.

In Table 23.2 we present data in the same structure as in Table 23.1, but here the state is defined broadly and covers the NPF, other state agencies, and municipalities. The numbers in Table 23.2a, are in a sharp contrast to those presented in Table 23.1. The extent of state presence is greater and decreases at a much slower rate over time. More importantly, the number of firms that are under the direct control of the broadly defined state steadily increases and the proportion of these firms in the sample reaches 56 per cent in 2005. As in Table 23.1, control through the pyramid with a 50 per cent voting right threshold enhances the control ability of the state only a little but the golden share drives considerable increases in control. In panel (b) we present the control potential for the 25 per cent threshold, where the direct control in the early period is doubled when compared to the 50 per cent benchmark, but declines somewhat towards the end of the research period. The importance of pyramidal control is only marginal throughout the period but the golden share enhances the control over about an additional 10 percentage points of firms. These findings are in line with evidence from both developed (Bortolotti and Faccio, 2006) as well as transition economies (Chernykh, 2008).

State control over total assets of firms

Since the simple number of firms under state control does not account for the size of firms and their importance we next analyse the control over the assets of the firms. The total assets of the firm can be considered as a proxy for the size of each firm in the NPF portfolio as well as firms were privatized based on various proportions of their assets (Hanousek and Kočenda, 2008).

In terms of the volume of assets of firms where the state had voting rights, a decreasing trend can be seen in Tables 23.3 and 23.4. This pattern is paralleled in the evolution of assets over which the state as the NPF had majority voting rights (Table 23.3). Needless to say, the broadly-defined state manages to control directly a larger share of those assets (Table 23.4). We see that the volumes of assets the state was able to control directly were decreasing over time from initially very high levels. The gradual decrease was at a slower rate in the case of the state defined broadly (Table 23.4) when compared to the position of the NPF (Table 23.3). An increase in controlled assets is evidenced only in 1996 for both definitions of the state (50 and 25 per cent). Increases in the property controlled through the pyramid and golden share are found to be more important, especially over the years 1997–2002. This finding hints at the

Table 23.2 State control over firms (state defined broadly as a combination of the NPF, municipalities, and state agencies)

(a) Majority voting rights of at least 50 per cent

Year	Total Number	Extent of the control		
		Direct	Pyramid	Pyramid and Golden Share
1996	889 [100%]	133 [15%]	136 [15%]	NA [NA]
1997	570 [100%]	122 [21%]	125 [22%]	213 [37%]
1998	436 [100%]	128 [29%]	131 [30%]	217 [50%]
1999	406 [100%]	143 [35%]	147 [36%]	228 [56%]
2000	413 [100%]	163 [39%]	166 [40%]	244 [59%]
2001	411 [100%]	180 [44%]	184 [45%]	237 [58%]
2002	404 [100%]	194 [48%]	197 [49%]	236 [58%]
2003	417 [100%]	206 [49%]	209 [50%]	241 [58%]
2004	411 [100%]	215 [52%]	218 [53%]	245 [60%]
2005	394 [100%]	221 [56%]	224 [57%]	253 [64%]

(b) Voting rights of at least 25 per cent

Year	Total Number	Extent of the control		
		Direct	Pyramid	Pyramid and Golden Share
1996	889 [100%]	262 [29%]	262 [29%]	NA [NA]
1997	570 [100%]	213 [37%]	214 [38%]	296 [52%]
1998	436 [100%]	188 [43%]	188 [43%]	262 [60%]
1999	406 [100%]	191 [47%]	191 [47%]	262 [65%]
2000	413 [100%]	214 [52%]	215 [52%]	282 [68%]
2001	411 [100%]	236 [57%]	237 [58%]	279 [68%]
2002	404 [100%]	240 [59%]	242 [60%]	276 [68%]
2003	417 [100%]	251 [60%]	254 [61%]	288 [69%]
2004	411 [100%]	260 [63%]	262 [64%]	291 [71%]
2005	394 [100%]	260 [66%]	263 [67%]	293 [74%]

Source: Springer, *Economic Change and Restructuring*, Aug. 2011, 'State ownership and control in the Czech Republic', Kočenda, E. and J. Hanousek, with kind permission from Springer Science+Business Media B.V.

Notes: Total Number denotes number of firms where state has any voting rights. Direct defines control through 50% and 25% voting rights, respectively.

Numbers in brackets denote percentages with respect to the base that is Total Number in respective year.

Pyramid defines control through chain of successive voting rights of 50% and 25%, respectively. Golden Share defines control through this instrument.

preferences of the state to control the largest and most important firms directly rather than to engage in complicated schemes.

When we use the 25 per cent threshold the general results are similar to those for the 50 per cent one (Tables 23.3b and 23.4b). A specific feature to note is that the volumes of assets under state control are expectedly higher in the early years of the period under research but decrease to almost the same volumes as those measured with a 50 per cent threshold of voting rights. In both threshold cases the decrease is gradual during the 1990s and rapid after 2000.

Table 23.3 State control over total assets of firms (state represented by the National Property Fund)

(a) Majority voting rights of at least 50 per cent

Year	Extent of the control			
	Assets	Direct	Pyramid	Pyramid and Golden Share
1996	2310 [75%]	888 [29%]	895 [29%]	NA [NA]
1997	2230 [74%]	446 [15%]	446 [15%]	830 [28%]
1998	1850 [63%]	455 [16%]	455 [16%]	624 [21%]
1999	1780 [48%]	855 [23%]	855 [23%]	1020 [27%]
2000	1410 [33%]	966 [23%]	966 [23%]	1140 [27%]
2001	837 [18%]	520 [11%]	533 [12%]	676 [15%]
2002	768 [18%]	494 [12%]	494 [12%]	607 [14%]
2003	638 [13%]	438 [9%]	439 [9%]	484 [10%]
2004	552 [10%]	439 [8%]	439 [8%]	469 [9%]
2005	504 [7%]	395 [5%]	395 [5%]	426 [6%]

(b) Voting rights of at least 25 per cent

Year	Extent of the control			
	Assets	Direct	Pyramid	Pyramid and Golden Share
1996	2310 [75%]	1440 [47%]	1460 [47%]	NA [NA]
1997	2230 [74%]	1910 [63%]	1910 [63%]	1960 [65%]
1998	1850 [63%]	1650 [57%]	1650 [57%]	1710 [59%]
1999	1780 [48%]	1460 [39%]	1460 [39%]	1660 [45%]
2000	1410 [33%]	1090 [26%]	1090 [26%]	1330 [31%]
2001	837 [18%]	721 [16%]	721 [16%]	782 [17%]
2002	768 [18%]	565 [13%]	565 [13%]	670[16%]
2003	638 [13%]	453 [9%]	454 [9%]	552 [11%]
2004	552 [10%]	440 [8%]	440 [8%]	471 [9%]
2005	504 [7%]	396 [5%]	396 [5%]	427 [6%]

Source: Springer, *Economic Change and Restructuring*, Aug. 2011, 'State ownership and control in the Czech Republic', Kočenda, E. and J. Hanousek, with kind permission from Springer Science+Business Media B.V.
Notes: Assets denote amount of total assets of firms where state has any voting rights.
Numbers in subsequent columns represent total assets of firms (in billions CZK) that the state is able to control. Numbers in brackets denote percentages with respect to total number of assets where state holds voting rights in a given year (Assets).
Direct defines control through 50% and 25% voting rights, respectively. Pyramid defines control through chain of successive voting rights of 50% and 25%, respectively. Golden Share defines control through this instrument.

The detailed results on direct as well as integrated control of the state over the firms in the Czech Republic provide evidence that the state was primarily engaged in direct control. Arguably, the intention of the state to create special structures to effectively control firms and, hence, the economy was limited as opposed to empirical evidence from other transformation economies. Another realistic explanation for the less-than-optimal use of state control potential in Czech firms could be that the state bureaucracy in this particular era was not organized in a way to exploit all means of control that, for example, a corporate pyramid offers. Surely, the integrated control of the state via a pyramid as well as its enhancement by the golden share was found to be less extensive than for example in Russia or China. These two large countries have

Table 23.4 State control over total assets of firms (state defined broadly as a combination of the NPF, municipalities, and state agencies)

(a) Majority voting rights of at least 50 per cent

Year	Extent of the control			
	Assets	*Direct*	*Pyramid*	*Pyramid and Golden Share*
1996	2430 [79%]	1000 [32%]	1010 [33%]	NA [NA]
1997	2350 [78%]	563 [19%]	563 [19%]	946 [31%]
1998	2020 [69%]	618 [21%]	620 [21%]	789 [27%]
1999	1980 [53%]	1040 [28%]	1040 [28%]	1200 [32%]
2000	1680 [40%]	1210 [29%]	1210 [29%]	1380 [33%]
2001	1130 [24%]	778 [17%]	792 [17%]	935 [20%]
2002	1090 [26%]	741 [18%]	743 [18%]	855 [20%]
2003	1020 [20%]	732 [15%]	735 [15%]	777 [16%]
2004	929 [17%]	735 [14%]	737 [14%]	763 [14%]
2005	935 [12%]	784 [10%]	785 [10%]	812 [11%]

(b) Voting rights of at least 25 per cent

Year	Extent of the control			
	Assets	*Direct*	*Pyramid*	*Pyramid and Golden Share*
1996	2430 [79%]	1570 [51%]	1580 [51%]	NA [NA]
1997	2350 [78%]	2030 [67%]	2030 [67%]	2080 [69%]
1998	2020 [69%]	1820 [62%]	1820 [62%]	1880 [64%]
1999	1980 [53%]	1650 [44%]	1650 [44%]	1850 [50%]
2000	1680 [40%]	1350 [32%]	1350 [32%]	1590 [38%]
2001	1130 [24%]	998 [22%]	998 [22%]	1060 [23%]
2002	1090 [26%]	836 [20%]	836 [20%]	940 [22%]
2003	1020 [20%]	771 [15%]	772 [15%]	869 [17%]
2004	929 [17%]	760 [14%]	760 [14%]	788 [15%]
2005	935 [12%]	802 [11%]	802 [11%]	828 [11%]

Source: Springer, *Economic Change and Restructuring*, Aug. 2011, 'State ownership and control in the Czech Republic', Kočenda, E. and J. Hanousek, with kind permission from Springer Science+Business Media B.V.

Notes: Assets denote amount of total assets of firms where state has any voting rights.

Numbers in subsequent columns represent total assets of firms (in billions CZK) that the state is able to control. Numbers in brackets denote percentages with respect to total number of assets where state holds voting rights in a given year (Assets).

Direct defines control through 50 and 25% voting rights, respectively. Pyramid defines control through chain of successive voting rights of 50 and 25%, respectively. Golden Share defines control through this instrument.

run truly centralized economies, albeit not in all dimensions, while centralization in the Czech Republic was less strict. Chernykh (2008) shows that in Russia, both federal as well as regional governments participate actively and extensively in traded companies. A similar situation exists in China, where the state induced the emergence of business groups in state-owned sectors that have much in common with the classical corporate pyramid. These structures possess control over subsidiary companies and serve as government instruments to facilitate ownership reform and economic transformation as discussed in Ma and Lu (2005), and Yiu *et al.* (2005).

As our findings show, the Czech state bureaucracy apparently developed less efficient control enforcement methods than these two relatively more strictly centralized countries. Nevertheless, the control potential of the state in Czech firms remained substantial for a long period of time

(Hanousek and Kočenda, 2008) as the state has been giving up its positions in firms only gradually and through a lengthy process.

Concluding remarks

In this chapter we have analysed the extent of the integrated control of the state over privatized firms during the post-privatization decade (1996–2005) in the Czech Republic. During this period the integrated control potential of the state resembled a corporate pyramid, a corporate ownership structure found worldwide. We find that the control potential that a corporate pyramid offers is not large when the Czech state is considered as the ultimate owner at the top of the pyramid. The state favoured direct control provided by voting rights measured by a 50 per cent threshold and such control increased when a less conservative 25 per cent threshold was adopted. The use of the less conservative benchmark is fully justified since no other significant subject with a consistently higher share of voting rights was detected at the same time. While pyramidal control was not fully utilized, the golden share in the hands of the state substantially enhanced its ability to control firms in terms of their numbers as well as in terms of the assets they represent.

The state pyramid in the Czech Republic likely suffered from the dispersed nature of the state at the top of the pyramid, where various state bodies could not efficiently interact to pursue control. This is opposed to, for example, institutional arrangements in China, where state-owned business groups, when compared to government agencies, have direct rights to collect the economic income generated by their affiliated companies and also have greater incentives and capability to closely and effectively monitor the managers of the group members (Ma *et al.*, 2006).

The results inferred from our extensive data set provide hard evidence that the state indeed remained an important owner of privatized firms for a considerable period of time. Its reluctance to vacate its ownership positions is in striking contrast with the lack of capacity to push corporate performance evidenced in Kočenda and Hanousek (2009). Lack of focus and inter-agency cooperation as well as the simple inefficiency of the state bureaucracy are the most likely reasons behind our findings.

Our results are relevant to ownership and corporate governance issues in transition economies in general. State pyramids can be quite effective tools of control in economies where the state promotes their existence with the clear objective of using the pyramid structures for various purposes including control of managers, push for increased and improved tax collection, influence on corporate governance, etc. This is counterbalanced by the fact that well-functioning state pyramids signify less than complete privatization and economic transformation, though. These features might affect the decisions of foreign investors, rating companies and financial institutions. Future developments will show what course countries with state pyramids will take.

Appendix 23.1

Following Chapelle and Szafarz (2007), we compute the extent of state control in firms. First, let d_{ij} denote the share of direct cash-flow rights that firm i holds in firm j. Then the n-square matrix $D = (d_{ij})$ represents the *direct cross-ownership rights* in the data set of n firms. To prevent potential errors owing to dispersed ownership we limit the ownership rights calculation by stating that:

$$\sum_{i=1}^{n} d_{ij} \leq 1$$

for $j = 1, \dots, n$.

An integrated ownership via a structure such as a corporate pyramid can be constructed as a sum of all direct and indirect ownership links via a matrix approach. The matrix of integrated ownership $P = (p_{ij})$ is defined as:

$$P = diag\left\{I - \sum_{i=1}^{n} d_{ij}\right\} \sum_{s=1}^{\infty} D^s = diag\left\{I - \sum_{i=1}^{n} d_{ij}\right\}(I - D)^{-1}$$

In the above equation the diagonal matrix factor is a necessary scaling factor of

$$\sum_{s=1}^{\infty} D^s = (I - D)^{-1}$$

that prevents an implausible extent of control greater than 100 per cent.

We suggest measuring the direct control over companies by using a conservative majority threshold of 50 per cent and specify the following ownership-control matrix:

$$c_{ij} = \begin{cases} 1, d_{ij} > 0.5 \\ 0, if \exists k \neq i : d_{kj} > 0.5 \\ d_{ij}, otherwise \end{cases}$$

In the above definition we also control for the existence of a majority owner k and in this way we eliminate the double counting of controlling stakes. Simply said, in the case of a 50 per cent majority owner, other stakes have no real controlling power. The rule can be generalized to different controlling thresholds. Finally, we define the control extent P of the integrated, or ultimate, owner in a corporate pyramid as:

$$P = diag\left\{I - \sum_{i=1}^{n} c_{ij}\right\} \sum_{s=1}^{\infty} C^s = diag\left\{I - \sum_{i=1}^{n} c_{ij}\right\}(I - C)^{-1}$$

The above approach is versatile enough to enable analysis of the true extent of control of any type of owner, including that of the state in partially privatized companies.

Note

1 A substantial part of this chapter was written while Evžen Kočenda was a Visiting Fellow at the Center for Economic Studies (CES) at the University of Munich, whose hospitality is warmly acknowledged. We are grateful to Lucy Chernykh, Iraj Hashi, and presentation participants for valuable comments. Financial support from GAČR grant No. 403/12/0080 is gratefully acknowledged. The usual disclaimer applies.

Bibliography

Bortolotti, B. and Faccio, M. (2006), 'Reluctant privatization', *Center for Economic Institutions Working Paper Series* No. 2006–5.

Chapelle, A. and Szafarz, A. (2007), 'Control consolidation with a threshold: An algorithm', *IMA Journal of Management Mathematics*, vol. 18(3), pp. 235–43.

Chernykh, L. (2008), 'Ultimate ownership and control in Russia', *Journal of Financial Economics*, vol. 88(1), pp. 169–92.

Hanousek, J. and Kočenda, E. (2008), 'Potential of the State to Control Privatized Firms', *Economic Change and Restructuring*, vol. 41(2), pp. 167–86.

Hanousek, J., Kočenda, E. and Svejnar, J. (2007), 'Origin and Concentration: Corporate Ownership, Control and Performance in Firms after Privatization', *Economics of Transition*, vol. 15(1), pp. 1–31.

Khanna, T. and Yafeh, Y. (2007), 'Business Groups in Emerging Markets: Paragons or Parasites?', *Journal of Economic Literature*, vol. 45, pp. 331–72.

Kočenda, E. and Hanousek, J. (2009), 'State Ownership and Control in the Czech Republic', *CESifo Working Paper* No. 2801.

La Porta, R., Lopez-de-Silanes, F. and Shleifer, A. (1999), 'Corporate ownership around the world', *Journal of Finance*, vol. 54, pp. 471–517.

Ma, X. and Lu, J. (2005), 'The critical role of business groups in China', *Ivey Business Journal*, vol. 69(5), pp. 1–12.

Ma, X., Yao, X. and Xi, Y. (2006), 'Business group affiliation and firm performance in a transition economy: A focus on ownership voids', *Asia Pacific Journal of Management*, vol. 23(4), pp. 467–83.

Yiu, D., Bruton, G., and Lu, Y. (2005), 'Understanding business group performance in an emerging economy: Acquiring resources and capabilities in order to prosper', *Journal of Management Studies*, vol. 42(1), pp. 183–296.

24

THE BUSINESS ENVIRONMENT IN THE TRANSITION[1]

Wendy Carlin and Mark E. Schaffer

Introduction

When transition began, planning was abandoned, prices were liberalized and the new entry of firms was permitted. Although there was wide variation in the methods and speed of privatization of large firms, the privatization of small enterprises and shops was accomplished quickly in virtually every transition economy. The process of legalizing the start-up of new firms and the rapid privatization of small enterprises (mainly to managers) created the opportunity for new firms and new activities in existing firms to emerge across transition. This can be considered as a more or less uniform treatment effect of transition. In this contribution we investigate the interaction between the external environment such firms faced with the widespread opportunities for new business activities. The business environment for firms includes physical infrastructure, the availability of an educated labour force, the provision of administrative and judicial services, the control of corruption and crime, and the stability of the macroeconomic environment.

We address the following three questions. First, are the mainly new small and medium-sized enterprises (SMEs) in the transition economies different from firms outside transition in how their characteristics (such as their size and whether they are expanding their level of employment) affect their responses to the different elements of the business environment? Second, is there a difference at the country level between the average transition economy (TE) and the average non-transition economy (NTE) in how the seriousness of different elements of the business environment is rated? Finally, is there a systematic difference between TEs and NTEs at the country level in the relationship between the level of development or per capita income and elements of the business environment?

To answer these questions, we use data on TEs in the second decade of transition deriving from surveys of firms conducted in 2002–05, after the upheavals of early transition and of the Russian crisis. We would expect differences between TEs and NTEs to reflect both the legacy of the planning period and of the policies implemented during transition.

Two specific characteristics of the planned economies of the ex-Soviet bloc affected the supply of public goods at the outset of transition.[2] First, the economic history of the planned economies shows that some of these public goods – physical infrastructure and education – were provided in the planning era more universally across countries than is the case in market economies spanning the same levels of development. Associated with the more rapid industrialization of poor countries than would have occurred under market conditions were higher levels of physical infrastructure and schooling. Second, all of the planned economies lacked well-developed market economy institutions at the beginning of transition.

Economists anticipated that the abolition of planning, freeing up prices, allowing new firms to enter and the opening up of the economies to international trade would be followed by rapid catch up (e.g. Blanchard, 1997; Kornai, 2000). It was widely believed that the relatively good endowments of these countries with physical infrastructure and human capital would facilitate catch-up. Yet all of these countries experienced a period with output below its pre-transition level (Blanchard, 1997). After a decade of transition, a new consensus emerged that the quality of market institutions was central to convergence (e.g. Roland, 2000; Svejnar, 2002). We use data from inside and outside transition to test for the existence of the impact of differences in infrastructure and institutions between TEs and NTEs at the level of the firm.

Challenges in using firm-level survey data on the business environment

Since the late 1990s, the EBRD and the World Bank have systematically surveyed large numbers of firms in many different countries, asking managers about the quality of the business environment in which they operate. The standard question asked of managers is 'how much of an obstacle is X to the operation and growth of your business?', and the respondent rates the severity on a five-point scale of 0 (no obstacle) to 4 (very severe obstacle). The dimensions of the external environment asked about include the following: telecoms, electricity, transport, skills availability, macroeconomic stability, tax administration, customs administration, labour regulation, legal system, corruption and crime.

Acemoglu *et al.* (2001) and similar studies provide evidence that institutional quality matters for economic development, but are not very informative about which specific institutions are more important. The attraction of firm level data on the business environment is that they appear to greatly increase the sample size and therefore to make it possible to identify separately the effect of different institutions on growth. Commander and Svejnar (2011) and Commander and Nikoloski (2011) analyse transition economies and are the most relevant studies of this kind. However, the attempt to use firm-level data to test for the relative importance of a wide range of public inputs in the papers by Commander and co-authors did not produce clear results. The problem here is that the appearance of a large sample size is misleading: because all the firms in a country (or region) face the same set of institutions, the effective sample size is driven primarily by the number of countries rather than the number of firms. We use the same type of data as Commander *et al.* but propose a different framework in which to interpret them.

Before setting out our alternative, it is important to clarify the research strategy that uses firm-level data and is based on the estimation of an augmented production function (e.g. Commander *et al.*). The idea is that the business environment varies at the level of the firm and that this enables the researcher to get a handle on the effect of different aspects of the business environment on productivity by using a production function augmented by these indicators. However, as many of the papers using this approach make clear, their effect on performance can only be estimated if there is a way of isolating the quality of such a firm-level micro-business environment from the firm's characteristics.

A simple example illustrates the problems. It is plausible that a higher productivity firm will attract more attention from rent-seeking bureaucrats: a naïve regression of firm performance on the firm's report of the burden of business regulation would produce a positive estimate of the effect of bureaucratic attention on performance. The main research strategy adopted to get around this problem and uncover the effect of business regulation on firm performance separate from the effect of firm performance in attracting inspections has been to use the so-called 'cell averages' approach. Instead of using the firm's own report of the burden of business regulation, the average reports of firms with similar characteristics (such as firm size, industry and location) is used.

However, the cell averages approach does not necessarily solve the problem of the endogeneity of the measure of the firm's micro business environment. The reason is that unobservable characteristics that raise the productivity of the firm in question will also tend to raise the productivity levels of the other firms in the cell (e.g. a local demand or industry-specific shock will boost capacity utilization and performance). This will tend to raise the prevalence of inspections, expenditure on abatement such as bribes and the seriousness of this element of the business environment reported by the firm. This is an example of Manski's (1993) 'reflection problem' where a researcher tries to infer the impact on the individuals comprising a group of average behaviour in the group. As noted in Carlin *et al.* (2010), the econometric challenge in trying to tease apart differences in the institutional environment faced by firms in a single country while avoiding the problem of endogeneity is too much for the data to bear. And this may explain why the careful studies by Commander *et al.* that tried to do this found largely null results once country fixed-effects were included.

A framework for analysing firm-level evidence on the business environment

The problems with attempting to uncover the relevance of elements of the business environment by estimating a production function that includes business environment indicators can be avoided by taking a different approach. The approach outlined here is set out in more detail in Carlin *et al.* (2006, 2010), and has been applied to analysing the business environment in transition and developing economies by ourselves, the World Bank and the EBRD (Carlin *et al.*, 2012; Mitra *et al.*, 2010; EBRD, 2010; World Bank, 2012).

We take as our starting point that the business environment is external to the firm and that to an important extent, firms in a country share the same environment. This is especially obvious in the case of elements of the environment such as macroeconomic stability. In large countries there is likely to be substantial regional variation for some elements of the business environment, which, with sufficient data, could be tested. Thinking of the business environment as a public rather than a private input suggests that firm-level information be used in a different way from the augmented production function method. We look for a method of drawing inferences about the role of the business environment by using the indicators as dependent rather than independent variables.

Specifically, we formulate predictions as to how a firm's response to its business environment in terms of its evaluation of the costs imposed on it by deficiencies in infrastructure and institutions vary with its characteristics, including its performance. When taken to the data, these predictions indicate, for example, whether it is the case that improvement in a particular element of the business environment is likely to benefit well- or poorly-performing firms; and whether there are important differences between the constraints faced by internationally engaged firms as compared with those that are purely domestic in their inputs, markets and ownership. This is our 'within-country' analysis.

The key point here is that the survey responses on the seriousness of obstacles imposed by the business environment are not estimates of the quality or quantity of a country-wide public input or even of the public input supplied to the firm in question; they are *valuations* of the public input. A simple and intuitive interpretation is that the 'reported cost' RC_i to firm i of a public input is the gap between the firm's profit in the hypothetical situation where the public input provided is of such high quality that it poses a negligible obstacle to the firm's operations, and the firm's profit in reality, given the actual quality of public input provided.

In our previous work we show how these reported costs can be interpreted as the *shadow prices* of public inputs. Formally, we can think of the profit function π_{ij}^* as resulting from a constrained maximization by the firm, where the public input $\bar{B}_j$ is supplied to the firm at a level or quality that means the firm would prefer a higher quality or more of it. By the envelope theorem for constrained maximization, the derivative of the profit function π_{ij}^* with respect to a constrained or fixed input is simply the shadow price of the input.[3]

Figure 24.1 summarizes the predicted relationship between A_i, firm-level total factor productivity (TFP, or another indicator of firm quality or productivity) and the reported cost of a public input constraint, RC_i. In Figure 24.1a, as TFP rises, the reported cost goes up. More productive firms incur higher costs from inadequate quality or quantity of their business environment. In the right hand panel, we see that holding the firm's TFP constant, an improvement in the quality of public inputs is associated with lower reported costs.

To bring this framework to the data, we relate the reported cost of public inputs by firms to firm characteristics. The choice of firm-level characteristics to define the benchmark firm and to vary for the within-country analysis is fairly straightforward. Size is a standard control, motivated, for instance, by the standard finding that firm size and firm productivity are positively correlated. We also include a measure of firm performance, namely whether or not the firm has expanded permanent employment in the previous three years (TFP or some other direct measure of A_{ij} for firm i in country j is not available).

This allows us to test the basic prediction of the model that higher productivity firms report higher costs of public input constraints. International engagement is expected to be correlated with productivity and hence with higher constraints, with some possible exceptions where, for example ownership by a foreign firm may enable firms to avoid reliance on or reduce the costs of a low-quality public input. By looking at how shadow prices of public inputs vary with firm characteristics, we can see whether there are any systematic differences between firms inside and outside transition.

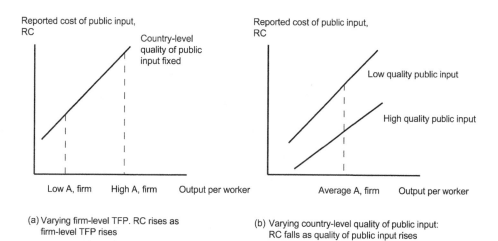

(a) Varying firm-level TFP. RC rises as firm-level TFP rises

(b) Varying country-level quality of public input: RC falls as quality of public input rises

Figure 24.1 Reported costs of public input constraints: (a) variation with firm-level TFP; and (b) country-level quality of the public input

We are also interested in understanding how different constraints are rated in terms of severity by the average firm, and how these ratings vary across groups of countries – here, between transition economies and their market economy peers. This is illustrated in Figure 24.2 for a single country (or group of countries). The two *RC* lines represent the relationship between firm productivity A_i and the shadow prices of the two public inputs. The vertical distance between the two lines captures the difference in the valuations by the average firm of the two inputs. This difference in valuation can be estimated separately for two different sets of countries and compared. This is the basis for the first part of the between-country analysis, where we compare how different constraints are rated by the average TE and NTE firms.

Lastly, we are also interested in how the effects of higher productivity and higher public input provision interact at the country level. Public input provision – the supply of $\bar{B}_j$ in country j – varies across as well as within countries. Causality runs in both directions: richer countries can afford better developed economic institutions, physical infrastructure, and human capital. Moreover, they are richer in large part because of the higher quality of their business environments. It is not possible to observe the flow of services from a public input to the firm. What the survey data provide is a window into how more or less burdensome a public input is, and we can look at how this varies as a country's income increases.

This is illustrated in Figure 24.3, where the level of development as measured by GDP per capita is taken to be synonymous with the average productivity of firms in country j, $\bar{A}_j$. The average cost of the public input constraint reported by firms in a country with low GDP per capita, which is characterized by low productivity firms and low quality of the public input, is shown in Figure 24.3a. Figure 24.3b shows a rich country with higher productivity firms and better quality public input, on the right. Figure 24.3a shows an example where the income-constraint locus slopes downward reflecting the fact that as the country becomes richer, it improves the quality of the public input ahead of the additional demands placed on it by higher productivity firms. In the right hand panel, the opposite is the case – improvement in productivity at the firm level and the associated greater intensity of use of the public input dominates the country-level improvement in its supply. We wish to analyse how the relationship between level of development and the average reported shadow price differs between TEs and NTEs, and across the different public inputs.

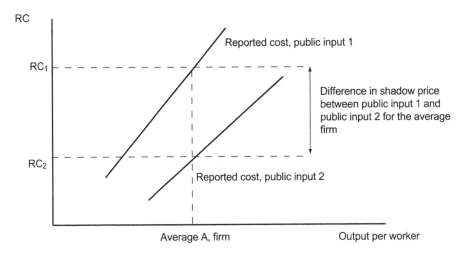

Figure 24.2 Difference in the reported cost of two different public inputs

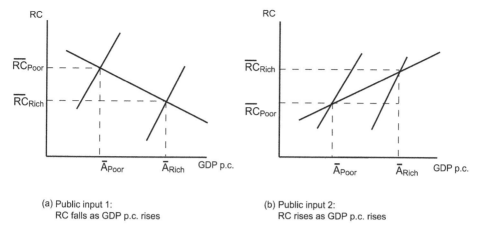

(a) Public input 1:
RC falls as GDP p.c. rises

(b) Public input 2:
RC rises as GDP p.c. rises

Figure 24.3 Variation of average reported costs of public input constraints with GDP per capita

Using the above framework, we address the following three questions:

- Are SMEs in transition countries different from firms outside transition in how their characteristics affect their responses to institutions and the business environment more generally?
- Is there a difference at the country level between the average TE firm and the average NTE firm in the relative importance of different elements of the business environment?
- Is there a systematic difference between TEs and NTEs at the country level in the relationship between level of development and elements of the business environment?

Data and empirical strategy

The surveys used here were conducted over the period 2002–10, and covered around 58,000 manufacturing firms in 175 separate surveys in 112 countries. Basic statistics on the surveys are presented in Table 24.1. Most of the surveyed firms are SMEs; mean log employment is 3.53, equivalent to 34 persons employed. Most of the data on firms in transition countries, and a small number of surveys of firms in market economies, were collected in the Business Environment and Enterprise Performance Surveys (BEEPS) conducted by the EBRD; data on firms from the rest of the world, and a handful of additional surveys for transition countries, come from the World Bank's Enterprise Surveys (ES). We limit the analysis to manufacturing firms only.

For our within-country analysis, we estimate two regressions for each public input k using data on firm i in country j:

$$RC_{ijk} = \alpha_{jk}^{TE} + \beta_{1k}^{TE}L30_{ij} + \beta_{2k}^{TE}FO_{ij} + \beta_{3k}^{TE}EX_{ij} + \beta_{4k}^{TE}IM_{ij} + \beta_{5k}^{TE}LGrow_{ij} + u_{ij}$$

$$RC_{ijk} = \alpha_{jk}^{NTE} + \beta_{1k}^{NTE}L30_{ij} + \beta_{2k}^{NTE}FO_{ij} + \beta_{3k}^{NTE}EX_{ij} + \beta_{4k}^{NTE}IM_{ij} + \beta_{5k}^{NTE}LGrow_{ij} + u_{ij}$$

(1)

where the variable *L30* is log(L/30) and the remaining variables are dummies corresponding to the following characteristics: *FO* denotes more than 10 per cent foreign ownership, *EX*, exporting more than 10 per cent of sales, *IM*, a direct importer of inputs, and *LGROW*, the firm has expanded permanent employment in the previous three years. The first question we ask is

Table 24.1 Summary data

	ALL	NTEs	TEs
Number of:			
Firms	57,832	52,000	5,832
Countries	112	84	28
Surveys	175	114	61
Means, firm characteristics:			
Log(L)	3.53	3.54	3.42
L (=exp(Log(L)))	34	34	30
Expanding	0.48	0.48	0.46
Foreign-owned	0.12	0.11	0.16
Exporter	0.29	0.28	0.34
Importer	0.25	0.24	0.33
Means, reported costs of public inputs:			
Electricity	1.46	1.56	0.65
Telecoms	0.68	0.72	0.47
Transport	0.92	0.96	0.59
Access to Land	0.83	0.84	0.67
Skills	1.17	1.18	1.09
Macroeconomic Instability	1.90	1.93	1.77
Gov. Policy Uncertainty	1.62	1.59	1.78
Tax Administration	1.41	1.39	1.62
Labour Regulation	1.00	1.00	0.98
Customs	0.99	0.96	1.19
Business Licensing	0.94	0.93	1.05
Courts	0.91	0.87	1.19
Corruption	1.56	1.59	1.29
Crime, Theft, Disorder	1.14	1.16	0.94
Access to Finance	1.48	1.47	1.58

whether the relationship between a firm characteristic and the shadow price of a public input k in a transition economy, captured by β_k^{TE}, is different from the same relationship in a non-transition economy, captured by β_k^{NTE}.

The same regressions are used for our between-country analysis. The reported costs of unreliable public inputs provide information on the importance of different elements of the business environment to firms in different countries. The simplest procedure would be to use the unconditional country means of the RC_{ijk} reported by firms (Table 24.1). However, the comparisons would be hampered by differing sample compositions such as different distributions of firm size. The estimations above address this problem by providing *conditional* country means in the form of the estimates of the intercepts α_{jk}. The conditional means α_{jk} can be interpreted as the estimated reported cost for public input k in country j for a 'benchmark firm' – a firm with a defined set of characteristics that is the same for every country. The benchmark firm here has 30 employees,[4] less than 10 per cent foreign ownership, is exporting less than 10 per cent of its sales, is not a direct importer of inputs, and has no reported change in permanent employment in the previous three years. These conditional means are the focus of our between-country analysis.

Our analysis calculates the estimated mean constraints as reported by the benchmark firm in TEs (captured by the estimates of α_{jk}^{TE}) and NTEs (α_{jk}^{NTE}) across the public inputs. We can see which public inputs are more burdensome to firms in TEs and whether these are the same as in NTEs.

Finally, we use the same estimates of α_{jk} to look at the relationship between the level of development and public input provision. The analytical technique is simple – we report simple scatterplots and regression lines of the estimated country conditional mean reported cost of constraint k, α_{jk}, versus GDP per capita.[5] We do this separately for TEs and NTEs.

In the analysis in this contribution, the data from transition come from the stable years of 2002 and 2005, after the Russian crisis and before the period of rapid growth prior to the global financial crisis. Another round of surveys was conducted in 2008 on the eve of the global financial crisis. We analyse how firms report their external constraints in a period of strong growth in Carlin *et al.* (2012).

Results

Our first question is whether firms in TEs differ from firms in NTEs in how they value elements of the business environment. Do characteristics of firms in TEs – size, growth, and international engagement – vary systematically with the shadow prices of public inputs? Does this systematic variation differ from what we observe in firms in non-transition economies?

The results of the estimations of (1) are presented in Table 24.2a, size; Table 24.2b, growth; and Table 24.2c, international engagement. The sample uses observations from transition economies in the 2002–05 period only (the BEEPS II-III surveys). Estimations of (1) employ survey-specific fixed effects; statistical tests are robust to arbitrary within-country correlation (clustering). In all cases we report the size and statistical significance (difference from zero) of the two estimated coefficients for the public inputs, β_k^{TE} and β_k^{NTE}, along with a test of whether they are different from each other.

The results in Table 24.2a and Table 24.2b are broadly consistent with the model's predictions. Larger firms generally report that public inputs are a greater obstacle to how they do business than is the case for smaller ones. The interpretation offered by the modelling framework is that the shadow prices of these public inputs are higher for larger firms; this is not surprising given the standard correlation in firm-level data between size and productivity. The findings are similar for firms that are expanding permanent employment; they too tend to report larger constraints – higher shadow prices – than firms that are not expanding. One

Table 24.2a Within-country analysis: reported cost of constraint by size of firm

	TE	NTE	Diff?	Obs	Countries
	Size (log L)	Size (log L)			
Electricity	−0.008	−0.012		55,964	110
Telecoms	−0.014	0.026★★	★★	36,345	99
Transport	0.008	0.023★★		55,452	109
Land Access	−0.042★★	−0.046★★		54,404	110
Skills	0.022★	0.035★★		55,692	110
Macro Instability	0.027★	0.038★★		37,455	100
Gov. policy uncertainty	0.021	0.046★★		31,603	79
Tax Administration	−0.012	0.001		55,301	110
Labour Regulation	0.044★★	0.054★★		55,256	110
Customs	0.038★★	0.050★★		51,759	110
Licenses	−0.003	0.004		54,747	110
Courts	0.043★★	0.037★★		44,712	100
Corruption	−0.006	−0.027		54,598	110
Crime	−0.028★	−0.005		53,540	107
Access to Finance	−0.036★	−0.063★★		53,859	107

Table 24.2b Within-country analysis: reported cost of constraint by whether firm expanded permanent employment or not

	TE Expanding	NTE Expanding	Diff?	Obs	Countries
Electricity	0.038	0.029		55,964	110
Telecoms	0.053	0.058★★		36,345	99
Transport	0.065★	0.037★★		55,452	109
Land Access	0.085★	0.072★★		54,404	110
Skills	0.135★★	0.072★★		55,692	110
Macro Instability	−0.038	0.031		37,455	100
Gov. policy uncertainty	−0.019	0.036		31,603	79
Tax Administration	0.030	0.003		55,301	110
Labour Regulation	0.035	−0.018		55,256	110
Customs	0.058★	0.054★★		51,759	110
Licenses	0.051	0.037★★		54,747	110
Courts	−0.007	0.001		44,712	100
Corruption	−0.016	0.043★		54,598	110
Crime	0.005	0.067★★		53,540	107
Access to Finance	−0.049	−0.022		53,859	107

constraint worth noting that does not follow this pattern is 'access to finance'. The negative relationship between size and the difficulty of obtaining finance is not surprising – unlike the other constraints in the analysis, access to finance does not fit into our modelling framework because it is not a public input. In both TEs and NTEs, larger firms find access to finance easier to obtain – a standard finding.[6]

The most notable results in Tables 24.2a and 24.2b concern what *isn't* there. With just a single exception (telecoms), the relationship between firm valuations of public inputs versus firm size and growth is statistically indistinguishable in transition and non-transition economies. This does *not* mean that the provision of these public inputs is the same in the two groups of countries; the finding relates to the demand for public inputs rather than the supply. Rather, it means that valuations of public inputs increase with firm size and firm growth in transition countries in much the same way they do in other economies.

The picture with respect to international engagement by firms is different. Table 24.2c shows that there *are* systematic differences in how internationally engaged firms value public inputs in TEs vs. NTEs. The most striking difference is in how importing firms value public inputs. In NTEs, importing firms are significantly more constrained – place a higher shadow price on – almost all public inputs compared to non-importing firms. In transition economies, this duality between importing and non-importing firms is absent. We note also that import activity by these SMEs in TEs is considerably more common than in NTEs (33 per cent versus 24 per cent; see Table 24.1). Our interpretation of this finding is that openness to trade has 'levelled the playing field' in transition economies more so than in other economies; importing firms in TEs, unlike those elsewhere in the world, are not significantly more constrained than firms that are not internationally engaged.

Our second set of questions asks whether there is a difference at the country level in how the average TE firm rates public inputs as constraints compared to the average NTE firm. Table 24.3 reports estimates of α_{jk}^{TE} and α_{jk}^{NTE} along with tests of the difference between them; we report results for TEs for both the 2002–05 period. The estimated levels of the individual coefficients are reported along with tests of whether they are different from the overall mean constraint of

Table 24.2c Within-country analysis: reported cost of constraint by international engagement

	TE	NTE	Diff?	TE	NTE	Diff?	TE	NTE	Diff?	Obs	Countries
	Foreign-owned	Foreign-owned		Exporter	Exporter		Importer	Importer			
Electricity	-0.008	-0.019		-0.013	0.018		-0.053	0.315**	**	55,964	110
Telecoms	0.008	0.096**	*	0.016	0.050*		-0.010	0.021		36,345	99
Transport	0.070	0.025		0.002	0.010		0.007	0.293**	**	55,452	109
Land Access	0.096*	-0.076**	**	-0.029	0.009		-0.015	0.092*	*	54,404	110
Skills	0.038	-0.107**	**	0.116**	0.005	**	0.074	0.366**	**	55,692	110
Macro Instability	-0.013	-0.056		0.078	0.107*		0.038	0.060		37,455	100
Gov. Policy Uncertainty	-0.058	-0.009		-0.004	-0.015		0.046	0.074		31,603	79
Tax Administration	0.019	-0.061		0.029	0.004		0.077	0.346**	**	55,301	110
Labour Regulation	0.007	-0.065**		0.094*	0.055*		0.021	0.268**	**	55,256	110
Customs	0.125**	0.089*	**	0.278**	0.202**		0.313**	0.685**	**	51,759	110
Licenses	0.085**	-0.034	**	0.018	0.007		0.057	0.251**	**	54,747	110
Courts	0.008	-0.030		-0.093	0.010		0.070*	0.303**	**	44,712	100
Corruption	-0.016	-0.072*		-0.035	0.002		0.065	0.459**	**	54,598	110
Crime	-0.013	-0.039		-0.042	-0.059*		0.020	0.257**	**	53,540	107
Access to Finance	-0.263**	-0.295**	**	-0.017	0.004		0.025	0.158*	**	53,859	107

Table 24.3 Reported costs of public input constraints for the benchmark firm: TEs versus NTEs

	TE		NTE		TE vs. NTE
	Level	*N*	*Level*	*N*	*Diff*
Electricity	**0.652★**	5,798	**1.468★**	50,166	**−0.815★**
Telecoms	**0.444★**	5,728	**0.655★**	30,617	**−0.211★**
Transport	**0.543★**	5,772	**0.863★**	49,680	**−0.320★**
Access to Land	**0.632★**	5,386	**0.798★**	49,018	**−0.166★**
Skills	**0.956★**	5,706	**1.068★**	49,986	**−0.113★**
Macro Instability	*1.749★*	5,674	*1.861★*	31,781	**−0.112★**
Gov. Policy Uncertainty	*1.783★*	5,667	*1.548★*	25,936	*0.235★*
Tax Administration	*1.566★*	5,690	*1.309★*	49,611	*0.257★*
Labour Regulation	**0.925★**	5,653	**0.929★**	49,603	−0.005
Customs	**0.925★**	5,306	**0.686★**	46,453	*0.240★*
Business Licensing	**0.992★**	5,577	**0.853★**	49,170	*0.139★*
Courts	*1.192★*	5,352	**0.792★**	39,360	*0.401★*
Corruption	*1.292★*	5,108	*1.472★*	49,490	**−0.180★**
Crime, Theft, Disorder	**0.949★**	5,521	1.090	48,019	**−0.141★**
Access to Finance	*1.640★*	5,682	*1.485★*	48,177	*0.155★*

Note: Mean constraint for subset of 13 constraints; All tests are robust to heteroscedasticity. Columns may not sum owing to rounding.

1.1. Bold-italic cells in the level columns indicate that the reported mean is significantly greater than 1.1; bold (non-italic) and shaded indicates the reported mean is significantly less than 1.1. The same coding is used for reporting whether $(\alpha_{jk}^{TE} - \alpha_{jk}^{NTE})$ is greater or less than zero.

There are some clear commonalities between how firms in TEs and NTEs rate public inputs as constraints. Macroeconomic and policy instability and tax administration are rated as very costly constraints; telecoms, transport and access to land are relatively less costly. However, clear differences between the two country groups are also apparent. When we compare TEs with NTEs, we see that transition economies are less constrained with respect to physical infrastructure and human capital: electricity supply, telecoms, transport, and labour skills are all less costly constraints as perceived by firms in TEs versus firms in NTEs. Conversely, the constraints which firms in TEs rate as more costly compared to NTE firms are primarily those relating to economic institutions: tax administration, business licensing, customs and courts.

We interpret this as reflecting the inheritance of central planning. The transition countries entered the transition with certain legacies of decades of socialism, not all of which were negative. The industrialization strategies followed by the planners left these countries well-endowed with public infrastructure such as electricity supply and a well-educated labour force. The persistence of this legacy – abundant supply of physical infrastructure and human capital – is why firms in these economies rated these constraints as relatively less costly when compared with firms in other economies. Conversely, the same decades of socialism damaged, destroyed or prevented the development of market economy institutions, and the lack of these institutions is why firms in these countries report the corresponding constraints as relatively costly. We explore this theme in more detail in Carlin *et al.* (2012).

Our third set of questions is whether these systematic differences between the valuations of public inputs reported by firms are related to the level of economic development. In Carlin *et al.* (2012) we argue the answer is 'yes', and we refer the reader to that paper for a detailed analysis. In brief the argument is that the experience of planning had different implications for countries that were already industrialized when planning was adopted (e.g. Czechoslovakia) versus those which had not yet industrialized and where central planning brought industrialization with it (e.g. the countries of Central Asia). The aforementioned advantages of central planning – large-scale investment in public infrastructure and education – were distinctly more advantageous for the latter group of poor and underdeveloped countries.

Figures 24.4 and 24.5 illustrate these patterns for the constraints of electricity and the operation of the courts. In each figure, we plot the average estimated α_k for constraint k for each country survey. NTEs are indicated by the symbol 'N'; TEs are indicated by 'T'. OLS regression lines are also plotted – in each case, the TE line is the shorter one, reflecting the narrower range of levels of GDP per capita in the transition economies.

Figure 24.4 shows that the cost to firms of electricity as a constraint declines in non-transition economies as the economy develops: demand by firms grows, but the quality of the public input improves still more, so that the shadow price declines. It also shows how in 2002–05, more than a decade after the collapse of central planning, the electricity infrastructure in poor TEs was still abundant compared to other economies at a similar level of development, but the advantageous legacy was essentially absent for the richest of the TEs.

In Figure 24.5, for the operation of the courts, we see a less clear relationship between level of development and the reported cost of the constraint for the non-transition economies. Transition economies report a higher cost of this constraint compared to NTEs of similar income; the cost reported by firms is higher relative to NTEs for the richer countries. The interpretation we suggest is again in terms of the legacy of central planning. The inheritance of weak institutions, in this case the court system, was still visible almost two decades after the collapse of socialism in how firms reported the shadow price of this public input, and it was more evident in the richer TEs.

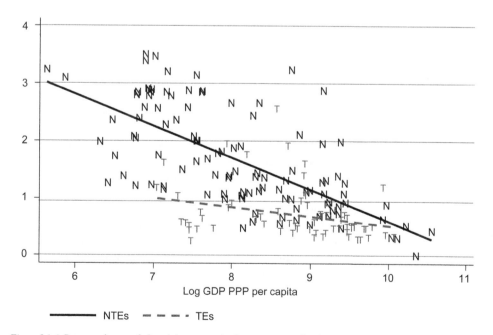

Figure 24.4 Reported cost of electricity constraint by country and GDP per capita: TEs vs. NTEs

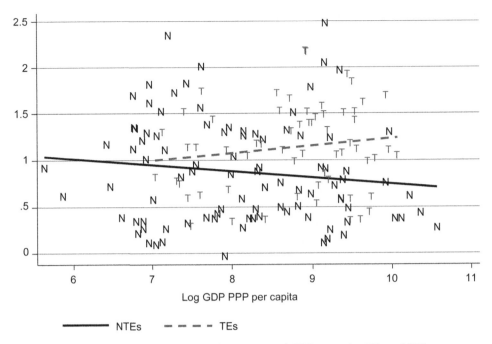

Figure 24.5 Reported cost of courts constraint by country and GDP per capita: TEs vs. NTEs

Conclusions

Did the new population of SMEs firms in the transition economies encounter more or less serious obstacles to their activities from their surroundings than was the case for similar firms outside transition and is there evidence of legacy effects from the planning era? In a first step, we tested whether firms with different characteristics (size, growth, international engagement) experienced different constraints from their business environment. Our model predicts that higher quality firms report higher shadow costs of constraints. This finding is confirmed for firms both inside and outside transition. The one notable difference related to transition was that importing firms in the transition economies were indistinguishable from non-importing firms whereas outside transition, importing firms reported themselves more constrained. This may reflect the greater openness of the transition economies.

In the cross-country analysis, we found clear evidence consistent with legacy effects of planning extending well into the transition period. The benchmark transition firm was less hampered by inadequate physical infrastructure and education among the workforce than was the case outside transition. This is consistent with the emphasis on industrialization of the planning regimes. Unsurprisingly, it was the poor transition economies that benefited most from the investments in physical infrastructure and schooling undertaken under planning. Conversely, in transition, it was the inadequacy of market institutions that were rated more significantly troublesome than was the case for firms outside transition – and this legacy of separation from the market had a higher cost for the richer transition economies.

Notes

1 We are very grateful to Paul Seabright for discussions on our related work which have influenced this paper. Some of the analysis in this paper builds on work in Carlin and Schaffer (2009), which was

prepared as a background paper for Mitra *et al.* (2010). An earlier version of this paper was given as the keynote lecture at AISSEC, Macerata, Italy, 2011.

2 See Carlin *et al.* (2012) for a detailed analysis.

3 More precisely, the reported costs in these surveys correspond to evaluations of discrete changes in quality of public inputs faced by firms. The marginal analogue to these discrete changes is the shadow price of the public input. See Carlin *et al.* (2012).

4 It is for this reason that our measure for firm size is defined as $L30 \equiv \log(L/30)$; it is zero for a firm with 30 employees.

5 GDP per capita is measured at PPP in 2005 US\$; the source is the World Bank's *World Development Indicators*.

6 The same pattern is visible in Table 24.2c with respect to foreign ownership. Foreign-owned firms in both TEs and NTEs find access to finance to be less of a problem, and the degree to which foreign ownership eases access to finance is no different in the two groups of countries.

Bibliography

Acemoglu, Daron, Johnson, Simon and Robinson, James A. (2001), 'The Colonial Origins of Comparative Development: An Empirical Investigation', *American Economic Review*, vol. 91(5), pp. 1369–1401.

Blanchard, Olivier (1997), *The Economics of Post-Communist Transition*, Oxford: OUP.

Carlin, Wendy and Schaffer, Mark (2009), 'Public infrastructure constraints on growth in the transition economies: the legacy of communism and evidence from enterprise surveys 1999–2008', Background Paper, Washington, DC: World Bank.

Carlin, Wendy, Schaffer, Mark and Seabright, Paul (2006), 'What are the Real Bottlenecks? A Lagrangian Approach to Identifying Constraints on Growth from Survey Data', *CEPR Discussion Paper* No. 5719.

——(2010), 'A framework for cross-country comparisons of public infrastructure constraints on firm growth', CEPR Discussion Paper No. 7662.

——(2012), 'Soviet power plus electrification: what is the long-run legacy of communism?', *CEPR Discussion Paper* No. 9003.

Commander, Simon and Svejnar, Jan (2011), 'Do Institutions, Ownership, Exporting and Competition Explain Firm Performance?' *Review of Economics and Statistics*, Vol. 93(1), pp. 309–37.

Commander, Simon and Nikoloski, Zlatko (2011), 'Institutions and economic performance: what can be explained?', *Review of Economics and Institutions* Vol. 2(2), Article 3.

EBRD (2010), *Transition Report: Recovery and Reform*, London: EBRD.

Kornai, János (2000), 'Ten Years after "The Road to a Free Economy:" The Author's Self-Evaluation', *Economic Systems*, vol. 24(4), pp. 353–59.

Manski, Charles (1993), 'Identification of Endogenous Social Effects: The Reflection Problem', *Review of Economic Studies*, Vol. 60(3), July.

Mitra, Pradeep, Selowsky, Marcelo and Zalduendo, Juan (2010), *Turmoil at Twenty: Recession, Recovery, and Reform in Central and Eastern Europe and the Former Soviet Union*. Washington, DC: World Bank.

Roland, Gérard (2000), *Transition and Economics: Politics, Markets and Firms*, Boston, MA: MIT Press

Svejnar, Jan (2002), 'Transition Economies: Performance and Challenges,' *Journal of Economic Perspectives*, Vol. 16(1), pp. 3–28

World Bank (2012), *More and Better Jobs in South Asia*, Washington, DC: World Bank.

Part VII
People

25

PEOPLE AND TRANSITION

Life in Transition Survey

Peter Sanfey[1]

Introduction

In 1989, when the communist system that had predominated for more than 40 years in central and eastern Europe and for more than 70 years in the Soviet Union began to collapse, few could have imagined the extent of the upheaval that would hit people's lives in the following 20 years. To say that transition has had a profound effect on ordinary individuals in this region is both a cliché and an understatement. The 'transition recession' that all countries suffered in the early 1990s caused widespread hardship, poverty and unemployment. The subsequent recovery and period of strong economic growth in the second decade, combined with increasing political and economic integration of many countries into gl obal structures, created new opportunities and better living standards for many. The economic crisis that hit the region with full force in 2009 has been a serious setback. While a partial recovery has taken place in 2010 and 2011 in most countries, the global outlook as of mid-December 2011 is highly uncertain and a return to recession cannot be ruled out. Encouragingly, however, few of the reforms introduced during the transition have been reversed.

There is a wealth of data and research on how the transition has affected people's material well-being and labour market status. Living standards assessments by the World Bank and other institutions have used household survey data to document poverty and unemployment levels, the degree of access to public services and the level of informality in the labour market. The EBRD has analysed extensively the climate for business start-up and development and has provided substantial support to entrepreneurs, mostly channelled through financial institutions on the ground, for the establishment of micro and small businesses.

But until a few years ago there was a dearth of information on what people really thought about the transition. Did they think their situation had improved relative to pre-1989? Were they satisfied with their lives and optimistic about the future? Did they support the notions of democracy and the market economy? To what extent did they trust people in the new circumstances? Had corruption gone up or down?

Prior to 2006 there were limited data on which to base answers to these fundamental questions. Research on life satisfaction showed generally low levels across the region, with several transition countries being among the lowest in the world.[2] Cross-country studies of corruption and declining trust, carried out by institutions such as the World Bank and Transparency

International, suggested that these problems had become endemic in parts of the region. What was lacking was a systematic survey of these issues that covered the whole transition region in a consistent way.

The life in transition survey

The EBRD-World Bank Life in Transition Survey (LiTS) was designed to address the major information gaps identified above. First carried out in autumn 2006 when most countries were growing strongly, it is an ambitious attempt to get inside the minds of ordinary people, randomly chosen across the whole region from central Europe to central Asia, and to find out how they feel about the transition process. The survey was repeated in late 2010, on a new sample of individuals and households, with a substantially modified questionnaire and an expanded country coverage that included five western European 'comparator' countries (see below). Both rounds included all EBRD countries of operations except Turkmenistan, where the prevailing political climate was not conducive to a survey like the LiTS, which includes a number of politically sensitive questions.

Methodology and design of questionnaire

In order to draw valid statistical inferences about the population, it is important to have a reasonably large sample size for each country and to ensure that individuals are randomly chosen. In the first round of the survey (LiTS I), 1,000 people were interviewed in each country, similar to the second round (LiTS II) although in the latter case up to 1,500 people were sampled in selected countries to allow for a telephone follow-up survey.

Briefly, the sampling methodology was as follows.[3] The first stage involved the establishment of Primary Sampling Units (PSUs) in each country. In some cases, census enumeration areas or electoral registers were used for this purpose, while alternative classification systems were used in other countries. Fifty PSUs were chosen randomly in each country, with selection probability weighted according to the size of the PSU.[4] Twenty households were then chosen in each PSU, again according to standard randomisation procedures. The person selected in each household to answer most questions was also determined randomly. Some questions relating to factual household matters (for example, the number of people in the household, access of family members to certain goods, and so on) were answered by the head of household, regardless of whether he/she was the person chosen to answer the rest of the questions. The questionnaire is lengthy and covers a range of topics. Each interview was meant to last approximately one hour but often took considerably more time.

Achieving a representative sample is a challenging task. The LiTS is a face-to-face survey and involves a lot of knocking on (random) doors, explaining to people the reason for calling and the nature of the survey, and asking them if they would be willing to participate. One problem that arose in most countries is that interviewers are more likely to find older, female people at home, especially if the house call was made during the daytime. Household members who are away permanently, either for work or studies, were excluded and this group is more likely to include young males. To correct for this problem, the data generated by the survey are weighted to adjust for the actual age and gender breakdown in the country's population.[5] All results referred to below are based on these weighted calculations.

In LiTS I, there were four broad areas investigated. First, the head of the household was asked about household characteristics such as income and possession of certain household and personal goods, as well the household's access to public services. Second, the selected respondent in the household was asked a series of questions concerning reforms, markets and democracy, life satisfaction and other attitudes and values. Third, the questionnaire contained a series of questions about people's experiences during the previous 15–20 years, including some of the important life events (jobs, marriages and the like) that took place during this time. Fourth, the questionnaire included a number of 'social capital' questions related to issues such as crime, corruption and trust.

In LiTS II, the questionnaire underwent an extensive revision. There were two main reasons for this. First, some questions from LiTS I had either not worked well, or were seen as less relevant from the perspective of 2010 rather than 2006. Many of the 'life history' questions were dropped as they had proved to be time-consuming and, because people's memories are fallible, the data they produced were rather suspect. Second, there was a desire on the part of both the EBRD and the World Bank to expand coverage of certain issues and to introduce new topics. LiTS II therefore includes questions on tolerance of minorities, on the experience of corruption in public services and on climate change. Given the timing, it also had a section on the impact of the global economic crisis – how it shaped people's attitudes and how individuals coped with the negative effects. One of the main reasons for carrying out a second round of the LiTS was to see whether the crisis had significantly altered people's views on the merits of transition, an issue of vital importance for institutions like the EBRD and the World Bank that try to promote reforms in the region.

LiTS II contains another important innovation. The survey was also carried out in five non-transition, western European countries: France, Germany, Italy, Sweden and the UK. The idea was to create a benchmark of advanced market economies and see how the transition region shapes up in comparison. As discussed below, the results from LiTS II show a striking divergence in many respects between these 'old EU' countries and the transition region.

LiTS I: main results

The first round of the survey revealed a number of new findings, some rather disturbing but others giving grounds for hope. The balance between negative and positive views is best captured by considering simultaneously the answers to three questions (Figure 25.1). When asked if they agree or disagree that their household lives were better now than in 1989, almost half of the respondents disagreed, and only 30 per cent agreed (the remainder said that they neither agreed nor disagreed). When it comes to life satisfaction, however, around 45 per cent of people proclaimed themselves satisfied with their lives, as against 32 per cent who are dissatisfied. Lastly, a majority of people (about 56 per cent), with only 25 per cent disagreeing, show a sense of optimism for the future, in the sense that they believe that children born now will have a better life than the respondent's generation.

People's views on transition in LiTS I were rather mixed. Two of the fundamental attributes of a successful transition – democracy and the market economy – attracted moderately strong support. More than one-third of people unequivocally favoured both concepts. However, 10 per cent of respondents said that, under some circumstances, they would opt for both a planned economy and an authoritarian political system. A further 20 per cent said that it did not matter to them which systems – democracy or authoritarianism, and market or planned economy – were present. (The remainder answered with some other combination – for example, some favoured democracy but also said a planned economy was preferable under some circumstances.)

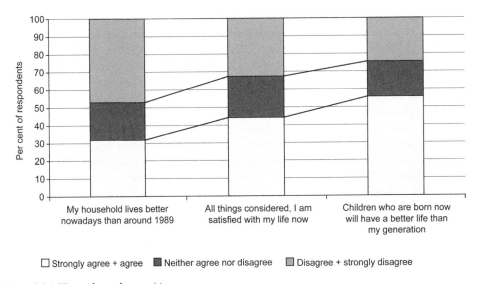

Figure 25.1 Views about the transition process
Source: EBRD/World Bank, *Life in Transition Survey.*

The results varied significantly according to different socio-economic factors, as well as by region. Subsequent econometric research by the EBRD showed that the better-off, professional classes and those with higher levels of education tended to favour democracy and markets.[6] This is hardly surprising, as these groups tended to have benefited most from the new system. The same patterns emerged when people were asked about the extent to which the state should intervene in the economy. In short, a divide appeared to have opened up between the winners and losers of transition, with the former group favouring democracy and a reduced role for the state, and the latter, consisting disproportionately of older, unemployed people, hankering after a return to the past. Support for democracy and the market economy was also strongest in the countries of central Europe and the Baltic states (CEB), and considerably weaker elsewhere, especially in the largest country in the region, Russia.

The questions on corruption and trust revealed a serious perceived deterioration relative to the pre-transition years. Two-thirds of respondents felt that the level of corruption was as bad as, or worse than, it was before the transition began. 'Irregular payments' appeared to be common in many areas of life, notably in gaining access to health services, providing acceptable education (and exam results) for one's children, and paying off the road police. The decline in trust was also striking. Only one-third felt that people could be trusted now, while two-thirds felt that they could be trusted prior to 1989. When it comes to institutions, people generally felt that they could trust the army, the presidency and the banks, but not political parties, the parliament or the courts.

Lastly, LiTS I provided a valuable snapshot of the extent to which different socio-economic groups were able to enjoy the benefits of the modern consumer society. There was particularly wide regional variation in some of the responses. For example, three-quarters of households in central Europe and CEB had a bank account and around 60 per cent a credit or debit card, compared to just 10 per cent (for both categories) in the Commonwealth of Independent States. Mobile phone and computer ownership had also penetrated widely by that point in CEB and south-eastern Europe (SEE) but much less so further east. The survey also showed the extent to which rural areas lag behind their urban counterparts in terms of access to certain public services such as a fixed telephone line.

LiTS II: main results

In LiTS II, people were interviewed in autumn 2010, at a time when memories of the worst global economic crisis in 70 years were still fresh. Many countries were still effectively in the thick of the crisis, or had only barely started to recover. Some of the key findings from LiTS I – on life satisfaction and optimism for example – remained broadly unchanged, despite the buffeting suffered by the region from mid-2008 onwards, but important regional differences emerged with regard to attitudes towards markets and democracy.

The crisis caused a big drop in GDP – more than 10 per cent on average between 2007 and 2009 – and affected huge numbers of people across the whole region. More than 40 per cent of respondents said that they had been affected 'a great deal' or 'a fair amount' by the crisis, compared to about 30 per cent in the western comparators. Interestingly, the perceived impact of the crisis, which is what the LiTS attempts to measure, had only a limited correlation with the actual impact, as measured by the fall in GDP. For example, the highest percentage of people affected in this way – more than 70 per cent in both cases – was in Bulgaria and Serbia, two countries where the drop in GDP in 2009 was no worse than the overall transition region average. In contrast, less than half of those interviewed in Ukraine replied the same way, notwithstanding a fall in real GDP in 2009 of 15 per cent. Interestingly, the crisis was felt quite strongly even in some countries that managed to avoid recession, such as Azerbaijan and Tajikistan. Further research may be needed to explain the apparent disconnect between subjective feelings about the crisis and actual outcomes.

LiTS II also provides valuable insights into the different ways in which people coped with the crisis. In some EU member countries, people who lost their job were able to draw on unemployment insurance; elsewhere, this was usually not an option. As a result, roughly 70 per cent of those respondents who said they were affected by the crisis had to cut back on their consumption of staple foods and healthcare. Most people also reduced spending on other, non-core items. Social safety nets were generally inadequate, in contrast to the western comparator countries where they had a strong influence in mitigating the effects of the crisis. More encouragingly, a significant proportion of people, especially among those with higher incomes and greater asset ownership, were able to adopt a more 'active' approach, by taking an extra job, for example, or by working longer hours. However, these options were not available to the majority of people in the region.

The crisis had a much smaller effect on life satisfaction than might have been expected, given the severity of the economic downturn. In LiTS I, 44.2 per cent agreed or strongly agreed that they were satisfied overall with their life. In LiTS II this figure dropped to 42.7 per cent, a minor reduction under the circumstances. However, the corresponding average figure for the five western European comparator countries was 72 per cent, highlighting the large satisfaction gap that persists between the transition region and western Europe. The biggest decreases in life satisfaction tended to be in countries that endured severe economic contractions, such as Romania, Slovenia and the three Baltic states. Levels of optimism held up reasonably well. Nearly 50 per cent of respondents in LiTS II think that children born now will have a better life than the current generation, versus 56 per cent in LiTS I. These two variables – life satisfaction and optimism – are positively correlated, even when other variables are controlled for.

The crisis is associated with some weakening of support for democracy and the market economy. In LiTS II approximately one-third of people gave unequivocal support to both concepts, a figure similar to that in LiTS I. Only 10 per cent would like a return – under some circumstances – to both authoritarianism and the planned economy. However, a closer examination of the data shows that fewer people favour either option relative to four years previously. Interestingly, the drop in support for both is most pronounced in EU members, with the sole exception of Bulgaria where the proportion in favour of democracy and the market economy rose slightly. Further east, however, people living in more state-dominated systems appear to be more receptive to these ideas. In a sense, therefore, the crisis seems to have encouraged people to 'turn against what they had'.[7]

Corruption remains a serious problem for many transition countries, and the results of LiTS II are far from encouraging. Only a small minority of respondents believes that the level of corruption has fallen in the past four years. In virtually all countries of the region, it is perceived to be much higher than in the western European comparators. The problem is especially acute when it comes to dealing with the road police, public healthcare and the courts. One interesting finding of LiTS II is that people who use services such as the courts are more likely to report that people like them typically encounter corruption.[8] Another is that people's perceptions of corruption may actually lag behind the reality. In a majority of countries, the percentage of respondents who said that they or a member of their household made an irregular payment in the past year to receive a service exceeds the percentage who say that people like them typically have to pay to get the service. A closer analysis, however, shows that some of these payments are actually voluntary rewards for good service, for example to doctors and nurses.

More encouragingly, the level of generalized trust appears to have held up or even increased since 2006. Thirty-four per cent of respondents in LiTS II said they have some trust or complete trust in other people, versus 30 per cent in LiTS I. The corresponding figure for the western comparator countries is 42 per cent. The rise in trust, albeit rather modest, is surprising when one takes into account the strong correlation between this variable and life satisfaction, which (as noted) dropped slightly between 2006 and 2010. The survey also shows how trust in institutions varies across the region and how it has evolved over the four-year period. Interestingly, people in a number of former Soviet countries tend to express high levels of trust in political institutions such as the presidency and government. Throughout the region, trust in banks and foreign investors has remained steady, suggesting that these institutions are not in general blamed for the economic downturn that most countries suffered in 2009.

LiTS II contains some interesting findings on issues not covered in the first round, some of which are worth mentioning briefly. One controversial issue explored in LiTS II is 'tolerance', as measured by the expressed willingness of people to have as immediate neighbours certain groups of the population. The attitudes vary considerably across the population and with regard to different groups. For example, the vast majority of people do not mind living next to people of a different religion, but significant minorities (above 10 per cent in most countries and reaching 30 per cent in some cases) are averse to living beside immigrants or people of a different race. A second issue explored in LiTS II is satisfaction with public services, which appears to be relatively high, and rising since 2006, though it is lower than in western European comparator countries. Lastly, LiTS II contains some questions on people's attitudes to climate change. More than half of the sample – 54 per cent – said they are concerned about the problem, exactly the same percentage as in the five western European comparator countries.

Research using the LiTS

The data in the two rounds of the LiTS constitute an extraordinarily rich source of information about the transition region. The second round was released in June 2011 and is only now starting to be exploited by the research community. However, LiTS I is increasingly being analysed by researchers. There is little space to do justice to this work here. However, it is worth mentioning a couple of 'hot' topics and several key papers that have appeared so far.

Historical legacy

One of the most exciting areas of economic research in the past decade has been into the ways in which historical institutions, sometimes going back hundreds of years, affect current economic variables, such as long-term growth, and socio-political attitudes such as support for democracy and markets and trust in institutions. The LiTS allows further investigation of these topics because of the wide variation in historical background across the region. Recent papers in this literature include Grosjean (2011), Grosjean and Senik (2011) and Becker *et al.* (2011). Grosjean (2011) shows that a history of occupation by the Ottoman empire in south-eastern Europe is associated robustly with lower levels of financial development today. The explanation proposed is that Islamic institutions forbade lending with interest for a much longer period than in other parts of Europe, and the lingering effects of this prohibition are still seen today.

Grosjean and Senik (2011) examine the two-way relationship between support for democracy and for the market economy. The LiTS allows them to get around identification problems in two respects. First, one can identify people who live close to the border of their country and hence may have a common market experience with, but a different democratic tradition compared to, those across the border. Second, within a given country, people experience a similar level of democracy wherever they live but may have very different exposure to markets and competition, depending on the particular region. The main finding of this paper is a significant causal relationship from democracy to the market, but no evidence of a reverse relationship. Becker *et al.* (2011) use similar techniques to identify a 'Habsburg effect', in the sense that those living today in areas once occupied by the Habsburg empire have higher trust in courts and the police.

Life satisfaction

Several researchers have begun to dig more deeply into the LiTS data to see what drives life satisfaction and how it is shaped by past events and other socio-economic variables. Econometric research from the EBRD (2007b) suggests that the correlates of life satisfaction often found in studies from other parts of the world also appear in the transition region. For example, life satisfaction is positively correlated with income and education and negatively with unemployment status. The U-shape relationship between satisfaction and age found in numerous other studies also emerges from these data. Interestingly, women in LiTS I seem to be less satisfied than men, *ceteris paribus*. Senik (2009) explores the relationship between satisfaction and different types of benchmarks. Her results suggest a hierarchy of importance. *Internal* benchmarks, meaning your own income or other variable at some time in the past, matter most for subjective well-being. They are followed by local *external* benchmarks such as the performance of your parents or colleagues/neighbours, and then more general benchmarks such as your self-ranking on a subjective income or wealth ladder. Dabalen and Paul (2011) link the level of satisfaction with certain life events, such as the loss of a job, and they also explore the correlations with social capital variables such as generalized trust and participation in civic groups.

Concluding remarks

One can take many messages from the Life in Transition Survey, both positive and negative. The survey conveys how difficult transition has been for many people, and how life satisfaction levels in even relatively successful countries in the region still lag behind prosperous western countries. It helps to explain the obstacles that face reform-minded policy makers. However, there is also an impression of resilience, which shows through clearly in the results of the second round. Despite the severity of the global crisis and its impact on the region, life satisfaction is almost unchanged from four years earlier, markets and democracy still attract more support than the alternatives, and people are generally optimistic about the future. The big question is whether attitudes and values in the transition region will converge on those in the west during the coming years. Future rounds of the LiTS will, one hopes, reveal the answer.

Notes

1 Comments from the editors, Paul Hare and Gerard Turley, and from Elena Nikolova, are gratefully acknowledged. The views expressed in this chapter are those of the author only and not of the EBRD.
2 See Sanfey and Teksoz (2007) and Guriev and Zhuravskaya (2009).
3 See EBRD (2007a, 2011a) for a more detailed description of the underlying methodology in each round.
4 The geographical coordinates of each PSU can be subsequently traced.
5 To give a simple illustration, suppose that in a given country, the male/female ratio is 50:50 according to the census, but in the survey, twice as many females as males are interviewed. The 'solution' is to give double weight to the male responses, thereby correcting the bias in the sample. A similar (slightly more complicated) principle applies to the age breakdown.
6 See EBRD (2007b).
7 This argument is developed in Chapter 3 of EBRD (2011b).
8 See EBRD (2011b, Chapter 4).

Bibliography

Becker, S.O., Boeckh, K., Hainz, C. and Woessmann, L. (2011), 'The empire is dead, long live the empire! Long-run persistence of trust and corruption in the bureaucracy', *CEPR Discussion Paper No. 8288*.

Dabalen, A. and Paul, S. (2011), 'History of events and life-satisfaction in transition countries', *World Bank Policy Research Working Paper No. 5526*.

EBRD (2007a), *Life in Transition. A survey of people's experiences and attitudes*, London: EBRD.

——(2007b), *Transition Report 2007: People in transition*, London: EBRD.

——(2011a), *Life in Transition: After the Crisis*, London: EBRD.

——(2011b), *Transition Report 2011: Crisis and transition – the people's perspective*, London: EBRD.

Grosjean, P. (2011), 'Long term institutional persistence: Ottoman rule and financial development in the regions of Europe', *Journal of Comparative Economics,* vol. 39, pp. 1–16

Grosjean, P. and Senik, C. (2011), 'Democracy, market liberalization and political preferences', *The Review of Economics and Statistics,* vol. 93(1), pp. 365–81.

Guriev, S. and Zhuravskaya, E. (2009), '(Un)happiness in transition', *Journal of Economic Perspectives*, vol. 23 (2), pp. 143–68.

Sanfey, P. and Teksoz, U. (2007), 'Does Transition Make You Happy?', *Economics of Transition*, vol. 15(4), pp. 707–31.

Senik, C. (2009), 'Direct Evidence on Income Comparison and their Welfare Effects', *Journal of Economic Behavior and Organization*, vol. 72, pp. 408–24.

26

THE STATUS OF WOMEN DURING THE EARLY TRANSITION PROCESS

Peter Luke

Introduction

This chapter examines the position or status of women in the transition process mainly within the labour market and not within broader civil society as a whole. In addition, we concentrate on the initial 10 years of transition for the former Soviet Union (FSU) and the countries of Central and Eastern Europe (CEE), since these were the crucial years for establishing successful transition paths or otherwise. We provide a brief summary of a few labour market indicators, which cannot hope to do justice to a large and expanding area of investigation, but which nevertheless give an insight into establishing a multifaceted picture of women's changing role within the labour market during those times.

Following Momsen (2009), 'gender' means the socially acquired notions of masculinity and femininity by which men and women are identified, while the term 'gender relations' refers to the socially constructed form of relations between men and women. We, however, do not aim to summarise gender or gender relations under transition. Our task is less complex inasmuch as we concentrate primarily on one half of the gender nexus only and refer to the male position during transition primarily as a reference point for the position of women.

The position of women under socialism

> ... democratization of society, which is the pivot and guarantor of *perestroika*, is impossible without enhancing the role of women, without women's active and specific involvement, and without their commitment to all our reforming efforts. I am convinced that women's role in our society will steadily grow.
>
> *(Mikhail Gorbachev, 1987, p. 117, quoted in Rhein, 1998, p. 354)*

On the surface at least, the status of women under socialism was superior to that for women in Western market economies. Female equality in comparison to males was enshrined in most of the constitutions of the socialist countries. Without necessarily stating it explicitly, this equality, however, was always equality outside of the home; it was an equality that gave women the right and, indeed, the duty to work in the economy. The result was a very high female labour force

321

participation rate (relative to Western market economies) combined with initial high levels of female education before entering the labour force. All of this went along with levels of fertility comparable or higher to women in Western countries, although usually with marriage and giving birth occurring at a much younger age.[1]

The above was supported by generous social and welfare provisions – again in comparison to Western market economies – often linked to the place of work. Maternity leave ranged from 18 weeks in the FSU to 28 weeks in Czechoslovakia with the job of the individual, or at least *a* job, guaranteed at the expiration of the maternity leave period. This return to work could be on a part-time and flexible basis with additional holidays granted when children were sick. Extra money or allowances were given depending on the number of children. 'In Bulgaria and Czechoslovakia, for example, additional allowances amounted to 40 per cent of the minimum wage.' (Metcalfe and Afanassieva, 2005a, p. 399).

Notwithstanding the above, gender-based stratification within the labour force did occur. Skilled jobs in industry were the preserve of men. These were the best paying jobs and the ones that carried the most prestige. Women tended to be found within what would be known in the West as public sector jobs such as education and health, and in general administrative and clerical positions which were lower paid. However, as noted by Metcalfe and Afanassieva (*ibid.*, p. 399) high female participation in the fields of political administration and scientific research were also notable in comparison to the West.

This was very much 'emancipation from above': there was no independent women's movement; no feminist currents independent of the Communist Party apparatus developed (and none developed inside the apparatus either). This emancipation from above was linked to an *extensive* development of the economy – bringing more and more factors of production into use without necessarily making better use of the existing factors of production (referred to as an *intensive* development of the productive resources of the economy).

The above is important since, 'There were pressures to bring women into the labour market but no pressures to bring men into household and care work' (Pascall and Kwak, 2005, p. 3); and 'Women were legally defined as workers and mothers but there was no equivalent definition of men as workers and fathers' (Metcalfe and Afanassieva, 2005, p. 399). In short, socialism stopped at the front door of the home, and domestic inequality inside the home was the norm. Patriarchal principles dominated the household, with women facing a triple-burden as worker, child-carer and home-maker.

With transition under way in the early 1990s in the FSU and the countries of CEE the opinion was expressed that there would be a 're-traditionalisation' of women's role within society and within the home. There would be a move back to the 'male breadwinner model' whereby the man would provide the necessary income to support the family and women would stay at home or focus on the home and any attendant childcare duties. This should be contrasted with the dual-earner model in the FSU and CEE which had existed increasingly and extensively from the end of the Second World War.[2]

The *a priori* result of this re-traditionalisation, it was thought, would be an increase in female inequalities in the labour market as the transition process proceeded. That said, while some have spoken and written of a feminisation of poverty in transition economies (and more generally in developing economies), as noted by Pascall and Kwak (2005, p. 6), ' … some statistical comparisons of the early transition period failed to find such consistent trends against women'.

As former state firms were privatized, the benefits which had been attached to the workplace – crèche facilities, housing, generous maternity conditions – were sold off or reduced, and the composition of the labour market along gender lines certainly altered. To what extent this occurred because of the lack of material support for women to work, leading to inactivity or a transition from full to part-time working, or to what extent women voluntarily selected the role of home-maker and child-carer is not completely clear.

Certainly, even if one accepts that the position of females within the labour market (and the home) deteriorated in comparison to men with the onset of transition (and the World Bank report cited below does not come to such a clear-cut position) it seems clear from a reading of other sources (the UNECE report cited below, for example) that the position of women (and men) in the labour force was deteriorating *before* the onset of transition. Despite the lofty ideal expressed by Gorbachev at the start of this chapter, a hint of the change in official position towards women was made clear in a later speech by Gorbachev where, not for the first time or last, he would attempt to look both ways at the same time.

> ... the contribution and selfless work (without which) we would not have built a new society nor won against fascism ... over the years of our difficult and heroic history, we failed to pay attention to women's specific rights and needs arising from their role as mother and home-maker, and their indisputable educational function as regards children ... What we should do is make it possible for women to return to their purely *womanly mission*.'
>
> *(Emphasis added. Gorbachev, 1987, p. 117*
> *quoted in Metcalfe and Afanassieva, 2005b, p. 432)*

Indeed, Metcalfe and Afanassieva (2005b, p. 433) make the point that, 'while political commentators are keen to interrogate restructuring in the transition context, gender reform and reconstitution in Soviet society cannot be socially and politically isolated within the transition era: gendered dynamics of transition must be seen as a process which started before 1989'.

Neither should it be thought that this reconstitution of gender roles was unwelcome by all women. The World Bank (2002, p. 13) report makes it clear that, 'the new principles of perestroika were shared by many Soviet women who saw "emancipation" as the right *not* to work.' (emphasis added)

The remainder of this contribution proceeds as follows. We first outline the position of females within the labour market in the first ten years of transition up to the end of the 1990s. This covers female activity rates, employment patterns, unemployment, and gender wage gaps. It is fully accepted that the position of women in many of the transition economies discussed below will have changed in the second part of transition, up to the present day indeed. However, the 1990s were the crucial years of transition and we feel it appropriate to focus our narrative here. We take the FSU and the transition countries of CEE as one grouping. To a lesser degree we separately discuss the situation in the People's Republic of China (PRC) where transition started earlier.

Women in (and out of) the labour market during transition

The former Soviet Union and central and eastern Europe

The beginning of the decade brought a sharp fall in GDP ... With respect to gender, the concern has been that worsening labor market conditions have had a disproportionate negative effect on women by increasing any pre-existing gender gap in employment and wages ... The findings of this study ... do not support this claim. There appears to be no empirical evidence that the treatment of women in the labor market has systematically deteriorated across the region.

(World Bank, 2002, Gender in Transition, p. xi)

323

A generalized concern exists that female participation has declined and that the gender gap in both participation and wages has grown. But this claim is not entirely supported by empirical evidence.

(ibid., p. 16)

It is widely acknowledged that women were hurt disproportionately by the deteriorating conditions in the labour markets because as a result of macroeconomic austerity they lost previous non-wage benefits and services that made their participation in paid employment economically worthwhile.

(UNECE, 2003, No.1, Chapter 7, p. 191)

... the loss of benefits and social services which previously had made it easier for women – especially those with children – to hold a job suggests that many of the adjustments that have been made under the pressures of transition have fallen most heavily on women.

(ibid., p. 142)

In what follows we make use of both the UNECE (2003) and the World Bank (2002) publications.[3] As the preceding endnote points out, the respective reports cover different countries with a large overlap (the countries of CEE and the Russian Federation); but use different data sources, again, however, with an overlap (e.g. labour force surveys); and in quite a few cases, with different comparison years.

Other differences of measurement exist between the two reports. For example, the population of working-age is defined by the UNECE report as anyone 15 years of age and over (no mention is made of an upper age limit). The World Bank report uses the World Bank database *Genderstats*, a casual glance at which reveals the age range 15 to 64 for those of working age. Yet both definitions are probably different from the methodologies of many of the national statistical agencies. In China the working age population has an upper age limit of 55 for women and 60 for men, the respective retirement ages. Hence both quotes above may have a degree of ambiguity about them!

Female Labour Force Participation

We define the labour force participation rate (or simply activity rate) as the number of people working added to those actively seeking work divided by the population of working age, or equivalently, the labour force divided by the population of working age.

The above are not mere esoteric points. The World Bank report concludes that, 'In no country of the region except Bosnia and Herzegovina has the ratio of female to male activity rates significantly declined, and in nearly two-thirds of the countries, women's activity rates increased relative to men's although only Armenia had an increase of more than 5 percent' (World Bank, 2002, p. 17). Here it needs to be pointed out that this statement refers to a comparison between 1990 and 1999. When we turn to the UNECE report, however, we read that, ' ... female activity rates in 2001 were everywhere lower than in 1985 except in Romania ... Male activity rates also fell, but by much less than those of females except in Slovenia where both rates fell by about one fifth' (UNECE, 2003, p. 200). As can be seen from the quote, the period covered starts in 1985.

In the first case, the World Bank is, presumably, interested to see how the activity rates of females have fared since the start of transition to a market economy with 1990, broadly speaking, being the year when transition started for many socialist countries. For UNECE, they are presumably, interested in comparing female activity rates from the definitive situation under central planning; in 1985 virtually all countries were still under central planning. Table 26.1 gives a more nuanced picture using the UNECE data.

As can be seen from Table 26.1 the major part of reductions in the female labour force or of employment occurred in the 1985 to 1994 period, with employment of females increasing in some countries in the late nineties to the early part of the new millennium. This reinforces the point that the beginnings in the deterioration of the status of women (and men) within the labour force pre-dated transition proper.

The People's Republic of China (PRC)

Turning briefly to the PRC we present Table 26.2. We note the distinction between men and women, but also between urban and rural China. For labour force participation we make use of Maurer-Fazio *et al.* (2005) who, in a comprehensive study of three Chinese population censuses of 1982, 1990, and 2000, examine female and male labour force participation in both urban and rural China. For 1982 the authors find participation rates of 86 and 71 per cent for men and women respectively.[4] In addition, they present Table 26.3 where labour force participation is broken down by both gender, age, and location.

While older women in urban areas saw little change in their participation rates, older women (and men) in rural areas saw a large increase in participation between 1982 and 2000. It is surmised that this is due to the large outflow from villages of younger workers (of both sexes) to work in the booming coastal economic zones, leading to a 'feminization of rural agriculture'. Another feature of the above data is the greater likelihood of urban young females and urban young males staying within the education system for far longer than previous generations and certainly in greater numbers and for greater duration than their rural counterparts, showing an unequal access to education for the young, regardless of gender, based on an urban-rural divide.

Employment in CEE and the FSU

While both male and female employment fell, female employment fell more than male employment if we take 1985 as our starting point. Given the cut back in public sector jobs, many of which were female dominated, combined with a large increase in inactivity, then as with the labour force data the share of women in total employment fell everywhere except Romania (owing to the large influence of agriculture in the economy).

In addition, part-time employment increased in transition economies for women, standing, for example, at 72.5, 70.1, and 68.5 per cent of all part-time employment in Slovakia, the Russian Federation, and Estonia respectively in 2001. Given the withdrawal of many benefits that allowed women with children to engage in full-time jobs, part-time employment allowed a degree of paid employment with unpaid domestic employment.

The degree to which this growth in female-dominated part-time employment was voluntary or forced on women who could not obtain full-time employment is not known with certainty. However, Standing (1996, p. 302), using labour force data for the Russian Federation in 1993, reports that 12.4 per cent of unemployed women wanted or preferred part-time employment; an additional 12.2 per cent said they wouldn't mind either part-time or full-time work, with 57.5 per cent saying they wanted only full-time work.[5]

Table 26.1 Labour force participation and employment in selected transition economies, various years (per cent changes)

	Labour Force								Employment							
	1985 to 2001		1985 to 1994		1994 to 1997		1997 to 2001		1985 to 2001		1985 to 1994		1994 to 1997		1997 to 2001	
	Male	Female	Male	Female	Male	Female	Male	Female	Male	Female	Male	Female	Male	Female	Male	Female
Bulgaria	..	..	..	..	-2.0	-1.8	-6.8	-4.9	..	..	..	..	5.2	5.5	-13.6	-9.8
Czech Republic[a]	1.8	-5.6	1.2	-5.6	1.5	–	-0.9	–	-5.2	-15.2	-2.6	-10.3	0.9	-1.9	-3.6	-3.6
Estonia	-7.9	-27.1	4.5	-21.5	-7.5	-5.5	-4.7	-1.7	-19.8	-36.0	-3.1	-27.8	-10.2	-6.8	-7.8	-4.9
Hungary	-22.0	-32.1	-20.0	-30.1	-3.1	-7.2	0.7	4.7	-26.9	-35.4	-29.4	-36.6	-0.6	-5.5	4.3	7.9
Latvia	-10.0	-29.5	..	..	..	..	-5.4	-4.9	-22.9	-37.7	-11.8	-31.0	-8.6	-8.5	-4.3	-1.3
Lithuania	1.6	-11.7	..	..	..	..	-6.5	-0.6	-18.4	-24.2	-5.8	-13.6	-1.0	-11.6	-12.5	-0.9
Poland	-1.9	-10.9	-3.7	-11.7	0.8	-1.3	1.0	2.3	-18.4	-28.6	-16.3	-25.8	4.9	1.9	-7.1	-5.5
Romania	5.6	11.2	9.1	16.1	0.1	-2.5	-3.3	-1.8	-1.9	4.6	0.8	6.0	2.2	0.1	-4.7	-1.4
Slovakia	..	..	..	..	1.1	4.1	4.3	6.1	..	..	..	..	3.7	5.6	-5.9	-1.1
Slovenia	-7.7	-10.4	-12.1	-12.6	3.2	3.2	1.7	-0.7	-13.0	-16.0	-20.5	-20.0	6.2	4.8	3.1	0.2
Russian Federation	1.5	-11.7	2.4	-13.7	-3.3	-3.5	2.6	6.1	-7.9	-19.2	-6.1	-20.5	-7.4	-7.3	6.0	9.7

Source: UNECE secretariat estimates, based on national labour force surveys, statistical yearbooks and direct communications from national statistical offices. Contained in UNECE (2003, p. 200). The labour force in 1985 is an estimate based on assuming that since no official unemployment existed, then the total number of those employed is also the size of the labour force.
Note: a Based on 2000 data and not 2001.

Table 26.2 Labour force participation by gender and location, PRC for selected years

	LFP by Gender and Location		
	1982	*1990*	*2000*
Total	78.7	78.8	76.9
Male	86.45	84.6	83.0
Female	70.56	72.6	70.6
Urban	77.8	75.7	65.9
Rural	78.9	79.9	80.6

Source: Maurer-Fazio *et al.* (2005) 'Economic Reform and Changing Patterns of Labor Force Participation in Urban and Rural China', *William Davidson Institute Working Paper*, Number 787.

By the second half of the 1990s, employment patterns had 'settled down', a point noted by the World Bank report (2000, p. 22). At the end of the 1990s and the start of the new millennium, both reports highlight two sides of the same coin: the fact that the age group 20 to 24 exhibited a low female share in total *employment* (*ibid.*), but that the female share in youth unemployment tended to be smaller than their share of total *unemployment* (UNECE, 2003, p. 201). Both reports attribute this in large measure to the higher percentage of females enrolled in higher education.

Unemployment in CEE and the FSU

Turning to unemployment (Table 26.4), at first glance the figures suggest that this was an issue primarily for men in the various transition countries in the 1990s. Indeed, the World Bank report states that for official unemployment data covering the years 1992, 1995, and 1998, ' … in nearly two-thirds of the countries in the region the increase was sharper for men, and in some countries considerably so' (*ibid.*, p. 20).

Acknowledging difficulties that exist with official unemployment data, the authors of the World Bank report go on to examine survey data between the two years 1995 and 1999: 'The trends that emerge are very similar to those described above. Poland, the Czech Republic, the Former Republic of Yugoslavia, and the Kyrgyz Republic are the only countries where female unemployment rates are higher than those of men' (*ibid.*, p. 20). There is one caveat added, where it is mentioned (and explained in more detail in a box) that non-employed women face a higher risk of being counted as inactive than their male counterparts.

The UNECE report takes this issue up in more detail. Directly linked to the question of activity rates, Hungary is given as one of the more extreme examples. Between 1985 and 1997 female employment fell by 1 million and yet the female share in total unemployment was less than 40 per cent, the lowest share of all the eleven transition economies that they study. In total, 135,000 women were officially unemployed in 1997, equal to 12.5 per cent of all the jobs lost by women between 1985 and 1997.

> This suggests that more than 900 thousand women left the labour market, the equivalent of more than one-third of the labour force in 1985. In fact in most of these economies there is a much larger withdrawal of women from the labour force once they become unemployed than is the case for men.
>
> *(UNECE, 2003, p. 142)*

327

Table 26.3 Male–female LFP by age category and urban–rural location[a] (per cent)

	Unmarried, Urban (Rural) Females			Married, Urban (Rural) Females			Unmarried, Urban (Rural) Males			Married, Urban (Rural) Males		
	1982	1990	2000	1982	1990	2000	1982	1990	2000	1982	1990	2000
15 to 22	72.7	60.2	46.4	86.7	86.2	69.3	70.6	59.6	43.8	97.2	98.9	96.4
	(84.3)	(73.1)	(67.3)	(85.6)	(91.2)	(85.3)	(78.3)	(69.3)	(67.0)	(99.2)	(99.4)	(99.2)
23 to 35	95.0	91.6	90.4	92.1	91.1	79.2	94.2	92.5	92.2	99.1	99.3	97.2
	(95.1)	(94.8)	(92.9)	(88.1)	(91.2)	(89.4)	(96.7)	(95.2)	(96.1)	(99.6)	(99.5)	(99.2)
36 to 49	80.9	83.9	78.2	83.2	87.4	74.5	88.3	92.2	85.6	98.7	99.0	94.9
	(72.4)	(83.9)	(86.4)	(80.3)	(88.0)	(88.5)	(93.7)	(93.9)	(92.9)	(98.9)	(99.2)	(98.6)
50 to 65	21.5	22.8	17.3	28.9	37.4	22.2	67.5	70.9	49.1	76.2	75.0	55.3
	(23.8)	(36.2)	(49.3)	(39.2)	(54.2)	(67.0)	(72.6)	(78.8)	(81.1)	(82.9)	(85.4)	(85.0)
Over 65	2.8	3.3	1.9	4.7	7.6	4.0	19.2	17.0	9.4	26.3	24.5	9.6
	(3.1)	(5.5)	(13.3)	(7.0)	(12.8)	(27.0)	(19.2)	(23.2)	(30.3)	(33.9)	(39.1)	(41.6)
Total	62.7	52.5	47.3	75.0	76.1	61.9	75.0	67.1	58.2	89.9	89.3	80.4
	(64.0)	(59.6)	(56.3)	(74.0)	(80.3)	(80.9)	(78.6)	(72.7)	(72.9)	(92.0)	(92.5)	(91.2)

Source: Maurer-Fazio *et al.* (2005) 'Economic Reform and Changing Patterns of Labor Force Participation in Urban and Rural China', *William Davidson Institute Working Paper*, Number 787.

Note: a It may seem odd that there appears to be a high percentage of LFP for the age categories 50 to 65 and 65 and over given that the retirement age for men is 60 and 55 for women. However, many face the necessity to continue working well into retirement. See OECD (2007) for further details of the pension situation in China. However, figures quoted within that document (table 5, p. 28) show that in 1990 the average pension as a percentage of GDP per capita and the average pension as a percentage of the average state owned enterprise wage was 94.1 and 67.7 per cent respectively. By 2005 these figures had dropped to 65.9 and 47.9 respectively. Further, the average pension coverage rate (defined as [contributors + recipients]/total population) was a mere 13.4 for the whole of China, although with large disparities between rural and urban areas (table 7, p. 30)

Table 26.4 Unemployment rates between the sexes (per cent)

Country	1992			1995			1998		
	Female	*Male*	*F/M*	*Female*	*Male*	*F/M*	*Female*	*Male*	*F/M*
Armenia	..	..	..	..	..	..	15	4.9	3.06
Azerbaijan	0.2	0.1	2.00	1	0.6	1.67	1.4	0.9	1.56
Belarus	0.7	0.2	3.5	3.3	2.2	1.50	..	..	
Bulgaria	..	..		16.8	16.2	1.04	..	..	
Croatia	20.1	14.8	1.36	..	..		12.1	11.9	1.02
Czech Republic	3	2.2	1.36	4.8	3.5	1.37	..	..	
Estonia	3.4	3.9	0.87	8.8	10.6	0.83	8.6	10.4	0.83
Hungary	8.7	10.7	0.81	8.7	10.7	0.81	7	8.5	0.82
Latvia	2.8	1.8	1.56	18	19.7	0.91	14.1	13.5	1.04
Lithuania	2.8	4.3	0.65	..	..		12.4	14.5	0.86
Macedonia, FYR	32.5	22.1	1.47	41.7	31.9	1.31	..	..	
Poland	15.5	11.9	1.30	14.7	12.1	1.21	12.3	9.1	1.35
Romania	10.3	6.2	1.66	8.6	7.5	1.15	6.1	6.5	0.94
Russian Federation	5.2	5.2	1.00	9.2	9.7	0.95	13	13.6	0.96
Slovak Republic	11.7	11.1	1.05	13.8	12.6	1.10	12.6	11.4	1.11
Slovenia	10.8	12.1	0.89	7	7.7	0.91	7.7	7.6	1.01
Tajikistan	0.4	0.4	1.00	2.1	1.9	1.11	..	..	
Ukraine	..	..		4.9	6.3	0.78	10.8	11.9	0.91
Uzbekistan	0.3	0.2	1.50	0.5	0.3	1.67	..	..	..

Source: International Bank for Reconstruction and Development/The World Bank: *Gender in Transition*, 2002, p. 20.

Thus little comfort should be taken from the relatively low unemployment rates for women relative to men. It appeared in many transition countries in the early to middle 1990s that men were bearing the brunt of unemployment, whereas this would not appear to have been the case, assuming that voluntary exit from the labour market by females did not predominate.

The Gender Wage Gap in CEE and the FSU

Whether under central planning or in market-based economies, women on average earn less than men. Given this, the issue during the transition period is not whether men earn more than women, it is whether the gap between the sexes has narrowed, stayed the same, or increased.

In addition, the absolute size of the differential between male and female wages, whether on average for the labour market as a whole, or by occupation or industry, may be the most important issue to the individual woman; but to economists it is the part of the difference which cannot be explained by the productivity characteristics of the individual that is of greater interest. In brief, if a man is paid more than a woman in a particular job because he is more productive owing to, say, a higher education, or innate ability, this is of no immediate concern from a market perspective or, indeed, perhaps, from society's point of view as the difference in earning power is justified.[6]

In order to calculate the part of the differential not due to individual characteristics, typically the differential is 'decomposed' into an explained and an unexplained part. The explained part is due to things such as educational attainment, age, work experience; whereas the unexplained part is assumed to be either discrimination or unobserved productivity characteristics of, in this case, the male worker. The size of the unexplained differential is usually taken as a measure of discrimination. Thus, there can be a large gap between male and female wages, but with only a small part due to the unexplained part of the decomposition. Alternatively, one can have a small absolute wage differential, but with most of this due to the unexplained part, i.e., to discrimination.

In Table 26.5 we report data on the gender wage gap in selected transition countries for various years. In this table the gap is presented as a ratio such that a ratio close to one indicates a low gap in earnings between the sexes whereas a low ratio indicates the converse.

After reviewing the evidence Newell and Reilly (*ibid.*, p. 14) concludes that, ' ... in general, the gap in pay between men and women in the transitional countries remains low by international standards'. However, as conceded by the authors and pointed out by others such as Jurajda (2005) the relative stability of the earnings gap may have been 'softened' by the exit from the labour market of women with low levels of human capital. These tended to be the lowest paid workers and so selection effects may have given a 'boost' to the perceived performance of women's earnings within the labour market vis-à-vis men's earnings. Further, Jurajda (2005), reporting other surveys, comments that while Newell and Reilly found the earnings gap to be stable over time, others find a dramatic rise in wage inequality and some a decrease in the gap *dependent* on the countries surveyed.

Two forces would appear to have been at work during the early transition period: the one mentioned above, i.e., female labour force exit either to unemployment or more likely inactivity, which helped to diminish the observed gender wage gap; and secondly, an increase in wage dispersion from the compressed state under communism, which tended to increase the gender wage gap given the predominance of females in lower paid jobs in contrast to the position of males. Little wonder different studies found varying results given that *a priori* there was nothing to suggest that these two forces would be the same in all transition countries.

As to the composition of the gender wage gap, Jurajda (2005, p. 599) comments:

> A typical finding in this literature is that gender differences in productive characteristics can 'explain' only a small part of the wage gap. Hence, within-job wage discrimination and gender segregation are likely to be important in transition economies. Alternatively, there is a large difference in the relative unobservable labor quality of employed women and men.

The gender wage gap in the PRC

Cai *et al.* (2008, p. 188) notes that there have been two forces at work: one which has been narrowing the gender wage gap and the other which increases it. Education over time has acted to narrow the gap, but not as much as unobserved skills or discrimination has done to widen it within China. Summarising the work to date, they report that Knight and Song (2005), using data from the China Household Income Project (CHIP), found that for urban data in 1988, less than 50 per cent of the difference in pay can be explained by observable characteristics. Cai *et al.* (2008) further report the work of Liu *et al.* (2000) and that of Gustafsson and Li (2000). The former researchers, using two data sets covering Shanghai and Jinan, find that gender pay differences widen as one moves from the state sector to the collective or private sectors. The latter authors, using CHIP urban household data, report that between 1988 and 1995 the female/male earnings ratio declined modestly from 0.844 to 0.825.

Table 26.5 Monthly gender pay ratios in transitional economies for selected years (female wage as fraction of male wage)

Country	Year	Ratio
Czech Republic	1987	0.661
	1992	0.730
	1996	0.813
Hungary	1986	0.743
	1992	0.808
	1996	0.789
Poland	1985	0.737
	1992	0.790
	1996	0.790
Slovakia	1987	0.661
	1992	0.733
	1996	0.782
Bulgaria	1990	0.740
	1995	0.700
	1997	0.691
Romania	1994	0.786
	1996	0.760
Slovenia	1987	0.870
	1991	0.905
	1996	0.869
FR Yugoslavia	1995	0.899
	1996	0.888
	1997	0.884
Estonia	1997	0.750
Latvia	1997	0.799
Lithuania	1997	0.650 (manual)
	1997	0.710 (non-manual)
Russia	1989	0.709
	1992	0.685
	1996	0.695
Ukraine	1996	0.777
Kazakhstan	1996	0.723
Kyrkgystan	1995	0.733
	1996	0.730
	1997	0.720
Uzbekistan	1995	0.805

Source: Newell and Reilly (2001) 'The Gender Pay Gap in the Transition from Communism: some empirical evidence', *Economic Systems*, 25 (4) and references contained therein.

Conclusions

The above information paints at first a seemingly contradictory picture of transition in the 1990s from the perspective of women. While the World Bank report does not downplay the difficulties experienced by women, the impression left is that compared to the difficulties that men experienced, there was no overall dominant trend of females being – in all transition countries and at all times during transition – at an overwhelming disadvantage compared to men; transition might have been difficult but it was difficult, more or less, for both sexes.

Indeed, Standing (1996, see Chapter 9, *The Impact of Restructuring on Women*) – admittedly looking only at one transition economy, albeit the very important one of the Russian Federation, *and* focusing on manufacturing industry – writes, ' … contrary to expectations, between 1991 and 1994 women were not marginalized in Russian industry, at least not in terms of their share of employment'.

The UNECE paper above, along with others such as Ruminskay-Zimny (2002) have, however, highlighted the gender asymmetry within the labour market as regards processes that tended to disproportionately affect women within the labour market in the first period of transition.

While this contribution has concentrated on the first period of transition, from the perspective of hindsight, EBRD (2007, p. 70) states, 'In conclusion, while women *may* have fared worse in the early years of transition and took longer to adjust to changes, they have been catching up with men' (emphasis added).

However, while there may be some discussion of how women have fared within respective labour markets, if one looks at the position of women from a societal view point then, at the very least, there have been major changes to the status, position, and role within transition economies of women, and these have not always been to their advantage.

Not covered here is the evolution of poverty during the first period of transition, and how this might affect single (mainly female) parents or female-heads of households. Likewise, the abrupt decline in fertility in many transition countries, along with a re-examination by some transition societies of female reproductive rights was beyond the limited scope of this piece. Other important issues not included here were: the growing (or perhaps simply more open?) discrimination faced by women pre- and post-entry into the labour market; the huge increase in female trafficking for the sex industry in Western Europe; and the dramatic reduction in female roles in the political process during the first period of transition.[7] On a more positive note, we also left out any examination of the growing role of female entrepreneurs in transition and former transition economies, albeit facing many practical obstacles; and the role of higher education, still benefiting many more women than men.[8] We leave these issues for later reporting.

Notes

1 As an example, and commented on by Sobotka (2002): 'In the Czech Republic, about half of the first marital births were conceived before marriage during the 1980s … In Poland, 49% of first children were born within 9 months following the marriage in 1990' (Footnote 9, page 9). And further, ' … in the 1990s, a sharp fall in the TFR (total fertility rate – *PL*) shifted the position of Eastern Europe on the European fertility map from the 'highest fertility' to the 'lowest fertility' region within one decade'

2 As noted by Rhein (1998, p. 353) the male breadwinner model, 'assumes that women are in fact nurturers by nature and interested in caring for children. It assumes that in changing times, men should be the economic providers for the family. And finally, it assumes that there is indeed a man to turn to for economic support.' It is true that in the mature market economies of Western Europe and North America after the Second World War, there was an increasing tendency for dual-earner households as the market economies grew and the need for more labour increased as a result of the drawing of many women into the workforce. However, the degree of female labour market participation was never quite on the same scale as the socialist countries and many of the jobs occupied by women tended to be part-time jobs as opposed to the predominantly full-time jobs under the socialist economic system. Finally, as has been increasingly noted there is yet another evolving trend in many countries of females – educated and financially secure – who never marry or marry at a much later age than hitherto. The rise of single occupancy households of both males and females is thus another possible variant, aside from the male breadwinner model or the dual-earner model.

3 The UNECE (2003) report covers the countries of Bulgaria, Czech Republic, Estonia, Hungary, Latvia, Lithuania, Poland, Romania, Slovakia, Slovenia and the Russian Federation. The data sources are from 'UNECE secretariat estimates, based on national labour force surveys, statistical yearbooks, and direct communications from national statistical offices', source note under all data tables in Chapter 7 of the UNECE (2003) report. Depending on the table, data can cover the period before the start of transition (1985) or after transition commences (1994) with comparison dates going to 1997 and in some cases to 2001.

The World Bank (2002) has as its Europe and Central Asia region, the former countries of the Soviet Union: Russia, Ukraine, Belarus, Moldova, Latvia, Lithuania, Estonia, Armenia, Azerbaijan, Georgia, Kazakhstan, Kyrgyz Republic, Tajikistan, Turkmenistan and Uzbekistan. Central and Eastern Europe consists of: Poland, Czech Republic, Slovakia, Hungary, Albania, Bulgaria, Romania, Slovenia, Croatia, Former Yugoslav Republic of Macedonia, Bosnia and Herzegovina, Serbia and Montenegro and Kosovo. The report uses as its primary data sources, World Bank databases, and the UNICEF Transmonee database. This is supplemented with data from labour force surveys, Living Standard Measurement Surveys, Demographic and Health Surveys, and country censuses. Referring to the first two primary databases, the World Bank report (2002, p. 2) notes that, 'These databases reply primarily on official data supplied from government statistical offices. They are predominantly administrative data and have come under increasing scrutiny in recent years, especially in the area of human development indicators, as the findings of an increasing number of household surveys have questioned their reliability'. The report uses various years in its tables – 1992, 1995, 1998, etc. – with 1999 appearing to be the most recent year used.

4 By way of international comparison, the authors, citing Szafran, (2002, Table 1, p. 32) give LFP rates of 77 and 53 per cent for men and women in the USA for 1982 and using the ILO Year Book 1983 give LFP rates in 1982 for men and women of 80 and 48 per cent in Japan, 71 and 44 per cent for South Korea, 83 and 30 per cent for Brazil, 87 and 13 per cent for Pakistan. For France in 1983, figures of 69 and 42 per cent are given.

5 The Russian Labour Flexibility Survey was launched in late 1991 when the USSR as an entity still existed. It focused on manufacturing in three Russian Oblasts and the field work involved the visiting and questioning of managers within factories. As such this was not a household labour force survey. The first round covered 503 industrial firms and covered a workforce of 529,250 people in Moscow City, Moscow Region, and St Petersburg. The surveys in July 1993 included Nizhny Novgorod and the survey of July 1994 included Nizhny Novgorod and Ivanovo. See Chapter 3 of Standing (1996, pp. 32–62) for more details.

6 We write the word 'perhaps' since if females within any society have deliberately had access to education curtailed for, say, cultural or religious reasons then the differential is not fair from society's point of view. The potential of the individual female has been stunted through no fault of their own but because of institutional norms, whether they be formal or informal; the individual female loses out, but so too does society in a reduced contribution to what could have been contributed by the female to society; there is a cost to the individual and one to society. The discrimination, however, is occurring not on the job but pre-entry, in the limited access to education. Other examples include society's attitude to childcare in the home. While work experience is a legitimate individual characteristic, which contributes to on-the-job productivity, and hence the wage of the individual, if society deems that women must be primarily responsible for the upbringing of children this will inevitably curtail the total amount of work experience and hence impact on the female wage. The individual owner of a firm will pay a wage according to the actual work experience of the female (along with any other productivity characteristics) but the female *could have had* more work experience if either society had prioritized the appropriate child care facilities (*à la* central planning) or the outlook of the partner of the female had been different (*à la* Scandinavian men). Again, the disadvantage to the woman is occurring off the job, in society at large.

7 To give but one example, 'From 1937 there existed an unofficial communist party policy to increase the number of women in political executive roles. This resulted in women accounting for 30 per cent of all deputies in USSR's Supreme Soviet Council and around 40 per cent in local Soviet Councils. This high figure for female representation existed until 1989 when these quotas were abolished.' (Metcalfe and Afanassieva, 2005b, p. 431) Notwithstanding this, it can be said of the former socialist regimes, that the elevation of a certain number of women to political roles was tokenism to demonstrate aspects of socialist ideology, rather than a genuine thrust of female involvement in the political process. It is a moot point as to whether the visibility of women at the (near) top of communist society

through token female representation pre-transition is more desirable than virtually no female representation during transition.

8 Space prevents us, however, from describing whether the highly educated nature of women in many transition and post-transition societies has also been reflected in corresponding wage levels. See, however, Newell and Reilly (1999). On female entrepreneurship in transition economies see the work of Aidis *et al.* (2007) and references therein.

Bibliography

Aidis, Ruta, Welter, Friederike, Smallbone, David and Isakova, Nina (2007), 'Female Entrepreneurship in Transition Economies: the case of Lithuania and Ukraine', *Feminist Economics*, vol. 13(2).

Cai, Fang, Park, Albert and Zhao, Yaohui (2008), 'The Chinese Labor Market in the Reform Era', in Brandt, Loren and Rawski, Thomas G. (eds), *China's Great Economic Transformation*, New York: Cambridge University Press.

EBRD (2007), *Transition Report 2007: People in transition*, London: European Bank for Reconstruction and Development.

Gorbachev, Mikhail (1987), *Perestroika: New thinking for Our Country and the World*, London: Collins Publishing.

Gustafsson, Björn and Li, Shi (2000), 'Economic transformation and the gender earnings gap in urban China,' *Journal of Population Economics*, vol. 13(2).

Jurajda, Štěpán (2005), 'Gender Segregation and Wage Gap: An East–West Comparison,' *Journal of the European Economic Association*, vol. 3(2–3).

Knight, John and Song, Lina (2005), *Towards a Labour Market in China*, Oxford: Oxford University Press.

Liu, Pak-Wai, Meng, Xin and Zhang, Junsen (2000), 'Sector Gender Wage Differentials and Discrimination in the Transitional Chinese Economy,' *Journal of Population Economics*, vol. 13(2).

Maurer-Fazio, Margaret, Hughes, James and Zhang, Dandan (2005), 'Economic Reform and Changing Patterns of Labor Force Participation in Urban and Rural China', *William Davidson Institute Working Paper*, Number 787.

Metcalfe, Beverly Dawn, and Afanassieva, Marianne (2005a), 'Gender, work, and equal opportunities in central and eastern Europe', *Women in Management Review*, vol. 20(6), pp. 397–411.

——(2005b), 'The woman question? Gender and management in the Russian Federation', *Women in Management Review*, vol. 20(6), pp. 429–45.

Momsen, Janet Henshall (2009), *Gender and Development*, London: Taylor & Francis.

Newell, Andrew and Reilly, Barry (2001), 'The Gender Pay Gap in the Transition from Communism: some empirical evidence', *Economic Systems*, vol. 25(4).

——(1999), 'Rates of Return to Educational Qualifications in the Transitional Economies', *Education Economics*, vol. 7(1).

OECD (2007), 'Pension Reform in China: Progress and Prospects', by Felix Salditt, Peter Whiteford and Willem Adema, Working Paper 53.

Pascall, Gillian and Anna Kwak (2005), *Gender Regimes in Transition in Central and Eastern Europe*, Bristol: The Policy Press.

Rhein, Wendy (1998), 'The feminization of poverty: Unemployment in Russia', *Journal of International Affairs*, vol. 52(1).

Ruminskay-Zimny, Ewa (2002), *Gender Aspects of Changes in the Labour Markets in Transition Economies*, United Nations Economic Commission for Europe.

Sobotka, Tomáš (2002), 'Ten years of rapid fertility changes in the European post-communist countries – evidence and interpretation', *Population Research Centre*, working paper series 02–1.

Standing, Guy (1996), *Russian Unemployment and Enterprise Restructuring – reviving dead souls*, Geneva: Macmillan Press.

Szafran, Robert (2002) 'Age adjusted labour force participation rates, 1960 – 2045', *Monthly Labor Review*, September, pp. 25-38.

UNICEF (1999), *Women in Transition*, MONEE Regional Monitoring Project No. 6. Florence: UNICEF.

United Nations Economic Commission for Europe (2003), *Some Aspects of Labour Market Performance in Eastern Europe and the CIS*, Economic Survey of Europe, No. 1.

World Bank (2002), *Gender in Transition*, Human Development Unit, Eastern Europe and Central Asia Region. Washington, DC: World Bank.

27

THE RURAL ECONOMY AND HOUSEHOLDS IN CHINA AND RUSSIA

A comparison

Michael Cuddy, Pauric Brophy and Hongmei Liu

Introduction

Dispersed population, or lack of population concentration, and heavy dependence on the primary sector are key factors in defining rural and its attendant endemic problems. Heavy dependence on agriculture with its low value added and declining terms of trade gives rise to low incomes per capita relative to non-farm activities. Low value added combined with productivity-enhancing technology gives rise to surplus labour and out-migration. Over a long-term horizon, changing technology, the evolving economic environment and policy intervention inexorably leads to a relative decline in the employment provided by the agricultural sector in most developed economies. The speed with which such structural adjustment takes place determines the level and extent of inequality between farm and non-farm and rural and urban households.

China and Russia were the two major societies that embraced communism as a political system and central planning as an economic mode of organization. The communist political system is still in place in China, although there are some interesting experiments in local democracy, while the central planning system has been gradually transformed over time toward a 'constrained' market economy. Both communism and central planning were simultaneously replaced by democracy and market capitalism in Russia in the early 1990s. The transition from a centrally planned system to a market system and from state/communal farms to private farms has been much more gradual and has extended over a much longer period in China than in Russia. In fact, the process was quite abrupt in Russia. Also the nature of the transfer of ownership/use of land from public to private has been quite different between the two countries.

These different approaches to the transition process have important implications for the rural economy and rural households. They influence the speed of structural change, which is part of the longer-term efficient sectoral allocation of resources, and thus the level and extent of income disparity between farm and non-farm and urban and rural households.

The aim of this contribution is to examine and evaluate the rural economy and the rural household in China and Russia under the still evolving transition process. The general political and administrative context within which the rural economy is developing is examined in the next section, followed by a statistical overview of the rural economy in both countries. The agricultural sector, which is normally the core of the rural economy, is examined next. The importance of non-agricultural activity and the sources of household income are then explored; finally, income disparities and migration are examined, prior to a short concluding section.

Political environment for economic development

The political and administrative system in China is communist, akin to what it was in the Soviet Union. There is a dual system: the Government structure, which includes the judicial, legislative and executive arms, extends from the national to the local level; there is the corresponding Communist Party structure, which includes the executive and legislative arms and the political arm, where the latter is synonymous with the legislative arm of government. The Party, in general, oversees all aspects of government administration. There is a relatively high level of autonomy at the provincial and local levels, although subject to central government legislation.

Some democratic processes have been introduced in recent years at the lowest administrative level. Six members of the seven-member village councils are democratically elected by its citizens, while one member is appointed by the Party. The village mayor is also elected by vote of the local citizens. At the national level, a meeting of the National Congress in 2002 agreed to broaden its membership to non-Party members, in particular the business community.

The transition process in rural China moved slowly through the 1970s, 1980s and into the 1990s. The breaking up of the communal or state farms into family household units began in 1978. The central government confirmed the land-use right for rural households for 15 years in 1983, then, lengthened this lease period to 30 years in 1993. In 2009 the central government made clear that the land-use right, obtained by farmers though contract with the village committee, will be permanent (Xu Xiaorui, 2011).

Four important institutional initiatives followed, which achieved the twin objectives of improving economic efficiency and at the same time not offending the centres of power (Qian, 2002). These four initiatives are: (i) a 'dual-track' approach which liberalized prices at the margin while retaining plan prices and quotas. This allowed producers to sell their excess production through the market once the plan targets were achieved; (ii) local governments were allowed to establish and operate enterprises, Township and Village Enterprises (TVEs), which were more efficient than state-owned enterprises (SOEs) and gave a greater share of value-added created to the local authorities, than would be the case with private enterprises; (iii) these TVEs generated funds for the local authorities, which were retained locally and used to stimulate local economic activity and provide local social infrastructure; and (iv) anonymous cash transactions were allowed and earnings and wealth could be hidden in anonymous bank accounts. This prevented the State from taking excessive amounts of privately earned money, which provided a huge local incentive to work and invest. By the mid-1990s, over 95 per cent of rural land belonged to the family household units for private use (rather than ownership), while the TVEs were predominantly transferred to private ownership.

The recent political and administrative experience in Russia has been quite traumatic. The Communist system of the Soviet period was replaced by a democratic system during the 1990s. The system of government, in principle, is somewhat akin to that of the US: there is a constitution, a President, who is elected by the people, with significant executive powers, and upper and lower houses of Parliament. There are regional and local governments, with chief executives and elected legislative bodies. Initially the chief executives were elected by popular vote. However, this was replaced by direct appointment by the President in 2005. Although the regional and local authorities are subject to the federal government, they have responsibility for certain functions, particularly in regard to the local planning and economic development. The central administrative system is structured according to the ministerial functions, which are exercised from the national to the local level.

However, despite this formal move to a democracy, the institutions required to support the working of the democratic process were only slowly put in place and still remain quite weak.

A privatization process had already commenced in Russia in 1990/91, towards the end of the communist period in the USSR. This process, mainly 'employee lease-buyout', was continued in Russia after independence and was replaced by 'mass privatization', based on the November 1990 Law of Land Reform, which was essentially completed over the period 1992–94. The privatization of state farms (*kolkhozes* and *sovkhozes*), which accounted for nearly 95 per cent of the land area, was completed over this period.

The brutal nature of the transition from the communist to the democratic system of government, combined with the massive privatization process (land, industrial and service enterprises and natural resources) led to a chaotic environment, where political influence was used to acquire economic ownership and control. The institutional structures capable of coping with private economic entities rather than state entities have only gradually adapted to the new demands.

Despite being elected to better the social and economic wellbeing of their citizens, heads of local authorities used the administrative areas under their jurisdiction as personal fiefdoms, the economic spoils of which could be used for personal enrichment, to be shared with their local business or personal associates (Cuddy and Gekker, 2002). The chaotic privatization process and its aftermath, combined with a drastic reduction in government expenditure, led to a cumulative decline in economic activity. Between 1991 and 1998 industrial output and agricultural output had declined by 42 per cent and 62 per cent, respectively (Thiromirov, 2000). In addition, the drop in value-added creation and the failure of the central government to put in place an effective tax collection system left government coffers empty and the consequent impoverishment of public service institutions. The old system of control was unable to adapt to the new demands and the putting in place of a new system could only take place over an extended period of time.

In contrast to China, the Russian local authorities had great difficulty extracting taxes from the newly created private enterprises. At the same time revenues generated at the local level were taken over by the regional or federal government. Consequently, there was no incentive to create additional local revenues or to create a positive environment for local enterprise, as the local authorities benefited little from the success of private business. Zhuravskaya (2000) suggests that local governments in Russia generally over-regulated business in contrast to their Chinese counterparts who actively promoted entrepreneurial activity.

Despite the achievements of Vladimir Putin (inaugurated as President of Russia in 2000) in rescuing the country from economic anarchy and re-establishing order and centralized control, the market environment is still quite hostile, with considerable risk involved in any private business venture. Although, a considerable amount of legislation has been passed in order to create a supportive market environment, the implementation and enforcement of this legislation is very often rudimentary. The current problems in Russia relate to extremely weak or non-existent institutional structures, which will require a considerable period of time to evolve.

A statistical overview

Overall, China is economically less advanced than Russia. Its GDP per capita is €2,485 compared to €8,953 for Russia (UNDP, 2010). China is four times more dependent on agriculture for employment of the labour force than Russia (Table 27.1). Industry is relatively less important and services are considerably less important in China than in Russia. Public services are, in particular, much more important in Russia than in China. The share of value added in the agricultural sector is low compared to the corresponding employment share in both countries, indicating the relatively lower incomes to workers in the agricultural sector in both countries. However, the position of the agricultural sector is relatively worse in China than in Russia. On the other hand, the earnings in the industrial sector in China are relatively better than in Russia.

China is considerably more dependent on the rural economy than Russia in terms of the percentage of the population, which lives there: 54.3 per cent in China versus 27 per cent in Russia (Table 27.2). The income per capita in rural areas in China is 30 per cent of that in urban areas while in Russia the corresponding figure is only 16 per cent. However, the income per capita in rural China is only about half that in rural Russia.

The sectoral structure of the rural economy is quite different between the two countries. There is a very high engagement in agriculture in China relative to Russia, a higher level of engagement in industry and a considerably lower engagement in services (Table 27.3). Off-farm employment provided by TVEs is very important in supplementing farm incomes in China, as will be shown below.

Taking the percentage of the workforce engaged in agriculture as an indicator of the level of economic development, the divide between the two countries is quite evident. On the other hand, the high dependence on agriculture in China indicates the very significant potential redeployment of labour into urban areas and alternative economic sectors, thus contributing to economic growth in China.

Agriculture

The areas of arable land in China and Russia are almost exactly the same at 122.5 and 123.4 million hectares, respectively (Table 27.4).[1] Given that the population in China is almost 10 times

Table 27.1 Sectoral shares (%) of GDP in China and Russia, 2008

Sector	China		Russia	
	Labour	*GDP*	*Labour*	*GDP*
Agriculture	39.6	11.3	10.0	4.2
Industry	27.2	48.6	31.9	33.8
Services	33.2	40.1	58.1	62.0

Source: NBSC, 2010; *Goskomstat*, 2011.

Table 27.2 Share of population and income per capita in rural and urban economy of China and Russia, 2008/09

	China		Russia	
	Population share	*Income per capita (€)*	*Population share*	*Income per capita (€)*
Rural	54.32	560	27.0	1015
Urban	45.68	1866	73.0	6336

Source: Derived from Goskomstat of Russia, 2011; National Bureau of Statistics of China, 2010, Zvyagintsev *et al.* (2007) and World Salaries, 2008.

Table 27.3 Sectoral shares of employment in rural China (2006) and Russia (2003)

	China	Russia
Agriculture	56.8	36.6
Industry	26.0	22.2
Services	17.2	41.2

Source: Adapted from NBSC (2010) and Bogdanovskii (2008).

Table 27.4 Total arable land area and land area per capita in China and Russia 2010

	China	Russia
Total arable land and permanent crops (Mil. Ha)[a]	122.5	123.4
Land area per capita (Ha)[b]	0.092	0.870
Land area per person engaged in agriculture (Ha)[b]	0.315	12.394

Source: a FAO (2010); b Derived from land area and data in previous tables.

that of Russia, the land area per capita in Russia is almost 10 times that in China. Also, given that China has a much higher percentage of its workforce engaged in agriculture, the result is that the land area per person in agriculture in Russia is nearly 40 times that in China. However, although the household distribution of agricultural land in rural China is quite equitable, it is quite the opposite in Russia.

The communal farms in China (the communes) created under the communist regime were broken up following a government decision in 1978. Family farms were created with each household being allocated land on the basis of the family size. Farmers were initially required to sell part of their harvest to the state at a fixed price and the remainder could be sold on the open market. This was subsequently replaced by a system of taxes, which was removed completely through legislation, which came into effect on 1 January 2006. Although the land is still formally in collective ownership, farmers now hold 30-year leases on the 'use' of the land. This land use privilege can be inherited or traded on the land market.

The state farms in Russia, which comprised the major part of Russia's agricultural land, were privatized in the early 1990s. They were originally vested in the farm workers, including the farm manager, pensioners and social service workers, all with an equal share. These farms operated initially as a form of workers' co-operative. Members of the co-operative were allowed to leave and take their land share of the farm. Only a relatively small number initially took this route. The majority of shareholders leased their land share to the enterprise (Serova, 2003). The lease of land shares became even more important after 1998. While approximately 5–6 per cent of farmland shares change between users annually, this is now predominantly among the large enterprises. On the one hand, farm land is transferring from financially weak or bankrupt farms to financially strong farms and, on the other, there are investors from outside of agriculture, agribusiness (distribution, factor inputs, use of outputs – vertical integration) and oil, gas and financial institutions, who are investing in the more profitable farms. Some of these companies lease up to 300,000 hectares each in several regions. Thus there is an increasing concentration in land use. Although the predominant corporate form of the farm enterprise is like a production co-operative (46 per cent), the more successful are joint stock companies or farms that have a strong manager.

The household 'subsistence' plot in Russia is a carry over from the Soviet period of the small family land holding for self-sufficient food production. In some cases, this household plot has been increased by adding a 'share' from the farm enterprise (the privatized state farms), which has been taken in the form of land. These individual farms now engage in commercial production.

Only 4.5 per cent of the arable land area of China is in State farms, with 95.5 per cent in individual family farm units (Table 27.5). The average size of the individual farm is about 0.67 ha (Eastwood *et al.*, 2004). In Russia, 86.1 per cent of the land is in 'farm enterprises'. The average size of these farms is about 5,000 ha. The individual farms account for about 7.9 per cent of the land area with farms which have an average size of about 50 ha. The household plots account for 6 per cent of the farmland with an average size of about 2 ha.

Despite the large share of the land area in farm enterprises, the output of these farms accounts for less than 50 per cent of the value of Russian agricultural production (Figure 27.1). Indeed, private household plots, with only 6 per cent of the land area, have challenged these large farms for the biggest share of total production. The share of output (by value) from the individual farms seems to have plateaued at less than 8 per cent, corresponding to its share of land area farmed.

Three factors explain this seeming anomaly. First, the financially stronger farms in Russia, approximately 40 per cent of all farms, produce 70 per cent of the total value added (Uzun, 2001). Indeed, at the very upper end, 7 per cent of farm enterprises account for nearly 50 per cent of the sector's sales. Second, the agricultural enterprises are engaged in extensive production in contrast to the highly intensive nature of production on the private household plots.

Table 27.5 Land use share (%) by type of farm in China and Russia (2000)

Type of farm	China	Russia
State-owned	4.5	
Farm enterprise		86.1
Individual farm	95.5	7.9
Household plot		6.0

Source: Adapted from National Bureau of Statistics of China (2010) and Serova (2003).

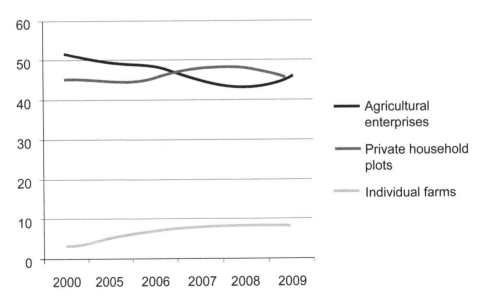

Figure 27.1 Share of agricultural output (value) in Russia by farm type, 2000–09
Source: Derived from *Goskomstat* (2010).

Thirdly, it is also partly explained by the higher unit value of output on the private household plots, for example vegetables and fruits. Nevertheless, the agricultural enterprises dominate production of the principal agricultural commodities in Russia, producing, for example, about 85 per cent of grains and over 75 per cent of sunflower seed (USDA, 2005). In 2003 private farms accounted for 14.4 per cent of Russia's total grain production (up from 6.8 per cent in 1995), 21.8 (10.9) per cent of sunflower seed, and 10.1 (4.0) per cent of sugar beet. Private household plots produce 93 per cent of the country's potatoes and 80 per cent of the vegetables, either for personal consumption or for sale in local markets.

Despite the fact that both countries have comparable arable land areas, agricultural production, across the top 20 products in both countries, is 8 times higher in China than in Russia (Table 27.6). This is because of the sheer human intensity of production on very small production units. Indicative of this is the fact that the top three agricultural commodities in China are pig-meat, rice and vegetables, which are intensively produced, in contrast to the top three in Russia, cow milk, wheat and beef, which are extensively produced. The fact that the number of persons engaged in agriculture in China is 66 times that in Russia and that output in China is only eight times that of Russia, suggests that the higher levels of technology used in the extensive production and land productivity in Russia have been able to narrow very significantly the gap that might otherwise exist on the basis of relative numbers engaged.

According to Huang and Pieke (2003), more capital intensive production combined with a decline in demand for agricultural produce has led to an increase in the underemployment or surplus labour in rural China from 33 per cent in 1988 to 60 per cent in 2000. However, under the *hukou* registration system introduced in the mid-1950s, peasants and their children (except

Table 27.6 Value of agricultural production in China and Russia by main products

Rank	China		Russian Federation	
	Product	*$m*	*Product*	*$m*
1	Pigmeat	47774	Cow milk	7822
2	Rice	36561	Wheat	6670
3	Vegetables	23807	Beef	3629
4	Hen eggs	19298	Potatoes	2829
5	Wheat	15806	Chicken meat	2319
6	Chicken meat	12957	Pigmeat	2034
7	Beef	12069	Hen eggs	1770
8	Cotton	11134	Sunflower seed	1549
9	Asparagus	10120	Sugarbeet	1318
10	Garlic	9706	Tomatoes	459
11	Cow milk	9535	Apples	421
12	Apples	8574	Vegetables	417
13	Potatoes	8486	Barley	394
14	Tomatoes	8035	Cabbages	337
15	Maize	6959	Onions	316
16	Groundnuts	6754	Sheep meat	308
17	Watermelons	6657	Currants	274
18	Cabbages	5178	Cucumbers	191
19	Tobacco	5172	Garlic	175
20	Spinach	5112	Rye	168
Total value		269694		33400

Source: FAO, 2010.

in certain circumstances) were not allowed to become city dwellers.[2] So migration was restricted, creating a very significant labour pool in rural areas.

Although the farm enterprises have shed labour, there is still a significant excess of labour on the Russian farms. While all farms are shedding labour, the outflow from insolvent farms is most marked, where insolvent farms have less than half the labour force of solvent farms of comparable size.

Non-agricultural activity and income sources

Employment in the agriculture sector is considerably more important in rural China than in Russia (Table 27.7). Employment in industry is broadly similar in both countries. Employment in commercial services is very similar in the two countries. The big difference is in the share of employment in the social services, which is considerably more important in Russia than in China, 28.3 per cent versus 1.7 per cent. This is because social services in rural China are generally very poorly developed with only limited state support. For example, basic education is financed mainly from household savings (Wang and Moll, 2010). Health services must, also, be paid for from rural household savings (Gustafsson and Li, 2004).

One of the important outcomes in the development of rural China has been the emergence of TVEs in the 1980s. These were enterprises established and managed by the town and village councils, primarily for the benefit of the local community. Profits from these enterprises were spent on growing the enterprises or on local social infrastructure. Although still so called, they are now mostly privatized. What remains in the hands of local administrations is mainly in the limited social services. Over 75 per cent of rural non-agricultural enterprises in 2008 were TVEs.

The harsh transformation of Russian rural society, which began in the early 1990s, is still working itself out. The privatization of the state farms has led to a very significant shedding of labour and the ancillary economic and social activities, which were internalized within the state farms during the Soviet period. These services which were shed are now developing as private entities or are being provided by the state. Consequently, the share of agricultural employment is rapidly declining while industry, trade and consumer and social services are increasing (Figure 27.2).

Table 27.7 Sectoral composition of rural employment in China and Russia

Sector	%		
	China		Russia
Agriculture	56.8		36.6
Non-Agriculture			
- *Township and Village Enterprises*	32.7		
- *Private and self-employed individuals*	10.5		
Industry		22.8	22.2
Construction		3.2	
Transport and storage		2.5	13
Wholesale and retail		7.9	
Hotels and catering		2.5	
Social Services		1.7	28.3
Other		2.5	
Total		100.0	100.0

Source: Adapted from *China Labour Statistical Yearbook*, 2009, and Bogdanovskii (2008).

Household income sources are quite different between the two countries as might be suggested by the sectoral composition of employment. However, some additional insights emerge. Dependence on agriculture is confirmed by the fact that 64 per cent of rural household income in China comes from household operations, primarily agriculture (Table 27.8). Twenty-eight per cent of income comes from wages and salaries, which are mainly in the non-farm sector. Transfers account for only 6 per cent of household income and these are predominantly through family remittances.

It is interesting to note the rapid growth in rural household income in China over a twenty-year period, by almost a factor of six over this period (Figure 27.3). Indeed, there has been almost a doubling of rural household income since 2000. These increases are driven by increases in food prices, raising the returns from household operations, and from increases in wages and salaries from non-agricultural activities.

The household income structure is very different in Russia where 58 per cent of household income comes from salaries, 41 per cent from non-farm and 17 per cent from farm sources (Table 27.9). The 17 per cent from farm sources arises from the salaried employees of the privatized state farms. While it is obvious that a very large percentage of rural households generate income from their household plots (91 per cent), it is surprising that 90 per cent of farm

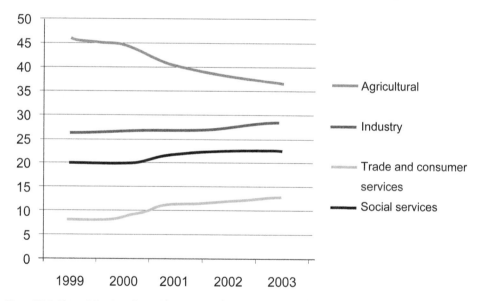

Figure 27.2 Share (%) of rural employment by sector in Russia, 1999–2003
Source: Derived from Bogdanovskii (2008).

Table 27.8 Structure of rural household income in China, 2008

Source	%
Household operations	64
Wages and salaries	28
Transfers	6
Property income	2
Total	100

Source: NSBC, Rural Household Survey, 2010.

Table 27.9 Structure of rural family income in Russia

Source	Share of income (%)	Share of households (%)
Income from household plot	17	91
Salaries from agricultural employment	17	90
Salaries from non-agricultural employment	41	
Salaries from off farm self-employment	2	18
Transfers	18	66
Other income	5	42
Total	100	

Source: Derived from Zvyagintsev *et al.* (2007).

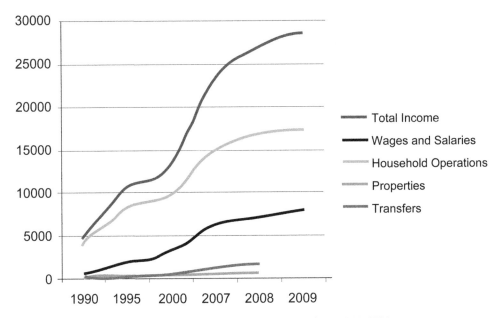

Figure 27.3 Total rural household income and its components in China, 1990–2009.
Source: NSBC, Rural Household Survey, 2010.

households have some sort of salary income. It is clear that a large part of the non-farm salaries come from employment in the social services while the second major component comes from industrial employment. It is also noteworthy that 66 per cent of rural households receive transfers of some sort, mostly from the state, in contrast to China. Finally, although accounting for only a small percentage of household income, 18 per cent of households are engaged in off-farm self-employment.

Income disparities and migration

The UN Gini indices[3] for China and Russia, respectively, are 46.9 and 39.9 (UNDP, 2010). Since incomes per capita in urban areas in both countries are multiples of the incomes per capita in rural areas, this significant difference in Gini indices is explained primarily by the large percentage of the population in rural China compared to rural Russia (Gustafsson *et al.*, 2007). The difference in Gini indices is mitigated by the fact that the urban/rural income divide is much smaller in China compared to Russia (a ratio of 3:1 versus 5:1). Whereas the Gini index is similar in urban areas in China and Russia, it is higher in rural China than in rural Russia. One of the big contributors to rural income disparities in China is off-farm income (Benjamin *et al.*, 2004, Cuddy *et al.*, 2008). Rural households with off-farm incomes have consistently higher incomes than those without any off-farm income. Given the continuing divergence between farm and non-farm incomes (Figure 27.4), this latter will be a continuing source of inequity between urban and rural and between those rural households with and without non-farm income.

A particular factor in Russia, which gives rise to declining regional and rural economic circumstances, is the former spatial distribution of industry, which was determined by political decisions rather than considerations of economic advantage. Market forces are now sweeping away those industries which are in non-competitive locations and sectors.

Public policy has contributed to income inequality in China and to greater equality in Russia. The first example is through income transfers. The rural population in China is not covered by pensions whereas the urban population is; all citizens are eligible for pensions and social welfare in Russia. In addition, the Chinese urban population has obtained housing subsidies whereas the rural population is not afforded the same privilege. Transfers are very important in rural Russia: transfers are received by 66 per cent of rural households and, on average, account for 18 per cent of rural household income (Zvyagintsev *et al.*, 2007). Transfers account for only 6 per cent of rural household income in China and these are primarily remittances from family members working in the cities.

Whereas rural industrialization in China is an important factor in closing the urban/rural income gap in China, this is not the case in Russia. However, a system of 'fiscal federalism' in Russia helps to redistribute regionally the revenues from localized natural resources, thus reducing the interregional and urban/rural income inequality (Mahler, 2011).

Although household income is the most important element in determining the standard of living of rural households, access to social services provided by the state is also extremely important. The introduction of the 'household responsibility' system in China in 1978 pushed

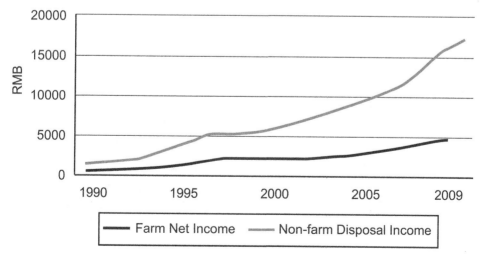

Figure 27.4 Disparities in farm and non-farm incomes in China
Source: Lijuan (2010), www.china.org.cn/opinion/2010-02/03/content_19362162.htm.

responsibility for education and healthcare onto the individual. This situation has effectively continued in China up to the present time (Gustafsson and Li, 2004). Something similar happened in Russia following the break up of the state farms, particularly with respect to healthcare. Also, throughout the 1990s, the weak public finances particularly affected the provision of health and education services and rural areas were most seriously affected. These difficulties have now been largely resolved with respect to the education sector. However, a significant reform of the health service has led to a hybrid system, which is a combination of central finance and health insurance (Gordeev, 2009). However, there is no distinction between the treatment of urban and rural areas with respect to the provision of education and health services and so this is not a contributing factor to disparities between urban and rural Russia.

The upshot of urban/rural income disparities is a migration from rural areas to urban centres. Despite the existence of local registration systems, the *hukou* in China and the *propiska* in Russia, migration continues to be one of the major demographic phenomena in China and Russia. Traditionally the migration movement in China was from the rural West and Central regions to the urbanized East. In general, this continues to happen but migration flows have also been heavily influenced by political encouragement for migration to ethnic minority regions in order to ensure political and social stability. Thus, whereas migrants as a share of the provincial population are highest in Beijing, Shanghai and the highly urbanized province of Guandong, they are also high in the Uygur province of Xinjiang (Figure 27.5). The major outmigration is now from the Central region, the main beneficiary being the East region and to a far lesser degree the West region.

Internal migration in Russia has been traditionally from the more rural east of the country to the more urbanized west. However, most rural regions in Russia are losing population to the urban centres. This internal migration in Russia has been compounded by the inflow of ethnic Russians from the countries of the former Soviet Union (Figure 27.6). The government has been quite successful in curbing both these migration flows through external and internal controls. However, some of this success may be due to an upturn in the internal local economies and external economies, post 1998.

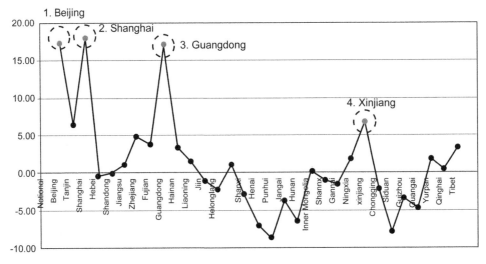

Figure 27.5 Net Migration to population by Province (2000)
Source: Bao (2008), with permission.

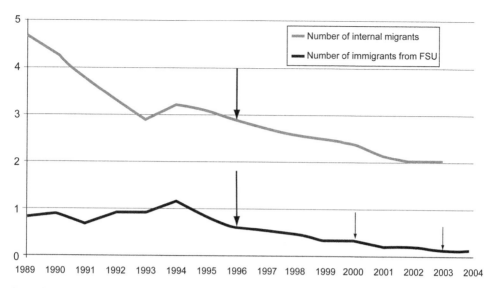

Figure 27.6 Migration flows in Russia and the impact of legislative restrictions
Source: Andrienko, Y. and Guriev, S. (2005), with permission.
Note: Arrows show changes in legislation.

Conclusion

China is in transition from a centrally planned to a 'constrained market economy' with some level of democratization at the lower administrative levels of the communist political system. Russia is in transition from a communist to a democratic political system and from a centrally planned economic system to a market driven system. Whereas the transition has been taking place in China over a very long period, the change in the political and economic systems in Russia was very abrupt, while the institutions supporting these systems have been adapting to these radical changes. The systemic transformations in both China and Russia, and their relative speeds, have had an important impact on the rural economy and rural households, which are central to long term structural change and sectoral resource allocation in these countries.

The two countries were at different stages of development at the beginning of the transition, with Russia already quite industrialized and, therefore, far less dependent on the rural economy and the primary sector than China. However, the political decision to break up the communal farms in China into individual extremely small private plots has important consequences for the efficiency of production and the long-term viability of farm households, in the absence of alternative income sources. In contrast, the state farms in Russia were not broken up but were mostly transferred into private ownership as going concerns. Although many of these farms have not yet achieved financial sustainability, a strong land market is gradually moving bankrupt farms into alternative viable corporate ownership. The potential shown by these farms which have achieved financial viability augurs well for agricultural production and efficiency in Russia. However, increasing numbers of rural households are becoming employees of corporate owners rather than farm holders. A special feature of rural Russia is the ownership by all households of the 'household plot'. The intensive cultivation of these plots has acted as a safety net for rural households during the more turbulent years of the transition.

Despite the very intensive cultivation of the family farm in China, only a subsistence livelihood can be realized from the farm alone. The TVEs heralded new income opportunities for

347

rural households in off-farm employment. Initially in public control, these enterprises have gradually moved into private ownership in a constrained market environment. In the absence of social welfare transfers, this off-farm income makes the difference between poverty and a more comfortable existence in rural China. Income from off-farm employment is the major factor influencing income inequality in rural China. Rural households in Russia live in far less precarious circumstances: most households have salaries from farm or off-farm activities; most households cultivate the household plot and two-thirds have some income transfer from the state. Consequently, there is a much higher level of income equality in rural Russia than in rural China. A further factor influencing the relative living standards in rural China and Russia is the access to social services. Whereas the access to education and health in rural Russia is primarily through state provision, in China rural households must pay for these services out of savings.

The inevitable migration from rural to urban areas due to living standard inequalities has been mainly from West to East in China and from East to West in Russia. Although migration in China has been essentially internal, in Russia there has also been significant migration from the former republics of the Soviet Union to Russia. The strong rural/urban migration is likely to continue in China, given the disparities in living standards between urban and rural areas and the low potential for agriculture in raising rural household income levels. However, this is likely to be influenced by government policy, which is currently addressing the urban/rural imbalance in a meaningful way. Developing urban centres in the more rural provinces, in order to stem migration to the East coast cities, is likely to be an important element in the policy mix. Government policy is also likely to continue to direct population flows to provinces with high levels of ethnic minorities.

Although Russia has taken some successful initiatives in curbing migration from external and internal sources, the same level of migration pressure does not exist in rural Russia as in China. Also, there is greater potential for labour absorption in rural Russia, as the current financially distressed farms gain financial viability through improved management, credit injections, and new ownership. This labour absorption can come from on-farm employment owing to expanded production and from off-farm employment in the food processing sector.

The challenges facing rural China and Russia derive from the stage of development of these economies when the transition process began, from the transformation process and the speed of the transformation. It is clear that the challenges facing rural China are far greater than those facing rural Russia, mainly because of the enormity of the rural population in China. However, the constrained market system and the continuing central political control are likely to favour China in addressing these challenges in the coming decades.

Notes

1 Arable land in China dropped dramatically from 130 million hectares in 1996 to about 122 million hectares in 2008 owing to rapid urbanization and natural disasters (*China Daily*, July 5, 2011).
2 The rule has been ignored at times when urban centres wish to increase their labour pool and it is re-imposed or enforced in times of high unemployment.
3 The Gini Index is the Gini Coefficient multiplied by 100. The Gini Coefficient is a measure of inequality derived from the Lorenz curve, which plots the cumulative share of the population, from lowest to highest income, against the cumulative share of income. The higher the Gini Index the greater the level of inequality.

Bibliography

Andrienko, Y. and Guriev, S. (2005), 'Understanding migration in Russia – a policy note', No. 23, *CEFIR Policy Paper Series*, Moscow.

Bao, S. (2008), 'The inter-regional migration in China', *China Data Centre*, http://chinadatacenter.org. Ann Arbor: University of Michigan.

Benjamin, D., Brandt, L. and Giles, J. (2004), 'The Evolution of Income Inequality in Rural China', *Working Paper* No. 654, William Davidson Institute, Ann Arbor: University of Michigan.

Bogdanovskii, V. (2008), 'Rural and Agricultural Labor Markets,' in Z. Lerman (ed.), *Russia's Agriculture in Transition: Factor Markets and Constraints on Growth*, Lanham. MD: Lexington Books, Chapter 7.

Cuddy, M. and Gekker, R. (eds) (2002), *Institutions and their change in transition economies*, Ashgate, London.

Cuddy, M., Liu, H. and Paulos G. (2008), 'Factors influencing poverty levels in rural households in Southwest China'. *Working Paper* No. 0136, Economics Department NUI, Galway.

Eastwood, R., Lipton, M. and A. Newell (2004), 'Farm size', Paper prepared for Volume III of the *Handbook of Agricultural Economics*, Brighton: University of Sussex.

FAO (2010), *Food and agricultural commodities production*, http://faostat.fao.org/

Gordeev, V. (2009), 'Analysis of the financial reforms in the Russian healthcare sector'. Paper read at *7th World Congress on Health Economics, Harmonising Health and Economics* 12–15 July, Beijing.

Goskomstat (2011), *Russia in Figures*, www.gks.ru/wps/wcm/connect/rosstat/rosstatsite.eng/

Gustafsson, B., Li, S. and Nivorszhkina, L. (2007), 'Understanding why household incomes are more unequally distributed in China than in Russia', Paper read at *International Conference on Experiences and Challenges in Measuring National Income and Wealth in Transition Economies*, Beijing, September 19–21.

Gustafsson, B. and Li, S. (2004), 'Expenditures on education and health care and poverty in rural China', *China Economic Review*, vol. 15(3).

Huang, P. and Pieke, F. (2003), 'China migration country study', Conference paper for *Regional Conference on Migration, Development and Pro-Poor Policy Choices in Asia*, 22–24 June 2003, Dhaka, Bangladesh.

Lijuan, Z. (2010), www.china.org.cn/opinion/2010–02/03/content_19362162.htm

Mahler, C. (2011), 'Diverging fortunes: recent developments in income inequality across Russian regions', *Opticon 1826*, Issue 10 (Spring).

National Bureau of Statistics of China, (2009), *China Labour Statistical Yearbook 2009*, November, Beijing: China Statistics Press.

——(2010), www.stats.gov.cn/english.

——(2003), *Statistical Communique 2002*, February 28, Beijing: National Bureau of Statistics.

——(2002), *Agricultural Census Communique 2 & 3*, Beijing: National Bureau of Statistics.

——(2010), *Rural Household Survey*, Beijing: National Bureau of Statistics.

Qian, Ying Yi, (2002), 'How Reform Worked in China', *William Davidson Working Paper*, No 473, Ann Arbor: University of Michigan Business School.

Serova, E. (2003), 'Evolution of the farm structure in Russia's agriculture: background and perspectives', mimeo, *Analytical Centre AFE*, Moscow.

Thiromirov, V. (2000), 'The second collapse of the Soviet Economy: myths and realities of the Russian reform', *Europe-Asia Studies*, March.

UN (2010), United Nations Statistical Division 2010, unstats.un.org/unsd/demographic/products/socind/inc-eco.htm.

UNDP (2010), *Human Development Report 2010*, New York: UNDP.

USDA (2005), 'Russia: agricultural overview', *Production Estimates and Crop Assessment Division*, Washington, DC: Foreign Agricultural Service.

Uzun, V.Y. (2001), 'Organisational Types of the Agricultural Production in Russia' in *The markets of production factors in Russia's agriculture*, Moscow: AFE

Wang, H. and Moll, H. (2010), 'Education Financing of Rural Households in China', *Journal of Family and Economic Issues*, vol. 31(3), pp. 353–60

World Salaries (2008), www.worldsalaries.org/total-personal-income.shtml.

Xu Xiaorui (2011), 'The analysis about rural economic development of China today', *Special Zone Economy*, Beijing (in Chinese).

Zhuravskaya, E. (2000), 'Incentives to provide local public goods: fiscal federalism, Russian style', *Journal of Public Economics,* vol. 76(3), pp. 337–68.

Zvyagintsev, D., Shick, O., Serova, E. and Lerman, Z. (2007), 'Diversification of rural incomes and non-farm rural employment: evidence from Russia', paper read at the *104th Joint EAAE-IAAE Conference on Agricultural Economics and Transition: what was expected, what we observed, the lessons learned.* Budapest, Hungary.

28

LABOUR MARKETS AND LABOUR MARKET INSTITUTIONS IN TRANSITION ECONOMIES[1]

Hartmut Lehmann and Alexander Muravyev

Introduction

This chapter concerns the evolution of labour markets and labour market institutions and policies in the countries of Central and Eastern Europe as well as of Central Asia over the last two decades. As the dynamics of labour market outcomes in these transition economies (TEs) have drawn considerable attention already in the early years of transition and resulted in a voluminous literature easily available elsewhere, we only provide here a brief summary of the topic. Instead, we focus on the much less explored issue of the evolution of labour market institutions, which are among candidate explanations for the very diverse trajectories of labour markets in the region. We consider recent contributions that attempt to assess the effect of labour market institutions on labour market performance of TEs, including the policy-relevant issue of the complementarity of institutions.

Labour market dynamics

The transition from plan to market, which countries of Central and Eastern Europe (CEE) as well as of Central Asia TEs embarked on in the late 1980s to early 1990s, implied profound changes in their labour markets. Until the late 1980s, most of these economies, apart from Yugoslavia, were characterized by large excess labour demand, no open unemployment and high labour force participation. For example, estimates of the actual unemployment in the USSR show numbers of the order of 1 to 2 per cent and the available statistics on employment show employment ratios among those aged 15–59 being as high as 83.6 per cent in the late 1980s. These very high employment rates and close to zero open unemployment came, however, at a price as extremely low labour productivity and substantial labour hoarding were pervasive features of the centrally planned economy (Granick, 1987).

The start of the transition saw a rapidly collapsing demand for labour. In part, it was a consequence of the inefficient use of labour resources during the central planning period, which became apparent once market forces were released in TEs. More importantly, it reflected the collapse of output that TEs were facing in the late 1980s and early 1990s. Indeed, from the start of transition in 1989 until the resumption of economic growth, these countries lost from between one-fifth and more than two-thirds of their pre-transition level of GDP (EBRD, 2000). Figure 28.1 illustrates this pattern. For presentational purposes, we distinguish between Central European economies (CEE),[2] south-eastern European (SEE)[3] economies and the Commonwealth of Independent States (CIS),[4] and compare them with the EU-15 and the US. Figure 28.1 shows a relatively modest and short decline in GDP in CEE occurring in the early 1990s and a much deeper and longer recession in CIS. SEE countries stand out as the region impacted by the conflict in the former Yugoslavia. Overall, at the end of the 1990s, robust economic growth came back to all the regions and remained until the 2008 financial crisis. During this period, TEs were growing faster than both the EU-15 and the US.

How did the labour markets of TEs respond to these dramatic changes in GDP? In general, the adjustment of the labour markets following the initial transition shock occurred with falling employment rates, rising unemployment, reductions in working hours, and decreasing real wages – the whole gamut of the available adjustment mechanisms. However, these different mechanisms played out with different intensity in the various transition regions (Svejnar, 1999). In particular, during the early transition, CEE experienced falling employment rates and growing unemployment, accompanied by a modest decline in real wages. The former Soviet Union (FSU) instead saw collapsing real wages with relatively limited rises in at least, official rates, of unemployment and falls in employment (Boeri and Terrell, 2002).[5] Figures 28.2 and 28.3 provide some support for this point. Despite a much more dramatic decline in GDP, employment in CIS fell less than in CEE while the unemployment rate remained lower than in CEE until the late 1990s. SEE experienced a large decline in employment and high unemployment, but this was largely

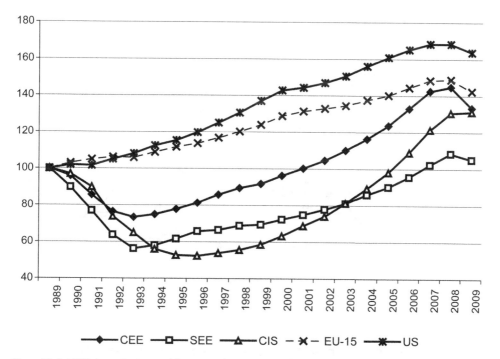

Figure 28.1 GDP dynamics in transition countries, EU-15, and US
Source: EBRD and OECD databases.
Notes: Unweighted averages for TEs and EU-15.

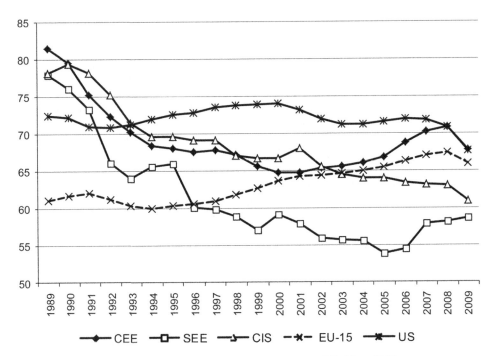

Figure 28.2 Employment-to-population ratios in transition countries, EU-15, and US
Source:TRANSMONEE and OECD databases.
Notes: 15-64 for EU-15 and 16-64 for US. Unweighted averages for TEs and EU-15.

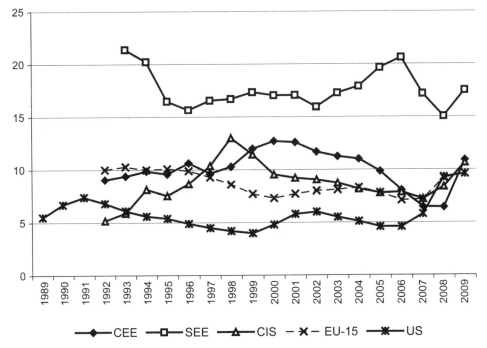

Figure 28.3 Unemployment rates in transition countries, EU-15, and US
Source: TRANSMONEE and OECD databases.
Notes: Unweighted averages for TEs and EU-15.

owing to the wars in the former Yugoslavia since the unemployment and employment dynamics in Bulgaria and Romania, not affected by the conflict, are quite similar to that in CEE.

Interestingly, the resumption of economic growth in CEE in the mid-1990s was not accompanied by increasing employment and falling unemployment. For example, Poland and Slovakia, while growing fast, experienced large declines in employment and increases in unemployment, which approached 20 per cent in the early 2000s. Only since then has there been a steady increase in the employment rate and a decline in the unemployment rate in CEE. CIS countries, which grew very fast between the late 1990s and 2008, did not, on average, see any increases in employment. It mostly remained flat (Kyrgyzstan, Russia, Ukraine) or even declined (Armenia, Georgia, Moldova) despite the robust economic growth in the region. The unemployment rate in CIS nevertheless saw some decline after its peak in the late 1990s. As for SEE, some upturn in employment occurred in the mid-2000s, albeit it remains rather low and unemployment very high in the region (except for Bulgaria and Romania).

Presented at the level of the three large country groups, the data suggest considerable heterogeneity in the evolution of labour markets in transition countries over the last two decades. The differences are even larger if one avoids aggregation and examines separate countries. The countries of CIS then appear by far the most diverse in terms of economic development and labour market dynamics, with increasing heterogeneity in the most recent years. On one side of the spectrum, there are resource-rich countries like Russia and Kazakhstan with modest, single-digit unemployment rates and a high employment rate (above 70 per cent). On the other side there are low-income countries like Armenia and Tajikistan, with higher unemployment and a very low employment rate (below 50 per cent as of 2009). Indeed, the recent data provide some support to the view expressed in Rutkowski and Scarpetta (2005) that a divide is emerging between labour markets of high- and upper middle-income European transition countries, particularly in CEE, and of low-income countries, especially those of Central Asia:

> Labour markets in European transition economies in many respects resemble those in developed economies of Europe, in both positive (for example, productivity growth) and negative aspects (for example, high and stagnant unemployment). In contrast, labour markets in low-income CIS countries seem to become similar to those in other low-income countries, with typical characteristics such as the dominant informal sector, underemployment, and low productivity employment.

Labour market institutions and policies

The diverse and often unconventional patterns of labour market adjustment in TEs have caused scholars and policy-makers to look for institutional explanations of these different labour market outcomes.

The set of labour market institutions that TEs had at the beginning of transition was rather atypical of mature market economies, but has changed considerably over the last 20 years. In the late 1980s, workers still felt well protected from unemployment in most parts of the region, but the protection stemmed from excess demand for labour, rather than from institutions such as employment protection legislation, an active role of trade unions regarding workers' rights, or unemployment benefits.[6] In fact, many of such labour market institutions and policies were simply missing. It was not until the late 1980s when, against the background of looming unemployment, TEs engaged in an active development of specific institutions and policies in order to ensure an effective functioning of labour markets. Two decades after the start of the transition process, most countries have established sets of labour market institutions and policies, similar to those existing in mature market economies.

Below we focus on the evolution of key labour market institutions and policies in transition countries over the last two decades and compare them with the respective institutions and policies in the EU-15 and the US. Similarly to studies of OECD economies, the focus is on employment protection legislation (EPL), union density, coverage and bargaining, the tax wedge on labour, the duration of unemployment benefits, the average replacement ratio and expenditures on active labour market policies (ALMPs).

Employment protection legislation

There is some debate in the literature concerning the evolution of employment protection in TEs over the two last decades. To a large extent, the debate stems from the lack of a commonly agreed measure of employment protection, which reflects the general difficulty of measuring institutions.[7] Some sources suggest that during the early transition period, employment protection in many countries, especially those of CIS and SEE, was quite tough, reflecting socialist legacies. These rigid regulations were subsequently liberalized over the course of transition, albeit to different degrees in different countries. However, a new study by one of the authors of this contribution suggests a more nuanced picture. For the case of the ex-USSR states, Muravyev (2010) shows that essential rigidities to national labour laws, such as restrictions on the use of fixed-term contracts and large severance payments, were not inherited from the Soviet time, but were rather introduced in the late 1980s to early 1990s, at the early stage of transition, when governments attempted to combat looming unemployment. The evolution of labour regulations thus followed an inverted U-shaped pattern with the peak of rigidity occurring in the 1990s.

Most sources nevertheless suggest liberalization of labour laws in TEs in the last decade, often quite dramatic as in the case of Georgia and Kazakhstan (Muravyev, 2010). As a result, most transition countries are in the middle of the labour market flexibility scale, at least as judged by the existing estimates based on the OECD EPL methodology (Venn, 2009).[8] Figure 28.4a illustrates these dynamics for the three regions. The data show considerable declines in EPL in SEE and especially CIS between 1995 and 2007, although not in CEE. Overall, TEs as a group now appear to be quite similar to EU-15. Still, in terms of EPL, of all TEs only Georgia is close to the USA, which has one of the most liberal sets of labour market laws in the world.

Union density, coverage and bargaining

Although trade unions (with almost universal membership) existed already at the time of the planned economy, in most countries (with the notable exception of Poland) they were *de facto* an integral part of the Communist party and state apparatus, transmitting policy directives to the workforce (Borisov and Clarke, 2006). It is fair to say that TEs did not have a system of industrial relations typical of mature market economies and such a system was only gradually taking shape during the first decade of transition. Perhaps the clearest manifestation of this development is the decline of unionization rates to the levels observed in mature market economies. Figure 28.4b illustrates this development.

Overall, CEE countries have achieved a more visible progress in establishing a system of industrial relations typical of Western democracies. For example, the effectiveness of trade unions in promoting the economic interests of their members increased already in the 1990s, although some scholars argue that even in CEE, industrial relations can be considered still in a process of flux.

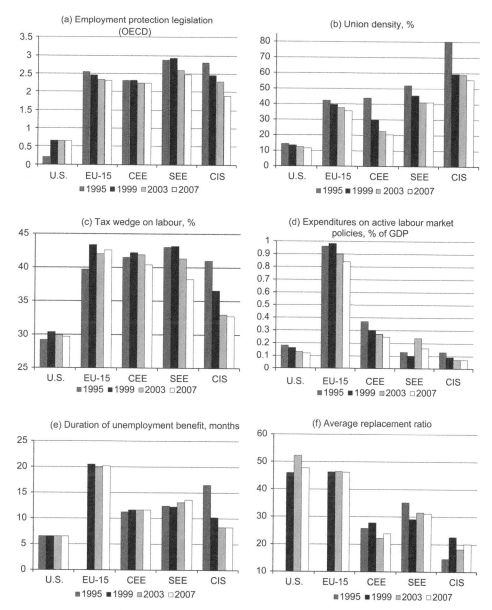

Figure 28.4 Labour market institutions by region (1995–2007)
Source: Lehmann and Muravyev (2010).

The picture emerging in CIS can be illustrated by looking at Russia. According to formal criteria, by the mid-1990s the country had an established system of industrial relations, characterized by a high unionization rate, multi-level collective bargaining, a high coverage rate, and a very high degree of coordination among both employees and employers (Cazes, 2002). More recent and more careful examinations of the country's industrial relations system, however, have revealed that many of the institutions created in the 1990s remained more like a form without content. In particular, decisions of the tripartite commission have no legislative status under Russian law and are therefore not binding; general agreements usually contain many purely declarative provisions, and violations of these agreements are typically left without sanctions (Borisov and Clarke, 2006). It is nearly impossible to define and classify wage co-ordination mechanisms in the Central Asian transition countries.

The tax wedge on labour

The early transition period was characterized by relatively high taxation of labour, especially in the form of high payroll taxes. By the early 1990s, TEs had progressive personal income taxes, although the highest marginal rates were generally below those in EU-15. A number of reforms, aimed at reducing the tax wedge on labour, which can be thought of as the difference between take home pay and the labour cost to the employer, were introduced since then. The most notable reform was the introduction of flat personal income taxes in most TEs, following the pioneering example of Estonia in 1994. However, the tax burden on labour has remained rather high in Central Europe, though not in most of the other transition countries. This can be seen in Figure 28.4c. Indeed, despite some reduction between 1999 and 2007, the tax wedge on labour in CEE is just a little below that in EU-15. In contrast, SEE and in particular the CIS have managed to reduce the tax wedge considerably. It is also noteworthy that the tax wedge is far lower in the US than in the other four regions.

Unemployment benefits

At the start of transition, even if substantial unemployment rates were foreseen, the governments, especially in Central Europe, adopted fairly generous unemployment benefits schemes mainly out of political considerations.[9] These were subject to cuts, sometimes dramatic, in the 1990s as the governments struggled to keep budget discipline in the face of a considerable and largely unanticipated decline in output. These cuts concerned both the unemployment insurance replacement rates and the maximum potential duration of unemployment benefit payments.

Figure 28.4e, f show benefit durations and the average replacement rates. CEE and SEE have maximum durations of roughly one year, whereas the CIS exhibits the shortest durations in the transition region. Compared to the EU-15 and the US, replacement rates are not very generous in CEE and the CIS, while SEE has somewhat higher rates. The EU-15, in contrast, combines long maximum duration with relatively generous unemployment benefit levels, while the USA has the shortest maximum duration of benefits combined, however, with a relatively high replacement rate.

Active labour market policies

While active labour market programmes have been introduced throughout the region, their share in GDP has been lower than in the old member states of the EU and substantially lower in SEE and the FSU. The EU-15 on average spends roughly one per cent of GDP on ALMP, while all transition regions spend far less (Lehmann and Kluve, 2010). Especially in the CIS, governments spend very little on such policies.

Minimum wages

Non-trivial minimum wages existed in some countries before the start of the transition process. For example, in the USSR, the ratio of minimum to average wage (the Kaitz index) was about 38 per cent in 1985. In the 1990s there was a remarkable erosion of minimum wages in CIS countries, with the Kaitz index falling below 10 per cent in some countries. In contrast, the level of minimum wages in CEE countries has been maintained at a much higher level. In the early 2000s, CEE and SEE had minimum wages around 40 per cent of the average wage.

Institutions as determinants of labour market performance

The evidence on how labour market institutions and policies have affected labour market outcomes in Eastern Europe and Central Asia is scarce. This is mainly caused by data constraints, especially regarding the early stages of the transition process. For example, it was only in the early 2000s when the first cross-country data on the stringency of labour regulations in the region appeared. In general, the quality of data is better in the new member states of the EU, and declines southwards and especially eastwards. The countries of Central Asia have by far the worst availability of data on labour market performance and labour market institutions.

As a result, most of the existing studies of labour market institutions in transition countries are based on data from the new member states and/or adopt a partial approach by focusing on particular institutions and policies, often within a particular country. A major problem of many studies that focus on specific institutions is thus that they do not allow for general equilibrium effects and interactions between institutions, a key issue in the modern literature on the institutional determinants of labour market performance. There is only a handful of cross-country studies that attempt to analyse the role of labour market institutions, including Cazes and Nesporova (2003), Fialova and Schneider (2009) and Lehmann and Muravyev (2010), which rely on standard linear regression models as in, e.g. Nickell (1997). Of these studies, most use data from OECD or EU-15 countries augmented with data from a handful of transition countries (typically, the Czech Republic, Hungary, Poland and Slovakia); to date, Lehmann and Muravyev (2010) remains the only study that provides a comprehensive analysis of over 20 TEs, which also looks at interactions between different institutions and policies. We, therefore, focus on the results of this work, drawing on other evidence when appropriate.

The impact of institutions on labour market performance in isolation

We organize our discussion of the impact of labour market institutions on labour market outcomes around Table 28.1, which gives a non-technical summary of the empirical evidence presented in the study by Lehmann and Muravyev (2010). Important insights are gained by looking at several measures of labour market performance, in this special case, at the employment rate, the unemployment, long-term unemployment and youth unemployment rates.

Table 28.1a shows which institutions impact on the four measures of labour market performance when each institution is looked at individually. EPL has a very strong negative impact on the employment rate and a strong positive effect on the youth unemployment rate. Therefore, on average, stricter employment protection legislation seems to reduce the employment rate in transition countries and increase youth unemployment. This result is in line with theoretical considerations: stricter EPL protects incumbent workers but firms are reluctant to hire new labour market entrants, thus possibly depressing overall employment and increasing youth unemployment. The empirical evidence on the impact of EPL presented before our study was based on more limited data with respect to the set of transition countries and to time, and is also rather contradictory and inconclusive and thus not very useful in buttressing the validity of the results shown in the first row of Table 28.1a.

Increasing expenditures on ALMP only seems to lower the youth unemployment rate according to the second row of Table 28.1a. This is not that surprising given how little

Table 28.1a Institutions and labour market outcomes (Lehmann and Muravyev, 2010)
  Panel 1. Baseline results.

	Employment rate	Unemployment rate	Long-term unempl. rate	Youth unempl. rate
EPL	—	0	0	++
ALMP	0	0	0	—
TAX	-	0	0	0
DENS	-	0	0	0
BEND	0	0	0	0
BENF	0	0	0	0

Note: -, – and —: negative impact and significant at the 10%, the 5% and the 1% significance levels, respectively; ++: positive impact and significant at the 5% significance level.

Table 28.1b Panel 2. Interactions between institutions and their complementarity

	Employment rate	Unemployment rate	Long-term unempl. rate	Youth unempl. rate
ALMP_TAX	0	Comp★★	Comp★★	0
ALMP_DENS	0	Comp★★	Comp★	Comp★★
ALMP_BENF	0	0	0	0
ALMP_BEND	Comp★★	0	0	0
ALMP_EPL	0	Comp★	Comp★	Comp★★
EPL_TAX	0	0	0	0
EPL_DENS	0	0	0	0
EPL_BENF	0	0	0	0
EPL_BEND	0	0	0	0
TAX_DENS	0	0	0	0
TAX_BENF	0	0	0	0
TAX_BEND	0	0	Comp★★	Comp★★★
DENS_BENF	0	0	0	0
DENS_BEND	0	0	0	0
BENF_BEND	0	0	0	0

Note: Comp★★★, Comp★★, Comp★: Complementary at the 1%, 5% and 10% significance levels, respectively.

transition countries spend on these policies and given that many governments, especially in CEE and SEE, have tried to fight the high incidence of youth unemployment by concentrating expenditures on this group of the unemployed. Overall unemployment and long-term unemployment do not seem affected by ALMP.[10] These general equilibrium results that are achieved with data covering most TEs and most of the transition period are corroborated, at least in part, by the microeconometric and macroeconometric evaluation literature on ALMP in transition countries summarized in Lehmann and Kluve (2010). For ALMP measures to work at the individual level, careful targeting is required; in addition, there seems to exist a hierarchy of measures with respect to their effectiveness: job brokerage and retraining and further training seem particularly promising in that they increase the average likelihood of a participant to find regular employment. Wage and job subsidies applied in TEs produce mixed results, while public works are nearly unanimously considered detrimental to a participant's chances to gain regular employment because of stigmatization or benefit churning mechanisms. The general equilibrium effects in individual countries produced by earlier macroeconometric work, on the other hand, are rather inconclusive since, e.g., in a low unemployment country, like the Czech Republic in the 1990s, researchers have found increased outflows from unemployment caused by increased expenditures on ALMP, while an insignificant impact was found in Poland where unemployment has been notoriously high throughout the transition period.

The third significant determinant of labour market performance is the tax wedge on labour. As we can see in the third row of Table 28.1a, an increase in labour taxation will lower the employment rate but will not affect the unemployment measures. This is in line with previous empirical evidence insofar as all previous studies that focused on TEs unambiguously hint at the detrimental effect of high taxation on labour market performance. However, in some studies increasing the tax wedge raises unemployment, in others it lowers employment and participation levels. When one looks at the average impact of the tax wedge across most TEs as is done in our study, the demand for labour seems to be the most important channel through which the tax wedge operates, since the employment rate will be strongly co-determined by labour demand while the three types of unemployment should be driven predominantly by labour supply decisions.

The fourth institution that has some impact on labour market performance in TEs is union density. Countries where more workers are enrolled as members of a trade union have on average a lower employment rate. Some corroborating, albeit relatively weak, evidence can be found in Ederveen and Thissen (2007) who show that higher union density increases unemployment. Unfortunately it was impossible to find data on collective bargaining for all TEs. Studies that analyse the impact of collective bargaining on labour market performance for a subset of transition countries in general find a positive impact.

The last two institutions shown in Table 28.1a, the duration of unemployment benefits and their level, do not have any effect with respect to all four measures of labour market performance. This result is very much in line with earlier evidence as Commander and Heitmueller (2007) as well as Ederveen and Thissen (2007) find no effect of the duration and generosity of unemployment benefits on unemployment. The apparently weaker link between unemployment benefit systems and labour market performance if compared to OECD countries can be explained, at least in part, by the low job creation capacity of most transition countries over most of the transition period. In other words, labour supply mechanisms are relatively unimportant when analysing outflows from unemployment as has been well demonstrated for example in the case of Hungary by Micklewright and Nagy (2010).[11] Analysing the impact of institutions on labour market performance in isolation, three of the six institutions and policies, namely EPL, tax wedge and ALMP seem to be of particular policy relevance implying, e.g. in the case of the tax wedge and EPL, that the liberalizing agenda promoted by the Bretton Woods institutions has some merit.[12]

The complementary nature of labour market institutions and policies

We finish our analysis by looking at what happens when institutions interact with each other. Some researchers suggest that institutions and policies interact in a systematic fashion and thus act in a complementary way when reforms of several institutions are tackled simultaneously. Complementarity can be explained with a classic example shown in Nickell (1997), discussing the level of unemployment benefits. *Ceteris paribus*, a high level of unemployment benefits should imply a higher unemployment rate, but when interacted with a short duration of these benefits and large expenditures on ALMP, generous unemployment benefits might result in better labour market performance. For OECD countries, several studies have pointed at this complementary interaction of institutions.[13] Lehmann and Murvayev (2010) is to date the only study that looks at the issue of reform complementarities in transition countries. They augment the baseline regression equation such as in Nickell (1997) with pairwise interactions of labour market institutions and policies for the full sample of transition countries. Their results are briefly discussed here.

Raising expenditures on ALMP will have a stronger impact on unemployment and long-term unemployment if the labour market is characterized by a relatively low tax wedge (row 1 of Table 28.1b). This result is intuitively quite plausible. If, for example, an ALMP measure targeted at the long-term unemployed is meant to rebuild their human capital, such a measure will result in larger outflows into employment if labour is taxed less. A similar argument can be made with the interaction of ALMP and EPL. ALMP measures are meant to make the unemployed fit for unsubsidized regular employment. If EPL is relatively unregulated, firms will be more willing to hire from the unemployment pool, a result that is shown in row 5 of Table 28.1b. The complementary effect of lowering the tax wedge and shortening benefit duration also seems to us rather convincing. According to row 12 of Table 28.1b, this complementarity will boost outflows from long-term and youth unemployment. It is these results that are particularly interesting from a policy point of view as they imply that broad reform packages that tackle more than one institution or policy will result in better labour market performance than reforming only one institution at a time.

Conclusions

The above analysis documents considerable heterogeneity in the evolution of labour markets in TEs over the last two decades, especially at the level of separate countries. The countries of the CIS appear by far the most diverse in terms of economic development and labour market dynamics, with increasing divergence in the most recent years.

The set of labour market institutions that TEs had at the beginning of transition was rather atypical of mature market economies, but has changed considerably over the last two decades. There has been considerable liberalization of labour regulations in TEs, more pronounced than in the old EU member states. By now, most TEs have established sets of labour market institutions and policies, which are similar to those existing in mature market economies.

A growing literature suggests the importance of labour market institutions in the determination of labour market outcomes in TEs. This is particularly true of EPL, the tax wedge and ALMP. Overall, data from TEs suggest that deregulation of labour markets improves their performance. There is also substantial evidence from TEs that reforming two institutions jointly or applying broad reform packages will generate larger benefits than a partial reform focusing on a single labour market institution.

This brief review leaves untouched several important issues that might have strong impacts on labour market dynamics in TEs. This is particularly true of inter-country (undocumented) migration and informal employment, which have apparently been more pronounced in transition than in OECD countries. The evidence on these phenomena in TEs remains scarce; it is still to be seen how they interact with and shape labour markets in transition countries.

Notes

1 The authors thank Paul Hare and Gerard Turley for valuable comments and suggestions. Financial support from the Volkswagen Foundation within the project 'The Political Economy of Labour Market Reform in Transition Countries: A Comparative Perspective' is also gratefully acknowledged.
2 The Czech Republic, Estonia, Hungary, Latvia, Lithuania, Poland, the Slovak Republic and Slovenia.

3 Albania, Bosnia and Herzegovina, Bulgaria, Croatia, Macedonia, Montenegro, Romania and Serbia.

4 Until recently, the CIS included 12 out of 15 constituent republics of the former USSR, namely Armenia, Azerbaijan, Belarus, Georgia, Kazakhstan, Kyrgyzstan, Moldova, Russian Federation, Ukraine, Tajikistan, Turkmenistan, and Uzbekistan, with Georgia officially leaving the organization in August 2009.

5 Non-standard mechanisms of labour market adjustment became widespread in CIS in the 1990s. These included wage arrears, forced leaves, reduction in working hours and in-kind payments in lieu of cash wages (Lehmann *et al.*, 1999; Earle and Sabirianova, 2002).

6 With respect to open unemployment, the former Yugoslavia seems to be the only important exception. For example, Macedonia suffered from double-digit unemployment rates as early as the late 1970s.

7 The most known indicators of employment protection are the OECD EPL indicator and the 'Employing workers' index from the Doing Business database.

8 This is especially true if an assessment of the rigidity of labour laws takes into account the issue of law enforcement, which is quite lax in many countries, especially in the former USSR (Gimpelson *et al.*, 2010; Rutkowski and Scarpetta, 2005).

9 For example, in Poland the strong political position of 'Solidarity' allowed the Mazowiecki government in December 1989 to introduce layoffs in labour legislation only in tandem with the introduction of a very generous unemployment benefit system that in its first, albeit short-lived, version did grant open-ended benefits to anybody, even if the person had no previous work experience.

10 Lehmann and Muravyev (2010) do find negative effects of ALMP on overall unemployment and long-term unemployment. However, given the small number of observations used in their macroeconomic regressions these effects are not significant at conventional levels.

11 The design of unemployment benefit systems, very different when we compare CEE and the CIS, had an important impact on labour market performance at the *beginning* of the transition, though (Boeri and Terrell, 2002). Relatively generous benefits in CEE created a wage floor that made labour costly, leading to large layoffs, which resulted in a rapid rise of unemployment. At the same time it caused a high reservation wage implying a 'stagnant' unemployment pool. In the CIS, having not very generous benefit provisions, no such wage floor existed, resulting in wage adjustment rather than employment adjustment. A more moderate rise in unemployment and larger outflows from unemployment were the consequences according to Boeri and Terrell (2002).

12 We do not discuss the effect of minimum wages on labour market performance, since there are no cross-country studies covering the majority of TEs that allow any generalizing inferences.

13 One such study is Bassanini and Duval (2009).

Bibliography

Bassanini, Andrea and Duval, Romain (2009), 'Unemployment, Institutions, and Reform Complementarities: Re-assessing the Aggregate Evidence for OECD Countries', *Oxford Review of Economic Policy*, vol. 25(1), pp. 40–59.

Boeri, Tito and Terrell, Katherine (2002), 'Institutional Determinants of Labor Reallocation in Transition', *Journal of Economic Perspectives*, vol. 16(1), pp. 51–76.

Borisov, Vadim and Clarke, Simon (2006), 'The Rise and Fall of Social Partnership in Postsocialist Europe: the Commonwealth of Independent States', *Industrial Relations Journal*, vol. 37(6), pp. 607–29.

Cazes, Sandrine (2002), 'Do Labor Market Institutions Matter in Transition Economies? An Analysis of Labor Market Flexibility in the Late Nineties', Discussion Paper 140/2002, *International Institute for Labor Studies*, ILO.

Cazes, Sandrine and Nesporova, Alena (2003), *Labor Markets in Transition: Balancing Flexibility and Security in Central and Eastern Europe*, Geneva, ILO.

Commander, Simon and Heitmueller, Alena (2007), 'Does Unemployment Insurance Help Explain Unemployment in Transition Countries?', Unpublished paper, London: London Business School.

Earle, John S. and Sabirianova, Klara Z. (2002), 'How Late to Pay? Understanding Wage Arrears in Russia', *Journal of Labor Economics*, vol. 20(3), pp. 661–660.

EBRD (2000), *Transition Report*, London: EBRD.

Ederveen, Sjef and Thissen, Laura (2007), 'Can Labor Market Institutions Explain High Unemployment Rates in the New EU Member States?', *Empirica*, vol. 34(4), pp. 299–317.

Fialova, Kamila and Schneider, Ondřej (2009), 'Labor Market Institutions and Their Effect on Labor Market Performance in the New EU Member Countries', *Eastern European Economics*, vol. 47(3), pp. 57–83.

Gimpelson, Vladimir, Kapeliushnikov, Rostislav and Lukyanova, Anna (2010), 'Employment Protection Legislation in Russia: Regional Enforcement and Labor Market Outcomes', *Comparative Economic Studies*, vol. 52(4), pp. 611–36.

Granick, David (1987), *Job Rights in the Soviet Union: Their Consequences*, Cambridge: Cambridge University Press.

Lehmann, Hartmut and Muravyev, Alexander (2010), 'Labor Market Institutions and Labor Market Performance: What can we Learn from Transition Countries?', *Working Paper* 714, Dipartimento di Scienze Economiche, Università di Bologna.

Lehmann, Hartmut and Kluve, Johen (2010), 'Assessing Active Labor Market Policies in Transition Countries', pp. 275–308 in Floro, E.C. and Pastore, F. (eds), *The Labor Market Impact of EU Enlargement: A New Regional Geography for Europe?* Heidelberg: Physica-Verlag.

Lehmann, Hartmut, Wadsworth, Jonathan and Acquisti, Alessandro (1999), 'Grime and Punishment: Job Insecurity and Wage Arrears in the Russian Federation', *Journal of Comparative Economics*, vol. 27(4), pp. 595–617.

Micklewright, John and Nagy, Gyula (2010), 'The Effect of Monitoring Unemployment Insurance Recipients on Unemployment Duration: Evidence from a Field Experiment', *Labour Economics*, vol. 17(1), pp. 180–87.

Muravyev, Alexander (2010), 'Evolution of Employment Protection Legislation in the USSR, CIS and Baltic States, 1985–2009', *IZA Discussion Paper* 5365.

Nickell, Stephen (1997), 'Unemployment and Labor Market Rigidities: Europe versus North America', *Journal of Economic Perspectives*, vol. 11(3), pp. 55–74.

Rutkowski, Jan J. and Scarpetta, Stefano (2005), *Enhancing Job Opportunities: Eastern Europe and the Former Soviet Union*, Washington, DC: World Bank.

Svejnar, Jan (1999), 'Labor Markets in the Transitional Central and Eastern European Economies', pp. 2809–57 in O. Ashenfelter and Card, D. (eds) *Handbook of Labor Economics*. New York and Oxford: Elsevier Science.

Venn, Danielle (2009), 'Legislation, collective bargaining and enforcement: Updating the OECD employment protection indicators', *OECD Social, Employment and Migration Working Papers*, No. 89, Paris, OECD.

Part VIII
Country studies

29

WHY HAS SERBIA NOT BEEN A FRONTRUNNER?

Milica Uvalic

Introduction

This case study is dedicated to Serbia, one of the countries born from the dissolution of the Socialist Federal Republic (SFR) of Yugoslavia, that over the last 20 years has changed its statehood five times. From being one of the six republics of SFR Yugoslavia, after its break-up in 1991 Serbia with Montenegro created the Federal Republic (FR) of Yugoslavia in April 1992, which became the State Union of Serbia and Montenegro in 2003. After the referendum in Montenegro in May 2006 when its citizens voted in favour of independence, in June Serbia and Montenegro became two independent states. Finally, Serbia's southern province of Kosovo unilaterally declared independence in February 2008, though by June 2011 Kosovo had not been recognized by 60 per cent of UN members. The focus of the chapter is primarily on Serbia, the preponderant part of the country in terms of territory, population and economic weight, though occasionally we will also need to refer to the country as defined at the time.

The paper discusses Serbia's economic history during 1989–2009, explaining why a country that had among the best starting conditions in 1989 to implement the transition to a market economy ended up lagging behind so much. Serbia is an interesting case for various reasons. Its 20-year transition has been more complex than in most other countries in Eastern Europe and in many ways unique. Still today, relatively little is known about the Serbian economy outside the narrow circle of experts and there are a number of controversial issues. There is no agreement among scholars when the transition in Serbia started, whether in 1989 or in late 2000 after the end of the Milosevic regime. There are also different assessments of the overall results achieved during the last decade.

We will recall the initial conditions in Serbia in 1989, while it was still part of socialist Yugoslavia, in the following section. The difficult 1990s in Serbia/FR Yugoslavia are analysed next. The new phase of Serbia's transition after the political changes in autumn 2000 is discussed in some detail, pointing to the main achievements and failures, and conclusions are drawn at the end.

Where was Serbia in 1989?

When the transition to a market economy and multiparty democracy was starting in 1989 in Eastern Europe, Serbia was still a constituent part of the SFR Yugoslavia, a federation composed of six republics (Bosnia and Herzegovina, Croatia, Macedonia, Montenegro, Serbia with its two autonomous provinces Kosovo and Vojvodina, and Slovenia). After Yugoslavia's break-up in June 1991, five independent states were created on its territory, mainly according to the geographical borders of the republics that existed in Yugoslavia; the only exception was the FR Yugoslavia that was created from two of its republics, Serbia and Montenegro.

The initial conditions in SFR Yugoslavia were somewhat different than in the other countries in Eastern Europe. The successor states of Yugoslavia inherited from their former country a number of advantages which had benefitted all its republics (including Serbia), but also some disadvantages.

SFR Yugoslavia had a long tradition of market-oriented reforms. In the 1950s the system of workers' self-management was first introduced, when enterprise ownership was also transformed from traditional state property into social property, intended as property of the whole society. Further economic reforms aimed at economic decentralization and greater reliance on the market mechanism through gradual price liberalization, a multi-tier banking system, foreign trade liberalization (Yugoslavia became a member of GATT in 1966), and legislation on joint ventures. SFR Yugoslavia also benefited from specific international relations: it was not a member of the Council for Mutual Economic Assistance (CMEA) or of the Warsaw Pact, but a non-aligned country, with privileged relations with the European Economic Community (EEC). Yugoslavia concluded several trade agreements with the EEC in the 1970s and a broad-based trade and economic cooperation agreement in 1980, which greatly facilitated its trade orientation towards primarily the West.

The beneficial effects of market-oriented reforms in SFR Yugoslavia were, however, limited by the unchanged nature of the political system. This is why the Yugoslav economy was also characterized by some features typical of the socialist economic system as described by Kornai (1980): the dominance of non-private property, 'soft' budget constraints, and state paternalism through state intervention in enterprise affairs (Uvalic, 1992). Nevertheless, extensive economic reforms in Yugoslavia brought many advantages with respect to the traditional socialist economic system. Yugoslavia's unique economic system of 'market socialism' stimulated considerable academic interest, as an example of a potential 'third way' between capitalism and socialism (Estrin and Uvalic, 2008).

Within the Yugoslav federation, Serbia was the largest republic in terms of the most important economic indicators (output, investment, employment). Although Serbia was less export-oriented than Slovenia or Croatia, in 1990 it accounted for the highest share of Yugoslavia's exports and imports. In 1990 Serbia already traded mostly with the OECD countries, that accounted for 57 per cent of its exports and 60 per cent of its imports. Foreign capital invested in Serbia through joint ventures was 21 per cent of the total invested in Yugoslavia (Uvalic, 2010, p. 33). Serbia was not among the most developed republics, since in 1989 it had a Gross Social Product (GSP) per capita at 88 per cent of the Yugoslav average. However, the central part of Serbia (without autonomous provinces) had a GSP per capita at the very same level, Vojvodina was at 118 per cent, while Kosovo stood at only 24 per cent of the Yugoslav average. In 1989 the joint GDP per capita (at Purchasing Power Parity) of Serbia and Montenegro was US $4,731 or around half of the GDP per capita of Slovenia, the most developed Yugoslav republic (Kekic, 1996, p. 15).

On the eve of transition, Serbia also inherited some disadvantages. The most serious was the ongoing political crisis. After unsuccessful attempts to find a compromise solution on how to reform the Yugoslav federation, the country effectively disintegrated in mid-1991 when Slovenia and Croatia declared independence. Another disadvantage were ambiguous property rights: given that enterprises were in social property defined as property of the whole society, privatization was more complicated – it was unclear who was to initiate the process of privatization and to whom the proceeds would go. There was also greater resistance to radical systemic changes in Yugoslavia/Serbia, owing to a higher degree of popular support of the regime.

Political and economic instability in the 1990s

Serbia started its transition within Yugoslavia with relatively good initial conditions. It also benefited from the first radical economic reforms implemented by the last Yugoslav government in 1988–90, aimed at liberalization, macroeconomic stabilization and privatization. The first multi-party elections in Serbia (December 1990) brought the victory of Slobodan Milosevic and his Socialist Party of Serbia (SPS), born from a marginally reformed League of Communists of Serbia. Since Milosevic's SPS remained the dominant party throughout the decade, there was ideological continuity with the previous regime.

The transition was interrupted by three groups of political shocks. The first shock was the disintegration of SFR Yugoslavia in mid-1991, which brought extreme political and economic instability to the whole Balkan region. The second shock was the military conflicts of the 1990s, in which the FR Yugoslavia was directly or indirectly involved – in Slovenia (1991), Croatia (1991), Bosnia and Herzegovina (1992–95) and Kosovo (1998–99). The third political shock was international sanctions: several UN resolutions introduced very severe and widely based international sanctions against FR Yugoslavia from 1992 onwards, and again in 1998–99. Throughout the 1990s, FR Yugoslavia had an unregulated status in the UN, its agencies and most international organizations, since the government insisted on the recognition of the 'continuity' between FR Yugoslavia and SFR Yugoslavia, which was never approved (in contrast to the Soviet Union, where Russia was immediately acknowledged as the legal 'successor state').

These political shocks have had profound economic consequences (Uvalic, 2010). With the break-up of the Yugoslav economic union, Serbia lost a wide, protected internal market. The military conflicts of the early 1990s heavily burdened the Serbian/Yugoslav government budget through war-related expenditure, contributing to extreme macroeconomic instability in 1992–93. The highly expansionary monetary and fiscal policies necessary to finance the wars led to one of the record hyperinflations in world history, an annual inflation rate in 1993 of 116.5 trillion per cent. The Yugoslav was the second highest recorded inflation after the Hungarian hyperinflation of 1945–46 (today third, after Zimbabwe's hyperinflation in 2008 became second). The Yugoslav hyperinflation lasted 24 months, making it the second longest in world history (after the Russian hyperinflation in the 1920s). Extreme monetary instability was additionally fuelled by inappropriate exchange rate policies, as the official fixed exchange rate of the dinar was only sporadically adjusted to the black market rate. FR Yugoslavia also went through a very deep recession: over 1990–93 it registered a cumulative decline in GDP of around 80 percentage points. Industrial production declined even more, contributing to a very marked process of deindustrialization. There were frequent shortages of basic products, the flourishing of the informal economy, rapid currency depreciation, and a high degree of 'marketization' – replacement of the dinar with the German mark.

Under such exceptional conditions, the economic reforms that started in 1989–90 were effectively suspended or reversed. After 1992 the government introduced emergency packages based on administrative measures – general or selective price freezes, wage limits or controls, and rationing of the most essential products. The international trade embargo reversed the trade liberalization measures implemented earlier. A government decree prohibited the lay-off of workers during the duration of international sanctions. Key Serbian firms considered of strategic importance for the economy were nationalized.

Following this period of extreme instability, a stabilization programme was implemented in January 1994 by the newly-appointed governor of the Yugoslav National Bank, Dragoslav Avramovic, based on a currency board. Although the programme was initially very successful – hyperinflation was eliminated virtually overnight – the results were short-lived. Tight monetary policy was relaxed by June 1994 and the currency board was abandoned. There was no willingness to implement fundamental changes of the economic system. Although a new privatization law was adopted in 1992, amendments to the law in 1994 introduced an inappropriate revaluation of enterprise assets, practically cancelling most of the privatizations.

The Dayton Peace Accords in December 1995 officially ended the war in Bosnia and Herzegovina, opening new perspectives. International sanctions against FR Yugoslavia were officially lifted, but owing to marginal changes in the political regime the so-called 'outer wall' of sanctions remained, preventing the re-entry of the country into international organizations and access to international financial markets. Economic performance of the Serbian economy after 1996 remained unsatisfactory. Although inflation never reached the dramatic levels recorded in the early 1990s, it remained high. There was economic recovery – GDP growth reached even 10 per cent in 1997 – but only limited revival of foreign trade. The lack of normalization of FR Yugoslavia's relations with international financial organizations impeded the inflow of badly needed foreign capital. There was only one important foreign direct investment in June 1997, when 49 per cent of Serbia Telekom was sold to the Italian STET and Greek OTE for DM 1.57 billion. The economy continued to be protected through high tariffs and a number of non-tariff barriers. The dinar remained non-convertible and inadequate exchange rate policy contributed to the continuous discrepancy between the official and the black market rate. A new privatization law was adopted in 1997, but since it did not render privatization obligatory its implementation was slow. Many new laws contained provisions which indicated the lack of willingness by the government to abandon pre-1989 institutions and practices.

These negative developments had profound social consequences. The UN economic embargo triggered smuggling, war-related illegal activities, and corruption. There was increasing poverty and social differentiation. Income redistribution often took place in favour of the economic and political elite, through various channels – the inflation tax, freezing of citizens' foreign currency bank deposits, and various pyramid schemes which involved para-state banks, where citizens lost their life savings after they had declared bankruptcy. A close relationship was established between the political and economic elite: the directors of the 30 most important enterprises were also the key politicians, members of the Serbian parliament, ministers in the Yugoslav government, and the closest political collaborators of president Milosevic.

The country was also facing rising political and social unrest. Mass demonstrations became the main method of open protest against the regime, as those organized in the winter of 1996–97 owing to the non-recognition of the victory of opposition parties at the local elections. In addition, after the 1990 Serbian constitution centralized Serbia's power over Kosovo, the political situation in this province progressively deteriorated. After 1996 the confrontation between the Serb and the Albanian community became more extreme, attempts to find a peaceful solution through the Serb–Albanian dialogue were unsuccessful, and the first violent clashes took place between the Yugoslav National Army and the Kosovo Liberation Army. Once the international negotiations with representatives of the Milosevic regime in Rambouillet failed, NATO's 78-day bombing of FR Yugoslavia started, despite lack of formal authorization by the UN Security Council. The military intervention destroyed Serbia's basic infrastructure, a number of bridges and the most important factories. In 1999 there was a 19 per cent drop in GDP and a 50 per cent decline in exports. Depending on estimates, the costs of the war range from US $30 – 100 billion (Uvalic, 2010).

Serbia's 'second' transition

Radical political changes finally took place in FR Yugoslavia in October 2000. The September 2000 elections brought the victory of Vojislav Kostunica, the candidate for president of FR Yugoslavia of the Democratic Opposition of Serbia (DOS). Political changes effectively took place only after 5 October 2000 when, following the non-recognition of the electoral results, there was a general uprising of the Serbian population. Milosevic had to give in and recognize the electoral results. Political changes in the Serbian government took place some months later, after the December elections.

In late 2000, the government had many difficult issues on its agenda. After 10 years of isolation, FR Yugoslavia had to regulate its membership in the UN, the IMF, the World Bank and other international organizations, but this required the prior settlement of its accumulated debt obligations. Another set of specific problems derived from the complex relationship between Serbia and Montenegro, among other reasons because Montenegro was represented in the Federal government by its main opposition party SNP (Socialist Peoples' Party), a party that for years had been a loyal collaborator of Milosevic. In late 2000 FR Yugoslavia was highly dependent on international aid, but was also subject to strict political conditionality related to war crimes. Within the government, however, there was no consensus on the delivery of Slobodan Milosevic to the International Criminal Tribunal for the former Yugoslavia (ICTY). Milosevic was imprisoned only in late March 2001 and was delivered to the ICTY much later, on 27 June 2001, the evening before the donors' conference for FR Yugoslavia – had he not been transferred to The Hague, the promised aid would not have been received. Regarding relations with the EU, FR Yugoslavia was included in 2001 in the new approach for the Western Balkan states – the Stabilization and Association Process – which offered preferential trade access, financial assistance, and the possibility of signing a Stabilization and Association Agreement (SAA) with the EU. However, mainly due to strict political conditionality – the alleged insufficient cooperation with the ICTY – Serbia was able to sign a SAA only in April 2008.

Despite all these political problems, the end of the Milosevic regime facilitated more radical economic reforms and gradual macroeconomic stabilization. Prices increased very fast after their initial liberalization, but the trend has been positive: average inflation declined from over 90 per cent in 2001 to around 10 per cent in 2008. This was sustained by prudent monetary and exchange rate policy. Restrictive monetary policy was accompanied by the unification of the exchange rate, the devaluation of the Serbian dinar, and the introduction of a managed float regime. During the 2001–08 period, the Serbian economy registered strong GDP growth, on average around 5 per cent (Figure 29.1). There was a fourfold rise in net monthly wages – from €90 in 2001 to €400 in 2008. By 2009 Serbia's GDP per capita reached US $6,000 (US $11,530 in PPP), corresponding to 37 per cent of the EU-27 average. Serbia finally started attracting FDI, particularly after 2003. Until the end of 2008 the cumulative net FDI amounted to US $15 billion, or US $2,005 on a per capita basis. Increasing capital inflows have also been secured through emigrants' remittances which have been even higher than FDI, and donors' financial assistance of various international organizations, the European Union (EU) and other western countries.

After 2001 Serbia experienced a strong acceleration of economic reforms, as suggested by the transition indicators of the European Bank for Reconstruction and Development (EBRD). The liberalization of prices and of the foreign trade system was implemented fast, while privatization was carried further through a new law adopted in mid-2001. Major reforms of the financial sector included the closing down of the four largest banks in 2001–2 and the privatization of most banks to multinational European banks after 2003, so today 80 per cent of banking assets

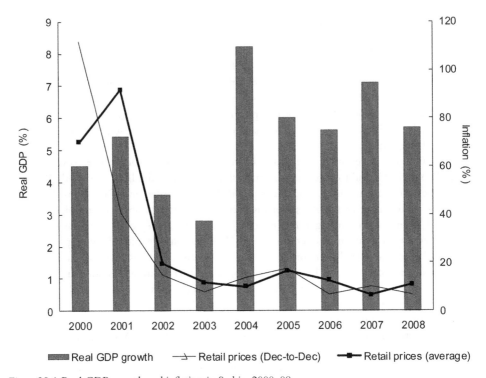

Figure 29.1 Real GDP growth and inflation in Serbia, 2000–08
Source: Uvalic, M. (2010), *Serbia's Transition. Towards a Better Future*, Palgrave Macmillan, p. 145, reproduced with permission of Palgrave Macmillan.

are foreign-owned. The setbacks regard primarily large-scale privatization, enterprise restructuring and corporate governance, competition policy, and securities markets and non-financial institutions, where Serbia still has a below-average EBRD score (2 or 2+).

There have been additional policy failures, however, not captured by the EBRD transition indicators. One of the most serious is the problem of 'jobless' growth. Despite relatively strong GDP growth during 2001–08, until 2006 employment declined while unemployment, whether measured by the official or the labour force survey rate, has continuously increased. There was a slight improvement after 2007, partly owing to methodological changes, which was practically cancelled by the effects of the global economic crisis in 2008–10. In October 2010 20 per cent of the active working-age Serbian population was unemployed.

Serbia has also been facing increasing external imbalances. Although foreign trade has recovered remarkably from 2001 onwards, the value of Serbia's imports has regularly been double that of its exports, determining a rising trade deficit. Exchange rate policy has kept the dinar overvalued, particularly during 2001–02 and in 2006–08, contributing to insufficient export growth. The rising trade deficit has led to an increasing current account deficit, which by late 2008 was close to 18 per cent of Serbia's GDP (Figure 29.2).

Moreover, the process of economic recovery in Serbia has been very slow. The recession of the early 1990s was more profound in Serbia than in most transition countries, while the NATO bombing caused another very deep recession, with a 19 per cent GDP fall in 1999. The relatively high GDP growth rates after 2001 have not been sufficient to compensate for the extreme loss of output in the 1990s. By 2008 Serbia's real GDP reached only 72 per cent of its

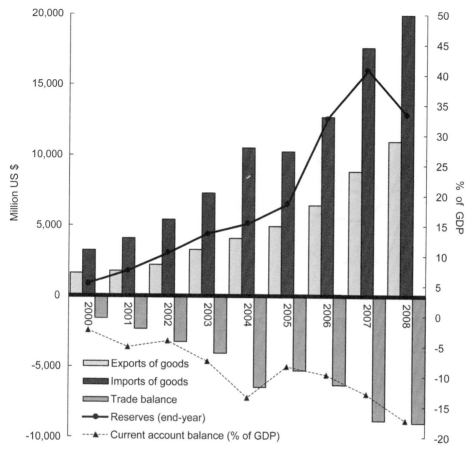

Figure 29.2 Serbia's external sector indicators, 2000–08
Source: Uvalic, M. (2010), *Serbia's Transition. Towards a Better Future*. Palgrave Macmillan, p. 156, reproduced with permission of Palgrave Macmillan.

1989 level, which is the most unfavourable position among all Balkan countries (Figure 29.3). There was a further setback in 2009 when Serbia, strongly affected by the global economic crisis, registered a negative GDP growth of 3.1 per cent. By mid-2010 Serbia was at only 70 per cent of its 1989 GDP level (EBRD, 2010).

At the basis of these failures are structural weaknesses in the real sector of the Serbian economy, which derive essentially from insufficient microeconomic restructuring. Serbia's 2001 transition strategy followed the prescriptions of the 'Washington Consensus' – the emphasis was placed on liberalization, macroeconomic stabilization and privatization, while a number of important microeconomic reforms were neglected. Although delays in microeconomic reforms proved to be fundamental in many Central East European (CEE) countries, causing setbacks even in the most successful countries like the Czech Republic (Svejnar and Uvalic, 2009), this was not taken into account in Serbia in 2001. Enterprise restructuring was expected simply as a by-product of liberalization, stabilization and privatization. In a liberalized and stable macroeconomic environment, it was assumed that enterprises, once privatized, would quickly and efficiently undertake economic restructuring. Such expectations have not been fulfilled owing to policy failures in several inter-related areas. The insufficient microeconomic restructuring of Serbian enterprises

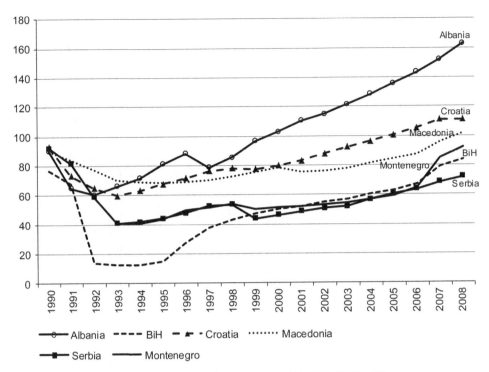

Figure 29.3 Real GDP in Serbia and other Balkan countries, 1990–2008 (1989=100)
Source: Uvalic, M. (2010), *Serbia's Transition. Towards a Better Future.* Palgrave Macmillan, p. 258, reproduced with permission of Palgrave Macmillan.

derives primarily from the inappropriate privatization strategy, but also from accompanying reforms which were substantially delayed.

The new privatization law adopted in 2001 was based on the method of sales to strategic investors of more than 2,000 enterprises through tenders and auctions. The law encountered serious delays in its implementation: although the initial deadline was 2005, by May 2009 there were still some 535 firms (23 per cent) that had not been sold. Moreover, there have been some 420 broken contracts since 2001, mainly due to the non-respect of obligations by the new owner such as illegal sale of assets, non-payment of wages and social security contributions, or simply no production. While firms bought by foreign companies have usually been restructured, this was not the case with those sold to domestic owners. Privatization proceeds, for the most part, have not been used for investment or restructuring.

The new privatization strategy relied heavily on FDI, but the expectations about its arrival were overly optimistic. FDI has been relatively modest, it has mainly been privatization-related, and its structure has not favoured industrial restructuring, since two-thirds has gone into services – banking, telecommunications, real estate, trade. Thus many industrial firms have not been modernized or restructured, although the manufacturing industry contributes around 90 per cent of Serbian exports. The privatization programme also excluded 550 public/state-owned strategic firms that were nationalized in the 1990s. The process of corporatization, restructuring and privatization of these state enterprises was effectively postponed until after 2006, when the new Serbian constitution finally clarified some ambiguities regarding their property status.

In addition to these weaknesses of the privatization strategy, there were also accompanying reforms that were unjustly delayed. Entry barriers were removed too gradually and there are areas, like registering property or obtaining building permits, where still today the conditions remain highly unsatisfactory (see www.doingbusiness.org). Regarding firm exit, a new bankruptcy law was adopted only in 2004, while the procedure for the write-off of enterprise debt was clarified even later, in 2006. As a result, there was a *slowdown* in net firm entry: for every closed enterprise, eight new firms were created in 2006, but only four in 2008 (Uvalic, 2010). A new Law on the Protection of Competition was adopted only in 2005, while the Anti-trust Commission, set up in 2006, has been ineffective. The hardening of enterprise budget constraints was implemented selectively, since government subsidies remain important in many sectors (mining, transport, metallurgy, textiles, chemicals, construction, wood). Serbia has officially adopted the OECD principles of corporate governance, but they are frequently not implemented due to insufficient skills of the new domestic owners to control managers, the lack of awareness of the new legislation or its deliberate non-implementation.

Ineffective employment policy has also contributed to limited microeconomic restructuring in Serbia. Employment policy was basically treated as exogenous to the reform process and reduced to a supporting labour market reform aimed at bringing more labour market flexibility (Arandarenko, 2009). The new system of labour taxation in force during 2001–07 introduced a highly regressive system of wage taxation, contributing to rigidities in the labour market and rendering the informal labour market more flexible.

Limited microeconomic restructuring in Serbia has contributed to two major macroeconomic consequences: (1) the relatively slow growth of the private sector; and (2) inadequate structural changes (Uvalic, 2010).

1 During 2001–10, Serbia's private sector share increased from 40 to 60 per cent of GDP. Among all 29 EBRD client countries, two countries today have the same relatively low share of private sector GDP as Serbia (Bosnia and Herzegovina, and Ukraine), while another four countries have lower shares (Belarus, Tajikistan, Turkmenistan and Uzbekistan). Somewhat paradoxically, Serbia's private sector expanded faster during the 1990s – when it rose from 10 per cent of GDP in 1991 to 40 per cent in 2000 – than after 2001.

2 Structural changes in Serbia have favoured the fast expansion of primarily services, which have had the strongest growth in recent years and by 2008 already contributed 64 per cent of GDP (considerably more than some of the developed CEE countries, like the Czech Republic). Industry has gone through a very strong process of deindustrialization in the 1990s and there was further relative decline after 2001. By 2008 Serbia's industrial sector had reached only 52 per cent of its 1989 production. The share of agriculture in GDP has also declined after 2001. As a result, Serbia's tradeable goods sector declined from 41 per cent of GDP in 2000 to 24.6 per cent in 2007, strongly contributing to the rising trade deficit.

Concluding remarks

In answering the question of why Serbia has not been a frontrunner in the transition process, there are three groups of reasons that ought to be stressed. The first regards the *adverse political conditions in the 1990s*. The re-emergence of nationalism, the break-up of the Yugoslav federation, the non-democratic political regime in Serbia throughout the 1990s and its involvement in several military conflicts, brought a decade of extreme political and economic instability. During the 1990s, political priorities rendered economic objectives secondary, so the transition was substantially delayed. The 1990s have also left a very heavy burden on the new government after the fall of the Milosevic regime. In late 2000, Serbia did not start its transition from scratch, but inherited many complex political problems, some of which – like the definition of the status of Kosovo – have not been resolved even today. After the turn in late 2000, the overall situation in Serbia was far worse than in the CEE countries in the early 1990s, which partly explains why the results have not been more impressive. The Serbian case shows how even particularly favourable initial conditions and institutional advantages can be undermined or definitely lost under unfavourable political conditions.

Second, Serbia *did not learn many lessons* from the more successful transition countries, but repeated some of the same mistakes. The Serbian government neglected many fundamental microeconomic reforms which should have been implemented early on. By the late 1990s the experience of some transition countries confirmed the importance of not only privatization but also of entry of new private firms; of not only the transfer of ownership but also of effective mechanisms of corporate governance; of increasing competition as even more important than privatization; of not only markets but also of active government policies (Kolodko and Nuti, 1997). The rich experience of transition countries from the 1990s was not sufficiently taken into account, although in 2001 Serbia's main advantage was precisely being able to learn from others (Uvalic, 2010).

Third, *external factors* have additionally contributed to delays in Serbia's transition – the very harsh international sanctions against FR Yugoslavia during most of the 1990s, the 1999 NATO bombing, the hesitant or inadequate policies of the EU and of the wider international community. Some of the international measures applied towards Serbia/FR Yugoslavia were frequently ineffective or counterproductive, in this way contributing to even greater delays in carrying forward the transition. During the 1990s, Milosevic was able to reinforce his undemocratic political regime at the expense of the population at large. Moreover, there was a dramatic deterioration in state capacity, spread of criminality and corruption, weakening of the rule of law and flourishing of the shadow economy, phenomena which are quite contrary to the objectives of the transition to democracy and a market economy.

Yet Serbia today is increasingly resembling other transition countries. During the last decade, it has become a more open economy with dominant private ownership, it has liberalized its trade with the EU and with its neighbours, it has reformed many of its institutions and its financial sector is dominated by foreign-owned banks. The more difficult challenges still lie in the political domain: the difficult issue of Kosovo and Serbia's future accession to the EU. Serbia has recently applied for EU membership and was formally granted candidate status in March 2012. At this point, the Serbian government should consistently implement its pro-Europe agenda, reconcile with its difficult past and look primarily towards the future.

Bibliography

Arandarenko, M. (2009), 'Zaposlenost izmedju tranzicije i ekonomske krize' in Cerovic, B. and Kovacevic, M. (eds), *Tranzicija u Srbiji i globalna ekonomska kriza*, Beograd: Ekonomski fakultet.

Estrin, S. and Uvalic, M. (2008), 'From Illyria towards capitalism: Did labor-management theory teach us anything about Yugoslavia and transition in its successor states?', *Comparative Economic Studies,* 50th Anniversary Essay, vol. 50, pp. 663–96.

European Bank for Reconstruction and Development (EBRD) (2010), *Transition Report*, London: EBRD, various issues.

Kekic, L. (1996), 'Assessing and measuring progress in the transition', in Economist Intelligence Unit, *Country Forecast – Economies in Transition – Eastern Europe and the former Soviet Union – Regional Overview*, 2nd quarter 1996, London: Economist Intelligence Unit, pp. 5–22.

Kolodko, G. W. and Nuti, D. M. (1997), 'The Polish alternative – Old myths, hard facts and new strategies in the successful Polish economic transformation', *UNU WIDER Research for Action Series,* 33.

Kornai, J. (1980), *Economics of Shortage*, 2 volumes, Amsterdam: North-Holland.

Svejnar, J. and Uvalic, M. (2009), 'The Czech transition. The importance of microeconomic fundamentals', *UNU WIDER, Research Paper no.* 2009/17. Also in A. Fosu (ed.) (2013), *Development Success Historical Accounts from the More Advanced Countries*, Oxford: Oxford University Press.

Uvalic, M. (1992), *Investment and Property Rights in Yugoslavia. The Long Transition to a Market Economy*, Cambridge: Cambridge University Press. Paperback Re-issue (2009).

——(2010), *Serbia's Transition. Towards a Better Future*, Basingstoke: Palgrave Macmillan.

30

ESTONIA

Did the strategy of deep integration fail in the 2008/09 crisis?

Pekka Sutela

Introduction

Estonia and the two other Baltic nations, Latvia and Lithuania, regained their independence in 1991. Instead of engaging in the building of a sovereign national economy, they – Estonia more consistently than the other two – engaged in *deep integration*, here defined as a conscious policy aimed at making the country part of a wider set of markets and other institutions, in this case those of north-western Europe (Sutela, 2002). While maintaining political independence, the right to issue money, national armies and control over borders, they adopted the European four freedoms (almost) overnight, abolished monetary policy sovereignty by establishing currency boards, gave over the banking sector to foreigners, privatized (in the case of Estonia) most of their industries to foreign strategic owners (thus leaving the domestic equity markets very small) and sought to become members of Western institutions as soon as possible. In doing all this, they accepted the strongest possible external policy anchors short of losing political sovereignty.

Until 2008 these small economies grew quickly. Large inflows of capital allowed huge current account deficits, and while incomes and consumption boomed the economies also overheated, especially in real estate and services. The ensuing collapse in the 2008/09 crisis was, at some 15–20 per cent of GDP, among the very steepest globally. Still, this contribution argues, there was little alternative to deep integration for these countries, it has generally served them well, and has facilitated not only a rapid welfare improvement, but also a thorough shift in their geopolitical position. The argument uses a stylized Estonia as the ideal type of a Baltic country, but also points out many of the important differences between the three economies.

Varieties of external anchor

Transition was bound to be a complex and multi-dimensional process extending over decades rather than years, when the needed development of formal and informal institutions was taken into account (Gelb and Gray, 1991). To maintain consistency across policies and over time, external policy anchors were found useful. Going beyond abandoning the old system of central planning, they would not only define the general goal of transition, but would also – if found credible and if supported by the electorate and elites alike – tie the hands of decision-makers, at least in broad outline. In the weakest cases the external anchors consisted of little more than a generally defined desire to become 'a normal country'. That could imply hugely different outcomes, especially as normalcy can be defined either normatively – the way things should be – or positively – the way things usually are.

A stronger kind of an external anchor was provided by dependence on external actors. This might just mean a willingness to maintain international goodwill, but more importantly, for instance, dependence on international sources of finance. Among them, the International Monetary Fund (IMF) was early on given the key role in financing transition economies. Traditionally, IMF clients are countries in deep trouble, facing a financial crisis with no access to private money. The prevailing view in the early 1990s was that credit programme conditions would therefore concentrate on the current account, money supply and budget balance. This part of what came to be called the Washington Consensus was based on Latin American experience in the 1980s.

Transition economies did not in the beginning typically receive private finance, but their predicament was much wider: it included the whole transition menu. Therefore, IMF programme conditions proliferated, often including tens of numerical conditions and qualitative targets. There was no way to ensure consistency between these goals and a programme bargaining process – very much like the plan bargaining in which the former centrally managed countries were past masters – followed. Therefore, the IMF conditionality was much weaker than might have been expected. Many countries used this weakness to avoid painful decisions, whereas a radical reformer such as Estonia went the opposite way. Thus, establishing a currency board was a solution the IMF originally objected to, and early capital account liberalization was against the prevailing IMF thinking.

What many saw as the decisive divide was between those who could credibly aim for membership of the core European and Euro-Atlantic organizations and those who could not. Membership in the European Union (EU), WTO, NATO, OECD, and so on, defined in the 1990s what it was to be a European, and their combined membership requirements (to be called for short, the *acquis*) ran into well over 100,000 printed pages. If credible, this web of conditions to be fulfilled tied the hands of an accession candidate in a huge variety of ways. The accession conditions for new and applicant states were monitored in much greater detail than the behaviour of long-established members could be. Though nobody would call these requirements in any sense optimal, they had a certain consistency and proven workability.

However, as Estonia showed, it was possible to go even further than the *acquis*. Doing that is here called deep integration. Under some circumstances it was possible to tie oneself not only to the *acquis*, but to go further by establishing very quickly the institutions, rules and regulations that established members had.

This could not be done wholesale. Some of the rules, like the Maastricht criteria for EMU accession, had been written for well-established and stable European countries. Achieving the Maastricht criteria for inflation was a major obstacle for a poor economy engaged in catching-up growth. Others were economically dysfunctional and/or politically disliked, like the Common Agricultural Policy and various social provisions. Estonia wanted to have deep integration with north-western Europe, not to become a Scandinavian welfare state. There was still much scope to integrate fast. This concerned in particular the four freedoms, monetary arrangements and privatization policies.

Why deep integration?

Stylized 'Estonia', the ideal-type Baltic country, had good reasons for choosing deep integration. It was a middle-income country, poor relative to its Western neighbours, with only 1.5 million inhabitants, one-third of them non-Estonians, whose loyalty was doubted (unjustifiably, as it later proved) by many. Politically, Russia's imminent collapse was feared, and Estonia therefore needed to anchor itself to the EU and NATO as soon as possible. Economically, the small domestic markets could support at best limited competition or access to finance. These features needed to be imported. Socially, decades in Soviet isolation left the country with little competence relevant for operating a successful market economy, democracy and European integration. The general development goal was clear, though. In 1938 Estonia had probably been wealthier than Finland and personal cross-border ties since the 1960s and Northern Estonian access to Finnish TV media since the 1970s reminded of what could and now should be, the faster the better. Baltic nationalism is legendary, but it was always of the defensive type. The task was to ensure national survival, and that could be ensured by lowering all walls to the West, not by trying to establish tiny nationalist fortresses. That conclusion was also supported by the generally liberal thinking of the new national elites. As elsewhere in European transition countries, political integration enforced the positive impact of financial integration on pre-crisis growth by affecting expectations (Friedrich *et al.*, 2010).

What is deep integration in practice?

How does one become, in effect, a region in a wider set of markets and institutions? First, one adopts the four freedoms (almost) overnight both inside the country and crucially across borders. Exceptions were always bound to exist, but principally freedom of trade in goods and services and mobility of capital and labour were reached very fast, in some cases also in contrast to the orthodoxy then prevailing in economic thinking. There were costs involved, for instance in the mobility of labour. Thus according to its 2010 census, Lithuania's population shrank by a fifth from 1989 to 2010. Similar findings are evident in Latvia's 2011 census. Not all out-migration is for legal employment, and neighbouring countries sometimes complain about drug-trafficking, prostitution and other crime. Mobility of labour also tended to push costs up, as wage demands could, even in the absence of unionization, be backed by credible threats of out-migration. At the same time cross-border mobility created a basis for the famed flexibility of Estonian labour markets: Finland acted as the over-flow valve. Estonian unemployment peaked at 19.8 per cent in the first quarter of 2010, but rapidly declined to 13.6 per cent in the last quarter of the year. An unknown share of this is due to increased working in Finland, especially in construction and services. It should also be noted that a part of the working population, especially industrial workers, remain non-citizens in Estonia and Latvia. In Latvia their share of the population is about 15 per cent, and less than 10 per cent in Estonia. Unable to vote in national elections, their voice remains weak. This is enhanced by the political process which has kept the parties voted for by the non-titular residents out of coalition governments. Many of those who bear much of the burden of adjustment thus have no access to national decision-making.

Immediate capital account liberalization (though limitations on buying fertile Lithuanian lands remained for years) abolished barriers of access to finance. Monetization, financial deepening and the urge to catch up in incomes created small but fast growing markets, where two Swedish banks and one Danish bank soon dominated. These banks were, after the Nordic banking crises of the early 1990s, well capitalized, effective and profitable. An anecdotal rule of thumb says that a bank's Baltic exposure in assets should be one-tenth, bringing in a third of profits. There seemed to be no reason to doubt the fixed exchange rates, which were crucial for early economic stabilization, credibility of the new currencies and the strategy of deep integration. Nordic in-house banking finance was free to flow into real estate and services. To complicate matters, bank regulation was uncomfortably divided between the Baltic and Scandinavian authorities. Still, the takeover of small markets by reputable foreign banks was much to be preferred to the Icelandic alternative of having competitive domestic banks go into less-regulated foreign niche markets to gain some critical mass. In Latvia one bank tried to gain critical mass through internationalization by acting as a go-between for Russians entering into international markets. Parex bank had to be duly bailed out during the crisis. In Estonia capital mobility was complemented by a major inflow of Finnish small businesses, often themselves going international for the first time. They were also an integral part of civil society integration. From the first one in 1967, the number of ferries sailing daily between Tallinn and Helsinki, both small cities of about 0.5 million inhabitants, has grown to some 35 million.

It has to be remembered that none of the three countries boasts major natural resources. Estonia has some oil shale, Latvia hydropower and Lithuania fertile lands. Together, the forest resources of the Baltic states would support one, preferably Latvia-based, modern large-scale pulp and paper plant, but for reasons not completely understood a Nordic company failed in its efforts over 10 years to establish one. As traditional Tsarist- and Soviet-era manufacturing plants have crumbled, round wood remains Latvia's biggest export item. There was thus not a self-evident specialization for these economies, but neither was there an evident basis for oligarchies and the resource curse. Estonia inherited little manufacturing from the Soviet Union, and though there are a few business men with political ambitions, no oligarchy emerged. Latvia has a long tradition of industrialization, but the inherited electrical and transport equipment industries had no chance to survive. Instead, a kind of resource curse emerged on the basis of the logistics infrastructure that had been important in the Soviet Union. Ventspils harbour became the economic basis for one of the three oligarchs who have cast a deep shadow of corruption over the political economy of Latvia. Lithuania's manufacturing and logistics, in contrast, proved unexpectedly competitive, and were privatized to domestic non-oligarch owners.

As Baltic independence was regained, outside well-wishers often pushed the Baltic countries towards intra-Baltic co-operation. More often than not that was seen as an alternative to the deep integration that was considered far too demanding. That alternative strategy, however, was unattainable. Even together, the three countries would form a small economic area. The countries are divided by history, culture, languages, religion and the finer points of outward orientation. What united them was recent history and their position between Russia and the EU. That was the basic fact determining their choices.

Various privatization methods were used. Restitution had to be limited to post-1938 claims. Otherwise the politically highly complicated claims of the Baltic Germans would have arisen. Vouchers were also used though there was little reason to believe in efficient secondary markets. Latvia tended to favour domestic oligarchs, while a more balanced domestic ownership emerged in Lithuania. Estonia favoured sales to foreign owners, often at low prices. Access to markets, technologies, know-how and brands was deemed more important. In a few well-known cases, especially in the energy sector, the Baltic states gave preference to Western owners for security and strategic reasons. In all cases the preference given to strategic owners implied that only very small domestic equity markets developed. As the governments strongly preferred to balance their budgets to gain credibility, there are also very limited markets for government bonds. Therefore the central banks have little possibility to impact market liquidity. Instead, this is largely determined by the in-house decisions of banks and their Scandinavian owners.

Currency boards – or currency board-like arrangements; there is 'theological' discussion on the exact definitions – are the best known Baltic peculiarity. Estonia was the first one in 1992; the other two soon followed. There were many reasons for adopting this exceptional institution. Currency boards are simple. The central bank is reduced to intervening in the currency market to maintain the exchange rate. Thus, demands on scarce central banking competence are reduced. Neither an interest rate nor a banking channel for monetary policy is needed, and thus the rudimentary character of the financial system does not matter. With capital mobility and a fixed exchange rate, the interest rate is determined by the markets. A currency board is also a credibility-enhancing institution. Devaluation, the usual threat, can be made difficult. In Estonia it would have needed a change of law in repeated parliamentary sessions. (Less emphasized was the fact that those sessions could have taken place over a weekend.)

A currency board is, in monetary policy terms, as close as a country becoming part of a region in wider markets can come to, short of actually adopting the foreign currency. However, the latter was never a realistic alternative. The Scandinavian or wider European central banks did not wish to take over the *de facto* responsibility for monetary policy in countries that remained outsiders. Still, as long as there are separate currencies, a currency risk always remains. Paradoxically, unilateral fixed exchange rates can be endangered by central banks being too credible. Trusting the fixed exchange rate commitment, economic agents, households, companies and financial institutions, undertake transactions and enter into commitments implying monetary mismatches that they assume carry no risk. In the end, too many Baltic households, especially in Latvia, had their revenue in the local currency and substantial liabilities in foreign ones. When the pre-crisis capital inflow was evidently excessive, creating overheating and current account deficits of some 15–20 per cent of GDP annually, the exchange rates could not be re-adjusted due to the existing mismatches. Furthermore, a re-alignment would necessarily have postponed the prized future adoption of the Euro.

The credibility of exchange rate pegs was further enhanced, as the strategy of deep integration implied that the usual market-based vehicles for currency speculation were absent. As companies had been sold to strategic owners, there was only limited trading in equity shares. As stabilization was prioritized, government bonds were almost non-existent. As banks were foreign-owned, they had little need for markets by themselves. What is often forgotten, however, is that a fundamental and traditional currency speculation vehicle did still exist: exporters could decide not to repatriate their revenues. To simplify, as even foreign-owned and -financed exporters had all their revenue in foreign currency and some of their costs in local currencies, they might in principle have been interested in devaluation, but the aggregate impact of any re-alignment in an economy based on currency mismatches and very major capital inflows was difficult to foresee. What the interests of foreign-based banking groups might be is unclear without access to their internal accounting. The pricing of internal transfers and head office services is not known.

The 2008/09 crisis

Baltic economic growth rates were, as is well known, extremely high in the 2000s. Estonia grew by more than 7 per cent annually, until growth peaked at more than 10 per cent in 2006. Intriguingly, overheating was slowing down already in 2007, as the dominant foreign banking groups grew worried about credit quality issues probably created by extremely high credit growth. The slowdown in credit growth may well have contributed to the steepness of the ensuing collapse of production, especially in Latvia (Åslund and Dombrovskis, 2011). Because credit growth was decided within the internationally owned and financed banking groups, there was little that the Baltic central banks could do to inject liquidity (IMF, 2010). Though the decline in production extended over two years and resulted in the loss of a fifth of GDP, Estonia was already recovering in 2010. During the first quarter of 2011, Estonia's growth was a very impressive 8.5 per cent on the back of fast recovery of exports and services.

Latvia's growth had been even higher in the early 2000s and exceeded 10 per cent for several years. The ensuing decline was also exceptionally steep, and growth just failed to resume in 2010. Lithuania's growth was also very impressive, though not quite as high as in the northern neighbours. Neither was the decline quite as steep as there, as Table 30.1 shows.

There were no huge differences in inflation, though Lithuania posted very low figures in the early 2000s, when it famously just failed to fulfil the Maastricht criteria for EMU accession. After that the inflation rate again increased, casting doubt on the sustainability of earlier price stabilization efforts, reaching 11.1 per cent in 2008. Since 2004 Latvia has been the high-inflation country, posting rates above 6 per cent in 2004–06 and double digits in 2007–8, but ending in slight deflation in 2010. The Estonian inflation rate was more modest, fluctuating below 5 per cent in 2002–06, but then also reaching 10.6 per cent in 2008. Disinflation in 2009 was a sudden stop to 0.2 per cent, but in 2010 inflation again reached a more sustainable speed at 2.7 per cent. Details are presented in Table 30.2.

The headline statistics most debated were those for the current account balance. As Table 30.3 shows, deficits were huge, especially in Latvia but also in Estonia, reflecting imports which were booming with exceptionally fast income growth. Estonia's trade deficit varied between about 13 and some 17 per cent of GDP in 2002–08, before dropping sharply. This was partially a competitiveness issue: average nominal unit labour costs increased by 14.2 per cent in 2007 and 20.1 per cent in 2008. Partly it was a supply-side problem of a more general nature. Many goods and services demanded in the new market economy were not produced at all in these very small economies.

If the exchange rate were perfectly credible, current account deficits would arguably not really matter. The economy was just becoming increasingly owned by foreign entities. The external debt-to-exports ratio increased in Estonia from 108.0 per cent in 2005 to 153.2 per cent in 2007 and further to 180.0 per cent in 2009. While the Lithuanian figure was more modest at 160.1 per cent in 2009, Latvia, where the ratio peaked at 369.1 per cent in 2008, was again in a class of its own. No exchange rate regime is perfectly credible, and the combination of increasing debt and spiralling unit labour costs spelled trouble. Even a region inside a country has to worry about competitiveness of jobs, for otherwise it will lose jobs, population, service providers and payers of taxes to other parts of the country. As productivity rarely jumps upward,

Table 30.1 GDP change in the Baltic states, 2001–10

	2001	2002	2003	2004	2005	2006	2007	2008	2009	2010
Estonia	7.5	7.9	7.6	7.2	9.4	10.6	6.9	-5.1	-13.9	3.1
Latvia	8.0	6.5	7.2	8.7	10.6	12.2	10.0	-4.2	-18.0	-0.3
Lithuania	6.7	6.9	10.2	7.4	7.8	7.8	9.8	2.9	-14.7	1.3

Source: Official statistics.

Table 30.2 Annual consumer price inflation in the Baltic states, 2001–10

	2001	2002	2003	2004	2005	2006	2007	2008	2009	2010
Estonia	5.6	3.6	1.4	3.0	4.1	4.4	6.7	10.6	0.2	2.7
Latvia	2.5	2.0	2.9	6.2	6.9	6.6	10.1	15.3	3.3	-1.2
Lithuania	1.6	0.3	-1.1	1.2	2.7	3.8	5.8	11.1	4.2	1.2

Source: Official statistics.

Table 30.3 Current account balances in the Baltic states in 2001–10, per cent of GDP

	2001	2002	2003	2004	2005	2006	2007	2008	2009	2010
Estonia	-5.4	-5.2	-10.6	-11.3	-10.0	-15.3	-17.2	-9.7	4.5	3.6
Latvia	-7.5	-6.7	-8.1	-12.8	-12.5	-21.1	-22.3	-13.0	9.4	5.0
Lithuania	-4.7	-5.1	-6.8	-7.7	-7.1	-10.6	-14.5	-13.1	4.3	1.8

Sources: EBRD, IMF.

the remaining alternative is cutting costs. In the Baltic states, this was also the only available option, as devaluation was excluded for the reasons discussed above.

Further, in a deep integration case the face value of the current account deficit hides more than it reveals. As pointed out earlier, it is essentially the counterpart of the capital account surplus. Estonian international reserves also increased, almost tripling from 2002 to 2009, but as their role in a currency board is to cover base money, the ratio of reserves to gross short-term debt actually declined from 0.7 to 0.4, while import coverage in months fluctuated around 2.5, to rise after 2008. Before 2009, net foreign direct investment corresponded annually to between 2.1 and 15.7 per cent of GDP, reinvested net earnings to between -2.2 and -6.6 per cent. As already pointed out, there is always great uncertainty over how well the book-keeping values of transfer pricing, (non-)pricing of head office services and distinguishing between credits to daughter companies and investments are actually handled.

The financial crisis started to hit the Baltic states in 2007 when banks started to limit credit growth. In Latvia, the extreme case, growth of credit to the private sector amounted to 58.3 per cent in 2006, but -6.6 per cent in 2009. Broad money that had boomed at 37.5 per cent in 2006 declined both in 2008 (-3.9 per cent) and 2009 (-1.9 per cent). There was little that the authorities could do to maintain liquidity. With the exception of the Latvian Parex bank, banking sector solvency was never endangered. The Nordic parent banks were well capitalized and dominated by wealthy – and relative to the Baltic states, not small – states. There was never a risk of another Nordic banking crisis, but a credit swap line was extended by the European Central Bank to the Swedish and Danish central banks – indirectly to support the Baltic states, in case the need arose (Åslund and Dombrovskis, 2011). There was a pioneering Nordic-Baltic memorandum of understanding on improved co-operation in bank regulation in 2010.

As noted, much of the adjustment was through increasing unemployment. In Estonia it increased from 4.7 per cent in 2007 to 13.8 per cent in 2008 and further in 2009. At the same time the previously very fast average nominal growth rate dropped to zero in 2009 and was clearly negative in 2010. The national private savings ratio surged from 16.9 per cent in 2007 to 24.6 per cent in 2009, and is bound to remain high as financial balances are further consolidated. At the same time the public savings ratio turned from 5.6 per cent to slightly negative following the fiscal balance. Without going into detail, a classic internal devaluation to regain competitiveness and credibility took place. The incumbent governments of Estonia and Latvia were rewarded by re-election to power for having continued the policy of deep European integration. Estonia entered the eurozone.

Conclusion

The Baltic experience in 1991–2011 is an exceptional one and cannot be understood properly without appreciating the political background. Still, it proves that deep European integration is not only possible but can also attract popular support in very difficult circumstances. In the crisis, countries with large reserves, low private sector credit and little financial openness fared better than others. After a crisis, floating exchange rate regimes may well recover faster (Cecchetti *et al.*, 2011), but this is a price the Baltic nations were willing to pay for deep integration – for which they anyway had little alternative. Post-crisis problems still remain (IMF, 2011). These are not perfect states. Many aspects of that have been noted above. Further, Latvia and Lithuania have the largest income inequalities in the EU, while Estonia is close to the medium. Loss of population is worrisome. Though regaining competitiveness through lower costs succeeded, this cannot be a desirable long-term solution. The long-term relative advantage of the Baltic states remains unclear. The share of high technology exports is among the lowest in the EU in Latvia and Lithuania, close to the medium (and improving) in Estonia. Scores in European patent applications are similar or even worse. Baltic universities do not figure in international rankings. Long-term success is thus not guaranteed, but these countries have already done what few regarded as possible two decades ago. Innovative solutions ought to be forthcoming in the future as well.

Bibliography

Åslund, A. and Dombrovskis, V. (2011), 'How Latvia Came through the Financial Crisis', Washington, DC: Peterson Institute for International Economics

Cecchetti S.G, King, M.R. and Yetman, J. (2011), 'Weathering the financial crisis: good luck or good policies', www.frbatlanta.org/documents/news/conferences/11fmc_cecchetti.pdf

Friedrich, C., Schnabel, I. and Zettelmeyer, J. (2010), 'Financial integration and growth: Is emerging Europe different?', *CEPR Discussion Paper No.* DP8137, London: CEPR.

Gelb, A.H. and Gray, C.W. (1991), *The Transformation of Economies in Central and Eastern Europe: Issues, Progress, and Prospects*, Washington, DC: World Bank.

IMF (2010), *Republic of Latvia Article IV Consultation*, IMF Country Report No. 10/356. Washington, DC: International Monetary Fund.

——(2011), *Republic of Estonia: Staff Report for the 2010 Article IV Consultation*, IMF Country Report No. 11/34. Washington, DC: International Monetary Fund.

Sutela, P. (2002), 'Combining the incompatibles: Fixed exchange rate, liberalization and financial development in Estonia', in Sepp, U. and Randveer, M. (eds), *Alternative Monetary Regimes in Entry to EMU*, Tallinn: Bank of Estonia.

31

RUSSIA SINCE TRANSITION

Philip Hanson

Introduction

Post-communist economic change in Russia has attracted a lot of attention. This is partly for the obvious reason that the country is politically important. Russia is after all the main successor state of a nuclear-armed former superpower. However, that is not the only reason. Russia's experience has been exceptionally chequered, and the Russian transformation has attracted the interest and active engagement of several leading economists. They, along with home-grown economic reformers, played leading roles in some titanic policy struggles. There has been no shortage either of drama or of expert witnesses.

In this chapter I shall provide a narrative of Russia's reforms and outcomes. Narratives are not highly regarded in economics. However, there is plenty of thematic comparative analysis elsewhere in this handbook. A (mostly) one-country story can shed some light on the influence of initial conditions and political and social background in one particular attempt at post-communist transformation.

What follows is organized chronologically. The next section deals with the 1990s, for almost all of which decade Boris Yeltsin was president. Then there is a shorter section devoted to the 'Putin period' covering Vladimir Putin's presidency (2000–08) and premiership (2008 to the time of writing in mid-2011). I start with the conjecture: that weak social and political support for private ownership and competitive markets has been a problem for reform; coupled with a lack of effective state administration, this made for an erratic course in policy-making in the 1990s; and the resulting harsh experience, for most Russians, in that first decade has encouraged support in more recent times for statist policies.

The Yeltsin years

Boris Yeltsin was elected president of the Russian Soviet Federative Socialist Republic (RSFSR) in 1991. At that time the RSFSR was still a component of the nominally federal USSR. Reform plans for the RSFSR, separate from and more radical than, those for the Soviet Union as a whole, were developed during that year. The three Baltic states achieved their independence by the autumn of 1991. When the USSR disintegrated in December 1991, Russia, now officially known as the Russian Federation, was the best-placed for economic reform among the 12 independent nations that emerged (excluding the three Baltic states). It had a group of dedicated reformers in senior policy-making positions and a leader who was both popular and anti-communist.

Those advantages evaporated in the next few years. Two circumstances contributed to this. One was that the initial extent of economic distortion and product shortages was exceptionally high. The other was that an IMF-supported attempt to follow the Polish example of rapid liberalization and stabilization soon revealed the lack of political support in depth for Yeltsin and his small band of liberal reformers.

There were several features of Russian institutions, as they existed in the early 1990s, which made systemic reform a very fragile process.

- There was, for practical purposes, no rule of law or control of corruption, and the government lacked effective authority.[1]
- In particular, the political heads of the 89 regions that then made up the Russian Federation had considerable formal and even more considerable informal autonomy, so that in effect conflicting economic policies were pursued at the sub-national level
- The considerable formal powers of the President did not extend to the Central Bank, which reported to the parliament.
- Parliament was hostile to systemic reform so most economic measures were pushed through by presidential edict (*ukaz*) rather than by the passing of laws. This weakened the legitimacy of the reform programme.

Liberalization and stabilization

The initial conditions in Russia at the start of 1992 were singularly unfavourable for quick liberalization and stabilization, even if the institutional defects listed above are put to one side.

In the course of Mikhail Gorbachev's *perestroika*, the planning system had been weakened by the introduction of quasi-market reforms. The resulting institutional mixture did not amount to a viable new system. The Soviet Union was entering what has been called a 'systemic vacuum'. One result was a loss of control over household money incomes. These rose, on official data, by 13.1 per cent in 1989 and 16.9 per cent in 1990, while output growth was slowing and then turning negative (Yasin, 2002, p. 103). Price control was somewhat weakened but was still largely in place. By the summer of 1990 shortages of goods in cities were extreme. Rationing had been introduced. In Moscow, for example, one had to show a residence permit before one could buy most items – and few were available.

This meant that when prices in Russia were mostly[2] decontrolled on January 2 1992, the immediate inflation was extreme: over 1500 per cent from December 1991 to December 1992, more than twice Poland's inflation of 1989. Foreign trade and the exchange rate were liberalized soon after, with a unified exchange rate, determined on the Moscow inter-bank foreign exchange market, in effect from 1 July.

The strain the January 1992 price liberalization placed on Russian households was huge, despite the exemptions from de-control (see Note 2). A political difference from Poland was also important: there the last communist government freed prices before the Mazowiecki-Balcerowicz reform team came into office. In Russia the Yeltsin leadership and its reform team led by Yegor Gaidar took all the blame.

Stabilization was correspondingly more of a problem for Russia. In retrospect it is clear that macro-stabilization was politically more fraught in Russia than privatization. The course of Russian GDP and inflation, illustrated in Figure 31.1, shows how high inflation remained for a lengthy period, while levels of economic activity plummeted.

Yevgenii Yasin, who was first a senior advisor and then for a time Minister for the Economy, identifies three stabilization attempts in the 1990s: one that lasted only a few months in 1992, a second attempt in 1993–94 and a third in 1995–97, which finally had some success (Yasin, 2002, Chapter 10). It was however the unplanned, enforced and massive devaluation of the rouble in 1998 that finally triggered a recovery of output.

The stabilization efforts can be briefly summarized as follows. In mid-1992 a brief attempt at an orthodox tightening of the money supply was put into reverse when the Soviet-era veteran banker, Viktor Gerashchenko, was placed in charge of the Central Bank of Russia (CBR). He made credit available to prop up enterprises that were otherwise approaching bankruptcy. The rate of growth of the broad money supply (Russian definition, rouble M2) accelerated in the second half of the year and inflation stayed high. Meanwhile tax collection was falling well behind the reformers' original projections and the budget deficit was rising. The second attempt was also abandoned after a few months, in the face of a continuing steep fall in output. In 1995 a policy was pursued (under IMF guidance) in which the CBR stopped financing (by the issue of money) the government deficit. This stance was maintained into 1997. Inflation fell sharply and industrial output levelled out, rising a little in 1997.

This stabilization was accompanied, however, by the growth of a debt pyramid. Enterprise closures and mass unemployment were fended off by improvised non-monetary settlement arrangements. These ranged from simple non-payment of suppliers (including not paying the wages of suppliers of labour); barter, and quasi-money in the form of bills of exchange. The government was itself a player in this 'virtual economy'. It accepted tax settlements in quasi-money and it allowed state utilities, particularly those supplying electricity and gas, to accept a build-up of debt on the part of customers. Enterprises that faced a lack of final demand,

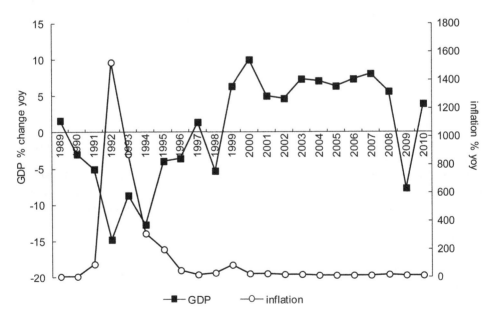

Figure 31.1 Russia: annual per cent changes in GDP and price level, 1989–2010
Source: European Bank for Reconstruction and Development (www.ebrd.com) and Rosstat (www.gks.ru).
Note: The measure of inflation here is the consumer price index, December to December. It peaked at a notional 1500%-plus in 1992 and was 8.8% in 2010.

whether for soft drinks or tractors or military aircraft, remained in operation, accumulating debt or settling accounts in barter or quasi-money with their suppliers, who did the same with their suppliers and so on down the production chain (Gaddy and Ickes, 2002).

These arrangements left enterprises just about afloat. However, the pressure on them to close down or to restructure was eased. To put it another way, they were able to preserve, after a fashion, the soft budget constraints to which Soviet state enterprises had been accustomed. They therefore were able to hold on to land, labour and capital that might have been more efficiently employed by newly-created firms (or by themselves if they had been able to re-structure). The chains of 'non-monetary settlements' left employees nominally employed but mostly unpaid, under-paid or paid in kind in whatever the enterprise happened to produce. They left the government increasingly in debt, which it financed by issuing a form of treasury bills (known in their Russian acronym as GKOs). The GKO issues created a debt pyramid that was sustainable only so long as new buyers of GKOs kept piling into the market, attracted by rates of return that in 1997–98 rose above 100 per cent.[3]

Therefore macro-stabilization, even when, in 1997, it began to show some positive results in falling inflation and a levelling-out of production, was a precarious business. It was conducted in a way that did not enforce enterprise restructuring or facilitate the growth of new firms. Its fragility was finally exposed in the summer of 1998 when investors began to take account, after the 1997 crisis in South-East Asia, of five developments: the fall in oil prices, reducing Russian government revenue; the continuing disarray in Russian state administration and the persistent budget deficit; the continuing flight of capital from the country; the loss of political support for stabilization and reform, and therefore the likelihood, arising from all this, that the Russian rouble was likely to be devalued, as the Thai baht had been the year before.

The Russian tycoon, Boris Berezovskiy, had in December 1997 forecast a major devaluation of the rouble (Yasin, 2002, p. 394). The exchange rate was being supported by the CBR between a regularly-adjusted floor and ceiling. On 17 August 1998 the government announced a partial default on debt and, in effect, let the currency fall. The rouble went quickly from about 6 to the US dollar to about 25.

This was the start of the Russian recovery. Enterprises hitherto unable to compete with imports suddenly found their foreign competitors' rouble prices rocketing. They demonstrated an unexpected ability to respond to price signals. Sales by domestic producers rose, and government coffers began to be replenished. The virtual economy began to turn real. Soon after that, in 1999, a recovery in oil prices assisted this process. Russia's GDP grew at around 7 per cent a year from 1998 to 2008 when a new and more global crisis intervened.

The response of Russian producers in late 1998–99 showed that the reforms, for all their deficiencies, really had created a population of profit-seeking business entities in place (or at any rate partly in place) of the Soviet-era state-owned enterprises.

Privatization, enterprise restructuring and the growth of new firms

Privatization was politically contentious in Russia but none the less was carried through more rapidly than stabilization. It was carried out, however, in a rough and ready fashion that left several time-bombs in the way of Russia's development.

Small-scale non-farm private enterprise developed in Russia with some impediments, but at first quite rapidly. When street trading was allowed, there was an explosion of market stalls and individual sellers in Russian towns and cities. There was a reaction against this in some cities, partly under pressure from existing, 'official' shops. Street trading was for a time abolished in Moscow, for example. However, the sale of previously state-owned shops and other small enterprises, often

to their managers, proceeded rapidly. Many larger enterprises, adjusting to the liberalization and stabilization measures just described, leased out parts of their premises to small concerns, including
stores.

In agriculture privatization faltered but in the longer run there was substantial restructuring.
Typically, the giant state and collective farms underwent a kind of quasi-privatization in which their
workers voted to re-label them companies but tried to keep them otherwise unchanged. Farm-
workers were encouraged to withdraw, taking land with them and creating private farm businesses;
few did. What did happen, gradually but extensively, was that the small 'household plots' that
rural residents and some urban residents legally operated during Soviet times, grew in importance.
Many were amalgamated (often without official registration) into *de facto* large or mid-size farms.

In one of the less conspicuous post-Soviet developments, Russian farming was eventually re-
shaped: specialization, impeded under the collective-farm system, developed, along with large
farm and wholesaling businesses and a general re-fashioning of the management of the food
supply chain. Foreign direct investors in the catering and retailing sectors, from McDonald's to
Carrefour, played a part in the last of these changes.

The simplest indicator of the transformation in the farm sector is that Russia is once again,
apart from an interruption in 2010–11, a major net exporter of grain. The Russian Empire had
exported grain. The Soviet Union under Lenin and Stalin endured famines and under
Khrushchev and his successors was a large net importer of grain.

The original privatization team, led by Anatolii Chubais, wanted large-scale privatization to be
quick. It was. One aim was to break the political resistance to reform on the part of the managers of state enterprises. Another, paradoxically, was to call a halt to the 'wild, spontaneous and often
criminal'[4] personal privatization that those managers were conducting as the old order collapsed.

Mass privatization, as it was called, involved in the Russian case the issue of vouchers to every
member of the population. These could be used in voucher auctions of shares in corporatized
state enterprises. In framing the legislation, the reformers bought the support of the 'red directors' by allowing an option in which managers and other employees could take ownership of 51
per cent of their enterprise's equity. The vouchers were tradeable, and many were bought up from
rank-and-file workers by the managers. Enterprise workforces could choose which privatization
option their workplace should pursue. The 51 per cent insider stake was the most popular
option, and ownership was quite rapidly concentrated in the hands of managers. Problematic
though some of the elements in Russia's large-scale privatization programme were, it did shift
assets into private hands at great speed: 16,500 large enterprises were privatized with the use of
vouchers between summer 1992 and summer 1994 – a remarkable organizational achievement.

Privatization from summer 1994 was supposed to continue through cash purchases only. This
stalled. It opened the way for the controversial 'loans for shares' auctions that were held in
1995–96. These have been the subject of a great deal of mystification. The auctions were corruptly
managed but the common perception that they entailed a small group of 'oligarchs'
acquiring major assets at well below their market value is misleading. Treisman (2010) estimates
that about US $850 million was paid for assets with a market value of US $1.5–1.9 billion, and
shows that the insiders ('red directors') were the ones who got the best deals while the new
entrepreneurs most commonly labelled oligarchs (Berezovskiy, Khodorkovskiy, Abramovich,
Potanin and others) obtained assets at the sort of discount commonly observed in emerging-
market privatizations.

In terms of ownership, the upshot of voucher and cash privatization was impressive. The economy
shifted from being overwhelmingly state-owned and state-run to being a predominantly privately-
owned economy. By 1996 the EBRD estimated that 70 per cent of Russian GDP originated
from production units that were wholly or mainly privately owned.

It did not follow, however, that existing enterprises were effectively restructured or that an abundance of new firms was created. It can be seen in Figure 31.2 that restructuring lagged behind privatization. (The figure also shows a later reduction in the EBRD's privatization score, but we shall come to that in the section on the Putin era.)

New firms are usually small. The officially reported numbers of small firms and their share in employment and output remain small. The numbers increased quite rapidly between end-1991 and end-1994, but then declined somewhat and thereafter stagnated (Kontorovich, 2005, p. 243, for the period through 2002). The density of small firms (number per 100,000 population) has remained low by international standards.

This picture of only modest enterprise restructuring and limited new-firm development reflects the persistent weakness of product-market competition in Russia, a defect that continued through the Putin era.[5]

It was none the less the case that a population of profit-seeking firms had been created. As has already been noted, these producers responded strongly to the 1998 rouble devaluation, and the inter-crisis boom of 1998–2008 was soon under way.

The nature of policy-making in the 1990s

Yegor Gaidar was the leader of the self-styled kamikaze reform team in 1992, yet he was never more than acting Prime Minister (the parliament refused to confirm him in office), and he lasted in that post barely a year. Yeltsin showed a clear inclination to support the market reformers but political pressures often led him to change his governments, sometimes bringing in members of the old political elite and sometimes recalling younger reformers. Opposition from the parliament was constant.

Figure 31.2 Russia: EBRD transition indicators for large-scale privatization and for enterprise restructuring, 1989–2010

Source: EBRD (www.ebrd.com).

Note: The scale for these indicators is from 1 (as in an unreformed centrally-planned economy) to 4+ (as in an advanced market economy).

When in 1993 the confrontation became acute, Yeltsin used the military, firing on the parliament. He then introduced a new constitution that increased presidential powers. Yet he did not impose autocratic rule. His popularity was low and his authority weak. It seemed to most observers, ahead of the 1996 presidential election, that there was a real possibility that the Communists might win and reverse the entire process of reform. This did not happen. Then, after the 1998 crisis, a government led by a veteran *apparatchik*, Yevgenii Primakov, was expected to put the clock back. It did not. Macroeconomic stability, at least, had come to be seen as desirable and private enterprise and the market as irreversible. Nonetheless, the reform process was a roller-coaster ride.

So was life for most Russian people in the 1990s. Real GDP, as officially measured, fell by 40–45 per cent between 1990 and 1998. Yasin (2002, p. 424) estimates that about half of this decline was made up of a reduction in military output and that the decline in economic welfare was more of the order of 15–23 per cent. Employment, certainly, fell much less than measured output. The informal or shadow economy probably propped up consumption levels without its extent being properly estimated, and military production and fixed investment fell more than consumption. However, there was extensive under-employment, non-payment of wages, a sharp rise in uncertainty about everyday life and a marked rise in age-specific mortality rates. Inequality rose steeply. The measurement of this phenomenon is problematic. Some assessments show a near doubling of the Gini coefficient between the late 1980s and the late 1990s. One major difficulty, however, is that measurements of inequality in a regime of central allocation, as in the 1980s, with privileged access arguably more important than prices and money incomes ('to each according to his official position') is especially difficult. Recovery, moreover, took time. The 1989 per capita level of real gross national income was not restored until 2003 (World Bank estimates, from Myant and Drahokoupil, 2010, Tables A.17 and A.1).

Russia transformed itself in the 1990s, but slowly, incompletely and at great human cost.

The Putin years

Putin, a former KGB officer, had served as a manager of external business relations under the reformist mayor of St Petersburg, Sobchak. The most effective of all Russia's reformers, Anatolii Chubais,[6] had a hand in bringing Putin to Moscow and installing him in the federal government, under Yeltsin's presidency. At the end of 1999 Yeltsin, in effect, selected Putin as his successor.

Putin, therefore, began his rule with some reformist credentials. In the early years, 2000–04, he imposed more 'order', by way of increased central political control. He also continued economic reforms. These included the introduction of a flat-rate income tax, the facilitation of a market in agricultural land and a serious attempt to reduce the corrupt bureaucratic impediments to the development of small firms.

The turn to statism

Then came a turn to more, and more opaque, intervention by the state: a way of supervising the economy that Russian liberals, who oppose it, call 'manual control'. The event that signalled the policy shift was the arrest of Mikhail Khodorkovskiy, the main owner of the Yukos oil company, in autumn 2003 (for a full account of the Yukos story see Sakwa, 2009).

Much of this 'manual control' was and continues to be corrupt. It has been facilitated by the weakness and venality of Russian courts and regulatory agencies. 'Corporate raiding' in Russia has a special connotation: assets are acquired by the use of corrupt assistance from the police, courts, licensing or regulatory authorities. Some foreign companies operating in Russia have lost, or come close to losing, assets in this way, but the syndrome is a general one, and is not confined to foreign investors. Foreign direct investment (FDI) has often, none the less, been commercially successful; there would however be more FDI if the risks were less. In the World Bank's 2011 *Doing Business* rankings, Russia was rated 123rd out of 183 countries – an unusually low position for an upper-middle-income country.[7]

Micro bad, macro fairly good

Microeconomic policy and institutional development, in other words, have lately been poor. That shows up in the stagnation of enterprise restructuring and a modest decline in the EBRD assessment of Russia's large-scale privatization (Figure 31.2). Macroeconomic policies, however, have remained robust. Russia's general government balance was in surplus from 2000 through 2008. Inflation slowly declined. The consumer price index finally dipped into single figures in 2006 and 2007. Economic activity boomed in the decade between the 1998 and 2008 crises.

The strength of this recovery, after the initial boost from devaluation, owed a great deal to terms of trade gains from a (mostly) rising oil price up to mid-2008. GDP grew as the Urals oil price rose, though the amplitude of fluctuations was much greater in the latter (Figure 31.3). Gross national income and real household income grew faster than GDP, but the windfall gains from oil revenue also contributed to rising demand for domestic production.

The link between hydrocarbon revenue and GDP was neither tight nor constant over time. Some of the inflow was sterilized, particularly from 2004, when a stabilization fund was established. Some of the un-sterilized inflow was spent on imports. However, by and large Russia's growth between the 1998 and 2008 crises could fairly be described as oil-fuelled, even if it would be misleading simply to regard Russia as a petro-state.[8]

The oil bonanza was managed with some prudence. Aleksey Kudrin, the Minister of Finance, appeared to have Putin's backing, most of the time, in resisting large increases in public

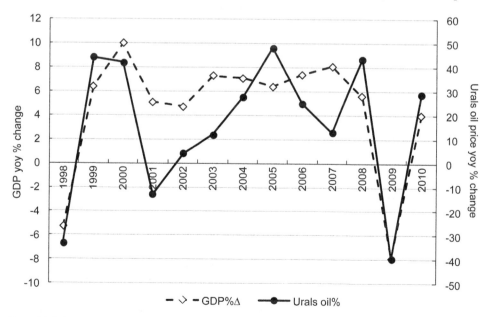

Figure 31.3 Russia: annual per cent changes in Urals oil price and GDP, 1998–2010
Sources: GDP: Rosstat; oil price: Central Bank of Russia (www.cbr.ru).

spending. In the election year of 2007,[9] however, the pressure to raise spending was stepped up and there was some loss of fiscal control. The break-even point, the average annual oil price at which the federal budget would balance, tended to creep up.

Russia in the global crisis

The global financial crisis brought Russia's boom to an abrupt end. There had been some claims in early 2008 that Russia would be a safe haven. It wasn't. Russia's GDP in 2009 was 7.8 per cent below the level of 2008. This was the largest year-on-year fall among the G20 nations. The reaction of the Russian economy contrasted with the continued, if slightly subdued, growth of the Chinese and Indian economies.

The accumulation of reserves during the boom now stood Russia's public finances in good stead. The downturn, though sharp, was relatively brief: four successive quarters. The Reserve Fund was drawn down in 2009 and 2010 to support deficit spending. Year-on-year growth in 2010 was 4 per cent and, at the end of that year, public debt had risen very little, to just 10 per cent of GDP.[10]

Russian policy debates in 2009–11 mostly concluded that the country's vulnerability to external shocks was explained by its heavy dependence on oil and gas. It is true that the average monthly Urals oil price peaked at US \$131/barrel in July 2008 and fell back to US \$38 in December of that year.[11] However, Saudi Arabia and most other oil-exporting nations experienced only a slowdown in growth, not an actual decline in GDP; Kuwait's GDP did decline, but only by a more modest 5.2 per cent.[12] It seems highly likely that other factors were at play.

In 2008–09 global capital movements displayed a flight from risk. That was bad news for Russia, but also for most other transition and emerging economies. Before the crisis Russia had seen a change in net private capital flows: up to 2006 these had been net outflows; in 2006 and 2007 net inflows of private capital were recorded for the first time. The crisis returned net private capital flows to what had been their default position – a net outflow.

Much of the gross outflow was of funds controlled by Russian companies. Weak protection of property rights has led large Russian private companies, with few exceptions, to be closely held through offshore holding companies registered in tax havens. It appears that in 2008–09 corporate borrowing from abroad, which had peaked in 2007, dropped, and stealth outflows of capital[13] rose. The flight of capital and the payment of dividends offshore appear to have been so extensive that they squeezed working capital in Russian industry. More than 90 per cent of the difference between 2009 and 2008 GDP in 2003 prices (a fall of 7.8 per cent) is accounted for by the difference between inventory accumulation in 2008 and the draw-down of inventories in 2009.[14]

In short, there is strong circumstantial evidence that Russia's output decline in the global crisis reflected the insecurity of property rights in the country, to the importance of which a large and abrupt fall in the oil price drew attention.

After the crisis: conclusions

The Russian economy has been making a recovery since mid-2009. GDP growth was 4.0 per cent in 2010. The IMF, the World Bank, Russia's own Ministry of Economic Development and private-sector analysts tend to concur in projecting growth at somewhere between four and five per cent a year, on average, in the medium term. This comparatively modest assessment reflects a less favourable external environment (sluggish recovery in Europe, Russia's main export market; tighter restrictions on lending by international banks) and Russia's changing demographics: the working-age population was still growing during the inter-crisis boom period; it is now declining, and it is likely that employment will be falling by about 0.4 per cent a year through 2020.

Russian policy-makers have been stressing the need to 'modernize' and diversify the economy. The need to improve the investment climate is widely discussed. The prospects for institutional change, however, are uncertain. With weak and corrupt courts and a great many predatory officials, Russia does not offer reliable protection of property rights. State-led development is still accepted as normal by most policy-makers, officials and indeed by many leading private business-people. Until further institutional transformation takes place, Russia is likely to remain a country in which returns to investment are not reliably appropriable by the investor, and consequently the investment rate (20.5 per cent of GDP in 2010) remains modest and below the savings rate. The Russian economy will most likely under-perform until there is a return to liberal reform.

Notes

1 The centrality of this problem was perceived at an early stage by the late Alec Nove. In a letter to Morgan Stanley of 15 January 1992, he noted that proposals for a large package of Western aid to Russia ahead of reforms 'underestimate[d] the government's powerlessness and the all-pervasive corruption' (Thatcher, 1998, p. 186).

2 Housing rents and most energy prices were not de-controlled. There was also a list of basic (mainly food) items on which local price controls could be maintained at the discretion of regional authorities. As late as 1 September 1993, the price of bread was still controlled in 40 per cent of 132 cities surveyed, and milk in 26 per cent (*Delovoi mir*, 18 September 1993, p. 7). The exclusion of rents and energy prices was common in other countries' early liberalizations; the regional-level opt-outs were not. If there is such a thing as dirty liberalization, Russia exemplifies it.

3 On IMF advice, foreign investors were allowed to buy GKOs (for roubles; capital convertibility was not established until 2006). The idea was the reasonable one of creating a wider market for government debt. The snag was that the GKO pyramid became subject to exchange-rate risk as well as its other risks.

4 Boris Yeltsin's words, from a speech reported in *Sovetskaya Rossiya*, 29 October 1991.

5 In 2008 the OECD's product market regulation (PMR) score, covering the extent of state control, barriers to trade and investment and barriers to entrepreneurship, was more than twice the OECD average (www.oecd.org/dataoecd/33/12/42136008.xls).

6 Chubais is a controversial figure, to put it mildly, in Russia. His effectiveness in getting an agenda implemented, however, is outstanding. This is suggested, *inter alia*, by his success in the partial privatization of the electricity industry under Putin, when the dominant trend in policy was towards statism

7 www.doingbusiness.org/data/exploreeconomies/

8 Oil and gas in the mid-2000s accounted for less than 2 per cent of employment (less than the Russian railways), about 20 per cent of GDP, 40–50 per cent of federal budget revenue and around 65 per cent of merchandise exports.

9 Parliamentary elections are held in December (in this case, December 2007) and the presidential election the following spring.

10 This is state debt in the usual sense. The figure would be somewhat larger if the quasi-state debt of state-controlled companies like Gazprom were included, but it would still be far below the levels now common in the developed West.

11 CBR data. www.cbr.ru.

12 IMF *World Economic Outlook database*, April 2011.

13 The CBR includes in its assessments of private capital outflows: (a) exports for which payment was not received (in Russia); (b) imports paid for but not received; (c) payments abroad for fictitious securities transactions; and (d) errors and omissions (a net item that is persistently large and negative). These can be loosely described as stealth outflows. They are presumably driven by money laundering and tax evasion, since capital convertibility has been in force since mid-2006.

14 Derived from Rosstat data at www.gks.ru/free_doc/new_site/vvp/tab25.xls.

Bibliography

Gaddy, C. and Ickes, B. (2002), *Russia's Virtual Economy*, Washington, DC: Brookings Institution.

Kontorovich, V. (2005), 'Small Business and Putin's Federal Reform,' in Reddaway, P. and Orttung, R. W. (eds), *The Dynamics of Russian Politics. Putin's Reform of Federal-Regional Relations,* vol. II, Lanham, MD: Rowman & Littlefield, pp. 241–67.

Myant, M. and Drahokoupil, J. (2010), *Transition Economies: Political Economy in Russia, Eastern Europe, and Central Asia*, Oxford: John Wiley.

OECD (1994, 1997, 2000, 2004, 2006, 2009), *Economic Surveys. Russian Federation*, Paris: OECD.

Sakwa, R. (2009), *The Quality of Freedom: Putin, Khodorkovsky and the Yukos Affair*, Oxford: Oxford University Press.

Thatcher, I.D. (ed.) (1998), *Alec Nove on Communist and Postcommunist Countries. Previously Unpublished Writings 2*, Cheltenham: Edward Elgar,

Treisman, D. (2010), '"Loans for Shares" Revisited,' *Post-Soviet Affairs*, vol. 26(3), pp. 207–27.

Yasin, Ye (2002), *Rossiiskaya ekonomika (The Russian Economy)*, Moscow: Higher School of Economics.

32

REBUILDING A TRADEABLES SECTOR

The binding constraint in the East German transition[1]

Wendy Carlin

Introduction

The two decades following the fall of communism have provided economists with a remarkable opportunity to study the consequences of radical changes in economic institutions, i.e. in the rules of the game and norms that underpin economic interaction. Transition has proved more protracted than anticipated – a rapid catch-up by the central and eastern European transition economies to European Union (EU) levels of productivity did not occur. A useful standard of comparison is with the phase of rapid catch-up by the southern European economies that began following the liberalization reforms around 1960.

Figure 32.1 presents Purchasing Power Parity (PPP) data on value added per employed worker, a broad measure of economy-wide labour productivity. It takes France as the comparator for two exercises: first for the catch-up of the southern economies from 1960, and, second, for the post-communist catch-up from 1991. Several points emerge from the comparison. First, with the exception of Slovenia, the leading Eastern European countries were further behind France in 1991 than were the Southern countries behind France in 1960 at the beginning of their catch-up; others including Bulgaria and Romania were even further behind. Second, the southern catch-up in the subsequent 17 years was mostly more rapid than that in the 17 post-transition years. Third, the southern productivity catch-up had virtually stopped by 1977 – in the subsequent 31 years, the labour productivity gap with France scarcely altered. Against the performance of its eastern European comparators, East Germany's performance was reasonably good and its catch-up to France was similar to that achieved by Greece from 1960 to 1977.

A substantial research effort has attempted to discover why well-educated labour forces with good levels of physical infrastructure in an era of financial globalization and trade integration were unable to take advantage of the apparently 'low-hanging fruit' available by introducing existing technologies, and to reap the rewards of rapid catch-up. Much of this research pointed to the neglect at the outset of transition of the challenges involved in creating market-economy institutions.

The East German transition provides a useful comparative case study. Unlike other transition economies, East Germany acquired high-quality and credible market institutions by virtue of

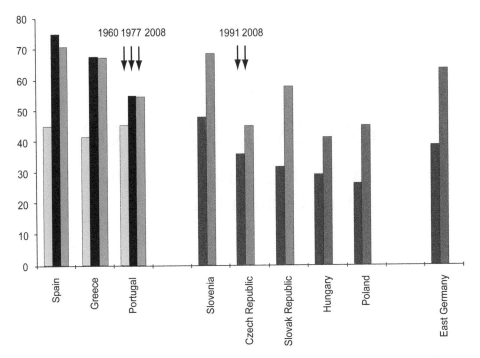

Figure 32.1 Two European Post-reform Catch-up Episodes: Southern Europe Post 1960; Transition
    Economies Post 1990
Sources: The Conference Board Total Economy Database, January 2010, http://www.conference-board.
org/economics/database.cfm;Volkswirtschaftliche Gesamtrechnungen der Länder (2009). Productivity is
measured as value added in PPP per employed worker.
Note: Productivity Index: France = 100.

unification. Yet its performance was in many ways similar to that of its central and eastern
European comparators: a transitional recession followed by slow convergence. East Germany's
experience of transition highlights the limited extent to which good institutions alone can
overcome 40 years of missing market experience, especially during a period of increasingly
integrated global markets.

What was the binding constraint on catch-up?

The framework of growth diagnostics proposed by Hausmann *et al.* (2006) can be used to analyse
the reasons for slow catch up in transition. The initial distinction is between a situation in which
the growth of private investment and entrepreneurship are inhibited by: (a) too low a rate of
return on private investment; and (b) too high a cost of finance. If there is evidence of an
abundance of profitable projects but the high cost of finance prevents them from being
undertaken, the question arises of whether it is poor access to international finance or poor local
finance that is at fault. In the case of poor local finance, this could be due to weak intermediation
or because of low savings.

In the left hand side of the tree (Figure 32.2), the availability of finance is not binding –
rather, it is the low rate of return on investment that is the problem. This could be because of
the effect of poor complementary factors such as unfavourable geography, inadequate physical

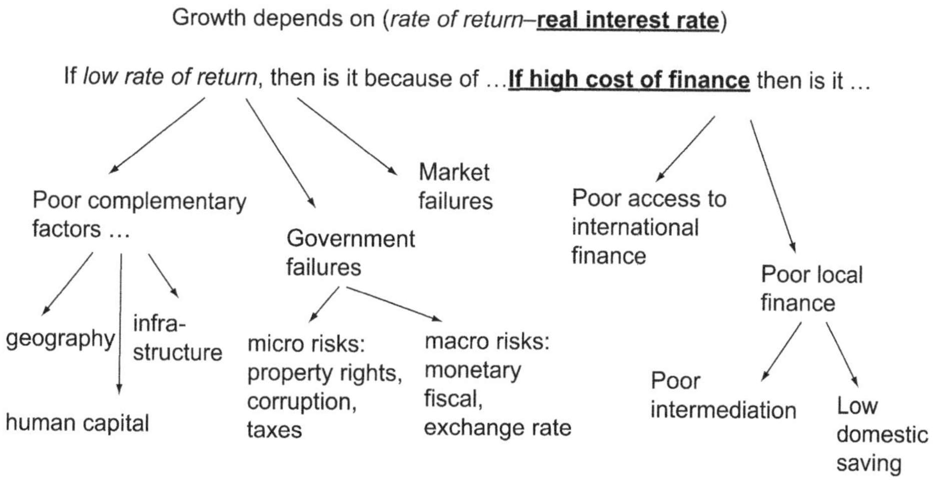

Growth depends on (*rate of return*–**real interest rate**)

If *low rate of return*, then is it because of ...**If high cost of finance** then is it ...

Poor complementary factors ...

Market failures

Government failures

Poor access to international finance

Poor local finance

geography infra-structure

human capital

micro risks: property rights, corruption, taxes

macro risks: monetary fiscal, exchange rate

Poor intermediation

Low domestic saving

Figure 32.2 Growth diagnostics: what is the binding constraint on growth where private investment and entrepreneurship are low?

infrastructure or weak human capital in reducing expected private returns. Alternatively, government failures could be responsible by raising micro or macroeconomic risk. The final branch points to market failures and the associated lack of good projects.

It is difficult to argue that the speed of catch-up of transition economies was hampered by lack of access to finance. On the contrary, a striking feature of transition was that unlike typical developing countries, the CEEC transition economies defied the so-called Lucas paradox: capital flowed to these economies and they did not have repeated balance of payments crises (e.g. Prasad *et al.*, 2007). Moreover international banks largely took over local banking networks, providing expertise and access to international capital markets. For the CEECs and East Germany, it seems reasonable to presume that we are in the left hand part of the decision tree: the rate of return, not the cost of or access to finance was the problem.

We can also rule out poor complementary factors – these countries were situated contiguous to the EU market and a positive legacy of communism was to leave levels of human capital and skills, and physical infrastructure, higher than those of the market economy benchmark at similar levels of GDP per capita (e.g. Mitra *et al.*, 2010, Chapter 5).

A large research literature has emerged in the past decade arguing that it was institutional weakness (government failure) that hampered the rapid catch up of the CEECs (see for example Rodrik, 2006). Effective legal systems, reliable and predictable tax and customs administration, norms and rules to control corruption, and so on, were not created – nor could they be – overnight. New owners had to be found for large enterprises and it became clear that privatization in the absence of adequate corporate governance failed to lift the performance of privatized enterprises above that of state owned ones (Estrin *et al.*, 2009). Foreign-owned firms performed notably better than those privatized to domestic owners.

Recent evidence suggests that political integration in the EU helps explain why the CEECs defied the Lucas paradox (Friedrich *et al.*, 2010). A plausible channel is that by creating expectations among foreign investors of a commitment to institutional reform, political integration facilitated the positive role of financial integration in promoting catch-up. If government failure or institutional weakness was a likely cause of slow catch-up in the CEECs, it was *prima facie* less plausible as a binding constraint in East Germany because of the transfer of West

German institutions. East Germany is at the extreme end of the political integration con-tinuum. However, institutions are not only 'rules on the books' but also norms, and recreating market economy norms was not immediate even in East Germany. Alesina and Fuchs-Schuendeln (2007) showed that East Germans continued to have different attitudes to state intervention than West Germans, and argued that such differences were likely to persist for another generation.

It is also possible that West German – as compared with generic – market institutions were mismatched with the needs of the transitional East German economy (e.g. Carlin, 1998). The core export-oriented sector of the West German economy is characterized by a number of specialized institutional arrangements involving among others unions, employers' associations, works councils, the commitment to transferable skills training by companies, technology transfer institutions, and various state-, quasi-state and private organizations at Federal, Land and local level. For example, it is argued that unions, employers' associations and works councils play important roles in delivering wage compression and employer commitment to training that lie behind the high-skills 'equilibrium' of the West German core economy (e.g. Hall and Soskice, 2001).

The most well-known example of institutional transfer to East Germany was the recruitment of East German workers by West German unions, and the participation of the *Treuhandanstalt* in wage-setting. Combined with the extension of social security entitlements, this placed a high floor under the wage. This rendered unprofitable much of the capital stock, producing the rapid deindustrialization of East Germany and raised the bar for the required productivity level of new projects if they were to be profitable. Once West German companies rapidly revised downwards their initial expectations of accessing buoyant markets in the former Soviet bloc via the expansion of production facilities in East Germany, it proved near impossible to replicate the West German core economy and its institutional context in the new *Bundesländer*. East Germany was left with the cost burden of the wage-setting and social security system without its micro-institutional benefits.

The federal government was forced to step in to deal with problems arising from the failure of the West German model to operate in the East. Combined with the associated fiscal burdens, this led to important changes in policy and institutions in the Federal Republic as a whole, culminating in the Hartz IV welfare reforms. Nevertheless, the export-oriented core of the West German economy retained its self-organizing capacity (as reflected in the substantial restructuring and real depreciation achieved over the post 2000 period, Carlin and Soskice, 2009). Yet in spite of the formal transfer of institutions, the export-oriented core did not extend its scale through replication in East Germany. The experience of East Germany over the past two decades was one of institutional adaptation – most obviously in the low membership of East German companies in employers' associations and the associated limited coverage of collective wage agreements in East Germany (Paqué, 2009).

In spite of these caveats, institutional quality, in the sense of the credibility and efficiency of the core market economy institutions of a functioning legal system, control of crime and cor-ruption, and the efficient administration of taxes and customs, were established quickly in East Germany. We are therefore led to turn to the final branch in the diagnostic tree diagram – market failures – in order to pin down the binding constraint on East German growth.

Hausmann *et al.* (2006) explained the 'market failure' problem in a less advanced economy as follows: 'the development process is largely about structural change: it can be characterized as one in which an economy finds out – self-discovers – what it can be good at, out of the many products and processes that already exist' (p. 18). In East Germany's case, this problem was compounded because the floor on real wages set by the political settlement (including the need to prevent mass migration to West Germany) meant it needed to 'self-discover' at a point much closer to the technology frontier than typical for a developing or transition country. New ideas for tradeables were required in order to replace the old activities rendered unprofitable by the real exchange rate and by openness to international competition. Opening up to international trade and capital flows does not *automatically* generate knowledge of profitable niches. Self-discovery is inhibited by learning and coordination externalities. In the core of the West German economy, a complex institutional matrix promotes the spillover of technological and marketing information and the co-ordination of lumpy upstream and downstream investments. However, as noted above, this was not reproduced in the East.

Moreover, East Germany faced problems of self-discovery even in non-tradeables. Normally in the sheltered sector, domestic firms have the opportunity to benefit from monopolistic innovation rents. But even in non-tradeables, the first-mover advantages for local suppliers in East Germany were often taken by West German firms – East German firms immediately faced 'foreign' suppliers and hence lower profits from 'innovation' in such markets.

What is the scale of the problem still faced by East Germany? The evolution of the 'export base'

Transition economies left the planning era with oversized industrial sectors relative to a market economy benchmark. East Germany's rapid deindustrialization following unification led it to overshoot the market economy benchmark. One reflection of this is its very low employment rate in industry. Figure 32.3 compares employment rates in industry (excluding construction) in East Germany with a number of transition economies, and with West Germany.

There is a scarcity in East Germany of 'export-base' jobs: these jobs are involved directly or indirectly in the production of goods and services sold beyond the region. A lagging region lacks sufficient jobs of this kind and is characterized by dependence on the central government to support living standards. Support arises from benefit payments and from the financing of

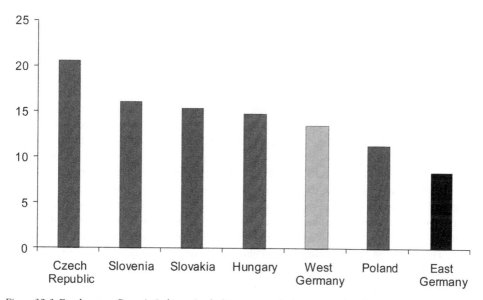

Figure 32.3 Employment Rates in Industry (excluding construction) per cent of working age population, 2007
Sources: ILO LABORSTA CE tables and St. Bundesamt VGR der Laender; Definition: ISIC 3 C+D+E.

government employment, where pay scales are set nationally. In principle there are two ways to eliminate such regional economic weakness – potential workers move to the other region, i.e. to West Germany and/or new jobs are created in East Germany.

For political reasons, it is implausible that all the adjustment would take place through the movement of population, and for economic reasons, it is infeasible for all the adjustment to take place through the creation of new export base jobs. A satisfactory adjustment path would therefore be likely to involve both processes (Rowthorn, 2000). What is an unsatisfactory outcome? An unsatisfactory outcome is a Mezzogiorno scenario, where excess population remains in the lagging region and local economic development is too weak to absorb it: productivity fails to converge and living standards are sustained by federal transfers. After a brief burst of adjustment in the 1960s, the Italian south was characterized by the Mezzogiorno scenario (Boltho *et al.*, 1997).

Using regional data for Germany, it is possible to make a crude calculation of the evolution of employment in tradeables, private non-tradeables and the government (i.e. non-market, non-tradeable) sector. Employment in tradeables is defined by employment in agriculture, mining, and manufacturing plus 'extra' employment in finance and business services. In each year, the region in Germany with the lowest ratio of employment in finance and business services to population was used to define the share of employment in this sector that could be viewed as non-tradeable, i.e. producing services required to support the local population. The remainder of employment in finance and business services in each region was defined as part of the 'tradeable' sector. Employment in the government sector was defined as that in 'public administration, defence and social security'. The results highlight the differences in the deployment of resources in East and West Germany – the employment rate deficit of East Germany is large in tradeables at some 8 percentage points. The employment rate in private non-tradeables is also markedly lower in East Germany.

Using 1991 as the base year, Figure 32.4 plots the evolution of the population of working age and employment in East Germany relative to Germany as a whole. The population of working age in East Germany fell by 5 per cent relative to Germany over the period. The chart makes clear that employment fell by much more. Following the end of the construction boom (reflected in the bulge in East Germany's share of employment in private non-tradeables), relative employment growth in both the government and in private non-tradeables evolved in line with relative population. This is what would be expected since employment in non-tradeables serves the local population. The normalization of the East German economy would involve bringing the employment in tradeables and population lines closer together: either by population draining from East Germany and/or by rising employment in tradeables, which would tend to stabilize the working age population and the associated non-tradeables employment. Given the loss of 'export base' jobs in the initial phase of the East German transition, this remains a substantial task. Nevertheless, Figure 32.4 indicates that both adjustment processes discussed above were present in East Germany from around the year 2000.

Figure 32.5 presents the employment rates in East and West Germany for tradeables and the two components of non-tradeables. In West Germany the rising overall employment rate was driven by private non-tradeables and a steady rise in the employment rate in the government sector. The upturn in East Germany's employment rate over recent years was the result of the recovery of the employment rate in private non-tradeables to a level similar to the peak achieved during the post-unification construction boom, the stabilization and slight upturn in tradeables, and the continued rise in the employment rate in the government sector.

A similar exercise can be conducted for each Land (Carlin, 2010). The clearest contributions to the amelioration of the regional problem are in Thüringen and Sachsen, where employment

Figure 32.4 Trends in East Germany relative to Germany as a whole: population of working age, employment in tradeables, in non-tradeables and in government, 1991–2007
Source: Calculated from data in Volkswirtschaftliche Gesamtrechnungen der Länder (2009).

rates in tradeables are rising towards the West German norm. However, Mecklenburg-Vorpommern appears to have the emerging characteristics of a Mezzogiorno region with little sign of closure of the huge employment rate gap in tradeables. It would appear that emigration is too weak to remove the surplus labour and local economic development is too weak to absorb the 'stayers'. The high employment rate in the government sector in this region is consistent with the decline of the region and its dependence on transfers.

Although the gaps in tradeables employment rates remain large, the achievements of East German development are tangible and suggest that designating East Germany as a whole as trapped in a Mezzogiorno scenario may be premature. Nevertheless, the challenges to creating an adequate export base remain substantial.

Buch and Toubal (2009) provide evidence of persistent differences between East and West Germany in their integration in *international* trade. They show that East German Länder trade much less with the rest of the world than West German ones, had fewer parents of multinational companies, and a lower share of inward FDI. Buch and Toubal (2009) showed that there was only slow convergence of East to West German levels along these dimensions. The methodology is well-designed to show a causal effect from lower openness to lower GDP per capita highlighting the consequences of East Germany's limited success in discovering its sources of comparative advantage.

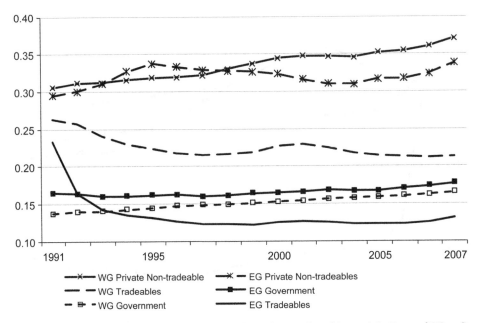

Figure 32.5 Trends in employment rates (per cent of population of working age) in East and West Germany: tradeables, non-tradeables and government, 1991–2007

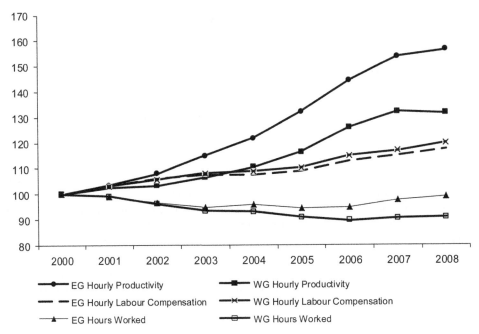

Figure 32.6 East and West German Productivity, Labour Compensation and Hours worked in Manufacturing, 2000–08

Source: Calculated from data in Volkswirtschaftliche Gesamtrechnungen der Länder (2009).

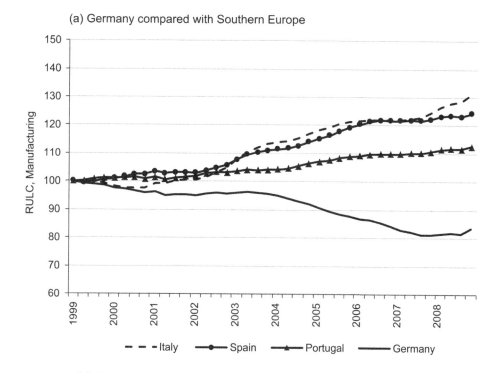

(a) Germany compared with Southern Europe

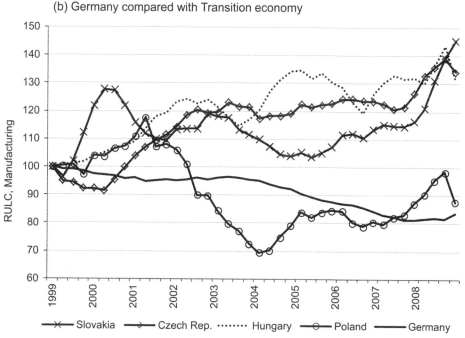

(b) Germany compared with Transition economy

Figure 32.7 Real exchange rates (EU-27) measured by relative unit labour costs in manufacturing, 1999–2008; 1999 = 100

Source: Eurostat (2010). Quarterly Real Effective Exchange Rates.

In the absence of policy instruments directly able to remove the market failures inhibiting the development of East Germany's export base, real depreciation is essential. Figure 32.6 shows that nominal wage restraint and more rapid hourly productivity growth both contributed to East Germany's improved competitiveness in manufacturing since 2000. It is productivity catch-up that made the greater contribution. The chart also makes clear that productivity improvement was accompanied by the stabilization of hours worked in manufacturing in East Germany. Money wage growth was below but close to that in West German manufacturing – reflecting the outcome in wage-setting of the conflicting pressures of a persistently weaker labour market in East Germany and the much more rapid growth of relative productivity.

The success of East Germany in achieving a substantial real depreciation vis-à-vis West Germany is all the more notable in the light of Germany's improved competitiveness versus other members of the eurozone since 1999. Figure 32.7 shows the evolution of real exchange rates among the EU-27 countries. Germany's real depreciation is evident both as compared with southern European eurozone members in the Figure 32.7a and as compared with central and east European transition economies in the Figure 32.7b.

The difficulty of achieving lower unit cost increases without the help of a nominal depreciation is reflected in the cumulative competitiveness gaps (and associated widening of trade deficits) that now exist in a number of eurozone countries. The adaptation of the wage-setting system and productivity improvements achieved in East Germany are a notable success.

Conclusions

East Germany's experience of transition highlights the limited extent to which good institutions alone can overcome forty years of missing market experience, especially during a period of increasingly integrated global markets. The East German case brings to the fore the problem of finding a niche in the international division of labour. However, there are signs of slow improvement in East German performance. For the region as a whole, it does not seem that the Mezzogiorno scenario is an appropriate characterization.

Setting East Germany's performance within a broader context highlights the contrast between its success in raising competitiveness and the erosion of competitiveness among a number of southern eurozone members. However, the speed of catch-up of East Germany is very slow and its continuation depends on the steady growth of its small poles of tradeables success. Given the evidence that agglomeration and networks are important, well-designed industrial policy to foster investment and job creation in the nodes of development that have established themselves is more likely to be successful than the application of 'watering can' support to the region as a whole.

Note

1 This contribution is based on the Keynote lecture delivered at the Conference '20 years of German Unification – From Transition to European Integration' of the Halle Institute for Economic Research (IWH). The lecture is published in Carlin (2010), where a full set of references can be found. A shortened version is published in Carlin (2011).

Bibliography

Alesina, A. and Fuchs-Schuendeln, N. (2007), 'Good-bye Lenin (or Not?): The effect of communism on people's preferences' *American Economic Review*, vol. 97(4), pp. 1507–28.

Boltho, A., Carlin, W. and Scaramozzino, P. (1997), 'Will East Germany become a new Mezzogiorno?', *Journal of Comparative Economics*, vol. 24(3), pp. 241–64.

Buch, C. and Toubal, F. (2009), 'Openness and growth: the long shadow of the Berlin Wall', *Journal of Macroeconomics*, vol. 31, pp. 409–22.

Carlin, W. (1998), 'The New East German Economy: Problems of Transition, Unification and Institutional Mismatch', *German Politics*, vol. 7(3), pp. 14–32.

Carlin, W. and Soskice, D. (2009), 'German economic performance: disentangling the role of supply-side reforms, macroeconomic policy and coordinated economy institutions', *Socio-Economic Review*, vol. 7, pp. 67–99.

Carlin, W. (2010), 'Good Institutions are not enough: Ongoing Challenges of East German Development' in *20 Jahre Deutsche Einheit: Von der Transformation zur europaischen Integration*, Tagungsband, 3/2010 Sonderheft Institut fur Wirtschaftsforschung Halle, pp. 9–31. This is also available as CES-ifo Working Paper No. *3204*.

——(2011), 'Good Institutions are not enough: Ongoing Challenges of East German Development' *DICE* 9(1), 28–34.

Estrin, S., Hanousek, J. Kočenda, E. and Svejnar, J. (2009), 'The effects of privatization and ownership in transition economies', *Journal of Economic Literature*, vol. 47(3).

Friedrich, C., Schnabel, I. and Zettelmeyer, J. (2010), 'Financial integration and growth: is emerging Europe different?' *CEPR Discussion Paper* No. 8137.

Hall, P.A. and Soskice, D. (eds) (2001), *Varieties of Capitalism: the Institutional Foundations of Comparative Advantage*, Oxford: Oxford University Press, Chapter 1.

Hausmann, R., Rodrik, D. and Velasco, A. (2006), 'Growth Diagnostics' in *Finance and Development*, vol. 43(1). and in Serra, N. and Stiglitz, J. (eds) (2008), *The Washington Consensus Reconsidered: Towards a New Global Governance*, Oxford: OUP.

Mitra, P., Selowsky, M. and Zalduendo, J. (2010), *Turmoil at Twenty*, Washington, DC: World Bank.

Paqué, K.-H. (2009), *Die Bilanz: Eine wirtschaftliche Analyse der Deutschen Einheit*. Munich: Hanser.

Prasad, E.S., Rajan, R.G. and Subramanian, A. (2007), 'Foreign capital and economic growth', *Brookings Papers on Economic Activity*, vol. 1, pp. 153–209.

Rodrik, D. (2006), 'Goodbye Washington Consensus, Hello Washington Confusion?', *Journal of Economic Literature*, vol. 44(4), pp. 973–87.

Rowthorn, R. (2000), 'Kalecki Centenary Lecture: The political economy of full employment in modern Britain', *Oxford Bulletin of Economics and Statistics*, vol. 62(2), pp. 139–73.

33

RESOURCE-RICH TRANSITION ECONOMIES

Richard Pomfret

Introduction

This contribution analyses the experience of the resource-rich southern Commonwealth of Independent States (CIS) countries and Mongolia during the transition. The seven countries faced similar challenges in the early 1990s: nation-building, transition from central planning, and realizing their resource wealth. Mongolia, as a nominally sovereign state and only informally the 'sixteenth' Soviet republic, faced an easier political task and could tackle macroeconomic problems (i.e. high inflation) faster. Tajikistan experienced civil war and Azerbaijan fought an interstate war against Armenia, while the other four Central Asian republics had a peaceful path to independence, with the Communist First Secretary becoming in each case the national President.

A central question is whether countries in transition from a centrally planned economy and Communist polity were particularly vulnerable to a resource curse owing to their fragile and changing institutions and to their inexperience with policy-making in a market-based economy. Esanov *et al.* (2001) argued that resource abundance was particularly harmful in the Soviet successor states because it allowed reform to be postponed and encouraged rent-seeking behaviour, while Brunnschweiler (2009) reaches the opposite conclusion, that among former Soviet and Eastern European countries in transition oil had a positive impact on growth between 1990 and 2006. The seven countries' comparative experience illustrates how a resource curse is possible and how it can be avoided.

The seven countries covered here are small open economies whose exports are concentrated in a few primary products. They had reasonably high levels of human capital in the Soviet era, as measured by literacy rates and life expectancy, and since 1991 have experienced an increase in per capita income at purchasing power parity (Table 33.1), although economic growth has been uneven.[1] The energy exporters, Azerbaijan, Kazakhstan and to a lesser extent Turkmenistan, attracted inflows of capital in the 1990s (Table 33.2) and enjoyed exceptionally rapid growth in the period 2000–07 (Table 33.3). Oil is the principal export of Kazakhstan and Azerbaijan. Natural gas is more important for Turkmenistan and Uzbekistan, and increasingly significant for Kazakhstan and Azerbaijan. Minerals (copper for Mongolia, gold for the Kyrgyz Republic and Uzbekistan) involve related issues of large capital requirements, technology, timing, rents and price volatility. In Central Asia water is a source of conflict between upstream countries, the Kyrgyz Republic and Tajikistan, wanting to develop hydroelectric capacity, and downstream countries, Uzbekistan and Turkmenistan, for whom water is a critical agricultural input.

Table 33.1 Demographic data, output and income, 1991 and 2007

	1991					2007			
	Population (million)	GDP (USD billion)	GNI per capita (PPP in current international $)	Life expectancy (years - 1991)	Adult literacy (per cent 1991)	Population (million)	GDP (USD billion)	GNI per capita (PPP in current I$)	Trade/GDP (per cent)
Azerbaijan	7.3	8.8	2,100**	65	97	8.6	33.0	6,630	97
Kazakhstan	16.5	24.9	4,680	68	98	15.5	104.9	9,520	92
Kyrgyz Rep.	4.5	2.6	1,690	69	97	5.2	3.8	1,980	133
Mongolia	2.2	2.0	1,987	61	98	2.6	3.9	3,160	130
Tajikistan	5.4	2.5	2,080	63	97	6.7	3.7	1,710	87
Turkmenistan	3.8	3.2	2,200**	63	98	5.0	9.5	5,510	153
Uzbekistan	21.0	13.8	1,290*	69	97	26.9	22.3	2,430	71

Source: World Bank, *World Development Indicators* at www.worldbank.org.
Notes: * 1992, ** 1993; trade/GDP = (exports + imports)/GDP. National accounts data should be treated with caution, especially for the 1990s; data for Turkmenistan are particularly dubious.

Table 33.2 Inward Foreign Direct Investment (US$ million)

	1992	1993	1994	1995	1996	1997	1998	1999	2000	2001	2002	2003	2004	2005	2006	2007	2008	2009
Azerbaijan	0	0	22	155	591	1,051	948	355	130	227	1,392	3,285	3,556	1,680	-584	-4,749	14	473
Kazakhstan	100	1,271	660	964	1,137	1,322	1,161	1,438	1,284	2,836	2,593	2,082	4,131	1,982	6,360	11,096	15,775	12,649
Kyrgyz Republic	na	10	38	96	47	83	109	44	-2	5	5	46	132	43	182	208	265	60
Mongolia	2	8	7	10	16	25	19	30	54	43	78	132	93	185	191	360	683	437
Tajikistan	9	9	12	10	18	18	30	7	24	9	36	32	272	54	339	360	376	8
Turkmenistan	na	79	103	233	108	108	62	125	131	170	276	226	354	418	731	804	820	1,355
Uzbekistan	9	48	73	-24	90	167	140	121	75	83	65	83	177	192	174	705	711	750

Source: UNCTAD at http://unctadstat.unctad.org/TableViewer/tableView.aspx (accessed 4 July 2011).

Table 33.3 Growth in real GDP 1989–2007 (per cent)

	1990	1991	1992	1993	1994	1995	1996	1997	1998	1999	1999; 1989 = 100
Azerbaijan		-1	-23	-23	-20	-12	1	6	10	10	45
Kazakhstan	0	-13	-3	-9	-13	-8	1	2	-2	2	63
Kyrgyz Republic	3	-5	-19	-16	-20	-5	7	10	2	4	63
Mongolia	-3	-9	-10	-3	2	6	2	4	4	3	
Tajikistan	-2	-7	-29	-11	-19	-13	-4	2	5	4	44
Turkmenistan	2	-5	-5	-10	-17	-7	-7	-11	5	16	64
Uzbekistan	2	-1	-11	-2	-4	-1	2	3	4	4	94

Source: European Bank for Reconstruction and Development, *Transition Report Update*, April 2001, p.15.

	1998	1999	2000	2001	2002	2003	2004	2005	2006	2007	2008	2009	2010
Azerbaijan	10	11	11	10	11	11	10	24	31	23	11	9	9
Kazakhstan	-2	3	10	14	10	9	10	10	11	9	3	1	6
Kyrgyz Republic	2	4	5	5	0	7	7	0	3	9	8	2	-4
Mongolia	4	3	1	1	4	6	10	7	9	10	9	-2	7
Tajikistan	5	4	8	10	9	10	11	7	7	8	8	3	6
Turkmenistan	7	17	19	20	16	17	15	13	11	12	11	6	11
Uzbekistan	4	4	4	4	4	4	8	7	7	10	9	8	8

Source: European Bank for Reconstruction and Development at http://www.ebrd.com/pages/research/economics/data/macro.shtml (accessed 4 July 2011).
Notes: 2010 = preliminary actual figures from official government sources.

Country experiences

The varieties of transition among the seven countries reflected differing resource endowments, and also the state of their resource sectors at the time of independence. Turkmenistan and Mongolia had recently developed gas and copper facilities, which meant that, as with the readily exportable cotton from Uzbekistan and Turkmenistan, the governments were under less intense pressure to reform the economy quickly. Tajikistan could also have been in a favourable position, with a modern aluminium smelter (benefitting from abundant hydropower) and the third-largest cotton crop in the region, but the economy was ravaged by a destructive civil war until 1997. Azerbaijan and Kazakhstan had abundant energy reserves, but needed foreign capital and expertise to develop them; the same applied to the Kyrgyz goldmines.

The varieties of transition were the result of these objective factors, as well as of political decisions by autocratic rulers. All but Mongolia have super-presidential regimes in which the personality of the president plays a role. Each president is concerned about personal power and survival, but demonstrations in 2005 met diverse responses in the Kyrgyz Republic, where a relatively liberal president exited peacefully, and Uzbekistan, where hundreds of civilians were killed. Corruption is a feature of all seven economies, but there is a distinction between Kazakhstan, where the sums were large in the 1990s but less blatant in the 2000s, and Turkmenistan where the President squandered the nation's resource revenues on monuments to

Figure 33.1 World cotton prices (Cotlook A Index), annual averages, January 1991 to June 2010, US cents per kilogram.
Source: World Bank Global Economic Monitor – at http://data.worldbank.org/data-catalog/global-econom ic-monitor.

himself, without concern for the future. The Presidents of Azerbaijan and Uzbekistan oversee less personalized regimes, displaying concerns that they be seen as wise and competent.

An important variation is between more dirigiste regimes (Uzbekistan and Turkmenistan) and more liberal regimes in the other resource-rich transition countries.[2] The dominant role of cotton in the Uzbek and Turkmen economies at the time of independence contributed to a rent-appropriating policy stance. Cotton was easy to redirect from Soviet to global markets, and during the 1990s the largest cotton exporter, Uzbekistan, had the best GDP performance of all Soviet successor states. With world cotton prices rising from under US $1.35 per pound in 1992 to over US $2.25 in mid-1996 (Figure 33.1), the cotton-producing countries were able to maintain public expenditure relatively well and were under less pressure to reform their economic and political systems. Turkmenistan and Uzbekistan are, with Belarus, the least-reformed Soviet successor states. Cotton required extensive government presence in maintaining irrigation channels and other functions, and this presence spilled over into the maintenance of state marketing monopolies which squeezed farmers' margins. Control over the economy was exacerbated after cotton prices fell and Uzbekistan in 1996 and Turkmenistan in 1998 resorted to foreign exchange controls, which in turn led to other restrictions on economic freedom. Slow reform contributed to a relatively shallow transitional recession during the 1990s, when Uzbekistan was the best-performing of all former Soviet republics, but also to a disappointing longer-term growth performance in the 2000s. Both governments used buoyant export earnings as an opportunity to promote import-substituting industrialization and other inward-oriented policies. Although Uzbekistan is a large producer of natural gas and a minor producer of oil, this meets domestic demand and Uzbekistan is roughly self-sufficient in energy.[3] Turkmenistan with large offshore energy resources was better placed to adopt a more outward-oriented policy stance, but rigid economic policies left it poorly placed to attract foreign investors to develop the oil and gas fields.[4]

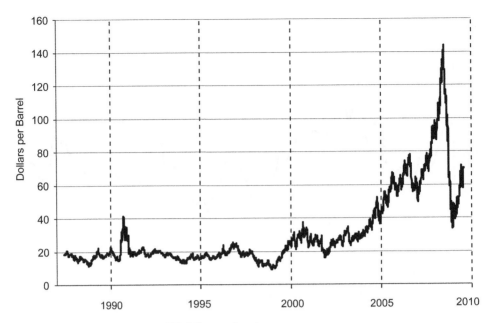

Figure 33.2 Oil prices 1987–2009, US dollars per barrel.
Source: US Energy Information Administration at http://tonto.eia.doe.gov/dnav/pct/hist/wtotworldw.htm
Note: Daily Europe Brent Spot price FOB.

The economies with abundant oil, gas and mineral reserves had poorer growth records than Uzbekistan during the 1990s. Apart from low world oil prices (Figure 33.2), they lacked the technical expertise to efficiently exploit their resources, especially offshore deposits in the Caspian Basin. Opening up new oil or gas fields or mineral deposits required a Production Sharing Agreement (PSA) with one of the few foreign firms with the necessary expertise (Pomfret, 2011). Azerbaijan and Kazakhstan negotiated with energy firms to exploit their oil and gas reserves, while Turkmenistan resisted foreign involvement. Similarly, the Kyrgyz Republic and Mongolia wanted to find foreign investors to exploit their gold, copper and other mineral deposits. All of these countries, especially the poorer non-oil producers, were under pressure to be market-friendly in their policies.

The most rapid exploitation of natural resources was in oil-rich Azerbaijan and Kazakhstan. In the early 1900s Azerbaijan produced half of the world's oil, but output stagnated in the second half of the 20th century as Soviet oil investment focused on Siberia. War with Armenia in 1992–93 over Nagorno-Karabakh further disrupted production, which by 1994 only just covered domestic demand. Military failure contributed to the overthrow of the Popular Front government, and Heydar Aliyev was elected president in October 1993. Aliyev negotiated a ceasefire in May 1994, and moved to kick-start oil production by signing the 'Deal of the Century' in September 1994; a consortium of foreign oil companies, committed to invest US $7.4 billion in offshore oilfields over 30 years. Oil production increased rapidly (Table 33.4), and oil accounted for almost 90 per cent of exports by 2002. The Baku–Tbilisi–Ceyhan pipeline to the Mediterranean was completed in 2005. Following the 2003 PSA for the Caspian Sea's largest gas field, Shah Deniz, a gas pipeline linking to the Turkish network was completed in 2006.

With increasing output of oil and gas and increasing energy prices, the state oil company SOCAR's financial position strengthened after 2003. Ilham Aliyev, who succeeded his father as

Table 33.4 Production of Crude Oil (million tons) and Natural Gas (billion cubic meters), Azerbaijan, Kazakhstan, Turkmenistan and Uzbekistan, 1985–2010

Oil	1985	1986	1987	1988	1989	1990	1991	1992	1993	1994	1995	1996	1997	1998	1999
Azerbaijan	13.2	13.1	13.9	13.7	13.2	12.5	11.8	11.2	10.3	9.6	9.2	9.1	9.0	11.4	13.9
Kazakhstan	22.7	23.3	24.1	25.0	25.4	25.8	26.6	25.8	23.0	20.3	20.6	23.0	25.8	25.9	30.1
Turkmenistan	6.8	6.6	6.5	5.7	5.8	5.7	5.4	5.2	4.4	4.2	4.1	4.4	5.4	6.4	7.1
Uzbekistan	2.3	2.5	2.7	2.4	2.7	2.8	2.8	3.3	4.0	5.5	7.6	7.6	7.9	8.2	8.1

Oil	2000	2001	2002	2003	2004	2005	2006	2007	2008	2009	2010
Azerbaijan	14.1	15.0	15.4	15.5	15.6	22.4	32.5	42.8	44.7	50.6	50.9
Kazakhstan	35.3	40.1	48.2	52.4	60.6	62.6	66.1	68.4	72.0	78.2	81.6
Turkmenistan	7.2	8.0	9.0	10.0	9.6	9.5	9.2	9.8	10.2	10.4	10.7
Uzbekistan	7.5	7.2	7.2	7.1	6.6	5.4	5.4	4.9	4.8	4.5	3.7

Gas	1985	1986	1987	1988	1989	1990	1991	1992	1993	1994	1995	1996	1997	1998	1999
Azerbaijan	12.7	12.3	11.3	10.8	10.0	9.0	7.8	7.1	6.2	5.8	6.0	5.7	5.4	5.1	5.4
Kazakhstan	4.9	5.2	5.7	6.4	6.1	6.4	7.1	7.3	6.1	4.1	5.3	5.9	7.3	7.2	9.0
Turkmenistan	75.3	76.7	79.7	79.9	81.4	79.5	76.3	54.4	59.1	32.3	29.2	31.9	15.7	12.0	20.6
Uzbekistan	31.3	34.9	36.0	36.1	37.2	36.9	37.9	38.7	40.8	42.7	43.9	44.3	46.4	49.6	50.3

Gas	2000	2001	2002	2003	2004	2005	2006	2007	2008	2009	2010
Azerbaijan	5.1	5.0	4.7	4.6	4.5	5.2	6.1	9.8	14.8	14.8	15.1
Kazakhstan	10.4	10.5	10.2	12.6	20.0	22.6	23.9	26.8	29.8	32.5	33.6
Turkmenistan	42.5	46.4	48.4	53.5	52.8	57.0	60.4	65.4	66.1	36.4	42.4
Uzbekistan	51.1	52.0	51.9	52.0	54.2	54.0	54.5	59.1	62.2	60.0	59.1

Source: BP *Statistical Review of World Energy*, June 2011 http://www.bp.com (accessed 5 July 2011).

president in 2003, appointed younger senior officials, and oversaw a closer integration of state company and government; SOCAR's activities shifted from resource–rent management to a more pro-active role in knowledge transfer and geopolitics. Oil revenues accrue to the State Oil Fund (SOFAZ), which became operational in 2001 with a mandate to transfer some funds to the government budget and invest the remainder overseas. In 2002 SOFAZ supported a commercial venture, the Baku–Tbilisi–Ceyhan pipeline. There was also debate over the extent to which the fund should support social welfare spending; in 2003 the Fund provided US $24 million to assist people displaced by the Nagorno–Karabakh conflict and transferred US $115 million to the state budget for other purposes. Azerbaijan had by 2008 saved less than one-tenth of its oil windfall, in contrast to Russia and Kazakhstan, which both saved over half of their 2003–07 windfalls in oil funds.

Kazakhstan has the Caspian Sea region's largest recoverable crude oil reserves, and accounts for over half of the oil currently produced in the region (Table 33.4). The modern Caspian oil industry dates from the Tengiz agreement signed between Chevron and the USSR in 1990; the largest foreign investment deal in Soviet history, which was inherited by Kazakhstan after the dissolution of the Soviet Union. During the 1990s, exploitation of the Tengiz oilfield and exploration for other oilfields was hampered by lack of technical expertise, lengthy negotiations with potential foreign partners, and Russian control over pipeline routes.[5] Despite the corruption, PSAs succeeded in developing energy resources, and foreign participation helped to ensure construction of new pipelines. Coinciding with the rapid rise in oil prices, Kazakhstan's oil exports drove growth rates of over 9 per cent per year in 2000–07, and accounted for a third of the country's GDP in 2005–07. The high growth was, however, associated with foreign borrowing based on a strong country credit rating and a real estate bubble, which led to a domestic banking crisis in 2007. When prices exceed reference prices extra revenues from oil, gas, copper, lead, zinc and chrome are transferred to the National Fund (NFRK), which must keep at least a fifth of its assets in the stabilization portfolio with specific criteria requiring investment in liquid foreign financial instruments. Following the 2007/08 financial crisis, NFRK funds financed a US$10 billion (or 9.5 per cent of GDP) anti-crisis plan in late 2008.

Concerned that earlier PSAs gave too much to foreign partners, Kazakhstan strengthened local content requirements in 1999, and mandated a minimum 50 per cent participation of state-owned KazMunaiGas (KMG) in PSAs in 2005. By 2009 KMG owned about 30 per cent of oil production and 40 per cent of proven reserves. KMG has some resemblance to Russian state-owned energy companies, Gazprom and Rosneft, although KMG has generally acquired larger shares of energy projects in a straightforward and transparent manner by purchase or the transfer of state-held licenses. Kazakhstan has also increased pressure on western participants in its energy sector by accepting Chinese participation. The Chinese and Kazakh presidents, together with their Turkmen and Uzbek counterparts, opened a gas pipeline in December 2009, and an oil pipeline from western Kazakhstan to China is under construction.

Tajikistan is the poorest of the former Soviet republics. Independence was accompanied by a civil war, which was not settled until 1997, and the government's hold over parts of the country remains tenuous. Tajikistan was a major cotton producer in the Soviet era, but the sector has declined since independence. The country also has substantial hydroelectric potential which has yet to be realized; the main use of existing hydro-power is in an aluminium smelter, which is by far the country's largest industrial facility. Tajikistan features little in this contribution because its main challenge continues to be the construction of a functioning state and economy.

The Kyrgyz Republic shares some of Tajikistan's characteristics – a poor mountainous country whose hydroelectricity development is stymied by opposition from downstream neighbours – but it has been more successful in nation-building. The Kyrgyz economy is the most liberal in Central Asia, although it does not function as well as a market economy should because institutional development is flawed and corruption remains a major feature. Uniquely in Central Asia, two presidents have been replaced by popular uprisings and in 2010 a constitution limiting presidential power and promising a parliamentary democracy was adopted.

The country's major resource is Kumtor, the eighth largest goldmine in the world. Kumtor was considered commercially non-viable by Soviet geologists, but in 1992 a Canadian company, Cameco, offered to take managerial control of the mine. The mine started operation in 1997 and accounted for about a sixth of the Kyrgyz Republic's GDP by the early 2000s; when the mine's production was disrupted in 2002, GDP growth dropped to zero. The mine was controversial, in part because, despite its substantial contribution to GDP, it appeared to contribute little to public revenues. Protests about environmental damage (e.g. a 1998 incident when a truck carrying 1,762 kg of sodium cyanide fell into a river) and mine safety (e.g. a 2002 death when part of the mine collapsed) were inflamed in 2005 when it turned out that compensation paid by the company to people suffering from the 1998 incident had ended up in a senior official's pocket. Between 2004 and 2009 the operation was restructured as a joint venture, Centerra Gold, between Cameco and the state gold agency. Concerns about who benefited contributed to the public unrest leading to the overthrow of President Akayev in March 2005 and to dissatisfaction with President Bakiyev's role. The atmosphere of uncertainty and renegotiation deterred foreign investment in other projects.

Mongolia was an independent country before 1991, and since 1990 has a democratic political system with rotation of power following elections. Mongolia has established a market-based economic system, but as in the Kyrgyz Republic this has not brought the anticipated level of prosperity. Unlike the Kyrgyz Republic, Mongolia failed to exploit its mineral resources, perhaps because its existing mineral industry included some modern facilities. Mongolia's largest enterprise, the Erdenet copper and molybdenum complex, was established with Soviet aid in 1978; by 1989 Erdenet had produced a million tons of copper concentrate, and was the largest copper mine in Asia. Domestic coal production met most of the energy requirements of the main towns and industrial and mining sites. Gold was produced in many small-scale operations, and the Mardai mine produced uranium for Soviet nuclear warheads.

Although Mongolia was believed to contain unexploited mineral resources, little exploration took place during the 1990s. Democracy in Mongolia has been associated with large swings in economic policy from freewheeling but corrupt capitalism to a dirigiste approach, neither of which encouraged the long-term capital inflows necessary to fund copper or coal mines. In 1990–92 many Soviet technicians departed. Development of the Mardai uranium mine by a Canadian-Russian joint venture was dogged by mutual recriminations; the Canadian partner pulled out in 1998 after investing US $6 million. During the commodity boom of the 2000s, Mongolia placed punitive taxes on foreign companies; in 2008 the World Bank estimated the effective tax rate was over 60 per cent, the second-highest in the world. The aim was to ensure that the state gained a large share of Mongolia's mineral wealth, but the effect was to deter investors.

Mongolia's first major new mining project should be the Oyu Tolgoi copper and gold mine located in the Gobi desert, and estimated to hold 45 million ounces of gold and 79 billion pounds of copper (nearly 3 per cent of the world's total supply). The mine was discovered by Canadian company, Ivanhoe, in 2001, but something always prevented an investment deal from being signed, notably laws passed by the government to capitalize on high metals prices. In October 2009, after the parliament revoked the most extreme tax laws, Ivanhoe and its partner Rio Tinto signed an investment agreement committing US $6 billion investment in Oyu Tolgoi to begin production in 2013.

The steps to avoiding a resource curse

Governments of resource-rich countries must decide how and how fast to exploit their natural resources, how to share the revenues between companies and the state, and how to use the state's revenues. These are interconnected. If the 'how' is unacceptable to any company with the technology to exploit the resource, then the other questions are irrelevant. If the terms are too attractive to a private-sector partner, then the country may achieve rapid resource exploitation, but not have revenues to spend. Moreover, this is not a one-shot game: either side may try to recontract, leaving the other to accept, renegotiate or give up on the deal; the government may win a battle over division of the spoils, but deter future investors concerned about the credibility of government commitments.

Speed versus caution

Host countries negotiating PSAs may want to proceed cautiously in the face of asymmetric information: operating firms have a better idea of upfront costs, and may overstate these so that

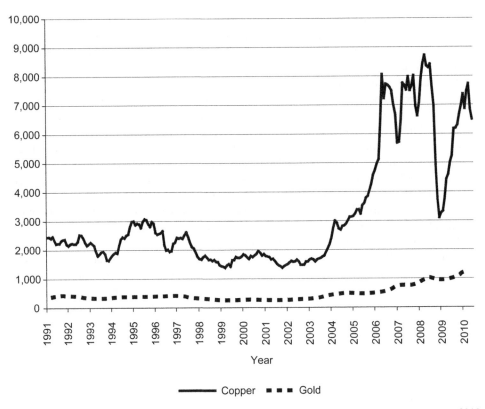

Figure 33.3 Copper (dollars per metric ton) and Gold (dollars per ounce) Prices, January 1991 to June 2010
Source: World Bank Global Economic Monitor – at http://data.worldbank.org/data-catalog/global-econo
mic-monitor.

they recoup more money before the state starts to collect its share of revenues. Speed may lead to mistakes in the choice of partner; Kazakhstan came to rue its choice of Eni as lead operator for Kashagan. If the state fails to hold the partner responsible for negative externalities (e.g. by specifying environmental or work safety obligations), then the partner may not feel obligated to spend money on these, as at Kumtor. Rapid exploitation of resources may also create an absorption problem due to lack of capacity to efficiently use the windfall.

The Hartwick–Solow rule that a country should not deplete total capital (i.e. physical, human and natural resource capital) provides a guideline for protecting future generations from resource depletion. However, it is desirable to transform natural capital into physical or human capital when the relative price of natural capital is high. Azerbaijan and Kazakhstan increased their oil output as oil prices surged from US $12 per barrel in 1998 to almost US $150 in 2008. Turkmenistan was less prepared to take advantage of the energy boom because it did not have the capacity to increase gas or oil output substantially, nor to export gas to any market other than Russia. The Kyrgyz Republic reaped substantial export earnings and local employment when gold prices were high in the 2000s, while Mongolia's drawn-out contractual negotiations meant that the country missed out on the boom in copper prices (Figure 33.3). In the worst-case scenario technical change can drastically reduce the value of specific minerals. Turkmenistan's failure to take advantage of high energy prices may be especially damaging, because EU gas markets are shifting towards liquefied natural gas, which will benefit producers with ocean ports (e.g. Qatar and Australia) and penalize land-locked gas producers.

Sharing the proceeds

Once a resource has been explored and is being exploited much of the revenue is rent, i.e. excess payment above that required to induce supply. The structure of PSAs and inclusion of arbitration are designed to limit opportunistic behaviour by host countries, which might be tempted, once the foreign partners have incurred the up-front costs, to revise the agreement. If the host tries to renegotiate for better terms, it may be challenged under arbitration, and ignoring an arbitration decision risks serious loss of future FDI. Yet, once revenues are flowing and costs recouped, the foreign partner may acquiesce in contract revision rather than risk harassment or even expropriation and forego a share of future revenues. A constraint on treating foreign partners too negatively is that such behaviour will discourage future foreign investment.

Nevertheless, there is flexibility in long-lived energy or mining PSAs, as relative bargaining strengths shift with market conditions. The energy-rich countries were in a weak position in the 1990s when world oil prices were low, but as prices soared in the 2000s their position strengthened. The challenge was to find a balance between asserting rights to a greater share of the proceeds which are grudgingly accepted as fair and deterring future foreign investment by being too grasping.

The activities of the state energy companies in Azerbaijan and Kazakhstan since the mid-2000s are a form of contract revision. If domestic companies are part of a consortium, then more revenues accrue domestically. Domestic energy or mining companies often have little to contribute, because absence of technology and skills is usually the principal reason for having involved foreign companies. Thus, their participation is primarily about rent extraction, although there may be positive externalities such as skill and technology transfer. At the same time, state energy companies are often highly politicized, and rents may be siphoned off through a non-transparent state entity or in Turkmenistan's case simply placed into off-budget accounts under presidential control.

Using the revenues

Once resources are being exploited governments face the question of how to use the revenues. As oil prices began to rise and then soared after 2003, revenues far exceeded domestic absorption capacity in Azerbaijan and Kazakhstan, which created sovereign wealth funds to manage the windfall. Both funds were established by presidential decree rather than by legislation which passed through parliament, thus leaving them subject to presidential discretion. For both countries a major issue has been making a credible commitment to avoid short-term plundering of the fund's assets, especially as both transition economies had reasons to increase social expenditures and to promote future growth.

Kazakhstan appears to have been more successful in this respect, at least before the 2007/08 financial crisis, whereas Azerbaijan saved little of the windfall revenues. Azerbaijan used its oil windfall to finance public expenditure, running a non-oil fiscal deficit equal to 30 per cent of GDP between 2003 and 2006 and borrowing abroad an amount equal to about 4 per cent of 2006 GDP. By contrast Kazakhstan was paying off external debts to reduce future obligations. The situation changed in Kazakhstan as the financial sector ran into serious problems in 2007; substantial funds were transferred from the NFRK in 2008–09 to help the ailing banking and construction sectors and to provide stimulus for small and medium-sized enterprises and fund public investment.

Reliance on resource revenues rather than taxes reduces the need for governments to seek popular support for spending, fostering undemocratic systems and lack of checks on executive power. An alternative is to redistribute resource rents to the population who can make private spending decisions, including voting on how much to devote to public expenditures through taxes. In Mongolia both major parties have promised cash handouts to the people, but doing this before earning substantial resource revenues looks like fiscal profligacy.

Conclusions

Realizing the benefits from resource abundance is an obstacle race, where falling at a hurdle may forestall any benefits or turn resources into a curse. The experience of the countries covered here illustrates the pitfalls, but also suggests that some are more serious than others.

The volatility of oil and mineral prices highlights the importance of timing when it comes to resource exploitation. At the negotiation stage governments may make mistakes such as choosing an unqualified partner, placing inadequate controls on the project or winning inadequate revenue shares for the state. Azerbaijan, Kazakhstan and the Kyrgyz Republic illustrate flawed outcomes following quick deals with foreign investors. The missed opportunities of Turkmenistan and Mongolia from not involving foreign partners are more clearly negative.

The shares of revenue streams are a prominent part of negotiations, but in practice the shares can be revised. Depressed world oil prices during the 1990s meant that Azerbaijan and Kazakhstan negotiated PSAs under unfavourable conditions, making substantial concessions in order to ensure foreign companies' investment. During the oil boom they were able to obtain improved terms using the state oil company as a vehicle. There are, however, constraints in that a too rapacious or capricious state will not be an attractive partner in future projects.

The final challenge once revenues are flowing to the state is to ensure that they are used wisely, for present and future generations. If leaders enrich themselves rather than promoting the public interest, the outcome may be a rent-seeking society with ruthless power-holders. Turkmenistan highlights the potential for institutional degradation, and Kazakhstan seemed to be on that path in the 1990s. Even well-intentioned governments can run into problems if their spending plans exceed the country's absorptive capacity, and then revenues fall.

The impact of resource abundance on institutions depends upon many factors, including path dependence and the conjuncture of circumstances. Kazakhstan in the 1990s was an example of rent-seeking institutional degradation, but a positive conjuncture in the 2000s (soaring oil prices, large oil and gas discoveries and new pipelines) triggered institutional and policy evolution. Uzbekistan, by contrast, had less resource–rent-driven institutional degradation in the 1990s, but avoided reforms and stagnated in the 2000s. Both Azerbaijan and Kazakhstan have super-presidential regimes with high levels of corruption, but the regimes are less rigid than those of Turkmenistan or Uzbekistan, where economic development has been stifled by an overpowering state administration. A general conclusion from the experience of the Central Asian countries is that a more open approach to trade and investment may be a catalyst for positive institutional change either directly through greater exposure to ideas and practices or indirectly through rising expectations of social and political inclusion.

The formerly centrally planned economies may be especially prone to a resource curse outcome owing to their inexperience with policymaking in market-based economies and the absence of strong economic institutions, but the malleability of institutions can also be an advantage as adverse institutional consequences of initial decisions can be corrected. The experience of the seven countries studied here is mixed and in most cases the jury is still out. The worst outcomes, apart perhaps from Turkmenistan, are due to poor policymaking or missed opportunities rather than a resource curse, while the more positive cases still face substantial challenges.

Notes

1 Pomfret (2006) provides more general background on the five Central Asian countries' economies. Tajikistan's high growth in 2000–04 was recovery from the civil war that ended in 1997. The seven countries' resource sectors are described more fully in Pomfret (2011).

2 Of the seven countries covered here, only Mongolia (in 1997) and the Kyrgyz Republic (in 1998) have joined the World Trade Organization (WTO). Uzbekistan (1994), Kazakhstan (1996), Azerbaijan (1997) and Tajikistan (2001) have applied for WTO membership, but accession negotiations are stalled or moving very slowly. Turkmenistan has not applied.

3 Uzbekistan has been reluctant to involve foreign firms in its resource sectors, but the economy is better managed than that of Turkmenistan and cotton remains a major export. Uzbekistan's second largest export is gold, in whose production foreign partners have played a role, but the arrangements and gold output are not publicized by the government.

4 At independence the resource base was cotton and a recently developed natural gas sector, neither of which was in urgent need of foreign expertise. Cotton provided the revenues in the mid-1990s to fund populist polices and grandiose buildings, but the government offered little incentive to farmers and production declined. As cotton exports diminished, revenues from gas exports began to increase after 2000, largely owing to external price changes; the volume produced was lower in the 2000s than it had been in 1990 (Table 33.4). Involvement of foreign firms was minimized, and almost all gas exports went to or through Russia until 2009 when a pipeline to western China broke Russia's monopoly. At independence oil output was small, but onshore and offshore reserves were believed to be substantial; large western firms signed PSAs, but after the turn of the century involvement of ExxonMobil and Monument was changed in favour of smaller companies. Oil output of just over 7 million tons in 2000 was not much higher than in 1985, and less than the 1975 peak, and by the mid-2000s it was becoming clear that to increase oil and gas output Turkmenistan needed foreign capital and know-how. Kalyuzhnova (2008, pp. 83–86) emphasizes lack of technical skills after the departure of Soviet specialists as the cause of falling revenues per cubic meter of gas exports, and also highlights how much time in exploiting offshore oil reserves has been wasted due to lack of expertise. Turkmenistan has not yet created a positive environment for foreign investors.

5 The 1990s in Kazakhstan were characterized by a series of deals between the government and the oil majors to revise the shareholdings in Tengiz and for the development of other large energy projects such as the Kashagan offshore oilfield and the Karachaganak gas field. The process was opaque, leading to drawn-out legal proceedings in New York and elsewhere and imprisonment in the USA of a Mobil Vice-President for failing to declare a 'commission' in his tax return.

Bibliography

Brunnschweiler, C. (2009), 'Oil and Growth in Transition Countries', *Center of Economic Research at ETH Zurich Working Paper 09/108*, Eidgenössische Technische Hochschule Zürich, May.

Esanov, A., Raiser, M. and Buiter, W. (2001), 'Nature's Blessing or Nature's Curse: The political economy of transition in resource-based economies', *EBRD Working Paper No.65*, London.

Franke, A., Gawrich, A. and Alakbarov, G. (2009), 'Kazakhstan and Azerbaijan as Post-Soviet Rentier States: Resource incomes and autocracy as a double 'çurse' in post-Soviet regimes', *Europe-Asia Studies*, vol. 61(1), pp. 109–40.

Jones Luong, P. and Weinthal, E. (2010), *Oil Is Not a Curse: Ownership Structure and Institutions in Soviet Successor States*, New York: Cambridge University Press.

Kalyuzhnova, Y. (2008), *Economics of the Caspian Oil and Gas Wealth: Companies, governments, policies*, Basingstoke: Palgrave Macmillan.

Olcott, M. (2007), *Kazmunaigaz: Kazakhstan's National Oil and Gas Company*, Houston, TX: James Baker III Institute for Public Policy, Rice University.

Pomfret, R. (2006), *The Central Asian Economies since Independence*, Princeton, NJ: Princeton University Press.

——(2011), 'Exploiting Energy and Mineral Resources in Central Asia, Azerbaijan and Mongolia', *Comparative Economic Studies*, vol. 53(1), pp. 5–33.

Part IX
Assessment

34

ECONOMIC GROWTH IN THE TRANSITION FROM COMMUNISM

Nauro F. Campos and Fabrizio Coricelli

Transition and growth

The two decades after the collapse of communism have witnessed large differences in terms of economic growth across transition countries. Figure 34.1 displays the dynamics of real GDP for central-eastern Europe (CEE) and for the Commonwealth of Independent States (CIS), during the period following the launch of market reforms, which started in 1989 in the CEE and 1991 in the CIS. Two main features stand out. First, the CEE countries have performed much better than the CIS. The initial output drop has been smaller and the recovery faster. As a result, in 2011 the level of real GDP in CEE countries was more than 80 per cent higher than before transition, whereas for the CIS the level of real GDP in 2011 was only 40 per cent above its pre-transition level. Second, both groups of countries have not performed particularly well in terms of the dynamics of real GDP vis-à-vis the rest of the world. Even though the CEE countries experienced a small loss in terms of output growth relative to the world economy, a large gap did open up for the CIS countries.

Both different initial conditions and different reform trajectories help explain these different performances. The growth performance of transition countries has been importantly affected by the initial 'transitional recession,' as defined by Kornai (1994). One might have expected that those countries initially harder hit would have displayed a steeper recovery. More generally, contrasting the experience of transition countries with that of other countries going through episodes of recession and crisis, one would have assumed that the specificity of transition would emerge in the form of a steep recovery following the output collapse, as the movement towards a market economy ought to have produced enormous efficiency gains. During the 1990s various explanations were provided for the persistence of the output decline and for the relatively poor post-recession performance (see Campos and Coricelli, 2002, for an overview). Here we focus on three main questions: (i) How did the 'transitional recession' compare with other episodes of deep recession in non-transition countries? (ii) What role did the 'transitional recession' play for the subsequent process of growth? (iii) What role did reform and liberalization policies play in transition countries, and more specifically, how important were the complementarities among reforms in terms of their impact on economic growth?

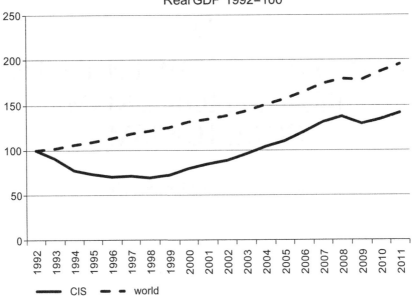

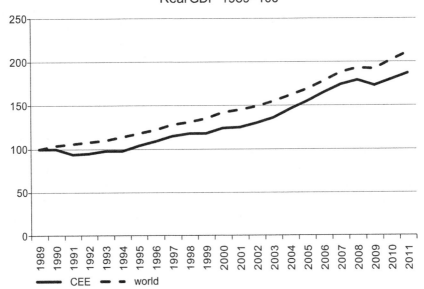

Figure 34.1 Real output during transition
Source: IMF, *World Economic Outlook Database*, June 2011.

The first question involves an assessment of the specificity of the transition experience. Is switching from a planned to a market economy radically different from, for instance, transforming a system from an agrarian economy into an industrial economy? The second question concerns the role of the initial output fall in explaining the subsequent recovery and growth. Did the depth and persistence of the initial output fall affect the characteristics of the output dynamics in the following period? The third question raises the issue of whether and to what extent the effects of structural reform policies depend on the magnitude and the pervasive nature of the initial distortions. Considering that planned economies were characterized by extreme distortions, linked to the absence of markets and the dominance of the state in the economy, should we expect that freeing the economy from these distortions would underpin a strong growth effect? Is there a role for policy complementarities in a world characterized by huge and widespread distortions?

Transition can be linked to the so-called 'unified theory of growth and development' by Parente and Prescott (2005). In this approach, growth and development go through different regimes, each characterized by institutional and policy factors which ultimately determine the growth performance of a country. The main idea is that countries can potentially exploit a 'world technology', which describes the technological frontier available in each period in history. Yet, national institutions and policies determine whether a country is capable of fully exploiting such a technological frontier. Defining a 'Malthus regime' as a regime under which output per capita stagnates, and a 'Solow regime' as the regime under which output per capita grows over time, the growth dynamics of a country can be analysed as a process characterized by a regime switch. Such switching occurs at different points in time for different countries. For this reason, a cross-section analysis would identify large differential productivity growth and productivity levels across countries. Furthermore, a time series of growth for a given country would identify structural breaks with accelerations of growth. Institutions and policies determine the timing of the regime switch and the extent to which a country is capable of moving closer to the world technology frontier. We believe transition fits rather well such a unified approach, because it is arguably the most important example of regime switch observed in the twentieth century.[1] From an empirical perspective, the transition experience accords with recent analyses of growth that emphasize the relevance of distinguishing periods of positive growth and periods of recession.

Transitional recession in a comparative perspective

Transitional recession is defined as the output fall that occurred after the launch of policies of liberalization and market reforms in formerly planned economies. The starting dates of transition differ across countries, with CEE countries launching their reform programmes during 1990–91, and the CIS countries launching such programmes after 1992. An additional complication for the cross-country comparison is that in the former Soviet Union, output began to fall before transition, namely with the start of *perestroika*. In Table 34.1 the recessions experienced by transition countries can be seen in a comparative perspective, over the whole period from 1960 to 2001.[2]

It is indeed remarkable that the cumulative decline for transition countries is by far the largest in the whole sample. Note that this is an average cumulative decline and thus it is affected by the milder drop in CEE. If we separate the CIS from CEE, we obtain even sharper results. Therefore, the first observation is that the 'transitional recession' is unique in its magnitude during the last half century. Furthermore, the duration indicates that the 'transitional recession' has also been the more persistent recession in a comparative perspective.

Table 34.1 Characteristics of recessions around the world (1960–2001)

Type/characteristics	Cumulative loss of GDP	Duration (years)	Number of observations
All country episodes	–7.5	1.62	637
Low income	–7.1	1.58	259
Low-middle income	–10	1.84	163
Upper-middle income	–8.6	1.67	97
High income	–4.1	1.38	118
Crisis	–6.8	1.64	182
Banking crisis	–11.7	2.19	104
Trade liberalization	–7.6	1.79	141
New government	–12.8	2.08	74
Civil wars	–17.4	2.42	60
Financial liberalization	–3.1	1.23	43
International capital flows	–3.6	1.32	53
Partial financial liberalization	–5.6	1.58	24
Partial capital liberalization	–6.0	1.53	43
Africa	–6.6	1.52	243
Asia	–6.0	1.39	93
Industrial country	–2.2	1.38	74
Latin America	–6.0	1.55	74
Middle East	–11.1	1.40	47
CIS[a]	–35.6	4.56	18
CEEs[a]	–19.3	2.88	16

Source: Cerra and Saxena (2008).
Note: a Authors'calculations.

The second observation is that the magnitude of the output decline in transition is comparable – actually deeper – than that observed during episodes of civil war in the rest of the world. The difference between CEE and the CIS countries has been huge: the average cumulative loss of GDP from peak-to-trough during the transitional recession in the CIS countries has been 35.6 per cent, and lasted 4.56 years, while in CEE it has been 19.3 per cent and lasted 2.88 years. It took the CIS countries an average of 10 years to return to their pre-recession output levels, while 3 years is the comparable figure for the CEE countries.[3]

Table 34.2 summarize econometric evidence on the effects of recessions on the immediate post-recession growth. It shows, by running two separate regressions for the period 1961–92 and for the period 1992–2007, that the magnitude of such negative effects is larger (or has significantly increased) in the later, more recent period. One reason may be the presence of transition recessions in the sample. This can be verified by including an interaction term for transition countries. Such an interaction term has indeed a significant negative sign, and although the estimated coefficients are still different before and after 1992, the difference is much smaller than in the regression without the transition countries dummy variable. This suggests that transition countries account for a substantial share of the increase in the negative effect of recessions found in the post-1992 period. These results further imply that recessions in transition countries have a strong negative and long-lasting effect on post-recession growth rates, pointing towards relatively shallow, if any, creative destruction in transition countries.

Table 34.2 Strength of recoveries before and after 1992

	Authors' calculations				Cerra and Saxena (2008, Table 3, page 26)	
	62–92	92–07	62–92	92–07	62–89	90–01
Dummy trough lagged	-0.375*	-1.017***	-0.380*	-0.601*	-0.39**	-1.2***
Trough$_{i,t-1}$	(0.240)	(0.313)	(0.243)	(0.855)	(-2.0)[a]	(-9.2)[a]
Trough$_{i,t-1}$ * transition			0.220 (1.549)	-2.618*** (0.855)		
Number of observations	3348	2366	3348	2366	3033	1714

Notes: *Significance at the 10%; **significance at the 5%; ***significance at the 1%.

Theoretical explanations

What are the main reasons that have been identified for this process? The theoretical literature on transition can be divided in two groups, one focusing on the initial fall in output, the other on medium- and long-term issues. The short time span that covers the experience of transition from a planned to a market economy makes it difficult for the analysis of economic growth to neglect the initial sharp, and largely unexpected, fall in output. Moreover, in some instances the initial collapse translated into a long and persistent depression.

Following the collapse of output, a lively debate started on its causes. Several observers claimed that such a collapse could be simply explained as a Keynesian recession, driven by a fall in consumer demand. Others argued that the fall in output could not be described as a simple Keynesian recession, as the timing and the magnitude of the collapse suggested a different interpretation, based on the concept of 'trade implosion'.[4] The phenomenon of 'trade implosion' can be ascribed to the break-up of the old system of coordination of production and exchange. The absence of market institutions implied that the old mechanisms of production and trade could not be quickly replaced by new well-functioning mechanisms. Kornai (1994) defined the output fall as a 'transformational' recession. This view appears relevant for a longer run perspective, as it pointed out the risks of a prolonged period of recession, or low-output equilibrium.

The sharp and unexpected fall in output is a puzzle for economic theory. Liberalization of prices, dismantling of trade barriers and the elimination of pervasive state intervention in economic activity, should have brought large efficiency gains. Within the literature on the initial output collapse, two main contributions stand out. One underlines the role of credit markets, the other the role of the so-called disorganization.

In a planned economy, the artificial structure of production and trade imposed by the planning system made credit markets, and to some extent even money itself, irrelevant, at least in connection with the enterprise sector. The dismantling of the planning system implied that production and trade were not only decentralized but that they would have to be carried out through monetary or credit arrangements. Development of credit markets takes time. The availability of cash for transactions by enterprises was constrained by official credit, given that firms initially lacked financial savings since these had been illegal in most centrally planned economies. Calvo and Coricelli (1993) single out credit markets as a fundamental institution missing in the former centrally planned economies. The collapse of CMEA trade can also be seen as an example, related to the abandonment of an old mechanism of trade and netting out of payments, without the substitution with a private credit market. The imposition of tight financial policies at the time of price liberalization likely determined a situation of credit crunch for enterprises. The contraction of central bank credit resulted in a contraction in the overall credit supply to the economy, as private credit markets could not develop overnight.

Liquidity shortages can in principle explain a temporary fall in output. Over time, firms can accumulate monetary balances and converge to the optimal level of output that would have been reached in the presence of perfect credit markets. Accordingly, the behaviour of output would follow a U-shaped pattern. An implication of this view is that the output decline should be accompanied by a decline in productivity. Moreover, real wages would drop as well, as enterprises attempted to generate liquidity to purchase inputs.

An alternative channel that shares some of the main elements of the above view is the so-called phenomenon of disorganization (Blanchard and Kremer, 1997). Disorganization is defined as the breakdown of economic relations of the old regime, relations that cannot be replaced overnight by new ones. The main concept underlying this view is 'specificity' in economic relations between firms. The period of central planning was one of extreme specificity, as firms were locked into relationships with a small number of firms, in many cases only one firm. Firms did not need to accumulate any information on other firms and in particular had no information on their customers' ability and willingness to pay. A high degree of specificity implies the presence of monopoly rents. Production chains link firms to several suppliers, depending on the degree of complexity of production. Higher complexity implies a larger number of inputs.

Under a decentralized system, prices are set through a bargaining process. Customer firms, generally state enterprises at the start of reforms, make an offer price to their suppliers. If such a price is below the reservation price of the supplier (e.g. the outside option for the supplier), the latter does not provide inputs to the state firm and thus output falls. Assuming strong complementarities in production, even the lack of one input implies the impossibility to produce. The reason for inefficient bargaining is that the reservation price is private information of the supplier.

An implication of the model is that the larger is the number of inputs, thus the higher is the degree of complexity of production, the larger will be the output fall. One could therefore expect that the output fall would be more pronounced in highly industrialized economies. This may be a reason for the different performance in output of highly industrialized countries of the former Soviet Union as against mostly agrarian economies such as that of China. Another implication would be that output decline would be worse in countries that started reforms from a more rigid system of central planning. In countries in which firms had already experienced decentralized mechanisms of bargaining, output decisions and even price setting, the adverse effects of inefficient bargaining are expected to be less acute.

Looking beyond the initial output fall, a popular view of transition describes output dynamics along a path determined by the sectoral reallocation of resources. As resources move out of the old state firms into the private sector, productivity increases. If there are adjustment costs, or other imperfections such as search costs, aggregate output is likely to drop initially and increase afterwards, when the private sector has reached a sufficient size. Accordingly, output follows a U-shaped path. The initial contraction in output is reminiscent of a phenomenon of Schumpeterian 'creative destruction'. Inefficient firms are weeded out, leaving room for the expansion of new, more efficient firms. A clear signal of such a Schumpeterian process would be the increase in productivity accompanying the initial decline in output: evidence shows that in the initial phase there was little dynamics in terms of job flows, thus indicating that Schumpeterian forces were slow to operate. At first sight, it would appear optimal to make the process of transition as fast as possible, by shortening the initial period of decline in output. However, if one takes into account possible adverse feedbacks, such as fiscal costs of the initial fall in output, or congestion effects in the labour market due to high unemployment, the normative implications of such views are less obvious. These reasons support the emergence of an important literature on the optimal speed of transition.

Perhaps, the most influential work in this area is Aghion and Blanchard (1994). They develop a two-sector search model, in which workers displaced from old state firms search for jobs in the new private sector. Job creation in the private sector is a function of profits, current and expected, which in turn depend on wages. The endogenous mechanism of job creation works through an efficiency wage model, in which the rate of unemployment, by reducing wages, stimulates the creation of jobs in the private sector. The shrinking of the state sector is considered a policy variable. Without macroeconomic feedbacks, the best policy would naturally be to shrink the state sector as fast as possible. However, job creation in the private sector depends on net profits, hence on tax rates paid by private firms. Given that the state pays for unemployment benefits out of its budget, the higher is unemployment, the higher would be the tax rate for private firms, not only because the needed public expenditure would be higher, but also because the tax revenue collected from state firms would be lower (as the state sector shrinks). This adverse fiscal effect counteracts the potential positive effect of unemployment on job creation in the private sector. As a result, there is the risk that too fast a speed of transition, i.e. an excessively rapid shrinking of the state sector, would derail the transition process, leading to an equilibrium with persistent high unemployment. By moderating the contraction of the state sector, the economy could achieve a successful shift of resources to the private sector that will ultimately absorb all workers in the economy.

Although relevant for a normative analysis of the speed of transition and for the role of unemployment, the basic model is less suited for the analysis of the growth process in transition economies. It implies a constant difference between productivity in state and private firms. In addition, the assumption of an exogenous decline of state firms discounts the important interaction between the increase of new private firms and the endogenous shrinking of the state sector.

Growth after the transitional recession

Campos and Coricelli (2002) provide, in the form of a list of stylized facts, a succinct summary of the economic growth performance in the first years of the transition. They claim that the unexpected and severe falls in per capita output were accompanied by both positive and negative events. Specifically on the latter, there was the collapse of the institutional framework, the emergence of significant costs (e.g. poverty), and capital stocks depreciated rapidly. On the positive side, the first years were marked by massive trade reorientation (unsurprisingly in light of the collapse of the Soviet Union) and radical structural change, with rapid increases in the share of services in GDP. A final element is that labour mobility was intense both during the transitional recession and in the subsequent positive growth years, but of a somewhat different nature (Campos and Dabušinskas, 2009). During the recession, labour did not move in the most obvious way, that is, geographically, yet labour mobility can be seen in that workers moved from 'full employment' in the late 1980s to inactivity or high unemployment at the end of the 1990s, from the state sector to the private sector (this is particularly true in the CEE countries); and in that workers have changed their occupations on an unprecedented scale. Underpinning the positive years of growth one finds the renewal of the process of accumulation of physical capital (with foreign direct investment playing a truly crucial role in many transition countries) and the gradual building up of institutional structures supportive of a vibrant market economy (rule of law, effective state bureaucracy, judicial systems, etc.). Yet one issue that has played a substantial role in growth terms is how structural reforms were chosen and actually implemented.

Reforms and growth

One of the most heated debates of the last two decades has been on the macroeconomic implications of structural reforms, or more specifically, on the economic growth pay-offs one should observe from the implementation of such reforms. Since the late 1980s, a large number of reform programmes were implemented across the world, with varying degrees of success. The reasons underlying this variation are still largely unknown and raise a number of questions. The transition experience provides an excellent setting to study such issues and unsurprisingly there is a large body of econometric evidence on the impact of structural reforms on economic growth in the transition economies. Babetskii and Campos (2011) put together a data set on more than 500 estimates of the effect of reforms on growth (from 46 studies) separated according to their effects: cumulative (or long term) and contemporaneous (or short run). They find a large variation across these different estimates, with the short-run effect tending to be negative, while the long-run effect tends to be positive. In addition to different types of reform effects, these authors use a general-to-specific modelling strategy to try to get at the reasons for the variation in the effect of structural reform on economic growth, taking into account both publication bias and perceived differences in the quality of the estimates/papers.

The main finding is that accounting for institutions and initial conditions are two major factors in decreasing the probability of reporting significant and positive effects of reform on growth, while focusing solely on trade liberalization significantly increases this probability. Note that initial conditions closely relate to a country's capacity to reap the potential benefits from (chiefly European) integration. Other noteworthy results include the observation that more influential papers (measured either by a dummy variable on whether it was published in a refereed journal or by Google Scholar citations), papers that do not use country-specific dummy variables (fixed effects) and with fewer degrees of freedom, tend to report smaller (or more negative) effects of reform on growth. They also find interesting differences among the variables that explain the variation in the long-run or cumulative vis-à-vis those for the contemporaneous or short-run effects. In particular, reform in terms of external liberalization still plays a significant yet not as prominent a role in the short-run as it does in the long-run case. The results suggest that this is because in the former the impact of macroeconomic stabilization seems to dominate.

The breadth of reforms that are needed to move from a planned to a market economy is undoubtedly much larger than any other experience of reforms in market economies. In this respect, transition has been a unique experience, as reforms had to be implemented in all eco-nomic and institutional areas typical of a market economy. Braga de Macedo and Oliveira-Martins (2008) constructed a coherence index of reforms based on the EBRD reform indicators. Their index captures the degree of co-movement in the various types of reforms. They find that the index has a positive effect on growth, controlling for the effect of the overall level of reform. Arguably more importantly, in addition to the effect of the extent of reforms, the implementation of reforms in areas that are likely to be complementary has a positive effect on growth, which in our view helps throw new light on the above mentioned growth differences between the CEE and the CIS countries and, to a lesser extent, between transition and the rest of the world (Coricelli and Maurel, 2011).

Concluding remarks

In this chapter we have analysed the growth experience in the first 20 years of transition from a comparative perspective. We followed the lead of recent theoretical and empirical analysis of growth and development and considered growth in transition in a unified framework including the initial transitional recession, the subsequent recovery and growth and the subsequent episodes of crisis experienced by transition countries. The empirical evidence reviewed suggests that in terms of growth, transition has been disappointing in the CIS countries, whereas it has produced more encouraging effects in CEE countries. We tried to link such results to the different reform paths followed by the two groups of countries. We conjectured that the still incomplete reform process, the piecemeal approach followed by the CIS countries, might be one of the explanations for the relatively poor results in terms of growth by the CIS countries in the first 20 years of transition (Campos and Coricelli, 2011).

From a methodological point of view, three main findings emerged. First, the comparative perspective provides useful information on the specific features of transition countries. Analyses based on samples composed solely of transition countries neglect potentially useful information and can thus be misleading. Second, analyses based on average rates of growth, as is typically done in the literature, may also produce misleading results, as the role of initial conditions and policies may vary significantly depending on whether countries are in periods of deep recession, periods of recovery or period of sustained growth. Finally, the impact of reforms crucially depends on the complementarity of reforms. Reform complementarity has an impact on output performance mainly through the depth and length of recessions, rather than the rebound of the economy following recessions.

Notes

1 It is remarkable that the model advanced by Parente and Prescott (2005) is very close in spirit to the models of transition proposed at the start of transition such as Aghion and Blanchard (1994) and, perhaps even more, Chadha and Coricelli (1997).
2 This section draws on Coricelli and Maurel (2011).
3 It is worth noting here that in the early transition years, measuring GDP for the transition economies was quite a challenging task, not least because these countries had formerly used the MPS system of national accounts rather than the standard UN–SNA system.
4 In the transition literature the term was first introduced by Calvo and Coricelli (1993).

References

Aghion, Philippe and Blanchard, Olivier (1994), 'On the Speed of Transition in Central Europe', in Fisher, Stanley and Rotemberg, Julio (eds), *NBER Macroeconomics Annual*, Cambridge, MA: MIT Press, pp. 283–320.

Babetskii, Jan and Campos, Nauro F. (2011), 'Does Reform Work? An Econometric Examination of the Reform-Growth Puzzle', *Journal of Comparative Economics*, vol. 39(2), pp. 140–58.

Blanchard, Olivier and Kremer, Michael (1997), 'Disorganization,' *Quarterly Journal of Economics,* vol. 112(4), pp. 1091–1126.

Braga De Macedo, Jorge and Oliveira-Martins, Joaquim (2008), 'Growth, Reform Indicators and Policy Complementarities,' *Economics of Transition*, vol. 16(2), pp. 141–64.

Calvo, Guillermo and Coricelli, Fabrizio (1993), 'Output Collapse in Eastern Europe: The Role of Credit', *IMF Staff Papers,* vol. 40(1), pp. 32–52.

Campos, Nauro F. and Coricelli, Fabrizio (2002), 'Growth in Transition: What We Know, What We Don't, and What We Should', *Journal of Economic Literature*, vol. XL, pp. 793–836.

——(2011), 'Financial Liberalization and Reversals: Political and Economic Determinants,' Brunel University and PSE, mimeo

Campos, Nauro F. and Dabušinskas, Aurelijus (2009), 'So Many Rocket Scientists, So Few Marketing Clerks: Estimating the Effects of Economic Reform on Occupational Mobility in Estonia,' *European Journal of Political Economy,* vol. 25(1), pp. 261–75.

Campos, Nauro F. and Kinoshita, Yuko (2010), 'Financial Liberalization, Foreign Direct Investment and Structural Reforms,' *IMF Staff Papers*, vol. 57(2), pp. 326–65.

Cerra, Valerie and Chaman Saxena, Sweta (2008), 'Growth Dynamics: The Myth of Economic Recovery', *American Economic Review*, vol. 98(1), pp. 439–57.

Chadha, Bankhim and Coricelli, Fabrizio (1997), 'Fiscal Constraint and the Speed of Transition', *Journal of Development Economics*, vol. 52(1), pp. 219–47.

Coricelli, Fabrizio and Maurel, Mathilde (2011), 'Growth and Crisis in Transition: A Comparative Perspective,' *Review of International Economics*, vol. 19(1), pp. 49–64.

Kornai, János (1994), 'Transformational recession: The main causes', *Journal of Comparative Economics*, vol. 19(3), pp. 39–63.

Parente, Stephen L. and Prescott, Edward C. (2005), 'A Unified Theory of the Evolution of International Income Levels,' in Aghion, Philippe and Durlauf, Steven (eds), *Handbook of Economic Growth*, London: Elsevier, pp. 1371–1416.

35

CENTRAL AND EASTERN EUROPE AND THE CIS

20 years on

Marek Dabrowski

Introduction

More than two decades have passed since the transition to market economy started in Central and Eastern Europe (CEE). There is a vast literature, including some contributions to this volume, which discusses strategic goals of transition, its historical, political and economic context, optimal transition strategies, major policy components of transition process (such as macroeconomic stabilization, liberalization, privatization and enterprise restructuring, building a market compatible social safety net, etc.), political economy of the reform process, reform results at various time points and in various countries/groups of countries, and many other important issues.

While the present author took an active part in the debate on many of the above issues in the past, the purpose of this contribution is different: trying to find out where the CEE countries and the former USSR are now, what is their role in the global and European economies, what kind of challenges they face in the coming years. Generally, we shall not be revisiting the historical controversy on an optimal transition strategy[1] and/or the superiority/deficiency of certain policies and reform variants compared to others. Neither shall we conduct a counterfactual analysis to find out what might have happened if individual countries or group of countries had adopted different policies or implemented them more rapidly or more slowly. Although intellectually exciting, this kind of analysis has to involve, by definition, a substantial speculative component.

The analysis below will cover the former communist CEE countries and the former USSR, leaving aside other formerly centrally planned economies in Asia (China, Vietnam, Laos, Mongolia and North Korea), Africa (e.g. Ethiopia, Angola or Mozambique), the Middle East (e.g. Iraq and Syria) or Latin America (Cuba).[2] We will provide the aggregate picture rather than an analysis of individual countries and try to use the already existing comparative analyses, databases and ratings.

This contribution falls into six sections. The next one is about the role of CEE/Commonwealth of Independent States (CIS) economies in the global and European economy and their development level. This is followed by two sections which analyse progress in economic transition and in political reforms. Then we discuss the role of external 'anchors', especially the European Union (EU) membership prospects. Finally, we present conclusions and an overview of forthcoming development and reform challenges.

431

The economic potential of CEE/CIS countries and their development level

The former communist economies of CEE and the CIS[3] do not play a leading role in the world economy or even in Europe. However, both regions together produce some 8 per cent of the world GDP, on a par with Latin America or the Middle East plus Africa (Table 35.1). According to IMF (2011, Table A, p. 167), the largest country of this group – Russia – contributed 3 per cent of world GDP in 2010, less than China (13.6 per cent) and India (5.5 per cent) but slightly more than Brazil (2.9 per cent), another BRIC[4] economy.

For the 10 CEE economies which joined the EU in 2004 and 2007, their share in EU-27 GDP amounted to 5.4 per cent in 2004 and to 7.4 per cent in 2010. The biggest country of this group – Poland – accounted for 2.9 per cent of EU-27 GDP in 2010, followed by the Czech Republic (1.2 per cent) and Romania (1 per cent).[5] In spite of a recorded increase, the share of NMS in EU-27 GDP remains marginal, with a rather peripheral role for the EU10 in the entire Union.

On a positive note, Table 35.1 demonstrates that shares of both the CEE and CIS regions in the global economy slightly increased over the last 15 years,[6] which, taking into consideration the declining share of the EU, the eurozone or the G7 in global output, provides us with indirect evidence of some income convergence. The same conclusion can be drawn from the above statistics on the share of EU NMS in EU-27 GDP.

The evidence of gradual income convergence of the transition economies can also be seen from Table 35.2, which presents gross national income (GNI) per capita calculated according to the World Bank Atlas method.[7] In 2010, the group of low and middle income countries of the World Bank region of Europe and Central Asia (ECA) was still below the world GNI per capita average (US $7,269 against US $9,116, i.e. 79.7 per cent) but this gap substantially diminished compared to previous periods. If one adds seven high-income countries, i.e. Slovenia, Czech Republic, Slovakia, Estonia, Croatia, Hungary and Poland, the entire region will reach the global average or even exceed it.

Nevertheless, the income gap has not disappeared completely. The seven high-income transition economies occupy the bottom end of the entire high-income group, much below its average GNI per capita. The same is true in respect to the EU. The highest-income EU new member state (NMS) (Slovenia) represents only 70.7 per cent of the entire block's average.

Table 35.2 also shows a 30-fold income difference between the richest (Slovenia) and poorest (Tajikistan) transition economy in 2010. However, this is not a new phenomenon. In 1995 this

Table 35.1 Shares in world GDP by regions/country groups (in per cent)

Country group	1995	2000	2005	2008	2010
G7	50.3	48.9	45.1	41.5	39.3
EU	26.0	25.0	23.0	21.8	20.4
CEE	3.2	3.3	3.5	3.6	3.5
CIS	4.0	3.6	4.1	4.5	4.3
Developing Asia	13.5	15.2	18.4	21.4	24.1
ASEAN-5	3.4	3.1	3.3	3.5	3.6
Latin America and the Caribbean	9.1	8.8	8.4	8.6	8.6
MENA	4.2	4.3	4.7	4.9	5.0
Sub-Saharan Africa	2.0	2.0	2.2	2.3	2.4

Source: IMF World Economic Outlook database, September 2011.

Table 35.2 GNI per capita, Atlas method (current US$)

Country name	1995	2000	2005	2008	2010	Income group[a]
Slovenia	8500	11090	18080	24210	24000	High income
Czech Republic	4470	5800	11330	17140	17890	
Slovakia	4120	5370	10880	16590	16210	
Estonia	3020	4220	9760	14410	14370	
Croatia	3530	5200	9730	13720	13780	
Hungary	4110	4700	10260	13010	12980	
Poland	2970	4590	7270	11870	12410	
Latvia	2050	3220	6810	12020	11620	Upper-middle income
Lithuania	2100	3200	7280	11910	11390	
Russia	2650	1710	4460	9630	9910	
Romania	1470	1690	3920	8290	7840	
Kazakhstan	1280	1260	2930	6140	7440	
Montenegro			3580	6370	6620	
Bulgaria	1360	1640	3640	5700	6250	
Belarus	1370	1380	2760	5590	6130	
Serbia		1400	3430	5520	5810	
Azerbaijan	400	610	1270	3790	5080	
Bosnia and Herzegovina		1510	3000	4530	4790	
Macedonia	1710	1850	2830	4180	4520	
Albania	670	1170	2580	3820	3960	Lower-middle income
Turkmenistan	610	650	1650	2830	3800	
Kosovo				3000	3300	
Armenia	450	660	1470	3340	3090	
Ukraine	920	700	1540	3210	3010	
Georgia	540	750	1360	2460	2690	
Moldova	470	370	890	1500	1810	
Uzbekistan	580	630	530	890	1280	
Kyrgyzstan	350	280	450	770	880	Low income
Tajikistan	200	170	340	620	800	
Memorandum						
World Bank ECA region [b]	1896	1781	3708	6960	7269	
European Union	18146	18946	28286	34762	33980	
High income	23699	25265	33920	38504	38517	
Low income	242	265	339	442	523	
Lower middle income	554	575	914	1397	1660	
Upper middle income	1608	1891	2935	4880	5876	
World	5065	5297	7142	8717	9116	

Source: http://data.worldbank.org/indicator/NY.GNP.PCAP.CD; http://data.worldbank.org/about/country-classifications/country-and-lending-groups.

Note: [a] The income groups are defined according to 2010 GNI per capita, calculated using the World Bank Atlas method: low income, US $1,005 or less; lower middle income, US $1,006–3,975; upper middle income, US $3,976–12,275; and high income, US $12,276 or more. [b] – It includes only low and middle income transition countries (plus Turkey).

difference was even higher (42.5-fold). Furthermore, in the period 1995–2010 several transition economies, e.g. Baltic and Southern Caucasus countries, Albania, Romania and Kazakhstan, recorded a spectacular income convergence. This convergence was facilitated by both internal reforms (market transition) and external factors such as economic integration with the EU (in CEE) and an energy and commodity boom (in the CIS).

All the former communist economies benefited from the global boom of the mid-2000s fuelled by low interest rates in the US and other advanced economies and an abundance of private funding. However, most of them suffered seriously when real estate, financial and commodity bubbles burst in 2007–08.

How much have economic systems changed since the early 1990s?

After analysing development levels and income convergence of the CEE/CIS countries, we next study their progress in transforming their economic systems over the last two decades. Is the transition from plan to market completed and can the analysed economies be considered to be capitalist ones?

The best comparative picture of economic reform progress can be obtained from the transition indicators of the European Bank for Reconstruction and Development (EBRD). Table 35.3 and Figure 35.1 present the evolution of sectoral scores for the period of 1992–2010. Indices for each area of reform have been constructed as unweighted averages of the individual scores of 27 transition countries (all but the Czech Republic and Kosovo which are not listed in the EBRD rankings), using the scale from 1 (no reform) to 4.33 (complete reform).

One can draw some interesting observations from this analysis. First, although the average scores for each reform area have been rising continuously, the 1990s brought much more rapid progress compared to the 2000s when reforms slowed down. In political economy terms this corresponds with the boom period of the beginning and mid-2000s, when high growth rates and an abundance of inexpensive funding discouraged policymakers from undertaking technically difficult and politically unpopular measures.[8] Second, the progress in individual reform areas has been uneven. As seen from Figure 35.1 the fastest progress has been achieved in the areas of price liberalization, trade and foreign exchange liberalization and small-scale privatization, all belonging to the early-stage transition agenda. Large-scale privatization and banking reform have lagged behind but, on average, the cumulative progress can be considered as substantial. Enterprise restructuring, competition policy, development of securities markets and non-bank financial institutions and infrastructure reforms are the less advanced areas which require continuous reform effort in most of the analysed countries.

Table 35.4 presents country scores built up as the unweighted averages of sectoral scores for each country in a given year, with an asterisk indicating years when the score was equal to or higher than 3, considered by us as the advanced stage of transition. One can see that the CEE

Table 35.3 EBRD average transition scores by sector, 1992–2010

Area of reform	1992	1995	1998	2001	2004	2007	2010
Large-scale privatization	1.36	2.23	2.68	2.82	3.04	3.14	3.21
Small-scale privatization	2.10	3.12	3.46	3.64	3.79	3.85	3.86
Enterprise restructuring	1.22	1.91	2.10	2.12	2.31	2.43	2.48
Price liberalization	3.05	3.59	3.78	3.95	3.99	4.00	4.04
Trade and forex system	2.23	3.01	3.27	3.58	3.73	3.82	3.91
Competition Policy	1.28	1.73	1.96	2.11	2.16	2.38	2.46
Banking reform and interest rate liberalization	1.27	2.14	2.26	2.42	2.77	2.94	2.98
Securities markets and non-bank financial institutions	1.17	1.72	1.94	2.03	2.26	2.40	2.46
Overall infrastructure reform	1.21	1.46	1.89	2.26	2.38	2.48	2.57

Source: http://www.ebrd.com/downloads/research/economics/macrodata/tis.xls.

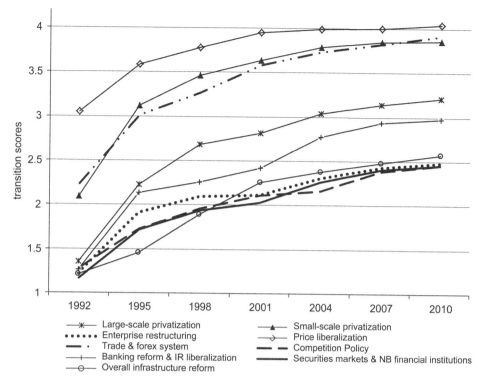

Figure 35.1 EBRD average transition scores by sector, 1992–2010
Source: http://www.ebrd.com/downloads/research/economics/macrodata/tis.xls

countries such as Hungary, Poland, Estonia and Slovakia had achieved the advanced reform level already by 1995.[9] They were followed by Slovenia, Latvia, Lithuania and Croatia whose 1998 average scores exceeded the level of 3. They were joined in the early 2000s by Romania and Bulgaria. Armenia, Georgia, Macedonia, Russia and Ukraine reached this level in the mid- or late 2000s, while Albania and Moldova only did so recently. Armenia and Georgia seem to be the most advanced reformers in the CIS region.

Other CIS and Western Balkan countries remain below the level of 3 even if some of them (Kazakhstan, Kyrgyzstan, Montenegro and Serbia) are pretty close to this level. Three countries can be considered as either non–reformer (Turkmenistan) or very limited reformers (Belarus and Uzbekistan) for the entire analysed period.

While the EBRD scores make it possible to compare the reform progress among transition economies on a systematic basis, they do not provide a benchmark to compare them with the outside world. To fill this gap, Table 35.5 presents the Heritage Foundation (HF) Index of Economic Freedom for transition economies which, with all its shortcomings, seems to be the best to offer global cross-country comparisons of the role of the market mechanism.

None of the former communist economies is ranked by the HF as 'free', i.e. representing a score of 80 or above. However, only six countries in the world fall into this category: Hong Kong (89.7), Singapore (87.2), Australia (82.5), New Zealand (82.3), Switzerland (81.9) and Canada (80.8). Estonia has the highest score among transition countries (75.2), behind Ireland (78.7), Denmark (78.6), USA (77.8), Chile (77.4) and Luxemburg (76.2) but ahead of the Netherlands (74.7), UK (74.5), Finland (74.0), Cyprus (73.3), Japan (72.8), Austria (71.9),

Table 35.4 EBRD average transition scores by country, 1992–2010

Country	1992	1995	1998	2001	2004	2007	2010
Albania	1.63	2.33	2.52	2.81	2.89	2.96	3.07★
Armenia	1.48	2.11	2.67	2.85	3.00★	3.11★	3.18★
Azerbaijan	1.19	1.70	2.33	2.44	2.59	2.63	2.63
Belarus	1.26	2.00	1.52	1.67	1.81	1.85	2.11
Bosnia and Herzegovina	1.22	1.11	2.04	2.22	2.52	2.70	2.82
Bulgaria	1.85	2.33	2.81	3.18★	3.37★	3.48★	3.56★
Croatia	1.93	2.70	3.04★	3.22★	3.44★	3.52★	3.55★
Estonia	1.85	3.15★	3.44★	3.70★	3.81★	3.93★	3.93★
Georgia	1.26	1.96	2.78	2.92	2.96	3.11★	3.11★
Hungary	2.63	3.48★	3.78★	3.85★	3.89★	3.96★	3.93★
Kazakhstan	1.30	2.26	2.81	2.85	2.93	3.00★	2.96
Kyrgyzstan	1.48	2.70	2.78	2.78	2.93	2.93	2.93
Latvia	2.00	2.81	3.11★	3.29★	3.56★	3.63★	3.63★
Lithuania	1.59	2.85	3.07★	3.37★	3.52★	3.70★	3.70★
Macedonia	1.81	2.44	2.67	2.85	3.04★	3.15★	3.26★
Moldova	1.44	2.52	2.70	2.81	2.78	2.96	3.00★
Montenegro	1.67	1.44	1.19	1.82	2.41	2.78	2.89
Poland	2.56	3.22★	3.52★	3.66★	3.66★	3.81★	3.89★
Romania	1.59	2.41	2.89	3.07★	3.22★	3.41★	3.48★
Russia	1.89	2.59	2.55	2.70	2.96	3.04★	3.04★
Serbia	1.67	1.44	1.44	1.85	2.44	2.74	2.93
Slovakia	2.52	3.11★	3.22★	3.41★	3.67★	3.74★	3.74★
Slovenia	2.04	2.93	3.22★	3.33★	3.37★	3.37★	3.41★
Tajikistan	1.30	1.70	2.00	2.15	2.30	2.37	2.48
Turkmenistan	1.00	1.26	1.45	1.30	1.30	1.30	1.44
Ukraine	1.19	2.19	2.48	2.63	2.81	3.00★	3.07★
Uzbekistan	1.19	2.22	2.11	2.11	2.08	2.15	2.15

Source: http://www.ebrd.com/downloads/research/economics/macrodata/tic.xls.

Note: ★ Years when the score was equal to or higher than 3, considered by us as the advanced stage of transition.

Sweden (71.9) and Germany (71.8). Apart from Estonia, only three other countries of the CEE/CIS region – Lithuania (71.3), the Czech Republic and Georgia (both 70.4) – are ranked in the 'mostly free' group (at its bottom), on a par with Taiwan (70.8), Norway (70.3), Spain and Belgium (70.2) and Uruguay (70.0). Fourteen transition countries belong to the 'moderately free' group, the same group where the Republic of Korea, Israel, Iceland, Jordan, Colombia, the United Arab Emirates, Mexico, Malaysia, Saudi Arabia, France, Turkey, Portugal, South Africa, Italy, Greece and Lebanon are ranked. Six transition countries belong to the 'mostly unfree' category and four – Belarus, Uzbekistan, Ukraine and Turkmenistan – to the 'repressed' group.

Summing up, two decades after the collapse of communism, the countries of CEE and the CIS can be considered largely as market economies, with a few exceptions such as Turkmenistan, Belarus and Uzbekistan. Nevertheless, they differ greatly between themselves in terms of the degree of market freedom, maturity of institutions, macroeconomic stability, etc. The Baltic countries and central Europe completed a basic transition agenda by the beginning of the 2000s, before joining the EU, and currently their economic systems do not differ greatly from the 'old' EU members. Other countries, especially in the CIS region, are less advanced and their model

Table 35.5 Heritage Foundation Index of Economic Freedom, transition economies, 2011

Category	Name	Rank	Overall score	Business freedom	Trade freedom	Fiscal freedom	Government spending	Monetary freedom	Investment freedom	Financial freedom	Property rights	Freedom from corruption	Labour freedom
Mostly free	Estonia	14	75.2	80.9	87.6	80.7	52.2	78.7	90.0	80.0	80.0	66.0	55.8
	Lithuania	24	71.3	81.7	87.6	86.1	58.0	74.5	80.0	80.0	60.0	49.0	55.6
	Czech Rep.	28	70.4	69.8	87.6	81.0	44.8	80.0	70.0	80.0	65.0	49.0	77.0
	Georgia	29	70.4	87.3	89.2	87.5	60.3	76.7	70.0	60.0	40.0	41.0	92.1
Moderately free	Armenia	36	69.7	82.4	85.5	89.2	85.7	76.0	75.0	70.0	30.0	27.0	75.9
	Slovakia	37	69.5	73.4	87.6	84.2	63.7	81.6	75.0	70.0	50.0	45.0	64.5
	Hungary	51	66.6	76.5	87.6	69.7	27.4	75.9	75.0	70.0	65.0	51.0	67.7
	Macedonia	55	66.0	64.6	83.6	90.0	64.3	84.5	60.0	60.0	35.0	38.0	79.7
	Latvia	56	65.8	72.8	87.6	82.5	55.5	73.5	80.0	50.0	50.0	45.0	61.3
	Bulgaria	60	64.9	75.8	87.6	86.9	58.3	75.5	55.0	60.0	30.0	38.0	82.0
	Romania	63	64.7	72.0	87.6	86.8	57.6	74.4	80.0	50.0	40.0	38.0	60.8
	Slovenia	66	64.6	83.6	87.6	65.1	41.1	80.5	70.0	50.0	60.0	66.0	41.8
	Poland	68	64.1	61.4	87.6	74.0	43.8	78.1	65.0	60.0	60.0	50.0	61.2
	Albania	70	64.0	67.1	79.8	92.1	68.7	79.9	65.0	70.0	35.0	32.0	50.4
	Montenegro	76	62.5	71.3	83.6	89.4	28.6	76.0	55.0	50.0	40.0	39.0	92.3
	Kazakhstan	78	62.1	74.3	80.9	87.3	78.5	69.9	30.0	50.0	35.0	27.0	88.4
	Croatia	82	61.1	65.2	87.6	74.6	50.3	78.5	70.0	60.0	40.0	41.0	44.1
Mostly unfree	Kyrgyzstan	83	61.1	75.4	63.2	92.6	74.2	68.6	55.0	50.0	25.0	19.0	88.1
	Azerbaijan	92	59.7	72.9	77.1	83.9	71.0	72.6	55.0	40.0	20.0	23.0	81.1
	Serbia	101	58.0	59.0	75.2	83.6	41.9	66.0	60.0	50.0	40.0	35.0	68.9
	Bosnia and Herzegovina	104	57.5	60.4	86.0	83.9	24.1	80.6	70.0	60.0	20.0	30.0	60.2
	Moldova	120	55.7	69.5	80.2	85.6	48.1	77.0	35.0	50.0	40.0	33.0	39.0
	Tajikistan	128	53.5	60.7	82.5	88.6	77.3	64.5	20.0	40.0	25.0	20.0	56.4
	Russia	143	50.5	50.7	68.2	82.7	65.1	63.1	25.0	40.0	25.0	22.0	62.9
Repressed	Belarus	155	47.9	70.6	80.3	83.6	26.2	62.2	20.0	10.0	20.0	24.0	82.3
	Uzbekistan	163	45.8	66.8	66.2	90.5	71.0	61.7	0.0	10.0	15.0	17.0	60.2
	Ukraine	164	45.8	47.1	85.2	77.3	32.9	63.2	20.0	30.0	30.0	22.0	50.0
	Turkmenistan	169	43.6	30.0	79.2	93.6	95.5	69.6	0.0	10.0	10.0	18.0	30.0

Source: http://www.heritage.org/Index/ranking, http://www.heritage.org/Index/explore.

of capitalism, with weak property rights, repressive government and a high level of corruption, is closer to that of many developing countries. Most of the analysed countries face the challenge of unfinished and incomplete reforms, as we discuss further below.

Political systems

Economic transition in the region was triggered by political changes, i.e. the collapse of communist regimes. Thus, simultaneously with building a market economy the former communist countries were expected to develop political freedom, pluralism and democracy. To assess progress in this field we use the Freedom House (FH) rating Freedom in the World (FIW) (Table 35.6). Each country in this rating is evaluated by two criteria: political rights (PR), and civil liberties (CL), both measured on a one-to-seven scale, with one representing the highest degree of freedom and seven - the lowest.

Based on FIW scores one can distinguish three groups of transition countries:

- countries that democratized their political systems in the early 1990s and sustained their 'free' status over the entire analysed period (this group includes countries that joined the EU in 2004 and 2007);
- countries that recorded limited progress in democratization in the 1990s but substantially improved their performance in the next decade (western Balkans);
- countries that, after the short period of political freedom and democracy in the early 1990s, moved back towards authoritarian or semi-authoritarian regimes (most of the CIS).

For the CIS region, even the wave of so-called colour revolutions (the 'Rose' revolution in Georgia in 2003, 'Orange' revolution in Ukraine in 2004 and 'Tulip' revolution in Kyrgyzstan in 2005) did not change the picture. Their outcomes proved unsustainable, with new authoritarian tendencies emerging after the revolutionary enthusiasm faded away.

Table 35.7 presents the results of another FH analysis Nation in Transit (NIT), which gives us a more detailed picture of countries' political systems by their major components. It is quite clear that even the best performers in these ratings (EU NMS) face problems in such areas as Judicial Framework and Independence (JFI) and Corruption (CO).

Finally we analyse the interrelation between political and economic reforms. Figure 35.2 plots the HF Index of Economic Freedom scores against the FH NIT scores (from the 2011 edition of both rankings). One can observe a certain degree of correlation in both spheres but not particularly strong (and obviously weaker than could be observed at the end of the 1990s and the beginning of the 2000s – see Dabrowski and Gortat, 2002). CIS countries (except Ukraine) are located above the trend line, indicating more economic freedoms than political ones. In the specific case of the Caucasus and some Central Asian countries this asymmetry is even stronger. In contrast, the EU NMS (plus Ukraine and Serbia) occupy the space below the trend line, i.e. they are relatively freer politically than economically. Other western Balkan countries are located close to the trend line.

The question of causality is more complicated. Democratization seems to facilitate market reforms as was empirically shown in the early transition period (when countries which experienced radical changes of political regimes and elites started their economic reforms earlier and conducted them in a more comprehensive and consistent way) and later episodes of both reform acceleration (election victories of democratic forces in Romania in 1996, Bulgaria in 1997 and Slovakia in 1998, collapse of Milosevic's regime in Yugoslavia in 2000, 'Rose' revolution in Georgia in 2003) and reform stagnation or reversal under authoritarian regimes

Table 35.6 FH Freedom in the World scores, transition countries, 1992–2010

Country	1992			1995			2000			2005			2010		
	PR	CL	Status	PR	CL	Status	PR	CL	Status	PR	CL	Status	PR	CL	Status
Albania	4	3	PF	3	4	PF	4	5	PF	3	3	PF	3	3	PF
Armenia	4	3	PF	4	4	PF	4	4	PF	5	4	PF	6	4	PF
Azerbaijan	5	5	PF	6	6	NF	6	5	PF	6	5	NF	6	5	NF
Belarus	4	3	PF	5	5	PF	6	6	NF	7	6	NF	7	6	NF
Bosnia and Herzegovina	6	6	NF	6	6	NF	5	4	PF	4	3	PF	4	3	PF
Bulgaria	2	3	F	2	2	F	2	3	F	1	2	F	2	2	F
Croatia	4	4	PF	4	4	PF	2	3	F	2	2	F	1	2	F
Czech Republic[a]	2	2	F	1	2	F	1	2	F	1	1	F	1	1	F
Estonia	3	3	PF	2	2	F	1	2	F	1	1	F	1	1	F
Georgia	4	5	PF	4	5	PF	4	4	PF	3	3	PF	4	3	PF
Hungary	2	2	F	1	2	F	1	2	F	1	1	F	1	1	F
Kazakhstan	5	5	PF	6	5	NF	6	5	NF	6	5	NF	6	5	NF
Kosovo	..	..	..	..	..	..	..	..	..	..	..	..	5	4	PF
Kyrgyzstan	4	2	PF	4	4	PF	6	5	NF	5	4	PF	5	5	PF
Latvia	3	3	PF	2	2	F	1	2	F	1	1	F	2	2	F
Lithuania	2	3	F	1	2	F	1	2	F	1	1	F	1	1	F
Macedonia	3	4	PF	4	3	PF	4	3	PF	3	3	PF	3	3	PF
Moldova	5	5	PF	4	4	PF	2	4	PF	3	4	PF	3	3	PF
Montenegro[b]	6	5	PF	6	6	NF	4	4	PF	3	2	F	3	2	F
Poland	2	2	F	1	2	F	1	2	F	1	1	F	1	1	F
Romania	4	4	PF	4	3	PF	2	2	F	2	2	F	2	2	F
Russia	3	4	PF	3	4	PF	5	5	PF	6	5	NF	6	5	NF
Serbia[b]	6	5	PF	6	6	NF	4	4	PF	3	2	F	2	2	F
Slovakia[a]	2	2	F	2	3	F	1	2	F	1	1	F	1	1	F
Slovenia	2	2	F	1	2	F	1	2	F	1	1	F	1	1	F
Tajikistan	6	6	NF	7	7	NF	6	6	NF	6	5	NF	6	5	NF
Turkmenistan	7	6	NF	7	7	NF	7	7	NF	7	7	NF	7	7	NF
Ukraine	3	3	PF	3	4	PF	4	4	PF	3	2	F	3	3	PF
Uzbekistan	6	6	NF	7	7	NF	7	6	NF	7	7	NF	7	7	NF

Source http://www.freedomhouse.org/images/File/fiw/historical/FIWAllScoresCountries1973–2011.xls.
Notes: a In 1992 – scores for Czechoslovakia.
b Scores for Yugoslavia until 2003 and for Confederation of Serbia and Montenegro in 2004–06.
PR, political rights; CL, civil liberties; NF, non-free; PF, partly free; F, free.

(Belarus since the mid-1990s, Russia since 2004). Generally, there is little evidence that market-friendly authoritarianism can be a promising option in the analysed group of countries.

However, the opposite causality can also hold true. There is a large body of literature (e.g. Lipset, 1959; Barro, 1996; Przeworski and Limongi, 1997) that claims that chances for democracy and its survival increase with a higher level of economic development and higher economic growth and both depend on better performance of economic systems based on market forces. Summing up, in spite of individual country deviations from the trend line in Figure 35.2, democratization and market reforms seem to reinforce each other in the long run.

Table 35.7 FH 'Nations in Transit' Scores, 2010

Country	EP	CS	IM	NGOV	LGOV	JFI	CO	DS
Albania	4.00	3.00	4.00	4.75	3.25	4.25	5.00	4.04
Armenia	5.75	3.75	6.00	5.75	5.75	5.50	5.50	5.43
Azerbaijan	7.00	5.75	6.75	6.50	6.50	6.25	6.50	6.46
Belarus	7.00	6.00	6.75	6.75	6.75	6.75	6.00	6.57
Bosnia and Herzegovina	3.25	3.50	4.75	5.25	4.75	4.25	4.50	4.32
Bulgaria	1.75	2.50	3.75	3.50	3.00	3.00	4.00	3.07
Croatia	3.25	2.50	4.00	3.50	3.75	4.25	4.25	3.64
Czech Rep.	1.25	1.75	2.50	2.75	1.75	2.00	3.25	2.18
Estonia	1.75	1.75	1.50	2.25	2.50	1.50	2.25	1.93
Georgia	5.00	3.75	4.25	5.75	5.50	5.00	4.75	4.86
Hungary	1.75	2.00	3.25	3.00	2.50	2.25	3.50	2.61
Kazakhstan	6.75	5.75	6.75	6.75	6.25	6.25	6.50	6.43
Kosovo	4.50	3.75	5.75	5.75	5.00	5.75	5.75	5.18
Kyrgyzstan	6.00	4.75	6.50	6.50	6.50	6.25	6.25	6.11
Latvia	1.75	1.75	1.75	2.25	2.25	1.75	3.50	2.14
Lithuania	1.75	1.75	1.75	2.75	2.50	1.75	3.50	2.25
Macedonia	3.25	3.25	4.50	4.00	3.75	4.00	4.00	3.82
Moldova	4.00	3.25	5.50	5.75	5.75	4.50	6.00	4.96
Montenegro	3.25	2.75	4.25	4.25	3.25	4.00	5.00	3.82
Poland	1.50	1.50	2.25	2.75	1.75	2.50	3.25	2.21
Romania	2.75	2.50	4.00	3.75	3.00	4.00	4.00	3.43
Russia	6.75	5.50	6.25	6.50	6.00	5.75	6.50	6.18
Serbia	3.25	2.25	4.00	3.75	3.50	4.50	4.25	3.64
Slovakia	1.50	1.75	3.00	2.75	2.50	2.75	3.50	2.54
Slovenia	1.50	2.00	2.25	2.00	1.50	1.75	2.50	1.93
Tajikistan	6.50	6.00	5.75	6.25	6.00	6.25	6.25	6.14
Turkmenistan	7.00	7.00	7.00	7.00	6.75	7.00	6.75	6.93
Ukraine	3.50	2.75	3.75	5.50	5.50	5.50	5.75	4.61
Uzbekistan	7.00	7.00	7.00	7.00	6.75	7.00	6.75	6.93

Source: http://www.freedomhouse.org/images/File/nit/2011/NIT-2011-Tables.pdf.
Notes: The ratings are based on a scale of 1 to 7, with 1 representing the highest level of democratic progress and 7 the lowest. The Democracy Score (DS) is an average of ratings for Electoral Process (EP); Civil Society (CS); Independent Media (IM); National Democratic Governance (NGOV), Local Democratic Governance (LGOV); Judicial Framework and Independence (JFI); and Corruption (CO).

The role of external anchors

The question of why some countries accomplished greater progress in both economic and political transition while others were less successful has been explored by many studies that investigated the initial political and economic conditions, reform strategies, interactions between the political and economic spheres, geographic location and many other factors. In this section we address just one factor, namely the role of external anchors.

The literature on the political economy of reforms explains why external anchoring is important for both reform design and reform implementation and, even more important, for sustaining reforms, in particular avoiding policy reversals (see, for example, Rodrik, 1996 and Fukuyama, 2004 for an overview). This may relate, among others, to insufficient domestic

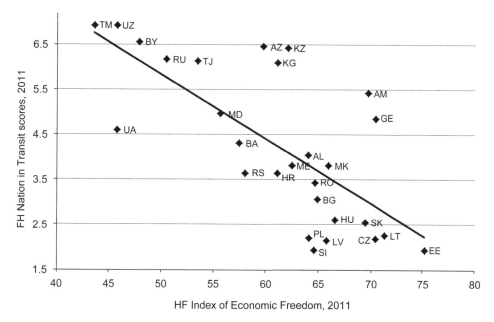

Figure 35.2 Interrelation between economic and political freedoms in transition countries
Source: http://www.heritage.org/Index/explore; http://www.freedomhouse.org/images/File/nit/2011/
NIT-2011-Tables.pdf; http://www.freedomhouse.hu//images/fdh_galleries/NIT2007/rating%20and%20d
emocracy%20score%20summary3.pdf

political consensus, high reform costs (in both socio-economic and political terms), uncertainty
about reform results and a lack of the technical skills needed to implement them. The external
incentives can have both a positive and a negative character (i.e. they can take the form of
'carrots' or 'sticks'). Among the former one can mention, for example, financial aid, technical assistance,
market access, perspectives of foreign investment inflows, international security guarantees and
membership of prestigious country clubs such as the EU. The 'sticks' may involve the danger of
a country experiencing economic and political isolation, downgrading its economic and geopolitical status and losing the external support enjoyed so far. In some extreme instances, lack of
reforms can even challenge a country's territorial integrity and existence.[10]

Among the various external anchors, the most important role has been played by either
actual or perspective membership in international organizations and regional integration blocks
and the 'rules of the game'/conditionality related to this membership. Since the collapse of
communism, the CEE and CIS countries became members of global financial institutions and
organizations such as the IMF, the World Bank, the WTO and the OECD,[11] regional development banks (EBRD and Asian Development Bank), regional integration blocks (EU, the CIS
and narrower integration initiatives within the CIS such as EvrAzES or custom union), geopolitical and security alliances (NATO, CIS Collective Security Treaty Organization) and
political organizations (Council of Europe, Organization for Security and Cooperation in
Europe). However, only a few organizations/blocks that have offered meaningful long-term
incentives and benefits have had a substantial impact on the transition process.

This relates, in the first instance, to the EU in all cases where it has opened its door to a
country's prospective membership. Table 35.4 gives us a hint on how the perspective of EU

membership helped to advance market reforms, first in Central European and Baltic countries, then in Bulgaria and Romania, and finally in the western Balkan state, on the one hand, and how the lack of such a perspective discouraged reforms in the CIS, on the other. This is even more visible in the case of political systems (Tables 35.6 and 35.7) with 'free' EU NMS, 'partly free' prospective EU candidates in western Balkans and mostly 'non-free' CIS.

Again one can raise the question of causality. Good economic and political reform scores can result from the presence of an EU membership perspective but the opposite may also be true: countries more advanced in these reforms have a greater chance and interest to meet the Copenhagen criteria and successfully join the EU accession process. None the less, the total absence of an EU accession perspective (even in a quite distant future) eliminates that important incentive for economic reforms and keeping them on track and makes political systems more vulnerable to authoritarian drifts. It is enough to compare the developments in the CIS versus South Eastern Europe. In the mid-1990s both regions represented, on average, a similar level of economic development and, as seen from Tables 35.4 and 35.6, exhibited comparable progress in their economic and political reforms. However, after offering the Western Balkan countries the EU membership perspective in the early 2000s, they moved quickly ahead in both areas while the CIS countries stagnated and some of them even regressed in the political sphere.

Neither the European Neighbourhood Policy nor the Eastern Partnership, the EU co-operation initiatives addressed to six Eastern European and Caucasus partners (Armenia, Azerbaijan, Belarus, Georgia, Moldova and Ukraine) have brought meaningful results yet. A similar co-operation framework launched between the EU and Russia has had a similarly disappointing outcome. These initiatives included the EU's offer of partial access to the Single European Market, but without a membership perspective.

Regarding other institutions there is some evidence of the positive impact of NATO membership, especially in the areas of political and institutional reforms, and a much weaker impact in respect to WTO membership (Schweickert *et al.*, 2007).

Interventions and surveillance by the Bretton Woods institutions (the IMF and the World Bank) seem to be important for short-term policy adjustments (like macroeconomic stabilization programmes) when some degree of domestic policy commitment ('reform ownership') is in place. However, they are unlikely to serve as the long-term external anchor, especially in the area of institutional reforms which require political changes.[12]

Looking ahead: reform agenda for the future

Two decades after the collapse of communism, all the CEE and most of the CIS countries completed the basic transition agenda in the economic sphere. This means they can be considered as market economies, but representing various development levels and various degrees of maturity and perfection of market institutions.

In spite of this completion of the basic transition agenda almost everywhere, further reforms are badly needed. The recent global financial and economic crisis revealed many shortcomings of existing policies and institutions which require correction. However, the reform agendas differ by individual countries and country groups/subgroups.

The formerly centrally planned economies never constituted a homogenous group. At the start of transition in the late 1980s/early 1990s they already differed in terms of development level, resource endowment, degree of openness, macroeconomic stability, external debt, structural distortions, role of market forces and non-public ownership, civil liberties, etc. However, the common institutional legacy and transformation challenges were strong enough to justify broadly similar policy agendas at the start.

Such an approach is not justified anymore. Ten CEE countries are part of the EU (and three of them have already joined the eurozone) and this restricts their freedom of choice in many important spheres of economic management in favour of the EU's common policies. Thus, apart from their national policy agendas they must participate in the process of intra-EU policy debate and institutional changes. Six countries of the western Balkan states are also at various stages of the EU accession process, and their priority is to adopt the EU *acquis communautaire*.

Due to their high level of trade and investment integration within the EU, the economic future of the CEE countries is strongly dependent on Europe's growth perspective and the EU's ability to make its institutions and policies more growth-friendly. At the national level, similarly to the 'old' EU members, most of them need to cut back their excessive welfare programmes and entitlements, increase labour market participation and its flexibility, reform their education and healthcare systems, stimulate innovation, continue deregulation of product and service markets, and public administration reforms. Some countries such as Hungary need substantial fiscal adjustments in order to avoid a sovereign debt crisis and to be able to meet the Maastricht criteria soon.

The reform agenda in the CIS region is much more complex and challenging. While countries of the former Soviet Union must also reform their pension, healthcare and education systems, their major development obstacle is related to the poor business and investment climate, which, in turn, is underpinned by the low quality of state institutions (especially public administration and the judiciary), widespread corruption and organized crime. These problems cannot be solved through technical economic measures, since they require a broader agenda of political reforms and overcoming authoritarian tendencies to be addressed. The second major challenge is related to the dominance of energy and raw materials in production and the export structure, which makes these countries vulnerable to shocks generated by commodity price volatility. However, this kind of 'monoculture' cannot be overcome without improving the business and investment climate, which would create more room for structural diversification.

It is also important to appreciate that the CIS region is becoming increasingly heterogeneous, not only in terms of the level of economic and social development but also with institutions and policies that are tending to diverge. Furthermore, geographic location may have an increasing impact on future development trajectories, directions of trade and investment flows, as well as on these countries' institutional design. The so-called western CIS countries (i.e. Belarus, Moldova, Russia and Ukraine), owing to their geographical proximity to major European markets, have the chance to build stronger economic and institutional ties with the EU, even in the absence of an EU membership perspective.

In contrast, the five central Asian countries suffer from being landlocked and from dysfunctional transportation networks inherited from the Soviet period. Their location makes them geographically closer to Russia, China, Iran or India than to the EU. In turn, the three Caucasus countries, although located closer to the EU and Turkey, suffer from their 'frozen' territorial conflicts, which limits their development options.

Notes

1 In particular, the question of optimal reform speed, i.e. the controversy over fast versus piecemeal reforms (or the so-called shock therapy *vs.* gradualism in more journalist-type debates) was hotly discussed in the 1990s.

2 Some of them, like North Korea and Cuba, have not yet started market transition.

3 In the IMF *World Economic Outlook* (WEO) country grouping, which we use here, the CEE region does not include the Czech Republic, Estonia, Slovakia and Slovenia (because of either their current income per capita level or membership in the eurozone, or both) but does include Turkey. The CIS

region in WEO also includes Mongolia, which is neither a CIS member, nor is covered by our analysis. It also includes Georgia which left the CIS in 2009 but is treated by both WEO and us as part of the CIS region for analytical convenience.

4 BRIC stands for the four largest emerging-market economies, i.e., Brazil, Russia, India and China.

5 See http://appsso.eurostat.ec.europa.eu/nui/setupDownloads.do.

6 The year 1995 has been chosen as the starting point of our comparison to exclude the period of dramatic GDP adjustment at the very beginning of transition. In 1995 most of CEE and some CIS countries had already ended this period while in Russia, Ukraine and Moldova output decline, although at slower pace, continued until 1999.

7 For the detailed methodology of the WB Atlas method – see http://web.worldbank.org/WBSITE/EXTERNAL/DATASTATISTICS/EXTDECSTAMAN/0,contentMDK:20877893~pagePK:641684 27~piPK:64168435~theSitePK:2077967~isCURL:Y~isCURL:Y,00.html.

8 However, there may be a methodological bias coming from the limited scale of the EBRD ratings. As a result, in some areas countries reached the upper ceiling pretty soon without measurement room to reflect further reform progress at the later stage. The same doubt applies to the country ratings presented in Table 35.4.

9 The same applies to the Czech Republic, which is not included in the EBRD rating.

10 Some regional conflicts in the early 1990s (in the former Yugoslavia and Caucasus region) triggered economic reforms in the countries involved to strengthen their capacity to deal with security challenges.

11 It relates to higher-income countries.

12 See Dabrowski and Radziwill (2007) for comparison of the role of EU membership perspective and IMF/World Bank conditionality as the external reform anchors.

Bibliography

Barro, R. (1996), 'Democracy and Growth', *Journal of Economic Development*, vol. 1, pp. 1–27.

Dabrowski, M. and Gortat, R. (2002), 'Political Determinants of Economic Reforms in Former Communist Countries', *CASE Network Studies and Analyses*, No. 242

Dabrowski, M. and Radziwill, A. (2007), 'Regional vs. Global Public Goods: The Case of Post-Communist Transition', *CASE Network Studies and Analyses*, No. 336

Fukuyama, F. (2004), *State Building: Governance and World Order in the 21st Century*, Ithaca, NY: Cornell University Press.

IMF (2011), *World Economic Outlook*, September, Washington, DC: International Monetary Fund.

Lipset, S.M. (1959), 'Some Social Requisites of Democracy: Economic Development and Political Legitimacy', *American Political Science Review*, vol. 53(1), pp. 69–105.

Przeworski, A. and Limongi, F. (1997), 'Modernization: Theories and Facts', *World Politics*, vol. 49(2), pp. 155–83.

Rodrik, D. (1996), 'Understanding Economic Policy Reform', *Journal of Economic Literature*, vol. 34(1)

Schweickert, R., Drautzburg, T., Gawrich, A. and Melnykovska, I. (2007), 'Institutional Convergence of CIS towards European Benchmarks', *CASE Network Reports*, No. 82.

36

COMMUNIST ASIA

Steven Rosefielde

Introduction

The Soviet Union, its satellites and communist Asia toyed with markets on and off, beginning as early as 1921 (Lenin's New Economic Policy). Some communist party members worried from the outset that free enterprise and communism were mutually exclusive, contending that the criminalization of private property, business and entrepreneurship were imperative to forestall the restoration of capitalism. Others, like Nikolai Bukharin, Josef Tito and Deng Xiaoping, counter-argued that markets and party control were compatible and best.[1]

The dispute was put to the test in the 1990s when the Soviet Union and its satellites overturned communism, with the stated intention of bringing about a transition to EU-type social democracy or American-style democratic free enterprise, while China, Vietnam, Cambodia and Laos set out to reform the command paradigm founded on state ownership of the means of production by building market communism. This chapter surveys the Asian communist party-controlled market experience over the period 1993–2011.

The decision to experiment with markets and other aspects of liberalization is often treated as the dawn of Asia's market communist epoch. The year 1993, however, provides a better benchmark, marking as it does the end of the command period and the beginning of a predominantly market-communist era. The tipping point was Deng Xiaoping's Southern Tour of Guangzhou, Shenzhen and Shanghai, where this *eminence grise* somehow successfully persuaded the party leadership that although their crackdown on the Tiananmen Square dissidents may have been appropriate, repression in the political sphere did not necessitate command planning of the economy. Deng urged them to proceed full-steam ahead with leasing-based marketization as the best strategy for catching up with, and perhaps overtaking, the West.

Beijing's decision to ride the market tiger, doubtlessly influenced by the Soviet Union's collapse in 1991, was quickly emulated throughout communist Indochina.[2] It was done while keeping dual options in mind. Asian communists could try to socialize markets for the advantage of their people's democratic republics, while keeping open the possibility of switching sides at the end of the day if capitalism on balance seemed best.

China

Deng and his supporters, like their command economy predecessors, did not have an elaborate blueprint for building market communism. Deng was a pragmatist, unperturbed by contradictions, who advised crossing rivers by feeling for the stones. There was no design for utopia. None the less, the inner logic of Chinese and Indochinese communist marketization is easily discerned as a strategy based on borrowing heavily from Western market institutions (*Gaige Kaifang* – reforms and openness), subject only to a few critical constraints.

First and foremost among these constraints was a policy of zero tolerance towards any challenges to communist party supremacy. There could be intra-party elections, with some non-party participation in selected activities, but regime change via the ballot was proscribed. Likewise, party edicts could not be overridden by independent judiciaries on constitutional or legislative grounds. There could be no rights that trumped the party, ensuring that people's democratic republics were governed by the rule of men, not the rule of law. Communist markets, accordingly, are founded on insecure property rights. Managers/owners are required to bear the risk that the communist party might choose to take control over their businesses without compensation, in addition to the more familiar market, counterparty and eminent domain hazards. The ideological prohibition on freehold ownership distorts entrepreneurship further.

Second, the communist party insisted on monopolizing state programming and management, with the exclusive right of determining taxation, public spending, monetary policy, state business and financial regulation, market access and foreign exchange rates. Unlike the West, communist party economic governance is intrinsically anti-competitive.

Third, the prohibition of freehold property, and the state's leasing powers, allowed the party to retain proprietary control over the economy's 'commanding heights', and to allocate lucrative leases preferentially, typically to party insiders and their families. This has led to the emergence of two *de facto* classes of property: 'state ownership' (including leasing) in the commanding heights, associated with state-owned enterprises (SOEs), and 'private leasing ownership' in the periphery. Both forms permit insiders to convert revenues informally into personal and private holdings of foreign assets, in violation of communist principles. Consumers are precluded from being sovereign in the public goods arena, and in the market too, because the party has the power to regulate commerce on its own behalf.

Fourth, the party placed itself in a position to create insider rents merely by granting contracts, subsidies and anti-competitive privileges to favoured leaseholders. This created a two-tier communist market: one that was competitive, where firms were too small to be noticed, or pickings too slim; and the other that was much more exclusive, where insider party interests determined market entry.

Fifth, the party reserved the right to police moral hazard. The leadership, on its own volition, could adopt stern measures to facilitate intra-party economic competition, repress regional and municipal economic fiefdoms, deter embezzlement, prevent insider capital flight abroad, and restrain income and wealth inequalities. These powers not only allow leaders to control corruption, but also to regulate the (remaining) communist content of Beijing's market system.

Sixth, domestic insider market rigging also applies to foreign trade. The party reserves the right to act as a discriminating protectionist by erecting import barriers and export subsidies (including, arguably, an undervalued renminbi, RMB) in violation of its World Trade Organization (WTO) obligations. These practices may be designed to beggar neighbours, or to amass colossal dollar reserves for diverse anti-competitive purposes, but regardless of their underlying motivation, they clearly infringe free competition.

Beyond these requirements, the sky is the limit in replicating Western market institutions and techniques. China has chosen, for instance, gradually to expand leaseholders' discretionary authority over asset use and the conduct of for-profit business, setting the example for its Indo-chinese imitators.

Deng's appointed successor, Zhu Rongji, devised a programme to transform red directors into managers of market competitive SOEs, and then ultimately into managers of leased private companies by expanding and codifying their powers in 'The Regulations on Transforming the Management Mechanism of State-Owned Industrial Enterprises', issued in July 1992. The document granted managers 14 specific control rights over: (1) production; (2) pricing; (3) sales; (4) procurement; (5) foreign trade; (6) investment; (7) use of retained funds; (8) disposal of assets; (9) merger and acquisitions; (10) labour; (11) personnel management; (12) wages; (13) bonuses; and (14) their internal organization. Managers were also given the power to refuse to pay unauthorized charges levied by the government at various levels.

These rules mimicked the rights of Western firms, but had less force because managers were not adequately protected by the rule of law (independent judiciary). The communist party, at its discretion, could violate its own administrative directives. Still, the new rules meant that under favourable circumstances firms could more efficiently supply other government entities and private consumers. The potential gains were obvious, but so too were the limitations. The command principle might still supersede the market. Managers might prefer to remain inert, accepting subsidies instead of competitively profit seeking, and Deng's reforms might be subverted by moral hazard. Instead of acting scrupulously on the state's behalf, red directors might detrimentally employ diverse means – fair and foul – to privatize usufruct and assets to themselves. Moreover, this situation can even result in a form of adverse selection, by providing incentives and the opportunity for 'bad' managers to take advantage. Thus, agents, who are supposed to serve the state, can serve themselves at the people's expense.

Zhu Rongji, Jiang Zemin and Hu Jintao, following in Deng's footsteps, however, were undaunted. They solved the moral hazard problem by capitulating to it, allowing red directors and others including the *taizidang* (sons and daughters of high party officials, often derogatorily called princelings) to lease state assets, close unsuccessful state enterprises and become billionaires while upholding Marxist communist principle by retaining the criminalization of freehold property. This 'solution' has produced a distinctive structure of asset control and ownership. China's major financial holding companies in the public sector (finance, transport and trade) are state, provincial and municipally owned/controlled, with substantial minority equity stakes held abroad and traded on the Hong Kong Stock Exchange. They are known as Red Chips (CITIC, COSCO, China Resources, Beijing Enterprises, etc.). There were 159 active SOEs of this type at the end of 2006, declining to about 100 by 2010; these companies can be considered China's commanding heights.

They coexist with other state companies controlled by the central government, operating in protected sectors, including defence, and more autonomous state and collective entities in competitive fields. Most sell equity shares, and therefore can be misleadingly classified as privately owned in a liberal freehold sense, even though they are under the state's thumb. The government also has substantial influence over the operations of foreign multinational companies participating in the Chinese market as joint ventures, including Alcatel-Lucent, Motorola and Volkswagen. Its sway, however, is less for small state and collective entities controlled by local governments and private groups in the competitive sectors, increasingly acting like conglomerates; and small private and family collective commercial firms in the urban and rural service sectors.

447

These developments have been accompanied by parallel stock market and banking reforms, allowing SOEs to increase equity (shares) sales to outsiders, and tighten credit discipline. They also have facilitated market-driven reshuffles of corporate structure through mergers and acquisitions (M&A), neither initiated nor controlled by the state.

The greater good in this permissive communist variant no longer depends on protecting the people's assets from private arrogation, preventing the diversion of government usufruct, and insider rent granting ('selling' privileged leasing rights to autonomous profit-seeking agents in return for service, taxes and support). Deng, echoing Soviet Politburo member Nikolai Bukharin in the 1920s, exhorted communists to enrich themselves in return for adding value. The game is not restricted to party insiders and the *taizidang*, although they are better positioned to acquire lucrative assets than ordinary lessees.

Everyone can compete in the cause of rapid development and modernization, until one fine fairy-tale day when the leadership decides to re-prioritize social justice over profit, terminating privileged leaseholds, imposing confiscatory inheritance taxes, and otherwise levelling income and wealth. Hu Jintao has dubbed the latest version of this dream, the harmonious society. He envisages subordinating development to a democratic order under the rule of law, featuring equality and justice, with an honest and caring government that assures rapid growth and social stability. Deng Xiaoping's pragmatism, as he always claimed, has led China away from Mao's terror-command to a more prosperous state-orchestrated, insider-privileged self-seeking economic order, searching for communist harmony. There can be no doubt that Hu Jintao's contemporary system permits citizens to pursue their livelihoods and fortunes through diverse means, including material incentive schemes, entrepreneurship, business, private investment, foreign trade, and negotiated wage, product and asset prices.

Leasing property, business, entrepreneurship, credit and finance have been decriminalized, and there is a semblance, if not the substance, of the rule of law. This seems to imply that Deng also has successfully marketized China's economy, and set the nation on a path-dependent course towards democracy, civic empowerment, the rule of law and a workable form of Marxist market communism under Xi Jinping, Hu's designated successor. China, in short, seems to have devised a Communist Party managed, self-regulating, normal, market regime that explains recent accomplishments and vouchsafes the future.

However, appearances are deceptive. The last two decades have witnessed the creation of production and supply that responds to consumer demands in a negotiated way in a multitude of Chinese sectors. These are genuine market exchanges. None the less, they differ fundamentally from the textbook neoclassical markets. Hu's markets are rent-granting, rent-seeking and rent-controlling (creation of fictitious values by overpaying insiders and agents who become recipients of unearned incomes) mechanisms serving the communist party and other privileged individuals, rather than competitively maximizing consumer utility.

Before 1989 Deng's markets advanced the communist cause first, and leaders' personal enrichment second, while restricting the scope of market participation. Hu's markets reverse this polarity, subordinating CPC statesmanship to the enrichment of party members, bureaucrats and allies who diversely exploit unprotected labourers, including 150 million migrant workers. Both paradigms support communist power, but for a different mix of purposes. Deng's markets were the handmaidens of egalitarian command; Hu's are the cornerstone of post-command, prosperity enhancing, but nevertheless inegalitarian, rent-seeking.

Extraction and apportionment systems are extreme forms of monopoly and oligopoly, where insiders acquire unearned income by denying market access to would-be competitors, manipulating supply and, in many instances, purchasers' demand. Textbook monopolists and oligopolists are restricted to maximizing marginal revenue by limiting supply, but Chinese rent-creators and rent-gougers can divert income and wealth for themselves through multiple channels to society's detriment. The behaviour is intrinsically corrupt from a neoclassical perspective, because insiders are paid more than the values of their marginal products, and rent-granting encourages other pernicious and productivity inhibiting attitudes. Rent-recipients often become lax and profligate, overpaying some factors, acquiring wrong input mixes and technologies, and squandering company assets. Like the Soviet Union, such regimes may outwardly appear successful, judged by various yardsticks, but nonetheless are degenerate.

Hu Jintao's China suffers from all these afflictions, but still has improved social welfare by keeping the worst aspects of rent-seeking at bay through a pragmatic admixture of material incentives, market competition and bureaucratic discipline. He and his post-Mao predecessors provided productive inducements to anyone willing to increase taxable or rent-appropriable income. All behavioural and institutional forms (household responsibility system, township and village enterprises (TVEs), special economic zones (SEZs), joint ventures before 1993, outsourcing, Red Chips, gambling, etc.) have become permissible (except freehold ownership), if they empower the Communist Party, the state and the privileged. In the same spirit, they have welcomed foreign direct investors, benefiting directly from Western technology transfer and the diffusion of foreign technology. Recently, Beijing has begun aggressively purchasing minerals and companies abroad with an eye to creating and capturing overseas rents. Moreover, the leadership has continuously pressured rent-recipients to run their operations as efficiently as rent-granting allows. Subsidies to state enterprises have been reduced, and many SOEs have been forcibly merged or disbanded. Market protections, including tariffs, and quotas (in accordance with China's entry into the WTO in 2001) have been lowered, although not enough, and firms with privileged charters have had to demonstrate some accomplishments to fend off rival insiders. Even the bureaucracy has been compelled to interest itself in various constructive activities, rather than perpetually seeking bribes.

The leadership has also been willing to share rents stemming from wage repression with foreign households (and relatedly, foreign businesses) by undervaluing the RMB in the international currency market. The state, in its capacity as opportunistic rent-seeker, could have tried to obtain imports for current consumption as cheaply as possible at the expense of reduced direct foreign investment by overvaluing the RMB, but the leadership instead gave priority to hot-housing national development.

These achievements may gradually be augmented until China completes its transition to an authentic, workably competitive, neoclassical market system, with democracy and civic empowerment; however, none of these outcomes seems probable any time soon.

Looked at from this perspective, China is a relatively efficient rent-granting regime that has avoided becoming completely dysfunctional by modernizing and improving economic efficiency on multiple fronts, including market competition. It has been predatory, and likely will remain so, but has ample room for further modernization and development.

Indochinese market communist latecomers

Contemporary Indo-chinese market communism is rent-seeking like its northern mentor, but the historical and institutional particulars differ. Although, Vietnam, Cambodia and Laos followed the dominant 20th-century communist sequence, passing through the terror-command and terror-free command phases before arriving at rent-granting/markets,[3] their communist parties did not consolidate their power within present boundaries until the Vietnamese War ended with the Fall of Saigon on 30 April 1975. Southeast Asian communism is younger than China's, and in the Laotian and Cambodian cases has shallower roots.

Vietnam

Vietnam's version of market communism called *Doi Moi* (renewal) began at the 6th Communist Party Congress in 1986 with the introduction of agricultural contracting in peasant co-operatives and the privatization of some commerce, although the material incentives and the family responsibility system had been tried briefly in 1960–62. It superseded the *Bao Cap* subsidy system (1975–86), which was gradually terminated by reducing food subsidies, and introducing cash salaries indexed to the cost of living.

Soon thereafter foreign investment, including joint ventures and outsourcing, was encouraged by the Foreign Direct Investment Law, 9 December 1987; inefficient agrarian co-operatives began being abolished by the Land Law of 1993, and farmers were given title to their plots, together with tilling rights. A Civil Code was established to define and protect these and other private property rights. Results were slight at first because the West boycotted Vietnam as long as its troops occupied Cambodia, but after 1989 the economy made notable headway.

The official objective of these reforms, replicating Deng Xiaoping's pragmatic experiment eight years earlier, was the creation of a socialist oriented market economy, with a strong state industrial presence including banking, and aspects of foreign trade (exports constituted 68 per cent of GDP in 2007), combined with agrarian cooperatives and private enterprise in the light manufacturing and service sectors.

The market dimension of Vietnam's *Doi Moi* socialism includes various material incentive schemes, the decriminalization of some negotiated transactions, the reduction of state price and wage fixing (regulation), and with it a lessened role for SOEs and central planning. The planning process has been decentralized with a concomitant increase in provincial and local economic power. The state owns all the non-tillable land, including resources, with private business being conducted mostly on a leasing basis. A stock exchange was established in July 2000 to expedite the partial privatization of SOEs, but foreigners are precluded from owning more than 49 per cent of any enterprise, and cannot purchase freehold land, including residential and commercial real estate. In 2005 banks were added to the list of *equitizable* SOEs (majority state owned firms with minority private equity stakes).

Vietnam joined the WTO in 2007, triggering an effort to protect intellectual property rights, but the initiative has been ineffectual. Overall, Vietnam has prospered by marketizing, liberalizing, globalizing (including the receipt of billions of dollars in remittances, transferred by post-Vietnam War refugees who settled in the West), and is viewed by many as being on a Chinese-style high road to workably competitive, neoclassical free enterprise.

However, this characterization is misleading to the extent that it assumes communism no longer matters, or that the Communist Party of Vietnam's (CPV) power will quickly evaporate. The Soviet Union's demise lends some credence to such conjectures, but not enough to carry the day. Vietnam's *Doi Moi* strategy has been a pragmatic exercise in devising a better mouse-trap; not a ploy for gradually relinquishing communist rule, or wholly abandoning its revolutionary agenda. The leadership from the outset has sought to kill several birds with one stone, including the retention of CPV power, the enhancement of Vietnam's wealth and influence, insider enrichment, modernization, development and improved living standards, with foreknowledge that these benefits could not be secured without ideological concessions. It understood, and agreed to accept the fact that material incentives, partial privatization, leasing and the decriminalization of private business and entrepreneurship would dilute insider rents, diminish communist legitimacy, reduce the CPV's span of control, increase pressure for civic empowerment and democracy, and raise the spectre of extreme inegalitarianism and social strife, placing CPV sovereignty at risk.

Central Committee members could not ascertain beforehand whether the rewards would exceed the risks, but opted to learn by doing. Their objective was certainly not to achieve neoclassical, democratic free enterprise with civic empowerment. They sought, and are still seeking to discover, an optimal mix that preserves CPV power, and the leadership's private ambitions, while securing as many communist ideological goals as possible. Egalitarianism, individual liberty and human empowerment are not high priorities, but the CPV does not spurn general prosperity and social harmony.

Their policies thus have boiled down to a masters first masses second strategy, with rising incomes and a social safety net. They have created a one-sided social contract that allows ordinary citizens to reap some of the fruits of their labour, sugar coated with revolutionary nostalgia, at the expense of egalitarianism, social justice, humanitarianism, civil liberties and political rights. For those who assign great weight to official GDP growth statistics, and domestic winners these 'birth pangs' seem a fair bargain, and no doubt will be broadly judged so by history, if blemishes fade with further communist development.

Vietnamese welfare will improve substantially if the country extends liberalization, unshackles agriculture, legalizes more aspects of private activity, reforms SOEs, embraces globalization (promoting FDI and exports) and restructures the financial sector. Corruption, too, may subside and rent recipients become more socially conscious. However, communist moral hazard and rent-granting could also endure, ensuring inequality (Gini coefficient estimates rose from 0.35 in 1990 to 0.43 in 2006),[4] unemployment, hardship, social injustice, authoritarianism and civic repression. Vietnamese average living standards are likely to improve for decades, given the country's relative economic backwardness and wage repression; none the less, both material and societal progress will be impeded if rent-granting, rent-seeking and rent-controlling are not constrained. Not only will Vietnam's Gini coefficient remain stubbornly high judged from the global norm, but the inequality will be largely attributable to insider power, rather than to competitively justified differences in marginal value-added.

This behaviour replicates contemporary China's in all essentials. Market communist regimes, it seems, are fundamentally alike. However, there are some significant differences. Both GDP and inequality have grown more slowly in Vietnam than in China (if one believes the statistics), and the CPV has permitted a freer flow of imports. This has led some to claim that governing coalitions are more diverse in Vietnam, that they constrain authoritarianism, are intrinsically more competitive and therefore superior to Beijing's brand of market communism. Others stress the weakening legitimacy of the current regime, contending that the CPV is effectively dead as a source of ideals or morality, prodding the Vietnamese to rediscover their Buddhist heritage. On the first view, Vietnam's brand of rent-granting/market communism has a better chance than China's of surviving, while on the second, this may not be good enough to prevent Vietnam's economic system from morphing in new cultural directions.

Laos and Cambodia

Market-oriented reform started in Laos and Cambodia at the same time that *Doi Moi* was officially promulgated in Hanoi, but with less substance. Laos's experience with command communism was brief (the Pathet Lao came to power under Vietnamese tutelage in the mid-seventies), and the Vietnamese-occupied Khmer Rouge ravaged Cambodia for 15 years. Both criminalized private property, business and entrepreneurship, created SOEs, and central planning before 1986. Then, under their versions of *Doi Moi*, called the *New Economic Mechanism* (in Laos), gradually introduced material incentives and rudimentary markets in agriculture and commerce, followed by the legalization of some forms of private property (including direct foreign investment, outsourcing and joint ventures), and institutions to enforce property rights. Managerial and financial autonomy were encouraged in SOEs, and prices liberalized.

It is claimed that this liberalization spurred rapid growth and development, but the results are invisible to the naked eye. Neither Laos nor Cambodia displays entrepreneurial vitality (Phnom Penh was still a virtual tourist ghost town in 2009), and direct foreign investment is limited because Laos is landlocked, and Cambodia's ports are in disrepair. In principle, Cambodia's electoral democracy should have some discernible effect on the performance of its rent-granting market communist–socialist system, and Laos eventually may display some novel aspects, but for the present all that can prudently be inferred is that the rent-granting, rent-seeking and rent-controlling could be milder and more haphazard in Cambodia and Laos than in Vietnam and China, and that each Asian market communist system may evolve separately in its own special way.

Asian market communist performance in (long-term) historical perspective

Living standards in Asia (China and Japan) and the West were similar until the start of the commercial revolution in 16th-century Europe (Figure 36.1), when per capita income began steadily improving in the West, while Asia stagnated. This divergence persisted for five hundred

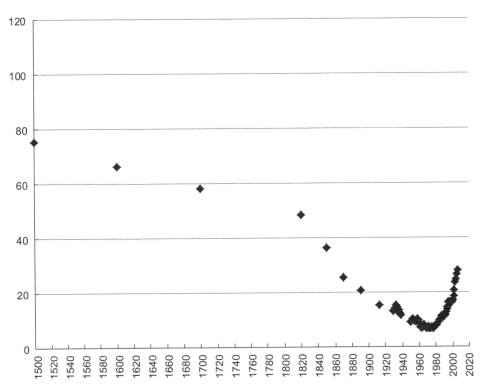

Figure 36.1 Chinese–EU Divergence and Convergence 1500–2006 per capita GDP (Western Europe = 100)
Source: Angus Maddison, *The World Economy: Historical Statistics*, OECD, Paris, 2003. http://www.ggdc.net/maddison/Historical_Statistics/horizontal-file_03-2009xls
Note: Western Europe includes Austria, Belgium, Denmark, Finland, France, Germany, Italy, Netherlands, Norway, Sweden, Switzerland and the United Kingdom.

years, creating an immense living standard gap. Per capita GDP in communist China, Vietnam, Cambodia and Laos fell to less than 20 per cent of the west European level by 1990. Its relative economic backwardness was even greater, judged from the American norm, making communist Asia ripe for rapid catch up after 1990, propelled by deepening market reforms.

OECD data compiled by Angus Maddison (Table 36.1) indicate that market communist Asia seized the day, especially during the first decade of the new millennium compared with the pre-Tiananmen Square benchmark. Per capita growth markedly accelerated, approaching double-digit magnitudes in China and Cambodia, and mid-single-digit rates in Vietnam and Laos, despite the 2008 global financial crisis. Although these claims may be exaggerated, evidence from multiple sources like Western import statistics nonetheless confirms that living standards rose significantly faster than the EU norm, enabling market communist China and Vietnam to close some of the per capita income gap with the West (Figures 36.1 and 36.2). Cambodia is supposed to have done nearly as well as China, but direct on-site observation does not corroborate what appear to be freely invented statistics.

Still, fuzzy data notwithstanding, communist market reform seems to have unleashed previously repressed economic potential even in Cambodia, despite strong communist party domination of public programmes, ownership, competition and foreign trade. Market communist Asia is dramatically out-performing command communist North Korea, and its own past benchmarks (Table 36.2). Although it might not out-perform democratic free enterprise in the very long run, Asian market-oriented communism is likely to continue recovering lost ground over the next few years, perhaps even decades, not least because much of these economies remains well behind the world technology frontier. Hence there is a great deal of catching up to be done.

Table 36.1 Asian Communist per capita GDP Growth 1985–2009

	1985–90	*1990–95*	*1995–2001*	*2000–09*
China	4.1	7.4	5.1	9.8
Vietnam	2.2	6.2	4.8	6.0
Cambodia	–2.0	1.8	2.4	9.2
Laos	0.2	3.0	1.8	4.0
North Korea	0.0	–11.8	–4.5	–1.2

Source: http://www.ggdc.net/maddison/Historical_Statistics/horizontal-file_03-2009xls
Statistics on World Population, GDP and per capita GDP 1-2006AD (last update: March 2009, horizontal file; copyright Angus Maddison).

Table 36.2 Communist GDP growth, command era 1929–2000 (GDP growth, per cent)

Years	USSR	North Korea	China	Cambodia	Vietnam	Laos
1929–1937	6.2					
1951–2000		3.0				
1953–1957			4.9			
1957–1962			–2.0			
1967–1976			3.7			
1975–1979				2.3		
1975–1985					4.0	3.0

Source: Angus Maddison, *The World Economy: Historical Statistics*, OECD: Geneva, 2003, Table 3.b, p.98, and Table 5.b, pp.174, 178.

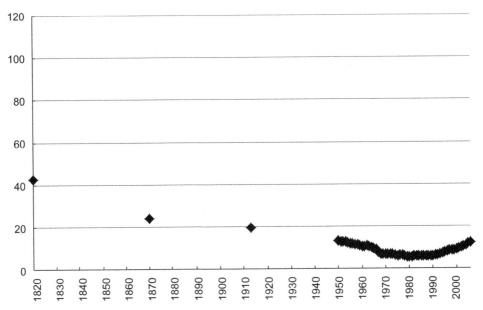

Figure 36.2 Vietnam–EU Divergence and Convergence 1820–2006 per capita GDP (Western Europe = 100). Source: Angus Maddison, *The World Economy: Historical Statistics*, OECD, Paris, 2003. http://www.ggdc. net/maddison/Historical_Statistics/horizontal-file_03-2009xls. Western Europe includes Austria, Belgium, Denmark, Finland, France, Germany, Italy, Netherlands, Norway, Sweden, Switzerland and the United Kingdom.

Notes

1 Steven Rosefielde, *Russian Economics From Lenin to Putin*, New York: Wiley, 2007; Rosefielde, *Red Holocaust*, New York: Routledge, 2010.
2 Deng could have blamed the Soviet Union collapse on Gorbachev's *perestroika*, but he rightly concluded that Gorbachev's ineptness, not the market was at fault.
3 Rosefielde, *Red Holocaust*.
4 http://www.euromonitor.com/vietnams_income_distribution Cf. Regina Abrami, Edmund Malesky and Yu Zheng, 'Accountability and Inequality in Single Party Regimes: A Comparative Analysis of Vietnam and China,' unpublished pdf, 5/16/08. China's Gini coefficient was 0.47 in 2004. See World Bank, *World Development Indicators*, Washington, DC: World Bank, 2007.

Bibliography

Blanchard, Olivier (1998), *The Economics of Post-Communist Transition*, Clarendon Lectures in Economics, Oxford: Oxford University Press.
Chien, Thang Le, and Truong, Quang (2005), 'Human Resource Management Practices in a Transitional Economy: A Comparative Study of Enterprise Ownership Forms in Vietnam,' *Asia Pacific Business Review*, vol.11(1).
Chol-Hwan, Kang, and Rigoulot, Pierre (2001), *The Aquariums of Pyongyang*, New York: Basic Books.
Chow, Gregory (2012), *China As a Leader of the World Economy*, Singapore: World Scientific Publishers.
Gainsborough, Martin (2007), 'From Patronage Politics to "Outcomes": Vietnam's Communist Party Congresses Reconsidered,' *Journal of Vietnamese Studies*, vol. 2(1), pp. 3-26
Haggard, Stephan and Noland, Marcus (2007), *Famine in North Korea: Markets, Aid, and Reform*. New York: Columbia University Press.

Hare, Paul (2007), 'Industrial Policy for North Korea: Lessons from Transition,' *International Journal of Korean Unification Studies*, vol.16(2), pp. 29–53.

Lee, Hy-Song (2001), *North Korea: A Strange Socialist Fortress*, New York: Praeger Publishers.

Naughton, Barry (2007), *The Chinese Economy: Transitions and Growth*, Cambridge, MA: MIT Press.

Ngan Thuy Collins (2009), *Economic Reform and Employment Relations in Vietnam*, London: Routledge.

OECD, *Economic Surveys: China*, Paris: OECD.

Rigoulot, Pierre, (1999), 'Crimes, Terror and Secrecy in North Korea,' in Courtois, Stefane *et al.* (eds), *The Black Book of Communism*, Cambridge, MA: Harvard University Press.

Rosefielde, Steven (2010), *Red Holocaust*, London: Routledge.

Rosefielde, Steven, Kuboniwa, Masaaki and Mizobata, Satoshi (eds) (2011), *Two Asias: The Emerging Postcrisis Divide*, Singapore: World Scientific Publishers.

Vu, Khuong (2009), 'Economic Reform and Growth Performance: China and Vietnam in Comparison,' *China: An International Journal*, vol.7(2), September.

Woo, Wing Thye (2007), 'The Challenges of Governance Structure, Trade Disputes and Natural Environment to China's Growth,' *Comparative Economic Studies*, vol.49(4), pp. 572–602.

World Bank (2012), *Building a Modern, Harmonious, and Creative High-Income Society*, Washington, DC: The World Bank.

37

THE GREAT TRANSFORMATION 1989–2029

Grzegorz W. Kolodko

Introduction

Rarely does so much change so rapidly as during the post-socialist system transformation that occurred between 1989 and the present time. For the 10 East Central European countries already belonging to the European Union (Bulgaria, the Czech Republic, Estonia, Hungary Latvia, Lithuania, Poland, Romania, Slovakia and Slovenia), many claim that the transformation has already succeeded because the region has institutionally matured to become a fully fledged market economy. Others, however, argue that there is still a long way to go.

I share the latter view. Although the very fact of formal membership in the European Union – in accordance with the Copenhagen Criteria established as early as 1993 – means that each new member is considered a 'functioning market economy' able to compete within the Union, yet this does not imply real systemic maturity. Such maturity requires qualitative advancement of the market culture and the reliability of market institutions, i.e., the rules of the market economy game, to ensure the effective operation of mechanisms for creating and allocating capital, and for distributing output. Effective operation of those mechanisms depends on the dynamics of complex economic processes, and their balance. Hence to achieve a state of market institutions and culture that meets these conditions, further development over a much longer period is needed.

As for other regions, especially in post-Soviet Central Asia, there are still some countries that would hardly be called post-socialist if it were not for the general transformation process that has gone on since 1989 or 1991. After all, there is no doubt that in 1989 Hungary, Poland or Yugoslavia of the time were already far more marketized and liberalized than countries such as Azerbaijan, Uzbekistan or Turkmenistan were 20 years later. Then, however, because of the context, nobody even thought of calling the former 'transformation economies', just as now the latter are not referred to, also because of the context, as 'reforming socialist (communist) economies'.

The cascade

In Poland the historic Round Table debate of spring 1989 culminated in a compromise agreement. Representatives of the governing authorities and opposition groups, intellectuals and businessmen, politicians and economists gathered at the Table. That agreement became the catalyst for a process of massive systemic transformation covering a great part of the world: first, Eastern Europe, and soon after that, the territories of the former Soviet Union (FSU). It also influenced the market orientation and pace of structural and institutional transformation both in China and in the Indo-china region, notably Vietnam.

Over thirty countries, stretching from the Elbe River to the Pacific Ocean and currently inhabited by over 1.8 billion people, over a quarter of the world's population, embarked on the path to more or less liberal market and democratic transformation. After 20 years of transformation, this process, taking place against a background of globalization and another phase of the scientific and technical revolution, as well as dramatic cultural and political changes, has given rise to a completely new world. For as it turned out, 1989 was a historically significant year for many other regions of the world as well – from South and Central America through Africa and the Middle East to South and Eastern Asia. This can be observed, *inter alia*, in such countries as Chile and Nicaragua, Ghana and South Africa, Yemen and Syria, India and Sri Lanka.

1989 also meant the end of the Cold War, the end of clashes between the two sides of that war, i.e., the First World (advanced capitalist countries led by the USA and the former colonial metropolitan countries) and the Second World (led by the USSR and China) on the territory of the Third World countries. Interestingly, twenty years later, China's influence is much greater, and in some parts of the differently divided world still growing.

The collapse of real socialism, the end of the Cold War, the post-socialist transformation and the expansion of neoliberalism, the markets 'emerging' from the post-colonial and post-socialist countries, the advance of globalization, the information revolution, mass migration and the devastation of the natural environment are the most important factors cumulatively causing the *cascade* of cultural, political, social, economic, technological and environmental transformations of the past two decades. The cascade of changes is rolling with great force through societies and economies, causing something that could be called a tectonic shift. A new quality is being created, which can be explained on the basis of the *coincidence theory of development* (Kolodko, 2011). It is against that background that the entire process of post-socialist market transformation, *per se* historic, should be perceived.

The sentence

If we had asked people, including outstanding economists, what the average standard of living and production level would be after two decades of systemic transformation (excluding China and Indochina, whose development is very specific), no one would have suggested that it would be only 20 per cent higher than in 1990. For such slow growth makes the enormous systemic transformation almost pointless from the strictly economic point of view. After all, why transform the system only to sentence the next generation (400 million people) to barely noticeable growth of 0.9 per cent per annum on average? Yet that is what was done.

Twenty years ago no one was bold enough to forecast that China would increase its GDP per capita not by one-fifth but by a factor of five. Yet over that period the huge country, still widely regarded as communist, increased its production level by more than 420 per cent. It achieved that by following its own chosen path, ignoring Western pressures and advice, unlike the countries of Eastern Europe and some republics of the former Soviet Union, which accepted such advice to varying degrees. China managed surprisingly well to ensure the cooperation of the invisible hand of the market with a highly visible head of state. The synergy between those two regulators of the social reproduction process determined China's unprecedented success, as the country quietly advanced from the phase of reforming the socialist planned economy to the gradual creation of a capitalist market economy. Although it still does not admit that, and nowadays advances the thesis of constructing 'a harmonious society', intentionally still socialist, in fact China is already well down the road of building a market economy. The latter is capitalist by nature, with all the long-term implications that has, including political ones.

We will never get a satisfactory answer to a counterfactual, or alternative history question: what would have happened if … ? What would have happened if China had followed the path of chaotic political and economic liberalization, like Russia did in the decade of Yeltsin's administration? Would it have a bigger population than it has now and a lower standard of life than in 1989, at the same time flooding the world with tens of millions of additional miserable migrants?

What would have happened if, first in Eastern Europe, beginning with Poland, and then in the Soviet Union, the political conditions for complex, profound systemic transformations had not appeared, and if this part of the world had then followed a path of gradual but effective market reforms, like China and Indochina did, instead of the rapid post-socialist transformation that they actually followed? We can speculate that the pace of economic growth in the 1990–2009 period might have been significantly faster than the disappointing average of 0.9 per cent yearly, as it had been in the previous 20-year period, 1970–89, and even more so in the two earlier decades, 1950–69.

Alternatively, one might imagine, as a result of the crisis at the turn of the 1980s and 1990s and the systemic inability to steer these economies along a path of fast and balanced growth, that the region might have descended into secular stagnation and, possibly, would now have an even lower production level than then. However, noting the engagement with market reforms at the end of 1980s, especially in Hungary and Poland, as well as Gorbachev's policies of *glasnost* and *perestroika*, the first option is surely more probable: with a higher average pace of growth than actually occurred.

Certainly, in the framework of a more profoundly reformed socialism, redistribution mechanisms would have also worked differently. The range of income inequality would surely be greater than at the time of the so-called real socialism, yet less than it has actually turned out to be (Kolodko, 2000). Yet, that supposition could be questioned as well since, for example, the Chinese and Vietnamese experience suggests otherwise. In these countries, advanced reforms of the socialist economic system have triggered a gradual increase in inequality, even more so than in countries that chose a path of systemic transformation. Suffice to say that the Gini coefficient, measuring the extent of income inequality, was 0.47 in China (as of 2007) and 0.37 in Vietnam (2004), while in Poland it was 0.35 (2005) and in Hungary only 0.28 (also 2005) (CIA, 2009).

Reforms versus transformation

There is a substantial difference between market reforms within a real socialist economy and a post-socialist market transformation. In the first case, the focus is on changing how the existing system functions in order to preserve its essentials. Attempts to make the socialist system more flexible and to increase its ability to adjust to changing cultural and technological conditions were made with that end in view. Their purpose was to enhance enterprises' effectiveness and gain social support, or at least acceptance, for the system's continued functioning. So with reforms, the changes – although at times profound and advanced – were by assumption designed to serve the purpose of retaining the established economic and political system, and not its rejection. That was the objective of the Soviet *perestroika* at the end of the 1980s; it was also the goal of the Polish reforms of that decade. Likewise, the economic transformations in Hungary that started in 1968, and the very different Yugoslavian model of self-governing socialism, initiated as early as the 1950s, can be viewed in the same light.

As for the second option – post-socialist transformation – its aim is to eliminate the former system and replace it – through substantial, qualitative institutional reconstruction – with a new system, *de facto*, a market capitalist economy. The fact that the term 'capitalism' is still used surprisingly rarely to refer to the system created on the territory of Eastern Europe and the FSU does not change anything. Although euphemisms such as 'market economy' are more frequently used, its capitalist nature is obvious.

The former 'communism' with all its disadvantages, including some imaginary ones, is often contrasted with the 'market economy', with its advantages, some of which are only hypothetical. Comparing such a non-existent 'communism', presented in the most gloomy terms, with an idealized 'market economy', actually also non-existent, is both methodologically erroneous and factually confusing. Valid comparisons entail confronting the existing realities – the former and the present one – rather than a slandered image of the past and a rose-tinted image of the present or imagined future.

Therefore, the so-called real socialism as it really was, especially in its economic aspect, and the so-called real, contemporary post-socialist capitalism, as it really is, should be juxtaposed (Główczyk, 2003). What is amazing is that neither economists nor economic historians are yet ready to make such an objective, comprehensive comparison. So we must wait for it, maybe another 20 years or more.

Emerging markets

The commonly used term, *emerging markets*, was not created to describe the new, complex economic reality of countries undergoing systemic transformation. The term relates to the expansion of the neoliberal model of capitalism that has been going on for as long as the now more than 20-year episode of post-socialist transformation (Harvey, 2005). These so called 'emerging' markets are not evolving and maturing market economies, civic societies and political democracies but emerging new fields of economic activity, particularly speculation, for the richer part of the world – that which 'emerged' long ago as a capitalist economy, and which has institutionally and financially matured. The rich world is now sufficiently strong and affluent that it seeks to use that affluence in other regions beyond its traditional zones of domination. Considering the map of the world before 1989, with the division then existing, the situation called for the non-market part of the world to 'emerge' and open up for capital penetration. That, in turn, was and still is only possible through transformation from socialist planned economy to capitalist market economy.

From this neoliberal point of view, 'emerging markets' are treated instrumentally as one more opportunity to do good business, not necessarily taking into consideration the social costs in the places where the business is done. However, from the point of view of the countries and economies interested in 'emerging', the purpose is basically different: it is the appearance of a market economy system, effective and competitive internationally, which would be able to fulfil the needs of their own societies in a satisfactory way.

Briefly, that is the fundamental difference between a neoliberal approach to the post-socialist systemic transformation and that represented by the notion of the social market economy. The first approach concentrates on emerging opportunities to do business. One should not be surprised at that, but it is necessary to understand it and react properly. The other approach concentrates on creating and developing a new type of social bond, based on new market

459

management principles. Hence, it is not just 'markets' that emerge but a market economy based society, and that is something quite different.

Therefore, the declared Western concern for democracy and progress, for development and wealth of the post-socialist societies, is mainly rhetoric, covering concern for their own interests, not only political but above all economic, particularly the interests of the financial elites of the rich countries. We must not take offence at this fact, yet failing to acknowledge it would be most naive. We need to adjust to it practically as a new challenge that creates both new dangers and risks, as well as significant new opportunities. However, to be beneficial for long-term social and economic development, an effective strategy, determining the aims of development and based on a sound economic theory, is necessary.

Over two decades ago, the real socialist system – the economy functioning without political democracy and based on state property domination, central capital allocation and bureaucratic control – was heading towards its end, as it had exhausted its development capacity. People were more and more dissatisfied in all the three social functions that they always undertake:

- producers – frustration was increasing, which resulted from wrongly organized production that did not bring the expected effects;
- consumers – in the face of increasing deficiencies and a deepening shortageflation syndrome (Kolodko and McMahon, 1987), the level of consumer satisfaction was relatively low (against the background of increasing production), and sometimes absolutely lower, because it was difficult not only to earn money but also to spend it;
- citizens – the so-called people's democracy and more or less liberalized one-party system were far from giving people the possibility to express opinions in an organized and creative way, enabling them to have an impact on public matters.

In that situation, when the system was clearly creating more problems than it was able to solve, the 'material fatigue' was so great that the system was bound to collapse under the weight of its own dysfunctionality. This is what finally happened in 1989 in Poland and much of Eastern Europe, although it could easily have happened up to a dozen years earlier or later, but it definitely had to happen. First of all, there was increasing social pressure for change, most clearly expressed in Poland, mainly, though not only, by the 'Solidarity' movement, which, with the passing of time, contradicted itself, turning to populist or neoliberal positions (Ost, 2005). It was also in Poland that the authorities, already supporting reforms, agreed to share the power at the Round Table. In Romania, the authorities behaved in a completely different way, resisting change for as long as they could. The processes in the other countries took forms between those two extremes.

Obviously, external pressures played their role here, yet, basically, it was an internal process in each country. The external forces took advantage of the internal decomposition processes rather than imposing the direction or pace of change. Even if in the USA the Democrats had held power, supporting reforms and looking for 'socialism with a human face', instead of Republicans with their confrontational outlook; and even if in the UK power had been with the Labour Party, favouring the social market economy and looking for the 'third way', instead of the Tories, perceiving the East with hostility; still the real socialism was doomed to fail. If it had not happened at the end of the 1980s, it would have happened a little later. However, it was not doomed to follow the path that then unfolded and which, to a great extent, is still evolving. Other paths of development might have been found, possibly involving lower social costs and higher living standards for the populations of the countries in transition.

Facts, Interpretations, Speculations

While the past is a matter of facts and their interpretation, the future – except for shaping it actively, which is the most important – is a question of speculations and their interpretation. The former is more difficult; the latter is more appealing, as the future knows no facts. It will provide them. However, what kind of facts they will be greatly depends on the assumptions made *ex ante*, and their consequences: theoretical and practical, intellectual and political. Therefore, hypothetical deliberations on the future, with certain intellectual and formal limitations, are not only interesting but may also be creative and fertile. Those who do not speculate do not predict, and without predictions, participation in creating the future is impossible.

The assessment of the previous course of post-socialist transformation is still controversial, and will remain so for many years. Yet, certain areas of theoretical generalization, hard to challenge intellectually, have already appeared (Blanchard, 1997; Csaba, 2007). At the same time, more could have been achieved in terms of economic growth, although sometimes there are fundamental controversies over the possible paths that could have been followed. There is no doubt, however, that 20 years after the transformation, its results, measured in terms of economic growth, could be much greater and its social costs (unemployment, inequalities, margin of exclusion, poverty, excessive death rates, etc.) could be substantially smaller. A similar pattern is likely to be observed in the future.

In the face of neoliberal propaganda typically offering a false path of transformation (one without an alternative) *ex ante* and its image *ex post,* attempts to estimate the economic growth that could have occurred in the years 1990–2009 are rarely made. Obviously, even an accurate result of such a complex estimation of the growth of production and consumption cannot be sufficient to assess the existing situation, as the gross domestic product (GDP) indicator normally used does not cover all the relevant aspects of the socio-economic situation. The UNDP Human Development Index (HDI), widely used in practice, is better, though also not perfect. However, that index also omits from consideration the natural environment or any evaluation of free time and its use. Eventually, these and other aspects of socio-economic development (such as cultural values, relations between political power and the economy) will be given their due attention in a synthetic way, for example by using an Integrated Well-Being Index (ZIP – *Zintegrowany Indeks Pomyślności*) (Kolodko, 2011).

Let us take the example of Poland – the largest economy of the new member countries of the European Union (EU) – whose real GDP in 2009 was about 180 per cent of its 1989 value. Excluding China and Vietnam, this was the best result in the post-socialist countries, aside from the specific case of Turkmenistan where the index was about 220 per cent (EBRD, 2008), stimulated by a boom in energy resource prices in recent years. Poland's growth of GDP by 80 per cent over two decades basically happened due to fast growth in the periods 1994–97 and mid-2002 to mid-2008. In the periods 1990–93 and 1998–2001, in contrast, overall GDP growth was close to zero. These changes in dynamics and the level of production were clearly correlated to the employment and unemployment rates (Figure 37.1).

There has been an attempt to estimate the hypothetical pace of growth over the past 20 years in Poland. The basis for the estimation is the assumption that the changes of GDP in the years 1990–93 could have complied with the original government's plans (a decline of 3.1 per cent in year 1990 and then further growth), and in the years 1998–2001 they could have been similar to the real dynamics observed in the period 1994–97, as assumed by the contemporary government's policy *ex ante* (Kolodko, 2009). That was possible. Implementing such a scenario only required avoiding obvious mistakes: firstly, devastating stabilization policy at the beginning of the first decade (Kolodko and Nuti, 1997); secondly, unnecessary cooling of the economy at

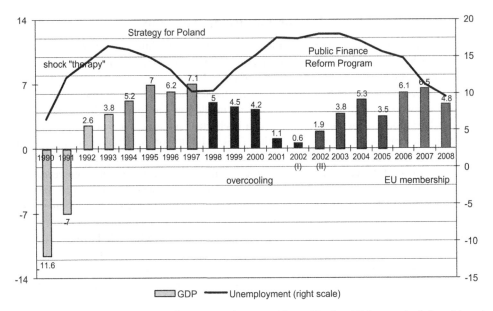

Figure 37.1 From Shock without Therapy to Therapy without Shocks: GDP growth (left scale) and
unemployment rate (right scale) in Poland, 1990–2008

Source: GUS (Central Statistical Office), Warsaw (various years).

the end of the decade, when the pace of growth was brought from the maximum (considering
the transformation period) level of 7 per cent in 1997 to the stagnation level of 0.2 per cent at the
end of 2001 (EBRD, 2008).

If the events had followed that scenario, based on the assumption of sound policies for
building market institutions and a responsible strategy for economic development, and if we had
reacted more effectively to the world's economic crisis of 2008–9 and managed to keep GDP
growing at about 4–5 per cent, then in 2009 the GDP level would not be 180 per cent of the
value from 20 years ago but half as big again: over 280 per cent of that value (Figure 37.2).

Presented in absolute values, it would mean not around 18 thousand dollars *per capita* (calculated according to the purchasing power parity, US$PPP), as in Latvia, but over 28 thousand
US$PPP, more than in Portugal. That illustrates the range of the unexploited possibilities and,
at the same time, irretrievably lost income. This loss, moreover, is the result of allowing economic
policy at certain times to be over-influenced by neoliberal thinking.

As for other transformed economies which, taken together, only in 2007 returned to the
production level of 1989, the range of policy mistakes was even greater than in Poland, hence
the failure to exploit their full growth potential was even more significant there. There were
various causes, usually of a political rather than an economic character, with endless political
disputes – sometimes turning in a populist direction, sometimes in a neoliberal one – making it
difficult to exercise rational and practical policy to promote balanced economic growth.

Still, it must be emphasized that in Poland the achieved pace of growth at 3 per cent per
annum was not inevitable, as at least 5 per cent was clearly achievable. Similarly, the transition
countries as a whole were by no means doomed *ex ante* to achieve the slow growth of just 0.9 per
cent annually. Fundamental mistakes in economic strategy, concerning both structural changes
and the creation of new institutions necessary for the efficient functioning of a market economy, and in economic policy as conventionally understood, have high costs. The price we now

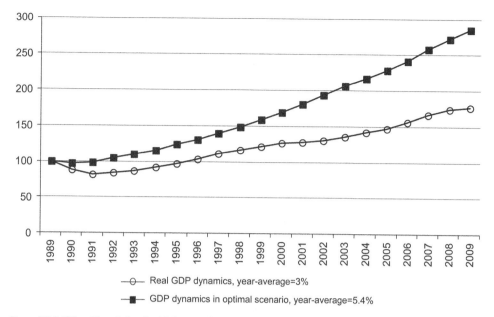

Figure 37.2 What if … Poland's GDP growth in 1990–2009 (1989=100). Actual and counterfactual (optimal policy) GDP growth

Source: Data for real GDP growth – GUS, Warsaw (various years). 2009 – Author's forecast. Hypothetical rates of GDP growth – Author's calculation.

have to pay is shown in the poor competitiveness of companies and the relatively low standard of living, as well as in excessive foreign debt and dependence on external capital and politics.

Will we have to pay a similar price in the future too? Let us hope not, though we cannot be sure, especially when we see how slow the process of learning from our own mistakes is. The observed inertia partly results from the post-socialist establishment's attachment to ineffective doctrines, and partly from the pressures exerted by national and foreign lobbies to secure their particular interests.

In 2008 the 10 post-socialist member countries of the EU were inhabited by 103 million people, which is 1.53 per cent of the world's population. They created GDP of about US $1.86 trillion (US$PPP), which is 2.6 per cent of gross world product (GWP) and at the same time 12.4 per cent of the gross product of the whole European Union. This share is relatively less – yes, less, not more – than 20 years ago, because production growth over the period 1990–2009, both at world level and in the wealthy countries of the world, including the Western part of the EU, has been much higher than in the post-socialist countries.

In the next 20 years (2010–29), though, it can and should be different. Post-socialist economies, even in the 2000–2009 decade – until the outbreak of the economic crisis – have demonstrated much stronger growth than the highly developed countries, partly making up for the differences between those countries. Enormous institutional progress, combined with technological advancement and raising employees' qualifications and managerial skills, is resulting in a pace of growth of labour productivity faster than in the West. That tendency, accompanied by improvements in the quality of microeconomic management, ought to be continued in the future. Obviously, this also requires an effective macroeconomic policy, as microeconomic changes alone are not sufficient.

The years since 2007 are characterized by particularly great uncertainty, connected with successive stages of the world financial crisis and recession. Certainly, it is difficult to forecast economic growth rates for the next few years against that background, yet the whole long-term analysis of systemic change suggests that, in the long run, post-socialist economies have good reason – related to global politics, institutions, culture, populations and technology – to expect faster growth than the 'old' members of the EU.

In the long-lasting process of eliminating historical differences in development levels, each fraction of a percentage point counts, as compound interest works with the passing of time. However, first of all, the proper strategy of long-term, fast economic growth must work. It must be based on a new pragmatism (Kolodko, 2011), turning away from the threat of populism and from the 'neoliberal deviation' of the market economy model. What is particularly harmful for economic balance and sustained growth is the combination of these two – populism and neoliberalism – which still sometimes happens in post-socialist countries.

The future

Looking into the future, let us analyse the example of Poland once again. Nowadays, just as in 1989 and thereafter, we are *ex ante* facing the opportunity of following various paths of economic growth. They range from a very high (but not impossible to achieve) average annual rate of growth of about 5 per cent and a more modest pace of about 3 per cent, rather low given the real possibilities and, especially, ambitions. Now we compare the estimated GDP levels after another 20 years, in 2029, achieved: (a) with growth at 3 per cent per annum, as it turned out in the period 1990–2009; and (b) with growth at 5.4 per cent, as it could have been if the economic policy mistakes noted above had been avoided. It seems that the higher 5 per cent growth rate may well prove achievable over the next two decades, but it will be critically important to base long-term strategy on the proper economic theory.

If all 10 post-socialist countries in the EU succeeded in growing rapidly at 5.4 per cent per annum for the next twenty years, their total GDP in 2029 would be US $5.33 trillion (US $PPP), nearly three times more than in 2009. Assuming that the average growth rate of world GDP will be about 3.5 per cent over the same period, and for the 'old' 15 countries of the EU it will not exceed 1.5 per cent, then after another two decades the ten countries' GDP will grow from the current 12.4 per cent of European Union GDP and 2.6 per cent of world GDP, to around 30 and 3.8 per cent respectively. That would greatly strengthen the relative position of the Eastern Europe region, especially within Europe.

By 2029 a further ten post-socialist countries might well have joined the EU: all the Balkan countries (Albania, Bosnia and Herzegovina, Croatia, Kosovo, Macedonia, Montenegro and Serbia) and some post-Soviet republics (Belarus, Moldova and Ukraine). In 2008 their total GDP was US $729 billion (US$PPP) (half of which, US $360 billion, is Ukraine). This is only modestly higher than Poland's GDP in the same year, US $685 billion (US$PPP) (Table 37.1).

Starting from a lower level, the GDPs of the European post-socialist economies still outside the EU may grow faster than the relatively more advanced countries. Therefore, the assumption of threefold growth by 2029 – up to around US $2 trillion (US$PPP) – seems realistic. Hence the combined GDP of all 20 post-socialist European countries (the 10 already in the Union and the 10 that should join later) would be approximately 5.3 per cent of the world's production. The world's population will then be around 8 billion, while in Eastern Europe there will be more or less the same number of people as now, i.e., 190 to 200 million. So this one-40th of the global population, 2.5 per cent of all mankind, will produce one-twentieth of GDP. Currently, the population of Central and South Eastern Europe, being 2.84 per cent of the Earth's population, produces about 3.7 per cent of world GDP.

Table 37.1 Population and GDP (in US$PPP) in Central and South Eastern Europe in 2008

Country	Population (in million)	GDP (in billion US$PPP)	GDP per capita (in US$PPP)
Bulgaria	7.3	95.9	13200
Czech Republic	10.2	273.7	26800
Estonia	1.3	28.6	21900
Hungary	9.9	205.7	20500
Latvia	2.2	41.6	17800
Lithuania	3.6	65.8	18400
Poland	38.5	684.5	17800
Romania	22.2	278.4	12500
Slovakia	5.5	123.1	22600
Slovenia	2.0	61.8	30800
EU-10	*103*	*1859*	*18100*
Albania	3.6	23.1	6400
Bosnia and Herzegovina	4.6	30.5	6600
Croatia	4.5	73.4	16900
Kosovo	2.1	5.0	2300
Macedonia	2.1	19.0	9200
Montenegro	0.7	7.2	10600
Serbia	10.2	83.1	8200
Belarus	9.7	116.7	12000
Moldova	4.3	10.8	2500
Ukraine	46.0	359.9	6900
SEE-10	*87.7*	*728.6*	*8300*
ECE-20	*190*	*2588*	*13600*
EU-27	*491*	*14960*	*34000*
World	*6707*	*70650*	*10500*

Source: CIA (2009).

Adopting the optimistic scenario of annual GDP growth at 5.4 per cent for the ten post-socialist countries already in the European Union, their *per capita* GDP would increase by as much as US $34,000 (from the average US $18,000 now to US $52,000 in 2029, all in US $PPP), or nearly 190 per cent per head, as the future population will be no larger than at present. Most importantly, living standards will be much improved. Surely that is what the post-socialist systemic transformation should amount to, rather than mistaking the means of action with its ends, as unfortunately sometimes happens.

Conclusions

Could it have been better? Will it be better? Obviously it *could* have been better – to varying degrees in the different countries. It would have been better if the objectives had been more carefully determined and the systemic transformation had been treated not as a self-contained aim but as an instrument to achieve the superior aim, namely rapid socio-economic development, enabling the region to make up for historical lags (Kolodko, 2002).

Will it be better? In the absolute sense, of course, yes. After two more decades of transformation, the levels of production and consumption will double and in some cases even triple. Will GDP per head in the new post-socialist member countries of the EU be around US $50,000 (US$PPP) in 20 years? This is not very probable overall, but it is possible for certain countries and sub-regions (more and more often now, one needs to think in terms of regions, not countries) able to sustain economic successes. Where this happens, it will mean even more than the GDP presently enjoyed by a resident in the 'old' 15 countries of the EU. And although the latter will also advance, increasing their production and consumption at least by one-third, the countries of Eastern Europe will differ less from Western Europe. However, even after 20 years, in many cases those differences will be substantial, still causing social tensions and political problems.

However, the situation may not actually *feel* better, because subjective opinions do not depend on objective assessments of differences between past and present, or on catching up with more affluent societies and richer parts of the world, but predominantly on self-evaluation of one's individual, group, social and national situation – as perceived in relation to one's desires, expectations and ideas. There is no doubt that these will always exceed the realistic opportunities of fulfilling them. Hence people's perceptions will be both the driving force of further changes and development, but also the reason for endless frustration.

Given the dynamics of growth and development and the progress likely in the future in those fields, the situation will still be worse than it could be. As usual, the potential will not be fully used, for the same reasons as in the previous twenty years. For the coming period, too, is bound to be full of policy errors, resulting from poorly resolved conflicts of group interests, based partly on inaccurate theoretical assumptions and, more generally, on economic theory lagging behind reality. There will be endless problems: first with formulating and focusing the general aim of development, and then decomposing it into concrete sub-goals. It has been like this, is like this now and will be like this in the future.

The conclusions from the past 20 years, as well as from the preceding years, should facilitate some reduction of the difference between potential and reality for the next two decades, 2010–29. However, even in 2029, just as in 1989 and in 2009, there will be people who, when asked: 'When, finally, will it be better?' will answer sarcastically: 'It's already happened …'

Bibliography

Blanchard, Olivier (1997), *The Economics of Post-Communist Transition*, New York: Oxford University Press.

CIA (2009), *The World Factbook 2008*, www.cia.gov/library/publications/the-world-factbook/index.html

Csaba, Laszlo (2007), *The New Political Economy of Emerging Europe*, Budapest: Akadémiai Kiadó.

EBRD (2008), *Transition Report 2008. Growth in Transition*, London: European Bank for Reconstruction and Development.

Główczyk, Jan (2003), *Szalbierczy urok transformacji (The Obstinate Charm of Transformation)*, Fundacja Innowacja, Warszawa: Wyższa Szkoła Społeczno-Ekonomiczna.

Harvey, David (2005), *A Brief History of Neoliberalism*, Oxford and New York: Oxford University Press.

Kolodko, Grzegorz W. (2000), *From Shock to Therapy. The Political Economy of Postsocialist Transformation*, Oxford and New York: Oxford University Press

——(2002), *Globalization and Catching-up in Transition Economies*, Rochester, NY and Woodbridge, Suffolk: University of Rochester Press.

——(2009), 'A Two-thirds Rate of Success. Polish Transformation and Economic Development in 1989–2008', *WIDER Research Paper*, No. 2009/14 (March), Helsinki: WIDER.

——(2011), *Truth, Errors, and Lies: Politics and Economics in a Volatile World*, New York: Columbia University Press.

Kolodko, Grzegorz W. and McMahon, Walter (1987), 'Stagflation and Shortageflation: A Comparative Approach', *Kyklos*, vol. 40(2), pp. 176–98.

Kolodko, Grzegorz W. and Nuti, D. Mario (1997), *The Polish Alternative. Old Myths, Hard Facts and New Strategies in the Successful Transformation of the Polish Economy*, Research for Action No. 33, UN-WIDER, Helsinki.

Ost, David (2005), *Defeat of Solidarity. Anger and Politics in Post-communist Europe*, Ithaca, NY: Cornell University.

INDEX

Taylor & Francis

eBooks
FOR LIBRARIES

ORDER YOUR FREE 30 DAY INSTITUTIONAL TRIAL TODAY!

Over 23,000 eBook titles in the Humanities, Social Sciences, STM and Law from some of the world's leading imprints.

Choose from a range of subject packages or create your own!

Benefits for you
- ▶ Free MARC records
- ▶ COUNTER-compliant usage statistics
- ▶ Flexible purchase and pricing options

Benefits for your user
- ▶ Off-site, anytime access via Athens or referring URL
- ▶ Print or copy pages or chapters
- ▶ Full content search
- ▶ Bookmark, highlight and annotate text
- ▶ Access to thousands of pages of quality research at the click of a button

For more information, pricing enquiries or to order a free trial, contact your local online sales team.

UK and Rest of World: **online.sales@tandf.co.uk**

US, Canada and Latin America:
e-reference@taylorandfrancis.com

www.ebooksubscriptions.com

ALPSP Award for BEST eBOOK PUBLISHER 2009 Finalist

Taylor & Francis **eBooks**
Taylor & Francis Group

A flexible and dynamic resource for teaching, learning and research.

For Product Safety Concerns and Information please contact our EU representative GPSR@taylorandfrancis.com Taylor & Francis Verlag GmbH, Kaufingerstraße 24, 80331 München, Germany

Printed and bound by CPI Group (UK) Ltd, Croydon, CR0 4YY

01/05/2025

01858412-0002